The ANC's Early Years

hidden histories series

Published in this series

The Making of an African Communist:
Edwin Thabo Mofutsanyana and the Communist Party of
South Africa, 1927–1939
Robert Edgar

Writing Left: The Radical Journalism of Ruth First
Donald Pinnock

50 Years of the Freedom Charter
Raymond Suttner & Jeremy Cronin

Rebellion and Uproar: Makhanda and the
Great Escape from Robben Island, 1820
Julia Wells

The Guardian: The History of South Africa's
Extraordinary Anti-Apartheid Newspaper
James Zug

'Deaf Me Normal': Deaf South Africans
Tell Their Life Stories
Ruth Morgan (ed)

The Corner People of Lady Selborne
John Mojapelo

I Listen, I Hear, I Grow: The Autobiography
of Ramaphakela Hans Hlalethwa
Ramaphakela Hans Hlalethwa

Christianity and the Colonisation of South Africa,
1487–1883. A Documentary History, Vol I
Charles Villa-Vicencio and Peter Grassow

Christianity and the Modernisation of South Africa,
1867–1936. A Documentary History, Vol II
John W. de Gruchy

Between Empire and Revolution: A Life
of Sidney Bunting, 1873–1936
Allison Drew
(co-published with Pickering & Chatto Ltd.)

Robben Island to Wall Street
Gaby Magomola

The ANC's Early Years

Nation, Class and Place in South Africa before 1940

Peter Limb

hidden histories series

Series editors:
Johannes de Bruyn, Nicholas Southey,
Russel Viljoen

UNISA PRESS
Pretoria

· **ISBN 978-1-86888-529-9**

Published by Unisa Press,
PO BOX 392, Muckleneuk Pretoria,
South Africa

Editor: Jeanne-Marie Viljoen
Cover design: Dawid Kahts
Typesetting: Pamset, Johannesburg
Printed by: Harry's Printers, Pretoria
Cover acknowledgement: UWC-Robben Island Museum Mayibuye Archives and University of
the Witwatersrand Cullen Library

Contents

Abbreviations and Acronyms

ABC	Advisory Boards Congress	NEC	Native Economic Commission
AFTU	African Federation of Trade Unions	NNC	Natal Native Congress
ANC	African National Congress	NRC	Natives' Representative Council
ANC-TT	ANC Transkeian Territories		
ANCWL	ANC Women's League	OFS	Orange Free State
ANC (WP)	ANC Western Province	OUP	Oxford University Press
APO	African Political (People's) Organisation	SACP	South African Communist Party
CAC	Cape African Congress	SAHJ	*South African Historical Journal*
CNC	Chief Native Commissioner		
CPSA	Communist Party of South Africa	SAIRR	S.A. Institute of Race Relations
CUP	Cambridge University Press	SAJE	*South African Journal of Economics*
I-ANC	Independent ANC		
ICU	Industrial & Commercial Workers Union	SALP	South African Labour Party
		SANAC	South African Native Affairs Commission
JAH	*Journal of African History*		
JJC	Johannesburg Joint Council	SANC	South African Native Congress
JNZH	*Journal of Natal & Zulu History*		
		SANNC	South African Native National Congress
JSAS	*Journal of Southern African Studies*	SSA	*Societies of Southern Africa*
KC	Karis-Carter, *From Protest to Challenge*	TAC	Transvaal African Congress
		TNC	Transvaal Native Congress
NAC	Natal African Congress	VA	Vigilance Association
NC	Native Commissioner		

Illustrations

Sources of illustrations

Mayibuye Centre, University of the Western Cape: numbers 1, 2, 4, 10, 11, 12, 13, 16, 17, 20
National Archives and Records Service of South Africa, from the Department of Justice Files JUS 3/527/17: owner/custodian, 6, 7, 8, 9
University of the Witwatersrand Cullen Library, Historical Papers: 3, 22
S.A. Rochlin Collection of South African Political and Trade Union Organizations, Concordia University, Montreal: 15, 19
SOAS Library, University of London: 5
Robert Edgar collection: 21
Author's collection: 14, 18

Tables

Preface

The African National Congress (ANC) is the oldest and most durable of African nationalist movements, not only in South Africa but also across the continent. Since 1994, it has governed the country as leader of the Tripartite Alliance with the Congress of South African Trade Unions (Cosatu) and South African Communist Party (SACP). A decade and a half ago, at the joyful celebration of the "New South Africa", the ANC and its allies had just buried apartheid for good. Today despite contradictions and strains, the alliance remains intact, its continued potency apparent in the rise of Jacob Zuma and fall of Thabo Mbeki. Behind the glamour of leaders lies the fact that working peoples of one form or another comprise the overwhelming majority of the ANC's constituency. Explaining the roots of this Alliance is important.

The immediate origins of this alliance in the passive resistance and defiance campaigns of the 1940s and 1950s, in underground and exile politics from the 1960s, and UDF-led struggles of the 1980s are widely, if not always precisely, understood. Yet, what of its longer-term roots? What made the ANC amenable to such an alliance in the first place? How did it first experiment with loose coalitions or even looser forms of "unity in action"? How did the early ANC combine political and labour issues and what were its policies and actions? What were the views (where recorded at all) of workers themselves towards Congress? Previous analyses tend to be fragmentary, but answers to these questions enrich our understanding of the deeper causes that have cemented this "unity in action" which continue to influence South African politics today.

My focus is the formative period of engagement of these political and socio-economic forces before permanent alliances emerged. The spotlight is squarely on the ANC but seen in its attitudes to, and relationships with the nascent formations of the black working class and in particular the most politically conscious and active workers. Where scanty records permit, I widen the scope to include migrant, rural, domestic, and women workers not always then clearly identified as part of a formal "working class".

Effective political unity across social classes needs common ground and shared interests. In anti-apartheid and anti-colonial struggles, common ground was firstly the mutual experience of racism and colonialism. Another unifier was the combination of broad geographic proximity and common obstacles to black empowerment that tended to push different black classes together spatially and economically despite a limited degree of class stratification. Political unity was never easily achieved, never simple or without tension. Proponents of unity had to forge lasting ties over time and on the ground; unity does not operate automatically—and many other political organisations fell by the wayside for want of support or inability to survive. That the ANC did survive and eventually flourish was due in no small part to both social and individual agency, to the dedication and labours of collectives and members, famous and forgotten.

Ordinary people, workers, have always held some place in ANC ranks, particularly at provincial or local levels. At first, their direct influence and membership was very limited but in the decades after World War II, when the black working class consolidated, workers exerted increasing political influence. The labour movement more and more became a significant component of anti-apartheid alliances that stood the test of time and contributed to the ANC's 1994 election victory. This is well known. Less acknowledged are deeper ANC connections with working peoples.

The early decades of the twentieth century saw the establishment, survival, and growth of ANC and black labour organisations. Unlike in Western countries, African political bodies in South Africa *preceded* African unions that faced huge obstacles. The slow and precipitous growth of black trade unions tended to make the early ANC (by default) a de facto, if not always effective or consistent articulator of labour rights. In colonial-like conditions largely denying black political rights, the ANC would sooner or later be obliged to relate its policies and practices to the people who formed its natural constituency, the overwhelming majority of whom were wage earners or other toilers.

ANC history can be controversial. In a recent seminar to African History postgraduates, my views seemed to some of them on the one hand too moderate, on the other hand too extreme. Might there be a danger some readers could (mis)interpret this book as somehow uncritically supporting the African nationalist hagiography typical of the immediate post-colonial period in many countries? After all, increasingly pro-business policies of ANC governments in recent years seem to confirm a picture of ANC alienation from workers, just as during national liberation struggles across Africa nationalist politicians invariably made good use of workers, and then abandoned them.

It is certainly true that many politicians in many countries, including South Africa, have left behind policies such as those enshrined in the Freedom Charter and Reconstruction and Development Programme that aimed to create jobs, safeguard health and the environment, and protect worker rights. My aim, though, is not the defence of a political party or leader but rather the uncovering of a local and provincial history hitherto largely neglected; a neglect all the more remarkable given the prominence of the ANC and black working class in South Africa. One might also ask whether my emphasis on the complex ties between Congress and workers obscures important relations with other social strata such as business, professionals, and intellectuals. However, other writers whom I discuss below already have treated such relationships. What is missing in the history of the ANC is a comprehensive analysis of early ANC attitudes to workers. I therefore ask readers to put aside for a moment any stereotypes of the ANC in its early days (or today) and examine the evidence I present.

It is useful to situate my comments in the wider field of African history. If one compares the political historiography of Africa with that of Europe, America, or India then there is a remarkable contrast. The latter all have great depth of regional political histories whereas Africa does not. There are relatively few scholarly histories of African parties reaching down to the local level. In part, this contrast flows from richer and more extensive publishing worlds outside of Africa. Yet even given South Africa's developed publishing and university systems, the literature on regional South Africa often does not accord with the complexity of African political history. The contrast also reflects responses to nationalist hagiography and crises of political rule in many African countries and subsequent abandonment of political history by many historians in favour of exciting new socio-cultural histories. This book seeks to encourage greater synthesis between political and socio-cultural history. There is a need to put revisionist political history, but one informed by advances in social history and cultural theory, back on the agenda. As South African historians build a densely layered corpus of knowledge about the past they are obliged to survey the entire range of relevant sources. Political narratives cannot neglect local or cultural spheres, just as socio-economic histories grounded in particular classes or communities need integrating into national histories.

This book is arranged into four parts. The introduction details writings on the ANC, the conditions and struggles of black labour, and emergence of African political and labour organisations. Parts two to four correlate roughly with decades that delineate broad phases of ANC history: the 1910s, formation; the 1920s, a time of experimentation; and the 1930s, a period of quiescence but also re-building.

The first chapter surveys writings on both the ANC and black workers. Workers and political activists, like most black people, faced harsh socioeconomic conditions. Chapter two outlines the growth of the working class and its organisations and struggles, to show that despite formidable obstacles that rendered impermanent most black unions and influenced the depth of ANC-worker relations, there were objective conditions favouring alliance with the ANC. Subsequent chapters provide case studies of ANC attitudes to labour at all levels of the organisation and examine the whole range of interactions between ANC and workers. I show how subjective factors either impeded or advanced contacts. Here I propose a new interpretation of the history of ANC attitudes to and connections with workers. I detail chronologically the history of these interfaces and demonstrate specific features of Congress that encouraged ties.

This history is of necessity incomplete because the histories of component parts are incomplete. The poorly developed administrative apparatus of the early ANC and the ephemeral nature of the first black unions produced an extremely dispersed and fragmentary organisational record. We can count on one hand the published autobiographies of black workers before 1940. To retrieve this hidden history I plot complex relationships using extant archival and written sources: ANC and union records; press articles; letters and official reports, published and unpublished; state and private archives; and, where available, oral sources.

A complicated and tortuous, often offensive, terminology of race has bedevilled South African history. Indigenous peoples not only lost their lands and livelihoods, but also sometimes their names. White rulers prescribed names to conquered peoples who, in turn, rejected "Native" and "Bantu" and developed their own terms of self-identification. Terminologies of identification changed. "Black" could refer both in written and popular discourse to wider groups of people, not just Africans. During the anti-apartheid era "Black" often included all oppressed peoples. In this book I use the most appropriate form for the period or organisation under discussion. Hence, "African political organisation" is used. The working class movement was segmented and its components at various times described themselves as "black workers" or "African workers" or simply workers. State legislation often aimed specifically at African, rather than wider black workers, and so it is often necessary to refer to "African unions".

There are many people to thank for realising this work. Comments by Paul La Hausse of Cambridge University, a further anonymous reader, and Raymond Suttner helped sharpen my focus. My debt to writers is clear from the footnotes but I should single out inspiration from works of Peter Walshe, Philip Bonner, Paul La Hausse, and Helen Bradford, though I expect few will agree with all I have written. Norman Etherington and Penelope Hetherington provided essential support at earlier stages. From Norman came greater appreciation of the need for rigour in historical writing and the revelation that history ought to be not only authoritative but also enjoyable.

Perceptive criticisms by readers of earlier drafts, including Phil Bonner, Paul Rich, Rob Lambert, Donald Denoon, and Cherry Gertzel saved me from inexactness and exaggeration. Colleagues at seminars at the Universities of South Africa, Western Cape, Rhodes, Fort Hare, North-West, Michigan State (MSU), Michigan, Wayne State, Toronto, Laval, Bruxelles, Western Australia, Melbourne, LaTrobe, and Deakin, and in Washington DC and Durban, gave thoughtful comments, as did referees of my journal articles. Material from "Sol Plaatje Reconsidered" (*African Studies* 62(1) 2003) is used by permission of Taylor and Francis, and from "'Representing the Labouring Classes': African Workers in the African Nationalist Press 1900-60" in Les Switzer and Mohammed Adhikari (eds.) *South Africa's Resistance Press: Alternative Voices in the Last Generation under Apartheid* is used with permission of Ohio University Press, Athens (www.ohioswallow.com). An extract of poetry from *The Nation's Bounty: The Xhosa Poetry of Nontsizi Mgqwetho* (Wits University Press, 2007) is reproduced by kind permission of Jeff Opland, the editor and translator. Graduate and undergraduate South African history students at MSU forced me to make plainer and more entertaining my ideas and their own research made me ponder more deeply the implications of nation, class, and place.

André Odendaal kindly facilitated my visit to Cape Town as a visiting fellow at Mayibuye Centre. The University of Western Australia History Department provided grants for travel to Zambia, Zimbabwe and Britain. A SADET grant for another project, on the international anti-apartheid movement, enabled me whilst in South Africa to tie up loose ends, as did trips supported by MSU. Robert Edgar, Christopher Saunders, John Wright, Chris Lowe, and Veit Erlmann kindly made available obscure works. Fred Morton, Deborah James and others shared their knowledge of regional South Africa. Joseph Lauer, MSU Africana Librarian extraordinaire, was always as supportive professionally and logistically as he was sceptical of half-baked ideas.

I highly appreciate the assistance and kindness of librarians and archivists at Wits, Unisa, ICS London, SOAS, UWA and MSU and in York, Oxford, Cape Town, Fort Hare, Pietermaritzburg, Durban, Bloemfontein, Johannesburg, and Tshwane (Pretoria). Finally, I wish to thank Sandra Dambaza for personal support at the start of this project and especially Nicole Livar for helping me see it through to the end.

Given this book's chronology and geographical breadth I have been unable to draw as much as I would have liked on oral history. I would like to thank Ashanti Nhlapo, Jabulane Matsebula, Lopang Kgomotso Motshegwa, Glen Mashinini and Nomalanga Grootboom for assistance with isiZulu, seTswana, and isiXhosa translations, and especially those ex-workers and ANC members who gave generously of their time. The South African Congress of Trade Unions in Lusaka and London, Mark Shope, "Mzala," Jack Simons, Ray Alexander, Stephen Dlamini, John Nkadimeng and Eric Mtshali kindly agreed to interviews at a busy and tense time. Over the decades, anti-apartheid activists provided inspiration. The late Govan Mbeki was particularly insistent that I should complete this work. I hope a deeper study of the ANC past will assist future researchers—and all South Africans—to appreciate this rich heritage.

1

Introduction

This is a book about the ANC in its early days, about how its politics related (or at times did not relate) to ordinary South African working peoples. It also has lessons for today's struggles, as seen in the recent leadership tussles within the ANC in which issues of class and alliance have been prominent. I paint this complex story onto a nationwide canvas but also bring to life the active agents of this history at regional and local levels. It is a story that needs to be told, because many parts of it, especially at the local level, remain hidden or largely forgotten, and because the theme has continuing significance in South Africa.

Between 1912, when the ANC formed, and the 1950s when it launched widespread defiance campaigns that greatly increased its mass support, both its membership and the number of black workers in South Africa underwent enormous growth. Writers often have chosen to emphasise the differences between these seemingly disparate political and economic spheres, but many ANC members had strong sympathies for the rights of black workers, with whom they shared common national oppression. Those more politicised workers aware of Congress viewed the ANC in different ways. Some viewed it as an important presence on the political scene; many who rose to leadership in unions and civic bodies maintained close working relations, becoming active in provincial and national ANC structures. The respective organisations at times formed temporary tactical alliances. The intensity of these interactions fluctuated greatly, from place to place, and over time.

Commentators tend to see a watershed in ANC history in the late 1940s to early 1950s, when the ANC led location discontent among township dwellers and workers into large-scale boycotts and became a mass organisation and—supposedly for the first time—forged ties with workers. But whilst ANC history and labour history have, separately, been treated extensively in South African historiography, their relationship before 1940 rarely has been subjected to detailed analysis. Generally, and sometimes with good reason, historians refer to this early period of ANC history as a time of moderation. ANC contacts with workers often seem a mere curiosity or temporary aberration.

A different story unfolds in the following pages, which is essentially a new history of the early ANC and its attitudes to workers. The paucity of historical sources on early black workers makes this book much more a history of ANC attitudes to workers than vice versa. No one has been able to write a comprehensive history of early black workers and politics, even more so of rural, domestic, or women workers and politics, because the extant sources just do not allow it. Similarly, there are very few autobiographies or even biographies of black industrial or rural or women workers at this time. Those writers, such as Helen Bradford, William Beinart, and Colin Bundy, who have toiled long in the archives and field to recapture what remains of these hidden histories, are still not able to tell us a great deal about rural or women workers' complex attitudes to, or interaction with, African politics as it relates to the ANC.[1] It is easy to allege that there were no such interactions. In the pages that follow I show that there were, and future research should uncover more.

It is symptomatic of the invisibility of workers' individual lives that actual names of African workers are virtually absent from the indexes of the two magisterial works on the Kimberley mines, and in this respect things do not improve much in the historiography of gold miners of the twentieth century. Mine workers are anonymous actors, and if academics recently have probed delicately their sex-lives and other cultural practices, then their politics before the 1940s remain hidden from view.[2]

Given the paucity of sources and the fact that those working 80 years or so ago are now largely no longer alive, it is therefore unrealistic to imagine one could write a detailed history of rural-based workers and their attitudes to the ANC, if indeed they knew of it in any detail. Nevertheless, where the sources do allow workers to speak about African politics, I give voice to this much-neglected dimension of South African history. This enables me to weave into the narrative themes of diverse identities and of regional and gender particularity, although this picture is still incomplete.

I then aim to demonstrate that ANC-worker relations were neither as one-dimensional nor as distant as many assume. When conditions favoured their interaction, some ANC members gravitated to the black labour movement and some politicised black workers tended to enjoy close ties with the ANC. By this, I do not suggest contradictions did not develop or fluctuations did not appear in these loose relations. It could not have been otherwise; contradictions and ambiguity were typical of the day.

The limited extent of black education and of class formation in early twentieth-century South Africa meant black workers (most especially mine, or farm, labourers) and ANC leaders (more particularly national figures) often were strangers to each other. The world of petitioning government was as remote for most workers as the world of the underground mineshaft was for ANC founders —but see Chapters 2-4 for instances of workers' petitions. Nonetheless, some workers looked to Congress as a political voice, and Congress often sought to articulate the nascent demands of black workers. In general, they maintained a continuing, cordial, and lively relationship even if at times specific conditions made this difficult. More often than not, the vicissitudes of these tie-ins related specifically to the nature of leadership or levels of repression.

The ANC, in theory and in practice, sought to articulate (if not always to implement) worker aspirations. Often it did this indirectly, in the sense that Congress saw black workers primarily as *Africans*, as part of its natural, national constituency, and not necessarily as *workers*. However at times Congress specifically addressed workers *qua* workers. In these senses, the articulation of labour interests that intensified in the 1950s was a continuation of looser, yet recurring, ties of previous decades. There is, I argue, more continuity in ANC-labour relationships than most historians have conceded.

By relationships, I mean the sum of a complex web of ties between the main actors in this historical drama—ANC leaders, members, supporters, and workers, labour movement activists, and union officials. The position of an ANC member relative to a worker, or attitudes of leaders to workers, could reflect diverse social forces or interdependences: class-occupation; race; ethnicity; culture; generation; ideology; fellowship; shared experience. This is important, for at times the formal organisations of workers, and Congress itself, virtually disappeared. In such periods, more subtle forces of shared ideas and traditions, the intimacies and sympathies felt for fellow oppressed Africans, came to the fore.

This book cannot claim to provide an exhaustive coverage of all ANC members or branches. But it does examine the attitudes to workers and their conditions of many leading and grassroots members with a variety of ideological views, over a considerable period of ANC history. The ANC always has had a nation-wide approach. This perhaps inclined most historians to view it as a top-down affair. Instead, reaching down to its branches precludes a focus on just a few "great men". I broaden conceptions of ANC history to challenge currently dominant interpretations that tend to reduce this rich history to that of a few *petit bourgeois* men in "top hats". I re-interpret those views not only by revisiting central leaders of the early twentieth century but also by rediscovering long-forgotten activists. In this way, I connect elite and subaltern currents of everyday accommodation and resistance. In establishing such connections, many early ANC activists acted as intermediaries. Their role was not just, as most writers on African intermediaries have imagined, an upwards mediation of the colonial state but also a downwards mediation by ANC-aligned interpreters, headmen or clergy to try to mitigate the harsh lives of African working people.[3] Similarly a single book cannot cover all workers and their attitudes to the ANC, nor deal with the totality of working class culture. Yet whilst my chief focus is on the ANC, I re-capture the views of a broad range of politically or industrially active, organised workers, especially those involved in various ways with the ANC.

Readers interested in traditional views of the early ANC as essentially "middle class" should consult works discussed below. When placed side by side with my own, these interpretations allow a nuanced appreciation of ANC history to explain continuity and change, moderation and radicalism, and middle-class and working-class input into African politics. Before analysing these themes, it is necessary to survey theoretical approaches to nation, class, race and other social forces that moulded South African history.

Notes

1   H. Bradford, *A Taste of Freedom: The ICU in Rural South Africa 1924-1930* (New Haven: Yale University Press, 1987); W. Beinart and C. Bundy, *Hidden Struggles in Rural South Africa: Politics and Popular Movements in the Transkei and Eastern Cape 1890-1930* (Johannesburg: Ravan Press, 1987).

2   R. Turrell, *Capital and Labour on the Kimberley Diamond Fields 1871-1890* (Cambridge: Cambridge University Press, 1987); W. Worger, *South Africa's City of Diamonds: Mine Workers and Monopoly Capitalism in Kimberley, 1867-1895* (New Haven: Yale University Press, 1987); V. Allen, *The History of Black Mineworkers in South Africa* (Keightly: Moor, 1992), v. 1; T.D. Moodie, *Going for Gold: Men, Mines and Migration* (Johannesburg: Wits UP, 1994).

3   B. Lawrence, E. Osborne and R. Roberts (eds), *Intermediaries, Interpreters, & Clerks: African Employees in the Making of Colonial Africa* (Madison: University of Wisconsin, 2006); P. Limb, "Intermediaries in South African Labour Relations, 1890s–1920s: Class, Nation, Gender" in P. Limb, N. Etherington and P. Midgley (eds), *Grappling with the Beast: Indigenous Southern African Responses to Colonialism* (Leiden: Brill, 2010).

Part 1

Nation, Class and Place in South African History

Perspectives on ANC-Labour History

Ideologies, Identities, and Place in South African History

The geo-spatial proximity of different black social strata and their shared national oppression and history—including resistance to oppression—facilitated ANC-worker contacts. The ANC presented its claims to political leadership as a string of implicit memories, images and shared traditions, wrapped in various ideologies. These ideologies are discussed below, and then related to class issues as they affected black labour.

The history of the ANC and black workers usually has been posed in terms of ideologies or class or, more recently, of identities.[1] They often had different ideologies, identities, or class backgrounds, but they also shared features and sought unity across differences. Identities can take diverse forms—including national, social, cultural, political, gender, imperial, and others—and can be flexible, socially constructed, and multiple. Historians of Africa agree pre-colonial Africans moved in and out of multiple identities[2] and colonial and post-colonial identities were crucial to the nationalist project. The investigation of identity helps us frame the history of movements such as the ANC in their widest sense and to see how national and other identities might be viewed from the perspective of the colonial subject or subaltern. The clarification of identities of ANC leaders helps better explain why they related to workers in ways they did. We still know relatively little about the totality of the identities of early leaders of the ANC, the most significant vehicle of African nationalism in South Africa. Important in this regard were African nationalist, liberal, imperial, and class identities.

The ANC was founded to bring together diverse cultural identities and political bodies. Colonisation had overlaid established African identities, ruptured the unity of African civil and political life, and encouraged divisions. A shared sense of British identity, respect for "British justice" and cultural sharing such as common use of English language facilitated colonial rule and helped mould outlooks of indigenous political leaders. Yet invoking of British values and liberalism by Africans did not take place without ambiguity or subversive sub-text. Unrewarded loyalty, racist attitudes, state violence, and African nationalist challenge gradually dissolved the legitimacy of colonial hegemony and encouraged African identities. The violence of colonial rule began to dissolve the "moral economy" cementing faith in Empire. ANC leaders began to understand or feel more acutely the inferior status of the subaltern even if, at first, they did so by blaming settler colonialism, not Britain. After 1910, they made Pretoria their main enemy, reserving for Britain a favoured place, either out of tactical consideration, or out of cultural loyalty.[3]

Comparative insights here are instructive. Whilst there are big differences in the nature of colonialism in South Africa and British colonies such as India or Zimbabwe, notably in the specific nature of colonial rule and form of identities, there are similarities. The forging and meshing of new identities in emergent labour and national liberation struggles was not dissimilar. In the 1920s there were similar experiments in Rhodesia and South Africa to mobilise and politicise workers who often combined class and national identities. Another similarity was the mixed identities of leaders. Mahatma Gandhi, like early ANC leaders, expressed faith in ideals of Empire and liberalism. Gandhi's assertion by the 1920s of an Indian national identity, seen for example in his turn to Indian culture and support for hand woven *dhoti* against British textiles by wearing traditional khādī, had no direct parallel in the "correct" dress of ANC leaders; a dress exhibiting "the aura of respectability" early Congress leaders "were eager to present to white and British political opinion". In this respect, the emergence of African identity was delayed by the persistence of imperial and colonial power structures. On the other hand, there was a parallel striving by the Indian National Congress and ANC to mobilise (and exert hegemony over) subaltern social strata during liberation struggles.[4] This was marked by identities of mutual solidarity in the context of economies marked by partial proletarianisation. If different class interests influenced the rate and nature of involvement in political action then nevertheless the logic of common struggle built around common identities served to unify.

Among historians the last decade has seen much preoccupation with identities, often to the exclusion of relationships between classes. But as Rajnarayan Chandavarkar and Nandini Gooptu persuasively argue for India, when the fluidity of relationships of power and political practice, and subaltern modes and perceptions of political action and power are factored into the equation, the salience of class re-emerges (see below). Similar problems of evidence recur in Indian and South African historiography with regard to workers' views of the Indian National Congress and the ANC. "Letting the subaltern speak", as Chandavarkar astutely observes in discussing the rise of the notion of "popular culture" in response to the perceived elitism of nationalist hagiography, in turn often has meant historians relying on discourses of dominant classes *about* working peoples. Moreover, no inherent solidarity existed among "subordinated classes"; divisions also were important. Thus, the emphasis of the Subaltern School on the "autonomy" of the poor and on "popular culture" explains little about the nature of relationships between Congress and the working masses, or the appeal of the former to the latter at various times; an appeal that often varied from period to period and from place to place. Such comparative insights can alert South Africanists to wider patterns. In the end, however, South Africa had its own particular historical trajectory, to which I now return.[5]

Historians often have interpreted ANC history in terms of ideologies such as liberalism, populism, and nationalism. Congress, especially before 1940, certainly employed liberal ideas in profusion. Peter Walshe stresses the multiple influences of liberalism, Christianity, and labour politics on ANC policies; Paul Rich argues that from the late 1940s it developed a new nationalism, more populist in thrust and less based upon liberalism. Many people had thought this theorising on nationalism done, but as Ivor Chipkin reminds us, debates about nationalism are very much alive in South Africa today.[6]

Yet Congress members also encountered other ideologies as divergent as Garveyism, ethnic nationalism, social democracy, and communism. They made use of such ideas and their imagery. Some ANC branches experimented with a range of ideologies and sought to articulate the desires and invoke the traditions of disparate black social formations. ANC leaders were not all cast from the same monolithic *petit bourgeois* liberal mould invoked by some historians, but came from a range of social backgrounds. Neither was ANC nationalism necessarily exclusive.

African national unity (later "African nationalism") was the ANC's *raison d'être*. Under colonial rule, this has its own multifaceted history. Explanations of this trajectory posit the emergence of a middle-class intelligentsia that articulates a nationalist ideology subsuming working classes, a model on the surface apparently confirmed by recent African history. The elite or intelligentsia, as Benedict Anderson argues, played a pivotal role in developing nationalism, particularly through the medium of print and in colonies with a stunted indigenous bourgeoisie such as South Africa, where this trend took a particular path. However, whereas Anderson, in reconsidering his analysis of nationalisms, gives closer attention to the role of the colonial state and its imaginings by way of censuses, maps, and museums, the rise of African nationalism owed as much to its own theorists and tacticians as to any external influences. Asserting this does not deny the influence of "imported" ideologies such as liberalism (and later socialism), but it does highlight African agency instead of positing a crude diffusion from the metropolis. A nascent African intelligentsia in the period from 1860 to 1910 developed letter-writing networks—and later, black newspapers—to help "contest the control of the colonial state", as Vukile Khumalo shows. Moreover, a "stunted indigenous bourgeoisie" suggests the presence of a large population of toilers. Workers were not mute. Migrant workers adopted an epistolary mode of communication; despite illiteracy, they made extensive use of letters via literate worker amanuenses and inhabited a "working-class private sphere" that was "simultaneously personal and collaborative", as Keith Breckenridge demonstrates.[7]

Such connections between workers and literate "elites" could link to the ANC, as the educated African often was a supporter of Congress. In this regard, face-to-face or organisational contacts complemented intellectual pastimes. One should not exaggerate the role of the intelligentsia in "inventing" nationalism to the total exclusion of other forces, such as "pre-modern ethnic ties".[8] Whilst intellectuals were prominent in ANC ranks there were other social strata, including workers, who had an input into ANC policy and action.

Whereas it may be valid to characterise the main tendency of pre-1949 ANC politics as liberal, it also drew upon thoughts and actions "from below". The nature of the ANC lies in the complex interplay of socio-economic and political forces. Analysis of the ANC as wholly "middle class", or wholly populist, or wholly nationalist is problematic as the colonial setting in South Africa set peculiar parameters, oppressing *all* black social strata. The ANC, in all its ramifications—branches, leaders, members, supporters, and traditions, as a *movement*—was rather *more* than middle class. It is class reductionism to try to compress the ANC, for the sake of ideological or epistemological "clarity", into a single-class mould. I do not argue here in a teleological way for schematic cross-class unity, but rather insist that it is necessary to investigate thoroughly the history of the ANC.

African nationalism became a prominent and coherent component of ANC ideology from the 1940s, but ANC leaders had earlier expressed nationalist sentiments. Objectively, the ANC before 1940 was a national movement akin to other nationalist organisations. But specific conditions in South Africa since the establishment of Union in 1910 inclined it to either seek greater influence within the state or promote basic restructuring that incorporated national aspirations of the African nation(s). Sandwiched between white colonial nationalism and British imperialism and drawing upon, but in competition with, rival ethnic nationalisms, African nationalism was indeed a complex phenomenon. I use the term to refer to the various ideological currents circulating among Africans who experienced common political oppression and articulated a countrywide striving for unity.

Nationalism exists only in relation to the state and the invention of social forces, able to be analysed "from below" to see how common people influence the principle, argues Eric Hobsbawm. Because nationalism links closely to class domination it is "not ideologically neutral", acknowledges Anthony Giddens. Nationalisms therefore rarely emerge without involvement of *both* elites and masses. John Lonsdale shows their dialectical relationship in his study of "ordinary Africans" in national movements; Basil Davidson argues it "was always the 'labouring poor' whose involvement ... gave the tribunes of the 'national struggle' ... their ground to stand on".[9] Viewed thus, nationalism is not necessarily a lofty political movement always divorced from working lives but rather a multifaceted web of ideas that might naturally find followers among workers.

The correlation of nationalism to labour is similarly complex. If we stress class differences, then we might see the ANC and black worker movements as competing struggles. Equally, we could view them as complementary movements. Merely positing class bases in worker-nationalist alliances, argues Ari Sitas, is inadequate to understand variations. He stresses that the over-emphasis on nationalist imaginings "from above" fails to explain how horizontal national identities absorb influences from "below".[10]

There were influences from above and below on emergent African nationalism. Writers often have viewed the ANC in Western terms as a movement remote from workers. There is empirical evidence to support such a view, but when the ANC is seen through black worker eyes the ties between it and workers can be more pronounced. This does not mean there was not then, or today serious disjuncture between African nationalism and the needs of workers. The ANC in its early stages can be characterised as dominated by professionals. But I show that its policies attracted other strata, including workers. Common oppression of Africans inclined the embryonic force of African nationalism towards a form of organised political resistance to racism and exploitation. This political resistance was rooted in a mass constituency largely made up of toilers even if its most vocal actors were professionals. The coercive power of the South African state created a seemingly impenetrable barrier to the flourishing of black nationalisms. This political impassability combined with economic levelling of diverse black strata to induce the sort of cross-class alliances that characterised much of ANC politics. In this context, the concept of an "elite" ANC requires closer analysis.

The term elite is relative. To some people its application to earlier years may have a nice ring of continuity with contemporary politics. However, emphasis on dissimilarities can obscure national, ethnic and regional solidarities that can cut across, or link up, different social strata. In South African history, overemphasis on a "black elite" can obscure other social forces. The concept of elite does have an empirical basis: in educational levels and property holdings or minor capital accumulation of some leading African figures—though often this was a temporary phenomenon and some of them died with modest estates, or even in poverty. Moreover, I argue that no elite is a monolith. With some African primary teachers earning less than factory workers, the mere accretion of literacy does not guarantee membership of a privileged elite, any more than, say, a literate trade union shop-steward such as Moses Kotane, also a communist, necessarily shares an "elite" membership with a budding African entrepreneur like Richard Baloyi.

This idea points to a certain weakness of concepts and their application in African history. Frederick Cooper argues that scholarship on colonial Africa influenced by post-colonial or subaltern critiques is important, but at times convoluted, logically contradictory, and conformist. Some terms often are not specified, and thus become empty of analytic power. I argue similarly in the context of South African historiography against the willy-nilly use—without regard for place, period or person—of terms like "elite" and *petit bourgeois*. Bradford in 1987 likewise warned against "strait-jacketing of struggles within extremely schematic categories … [such as] *petit bourgeois*". Indeed, those writers—notably Bonner, Bradford, and La Hausse—who have most expertly detailed and analysed the intricate texture of the intersection of class, race, and place in South African politics of the period, and upon whom I draw in this book, eschew such simplistic schemas.[11]

Even so, many if not most historians view Congress as elitist and dismiss its early history as fractured. Yet, this was a grossly deformed "elite", certainly not a *power* elite. Many regional ANC officials were not particularly elitist. Relations between ANC and African elites or between elite and subaltern strata were neither straightforward nor unchanging. A careful reading of discourses in and around Congress points to contradictory attitudes and ambiguous identities that lingered and contributed to the multifaceted social mix of contemporary South Africa. Whether seen as belonging to an African *petit bourgeoisie* (a very inexact term, as many Africans lacked effective access to the means of production), an African "elite" (but without power and, progressively, the vote), an African intelligentsia (without academies or publishing houses), or an African peasantry (without land), a more complete understanding of the life and work of African political leaders helps us better appreciate their place in history.

In this book, I use terms such as "elite" and "class" but try to define and qualify them and where possible use more precise terms such as social strata. But one thing should be made clear from the start. One could ask whether the stance in the statements about workers by ANC leaders that I cite in this book amounts to mere rhetoric. It certainly does not imply any proletarianisation process among ANC leaders, except in terms of a general decline of political and economic power of educated Africans. Even so, it does point to a process of political mobilisation. Cooper argues there "is much to learn by looking at political mobilisation within and against empire, not just in terms of a community or nation rallying against [empire]" as political movements "developed more varied repertoires, including … pan-Africanism … [or] proletarian internationalism".[12] Wherever possible given the empirical evidence, I measure ANC rhetoric against its varied actions.

Central to the process of African political mobilisation in South Africa was the attempt to forge unity in action. In the early days of the ANC, this was hardly the grand Congress Alliance of the 1950s, yet the yearning for unity could take various forms, from shaky electoral coalitions or lobbying of ginger groups to the simple assertion of a shared dignity and identity. For example, Reverend Z. R. Mahabane's Presidential Address to the 1920 Cape Congress, referring to the job colour bar, urged "restoration of our national solidarity and identity as a distinct people in the political economy of South Africa". In the pages that follow I investigate the relationships, ties, connections, solidarities—but also tensions and contradictions—between early African political leaders and their organisations on the one hand, and workers and their organisations on the other. I am concerned with both continuities and transformations in these interactions.

Africans expressed solidarity with those with whom they identified. Scholars have written little about solidarity in African history, yet it was implicitly a central pillar of anti-apartheid campaigns and rhetoric. The origin of the term lies in social obligation or legal liability. In nineteenth-century Europe, people came to equate it first with *fraternité* and then more particularly with working-class unity. What distinguishes "solidarity" from mere "co-operation" is the idea of meaningful and *ongoing* reciprocity.[13] African societies, both pre-colonial and colonial, displayed a high degree of social cohesion and mutual obligation—as seen in kin relations. These mutual obligations did not evaporate under colonialism. The ANC, I suggest, strove to bring together these social contracts.

The overlap of race and class marked intense national oppression in which potential for labour market mobility by African workers was minimal. The ANC developed in just this context. Various terms—some more analogy than precise analysis—explain this intra-national domination: "settler capitalism" or "internal colonialism" for example.[14]

The duality of cultures and powers created a deeply ambiguous context in which African political culture developed. To appreciate this, consider that ANC leaders were under enormous state pressure and scrutiny. They carried a heavy Christian-liberal ideological baggage. Yet they also employed irony and ambiguous metaphors. We can adduce cultural data to "prove" so and so was "Englished". I have dealt with the ambiguity of these matters in my works on Sol Plaatje and on how ANC leaders navigated the British World. If many top ANC figures spoke English and devoured Shakespeare then they also wrote profusely in African language columns of the black press. Founders John Dube and Pixley Seme both were hauled before the government on charges of virtual sedition for what they wrote in Zulu. Cultural accretions per se do not prove a great deal, and the way in which ANC leaders combined religion, ethnicities, cultures and politics is testimony not only to the complexity of the time and the great transitions underway, but to their ability to synthesise such diverse forces.

"Congress" (or "Kongelesi") itself became a deeply ambiguous term, implying a political gathering typical of, simultaneously, traditional African polities and modern Western parliaments, and a broad movement for equality (and later liberation). The ANC was a coming together of such approaches in which different ideologies contested in a range of discourses and struggles. These ambiguities and plural discourses perforce require that ANC documentary sources be scrutinised to transcend merely apparent meanings.

Because socialism influenced South African political bodies with close ties to workers in the period under consideration, it is germane briefly to review socialist views on nationalism. Bearing in mind Marxism's internationalism that placed class struggle above nationalism, it represented a new approach. But there was now and then a Eurocentric vein in the midst of this internationalism. *The Communist Manifesto* states: "Though not in substance, yet in form, the struggle of the proletariat with the bourgeoisie is at first a national struggle." Marxism at first was little known in South Africa. But from the 1920s, it generated intense debate among black communists. At first, some of them viewed nationalism as an affliction of a "black bourgeoisie". J. B. Marks, an ANC and Communist Party of South Africa (CPSA) leader wrote, "I fully realised the harmfulness of nationalist sentiments to which I had not been entirely immune."[15] Sometimes a distinction was made between oppressed and oppressor nationalisms. In general, articulation of such ideas and growing awareness of the wider effects of colonialism on oppressed peoples led communists, after a period of confusion, to support African national liberation.

The spread of settler capitalism involved subjugation of the colonised. It also promoted their interaction, pushing together different oppressed social strata even as reproduction of capitalist relations of production created new, antagonistic classes among them. Accompanying this trend was racial discrimination that set restrictive parameters on mobility of indigenous classes. Black workers and African nationalists found themselves in a society notorious for racism, which would lock black workers into the need for race-class alliances. This became even more necessary as white wage earners deployed invented traditions of craft exclusivism to ostracise black people from white trade unions and from the official definition of workers.[16] The effects on Africans were paradoxical—white employees were an "inspiration" with their weapons of unions and strikes, but an obstacle to black progress with their racism. This slamming of the door on joint class action—or for that matter on joint membership of social democratic parties and unions—left African workers few other potential allies than fellow black social strata and, perhaps inevitably, the ANC. The failure of (white) social democracy in South Africa created a vacuum the ANC filled. An understanding of this context is crucial to black labour history. Intense social and legal barriers, reinforced by racism, retarded the job mobility, conditions, and organisation of black workers—and made the work of the ANC harder.

ANC members therefore had to come to terms with a range of ideologies. The ANC at different times articulated its own nationalism in various ways. In *Africans' Claims* (1944), it demanded "full citizenship rights and direct participation in all the councils of the state" for Africans. The Congress Youth League (CYL) in 1946 saw African nationalism as consisting of not only philosophical, historical, democratic and ethical, but also economic elements, including "African socialism". Pallo Jordan argued in 1988 that in South Africa an African "national consciousness" was made possible when black people "were brought together into the same socio-economic milieu".[17]

This notion of a shared social landscape resonates with recent work. Hilary Sapire's description of Brakpan location encapsulates the social proximity of black strata, symbolising all black South Africa. "The small size of the ... petty bourgeoisie, the strangling of their social aspirations ... meant ... middle-class leaders were remarkably perceptive" to mass opinion. The obvious corollary is "vast areas of shared experience" with working-class neighbours. Similarly, spatial parameters and population density of the dense square mile of Alexandra combined with its local tradition of protest to facilitate African resistance to apartheid.[18] This shared experience was significant in moulding ANC-worker relations, and reinforces just how important place (or space) can be. However, consideration of inter-class association requires a clear conception of social classes.

Classes and South African History

Precise definition of social classes is crucial to my argument on ANC-worker relations, yet there is no scholarly consensus on what exactly constitute classes. For example, Poulantzas sees clerical-service workers as a "new petty bourgeoisie" whereas Braverman includes them within the working class, arguing clerical workers have long ceased to have inherent ties with capital. In South Africa, Africans worked as both manual and clerical workers. Only when the apartheid economy required a significant increase in bureaucracy did they enter clerical positions in large numbers. Whilst the harshness of labourers' working lives stands in sharp contrast to the "easy" lives of, say, teachers, racist practices impeded the upward mobility of *all* black workers. If one adopts Braverman's broader definition of working class, then the sometimes-artificial barriers supposed to exist between black *wage earners* and a (not yet fully formed) black proletariat largely evaporate.[19]

I concur with Braverman but incorporate insights of other approaches, particularly those that emphasise social dynamics. One way around the definitional problem is to stress, as do Balibar and Wallerstein, the working class as not an ideal type but a *process* of proletarianisation. Another is to emphasise, as Bourdieu does, the transverse mobility of class or, as Stedman Jones does, the lack of a "great political, cultural and economic divide" between middle and working classes so apparent in changing political discourses. Hence, it should not be assumed workers *inherently* thought or acted differently from *petit bourgeois* leaders on crucial political questions. Different black strata shared joint repression and intertwined to some extent. Working and "middle" classes accepted institutions such as churches or the ANC as their own and jointly took part in what Bourdieu terms "competitive struggle": the "form of class struggle which the dominated classes allow to be imposed on them".[20]

I define "working class" primarily in terms of its involvement in production, distribution and exchange of commodities or services; workers sell their labour power and lose control of their labour and its product. In South Africa, where many Africans retained ties to land, formation of a working class was drawn-out. Proletarianisation also involved the "making" of a working class "by itself" in the sense workers took up and fashioned culture and politics for their own use. This could involve different forms of awareness: worker consciousness, manifested in strikes; union consciousness, manifested in labour organisation; political class-consciousness, manifested in alliance with the ANC. Strikes tend to integrate into working class culture; political protests merge into political culture; when both are repressed in a colonial situation there is overlap fertile for alliance.[21]

Working class therefore refers to that body of people forced to labour for a living, having lost control of essential means of production. The industrial working class, or *proletariat*, comprises workers employed permanently or temporarily in manufacturing, mining and related sectors. *Intelligentsia* refers very specifically to people carrying on intellectual work for their living. The South African working class has various strata: urban, rural, skilled, unskilled, manual, mental. *Petit-bourgeois* own small-scale means of production. Here it will *not* refer to non-industrial wage earners simply happening to articulate "middle-class" ideology. The South African state's propensity to cultivate these social strata as an "elite" and the tendency of such people to seek upward social mobility can obscure a clear delineation of white-collar employees as workers. Moreover, this "elite" was quite powerless. I qualify these largely economic categories of class by recognition that members of any class may espouse the ideology of another class.[22]

A further important point relates to the difference between mere definitions of class and the dynamic nature of *labour movements*. As labour movements developed, they combined in dynamic tension worker activists with union representatives and labour or socialist political parties. Most labour councils, including national or regional union federations, that developed in Europe, Australia, or South Africa combined artisan with labouring unions. This became important in the political sphere. As labour movements grew, differences between artisans and labourers, whilst not disappearing, merged for political unity. Because racism skewed such bodies in South African history, historians of black labour naturally sought their sources elsewhere, but most neglected the continuing mutual needs of black labour and African nationalists when it came to the arena of politics.

Class and ideology influenced the evolution of ANC-worker relations but it also followed a synthesis of intricate political and intellectual patterns. ANC members and workers could communicate through shared languages and cultures, at meetings, via the press, through political campaigns, in fraternal bodies, even at football matches. In these diverse arenas, the ANC often claimed to represent black workers. Representation is an ambiguous term. In political science, it can refer to how representative government speaks *for* people. In a non-governmental sense, it can refer to how political bodies speak on behalf *of* their claimed constituency. Labour history, notes Reid, shows that competing social classes "brandish their own representations". I use representation to refer to how the ANC claimed to speak on behalf of black workers. The State denied the ANC participation in parliament to represent Africans, but Congress had to generate legitimacy among Africans if it was to grow. Legitimacy involves appraisal of authority expressed in terms of community values but ANC appeals to be a legitimate movement of Africans had to confront rival imperial, state, and ethnic authorities all claiming a measure of legitimacy. Moreover, as Bonner shows, ANC politics has involved ethnic dimensions.[23]

In its claim to legitimacy, the ANC simultaneously asserted its inheritance of the African past and its role as harbinger of modernity. In so doing, it claimed to represent all Africans, including workers. Because ANC leaders and activists at all levels across the country identified as Africans and also were stakeholders in various regional, ethnic, generational, and even religious and gender-based institutions or identities, class was rarely their main expression of identity. This fact, and the peculiarly incomplete nature of the process of formation of the South African working class helps explain the limited appeal of radical or socialist ideology to both black workers and other social strata; it also helps account for the inconsistency of many ANC leaders in following through on their promises of solidarity with workers. Yet, mere membership of educated or *petit bourgeois* strata did not preclude such leaders from identifying strongly with black workers' grievances.

The following chapters suggest to what extent the ANC was a legitimate vehicle of worker aspirations. Given the complexity of class and national forces, even if one assumes the ANC was a "middle-class" body, it does not follow axiomatically that it must have been isolated from workers. Detailed analysis of the extant evidence of ANC-worker interactions is required to establish firmly these claims. First, it is necessary to analyse how writers have treated the ANC and workers.

The Historiography of the ANC and of Black Workers

The extant records left by the ANC and black workers in the first part of the twentieth century are a heterogeneous and incomplete mixture of official records, journalism, and oral history. In interpreting these texts, historians have dissected class stratification within the ANC but often viewed its dealings with workers as at best irregular and based on a wish to subordinate labour to the interests of African nationalism. In doing so, they have been more concerned with analysing the fate of political tendencies within the ANC than actual ties with workers. For example historians often read the absence of socialists as confirmation of lack of proletarian credentials, yet there was no strong organic tradition of such movements among black workers. Writers portray the ANC as having developed closer labour ties only after 1940 and if recent research confirms its structures then underwent substantial reformation, pre-1940 ANC history still tends to be viewed as a long period of moderation with scant contact with workers, save in brief periods of crisis. These writers often use imprecise conceptions of class; for instance referring to any black wage earners with an education as *petit bourgeois*. The ANC is so dressed up as "middle class" that workers in its ranks are easily mistaken as *petit bourgeois*.

Before discussing how writers have portrayed the ANC and workers in South African historiography, it is necessary to explain the specific context in which this developed. Restrictions on the free growth of a black intelligentsia and literate worker culture stifled black writing and reading. By 1936, there were no major African-owned publishing houses, with the field dominated by mission presses. The ANC did not include *professional* historians in its ranks. However, in a colonial-like situation it is reasonable to view the scattered and disparate accounts by black writers as "people's history". Many early black writers, in the face of national repression and difficulties in obtaining higher education, and with few publication outlets, adopted overtly political approaches. These writers often linked up with Congress and employed black newspapers as their vehicle, publications that in turn provided a central platform for articulation of ANC policies.[24]

Contemporary Africans often were more aware of the composite mix of class and nation than later commentators were. Herbert Dhlomo, a prominent poet and CYL figure, spoke in 1945 of a "New African" class that "consists mostly of organised urban workers who are awakening ... to the power of intelligently-led mass action ... workers' strikes; organised boycotts; mass defiance of injustice—these and many more are but straws in the wind heralding the awakening of the New African masses". Dhlomo, as Tim

Couzens perceives, was quick to point to how, within this class, it was the "the rising capitalist and the highly-salaried professional men—who, feeling the pinch and frustration first, rise and lead the people". I show below how even earlier ANC leaders grappled with these issues. Whilst in much of the literature of the 1970s and 1980s the emphasis was on the prevarication of the black elite, there was little focus on their ties with workers, or to workers themselves. In part this was due to fluid—if within constricted walls—black class mobility. Couzens' splendid short survey of African leaders, based on a reading of the biographical directories of Skota and Mancoe published in the 1930s, emphasises how people like Mapikela and Mancoe moved up out of the black working class to a cosier middle stratum. Yet such people were, as Dhlomo reminds us, first to feel "the pinch and frustration" of a white state desperate to deny them political power or substantial capital accumulation. The resultant politicisation was not a novel tendency, as Etherington shows for late nineteenth-century *kholwa* (educated strata) who constituted the founding ranks of African nationalism.[25]

Historians have not always grasped the power of community, kin, and nation. The politicised black *nouveaux riches*, if quick to build bigger houses for themselves, largely inhabited the same dusty neighbourhoods, read the same newspapers, gave allegiance to the same political bodies and suffered the same repressive laws as the less "respectable". Memories of their own working days and association with less respectable compatriots could linger, whilst their wider respectability soon vanished as the state dubbed them "agitators" and had secret police tag their movements.

One way to categorise historians' views of ANC-worker ties is to contrast "insider" and "outsider" views. There is a more or less hagiographic view within ANC ranks that stresses the strategic inter-connectedness of labour and national movements, yet still paints early ANC leaders as middle class. A more self-critical approach also depicts the ANC as remote from workers. Within the latter it is possible to identify a more recent, syncretic trend that pays greater attention to ANC ties with workers, whilst remaining critical of *petit bourgeois* aspects of the organisation. Another mode of classification contrasts those who stress continuities with those stressing abrupt changes.

The contributions of ANC members to ANC historiography often were indirect. They addressed crowds and drafted brusque leaflets and submissions to commissions on behalf of Africans in general and, at times, of black workers in particular. They pondered, at ANC conventions and in the press, the ANC's potency. Together these outpourings of thought constitute African views of events. Early ANC history largely was a history of representation of black grievances. In making representations, not only did Congress insert African voices into the archives, but voices of black workers also indirectly came into earshot, though often in forums remote from worker lives such as newspapers and to government commissions—although oral communications could transmit the contents of both. ANC historiographical traditions have tended towards hagiography, seeking to minimise, for reasons of political unity, black class divisions. Within this tradition, there was room for critical propaganda. Writings on ANC history by its members chiefly explored political dimensions of this history, but also cast light on ANC-labour relations.

ANC writers gave their views on ANC—and at times, labour—history. Autobiographies by Nelson Mandela, Selby Msimang, and Alfred Bitini Xuma mention labour. Msimang, Sol Plaatje and Richard Selope Thema wrote in the black press about workers. In the 1920s, J. T. Gumede gave close support for labour rights in ANC publications. In the 1930s, Xuma wrote pamphlets on socio-economic problems affecting workers. Autobiographies of workers associated with the ANC speak directly to ANC-labour connections. Frances Baard recalled in the 1950s Africans "suffering with low wages ... joined the ANC to make these things better". Naboth Mokgatle's autobiography expressed a militant worker's frustration with timidity of ANC leaders. Ben Baartman claimed that in Worcester a worker invariably was an ANC member and vice versa.[26]

Historians often neglect the contributions of left-wing ANC members to ANC historiography. Some wrote as communists, but also addressed ANC issues. Moses Kotane, Albert Nzula, John Gomas and J. B. Marks (all with wage-earning experience) penned articles for the labour and ANC press. Kotane wrote that the "white" version of black history was "a multitude of nameless, faceless ordinary people". Elsewhere he argued ANC leadership had "always been collective". Nzula in the early 1930s wrote on ANC-worker relations. In a 1934 pamphlet Gomas reviewed the history of black workers since emancipation, noting the almost defunct ANC eventually must revive.[27]

ANC writers after 1940 took up these themes. Walter Sisulu and Nelson Mandela sought inspiration from national *and* class sources. Activist writers Jack and Ray Simons—who became ANC members when the movement opened membership to white people in 1969—expressed critical appraisal of ANC history in their synthesis of labour and political history. Their assessment of the ANC is ambiguous: a "radical liberal movement" whose petitions had "educative value, yet brought no relief". ANC leaders were "intellectuals and trade unionists". In his last published work, Jack Simons re-iterated: "The founders of the ANC were radical liberals; the ANC has never been a workers' party with a socialist programme." Ben Magubane stressed class influences on ANC politics.[28]

Francis Meli's unofficial ANC history posited a close connection between class and African nationalism. Class formation inclined black workers to see themselves as Africans "drawn into a single fraternity by their economic interest". However, early ANC leaders, if progressive for their time, were middle class; the "social composition of the ANC and its leadership ... was definitely not working class". Elsewhere Meli argued workers later "became an active factor" in the creation of African nationalism. Another contemporary ANC activist, Jabulani "Mzala" Nxumalo, characterised the early ANC as a "loosely bound" body, "out of touch with ... the masses".[29]

After 1990, ANC writers such as Govan Mbeki and John Pampalis continued to write ANC history. Pampalis' conception of classes was ambiguous; he included skilled workers as part of a *petite bourgeoisie*. Mbeki, if acknowledging intellectuals provided early ANC leadership, maintained in *Learning from Robben Island* that it was representative of *all* classes of African society. He argued that by the late 1950s most members were "urban working class". He also suggested that earlier lack of access to ANC archives inclined historians to stress discontinuities in its history.[30]

Some of these writers claim close ties between the ANC and workers; others stress their social distance. Most are ambiguous about continuity of class influences in ANC history. They emphasise continuity of ANC struggles but do not pay close attention to the nature of ANC-worker interactions before 1940. Rather they stress the shift to a more mass-based ANC in the 1950s. Hence many of them tend to perpetuate the idea of a "middle-class" Congress despite their wish to highlight its broad, multi-class appeal. Neither do they show great precision in definition of classes. These problems also appear in commentators on ANC history outside of Congress Alliance ranks.

Peter Walshe's *Rise of African Nationalism in South Africa* remains the most detailed history of pre-1952 ANC structures and politics. He charted the diverse ideological and class forces in Congress, stressing that the early ANC drew "the great proportion of its members from the new 'middle class'", without ever clearly defining this class, but appreciating the ebb-and-flow of contacts between ANC and labour. African nationalism, in his view, was a political movement largely promoted from above, but with working class influence noticeable and growing more pronounced by the 1950s. Yet he is more concerned with ideologies and incompletely renders the complex "hidden histories" of many lower-level ANC figures and structures.[31]

Other writers stressed ANC alienation from workers. The ANC, claimed Edward Feit, was unsympathetic to workers and only reluctantly became involved in their struggles in the 1950s. A reluctance to probe worker conceptions of nationalism or detailed responses of lower-level ANC structures to labour struggles means such liberal views often fail to explain the warp and weft of class-national alliances. Other, more radical, writers share the view that ANC leaders deleteriously influenced the growth of black unions. Robert Fine blamed the ANC-led Congress Alliance for retarding black unionisation. Rob Lambert concurred, but perceived that workers increasingly influenced the ANC.[32]

Some writers have contested such views. André Odendaal pointed to the sometimes-close ties between political groups and different social strata, including workers. He argued the historiography has neglected continuity of "African national orientation" in black politics. David Carter rejected Feit's assertion that higher education levels of ANC leaders equate mechanistically to "bourgeois" influence. He showed workers were the largest occupational group in the 1952 Defiance Campaign in the Eastern Cape and Transvaal.[33]

These debates should remind researchers we should not assume labour was inherently "radical"; even if the racial-capitalist regime in South Africa *objectively* situated black workers at the centre of exploitation, *subjectively* wage earners might adopt a range of opinions on politics and industrial relations depending on their particular consciousness, their various identities, and their perception of their freedom to organise themselves.

The varied ideological influences on the ANC also have been explicated. Tom Karis saw subtle changes taking place in ANC structures from 1937-49 that were to see its gradual re-organisation and then, in 1952, transformation "into an embryonic mass movement". Gail Gerhart argued that the "middle class" dominated ANC leadership by 1950 but observed it had a "sprinkling of Marxists". Paul Rich drew out gradual changes in ANC ideology over the decades in his study of liberal influences on a section of the "African petty bourgeoisie". The ANC was radicalised under the impact of the CYL and unionisation but its liberal aim of incorporation of Africans into a common society remained influential; during the Congress of the People campaign of the 1950s the ANC was only able to gain sporadic involvement of workers, he argues – 1950s politics proved fertile ground for others to plumb the short-term origins of the Congress Alliance.[34]

If scholars have extensively charted ideological influences on the ANC then we cannot say the same of the lives of its diverse members, a lacuna that this study seeks to partly rectify. Nevertheless, extant biographical studies of ANC leaders do reveal class influences at work. Shula Marks focused on the political ambiguity of A. W. G. Champion and John Dube in the face of state domination and mass pressure. Brian Bunting's biography of Moses Kotane captured the simultaneous pull of nationalist and socialist thought. Brian Willan's magisterial study of Sol Plaatje concluded early ANC leaders were "not seriously concerned" with workers. Doreen Musson's life of John Gomas incorporated his role in the ANC, which she identified with the "black petty bourgeoisie". Steven Gish's splendid biography of A.B. Xuma did depart from the view of a middle- class leader by stressing his transcendence of narrow class interests in support of the rights of Africans but, beyond Xuma's nationalistic inclusivity, does not fully explain his interest in workers, and at times speaks of class in imprecise terms, such as an "African educated class".[35]

Studies of ANC nationalism commented on broader social ties of the movement. Apollon Davidson argued that early ANC intellectuals remained close to the people; Adam Kuper claimed class differences between workers and ANC ensured it was not deeply involved with labour. Marks and Trapido, if aware that "in a colonial situation a group's class position offers no certain guidance to its political affiliation", nevertheless painted the ANC of the 1940s as dominated by an "urban-based intelligentsia" that *constituted* the ANC—without delineating the precise nature of ANC membership.[36]

Tom Lodge, in an impressive series of studies, located ANC nationalism more within community-class struggles. He showed its leaders tended to be drawn from relatively more prosperous social strata. Early leaders feared being driven back into the ranks of workers; rank-and-file were "lower middle class". ANC urban growth was erratic but increased to acquire a working-class social base in the 1950s. Surveying the history of ideologies in the ANC he spoke of the rupturing effect of abrupt changes on "middle-class" intellectual tradition; yet the ANC represented "a nascent African bourgeoisie".[37]

ANC engagement with workers often is dated from the late 1940s or early 1950s. O'Meara portrayed the ANC of the 1930s as "a disorganised organ of petty bourgeois protest", yet capable of being transformed in the 1940s "into the political movement of a class alliance". Luli Callinicos saw ANC mobilisation of "the masses" as dating from 1949; before then it was a "middle class elite party". Fine argued that in the 1930s it "had little support outside a small middle class circle". Baruch Hirson asserted that in the 1930s-40s its leaders were isolated from workers.[38]

This tendency to portray the pre-1949 ANC as "middle class" is not restricted to outsiders. I have already noted the views of Meli and Simons. Mary Benson, who worked with the ANC, saw its forerunners as "an élite party of middle-class intellectuals". Today authors generally accept the early ANC *must* have been middle class. In a recent collection, Phil Mtimkhulu characterised the pre-1940 ANC as having a "poor mass base"; Devan Pillay called it "moderate and passive". To James Zug, the ANC "refrained from direct political action", and its work, apart from annual conventions, was marked by "silence".[39]

Among writers who focus on the pre-1940 period, terms such as "middle class" often are used in ways that contradict these writers' own appreciation of the commonality of black conditions. Alan Cobley elucidated the internal stratification of African middle strata, showing that many early ANC leaders were involved in business. He included in this "occupational elite" not only doctors and other professionals but also senior clerks, journalists and certificated teachers but was careful to place "lesser white-collar jobs and skilled manual jobs" (such as uncertified teachers, shop assistants, and printers) on the *margins* of the elite. The term is doubly appropriate, as Paul La Hausse's use of "marginalised elite" suggests. I exclude them from the elite proper.[40]

Many of these historians can misread ANC historic ties to workers, which they may see as one-dimensional: workers *versus* nationalists, instead of workers both allying and arguing with nationalists or vice versa. Yet the most detailed histories of the ANC, by Walshe, Lodge, and Meli, acknowledge the role of workers within the ANC—with due recognition of their limited power. Moreover, writers dealing with the ANC's origins, such as Odendaal, emphasise continuities in ties between Congress and different social strata.

There is no need here to recapitulate the works of these fine writers: the middle-class credentials of many ANC leaders of the pre-1940 period and their political twists and turns are well known. However new trends in ANC and regional historiography give more attention to working-class influences at local levels, widening the appreciation of the ANC's contacts with workers and gradually pushing back the date of these influences. Bonner's analysis of the volatile nature of early Transvaal Congress leadership and its ties to workers at a time of economic crisis during and after World War I revealed how many-sided class and political forces impacted upon the movement. Willie Hofmeyr argued that ANC branches in Western and Southern Cape rural towns in the late 1920s and early 1930s "became fully involved in popular struggles" of workers; the ANC cannot be dismissed as "just another petty bourgeois nationalist movement". Peter Delius revealed that some migrant workers retained rural links via the ANC in the 1940s.[41]

This rural dimension is important in any attempt to write a national history of these interactions. In the pre-World War II period, rural-based social forces, if only occasionally and irregularly, at times linked up with ANC structures or individuals. Yet, already in the 1930s, Govan Mbeki detected in the lack of a firm countryside base a basic weakness of the liberation movement, which he felt "must go and organise in the rural areas". Congress did try and cultivate rural ties but in general its lack of a strong rural base was a nationwide trend that persisted for decades. In any case, the "working class" in rural areas was itself in a very formative stage; and so was the ANC: neither could rely on permanent structures. It is not surprising therefore, as Beinart and Bundy have shown, that parochialism and misunderstanding often prevented the ANC from consummating nascent ties.[42]

Still, the forging of tentative working relations in joint resistance to oppression, or in acts of solidarity, had the potential to establish a symbolic presence enabling the memory of Congress to linger. This could encourage individuals to join the movement. A good example of this process was the joining of Congress in the 1920s by young activists who remembered its vigorous protests in 1918-20. In turn, leaders of those protests themselves had been inspired by a previous generation of Congress-aligned protestors. Therefore it can be inexact to point to single "flash" of Congress history to prove more general inactivity.

Similarly, ANC urban history needs close reading. Sapire astutely observed that an overly "institutional focus" and neglect of "economic and social matrixes of urban social and political movements" obscured from history "urban constituencies, idioms of protest, ideologies and forms of consciousness which fed into the overall mass political culture". In her regional study of Brakpan in the 1940s-50s, she pointed to growing ANC contact with workers. Janet Cherry argued that in the same period there was a meshing of ANC and union struggles in Port Elizabeth where the ANC "was working class in its leadership, its mass base, and its style of organisation".[43]

This meshing of histories of class, nation, region, and race has created a more realistic and nuanced narrative of African politics that highlights the influences of social identity, culture, and place. Recent general histories indicate a growing acknowledgement by historians that even if the ANC was "suspicious of mass politics" then "nevertheless, they were drawn into broader representations". However, there is still a tendency to highlight the role of external bodies, notably the CPSA or ICU, rather than comprehensively to analyse the ANC's own interconnections to workers.[44]

Provincial and biographical studies can bring together rural and urban histories. La Hausse's biography of local ANC activists in Natal integrates African and Zulu nationalism, land, class, elites, religion, and traditionalism. He takes issue with historians whose over-arching characterisations of a black *petit bourgeoisie* have induced neglect of their wider political culture.[45] Yet, ironically, despite his magnificent portraits of two hitherto obscure figures, we still await full-blown biographies of more seminal ANC figures. And we still lack scholarly histories of the ANC in the provinces. To this end, in the chapters that follow, I stitch together social and biographical portraits of a myriad of ANC and labour figures and connect them in the history of ANC regional and national bodies. There is good reason to structure the narrative in this way as it was along these lines that the ANC organised, and it was mostly at this level that they made contact or appeals to workers.

There are some excellent studies of urban and rural-based regional ANC leaders, notably by Beinart and Bundy. Lungisile Ntsebeza also uncovers aspects of Cape African political history, yet his recent study of local politics and chiefs in Xhalanga, Transkei, fails to notice the presence of the Transkeian ANC in the 1920s. In part, the continuing lack of awareness of historical continuities reflects the dearth of regional political histories, the rectification of which this study partially seeks to correct.[46]

Many historians seem satisfied with the simple axiom that the ANC before the turn to mass action in 1949 was "middle class". But by exaggerating pre-1940 ANC timidity and aloofness from workers, writers adopt a somewhat mechanistic argument about wartime changes stimulating working class expansion and political ferment to explain the ANC's later move to the "masses". If ANC-oriented historiography has emphasised "organised national struggles with a focus on heroes" and downplaying class, then conversely, labour history has tended to ignore national resistance, suggests Callinicos. Indeed, the story of black workers, observed unionist J. Phendlani in 1967, simply was "not told in school history books". Instead, memories, books written chiefly by white people, and scattered reminiscences and analyses by unionists kept this history alive.[47]

Early labour histories, such as that by E. Gitsham and J. Trembath, were influenced by prevailing white worker racism and tended to depict labour history merely as a chronology of white strikes. Early Marxist writers on South Africa, including Tom Mann, D. I. Jones and S. P. Bunting, began to see black workers as the central political force. By the late 1920s, black communists were writing on these issues in the left press. Communist veterans Eddie Roux, and then Jack and Ray Simons, explored in more detail connections between labour and the ANC. Roux's pioneering work, at first in the communist press and later as books, not only chronicled for posterity many interesting intersections between the ANC and the labour movement, but also began to raise some problematic issues of this history. Marxist-influenced writers within the ANC, such as Govan Mbeki and Meli, incorporated class themes into ANC history.[48]

These "writer activists" engaged more with politics than history writing. Moreover, as Premesh Lalu argues, the framework of the CPSA press remained Eurocentric and did not transcend state discourses in the sense of positing a purely urban, male, industrial proletariat. However, this does not mean all these early writers were of a drab, uniform mould or necessarily wrote hagiographic African nationalist histories—indeed, some of them give as much, if not more attention to class as nation, but all were thoroughly committed to the national liberation struggle. Some, such as Roux, began to explore the role of language, others such as Mbeki (as noted above) began to analyse rural societies, and Simons later wrote on African women. At times, their intimacy with African liberation and labour movements enabled them to better understand the texture of struggle on the ground.[49]

Professional historians continued to engage, in a more detached way, with the intersection of nation and class. A wave of radicalism, influenced by the light shed on Marx's own conceptualisation of classes by the work of E.P. Thompson, Nicos Poulantzas and Louis Althusser, swept over South African labour historiography in the 1970s and early 1980s. Frederick Johnstone and others explored job colour bars and proletarianisation, uncovering a great deal about state labour policies and proposing new periodisations of economic history. Yet little emerged of workers' attitudes to the ANC. Writers such as Bradford and Peter Wickins on the ICU, and Lambert and Bonner on the politics of unionism did, however, further elaborate union history and this now encompassed its ties with community and ANC struggles. Still, most writers emphasised the social distance between workers and ANC.[50]

Meanwhile, historians such as Tim Keegan and Dunbar Moodie fused class analysis with a social history approach stressing African agency, culture, and history "from below" that helped them re-create individual working lives with great sensitivity. The combination of these insights with research into ethnic or kin-based networks and localised instances of worker protest revealed subtle nuances of class, community, and national consciousness. More recently, the history of generational and gender contradictions *within* African societies, and how this relates to labour issues, has been explicated. There were, in some of these studies, treatments of the ANC. Beinart, in a case study of a migrant worker, argued that the worker's rural-urban, class-national ideas "proved most useful" to the ANC.[51]

These rural-urban connections are important. Many urban workers retained ties with rural areas, some preferred payment in cattle; others combined wage labour with farming. However, the level of industrialisation in South African meant there is considerable evidence of gradual proletarianisation, much more so than in other African countries. The historical record has left relatively little trace of the views on ANC politics of rural dwellers or mineworkers. Wage earners in areas such as manufacturing, clerical work, and teaching were among those who tended to hear about the ANC, if sporadically, but I also present cases where the ANC sought, even less regularly, to reach rural dwellers.

Historians have incompletely documented the history both of women involved with the early ANC and African women workers. Exceptions include Iris Berger's study of factory workers and Julia Wells's analysis of the role of women in anti-pass actions. Insights come from Frances Baard's memoirs. Belinda Bozzoli's study of educated Bafokeng domestic workers probed their lives and attitudes to the ANC. Despite a reluctance to abandon prevailing notions of a "middle-class" ANC, Bozzoli conceded that in the 1950s it was able successfully to enter "into the mind" of some working-class women. But overall there is little on pre-1940 struggles; Cynthia Kros begins her study

African women protest passes, 1913

(that excludes unions) of African women's organisations in Johannesburg only in the later 1930s for this reason. She observes that in South African society black middle-class women have only "marginal advantages" over working class women, who share geographical near-proximity and with class interests often blurred in politics. Wells does treat women workers as part of the 1913 anti-pass protests. It is indicative of this gap that a recent chapter by Berger on women and unions from 1930 to 1960 barely mentions *African* women before World War II.[52]

One of the great unknowns of South African historiography remains the intersection of women with early ANC politics. Women are largely absent from early ANC history, largely due to the paucity of sources but also because the organisation did not facilitate direct female membership until the 1940s, limiting women's potential involvement. Even so, and as Frene Ginwala and Nomboniso Gasa show, women (including workers) became involved in protests, and in actions *around* Congress, often through the medium of bodies established as women's self-help groups. Below I highlight such occasions but more work is needed in this area. As Cherryl Walker observes, across Africa women's solidarity appears more pronounced among working, than middle, strata. Susan Geiger finds that in colonial Tanzania, ordinary women formed a vital, if not chronicled, component of African nationalism and that women need to be seen not just as *women* nationalists, but as nationalists in their own right. In this regard, a thorough history of the Bantu National Women's League and its involvement with working women is long overdue.[53]

African workers and their early unions left few written records and these are chiefly in English, though this was rarely the language most workers spoke. However, oral history increasingly fleshes out workers' hidden lives. For example, Eddie Webster let foundry workers speak for themselves. Luli Callinicos employed interviews with workers such as Elias Motsoaledi to illustrate how they regarded the ANC. Thiathu Nemutanzhela dealt with how ANC-CPSA leader Alpheus Maliba exploited oral traditions in a style that enabled rural workers to relate better to working class and national movements.[54]

Despite such epistemological and theoretical advances, ambiguous definitions of class continue to bedevil the historiography. For many writers, "middle class" still includes skilled workers such as artisans, or occupations with considerable internal wage differentials, such as black teachers. There are good reasons to reconsider such categorisation. The contemporary chasm between the poor/ unemployed and wage earners, played out in economic crises, reinforces this notion. Yet it is not always clear in such crises at what stage say, a "middle class" employee becomes déclassé or a worker. Moreover, the changing nature of the economy (such as the need for more clerical or skilled labour) is not always factored into such classifications. As Jocelyn Kirk cogently argues, we need to be alert to the changing meaning of class categories over time and understand the tenuous nature of "economic separation between and among the African working and middle class". Kirk's case study of late nineteenth-early twentieth-century Port Elizabeth may not be applicable across South Africa, but she demonstrates how black middle *and* working classes united in opposition to racism and exploitation. Here, Maynard Swanson's suggestion is apposite: perhaps the argument over the petit-bourgeois nature of African leaders is not necessary, for at the time they envisaged "a broader social purpose" in realisation of their aims.[55]

Most studies surveyed above view the ANC as remote from workers, often sharing the notion, at times ill defined, of the ANC's unproblematic "elite" class nature. Many prefer to talk in terms of *petit-bourgeois* leaders without clarifying class definitions, yet use class orientation freely to characterise ANC politics. There is a tendency to conflate the ANC as a wider movement with a small coterie of more elitist leaders. Rarely have historians given systematic analyses of the full class influences on ANC leaders; nowhere is this more glaring than in the dearth of scholarly social biographies of early ANC activists. Gaps abound in our understanding of the workings of local ANC branches and few writers comprehensively integrate the totality of ANC contacts with workers into ANC history or account for marked regional variations in such ties.

What then would have been the motivation for ANC interest in workers? Was it simply political expediency, a tactical need for African nationalism to garner all possible support, a motive enhanced by the strategic position of African workers in the economy? Or was it the desire of the mission-educated African liberal elite to "uplift" their less-educated compatriots?[56] Alternatively, perhaps, was it an article of a different kind of faith, of solidarity rooted in nation and nourished in common oppression across class?

African nationalism (and its predecessors) in South Africa had great need for allies and I will describe in some detail the form this search for support took. It is similarly undeniable that Cape liberalism and the deeply religious persuasion of much of the black elite gave early black political leaders an almost condescending approach wanting to "uplift" their compatriots. And yet, the position of this elite, as we shall see, was itself most precarious. To imply a simplistic motivation to Congress as a whole is not only to ignore other important ideological influences on the ANC. It also is to misunderstand the complex relations between different social classes in a colonial society marked by deep cleavages. It sets up a virtual parody of African leaders, one that denies them a more secular view of national or "race" solidarity, and can even deny them agency in some social arenas.

The extant historical sources on this period are much richer on the ANC than workers. I try to compensate for this by focusing squarely on ANC labour policy and *relationships* between ANC and working peoples. If in the end I write more about ANC personalities than "true" workers then this reflects just these sources. Elsewhere, I have written of the broader identities of the ANC of this period and above-mentioned writers, notably Walshe, have detailed its broader policies and ideologies. I do not therefore repeat these narratives, except to situate the study, but I do relate the ANC-labour relationship back to these wider concerns.

South Africa Today

The unbanning of the ANC and its assumption of state power blew away the censorship that had prevented some aspects of the serious study of ANC history. Since 1994, the new political dispensation in pursuit of non-racial democracy has encouraged research into the multiple identities of citizens and there has been a wealth of recent studies of ANC figures, most notably in the form of memoirs. However, there are still big gaps in ANC and labour history, and obstacles to effective further research.

We still know relatively little of the lives of provincial leaders and rank-and-file of the ANC, the most significant vehicle of African nationalism. There are no comprehensive provincial ANC histories, with the pre-history of ANC Women and Youth sections not chronicled. These lacunae are odd, given the reliance of the liberation movement on "people's history", but I ascribe it several causes. Firstly, in the 1990s many historians (most of them white) were reluctant to embrace ANC history. This was a period marked by the joy and trauma of reconciliation and the temporary relegation from school curricula of Historical Studies. Ironically, the Rainbow Revolution and reconciliation of the 1990s simultaneously confronted these traumas whilst turning its back on history. There was an understandable need to forget the past and let wounds heal. Secondly, the inevitable "turn" of intellectual fashion saw the triumph in the Academy of a cultural history relatively uninterested in either labour or political history, and certainly not the nationalism "tainted" by hagiography of the 1960s and 1970s. Thirdly, the persistence of certain stereotypes among some historians of African political movements—notably the view of a largely "elite" ANC—inclined many authors to ignore its wider socio-political dimensions. Fourthly, early ANC and labour history has tended to be *separately* treated; their relationships rarely brought together and subjected to detailed analysis. Fifthly, the decline of socialism and alleged "end of history", together with a relatively peaceful transition in South Africa in the 1990s, meant classes were no longer so important to study. Finally, "resistance" was now somehow old-fashioned, tainted by prior African nationalist hagiography, even if the detailed history of resistance had barely begun.[57]

All this produced a situation where, at the very time one would have expected an upsurge in black interpretations of the ANC, there were few. Regrettably, black voices are still somewhat absent from the chorus of historians. Without the development of a whole new generation of black historians and political scientists, prospects for further research into the ANC in all its facets will stagnate. However, now history is back on the curriculum, with some new black appointments made, and the SADET Project[58] giving guernseys to up-and-coming young black historians still outside the Academy.

In the context of a free South Africa, it is more necessary than ever to *synthesise* the work of four decades of history writing, especially on class and nation, but also dealing with gender and place. Some may disagree with my focus, or my insistence on detail; some will accuse me of bringing grist to the nationalist mill. Others may say I present too little of the voices of rural peoples or women about African politics. However, let us first view the empirical data so long hidden, and for those with more evidence of such voices, please step forward. Bernard Magubane points to the backhanded dismissal of the history of African nationalism by many liberals and neo-radicals. At the same time, South African history writing, as Christopher Saunders observes, is now much more diffuse and hard to categorise.[59] In this tangled web, there is a danger not only of neglecting the class but also the national dimensions of history, and of throwing out the gains of the radical baby with the liberal bathwater.

It is therefore timely to examine who in the ANC claimed to speak on behalf of workers and why. ANC-labour connections need plotting carefully over the decades. The formative period 1912–1940 especially stands in need of such a corrective. We should see ANC attitudes and policies towards labour in all their diversity, as previous studies have been sketchy or partial. More understanding is required of the ANC as a dynamic movement, not as a monolithic structure. There is still no detailed survey of ANC-worker interactions, no explanation of shifts in these relations over time. Historians have well treated discontinuities in these ties, but not continuities. There is, therefore, no good reason to rehearse the well-known contours of ANC history. Instead, I adduce below much evidence to show the ANC as very much interested in the whole question of black labour. When I map these viewpoints, policies, and actions on a large, nationwide canvas and across time, relations are far less hegemonic than previous writers have suggested. Before doing so, and to underline the rationale for this book, it is necessary to appreciate the centrality of black labour in South African society.

Notes

1   P. Walshe, *The Rise of African Nationalism in South Africa: The African National Congress 1912-1952* (London: Hurst, 1970); P. Limb, "Early ANC Leaders and the British World: Ambiguities and Identities", *Historia* 47 (2002), pp. 56-82.

2   T. Ranger, "The Invention of Tradition in Colonial Africa", in E. Hobsbawm and T. Ranger (eds.), *The Invention of Tradition* (Cambridge: Cambridge University Press, 1983), pp. 211-262, p. 248.

3   C. Saunders, "African Attitudes to Britain and the Empire before and after the South African War", in D. Lowry (ed.), *The South African War Reappraised* (Manchester: Manchester University Press, 2000), pp.140-149; R. Ross, *Status and Respectability in the Cape Colony 1750-1870* (Cambridge: Cambridge University Press, 1999), pp. 43, 119.

4   G. Vahed, "'African Gandhi': The South African War and the Limits of Imperial Identity" *Historia* 45 (2000), pp. 201-219; R. Ross, *A Concise History of South Africa* (Cambridge: Cambridge University Press, 1999), p. 86; B. Raftopoulos and I. Phimister (eds.) *Keep on Knocking: A History of the Labour Movement in Zimbabwe 1900-1997* (Harare: Baobab, 1997); R. Guha, "Discipline and Mobilize" in P. Chatterjee and G. Pandey (eds.) *Subaltern Studies VII* (Delhi: Oxford University Press, 1992) pp. 69-120.

5   N. Gooptu, *The Politics of the Urban Poor in Early 20th-Century India* (Cambridge: Cambridge University Press 2001); R. Chandavarkar, *Imperial Power & Popular Politics: Class, Resistance and the State in India, c1850-1950* (Cambridge: Cambridge University Press, 1998), pp. 266-273. Cf. P. Limb, "The ANC and the Indian National Congress: A Comparative History", African Studies Association conference paper, Washington DC, 2002.

6   Walshe, *Rise of African Nationalism*; P. Rich, *Hope and Despair: English-Speaking Intellectuals and South African Politics 1896-1976* (London: British Academic, 1993), pp. 92-93; I. Chipkin, *Do South Africans Exist? Nationalism, Democracy and the Identity of 'The People'* (Johannesburg: Wits University Press, 2007), p. 11.

7   B. Anderson, *Imagined Communities* (London: Verso, 1983), pp. 13-15, 137, and 2nd edition (1991); A. D. Smith, *Nationalism: Theory, Ideology, History* (Oxford: Polity, 2001), p. 68; V. Khumalo, "Epistolary Networks and the Politics of Cultural Production in KwaZulu-Natal, 1860 to 1910", Ph.D. thesis University of Michigan, 2005, p. 189; K. Breckenridge, "Love Letters and Amanuenses: Beginning the Cultural History of the Working Class Private Sphere in Southern Africa, 1900-1933," *Journal of Southern African Studies* [hereafter *JSAS*] v. 26 (2000), pp. 337-348, p. 348.

8   A.D. Smith, "The Nation: Invented, Imagined, Reconstructed?", in M. Ringrose and A. Lerner (eds.), *Reimagining the Nation* (London: Open University, 1993), pp. 9-28, p. 23.

9   E. Hobsbawm, *Nations and Nationalism since 1780* (Cambridge: Cambridge University Press 1990), pp. 5-11; A. Giddens, *The Nation-State and Violence* (Oxford: Polity, 1985),

p. 121; J. Lonsdale, "Some Origins of Nationalism in East Africa," *Journal of African History [hereafter JAH]* v. 9 (1968), pp. 119-146; B. Davidson, *The Black Man's Burden* (London: J. Currey, 1992), pp. 163-166.

10   A. Sitas, "Class, Nation, Ethnicity in Natal's Black Urban Working Class", *Societies of Southern Africa in the 19th and 20th Centuries Collected Seminar Papers [hereafter SSA]* 38 (1990), pp. 257-278, p. 267.

11   F. Cooper, *Colonialism in Question: Theory, Knowledge, History* (Berkeley: University of California Press, 2005); Bradford, *Taste of Freedom*, pp. 15-16; P. Bonner, "The Transvaal Native Congress 1917-1920: The Radicalisation of the Black Petty Bourgeoisie on the Rand," in S. Marks and R. Rathbone (eds.), *Industrialisation and Social Change in South Africa* (London: Longman, 1982), pp. 270-313; P. La Hausse, *Restless Identities: Signatures of Nationalism, Zulu Ethnicity and History in the Lives of Petros Lamula (c. 1881-1948) and Lymon Maling (1889-c. 1936)* (Pietermaritzburg: University of Natal Press, 2000).

12   Cooper, *Colonialism in Question*, Introduction.

13   A. Wildt, "Solidarity: Its History and Contemporary Definition" and K. Metz, "Solidarity and History" in K. Bayertz (ed.), *Solidarity* (Dordrecht: Kluwer, 1999), pp. 209-220, 191-207; P. Limb, "Apartheid, Solidarity, and Globalisation: Lessons from the History of the Anti-Apartheid Movements", paper to International Conference on a Decade of Freedom, Durban, Oct. 2004.

14   D. Denoon, *Settler Capitalism* (Oxford University Press, 1983); H. Wolpe, "The Theory of Internal Colonialism: The South African Case", in I. Oxaal (ed.), *Beyond the Sociology of Development* (London: Routledge, 1975), pp. 229-252; *Apartheid South Africa: Colonialism of a Special Type* (London: ANC, 1980).

15   E. Nimni, "Marx, Engels and the National Question", *Science & Society* v. 53 (1989), pp. 297-326; K. Marx and F. Engels, *Manifesto of the Communist Party, Selected Works* v. 1 (Moscow: Progress, 1969), pp. 100, 118-120; J.B. Marks, "Breaking the Shackles", *African Communist [hereafter AC]* 51 (1972), pp. 10-11.

16   E. Bonacich, "Capitalism and Race Relations in South Africa: A Split Labor Market Analysis", *Political Power and Social Theory* v. 2 (1981), pp. 239-278; H. Wolpe, *Race, Class and the Apartheid State* (London: Currey, 1988), p. 52; R. Davies, *Capital, State and White Labour in South Africa 1900-1960* (London: Harvester, 1979), pp. 361-365.

17   *Africans' Claims in South Africa* (Johannesburg: ANC, 1944); A. Lembede, "Some Basic Principles of African Nationalism", *Inyaniso* (Feb. 1945); P. Jordan, "The South African Liberation Movement and the Making of a New Nation", in M. van Diepen (ed.), *The National Question in South Africa* (London: Zed Press, 1988), pp. 110-124, p. 112.

18   H. Sapire, "African Political Organisation in Brakpan in the 1950s", *African Studies* v. 48 (1989), pp. 183-207, pp. 184, 199, "African Urbanisation and Struggles against Municipal Control in Brakpan 1920-1958", Ph.D. thesis, University of the Witwatersrand [Wits], 1988 p. xi; T. Lodge, *Black Politics in South Africa since 1945* (London: Longman, 1983); B. Bozzoli, *Theatres of Struggle and the End of Apartheid* (Edinburgh: Edinburgh University Press, 2005); D. Curry, "Community, Culture and Resistance in Alexandra, South Africa, 1912-1985", Ph.D. thesis, Michigan State University, 2005.

19   N. Poulantzas, *Classes in Contemporary Capitalism* (London: Verso, 1978); H. Braverman, *Labor and Monopoly Capitalism* (New York: Monthly Review, 1974), pp. 316, 355-378; E. Webster, *Cast in a Racial Mould: Labour Process and Trade Unionism in the Foundries* (Johannesburg: Ravan Press, 1985).

20   E. Balibar and I. Wallerstein, *Race, Nation, Class: Ambiguous Identities* (London: Verso, 1991), p. 11; R. Jenkins, *Pierre Bourdieu* (London: Routledge, 1992), pp. 140-141;

G.S. Jones, *Languages of Class: Studies in English Working Class History 1832-1982* (Cambridge: Cambridge University Press, 1983), pp. 183-185.

21 E.P. Thompson, *The Making of the English Working Class* (London: Penguin, 1968), pp. 8-10, 211-213; J. Krikler, *Revolution from Above, Rebellion from Below: The Agrarian Transvaal at the Turn of the Century* (Oxford: Clarendon Press, 1993), pp. vii, 2-3; F. Fisher, "Class Consciousness among Colonized Workers in South Africa" in T. Adler (ed.) *Perspectives on South Africa* (Johannesburg: African Studies Institute [hereafter ASI], 1977), pp. 300-352; M. Perrot, *Workers on Strike: France, 1871-1890* (New Haven: Yale University Press, 1987).

22 B. Nzimande, "Class, National Oppression and the African Petty Bourgeoisie: The Case of the African Traders", in R. Cohen, Y. Muthien and A. Zegeye (eds.) *Repression and Resistance: Insider Accounts of Apartheid* (London: Zell, 1990) pp. 165-209 p. 182; T. Nyquist, *Toward a Theory of the African Upper Stratum in South Africa* (Athens, OH: Center for International Studies, 1972), p. 55: cf. L. Dreyer, *The Modern African Elite of South Africa* (London: Macmillan, 1989).

23 J. Dunn, "The Politics of Representation and Good Government in Post-Colonial Africa", in P. Chabal (ed.), *Political Domination in Africa* (Cambridge: Cambridge University Press, 1986), pp. 158-174; B. Berman and J. Lonsdale, *Unhappy Valley* (London: Currey 1992), Chapters 9, 12; D. Reid, *Paris Sewers and Sewermen* (Cambridge Mass.: Harvard University Press, 1991), p. 87; A. Ashforth, *The Politics of Official Discourse in Twentieth-Century South Africa* (Oxford: Clarendon, 1990), p. 43; P. Bonner, "Kgatla Conspiracies, Pedi Plots: African Nationalist Politics in the Transvaal in the 'Dead' Decade of the 1930s", Paper, UKZN History Seminar, 2002.

24 R.H.W. Shepherd, *Literature for the South African Bantu* (Pretoria: Carnegie Corporation, 1936), p. 6; P. Morris, "The Early Black South African Newspaper and the Development of the Novel," *Journal of Commonwealth Literature* v. 15 no. 1 (1980), pp. 15-29, p. 16; J. Peires, *The House of Phalo* (Johannesburg: Ravan, 1981), p. 176; B. Bozzoli and P. Delius, "Radical History and South African Society", *Radical History Review* 46 (1990), pp. 13-46, p. 16; J. Starfield, "The Lore and the Proverbs: Sol Plaatje as Historian," ASI seminar paper, Aug. 1991, p. 3. For a similarly non-elitist view of historians as inclusive of public intellectuals, workers and journalists see S. Ndlovu, "The Changing African Perceptions of King Dingane in Historical Literature", Ph.D. thesis, University of the Witwatersrand, 2001, p. 267.

25 H.I.E. Dhlomo, "Racial Attitudes: An African Viewpoint", and "African Attitudes to the European", *The Democrat,* 17 Nov., 1 Dec. 1945, cited in T. Couzens, *The New African: A Study of the Life and Work of H.I.E. Dhlomo* (Johannesburg: Ravan Press, 1985), pp. 33, 35; N. Etherington, *Preachers, Peasants and Politics in Southeast Africa, 1875-1880* (London: Royal Historical Society, 1978).

26 N. Mandela, *Long Walk to Freedom* (New York: Little Brown, 1994), pp. 110-113; H.S. Msimang, "Autobiography", SOAS Ms. 380077; A.B. Xuma, "Autobiography", 1954 ms., Xuma Papers, Cullen Library, University of the Witwatersrand, AD 843, P24; J. Starfield, "'Not Quite History': The Autobiographies of H. Selby Msimang and R.V. Selope Thema and the Writing of South African History," *Social Dynamics* v. 14 no. 2 (1988), pp. 16-35; J.T. Gumede, "To All Leaders of the African People," *National Gazette* 7 Sept. 1927; A.B. Xuma, *Bridging the Gap between White and Black in South Africa* (Lovedale, 1930); F. Baard, *My Spirit is Not Banned* (Harare: Zimbabwe Publishing House, 1986), pp. 31-56; N. Mokgatle, *The Autobiography of an Unknown South African* (Berkeley: University

of California Press, 1971), pp. 281-284, 305-307; B. Baartman, *The Autobiography of a South African Textile Worker* (London: Sactu, 1988).

27   M. Kotane, "How a Non-European Looks at Afrikanerdom," *Freedom* 6 (1945); Kotane, "Landmarks of the ANC", *Sechaba* v. 2 no. 8 (1968) pp. 10-11; A. Nzula, "The Struggles of the Negro Toilers in SA" *Negro Worker* v. 5 nos. 2-6, 10 (1935); J. Gomas, *100 Years: "Emancipation of Slaves"* ([Cape Town]: CPSA, 1934).

28   W. Sisulu, "The Development of African Nationalism," *India Quarterly* v. 10 (1954), pp. 206-214, p. 210; N. Mandela, "Freedom in Our Lifetime," *Liberation* June 1956, pp. 4-8; H.J. Simons and R. Simons, *Class and Colour in South Africa 1850-1950* (London: Penguin, 1969), pp. 621-623; H.J. Simons, *Struggles in Southern Africa for Survival and Equality* (London: Macmillan, 1997), p. 121; B. Magubane, *The Political Economy of Race and Class in South Africa* (New York: Monthly Review Press, 1979), pp. 258-330.

29   F. Meli [A. Madolwana], *South Africa Belongs to Us: A History of the ANC* (Harare: Zimbabwe Publishing House, 1988), pp. xi, 2, 6, 36-44; Meli, "A Nation is Born," *AC* 48 1972, pp. 17-36, p. 20; J. Nxumalo, "The National Question in the Writing of South African History", *Journal of Social Studies* v. 58 (1992), pp. 17-91; interview of the author with Mzala [J. Nxumalo], London, Apr. 1989.

30   J. Pampalis, *Foundations of the New South Africa* (London: Zed, 1991), p. 81; G. Mbeki, *Learning from Robben Island* (London: Currey, 1991), p.127; G. Mbeki, *The Struggle for Liberation in South Africa: A Short History* (Cape Town: David Philip, 1992), pp. 50-54, 70-74, G. Mbeki, *Sunset at Midday* (Johannesburg: Nolwazi, 1996), p. 31.

31   Walshe, *Rise of African Nationalism,* pp. 10, 15, 32, 243. S. Trapido, "A Preliminary Study of the Development of African Political Opinion 1884-1955", BA (Hons.) thesis, University of the Witwatersrand, 1959, p. 200 similarly concludes that until the 1950s most ANC leaders were "drawn almost entirely from the middle class professional elite".

32   E. Feit, *South Africa: The Dynamics of the ANC* (Oxford: OUP, 1962), pp. 1-9, 26-36; E. Feit, *African Opposition in South Africa: The Failure of Passive Resistance* (Stanford: Stanford University Press 1967); R. Fine and D. Davis, *Beyond Apartheid: Labour and Liberation in South Africa* (London: Pluto, 1991), pp. 212-213, 266-289; R. Lambert, "Trade Unionism, Race, Class and Nationalism in the 1950s Resistance Movement", in P. Bonner, P. Delius and D. Posel (eds.), *Apartheid's Genesis, 1935-1962* (Johannesburg: Ravan, 1993), pp. 275-295, p. 289.

33   A. Odendaal, *Vukani Bantu! The Beginnings of Black Protest Politics in South Africa to 1912* (Cape Town: David Philip, 1984); A. Odendaal, "'Even White Boys Call Us "Boy"': Early Black Organisational Politics in Port Elizabeth", *Kronos* 20 (1993), pp. 3-16; D. Carter, "The Defiance Campaign: A Comparative Analysis of the Organisation, Leadership and Participation in the Eastern Cape and the Transvaal", *SSA* 12 (1970), pp. 76-97, p. 84; Thomas Dube, "A Study of African Reaction to Apartheid 1910-66", MA thesis, University of Chicago, 1972, pp. 13-24 claims Congress maintained mass support.

34   T. Karis, "The ANC, 1937-1949" and "The Defiance Campaign" in T. Karis and G. Carter (eds.), *From Protest to Challenge* (Stanford: Hoover Institution, 1972) [KC] v. 2, pp. 81-91, 426; G. Gerhart, *Black Power in South Africa: The Evolution of an Ideology* (Berkeley: University of California Press, 1978), pp. 39, 86; P. Rich, *White Power and the Liberal Conscience: Racial Segregation and South African Liberalism 1921-1960* (Manchester: Manchester University Press, 1984); P. Rich "Reviewing the Origins of the Freedom Charter", in N. Etherington (ed.), *Peace, Politics and Violence in the New South Africa* (London: Zell, 1992), pp. 254-283; P. Rich, *State Power and Black Politics in South Africa*

1912-1951 (London: Macmillan, 1996); D. Everatt, "Alliance Politics of a Special Type: The Roots of the ANC/SACP Alliance, 1950-4", *JSAS* v. 18 (1991), pp. 19-39.

35 S. Marks, *The Ambiguities of Dependence in South Africa: Class Nationalism and the State in Twentieth-Century Natal* (Baltimore: Johns Hopkins University Press, 1986); B. Bunting, *Moses Kotane* (London: Inkululeko, 1985); B. Willan, *Sol Plaatje: South African Nationalist, 1876-1932* (London: Heinemann, 1984), p. 211; D. Musson, *Johnny Gomas* (Cape Town: Buchu, 1989), p. 21; S. Gish, *Alfred B. Xuma: African, American, South African* (New York: New York University Press, 1999).

36 A.B. Davidson, *Iuzhnaia Afrika: Stanovlenie sil protesta 1870-1924* (Moscow: Nauka, 1972), Chapter 3; L. Kuper, "African Nationalism in South Africa, 1910-1964", in M. Wilson and L. Thompson (eds.), *The Oxford History of South Africa* (OUP, 1969-71), v. 2, pp. 424-476, p. 447, 470-471; S. Marks and S. Trapido, "The Politics of Race, Class and Nationalism", in S. Marks and S. Trapido (eds.), *The Politics of Race, Class and Nationalism in Twentieth-Century South Africa* (London: Longman, 1987), pp. 1-70, pp. 2-4, 36, 45. V. Mahali, "Contradiction, Conflict and Convergence of Class and Nation in Black South African Politics, 1925-1985", Ph.D. thesis, Illinois University, 1996, pp. ix, 31 argues that the "deliberate stunting of the black bourgeoisie" lent the ANC a mass base but its involvement in labour struggles essentially was tactical.

37 Lodge, *Black Politics*, pp. 2-10, 68, 78-110; T. Lodge, "The Destruction of Sophiatown", *Journal of Modern African Studies* v. 19 (1981), pp. 107-132; T. Lodge, "Political Mobilisation during the 1950s: An East London Case Study", in Marks and Trapido, *Politics of Race*, pp. 310-335: T. Lodge, "Political Organisations in Pretoria's African Townships, 1940-1963" in B. Bozzoli (ed.), *Class, Community and Conflict* (Johannesburg: Ravan, 1987), pp. 401-417; T. Lodge, "Charters from the Past: The African National Congress and its Historiographical Traditions", *Radical History Review* 46/47 (1990), pp. 161-188.

38 D. O'Meara, "The 1946 African Mineworkers' Strike in the Political Economy of South Africa", *Journal of Commonwealth and Comparative Politics* v. 12 1975, pp. 146-173; L. Callinicos, "'We Are Not Alone': The Making of a Mass Movement, 1950-60", *Staffrider* v. 8 no. 3 (1989), pp. 88-104, pp. 93, 101; Fine, *Beyond Apartheid*, pp. 48, 212, 266; B. Hirson, *Yours for the Union: Class and Community Struggles in South Africa, 1930-1947* (London: Zed Press, 1989), pp. 162, 183, 198.

39 M. Benson, *South Africa: The Struggle for a Birthright* (London: Penguin, 1966), pp. 150-159, 163-164, 186-189; P. Mtimkhulu, "Mass Movements of the 70s and 80s and the Liberation Struggle" and D. Pillay, "The Congress Movement in Historical Perspective 1912-92", in S. Buthelezi (ed.), *South Africa: The Dynamics & Prospects of Transformation* (Harare: Sapes, 1995), pp. 93-110, p. 97 and pp. 23-41, p. 23 respectively; J. Zug, *The Guardian: The History of South Africa's Extraordinary Anti-Apartheid Newspaper* (Pretoria: Unisa Press; MSU Press, 2007), p. 12.

40 A. Cobley, *Class and Consciousness: The Black Petty Bourgeoisie in South Africa, 1924 to 1950* (New York: Greenwood, 1990), pp. 40-49; A. Cobley, "'On the Shoulders of Giants': The Black Petty Bourgeoisie in Politics and Society in South Africa, 1924-1950", Ph.D. thesis SOAS, 1986, p. 19; La Hausse, *Restless Identities*.

41 Bonner, "The Transvaal Native Congress"; W. Hofmeyr, "Agricultural Crisis and Rural Organisation in the Cape 1929-1933", M.A. thesis, University of Cape Town, 1985; P. Delius, "*Sebatakgomo* and the Zoutpansberg Balemi Association: The ANC, CPSA and Rural Organisation, 1939-1955", *JAH* v. 34 (1993), pp. 293-313.

42 Bundy, "Introduction" to Mbeki, *Robben Island* p. xii; Beinart and Bundy, *Hidden Struggles,* p. 39.

43 Sapire, "Brakpan", pp. 184, 199; J. Cherry, "The Making of an African Working Class, Port Elizabeth 1925-1963", M.A. thesis University of Cape Town, 1992, p. 220.

44 W. Beinart, *Twentieth Century South Africa* (Oxford: OUP, 1994), p. 87. See also S. Dubow, *The African National Congress* (Sutton: Thrupp, 2000).

45 La Hausse, *Restless Identities.*

46 L. Ntsebeza, *Democracy Compromised: Chiefs and the Politics of the Land in South Africa* (Leiden: Brill, 2005).

47 L. Callinicos, "'People's History for People's Power': Representing the Past in a Divided South Africa", *South African Historical Journal [SAHJ]* 25 (1991), pp. 22-37; Food and Canning Workers Union. *Annual Report,* 1967; C. Kadalie, *My Life and the ICU: The Autobiography of a Black Trade Unionist in South Africa,* ed. S. Trapido (London: F. Cass, 1970); Mokgatle, *Autobiography.*

48 E. Gitsham and J. Trembath, *A First Account of Labour Organisation in South Africa* (Durban, 1926); T. Mann, *Memoirs* (London: MacGibbon, 1923); D. Jones, "Communism in SA", *Communist Review* v. 1 no. 3-4 (1921), pp. 15-17, 63-71; S.P. Bunting, *Imperialism and South Africa* (Johannesburg: CPSA, 1928); E. Roux, *Time Longer Than Rope* (London: Gollancz, 1948); Simons, *Class and Colour.*

49 P. Lalu, *The Communist Party Press and the Creation of the South African Working Class: 1921-1936* (Cape Town: Centre for African Studies, 1993), p. 31.

50 F. Johnstone, *Class, Race and Gold: A Study of Class Relations and Racial Discrimination in South Africa* (London: Routledge, 1976); J. Lewis, "South African Labor History: A Historiographical Assessment" *Radical History Review* 46 (1990), pp. 213-257; D. Hindson, *Pass Controls and the Urban African Proletariat in South Africa* (Johannesburg: Ravan Press, 1987); P. Wickins, *The Industrial & Commercial Workers' Union of Africa* (Cape Town: OUP, 1978); Bradford, *Taste of Freedom*; E. Webster (ed.), *Essays in Southern African Labour History* (Johannesburg: Ravan Press, 1978); P. Bonner and R. Lambert, "Batons and Bare Heads: The Strike at Amato Textiles, February 1958", in Marks and Trapido, *Politics of Race,* pp. 336-365.

51 T. Keegan, *Facing the Storm* (London: Zed, 1988); D. Moodie, "The Moral Economy of the Black Miners' Strike of 1946," *JSAS* v. 13 (1986), pp. 1-35; T. McClendon, *Genders and Generations Apart: Labor Tenants and Customary Law in Segregation-Era South Africa, 1920s to 1940s* (Cape Town: David Philip, 2002); W. Beinart, "Worker Consciousness, Ethnic Particularism and Nationalism: The Experience of a South African Migrant, 1930-1960", in Marks and Trapido, *Politics of Race,* pp. 286-309.

52 Baard, *My Spirit*; J. Wells, *We Now Demand! The History of Women's Resistance to Pass Laws in South Africa* (Johannesburg: Wits University Press, 1993); B. Bozzoli, *Women of Phokeng: Consciousness, Life Strategy, and Migrancy in South Africa, 1900-83* (Johannesburg: Wits University Press, 1991), pp. 239-241; I. Berger, *Threads of Solidarity: Women in South African Industry, 1950-1980* (Oxford: Currey, 1992), "Generations of Struggle: Trade Unions and the Roots of Feminism, 1930–1960", in N. Gasa (ed.), *Women in South African History: They Remove Boulders and Cross Rivers = Basus'iimbokodo Bawel'imilambo* (Cape Town: HSRC, 2007), pp. 185-205; C. Kros, *Urban African Women's Organisations, 1935-1956* (Johannesburg: Africa Perspective, 1982), p. 6.

53 F. Ginwala, "Women and the ANC 1912-43" *Agenda* 8 (1990), pp. 77-93; N. Erlank, "Gender and Masculinity in South African Nationalist Discourse, 1912-1950", *Feminist Studies* v. 29 (2003), pp. 653-657; R. Suttner, "Masculinities in the African National

Congress-led Underground Organisation", *Kleio* v. 37 (2005) pp. 71-106; N. Gasa, "'Let Them Build More Gaols'", in Gasa, *Women in South African History*, pp. 185-205; S. Geiger, "Tanganyikan Nationalism as 'Women's Work': Life Histories, Collective Biography and Changing Historiography", *Journal of African History* v. 37 (1996), pp. 465-478; C. Walker, "Women and Gender in Southern Africa to 1945: An Overview", in C.Walker (ed.), *Women and Gender in Southern Africa to 1945* (Cape Town: David Philip, 1990), pp. 1-33, p. 24.

54 Webster, *Racial Mould*, pp. 270-276; L. Callinicos, *A Place in the City* (Johannesburg: Ravan Press, 1993); T. Nemutanzhela, "Cultural Forms and Literacy as Resources for Political Mobilisation: A. M. Malivha and the Zoutpansberg Balemi Association 1939-1944", *African Studies* v. 52 (1993), pp. 89-102.

55 S. Redding, "Peasants and the Creation of an African Middle Class in Umtata, 1880-1950", *International Journal of African Historical Studies* [*IJAHS*] v. 26 (1993), pp. 513-539; J. Kirk, *Making a Voice: African Resistance to Segregation in South Africa* (Boulder: Westview, 1998), pp. 19-21, 162; M. Swanson, "The Joy of Proximity: The Rise of Clermont", in P. Maylam and I. Edwards (eds.), *The People's City: African Life in 20th Century Durban* (Pietermaritzburg: University of Natal Press, 1996), pp. 274-298, p. 277.

56 As suggested by M. Tetelman, "We Can: Black Politics in Cradock, South Africa, 1948-85", Ph.D. thesis, Northwestern University, 1997, p. 32.

57 For an interesting re-think of "resistance" in historiography see J. Abbink, M. de Bruijn, and K. van Walraven (eds.), *Rethinking Resistance: Revolt and Violence in African History* (Leiden: Brill, 2003).

58 *The Road to Democracy in South Africa* (Cape Town: Zebra; Pretoria: Unisa, 2004-2006) v. 1-2.

59 B. Magubane, "Whose Memory – Whose History? The Illusion of Liberal and Radical Historical Debates" pp. 251-279, p. 276 and C. Saunders, "Four Decades of South African Academic Historical Writing: A Personal Perspective", pp. 280-291, p. 290, both in H.E. Stolten (ed.), *History Making and Present Day Politics: The Meaning of Collective Memory in South Africa* (Uppsala: Nordic African Institute, 2007).

Black Labour in South Africa to 1940

In the period until 1940 (and even more so afterwards), black workers were central to the South African economy. The formation and growth of these working strata and the conditions and protest actions of workers exhibited deep contradictions. Given harsh restrictions and discouragement of free African labour organisation, the emergence of strong, stable black unions was blocked. In their absence, worker protests remained uncoordinated and ultimately unsuccessful. Yet the same socio-economic and political forces that militated against free African labour association favoured worker alliance with African political bodies, such as the ANC—if conditions were right. Coercive labour structures engendered intolerable conditions that stimulated worker resistance—and condemnation by black political leaders. This encouraged some labour activists to gravitate to political movements; similarly, some ANC figures attempted to articulate the viewpoints or publicise the difficult conditions of workers. Before discussing these cases, it is crucial to appreciate socio-economic changes influencing potential mutual support by the ANC and workers and how conditions changed, or remained the same in the period so that analysts might better understand the forces or lack of forces underlying such ties.

Formation and Growth of the Black Working Class

Three main, interrelated, forces gave rise to a black working class: colonial conquest, expansion of mining and later manufacturing, and the active agency of workers themselves. Colonial conquest by Holland and Britain stimulated a limited degree of capitalist growth. More concentrated development of capitalist classes—bourgeoisie and proletariat—was uneven and lengthy. Destruction of Khoekhoe societies from the late seventeenth century gradually spawned an underclass of black farm, domestic, and building workers, yet employer use of slave labour and violence curtailed the ability of these labourers to compete in the labour market. By the 1830s, formal slavery disappeared and migrant workers increasingly assumed the central role of a cheap labour supply. By the turn of the century, colonial conquest was complete. Large territorial losses and subsequent loss of control over their land and economies pushed many Africans into migrant labour, with subsequent disruption to social structures, including patriarchal and elder hegemony.[1]

The class of wage earners increased with penetration of British capital and industrial development. There was a slow but steady growth of small-scale manufactures and transport infrastructure. In 1865, the major non-agricultural occupations of black men in the Cape were labouring (18,627), domestic (5,133), transport (1,231) and building (987); for black women, domestic (22,413), laundry (2,177), and tailoring (425) work predominated. Things soon changed. Rail workers constructed only 69 miles of rail in the Cape by 1874 yet stimulated by mining expansion, laid a further 2,014 miles between 1880 and 1890. Two-thirds to three-quarters of an estimated 12,500 rail workers in 1877 were black. By 1902, of an estimated 201,640 African wage earners, 83,000 were domestic, 31,860 rail, and 29,000 rural labourers; the rest worked on the land and mines.[2]

Many black wage earners were migrant workers. They were not quite what Marx termed "free labourers in the double sense that neither they themselves form part and parcel of the means of production … nor do[es it] belong to them". They were far from constituting a class-conscious class "for itself" in the sense that migrant labour tended to make the proletarianisation process temporary and uneven. Yet as taxes, disease, military defeat, and decline of homestead economies drove more Africans to (partial) dependence on wage (or forced) labour, they began to develop consciousness of common interests. Africans in a "constant and steady flow of men in search of work" left rural areas, drawn into a capitalist economy on mines, farms and, progressively as the new century unfolded, factories. An inexorable, if irregular, forced march to wage labour had begun.[3]

The greatest cause of labour migrancy was mining expansion. In 1877, Anthony Trollope observed that at Kimberley diamond mines the "independent black man who owned the land has been expelled—but the working black man has taken his place." Diamonds, and from 1886 gold, transformed the rate and nature of economic growth, stimulated by inflow of imperial capital and skilled white labour. However, black labour-power, now increasingly concentrated, lay at its base. As a result, its role in the economy became so central that in 1937 a prominent historian declared: "The greatest social and economic fact in the history of the country is not gold ... but the universal dependence upon black labour." By 1916, mining employed 238,054 workers, manufacturing 91,335.[4]

Growth of a permanent black industrial working class was slow and tortuous. In the later nineteenth century some enterprising *kholwa* (Christian educated) individuals had temporary success as artisans, often using wages as a springboard for small-scale capital accumulation. Evidence presented to state commissions indicates a definite, if irregular, proletarianisation across the country. The Engcobo Magistrate reported in 1883: "Civilised natives are beginning to find out the value of learning trades." In Kokstad, "numbers of natives" were "employed in ... bricklaying, carpentering, and blacksmith's work". There were "a good many" black workers in Albany. Evidence to the 1893-1894 Cape Labour Commission testified to steady growth of black urban wage labouring classes not just in cities but also in rural dorps. Labour themes were prominent in questions and answers to the South African Native Affairs Commission (SANAC) of 1903-1905. The King William's Town Magistrate noted a wide range of urban occupations for urban men and women.[5]

However, very few such people became *permanent* artisans; still fewer penetrated the ever-intensifying job colour bar. Trollope noted that due to racism, apprentices from Lovedale College "could not often find employment". Some lost their positions whilst still at Lovedale: James Botoman was dismissed for "insubordination". These barriers pushed many artisans back into labouring: blacksmith William Africa turned to boundary riding.[6]

By the turn of the century, imperial observers pointed to a still meagre manufacturing base. In 1904, most of South Africa's 4,778 factories were small. Modest manufacturing growth occurred in Cape Town, Johannesburg and Port Elizabeth, aided by an increasingly uniform labour policy. World War I generated higher demand for black labour as the economy moved toward import substitution. Gross manufacturing value rose from £17 million in 1911 to £98 million in 1920-1921. The number of black urban workers increased from 243,509 in 1914 to 268,412 in 1918. A 1918 Natal report pointed to "a large class of natives permanently engaged ... in industrial pursuits".[7]

Africanisation of labour markets increased following the failure of short-lived experiments with Indian and Chinese indentured labour. African miners, bit by bit, learnt semi-skilled tasks: in 1907, Henry Hay, Wit Deep Mine manager, observed they were now doing work like drilling to such an extent that white people had become mere supervisors. However, they lacked formal organisation. By 1905, Natal sugar growers employed 8,000 "entirely unorganised" Africans. Nationwide, the number of Africans in manufacturing rose from 61,000 in 1915 to 113,000 in 1920, but was still largely unskilled. The 1921 census listed 96.5 per cent of black people as unskilled, of which farm labourers comprised 33.3 per cent, miners 21.3 percent and domestic workers 22.8 per cent; 6,729 were listed as "skilled labourers". African mine employment increased from 255,897 to 312,123 between 1918 and 1930. By the early 1930s, Africans comprised 90 per cent of the mine workforce, 60 per cent in manufacturing, and nearly all domestic workers.[8] Black labour was the linchpin of the economy.

Behind this growth were expanding steel, engineering, construction, and clothing industries encouraged by protectionism. The Iron and Steel Corporation (ISCOR) was inaugurated in 1928; the Electricity Supply Commission (Escom) in 1922—though most Africans remained without electricity. This was a period of limited industrial "take-off", and of a limited, but growing, state role in industry.[9]

Industrial growth continued, accompanied by related urbanisation trends. The number of Africans recorded as urban dwellers rose from 336,800 in 1904 to 1,146,700 in 1936. However, the persistence of casualisation and migrant labour meant the working class was stunted and uneven: in Durban from 1923 to 1927, at least 50 per cent of the workforce was casual. Gender imbalance was acute with only 147,293 African women of a (non-mine) African urban national population of 587,000 in 1921. Their role in industry was negligible but changing: from 1921 to 1936, the number of urban African women increased 142 per cent.[10]

The peculiar spatial patterns of settler capitalism rooted in institutionalised racial prejudice engendered shared experiences *across* classes. Poverty and segregation encouraged by white paranoia over sanitation and health induced a compression of black social strata—producing for example in East London what Keith Tankard terms a community that "evolved almost entirely as a labouring class". Margaret Ballinger in 1938 could not but be struck by the persistence in towns of the sharing typical of "a spirit of tribal communism" as workers disappeared from the workplace back to location "slums".[11]

This pushing together of diverse social classes was to be a recurring feature of urban life. Whilst it did not entirely block black capital accumulation—the statelier residences of some black leaders such as John Dube at Ohlange, or A. B. Xuma in Sophiatown being cases in point—this flattening effect tended to make cross-class political alliances more likely. If there was some minor capital accumulation among peak leaders, then this was irregular. A good number of ANC activists, especially at the local level, lived modestly or in some cases died virtual paupers. Moreover, many black leaders not associated with the ANC, such as J. T. and D. D. T Jabavu, lived as sumptuously as wealthier ANC leaders. Viewed as a whole, ANC activists had no monopoly on either wealth or poverty. For brief periods, some politicised poor rural or urban peoples found a home in the ICU or CPSA, but some of these also found a place in supporting the ANC. The economic trends behind these socio-political features continued in the 1930s.

The role of black labour in the economy continued to grow. Whilst the Great Depression saw the numbers of African workers in private industry decline from 81,000 in 1929 to 67,000 in 1932, by 1937 this rose again to 134,000 (Table 1), an increase related to labour-intensive industrial expansion after departure from the gold standard in 1932 generated income from higher gold prices, providing capital investment in manufacturing. Net industrial productive output increased 60 per cent from 1932 to 1937, by which date ISCOR employed more black people (2,876) than white (2,511). It achieved an output of 334,000 tons of raw steel in 1938 stimulating engineering growth. Africans gained greater access to semi-skilled positions such as machine-operators. In 1936, the number of African workers in textiles (3,695) and building (4,692) was still dwarfed by that of unskilled labourers (189,790) but between 1932 and 1939 the ratio of black industrial workers as a percentage of the workforce rose steadily: Southern Transvaal from 75,478 (53.6 per cent) to 157,754 (59.4 per cent); Durban from 35.6 to 41.5 per cent; Western Cape from 10.3 to 13.9 per cent. Africans employed in industrial manufacturing increased by 60 per cent from 1933 to 1936. Africans comprised 55 per cent of construction workers in the five major cities by 1938. By 1939, they comprised the largest ethnic group of workers in private factories, numbering 141,804.[12]

Table 1. Africans Employed in Private Industry and Their Wages

Year	Number	Annual wage (£)	Year	Male	Female
1929-30	81,233	45.00	1938-39	126,067	1,154
1932-33	66,757	46.00	1939-40	130,597	1,254
1937-38	134,233	44.00	1940-41	149,031	1,713

Sources: *Union Statistics for 50 Years*, p.G-6; S. van der Horst, *Native Labour* (1942) p. 263

Further urbanisation accompanied this expansion of wage labour. Census data in 1936 indicates 19.4 per cent of Africans were located in urban areas. The recorded black population of Johannesburg increased from 115,720 in 1921 to 191,338. The number of urban African women rose from 147,293 to 356,874 (a

142.3 per cent increase). Women only gradually entered private manufacturing (Table 1); by 1936, they numbered 3,372, chiefly in textiles or canning.[13] By 1940, despite continuing casualisation and migrancy, black people comprised a significant and rising proportion (Table 2) of the workforce.

Table 2. Total Wage Earners in Manufacturing, 1925–1939

Year	African	White
1925	82,608	56,433
1933	74,362	68,509
1939	156,550	115,424

Source: *Report of the Industrial Legislation Commission* (1951), p. 18

The Conditions of Black Workers

Proletarianisation and urbanisation brought together black workers. It was their working and living conditions that would largely determine their inclination to engage in industrial or political action. African wages were uniformly very low. Congress leader Walter Rubusana in 1900 stated that farm workers received only a nominal 10 shillings[14] a month; by 1925 they still only received between 6 shillings and 50 shillings a month; women farm workers between 2 shillings and 5 shillings a month according to black unions. African miners in 1903 earned an average of £2.14.4d a month, an amount that barely rose over the next three decades; in 1913 average mine wages had slipped to £2.12.6d, with mine clerks receiving a little more, from £3.15 to £5. In 1924, African wages generally averaged less than one-eighth of white wages. When the communist T. W. Thibedi visited the mines in 1926, he reported wages of only 1/4d a day for black miners. In periods of crisis, employers first cut black wages. African manufacturing wages in Cape Town from 1921-1924 declined from 30 shillings to 26/7d per week; on the Rand they lurched from 104 shillings a month in 1921 to 84/4d in 1922.[15]

Such low wages induced widespread suffering and resentment. A survey in the late 1920s of budgets of three strata of Durban Africans—teachers, artisans, and labourers—revealed that even teachers had to supplement a £5 monthly income with night tuition. A shoemaker barely made ends meet; a ricksha-puller spent most of a £7 a month income on food, rent and license. Making things worse, the index of retail prices rose from 152 in 1919 to 198 in 1920 (index 1900=100). Subsequent deflation did not help, as weak black labour organisation was unable to ward off pressure for wage cuts that returned in 1929.[16]

Through the 1930s, black wages remained low. Gold receipts cushioned somewhat the effects of the Depression but many black people suffered wage and job cuts. Average annual black wages declined by 6 per cent from 1929 to 1936. Unemployment hit black people hardest: in 1932, some 2,000-3,000 of 9,000 male Africans in Cape Town were unemployed.[17]

In 1930, Charlotte Maxeke estimated most African workers in Johannesburg earned only £3 10s per month. Missionary Ray Phillips later in the decade surveyed 3,654 African wage earners in 49 occupations, concluding they could not make ends meet. In 1932 the East London Medical Officer wrote that if low wages continued the "end result can be only a white capitalism exploiting a black proletariat". The African family monthly poverty line of the mid 1930s was £5.6.11d yet the average monthly wage of a sample of 100 Africans was £3.18.9d. By 1938, the Urban Areas Act had driven 55,000 Africans into segregated towns, adding considerably to transport costs, already 10-35 per cent of wages.[18]

Some rural workers received no cash wages at all. Rosalina Shongwe recalled farm labouring in the 1920s: we "used to not be paid". Paulina Nzuza, a Midlands farm worker born in World War I, received only 5 pence a day and recalled children driven to work. Chief Cornelius Mahlangu (Mapocho) in 1925 stated that farmers forced squatters around Welgelegen to render unpaid work for up to six months. E. Mahlangu noted child farm labour was rife in Witbank. A Vryheid magistrate remarked that many farm youths received no pay; a Standerton magistrate observed Africans regarded the Masters and Servants' Act as reducing them "to a state bordering on serfdom". Prison labour was widely used on farms, forcing down wages, restricting unions. The ILO concluded that South Africa practised forced labour. In such situations, Africans were truly powerless.[19]

In general, African wage earners shared common living standards, shown by figures on average monthly wages from 1927 to 1929. Rand mine wages remained static at £2.18. Rail and dock labourers received £2.15, £2.13 and £2.14 over the same period. Uncertified teachers received only £3 in 1928; qualified low-level primary teachers won only £3-£9. This commonality established the potential for shared interests between the ANC and wage earners. Room for different class interests did emerge in the limited growth of black middle strata. However, despite internal class differentiation among workers, few achieved even the status of artisan; white-collar workers being the chief exception (Table 3).[20]

Table 3. Occupations of Africans, 1921 and 1936

Occupation	Male 1921	Male 1936	Female 1921	Female 1936
Professional	7,444	9,557	2,312	4,253
Teachers	-	4,758	-	3,441
Clerical/Sales	14,588	24,778	469	372
Agriculture	1,338,110	1,441,497	1,412,289	1,659,349
Peasants	1,036,856	814,282	1,345,421	1,618,746
Farm workers	301,254	621,002	40,232	144,096
Mining	235,134	388,894	531	-
Industrial	203,776	272,641	15,814	3,372
Domestic	88,953	114,502	162,905	242,405

Source: *Union Statistics for 50 Years,* p. A-33

Talk of class stratification can mask basic commonalities. Only 92 of 200,000 African mine employees earned more than £6 a month, making it hard to define such a small group as a *separate* class. In any case, the Chamber of Mines blocked wage increments for clerks, pushing some of them into politics. Authorities delayed African teacher salary increments agreed in 1928 until 1946, contributing to a similar politicisation in their ranks. Hyman Basner described African primary teachers of the 1930s as "near-poverty stricken". By then the maximum salary of lower-level African teachers was only £6 a month; many suffered periods of unemployment. The 1936 census lists only 1,221 African carpenters, 2,332 boot-makers and 62 plumbers. The African "middle class" in 1936 had 8,199 teachers, 1,950 shop assistants, seven lawyers and one lecturer; not only a minuscule but also an impoverished class. Peter Abrahams, who experienced poverty, estimated "no more than a dozen" black families "knew the meaning of economic security".[21]

The above evidence confirms Cobley's argument that an "emergent black petty bourgeoisie and the black working class lived cheek by jowl"; a "'squeezing together' of classes ... provided a basis for effective cross-class political action",[22] suggesting it is not possible to equate the gradual stabilisation of a more permanent African urban community with growth of a *petit bourgeoisie*. The consolidation of families or securing of property titles itself constitutes no more than *stabilisation* of employee strata. Evidence of *petit bourgeois* development should reflect a degree of control or ownership of means of production and some capital accumulation. In South Africa, the *main* tendency was for "marginal" black employees to remain within the ranks of the working class.

Shared poverty, poor conditions and discrimination was to be conducive of cross-class alliance. Africans faced an array of debilitating social ills. Epidemics, work accidents, unhealthy housing and poor diet contributed to high labour and general mortality, a trend denying experienced workers to nascent black labour and nationalist movements

Many Africans lived in poor housing. In Cape Town only after severe bubonic plague in 1901 were attempts made even to monitor their housing. Miners worked in unsafe mines and slept on concrete bunks. Between 1916 and 1921, there were 15,954 African casualties and 2,936 deaths on mines. In 1929 alone, 2,661 African miners died from diseases contracted at work, 651 from accidents. Workers decimated by tuberculosis spread it in the Reserves. Black mortality rates consistently were over 500 per 1,000 births.[23]

Conditions remained harsh. In 1934, "Rooiyard", a slum shared by 376 people, had only one water tap, whose use cost tenants 40 per cent of wages. Poverty fed high infant mortality rates: 557 per 1,000 in Germiston in 1932, 898 per 1,000 in Benoni in 1930-1936. Removals under the 1934 Slums Act led to severe overcrowding. Ndabeni in 1935 comprised "dilapidated, dirty, tumble-down tin-shanties". Rail- and dockworkers in 1937 described their housing as "infested with vermin, the roofs leak". Labourers at Doornkop Estate, surrounded by malarial areas, had no hospital and suffered poor food and houses.[24]

These harsh conditions posed both a challenge and opportunity to the ANC if it was to gain support. The largely urban-based body gradually sensed opportunities presented by an increase in the urban work force, which reached 400,000 in the 1930s. Resentment at persisting poor conditions made people angry; growing urbanisation and compressed spatial patterns concentrated them at work and home. Both trends could aid political activity. Yet poor people lacked resources to build either industrial or political structures. A further impediment to organising workers was the state's restrictive black labour policy.

Restrictions on Black Labour Organisation

An arsenal of laws secured cheap labour. The state introduced pass laws as early as 1760. An 1812 Proclamation legalised ten years of unpaid labour of black children born on white farms. After the formal emancipation of slaves, black labour remained tightly controlled. At the first legal Khoekhoe protest meeting, in 1834 at Kat River against re-imposition of slave-like conditions imposed by vagrancy laws, M. Pretorius stated: "One ordinance comes in their favour to raise them, another soon follows to degrade them." Liberal white people advocated free labour but an 1841 ordinance legalised penal sanctions merely for leaving a job. The 1856 Masters and Servants Acts (in force until the 1970s) made it a crime to strike or change employment without consent. Anti-squatting and land laws and hut and labour taxes forced the pace of proletarianisation. Ruthless application of harsh criminal statutes created a steady supply of unfree labour and convict labour, used extensively on public works and farms, which existed well into the apartheid period.[25]

In the second half of the nineteenth century, white employers compelled black children captured by commandos to become "apprentices" (*inboekelings*), a euphemism for thinly disguised slavery legalised in the Boer Republics, where unpaid labour was rife. They left few extant voices but farm labourer "David" told the 1871 Transvaal Commission on African Labour: "We have always worked without payment."[26]

As the years rolled by more discriminatory laws further regulated black labour. A system of statutory control and codification of provincial ordinances ensued with the emergence of a politically independent South African state in 1910, directly via labour laws such as the 1911 Native Labour Regulation Act and indirectly through laws restricting black rights in general. The Mines and Works Act introduced a statutory colour bar reserving 32 categories of work for white people. The 1914 Riotous Assemblies Act banned union organisers from work areas. Regimentation of contracts added to the unfree nature of labour markets. In 1914, the *Natal Mercury* observed the "continuous expression of the police element" in managing the African worker.[27]

The 1922 Apprenticeship Act and 1924 Industrial and Conciliation Act restricted black workers' freedom of movement and organisation. The latter co-opted white (and in theory Indian and "coloured") unions but excluded "pass-bearing natives" from the very definition of employee, effectively thwarting African union recognition until 1979. The 1923 Natives (Urban Areas) Act sought to tighten the influx of Africans into towns and channel labour. The 1925 Wage Act endorsed "civilised labour" policies privileging white people. The 1926 Mines and Works Amendment Act extended the job colour bar. Amendment in 1926 of Transvaal and Natal Masters and Servants' ordinances tightened legal sanctions against freedom of movement by rural labourers. The 1927 Native Administration Act made it a trespass offence for union officials to enter work areas and made inciting "racial hostility" an offence. The Chamber of Mines and Native Recruiting Corporation wasted no time in intensifying policing of the mines to smash the incipient threat from unions.[28]

In the 1930s, repression continued. Across the British Empire, the view persisted among capitalists and government alike that subject labour was expendable. Tanganyika Labour Commissioner Orde-Browne summed this up: "mine labourers were better fed but acquired subversive ideas. Which was better: a sick savage or a healthy Bolshevik?" South Africa answered decisively in favour of the former. The 1932 Native Service Contract Act extended the definition of labour tenant to include dependents. Amendments to Masters and Servants' Acts legalised whipping. The 1937 Native Laws Amendment Act made urban habitation dependent on registered employment. Eventually, however, rising black employment compelled some revision of strategy. A 1935 government report toyed with the idea of increasing wages but concluded the solution lay in preventing "undesirable drift" to cities. The Minister of Labour in 1939 proposed non-statutory recognition of African unions and the Secretary of Native Affairs conceded their existence "demands some form of recognition" but this was to be in a form to prevent workers "from becoming the dupes of ... unbalanced, semi-educated" Africans. Such attempts to form "tame-cat" unions foundered on African resistance. Some unions gained small rises by using 1937 amendments to the Industrial Conciliation Act but in general, Africans remained excluded from definitions of employee and wage committees failed to represent them.[29]

Unionisation was difficult in such conditions. Yet if the plethora of repressive laws succeeded in constricting African unions, then events did not entirely prevent politicisation. The holding down of wages tended to unite rather than stratify workers, whose repression sometimes led to protests and heightened class-consciousness. This tended to encourage them to search elsewhere for a vehicle for their demands and in the absence of unions they could incline towards the most viable, persistent, African political organisations.

Growth of Protest and Strike Action and Black Industrial Organisations

The nature of black workers' organisations influenced their relations with the ANC. In the face of the numerous obstacles detailed above, such organisations tended to be weak and short-lived. There simply was no place for black trade unions in the South African labour or political systems. Nevertheless, this did not stop strikes, nor prevent development of worker consciousness. To understand better the possible relationship between workers and the ANC it is necessary to gauge the mood of workers and get an idea of their organisation through an outline of their workplace actions and structures.

Strikes across southern Africa were "an essential part of the conscientising process in the proletarianisation of labour". Strikes, in Lenin's terms, "signify the beginning of the working class struggle … when the workers state their demands jointly", but "can only be successful where workers are sufficiently class-conscious … [and] have connections with socialists". Evidence adduced below shows that by 1920, African workers had begun to state their demands jointly and even forge tentative ties with socialists.[30]

Black workers adopted diverse forms of resistance. There is only sketchy data on their early actions. Slaves developed a range of direct, informal and, towards the end of slavery, legal forms of resistance. Strikes began almost as soon as slavery ended. Mfengu beach labourers at Port Elizabeth struck in 1846. There were many dock strikes, for example in Cape Town in 1854, 1889, 1891-1893, 1896 and 1901, in Port Elizabeth or East London in 1854-1857, 1872-1873, 1877-1878, and 1903, and Durban in 1875 and 1901-1903. A three-day strike in Port Elizabeth in 1901 involving dockers and women domestic workers was led by Frank Makwena (Mokwena), a teacher and carpenter later active in the ANC. These strikes defended worker conditions and showed workers were not powerless; if they could link up with political forces, then empowerment loomed, but this was not yet possible.[31]

Mine strikes were a major challenge to white supremacy due to mining's strategic place. There were eight strikes at Kimberley in the 1880s. At nearby Wesselton, when 800-900 miners vigorously resisted wage cuts and restrictions on their movement, police killed three workers. Black gold miners stopped work, for example in 1877, 1885 and 1887, and 6,000 struck in 1896 when reduction of wages prompted worker meetings; the government deployed troops. Yet they had no formal organisation to mobilise or negotiate on their behalf, no political body to champion their cause. J. T. Jabavu's moderate *Imvo Zabantsundu* newspaper could only muse that it was "momentary excitement".[32]

Sensing the futility of front-on resistance and confined in compounds, migrant labourers used diverse tactics to resist proletarianisation and wage cuts or protect their interests. Ciskei labourers in the 1880s-1890s simply refused to migrate, relying on their ties to the land. Despite rinderpest, Transkeian migrant labourers displayed, in Phoofolo's words, "adaptation and resistance" and chose to work where wages were higher.[33]

The ability to use such weapons declined appreciably with the effect of droughts and wars after 1882 and passage of the 1913 Natives' Land Act, which effectively stripped Africans of land-owning rights in 87 per cent of South Africa. Still, the rate of farm mechanisation was uneven, and rural labourers took part in scattered forms of resistance to exploitation from small-scale individual acts of avoidance, stock theft and arson, to more collective actions such as strikes. An apt characterisation of this period (if of neighbouring Southern Rhodesia) is that by Charles van Onselen: "Black workers did not require meetings, pickets, leaders and ideologies to make them understand who was oppressing them."[34]

Black workers in the early period of industrialisation used other methods to defend their living and working conditions. Titus Lergele and 58 other workers at Genadendal Mission lodged a petition in 1871 praying for relief from laws "which injuriously affected the labouring classes". Labourers and gangers on the Cape railways in the early 1890s twice sent successful delegations to reduce hours of work. In the same decade, workers in compounds clubbed together to collectively purchase necessities, whilst farm workers complained to the Protector of Natives about non-payment of wages. Natal workers made use of the courts in 1899 to gain overtime payments.[35] Interestingly, historians point to the ANC's use of such tactics as petitions, delegations, and courts as evidence of its *petit bourgeois* nature, yet workers themselves used such tactics.

Black workers giving evidence to government commissions drew attention to their conditions. Labourer Marthinus Davids of Prince Albert told the Cape Labour Commission of 1893-1894 he felt "better off in town" than working on farms where his movement was restricted. He articulated complaints of fellow farm workers about low wages, poor food, and beatings. Griqua unemployed farm worker "August" of Middelburg complained of unfair dismissal. Jan Mavukla, a Hope Town worker, criticised restrictive regulations and low wages that prevented him improving his housing. James Cochlin, a "coloured" printer in Colesberg, presented a petition of grievances drawn up after a meeting of workers. Workers in late Victorian Cape Town employed individual and group forms of protest, such as "desertion" and boycott, to pursue better conditions. They joined mass meetings over unemployment in 1884-1885 in Cape Town, and initiated legal action for non-payment of wages, at times employing the first generation of African lawyers such as Alfred Mangena, a Congress founder, who in 1901 worked on behalf of dock and harbour workers.[36]

Observers detected a growing class-consciousness. A strike by 200 African workers in Natal in 1895 prompted the white press to note: "It is evident that the natives are fully alive to the scarcity of labour and want to take advantage of it." Through trials and tribulations, workers increasingly saw themselves as constituting a class. Daniel Daniels, a "coloured" blacksmith in Carnarvon, told the Cape Labour Commission that "our class" wished to work and that many of those that did not objected to low wages and mistreatment. The Commission remarked that African wage earners across the Colony increasingly perceived the value of sticking together to avoid exploitation. Grahamstown labourer Charles Iafele articulated complaints of "us servants", telling the Commission that a bargaining tactic was simply leaving bad employers. The Port Elizabeth Magistrate noticed a similar tactic of domestic workers to assert dignity and achieve better wages and conditions. In 1908, white union leader John Ware conceded the effectiveness of indirect resistance: "If things do not suit [a black worker], he goes home and stays there; he does not go on strike; that is better than any strike."[37]

Evidence of gross labour exploitation also came from educated black people who, acting as labour intermediaries, established a tradition of labour "representation from above" that the ANC later adopted. Often these people had experience of wage labour. Gideon Fortuin, a black contractor aged 62, had worked as a farm labourer and remained in touch with labourers around Oudtshoorn who complained bitterly of under-payment. James Pellem, a labour agent in Queenstown, testified that workers avoided work on farms due to "bad payment and ill treatment", as did Mfengu teachers Hans Zwartboy of Middelburg and Charles Hlati of Queenstown. Reverend Gana Kakasa of Grahamstown passed on worker complaints of bad housing and wages in Fort Beaufort, whilst Reverend Benjamin Dlepu in Port Elizabeth was well aware of worker objections to bad overseers on mines and farms. A Basuto constable in Richmond related that for ten years he had heard many farm worker complaints of irregular wages. Some representations of labour grievances were more political. Store worker Jakob Meyer in Graaff-Reinet, delegated by a "Natives' Political Association" to give evidence on farm workers, detailed inadequate wages and poor housing. Such word of mouth communication networks helped identify employers noted for ill-treatment. Robert Francis, a Transvaal merchant employing 30-40 workers, complained before SANAC that his worker Job Nkosi, an educated man who subscribed to newspapers, fomented work stoppages and strikes, telling fellow workers they would be owners of the land. Unlike Francis's other workers, Nkosi worked full time and under each new contract sought higher wages. Networks helped workers build solidarity; an 1889 report noted rural workers had "friendly connections all about" if discharged.[38]

Small business owners and clerical workers also opposed harsh conditions. African witnesses before SANAC attacked working conditions in the Transvaal. James Mama, who worked in a lawyer's office for £4 a month, stated that work on the Rand "is carried out under pressure and is a hardship" due to oppressive pass laws that gave only four days to find work, forcing black people to take work at lower wages. Marabastad butcher John Makue had a small shop but could not afford to employ labour, lamenting: "Our earning power is very small ... It is not good under any circumstances to be forced to work."[39]

During the South African War of 1899-1902, strikes and "desertions" took place among black people sent to work on railways and employed as labourers and drivers. Magistrates recorded strong objections of migrant labourers to the contract system. After hostilities, African workers voted with their feet against reduced mine wages and when white people attempted to reclaim lost property, some labourers refused to work on their farms. These protests may have expressed, as Krikler argues, more the consciousness of peasants to class exploitation than working-class consciousness, but as Nasson observes, "localised, small-scale forms of organisation" nevertheless grew.[40]

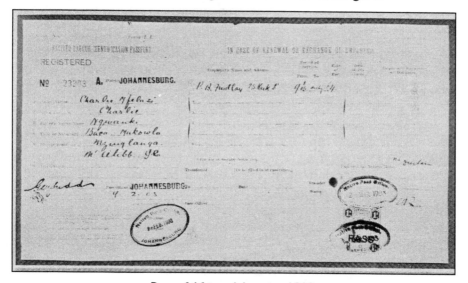

Pass of African labourer, 1903

Efforts to cut wages and extend pass laws provoked more strikes. Black miners struck in 1901 and again in April, May and June 1902. In September 1902, 61 Brakpan Electrical Works labourers struck. Strikes could be violent: 400 workers attacked police in January 1902; a Langlaagte Mine strike in June saw 1,100 workers take up arms. Strikers forged ties with their kin in rural areas and traditional leaders. Transkeian labourers on the Cape Town docks numbered 1,800 in 1902 and, as they saw their wages reduced, came out on strike for three days. One striker told the Docks Location Superintendent: "We are not only fighting for ourselves, we are fighting for our brothers at home." In 1904, headmen who, if serving as labour recruiters and a (poorly paid) part of the civil service, nevertheless perceived injustice in wage cuts, called these labourers out on strike.[41]

Headmen such as Mkatshana Veldtman had the job of explaining working conditions to migrant labourers and accompanying them to cities. Transkei workers, he noted, avoided low wage farms, preferring work in large groups under a headman for protection. Employers found it advisable to employ headmen along with workers; they used them as supervisors and paid them accordingly. In 1903, a dock agent in Cape Town noted worker discipline under headmen was "very good. You must engage the headman with the [work] men, for if you say a word to them the whole gang is apt to stand around to one side." On the other hand, headmen in 1901 supported workers facing a loss of travel money.[42] In a way, many Congress leaders later assumed an analogous position to headmen as an ambiguous intermediary between labour and employers or the state.

All these protests were destined to fail due to lack of effective labour organisation and weak, wider political support. A "coloured" printer and ex-farm worker remarked in 1893 that before then he had not complained of harsh working conditions as he lacked knowledge; yet an intimation of looming change was his disclosure that labourers now knew more of their rights. In that year, a building contractor was still disdainful of a threat by some of his workers to strike as "they have no society and no fund to fall back upon", with unskilled workers unlikely to join them. In many industries, plentiful labour made striking risky. When Table Mountain labourers threatened to strike in 1890, farm labourers from Worcester, to whom any urban wage rates seemed attractive, promptly replaced them.[43] There were other aspects of weak industrial organisation.

A workforce divided into ethnic contingents limited effective black unions, as did the partial nature of proletarianisation induced by retention of rural ties. The highly stratified and segmented South African work force privileged white, and to a lesser extent, "coloured" workers who had more chance of becoming small contractors or artisans. Further constrictions on unionisation included legal constraints on black organisation, low wages, white cultural reluctance to share knowledge about union building, and the coercive nature of the recruitment process and control of housing and workplaces.

The mining industry threw together labourers from diverse regions, housed in authoritarian compounds, shuttled around the sub-continent on the migrant-labour roller coaster. Mine accidents, overseer brutality and diseases debilitated worker potential for independent organisation. The compound system exploited or generated ethnic tensions to foster vertical divisions, induced paternalism, and isolated labour leaders. Such divisions undoubtedly remained significant but as Terence Ranger notes for the Jagersfontein mine, reports of "faction fights" could disguise emergent class consciousness. Nevertheless, labourers' varied identities and loyalties made it difficult to mobilise them industrially, just as state and company regulations and policing made compounds almost impregnable.[44]

Compound life obstructed union formation and made cross-ethnic class solidarity difficult. Yet high concentration of workers in compounds could favour strike action and organisation. Workers and their urban communities found ways to penetrate barriers. Workers combined informally through ethnic or kin-based networks of mutual aid that could share data on workplaces and be a support-base in industrial action. The 1903 Transvaal Labour Commission observed a "good deal of desertion ensured from the mines to the towns due to higher wages", testifying that the African "knows how to sell his labour on the market". In the production process, Africans made use of go-slows and complaints. In 1905 alone, there were 3,585 complaints lodged on the Rand. In 1907, the Government Native Labour Bureau saw its greatest problem as recovering absconders. "Desertions" declined with standardisation of labour laws but by 1911, there were still 62 desertions per 1,000 labourers. With Union in 1910, the Bureau still complained of numerous mine strikes, which it attributed to "agitators", but which had roots in attacks by white overseers and worker solidarity in defence of their comrades.[45]

A major cause of class formation was the conscious, active process of working and acting together as workers seen in all these struggles. Even so, this was not a fully formed class consciousness. On the Cape Town docks, as Saul Dubow argues, demands made by workers "indicated a desire for justice … rather than a class consciousness". Yet a change from individual to more collective forms of resistance started to occur.[46]

The transformation of collective resistance into unions faced severe obstacles. The first permanent trade unions were branches of British craft unions. They operated in a society fed by reliance on cheap black labour, influenced by prevailing racist social attitudes, and class stratification based on skill divisions. A white labour aristocracy, feeding on mobile, imperial racisms, flourished and fashioned new variations of racism in restrictive apprenticeship systems, white-only unions and colour bars. Before World War I, one can speak of an imperial rather than a truly *national* white "working class".[47]

Occasionally white unionists condemned exploitation of black workers. F. D. Smith, Diamond Fields Union Kimberley Secretary, in 1893 drew attention to the perilous state of disabled black miners. Miner Alfred Musson in 1908 declared the African worker a "very good labourer" who should be well paid. However, by 1914 only four unions were prepared to accept black members. James Riley, Trades and Labour Council President in 1908, saw no threat from black workers if they got the same wages as white people. Yet his colleague John Ware saw black labour as "the very worst". Congress leader Rubusana observed that Africans' "admission to trades-unions … is extremely rare". Communist David Ivon Jones in 1921 stated that the idea of the "native as a fellow-worker … never entered into any [white] Labour calculations".[48]

This problem would mean that the opening of dialogue between Congress and the mainly white socialist movement was not easy. Mainstream social democracy made no major attempt to open a dialogue with Africans. There were only isolated efforts to organise African workers. Employer H. W. Struben noted in 1903 that in the Cape Peninsula "a class of labour agitator" was "trying to get at the native and organise him into labour unions", but often only "so that they can get better wage for themselves".[49]

Attempts at cross-race class solidarity were scattered and ineffective. One such was the 1909 call by Archie Crawford, a fitter and editor of Johannesburg socialist newspaper *Voice of Labour* (1908-1912), for a socialism "irrespective of colour", or George Mason's cry for African workers "as fellow workers to come out" in a 1913 strike. More typical of organised white labour was H. W. Sampson, a printer from London who, when chairing the South African Labour Party's 1909 conference, refused a motion that class, not race, should guide party policy. In general then, whilst Crawford was willing to give some editorial voice to black leaders such as John Dube and Abdullah Abdurahman, early South African socialists had no coherent theory of black rights upon which to guide their relations with Africans. For their part, black political activists were at first inclined to be sceptical of their intentions, and remained largely unaware of socialist doctrines.[50]

Nevertheless, a minority of social democrats was awakening to the incipient power of black labour. Left-wing radicals split from the Labour Party in 1915 to form the International Socialist League (ISL). Its leaders, D. I. Jones and S. P. Bunting, emerged as champions of black rights and were instrumental in the 1921 establishment of the Communist Party of South Africa. Some members of these early socialist organisations privileged class over national issues (analogous to 1980s "workerists").[51]

Coloured and Indian workers shared poor conditions with African workers but when offered fringe benefits they began to organise separately. Work processes segregated workers from different backgrounds, rendering inter-racial class solidarity difficult. Policies of influx control and employer preference drove further wedges between workers. For example, Indian workers at Falkirk engineering, fearing replacement, failed to mobilise Africans in a 1937 strike. To take another example: African coal miners at Dundee, Natal, were isolated, largely unorganised, and divided racially, with strikes ending in failure. Such labour market ethnic segmentation hampered solidarity.[52]

Despite this segmented work force, capitalist exploitation and depressions still provoked industrial action among more privileged segments. In 1911-1913 strikes, Indian workers showed a level of class and political consciousness that some Africans noticed. White employees rarely expressed any kind of solidarity with black people. They stood by when police repressed a strike by 6,000 African people at Kimberley in 1905; De Beers had many alleged strike "ringleaders" jailed under Masters' and Servants Act. Yet, examples of vigorous and at times effective strikes and of tight industrial and political organisation offered models to both African workers and political activists.[53]

During the July 1913 white miners' strike, according to official reports, white people intimidated Africans who were "incited to strike and to demand more money". Africans, who had seen their wages recently cut, saw white workers in action, exerting power. As a result, 9,000 African workers on five mines joined the strike, some wearing red strike rosettes or later withdrew their labour; some picketed or drew up grievance manifestos such as calls for higher pay. African miners turned on that paternalistic emblem of control, the mine managers, and chased them out of the City and Suburban mines with stones, the same weapon with which they then fearlessly confronted mounted police. The mine owners needed soldiers with bayonets to arrest "ringleaders" among the workers. At the start of the following year, there were the first strikes by African coal miners, at Natal Navigation and Glencoe collieries in Natal, localities that combined labour migration with more settled African workers' quarters, the latter trend testifying to gradual proletarianisation. Further strikes by African coal miners occurred in 1918, at eight Witbank mines and again in Natal in 1919, defeated by armed soldiers.[54]

In a 1914 investigation, a magistrate noted that in 1913 black miners of all nationalities had been "absolutely together". In one incident, a group of 600 Swazi workers attacked mine officials. An African worker recounted how he and his comrades had stopped work to "get more money". During the major white general strike of the same year, 90 African mine workers at Van Ryn Gold Mine refused to work and escaped from the compound into a field, where a force of burghers attacked them, killing one.[55]

By the time of the formation of the ANC, it was clear to both black and white leaders that the overwhelming majority of African workers went to the mines to work under economic compulsion. At this time, such radicalisation as noted above indirectly helped mould an outlook among Congress leaders to policies that were more radical.

White domination therefore did not totally exclude inter-racial contact. Development of class consciousness among black workers could involve learning tactical lessons from white people on strike or organised in unions. Neither was the African workforce totally bereft of organisation. On the mines, a range of religious and cultural groups formed. By 1884, there were benefit societies. In 1906, the Cape and District Zulu Association claimed to represent Zulu workers. Domestic workers had their "kitchen associations". A state inspector reported in 1914, "some natives are realising that it is in their interests to form a combination, and they are engaged in bringing into existence what they call 'the Native Workers Union.'" Thomas Zini, a migrant worker (and Congress member) proposed an African miners' union in January 1912. There is no record of such unions surviving.[56]

In the absence of viable African unions, the focus of class struggle could, and did, either shift to nationalist or socialist groups, as between 1918 and 1920 when pass protests and strikes erupted, or take the form of wildcat strikes. By this time, Africans increasingly were the motor of industrial action. In contrast, white (male) worker militancy slowed to a crawl after the last major white strike in 1922. State reports noted "a new and noteworthy feature": African "labourers throughout the Union have adopted the strike weapon". In 1918, there were 23 recorded strikes, involving 2,759 white and only 35 black people but in 1920 105,658 workers, chiefly black miners, struck. In 1927, 4,418 black people went on strike compared with only 740 white people. In one year alone, 1920, there were strikes by Rand, Ingagane and Rietkuil miners, Steenbras labourers, and Sandhills rail workers, Pietermaritzburg workers and Durban and Port Elizabeth dockers. Miners in Natal struck in 1921 and 1926-1927, refinery workers in 1928, Wolhuter miners in 1923, Ermelo miners in

1924, and laundry workers in 1928-1929. The African working class was flexing its muscles.[57]

Most African workers remained un-unionised but some black unions emerged. The first successful black general labour union, the Industrial and Commercial Workers' Union (ICU), formed in 1919. For a while, workers were emboldened. A "stay at home" with well-organised pickets took place in Waaihoek in 1925 under ICU auspices. In general, the ICU eschewed strike action though this did not prevent un-unionised workers from protesting: in the 1920s, farm workers burnt crops, sugar workers absconded to higher paying rail work, and working women took mass action over passes and beer-halls.[58]

Organisation spread among "white collar" workers. The Cape Native Teachers' Association emerged in 1920. In 1926, the Northern and Southern Transvaal Native Teachers' Associations merged to become the Transvaal African Teachers' Association. In Natal, African teachers began to organise. ANC members were active in these bodies.[59]

In the late 1920s, the emergence of the first black industrial unions was encouraged by the relative shortage of labour in cities, acquisition of work-place skills, and a move to industrial rather than craft unions. The CPSA, excluded from the ICU, strongly supported these unions. In 1928, 12 of these industrial unions united in the South African Federation of Non-European Trade Unions (FNETU) claiming, perhaps exaggeratedly, a membership of 10,000-15,000 members. Thibedi acted as General Secretary, in September 1930 calling a mass meeting at CPSA headquarters, 41A Fox Street, Johannesburg over the issue of wages. However, by late 1930 FNETU was in serious decline.[60]

These were daring experiments in labour organisation. However, the hostile attitude of the state, employers, and white employees, together with migrant worker instability and low wages, resulted in weak union resources and legal barriers to operating, restricting steady growth of black industrial unionism. There also were political divisions and inexperience in leadership. Not surprisingly, the ICU and FNETU were short-lived.[61]

Nevertheless, weak unions did not stop African workers protesting intolerable conditions. In the 1930s, strikes continued to be largely a black phenomenon (Table 4). Workers stopped work on the Durban docks in 1932 and again in 1935, 1937 and 1939. Miners downed tools on the gold mines in 1931 and from 1934 to 1938, and on coalmines in 1931 and from 1934 to 1939. In 1934, miners held a concerted five-day boycott of Randfontein stores. Striking Newcastle coal miners in 1934 elected their own spokespersons. In 1937, workers at Welgedacht killed a mine manager. In 1936, 200 workers stoned a Brakpan compound office. By 1939, the Native Affairs Commissioner warned of "the rise of an industrial class among the Bantu" now "learning the lessons of industrial combination and agitation".[62]

Table 4. Workers on Strike, 1930–1939

Year	White strikers	Black strikers
1930	387	4,663
1933	1,255	330
1935	1,005	1,362
1937	1,057	4,849
1938	92	3,706
1939	32	4,839

Sources: *Union Statistics for 50 Years* p.G-18; R. Davies, *Capital, State and White Labour*, p. 262

In the 1930s, black workers took part in other forms of action, ranging from peaceful petitions to township violence. A list of grievances by black rail workers in Queenstown enumerated their demands: higher wages; provision of houses; extension of sickness fund benefits; waterproof clothes; and an end to pass laws. African workers took part in violent community-based protests against police raids in Middelburg, Vrededorp, Springs, Benoni, and Vereeniging.[63]

African unions remained fragile. Periodic attempts by CPSA and ANC activists and unionists to organise miners failed. In 1937, unionist Gana Makabeni told visiting African-American Ralph Bunche that lack of organising on the mines was due to compound impenetrability. African unions still had no legal status and did not receive information about wage arrears due their members. African workers could not move freely and were subject to arrest if they refused work orders. In 1930, police arrested African Laundry Workers' Union Secretary James Shuba for servicing striking members. When workers at Sayle and Rossack company requested increased wages in 1937, bullets met them; the victims' sentence was hard labour. Max Gordon, African Commercial and Distributive Workers' Union Secretary, observed that at Middleburg Collieries "oppressive legislation" maintained low wages. A Pretoria steel strike in 1935 saw the arrest of all strikers. Police told 12 African laundry workers that management had every right to sack them.[64]

Many workers remained beyond the reach of unions to service effectively. The 1,650 Port Elizabeth dockers had no union. There were abortive attempts to organise an estimated 275,000 domestic workers: by ANC activist Bransby Ndobe in 1930, by the National Liberation League in 1937, and by an ephemeral African Domestic Servants' League in the late 1930s. There was little union co-ordination and sectarianism weakened unions. FNETU criticised Albert Nzula, a communist also active in the ANC, for calling strikes "without adequate preparation". The sectarianism plaguing the communist movement in the early 1930s is apparent in the call of FNETU's bulletin, *The Hammer*, for workers to oppose not only the ruling class but also "reactionary trade unions and the Social fascists". By 1932, weakened by such sectarianism, it was no more than a shell.[65]

Solidarity with black workers by white unions remained rare. The South African Trades and Labour Council, formed in 1930, did not endorse job colour bars and let three black unions affiliate, yet rejected further applications for affiliation of African unions. The Cape Garment Workers' Union effectively used a closed-shop agreement to exclude African people. The Amalgamated Engineering Union in 1930 urged concerted action to enforce the colour bar on the pretext of relieving white unemployment.[66]

Despite these problems, some black industry-based unions survived, often as parallel branches of white registered unions. Ray Alexander, a communist, organised rail and harbour, chemical, sweet, food, tin, and laundry unions. "As I organised the workers I helped to develop their own leaders," she recalled to me. In 1936-1937, small unions covering printing, dairying, building and meat workers formed on the Rand. The Railway and Harbour Workers' Union was formed in 1936 in Cape Town and survived restrictions. An African General Workers' Union formed in Port Elizabeth in 1937. In Natal in the late 1930s, the CPSA helped form unions among baking, twine, and chemical workers. The African Trade Union Co-ordinating Committee, with 12 unions, emerged in 1937; by May 1938, it claimed 8,000 members.[67] In general, however, these unions remained weak.

African "white collar" unions also faced obstacles in the 1930s. Teacher unions faced interference by missionaries and the stagnant salaries of members. Industrial awards governing white nurses excluded African nurses who were ostracised from the South African Trained Nurses Association until 1932. In that year, the Bantu Trained Nurses Association was affiliated, but by 1934 had only 24 members.[68] The vast majority of African working people on farms, mines, and domestic work, remained un-organised. If the above constitutes the formal architecture of the black working class, then diverse and vibrant urban African cultures also were emerging in its ranks.

The African Cultural Turn and Workers

Given its multi-cultural nature, the African working class thrown together on the mines and factories exuded a cultural syncretism. This was not merely the trappings of industrial modernity. Capitalism certainly imposed a time-regulated working day and regimented work discipline. Also, mission Christianity, as the Comaroffs remark, required Africans to "learn the political language of colonialism".[69]

Yet African cultures did not disappear. Rather, Africans retained, defended, and re-worked their culture under the influence of newly adopted habits and commodities such as literacy and western clothing and musical instruments to produce new forms of culture—dance clubs, masculine migrant workers' poetic work songs (*lifela* in Sesotho), female-dominated shebeens and *stokvels*, and urban *marabi* culture. African working-class cultures emerged in locations such as the Malay Camp in Kimberley and Doornfontein in Johannesburg in the late nineteenth/early twentieth centuries, marked by new patterns of adaptation for survival and blending of different cultures. Writers generally emphasise this culture as belonging to proletarian or lumpen-proletarian sectors of impoverished African townships, but it could also be a *bridge* between different social strata, a unifying theme allowing expression of national or class solidarities. Far from being completely aloof from each other, workers and *kholwa shared* culture in such places where, David Coplan notes, "people ranging from petty-bourgeois professionals to domestic servants and industrial migrants gathered for social recreation". As Frank Bridgman perceived at the time: "These slum districts constitute the rendezvous for all classes of Natives." Writers interpreting such a deeply segregated society have rarely made these connections, but as Coplan further observes, there were continuities in modes of communication and experience that connected rural and urban, and middle- and working-class African lives.[70]

Other cultural arenas where *kholwa* could meet worker included the football field, dance hall, weddings, funerals, shebeens, church and social club. There were successful efforts to screen off more elitist black property-owning strata from those looked down on as *amaqaba* ("red", pagan, or "blanket" people). Aspirant *petit bourgeois* appropriated to themselves "genteel" sports such as cricket, or more "civilised" forms of music. Such tensions are typical of social dynamics, but there were bridges between social strata, especially in such a colonial-like society that insisted on reducing all black people to a common subaltern status. As Ellen Hellman observed in 1935, urban residence brought a multiplicity of contacts whilst oppression gave a "greater unity in common suffering". The relevance of this cultural dimension to the emerging relationship between African politics and the black labour movement becomes clearer when we try to imagine life as it then existed. Cultural connections fuse with geospatial proximity to re-create a picture of African life in which the lives of the African nationalist and the African worker need not always be so distant. Moreover, the migrant worker could act as a go-between. The African working class was very different to that in England, for instance, but the role of popular culture and politics in the making of both was analogous.[71]

Conclusion

By 1940, black workers still remained weakly organised. Yet their rising numbers and continued repression made them a highly volatile potential ANC ally. Three causes would influence closer ties with political forces. Firstly, powerful economic and political trends created a vacuum in industrial representation. Secondly, the failure of black unions to fill this vacuum left many workers without leadership, encouraging the ANC to claim to represent their interests. Thirdly, influenced by their isolation from white unionism, black workers tended to *combine* political and industrial demands. A repressive, rigid society made virtually every attempt at black labour organisation also a political act in the sense it challenged white hegemony. Whilst this was a great obstacle to free unions, politicisation of the labour movement offered potential for unity. Mark Shope, ANC and union veteran, claimed Africans always "rejected the ... line of 'no politics'" in the union movement.[72]

When worker actions became political, they entered the realm of the ANC—politics. At the same time, due to the factors outlined above, relatively little deep black class differentiation emerged. Neither a self-sufficient black bourgeoisie nor a black labour aristocracy materialised. When it came to rival political ideologies, there was little deep penetration of black working-class communities. Social democracy as a black political force was stillborn. Communism remained small, liberalism the preserve of the educated. Various short-lived black unions came and went, but the ANC survived. Whether the ANC connected with black labour would depend largely on the policies and attitudes of its branches. It is to the story of Congress that we now turn.

Notes

1   R. Elphick and V. Malherbe, "The Khoisan to 1828", in R. Elphick and H. Giliomee (eds.), *The Shaping of South African Society 1652-1840* (Middletown: Wesleyan University Press, 1988), pp. 3-65; S. Newton-King, *Masters and Servants on the Cape Eastern Frontier* (Cambridge: CUP, 1999); N. Worden, *Slavery in Dutch South Africa* (Cambridge: CUP, 1985), pp. 7-16; B. Carton, *Blood from Your Children: The Colonial Origins of Generational Conflict in South Africa* (Pietermaritzburg: University of Natal Press, 2000).

2   H. Houghton, "Economic Development, 1865-1965", in Wilson, *Oxford History of South Africa*, v. 2, pp. 1-49; *Cape Census of the Colony 1865*; A. Mabin, "The Rise and Decline of Port Elizabeth", *IJAHS* v. 19 (1986), pp. 275-303, p. 289; H. Robertson, "150 Years of Economic Contact between Black and White", *South African Journal of Economics [SAJE]* v. 3 (1935), pp. 3-25, p. 12; S. van der Horst, *Native Labour in South Africa* (Oxford: OUP, 1942), pp. 140-142; A. Purkis, "The Terms of Labour on the Cape Railways 1871-1885", *Smalberger Collection UCT*, C.5.2; *Cape Blue Book on Native Affairs*, 1900-1902.

3   Marx, *Capital* v. 1, p. 667; P. Harries, *Work, Culture and Identity: Migrant Labourers in Mozambique and South Africa, c1860-1910* (Johannesburg: Wits University Press, 1994), p. 227; S. Marks, *Reluctant Rebellion* (Oxford: OUP, 1970), pp. 120-130, 237-240; C. van Onselen, "Reaction to Rinderpest in Southern Africa 1896-7", *JAH* v. 13 (1972), pp. 473-488; J. Lambert, *Betrayed Trust: Africans and the State in Colonial Natal* (Pietermaritzburg: University of Natal Press, 1995); I. Machin, *Antbears and Targets for Zulu Assegais: The Levying of Forced African Labour and Military Service by the Colonial State of Natal* (Howick: Brevitas, 2002); *Cape Blue Book on Native Affairs* 1900 (pp. 54-56), 1901 (p. 35).

4   A. Trollope, *South Africa* (London: Chapman, 1878), p. 366; C. de Kiewiet, *The Imperial Factor in South Africa* (Cambridge: CUP, 1937), p. 2; C. Newbury, *The Diamond Ring: Business, Politics, and Precious Stones in South Africa, 1867-1947* (Oxford: OUP, 1989); A. Mabin, "The Making of Colonial Capitalism", Ph.D. thesis, Simon Fraser University, 1986, pp. 44-47; Davies, *Capital, State & White Labour* p. 46; A. Jeeves, *Migrant Labour in South Africa's Mining Economy* (Montreal: McGill-Queen's University Press, 1985).

5   Etherington, *Preachers,* pp. 12-13, 126-127, 179-192. By 1900, over 1,000 of 6,640 Lovedale graduates worked in transport or labouring: B. Kennedy, "Missionaries, Black Converts, and Separatists on the Rand, 1886-1910", *Journal of Imperial and Commonwealth History* v. 20 (1992), pp. 196-222, p. 201; *Cape Report and Proceedings of the Commission on Native Laws and Customs,* 1883 v. 2, pp. 285-296, 300-303, 327, 346-357, 282; *Cape Report of the Labour Commission. Minutes and Proceedings* (1893-1894) (G39-93); *Report of the South African Native Affairs Commission 1903-1905* (hereafter SANAC), v. 2, p. 446.

6   Trollope, *South Africa* p. 398; *Lovedale Past & Present* (Lovedale, 1887), pp. xiv, 374, 533.

7   R. Solomon, "Economic Conditions and Communications", in A. Herbertson (ed.), *The Oxford Survey of the British Empire: Africa* (Oxford: OUP, 1914), pp. 121-123; B. Bozzoli, "The Origins, Development and Ideology of Local Manufacturing in South Africa", *JSAS* v. 1 (1975), pp. 194-214; *The South African Natives: Their Progress and Present Conditions,* (London 1908), Chapter 1; *Report of Local Natives' Land Committee (Natal Province)* (U.G.34-18), p. 10.

8   P. Richardson, *Chinese Labour in the Transvaal* (London: Macmillan, 1982); *Minutes of Evidence, Transvaal Indigency Commission 1906-1908*, p. 343; A. de Minnaar, "Labour

Supply Problems of Zululand Sugar Planters 1905-1939", *Journal of Natal and Zulu History [JNZH]* v. 12 (1989), pp. 53-72; J. Lewis, "The New Unionism", *South African Labour Bulletin [SALB]* v. 3 no. 5 (1977), pp. 25-49; *Report of Industrial Legislation Commission* (1935), p. 11; *Union Statistics for Fifty Years, 1910-1960* (Pretoria, 1960), L-3-2.

9   R. Christie, *Electricity, Industry and Class in South Africa* (London: Macmillan, 1984), pp. 50-78; G. Marais, "Structural Changes in Manufacturing Industry 1916-1975", *SAJE* v. 49 (1981), pp. 26-46; B. Freund, "The Social Character of Secondary Industry in South Africa 1915-1945", in A. Mabin (ed.), *Organisation and Economic Change* (Johannesburg: Ravan Press, 1989), pp. 78-119, p. 103.

10   P. Maylam, *A History of the African People of South Africa* (Cape Town: David Philip, 1986), p. 148; P. Maylam, "The Changing Political Economy of the Region, 1920-1950", in R. Morrell (ed.), *Political Economy and Identities in KwaZulu-Natal* (Durban: Indicator, 1996), pp. 97-118, p. 102; *Report of Select Committee on Native Affairs (Natives (Urban Areas) Bill)* (SC3-23), p. 87; F. Bridgman, "Social Conditions in Johannesburg" *International Review of Missions* v. 15 1926, pp. 569-583, p. 583; A. Mariotti "The Incorporation of African Women into Wage Employment in South Africa 1920-1970", Ph.D. thesis, University of Connecticut, 1980, pp. 120, 278; *Union Statistics*, p. A-33.

11   A. Christopher, "Roots of Urban Segregation: South Africa at Union, 1910", *Journal of Historical Geography* v. 14 (1988), pp. 151-169; M. Swanson, "The Sanitation Syndrome" *JAH* v. 18 (1977), pp. 387-410; K. Tankard, "Urban Segregation: William Mvalo's 'Celebrated Stick Case,'" *SAHJ* 34 (1996), pp. 29-38.

12   *Union Statistics* L-3, A31-6, G-15; C. Schumann, *Structural Changes and Business Cycles in South Africa 1806-1936* (London: King 1938), pp. 170, 22-44; S. Jones and M. Müller, *The South African Economy, 1910-90* (Basingstoke: Macmillan, 1992), pp. 72, 170; Freund, "Character" p. 90; M. Morris and D. Kaplan, "Labour Policy in a State Corporation: Case Study of the SA Iron and Steel Corporation", *SALB* 2, 6 (1976), pp. 21-33; C. Richards, *The Iron and Steel Industry in South Africa* (Johannesburg: Wits University Press, 1940), pp. 293-299, Table 8; J. Tinley, *The Native Labour Problem of South Africa* (Chapel Hill: University of North Carolina Press, 1942), p. 114; *Industrial Legislation Commission of Enquiry* (UG62-51), pp. 7-11; J. Nattrass, *The South African Economy* (Oxford: OUP, 1981), p. 170; "13 Pages of Statistics Relating to the South African Economy in 1920s-1940s," *Saffery Papers*, ICS.

13   *Census* 1936; *Native Urban Employment* (Johannesburg: Wits Dept. of Commerce, 1948), pp. 2-13; Berger, *Threads of Solidarity*, p. 63; Hirson, *Yours for the Union*, pp. 38, 55; *Union Statistics*, p. A-33.

14   Before decimalisation of the monetary unit in 1961 South Africa used pounds (£), shillings (/-) and pence (d).

15   South African Native Races Committee, *The Natives of South Africa: Their Economic & Social Condition* (London: Murray, 1901), pp. 256-258; *Report of the Economic and Wage Commission* (UG14-26), pp. 263-273; *Evidence to Economic and Wages Commission* September 19th, 1925 (ICWU, 1925), p. 6; SANAC v. 5 annex 4; *Report of the Native Grievances Inquiry 1913-1914* (UG 37-14), pp. 37-9; H. Houghton, *The South African Economy* (Cape Town: OUP, 1978), p. 169; *South African Worker* 23 July 1926; Johnstone, *Class, Race and Gold*, p. 42; Wilson, *Labour in the Mines*, p. 46; *Official Yearbook of the Union* 1922 (p. 305), 1923 (p. 329), 1930 (p. 190).

16   M. Palmer, "Note on Some Native Budgets Collected in Durban", *South African Journal of Science* v. 25 (1928), pp. 499-506; Palmer, "Some Problems of the Transition from

Subsistence to Money Economy", *South African Journal of Science* v. 27 1930, pp. 117-125; *Official Yearbook of the Union, 1930-1931*, p. 205.

17 Schumann, *Changes*, pp. 168, 175; Tinley, *Labour*, p. 116; South Africa Dept. of Labour *Report* 1933; *Report of Social & Economic Commission 1930-1932*, p. 121; Cape Peninsula Joint Council, "Native Unemployment in Cape Town Area", 14 Oct. 1932, in South African Institute of Race Relations B Box Collection [*SAIRR-B*], B.7.1.1.

18 . C. Maxeke, "Social Conditions among Bantu Women and Girls", in *Christian Students and Modern South Africa* (Fort Hare, SCA. 1930); R. Phillips, *The Bantu in the City* (Lovedale Press, 1938); P. Laidler, "The Relationship of the Native to South Africa's Health", *South African Medical Journal* 8 Oct. 1932, pp. 617-628; Johannesburg Rotary Club. Committee on Non-European Affairs to Minister of Railways 9 Feb. 1938, "Draft Memorandum on Native Wages in Johannesburg, Sept. 1938", *SAIRR-B*.

19 R. Shongwe interview, transcript of *Apartheid* (1986), ICS Archives; "T. McClendon Interviews with Labour Tenants, Mid-Natal, 1992", Campbell Collections; *Report of Select Committee on Subject-Matter of Masters & Servants Law (Transvaal) Amendment Bill* (SC12-25), p. 92; E. Mahlangu, "I Mpilo Yezisebenzi Kwela se Oggies", *South African Worker* 12 Nov. 1926; *Bantu World* 23 Apr. 1938; E. Haines, "The Economic Status of the Cape Province Farm Native", *SAJE* v. 3 (1935), pp. 57-79; Dept. of Labour Report 1933, p. 63; Wilson, *Labour*, p. 163; "Native Labour in Zululand", *ILO*, 1936.

20 *Official Yearbook of the Union* 1930-1931, p. 190; Cobley, *Class and Consciousness*, p. 46.

21 Phillips, *Bantu in the City*, pp. 420-421; Basner, *Am I an African?*, p. 51; Cape Ordinance 25 (1929) six p. 82; R. Shepherd, "Memo on the Work and Experience of Lovedale Institution", *Minutes of Evidence Native Economic Commission* [NEC] 1930-1932; *Census* 1936; P. Abrahams, *Tell Freedom* (London: Faber, 1954), p. 324. A. Cobley, "A History of Professional Elites in Africa and the Caribbean: A Comparative Perspective", paper to ASA conference, Houston, Nov. 2001 p. 6 notes that by 1936 there were only 7 African lawyers, 7 doctors and 10 journalists, with over one third of teachers uncertificated.

22 Cobley, *Class and Consciousness*, pp. 40-49.

23 *Report and Proceedings of the Cape Peninsula Plague Advisory Board* (1901), pp. 33, 44, 98-111; Allen, *Mineworkers* v. 1 p. 239; R. Packard, *White Plague, Black Labour: Tuberculosis and the Political Economy of Health and Disease in South Africa* (Berkeley: University of California Press, 1989), pp. 67-9, 688-692; J. Baker, "'The Silent Crisis': Black Labour, Disease and the Economics and Politics of Health on the South African Gold Mines, 1902-1930", Ph.D. thesis, Queens' University, 1989, pp. 13, 28, 191; R. Edgecombe and B. Guest, "The Coal Miners' Way of Death", *JNZH* 8 (1985), pp. 63-83, p. 83; Edgecombe and Guest, "The Black Heart of the Beautiful Mountain: Hlobane Colliery, 1898-1953", *SAHJ* v. 18 (1986), pp. 191-221, p. 199; Bridgman, "Social Conditions", p. 573.

24 E. Hellmann, *Rooiyard* (Lusaka: Rhodes-Livingstone Institute, 1948), p. 11; W. Sachs, *Black Hamlet* (London: Bles, 1937), p. 126; Phillips, *Bantu*, p. 110; J. Cohen, "*Twatwa*: The Working Class of Benoni during the 1930s", *Africa Perspective* 20 (1982), pp. 76-96; P. Laidler, *Locations: Health and Sanitation* (East London, 1936), p. 10; S. Parnell, "Racial Segregation in Johannesburg: The Slums Act 1934-1939", *South African Geographical Journal* v. 70 (1988), pp. 112-126; *Cape Times* 22 Apr. 1935; Non-European Railway & Harbour Workers' Union, *We Want to Live* (1937); E. Kuzwayo, letter to *Umsebenzi* 20 June 1930.

25 R. Ross, "Emancipations and the Economy of the Cape Colony" *Slavery and Abolition* 14 1993 pp. 130-134; E. Bradlow, "The Khoi and the Proposed Vagrancy Legislation of

1834", *Quarterly Bulletin South African Library* 39 (1985) pp. 99-106; *South African Commercial Advertiser* 6 Sept, 1834; V. Malherbe, "Indentures and Unfree Labour in South Africa: Towards an Understanding," *SAHJ* 24 (1991) pp. 3-30; *Report of Select Committee on Master & Servants Acts* (1889); C. Bundy "The Abolition of the Masters and Servants Act," *SALB* v. 2 no. 1 (1975), pp. 37-46; M. Motala, "Theories of the Rule of Law in South Africa with Special Reference to the Control of Labour", M.Phil. thesis, University of Warwick, 1981, pp. 157-179; *Commission of Enquiry into the Public Service of the Colony 1904-1906, Minutes*, v. 5, p. 1671; Cape. *Report of the Labour Commission* (1894), v. 2, p. 386ff; C. Feinstein, *An Economic History of South Africa* (Cambridge: CUP, 2005), pp. 54-55.

26   P. Delius and S. Trapido, "*Inboekselings* and *Oorlams*: The Creation and Transformation of a Servile Class", in Bozzoli, *Town and Countryside* pp. 53-88; J. Bergh and F. Morton, (eds.) *"To Make Them Serve": The 1871 Transvaal Commission on African Labour* (Pretoria: Protea, 2003), p. 104; F. Morton, "Female *Inboekelinge* in the South African Republic, 1850-1880" *Slavery and Abolition* v. 26 (2005), pp. 199-215.

27   D. Duncan, "Wage Regulation for African Workers 1918-1948," *South African J. of Economic History* v. 8 (1993), pp. 24-45; I. Ibokette, "Labour Strategies in the Transvaal Gold Mining Industry 1890-1910" M.A. thesis, Queens University, 1983, pp. 8-24; *Natal Mercury* 22 Aug. 1914. E. Katz, "Revisiting the Origins of the Industrial Colour Bar in the Witwatersrand Gold Mining Industry, 1891-1899", *JSAS* v. 25 no.1 (1999), pp. 73-88 shows mine colour bars involved not just pressure from white workers but also engineers and state officials.

28   SC3-23 p. 199; J. Lever, "Capital and Labour in South Africa: Passage of the Industrial Conciliation Act 1924" *SALB* 3 10 (1977), pp. 4-31; *Statutes 1913-1953* Act 11 1924/24, 816; D. Duncan, "The State Divided: Farm Labour Policy in South Africa 1924-1948", *SAHJ* 24 (1991), pp. 67-89; *Social and Economic Commission Report 1930*, p. 217; M. Chanock, *The Making of South African Legal Culture 1902-36* (Cambridge: CUP, 2001); K. Breckenridge, "'We Must Speak for Ourselves': The Rise and Fall of a Public Sphere on the South African Gold Mines, 1920 to 1931", *Comparative Studies in Society and History* 40 (1998), pp. 71-108.

29   Orde-Browne in "Conference on Africa", Minutes of First Meeting, Rhodes House, 9 Nov. [1929?], Ms. Fisher, 67 fols. 44-74, Bodleian Library; *Report of Industrial Legislation Commission* (1935), pp. 13, 41; M. Stein, "Max Gordon and African Trade Unionism on the Witwatersrand, 1935-1940", *SALB* v. 3 9 (1977), pp. 41-57; "Minutes of Meeting 9 Aug. 1939 Explaining Conditions under which Government is Prepared to Afford the Recognition to Organisations of Native Workers", *Saffery Papers* A5(iii), ICS; *Report of the Native Affairs Commission 1939/40*; *Report of Select Committee on ... the Wage Bill* (SC5-37) p. 111.

30   C. Perrings, *Black Mineworkers in Central Africa: Industrial Strategies and the Evolution of an African Proletariat in the Copperbelt, 1911-1941* (London: Heinemann, 1979), pp. 207-229; V.I. Lenin, "On Strikes", in Lenin, *On Trade Unions* (Moscow: Progress, 1978), pp. 57-67, pp. 61-66.

31   N. Worden and G. Groenewald (eds.) *Trials of Slavery* (Cape Town: Van Riebeeck Society, 2005); J. Mason, *Social Death and Resurrection: Slavery and Emancipation in South Africa* (University of Virginia Press, 2003); G. Baines, "The Port Elizabeth Disturbances of October 1920", MA thesis, Rhodes University, 1988, p. 57; Kirk, *Making a Voice*, Chapter 5; J. Smalberger and K. Gottschalk, "The Earliest Known Strikes by Black Workers" *SALB* 3 7 (1977) pp. 73-75; *Cape Monitor* 7 Mar. 1854; A. Mabin, "Strikes in the Cape Colony

1854-1899", African Studies seminar paper, University of the Witwatersrand, May 1983; D. Hemson, "Class Consciousness and Migrant Workers: Dock Workers of Durban", Ph.D. thesis, University of Warwick, 1979; V. Bickford-Smith, "Protest, Organisation and Ethnicity among Cape Town Workers 1891-1902", *Studies in the History of Cape Town* 7 (1994) pp. 84-108.

32 Worger, *City of Diamonds*, p. 287; P. Harries, Capital, State and Labour on the l9th Century Witwatersrand: A Reassessment", *SAHJ* 18 (1986), pp. 25-45, Harris, *Work, Culture and Identity*, p. 132; "Native Labour Crisis," *Imvo Zabantsundu* 1 Oct. 1896. For conscious mine owner policy of depressing wages, see evidence in *The Native Labour Question in the Transvaal: Extracts from the Industrial Commission of Inquiry: Report and Proceedings ... 1897* (London: PS King, [1901].

33 *Cape Argus* 20 Feb 1872; Mabin, "Strikes", pp. 8, 35; W. Beinart, *The Political Economy of Pondoland, 1860-1930* (Cambridge, 1983), pp. 9-25; P. Phoofolo, "Zafa! Kwahlwa! Kwasa! African Responses to the Rinderpest Epizootic in the Transkeian Territories 1897-1898", *Kronos* 30 (2004), pp. 94-117, p. 117.

34 J. Lewis, "Rural Contradictions and Class Consciousness", *Africa Seminar* 5 (1985), pp. 38-58; M. Mulaudzi, "'U Shumu Bulasi': Agrarian Transformation in the Zoutpansberg District of South Africa to 1946", PhD thesis, University of Minnesota, 2000; M. Murray, "The Formation of the Rural Proletariat in the South African Countryside", in M. Hanagan (ed.), *Confrontation, Class Consciousness and the Labor Process* (New York: Greenwood, 1985), pp. 97-121; P. Scully, "The Bouquet of Freedom: Social and Economic Relations in Stellenbosch District, 1870-1900", MA thesis, University of Cape Town, 1987, pp. 85-89, 128; C. Van Onselen, *Chibaro: African Mine Labour in Southern Rhodesia 1900-1933* (London: Pluto, 1976), p. 244.

35 J. Simons, "Masters and Servants", *Fighting Talk* Nov. 1956, pp. 3-4; C. Elliott (Manager Cape Railways), C. Lura (drill-worker), Protector of Natives (Kimberley), *Report of the Labour Commission* v. 1, p. 161, v. 2 pp. 367, 399; K. Atkins, *The Moon is Dead! Give Us Our Money: The Cultural Origins of an African Work Ethic, Natal, South Africa, 1843-1900* (London: Currey, 1993), pp. 90, 128, 134.

36 *Report of the Labour Commission* v. 2, pp. 156 (Davids), 461 (August), 362-363 (Mavula), 430 (Cochlin); Bickford-Smith, "Protest," pp. 86-88, 91; V. Bickford-Smith, *Ethnic Pride and Racial Prejudice in Victorian Cape Town* (Cambridge: CUP, 1995), pp. 108-111, 183, 207, 209.

37 *Natal Witness* 28 Nov. 1895; *Report of Labour Commission* (1894) v. 2 pp. 199-201 (Daniels), v. 3, p. xvii, v. 2, p. 548 (Iafele), pp. 574-577, 583 (Port Elizabeth); Transvaal. *Mining Industry Commission 1907-1908 Evidence* (TG2-08), pp. 1405, 1424-1425 (Ware).

38 *Report of the Labour Commission* v. 2, pp. 100-114 (Fortuin), 459 (Zwartboy), 542 (Kakasa), 585 (Dlepu), 284 (Richmond), 691 (Meyer), v. 3, pp. 17, 22 (Pellem, Hlati) v. 1 p. 128 (Veltman on De Beers workers); SANAC, v. 4, pp. 627-628 (Francis); *Report of Select Committee, Master and Servants Acts* (1889), p. 15.

39 SANAC, v. 4, p. 645 (Mama), 647 (Makue).

40 P. Warwick, *Black People and the South African War 1899-1902* (Cambridge: CUP, 1983) pp. 9-10, 124-138; *Blue-Book on Native Affairs* 1900 (p. 55 Mount Frere), 1901 (p. 9 Barkley; p. 47 St. Marks); J. Krikler, "Agrarian Struggle and the South African War", *Social History* 14 (1989), pp. 153-157, Krikler, *Revolution from Above*, pp. vii, 2-3; B. Nasson, *Abraham Esau's War* (Cambridge: CUP, 1991), pp. 1-29, 62, 170-182.

41 Warwick, *Black People*, pp. 169-74, "Black Industrial Protest on the Witwatersrand 1901-1902," *SALB* v. 2 8 (1976), pp. 22-35; Pritchard to SNA 21 July 1902, Report of G. Sirckin

28 June 1902, South African Materials 1913-1979 [SOU/I] file 6 SNA11/1308/1902, University of York; N. Lowe, Superintendent Docks Location to SANAC v. 2, pp. 105-107, 114; S. Dubow, "African Labour at the Cape Town Docks 1900-4", *Studies in the History of Cape Town* 4 (1984), pp. 108-134; J. Watson to SANAC v. 2, p. 231.

42 *Report of Labour Commission* v. 1 1893, pp. 126 (Veltman), 21 (McKenzie). Headmen received only £5 at appointment and a ceiling of £24 after 20 years: E. Dower, Native Affairs to *Commission of Enquiry into the Public Service of the Colony, 1904-1906, Minutes of Evidence,* v. 5, p. 1853; V. Bickford-Smith, "Black Labour at the Docks at the Beginning of the Twentieth Century", *Studies in the History of Cape Town* v. 1 (1979), pp. 75-125, pp. 103, 112.

43 *Report of the Labour Commission* v. 2 pp. 429, 489-492 v. 1 pp. 35, 113 J. Cochlin, W. Kitch, T. Cairncross.

44 S. Moroney, "Development of the Compound as a Mechanism of Worker Control 1900-12" *SALB* v. 4 3 (1978) pp. 29-49, p. 42; Turrell, *Diamond Fields*; J. Guy and M. Thabane, "Technology, Ethnicity and Ideology: Basotho Miners and Shaft-Sinking on the South African Gold Mines", *JSAS* 14 (1988) pp. 257-278; Moodie, *Going for Gold*; Harries, *Work, Culture and Identity,* Chapter 3, pp. 222-225; T. Ranger, "Faction Fighting, Race Consciousness and Worker Consciousness: A Note on the Jagersfontein Riots of 1914", *SALB* v. 4 no. 5 (1978), pp. 66-74.

45 S. Moroney, "Mine Workers' Protest on the Witwatersrand 1901-1912", *SALB* v. 3 5 (1977), pp. 5-24; S. Moroney, "Industrial Conflict in a Labour Repressive Economy: Black Labour on the Transvaal Gold Mines 1901-12" BA thesis, University of the Witwatersrand, 1976, p. 114; *Transvaal Labour Commission Report* 1903; TG2-08, p. 1310; Native Affairs *Report* 1911, p. 42, 1913-1918, p. 112: declining from 14,943 in 1912 to 11,483 in 1915 and 5,941 in 1918; Report of GNLB in *Blue Book on Native Affairs 1910* (U17-11), p. 392.

46 Dubow, "African Labour", pp. 109-111, 130-131.

47 H. Southall, "British Artisan Unions in the New World" *Journal of Historical Geography* v. 15 (1989), pp. 163-182; Simons, *Class and Colour* pp. 25-31; Davies, *Capital, State and Labour* pp. 72, 361; Johnstone, *Class, Race and Gold* pp. 23, 51; J. Hyslop, "The Imperial Working Class Makes Itself 'White': White Labourism in Britain, Australia and South Africa before the First World War", *Journal of Historical Sociology* v. 12 (1999), pp. 398-421, J. Hyslop, "The World Voyage of James Keir Hardie: Indian Nationalism, Zulu Insurgency and the British Labour Diaspora 1908-8," *Journal of Global History* v. 1 (2006), pp. 343-362.

48 *Report of Labour Commission* (1894) v. 2 p. 402 (Smith); TG2-08 pp. 1218 (Musson), 1430 (Riley), 1405, 1424-1425 (Ware); Rubusana in *Natives of South Africa,* p. 25; D. I. Jones, "Communism in South Africa", *Communist Review* v. 1 no. 3 (1921), pp. 15-17.

49 SANAC, v. 2 (Cape Evidence), p. 308.

50 *Voice of Labour* 31 July, 14 Aug., 16 Oct., 6 Nov. 1909, 7 Jan. 1910 (Dube), 4 Mar. 1910; E. Katz, *A Trade Union Aristocracy* (Johannesburg: Wits University Press, 1976), p. 310; J. Daniel, "Radical Resistance to Minority Rule in South Africa 1906-1965", Ph.D. thesis, SUNY, 1975, p. 47; Simons, *Class and Colour* pp.86-89, 106, 141-154

51 Simons, *Class and Colour* p. 204; D. Ticktin, "Origins of the South African Labour Party, 1880-1910", Ph.D. thesis, University of Cape Town, 1973; *International* 10 Sep. 1915, 7 Dec. 1917, 18 Feb. 1916; L. van der Walt, "'The Industrial Union is the Embryo of Socialist Commonwealth': The ISL and Revolutionary Syndicalism in South Africa 1915-1920", *Comparative Studies of South Asia, Africa & Middle East* 19 (1999), pp. 5-28.

52 P. Duin, "Artisans and Trade Unions in the Cape Town Building Industry 1900-24," in W. James and M. Simons (eds.), *The Angry Divide* (Cape Town: David Philip, 1989), pp. 95-110; F. Ginwala, "Class Consciousness and Control: Indian South Africans 1860-1946", Ph.D. thesis, Oxford University, 1975, pp. 430, 396-398; V. Padayachee, S. Vawda and P. Tichmann, *Indian Workers and Trade Unions in Durban 1930-1950* (Durban: ISER, 1985); R. Edgecombe and B. Guest, "Labour Conditions on the Natal Collieries: The Case of the Dundee Coal Company, 1908-1955", African Studies seminar paper, University of the Witwatersrand, May 1986, p. 31.

53 J. Beall and M. North-Coombes, "The 1913 Disturbances in Natal", *JNZH* v. 6 (1983), pp. 48-77; Worger, *City of Diamonds*, p. 301; M. Swan, "The 1913 Natal Indian Strike" *JSAS* v. 10 (1984), pp. 239-258.

54 *Report of Judicial Commission of Inquiry into Witwatersrand Disturbances*, pp. 7-16 and its *Minutes of Evidence,* pp. 235-237, 319, *Report of Witwatersrand Disturbances Commission* (1913) p. 16; Governor General to Sec. of State 20 July 1913, *British Documents on Foreign Affairs: Reports and Papers from the Foreign Office Confidential Print* (Bethesda MD: University Publications of America, 1995), v. 10, p. 371; P. Alexander, "Challenging Cheap-Labour Theory: Natal and Transvaal Coal Miners, c. 1890-1950", *Labour History* v. 49 no. 1 (2008), pp. 47-70, pp. 57-59.

55 C. Diamond, "The Natives' Grievances Enquiry 1913-1914," *SAJE,* v. 36 (1968), pp. 211-27; *Report Economic Commission 1914*; Johnstone, *Class, Race and Gold,* p. 169-71; *Report of the Native Grievances Inquiry 1913-1914* (UG 37-14), pp. 36, 64, 82; "Trouble with Natives" *Transvaal Leader* 19 Jan. 1914 reprinted in *Correspondence Relating to the Recent General Strike in South Africa* (Cd 7348), p. 136.

56 J. Kirk, "The Formation of an African Working Class in South Africa: Workers' Protest and Consciousness 1900-1930," MA thesis, University of Wisconsin, 1980, pp. 10, 122; J. Kirk, "A 'Native' Free State at Korsten: Challenge to Segregation in Port Elizabeth South Africa, 1901-1905", *JSAS* v. 17 (1991), pp. 309-336; L. Forman, *Black and White in South African History* (Cape Town, 1959), p. 5; Odendaal, *Vukani Bantu,* p. 62; Atkins, *The Moon is Dead,* pp. 122-135; *Report of Economic Commission 1914,* p. 179; Moroney, "Mine Workers", pp. 7, 15; "A Native Miner's Union," *Voice of Labour,* 12 Jan. 1912.

57 Native Affairs Report, 1919-21, pp. 10-11; Colonial Office (CO) 551/149 4892 Governor General's Report 10, 31 Jan. 1922; Dept. of Mines. Factory Division. *Annual Report* 1919, p. 27; South Africa. *Official Year Book* 1921, p. 320; *Cape Times* 2 Mar. 1922, 19 Aug. 1920; H.J. Ringrose, *Trade Unions in Natal* (Oxford: OUP, 1951), p. 14; Edgecombe, "Black Heart", p. 217; Hemson, "Class Consciousness, pp. 203-207; *South African Worker* 24 Oct. 1928; *Union Statistics* G-18; C. van Onselen, *The Seed is Mine: The Life of Kas Maine, a South African Sharecropper 1894-1985* (Cape Town: David. Philip, 1996), p. 151.

58 *International* 19 Dec. 1919; Kadalie, *My Life and the ICU,* pp. 31-35; B. Hirson, "The Bloemfontein Riots 1925", *SSA* 82/11; M. Murray, "'Burning the Wheat Stacks': Land Clearances and Agrarian Unrest along the Northern Middleburg Frontier, c.1918-1926" *JSAS* v. 15 (1988), pp. 74-95, p. 78; *Report on Suppression of Stock Thefts* (SC4-23), pp. 193-208; SC12-25, pp. 80, 92; H. Bradford, "'We Are Now the Men'", in Bozzoli, *Class and Conflict,* pp. 292-323; W. Beinart, "Women in Rural Politics: Herschel District in the 1920s and 1930s", in Bozzoli, *Class and Conflict,* pp. 324-357, p. 324.

59 R.L. Peteni, *Towards Tomorrow: The Story of the African Teachers Association of South Africa* (Morges, 1978), pp. 22, 52; Obituary of S.M. Makgatho, *Bantu World* 2 June 1951.

60 J. Lewis, "The New Unionism: Industrialisation and Industrial Unionism in South Africa 1925-1930" *SALB* v. 3 5 (1977), pp. 25-49; M. Stein, "African Trade Unionism on the Witwatersrand, 1928-1940" BA thesis, University of the Witwatersrand 1977, p. 14; W. Ballinger to W. Holtby 15 Jan. 1930, *W.G. Ballinger Papers 1920-1960*, Yale University microfilm; "Black Workers Fight for More Wages," FNETU flyer 15 June 1930, Glass Papers, Rochlin Collection of South African Political and Trade Union Organizations, Concordia University. FNETU numbers seem exaggerated: M. Roth ("The Wide-Ranging Influence of the 1928 Decree of the Communist International" *Acta Academica* 34 [2002] pp. 114-136) using CPSA sources, notes the Comintern came to see FNETU as a "paper" organisation, but skeleton unions probably existed.

61 G. Clack, "Changing Structure of Industrial Relations in South Africa with Special Reference to Racial Factors and Social Movements", Ph.D. thesis, University of London, 1962 pp. 232-243; [S. P. Bunting] "Statistics of SA Labour" intercepted letter [1930], Dept. of Justice (JUS) files, National Archives, Pretoria; B. Weinbren to E. Roux 27 Apr. 1929, *Roux Papers*, ICS.

62 *Umsebenzi* 15 Apr. 1932, 23 Jun. 15 Sep. 1934, 27 Mar. 1937, 12 Mar. 1938; *Midland News* 18 Aug. 1931, 5 Apr. 1932; Dept. Labour *Report* 1933, p. 42; Native Affairs Report 1935, p. 68; Hemson, "Class", p. 727; Allen, *Mineworkers*, p. 339; Ringrose, *Unions*, p. 23; *Rand Daily Mail* 1 Nov., 31 Oct. 1939; Hirson, *Yours for the Union*, p. 73; J. McNamara, "Black Workers Conflict on South African Mines 1973-1982", Ph.D. thesis, University of the Witwatersrand 1985, pp. 33-38, 64, 80; *Rand Daily Mail* 11 Feb. 1936; *Native Affairs Report 1939-1940*, p. 7.

63 Petition in *South African Unions Papers, 1927-1960* reel 9, ICS; Hirson, *Yours for the Union*, Chapter 6; *Vereeniging: Who is to Blame?* (Johannesburg: CPSA, 1937); *Report of Vereeniging Location Riots (1937) Commission*.

64 *Umsebenzi* 29 Aug., 17 Oct. 1930, 7 Aug. 1931, Apr. 14 1933, 5 Nov. 1932, 22 Sep. 1934, 18 May 1935, 4 Apr. 1936; Allen, *Mineworkers*, pp. 333-342; Simons, *Class and Colour*, p. 512; Hirson, *Yours for the Union*, pp. 40, 169; R. Bunche, *An African American in South Africa* (Athens, OH: Ohio University Press, 1992), p. 190; W. Ballinger, "Memo on African Industrial Organisations and Their Recognition", Mar. 1939, "African Trade-Unions, Activities and Disabilities in the Labour Movement", M. Gordon, "The Question of Recognition of African Trade Unions" [n.d.], *Saffery Papers*, ICS; *Cape Argus* 15 Dec. 1930; Friends of Africa Interim Industrial Report 28 Oct. 1937; M.Gordon to Wage Board Nov. 1939; ACDWU. "Memo to Wage Board July 1938" SAIRR-B reel 31; African Laundry Workers' Union to SA Police [SAP] 25 Jan. 1937, in "SA Unions Papers 1927-1960," reel 8.

65 Hirson, *Yours for the Union*, Chapter 5, p. 42; *Umsebenzi* 10 Oct., 25 July 1930, 15 Apr. 1932; A. Nzula, I.I. Potekhin and A.Z. Zusmanovich, *Forced Labour in Colonial Africa*, ed. R. Cohen (London: Zed Press, 1979: first published in Russian 1933), pp. 131-137; *The Hammer* Nov. 1931; Dept. of Labour. *Report* 1933, p. 42.

66 J. Lewis, *Industrialisation and Trade Union Organisation in South Africa 1924-1955: Rise and Fall of SATLC* (Cambridge: CUP, 1984); Friends of Africa Industrial Report Dec 1936, SAIRR-B reel 11; AEU to Boilermakers Ironworkers & Shipbuilders Society 20 May 1930, "South African Mining Unions Papers" ICS.

67 R. Alexander interview with the author, Lusaka, May 1989. See also her memoir: *All My Life and All My Strength*. ed. R. Suttner (Johannesburg: STE, 2004); M. Kiloh and A. Sibeko, *A Fighting Union: An Oral History of the South African Railway and Harbour Workers' Union* (Randburg: Ravan Press, 2000), p. 9; Phillips, *Bantu in the City*, p. 64;

Friends of Africa Industrial Report Dec. 1936, Adviser's Report Aug. 1937, *Saffery Papers*; *Umsebenzi* 27 Jun, 18 Jul, 8 Aug. 1936; R. Lambert, "Political Unionism in South Africa: The South African Congress of Trade Unions: 1955-1965"' Ph.D. thesis, University of the Witwatersrand, 1988 p. 483; *Bantu World* 18 Aug. 1938; B. Hirson, "Reorganisation of African Trade Unions in South Africa, 1936-1942" ICS paper 1975; M. Gordon, "Memo on Native Trade Unions", 20 Dec. 1938, *Saffery Papers*.

68 *Umsebenzi* 25 Jul. 1930; Cape Ordinance 25 1929 6, p. 82; R. Shepherd, "Memo on the Work and Experience of Lovedale Institution", in "Minutes of Evidence" Native Economic Commission 1930-1932, SOAS; N. Lubanga, "Nursing in South Africa: Black Women Workers Organize", in M. Turshen (ed.), *Women and Health in Africa* (Trenton: Africa World Press, 1991), pp. 51-78; Bantu Trained Nurses Association. 2nd Annual Meeting, 9 Dec. 1934 [Minutes], A. B. Xuma, Papers [XP], ABX 341209, reel 2.

69 Atkins, *The Moon is Dead;* J. and J.L. Comaroff, *Of Revelation and Revolution* v. 1 (Chicago: University of Chicago Press, 1991), p. 308.

70 D. Coplan, "The Emergence of an African Working-Class Culture", in Marks and Rathbone, *Industrialisation and Social Change*, pp. 358-375, pp. 359, 365; Harries, *Work, Culture and Identity,* Chapter 3.

71 Hellmann, *Rooiyard*, p. 114; Delius, "*Sebatakgomo*"; Harries, *Work, Culture and Identity*; E.P. Thompson, *The Making of the English Working Class* (London: Penguin, 1968).

72 R. Davies, "Capital Restructuring and the Modification of the Racial Division of Labour in South Africa", *SSA* 26 (1981), pp. 121-132; E. Webster, "Champion, the ICU and the Predicament of the African Trade Unions" *SALB* v. 1 6/7 (1974), pp. 6-13, p. 9; Mark Shope interview with the author, Lusaka, May 1989.

4

Early African Political Organisations and Black Labour

Early African political leaders could build bridges to black workers in a variety of ways: shared ideologies such as nascent nationalism or religion; shared history and culture; common oppression; policies that supported labour interests; and direct support for worker struggles. This chapter outlines the tentative and ambiguous, yet multifaceted and concerned policies towards black labour by incipient African political protest movements in the decades prior to the formation of the ANC in 1912. These antecedents are important because not only did many of these organisations become ANC branches, with their leading figures prominent in Congress, but also because traditions of concern for and interaction with labour laid down in this period are likely to have influenced ANC policies.

The emergence of early African (proto)-nationalism has been ascribed various origins, such as struggles over land, the influence of Christianity, and involvement of subaltern classes. Christian educated social strata (*kholwa*, or believers) such as Tiyo Soga first began to mention the idea of a wider African nation in the emergent black press of the later nineteenth century. These educated leaders began to present petitions of black grievances, for instance in Natal in 1863 and 1875, and in the Cape in 1869.[1]

Whilst radical historians from the 1970s sneered at this ultra-moderate petition-based politics, recent revisionist historians have begun to unpack the way in which petitions for black rights reflected the birth of a political culture of "evening meetings and social gatherings where people who wanted to discuss grievances turned their ideas into intelligible petitions".[2] Seen in this context, early Congress politics would be as much the reflection of an emergent black political agenda as any mimicry of white bourgeois politics. Moreover, as I noted in Chapter 1, petitions were also a weapon of black workers.

Traditions of resistance grew which, as Clifton Crais argues for the Eastern Cape, ranged from "meetings of the African elite to the daily struggles of farm labourers". Many political leaders, whom we shall meet below, raised labour issues. As early as 1888, Elijah Makiwane criticised low wages of black workers in Port Elizabeth.[3]

We must not exaggerate the ability of early black political leaders—or for that matter of black churches—to represent labour effectively. Yet often there was a correlation between urban growth, proletarianisation, and organisational growth. "Ethiopian" churches really "took off" in the Vaal triangle, where thousands of labourers joined; even in the 1920s, many local independent church leaders held "labourer's passes", indicating either they were workers or moved among workers.[4]

The African Methodist Episcopal (AME) Church's challenge to white authority influenced Congress. James Tantsi, Marshall Maxeke, and Henry Reed Ngcayiya, all Congress founders, were AME leaders. Later ANC radicals, such as Selby Msimang and James Ngojo, had similar ties. Preachers, some ex-mineworkers, began to penetrate compounds despite official sanction. AME ranks included carpenters and other workers.[5]

Such class interaction exacerbated colonist apprehensions about African resistance. Colonial official James Stuart worried over black miners now "acquainted with … insidious … propaganda called Ethiopianism".[6]

In the late nineteenth and early twentieth centuries, *kholwa* economic expansion and then the blocking of their advancement associated with fiscal crises and growing political exclusion helped push educated but marginalised African people into politics. An African "elite" (but one *without* power or, as La Hausse says, marginalised) took shape, whose leaders began to express their demands in political ideas through newspapers and organisations.[7]

New, often short-lived, political groups emerged, at first chiefly in the Eastern Cape. The Native Educational Association was established in 1879. In Port Elizabeth, *Imbumba Yamanyama* ("Inseparable Union", 1882-1884), and the African and American Working Men's Association (1890s), which combined black consciousness with mutual aid, expressed concern about black economic interests. In 1888 in Natal, *Funamalungelo* ("Demand Civil Rights") formed, and appears to have lasted until 1908. Native Vigilance Associations (VA) and Congresses, precursors of the ANC, arose: a loosely structured South African Native Congress (SANC) in 1898; the Natal Native Congress (NNC) in 1900; the Cape Native Congress and Transvaal Native VA in 1902, and the Orange River Colony (ORC) Native VA (later ORC Congress) in 1903. These groups formed at a time of growing economic and political crisis. Influenced by prevailing liberal ideology, they saw no automatic connection between their struggles and those of workers, but they articulated early forms of national consciousness and were rooted in local communities that included many workers. Eventually, most became ANC provincial branches.[8]

I discuss the history of these Congresses after 1912 in following chapters. Odendaal has splendidly detailed their history before this date but it is crucial to understand their complex relations with labour. They became quite widely known among Africans due to their advocacy of black rights, focusing on land and the franchise but also raising labour issues, creating an impression on some. In 1903, a writer in *The Friend* stated: "If Native organisations such as the Native Congress ... were granted power to control and supervise Native labour agency we would soon find this country on the highway to prosperity ... to the satisfaction of both master and servant."[9] This signalled awareness that Congress may have had both some power of control *over*, and empathy *with*, black labour.

The growth of political bodies went hand in hand with steady proletarianisation, so it should come as no surprise that labour concerns recurred in their deliberations irrespective of class identifications of particular leaders. This was the case when, from 1903 to 1904, African political figures gave evidence before the South African Native Affairs Commission (SANAC), one of whose briefs was to investigate labour issues.

The SANAC saw African workers as not yet constituting a class accustomed to and dependent on continuous wage labour, but conceded they were "becoming good workers in mines and more or less skilled in the industries"; their work was hard and dangerous, with exploitation by agents and "occasional harsh treatment". Commissioners (led by Sir Godfrey Lagden) rejected higher wages as a means to increase labour supply, preferring enforcement of vagrancy laws and rents, and on politics, they felt it better to allow open African parties than provoke "secret plotting".[10]

The SANC contested SANAC's assumption that government could best obtain data on African governance from replies to questions set by *white* rulers at meetings with *individuals*. SANC General Secretary Jonathan Tunyiswa presented resolutions from a 1903 Congress meeting in King William's Town requesting African representation on the Commission, public African meetings, and African input to frame questions—much along the lines of the Freedom Charter 50 years later. SANAC rejected the resolutions.[11]

There were limits to this concern. In 1909, SANC President Walter Rubusana joined with ORC Native Congress leaders in a protest letter to the Colonial Secretary over "degrading, harsh, arbitrary, [and] vexatious" regulations forcing African women in the ORC to carry passes. They had also raised this "standing grievance" in a 1908 royal petition. The SANC argued that African women in colonies lacking female passes were "better servants" and their "social scale" rose. It offered no challenge here to the subordinate role of labour in society: authorities could prevent desertion by "mere registration of contracts as between masters and servants". African leaders saw here an opportunity for their own advancement. Involving "standholders" and "headmen" in local government, they suggested, could ensure good conduct of women and workers. Nevertheless, their probable fear of sinking into the rigours of proletarian life balanced their condemnation of the role of force in the colonial labour system. Passes would "force women to go out and work", thus "introducing a pernicious system, viz.—compulsory labour, as sheer necessity will compel these people to go out and work". In this respect, the Congresses objectively articulated views that represented workers' interests—no worker consciously would favour forced labour! The paucity of enfranchised African citizens simultaneously weakened political organisations yet made them more likely to seek alliances with other social strata, such as workers, to bolster their fortunes.[12]

If there was condescension by men, this did not stop African women from finding ways to participate in early political organisations. Charlotte Manye (Maxeke) in 1902 was a Transvaal delegate to a SANC conference. "Her contribution was highly praised," but Congress "concluded that the time was not right for women to participate" in politics.[13] A closer examination of the ideas and actions of these provincial Congresses throws light on the origins of the ANC's later alliances with labour.

The Transvaal

The Transvaal Native Congress (TNC), the most radical provincial branch of what became the ANC, formed out of several earlier organisations. In 1902, activists of another early body, the Zoutpansberg Native Vigilance Association, established by 400-500 "mostly educated natives", formed the Transvaal Native Vigilance Association (TNVA). This organisation, observes Odendaal, soon attracted several hundred supporters, including chiefs, founded a short-lived newspaper, *Leihlo la Babathso* ("The Native Eye"), and championed African grievances such as land rights. Not long after, the South African Native Congress, founded in the Eastern Cape in 1898, established a presence on the Rand and began to attract members, including Saul Msane, a compound manager and Jesse Makhothe, a labour contractor. Also active were the Native United Political Association, Transvaal Basuto Committee, Bapedi Union, and the African Political Society of Pretoria. In 1906, the African National Political Union, led by S. M. Makgatho, formed and gained strong support— including from several chiefs—around Pietersburg and Pretoria. All these bodies, Odendaal observes, protested land, franchise, and labour grievances, and were "tolerated ... [but] largely unheeded" by government. Some of the leaders were wage earners. Paulus Molatje of the Basuto Committee of Johannesburg complained bitterly to SANAC of Africans' inability to buy land, of poor people forced to relocate, of police pass raids in the middle of the night and of young people not yet able to work forced to pay taxes. Molatje, himself an office worker, declared: "We are working men." Evening location curfews were a burden for all workers some of whom, he noted, did not leave work until 9pm.[14]

Some leaders of independent African churches linked up with these secular groups. The Independent Native Presbyterian Free Church's Reverend Edward Tsewu ministered to Rand labourers. He established *Iliso Lo Notenga* (Transvaal Native Landowners' Association) and won a legal action overturning prohibition on Africans buying land. Local-level organisations formed. As early as 1903, the Germiston Native Vigilance Association had deprecated the "policy of offering low wages" to black workers. By mid-decade, the TNC arose out of these bodies. It soon gained a wide following: a meeting in Rustenburg drew 56 delegates across the Transvaal from Pietersburg to the Rand.[15]

Educated Africans on the Rand began to take a greater interest in the political organisation of their people. Marshall Maxeke, educated in America, addressing a meeting of Africans in Johannesburg in 1903, asserted black dignity. The chairperson of the meeting lamented that the recent Transvaal Labour Commission had not deigned to call African witnesses. That soon changed. In October 1904, Tsewu forthrightly declared before SANAC that mining companies should give Africans "plenty of pay" and noted the cry of white farmers about labour "shortages" had become shriller when black wages had substantially decreased. Youth lacking work, or on low wages, should not pay high taxes, he argued. Tsewu attacked sub-standard municipal housing and sanitation and forced removals from locations to remote areas, which would dramatically increase worker transport costs, a scenario increasingly familiar to Africans.[16]

The TNC had well established itself by the time of the 1907-1908 Transvaal Mining Industry Commission, at whose hearings TNC leaders were prominent in defending the rights of black workers. This first substantial statement of TNC attitudes to labour is worth relating in detail. The TNC urged "amelioration of [labour] conditions" and removal of job colour bars. H. L. Phooko of the TNC demanded long-term African workers should receive commensurate wage rises. Phooko worked at the Driefontein mine as a Native Detective for the Criminal Investigation Department; thus, he was an odd labour champion, yet a decade later, another mine detective would head a feldgling mine clerks' union and go on to lead the first major black union in Natal. Phooko handed in a written statement asserting Africans were capable of learning skilled mine work. After all: "In the late strike they did all work done by white miners, and yet by the law of the country they are kept as unskilled even if skilled, and forced to work for low fixed wages, and not allowed freedom of contract as white people." He condemned as unjust the frequent use of corporal punishment on the mines and the lack of compensation to injured black mineworkers for lost workdays. Phooko, claiming to speak from his experience during a recent strike by white miners when he was required to mark wage tickets, protested that black drillers unable to complete a full stipulated shift to the depth of "six hands" received no pay whatsoever (their tickets were not marked even if they had drilled, say, 3-4 hands). Compound managers "should be made to listen to the complaints" of black workers; labour inspectors should not just gossip to compound managers but "go underground to solve the problem of the booted foot and sjambok". In his oral evidence, Phooko stated that workers' food was monotonous—mealie porridge—and inadequate. Therefore, workers spent much money buying extra food, especially meat. They received little medical treatment and housing was poor, often carelessly cleaned.[17]

TNC General Secretary Jesse Makhothe gave written and oral evidence to the same Commission in October 1907. He also showed great concern for mine safety and criticised the poor remuneration of African workers who performed skilled work with small engines and machine drills. Makhothe bluntly stated that Africans were not satisfied with their wages and preferred shorter-term piecework than longer-term contracts in case they had to leave a bad mine. All Africans disliked pass laws and wanted them abolished. He condemned their lack of housing; if the mines wanted permanent workers, then they should provide for their permanent residence. The evidence reflected Makhothe's personal circumstances: despite working on the Rand for seven years, he had no residence and lived in a compound. He criticised the rigidity of contract labour. Africans could not leave a "bad" mine until their contract expired. He condemned the whipping of African mineworkers by "Zulu police" in most mine compounds. He claimed to have worked on five mines—Geldenhuis Deep, Simmer & Jack East, Robinson Deep, Robinson Randfontein, and Witwatersrand Deep—and seen workers whipped severely merely for seeking to change employment. He was able to see this because he was a tramming contractor, earning only £12 a month of the £50 he received for his 38 contracted workers. He also worked with his team at the pit face. Educated at Lovedale and originally from Lesotho, from where he obtained many of his contract labourers, he knew Africans able to use complicated machine drills and clearly was in close contact with workers. Before coming to the Rand, he had worked as a "hammer boy" in Kimberley; his discharge after only one month of a three-month contract at Newbultfontein was typical of contemporary prejudice against educated Africans.[18]

As TNC Secretary, Makhothe claimed to "know all the natives of the Transvaal". Congress was an "association which has generally brought the complaints of the natives before the Government" and consisted of both educated Africans and some chiefs; its aims were "the education of the natives and the amelioration of their conditions". Makhothe's written statement as TNC Secretary was a comprehensive statement criticising the treatment of black labour, skilled and skilled. Harsh treatment from compound managers, white miners, and railways and pass-law officials all deleteriously affected unskilled labour. He detailed whippings of workers by compound police, the lock-up system, rigid wages, and the poor quality of labourers' food. He proposed practical alternatives. "Whipping should be discontinued and educated natives should take the place of the police boys"; officials should listen to worker complaints; "force should never, if possible, be resorted to"; piece-work should be reserved for heavier underground work; diet should be more appropriate for mineworkers—he contested the view that mealie meal porridge was expected by all Africans. Makhothe condemned the pass system as useless: an African worker could not even use a pass to go from one compound to another to visit his brothers, whilst the confusion caused by the need to register at the pass office yet have the pass signed by an employer when giving notice, led to many disputes.[19]

The Congress statement criticised exploitation by labour agents who recruited at inflated rates and then physically intimidated workers to accept a lower rate once they arrived at mines. Makhothe backed up these allegations with evidence he had witnessed. He criticised neglect of workers' complaints by "so-called inspectors who spend much of their time in chatting with the mine officials and neglect the people whom they are supposed to look after". From his own observations, "the very people who are supposed to be protectors of natives are the people who are persecuting them". He emphasised the need to ensure worker safety, again drawing on his own experience: "I am working in the mine; I know that there are bad mines where you can never be certain of your life."[20]

Makhothe defended skilled black labour but warned that the fact that public opinion was against it meant Africans had no incentive to develop such skills. The TNC had, the previous year, presented a petition to the House of Commons, proposing practical ways to revise pass laws, such as issuing gratis passports. The petition challenged prevailing notions on labour supply, urging the Chamber of Mines to start "effectually enticing their natives to follow mining as a profession".[21]

In one sense, TNC interest in workers was unsurprising; it flowed logically from the objective position of many Africans working in the Transvaal. It laid the foundation for a more militant TNC as opposed to some of those we shall meet later, such as Saul Msane who, if also becoming involved with Congress, had a rather different objective position.

The Cape

African political leaders in the Cape formed the South African Native Congress (SANC) in 1898. Like their colleagues in the Transvaal and Natal, SANC figures spoke out on labour issues, stimulated by growing racial discrimination and deteriorating economic conditions.

Migrant labour to Cape Town increased from the 1870s and by the turn of the century, several thousand Africans worked there, chiefly on the docks (1,500) but also on railways, brickworks, and other industries. As African workers began to settle in the Cape Peninsula, prospects for interaction with political forces rose. Some workers lived in the Docks Location but in 1901, the state established Ndabeni location, forcibly removing many Africans there on the excuse of a sanitation scare. In the absence of African unions, workers turned to strikes or educated Africans to seek redress. As labour shortages developed, dockers resisted employer efforts to reduce their wages through strikes, as in 1901 and 1903 but the tide began to turn in 1903, when employers deployed strikebreakers from Ndabeni. With their numbers growing and stabilising, and with concerns over poor housing rising, workers became more visible to African political leaders.[22]

Alfred Mangena, a lawyer and later a SANNC founder, taught dockers in Cape Town and lobbied on their behalf during a strike in 1901. In August 1901, he protested publicly in the black press against low quality and overcrowded housing of Ndabeni residents, chiefly workers, urging them to form "their own Council". He was "appointed by the natives at the Dock location to act as their senior secretary". One reason for this concern was his experience. Born in 1879, he worked for a time as a labourer in Cape Town where, Mweli Skota writes, he fought for "improvement of the conditions, wages and treatment of his fellow labourers. He started a workers' organisation and held meetings every week" which "grew bigger and stronger". In the rather romantic African nationalist prose of Skota, whenever there was trouble with employers, Mangena and his committee went in to fight for rights of workers, to "head and protect the masses". Yet as La Hausse soberly adds, he later took the opportunity to charge worker clients high fees.[23]

Other political activists, soon to become Congress leaders, helped workers. Reverend Henry Reed Ngcayiya, earlier active in the AME Church in Pondoland and Queenstown and later a SANNC founder, in 1901 vigorously led a protest delegation over lack of land and civil rights in Ndabeni location, Cape Town. Reverend Elijah Mdolomba (later Cape Congress President) who since 1901 had lived in Ndabeni where he had closely observed the habits of labourers, testified before the Select Committee on the Native Locations Act in 1903 where he tried to represent labour interests as best he could (as a non-worker). He was clearly more remote from workers than TNC leaders. He began with requests of educated Africans for their own neighbourhood, *separate* from labourers, and mentioned complaints of African shopkeepers against unfair competition. However, he moved on to speak of broader location grievances: high rents and bad housing—lack of floors and heating—and imprisonment of widows unable to pay rent. Mdolomba was well briefed on labourers' conditions: he recounted that dock workers earned only £4/16 shillings a month but had rail expenses of six shillings a month and might pay up to £2 a month for a room. Frank Makwena, a teacher later active in Congress who led a three-day strike in Port Elizabeth in 1901, complained to the Locations Committee of bad housing and high rents in that city, presenting detailed statistics on workers' conditions. African huts were healthier as they were not susceptible to sudden fluctuation of temperatures in draughty "wood and iron houses". Government should allow black widows to live rent-free.[24]

Some of these leaders were in touch with workers. When in the same year Mdolomba testified before SANAC, workers accompanied him: William Sipeka, a wood carter and dock labourer since 1895 and William Tshefu, a baker. To Mdolomba, Africans' harsh treatment under the Glen Grey Act seemed like slavery and needed correcting. Again well armed with statistics on labouring lives, he urged lower rents: £2 a month rent in Ndabeni plus six shillings for train fares left little from a dock worker's wage of £4.16.0. He asked for decent worker housing. This time he rejected Commissioner Samuelson's suggestion of separate areas for labourers and other African residents: "We must all be in one place." Mdolomba had assisted labourers to search for work. His vision of the future was of elegant black townships populated with artisans and labourers: "The people who will come here will be the working men." He saw two classes in Ndabeni: "the first consists of the workers who come to Cape Town and then go home again. For this class something must be done. And the second class consists of those who stay here permanently. For these also something must be done in their own way."[25]

Reverend Mdolomba was no radical socialist. Behind this racial solidarity was a relationship of economic symbiosis: more permanent dwellers such as traders, provided services to labourers so here was an interrelationship of mutual need related to the necessity of educated strata for capital accumulation that often stimulated them to undertake wage labour. State officials anxious to keep Africans in menial occupations were happy to encourage the trend: the King William's Town magistrate claimed that more educated Africans, especially those trained in trades, did not show any great "reluctance to engage in manual labour". Conversely, A. R. McKenzie, dock agent in Cape Town, observed in 1903 that educated black people worked well with pick and shovel.[26]

Another SANC leader to speak to the Lagden Commission was Nathaniel Mhala (Umhalla), educated in Zonnebloem and England, and now a Headman in Emncotsho and Under Labour Agent in King William's Town. He lamented that, lacking land, "our young people … subsist by working in the towns", on docks, railways, and mines. Mhala recently had been to Johannesburg where he visited workers on 15 mines, speaking to over 100 of them. He relayed complaints of young workers engaged at different mines and at lower wages than contracted through white labour agents. A clerk in King William's Town, William Nquameko Seti, whose job gave him "a fine opportunity of hearing these things" relayed similar worker views of ill-treatment on the mines. He noted reports of miners being "kicked about; pick-handles used against them", and of "bad food, bad treatment, the 'cat' being freely applied to the labourers and their not being properly attended to when sick". Mhala testified before the Transvaal Labour Commission in September 1903 on reports of mine labourers denied wages and being "kicked and bullied". Headman Thomas Zwedala from Lady Frere, who reported meeting 40 workers at Sterkstroom who complained of whippings on the mines, backed him up.[27]

In October 1903, Mhala and 16 other headmen spent eleven days visiting migrant labourers on 20 mines around the Rand, reporting their observations to W. T. Brownlee, Resident Magistrate of Butterworth District, who travelled with them. Workers complained of beatings and poor food, and especially of labour recruiters who misled them about wage rates. Headman Makubalo Ntlaboti of Queenstown spoke to workers who grumbled about forced work on Sundays with no overtime, and of crowded sleeping quarters and lack of ventilation. Mhala urged that workers jailed but subsequently found innocent should receive wages for their time in detention. Headman Bangiso Sangqu of Idutywa and one Langa of Engcobo heard workers complain of beatings from overseers and wages; Langa concluded that wages were the workers' chief complaint. Such African political leaders, observed Commissioner for Native Affairs Lagden, were "drawn from a class who are not manual labourers, and are rather inclined to look down upon [workers]". However, both labourers and elite suffered racism and repression. These headmen articulated workers' protests and proposed improvements to labour conditions: Langa and Sangqu for example, urged an end to exploitative labour agents and forced Sunday shifts; Sangqu, Paul Madubela of Kentani and Mtengwane Ludidi of Qumbu all called for higher wages, an end to beatings, and clear means of redress for labourers. Headman David Magodla of Nqamakwe felt "the labour done is more than the wages", with labourers badly treated, "packed like grain or coal bags in trucks. They are not regarded as human beings as Europeans are."[28] Headmen, who soon developed ties with emergent political bodies such as Congress, were thus sometimes effective intermediaries for workers and could form a vital channel of worker demands in the era before black unions appeared.

Leaders of Congress and Vigilance Associations (often closely aligned) were generally consistent in support for better conditions for black workers. Peter Mti, a lawyer's clerk and vice-chairman of the East London Native Vigilance Association called for the "highest possible wages" and better housing for Africans. Enoch Mamba of Idutywa was from 1901 Chairman of the Transkei Native Vigilance Association and, from 1906, prominent in Congress. He worked as a clerk, teacher, and from 1895 to 1898 as a labour agent; in 1896 he accompanied labourers to the mines. Mamba was particularly interested to protect the material interests of rural Africans (at first he distanced himself from the SANC, which he saw as urban-based) and to advance their political representation. In 1903-1904, he spoke out at government hearings against harsh conditions of mine labourers and high labour taxes, and told Lagden that employers and the state should not force Africans to work. Even after he ceased working as a labour agent, he maintained a close interest in labour questions, even visiting German South West Africa with Walter Rubusana to investigate the conditions of Cape migrant workers. Later, in 1911 Mamba addressed the Select Committee on the Native Labour Regulation Bill. He argued that mine labourers resented misrepresentation of working conditions by labour touts and called for better worker compensation and for workers to be free from coercion by creditors and able to appeal legal judgments against them, clearly indicating his continuing close contact with and sympathy for migrant workers.[29]

SANC aims, invariably expressed with protestations of imperial loyalty, were to "consider and represent all matters affecting" Africans: moderate and vague, but broad enough to encompass workers. In 1902, SANC leaders Rubusana, Tunyiswa, and Thomas Mganda sent a resolution asking the Crown to protect the interests of all African and "coloured" people in all South African colonies. They expressed solidarity with Africans in northern colonies facing ominous moves to limit their freedom. Tunyiswa told the Governor that SANC "represents the intelligence and culture of the educated classes in South Africa who are working for progress and advancement of the Native and Coloured people". In 1906, SANC sent a protest telegram to the Prime Minister asking for repeal of legislation on communal tenure law but adding that "labour clauses" should be "totally repealed". Despite its moderation, in 1906 SANC criticised the hostility of the "capitalistic press" and capitulation of the imperial government over black rights. It defended consumption of "kaffir beer", particularly by black workers who "feel the need of something to quench their thirst after violent exertions".[30]

Government approaches to SANC were dismissive. Sir Gordon Sprigg claimed in 1902 that a body sending resolutions with only a handful of signatures "cannot be said to possess any generally representative character". Native Affairs official W. G. Cumming alleged in the same year that its influence occurred only in East London and King William's Town. After a more representative gathering of 60 delegates attended a SANC Queenstown meeting in 1906, the state conceded that for "practical purposes" Congress constituted "as fairly representative a body of advanced Cape Colony" black people as "could at present be found in any organised form", and was a "useful safety valve for the feelings of a section of somewhat advanced natives". Ministers continued, however, to "regret an apparent want of moderation" in the tone of Congress.[31]

SANC leaders were better educated than manual workers, and whilst they never attempted to organise labour industrially, bonds with workers soon developed. Between 1896 and 1908, Rubusana raised labour, housing, water supply, and cooking grievances in deputations to East London authorities and supported demands by African women for washing and ironing facilities in

East Bank location. A meeting of 15 SANC delegates in King William's Town in 1902 included a printer, store worker, apprentice carpenter, editor, clerk, and two teachers. By 1906, meetings included delegates from the Transkei such as Mamba. In these early years, SANC even attracted the more moderate leaders, J. Tengo Jabavu and Meshack Pelem—although these two soon left the body.[32]

Congress expressed solidarity with black labour through regional newspapers. *Izwi Labantu* ("Voice of the People" East London, 1897-1909) editors included Nathaniel Mhala (Umhalla), 1897), George Tyamzashe, Samuel Mqhayi and Allan Soga. All were active in the SANC, which the paper supported to the extent of practically being its organ. In 1903 the government noted: "Representations of the Congress accord with the views expressed in the columns" of *Izwi*. In 1902, the SANC gave thanks to the editor. Soga saw Congress's role as confronting "all questions affecting the social problems and welfare" of black people. The labour reporting of *Izwi* well illustrates this emphasis on welfare.[33]

Soga, a SANNC founder, expressed ideas betraying some understanding of the significance of class struggle and labour's position in society. He characterised supporters of the Act of Union as "gentry (the capitalists)" and predicted: "This will be a glorious country for corporation pythons and political puff-adders, forced labour and commercial despotism." He saw growing labour conflict as "a phase of the coming struggle between capital and labour". Efforts to extend the black franchise foundered on the "superior strategy of the … capitalist class … playing their game for cheap labour".[34]

Izwi condemned the whipping of mine labourers and the "chapter of horrors" of their exploitation. It drew attention to the fleecing of migrant labourer wages by labour agents and lack of redress of labourers to employers who refused to grant good certificates of service. The "appalling" loss of black lives in collieries was linked to "conditions imposed by unfeeling capitalistic systems". *Izwi* stated: "The root of the evils that exist" with Master and Servant relations "lies with the Masters". It suggested: "The next war will be between labour and capital." In 1901 it criticised the "daily trudge of six miles" faced by labourers working in East London. Headmen in charge of 200 migrant labourers en route to Cape Town docks called upon the editor to complain about their conditions. "One can imagine the plight of these poor fellows sleeping out in the cold weather," the editor wrote. *Izwi* argued that any labour "shortage" in South Africa was due not to the "number of corpulent black men" but the low wages and harsh treatment of labourers. In 1906, *Izwi* saw the experiment in Chinese labour as alienating African labour from mine work, and urged Congress to take up the matter.[35]

Izwi pointed out that the labourer's "mouth is closed" due to his "ignorance of the English language". In 1908 it reported, "several letters sent to us for publication complaining of evil treatment" on Rand mines. The editor refused to publish them "as the interests affected [were] too great and the consequences too far reaching to be satisfactorily dealt with in the press". He qualified this refusal to take up the workers' cause by claiming a "responsible body" should first support labour complaints. Despite this prevarication, such reporting suggests the existence of lines of communication between workers and SANC political circles. Various letters by workers *were* published. Some workers used *Izwi* as an avenue to pursue their demands. Migrant labourer Jim Xholla addressed his labour agent in its pages to learn "if the money-order I can post right through to my home and let me know about the cattle".[36]

The complex rural-urban interests encapsulated in this message—an interest in cattle, land, and African families—point to what would be an enduring complication of relations between working peoples and urban African political leaders. It is not that African leaders would lack an interest, or stake in such matters—indeed over the years many of them sought to build their land holdings—rather it was that the ideological and structural framework of a largely Western-modelled and inspired Congress made its easy connection and identification moot among many ordinary working peoples.

The presence of regular mine advertisements directed at labourers suggests some workers read *Izwi*. Yet if it spoke *about* workers, then it made it clear it was "more intelligent and educated men and property holders" who led African opinion. At times, it reported workers unflatteringly. A meeting held to discuss a scheme for registration of servants was dominated by the very "insolent, loud mouthed, defiant, thieving, fraternity, whom the measure desires to reach". Moreover, "remedial measures" proposed by *Izwi* to mitigate excesses of mine recruitment centred on the role of the "press and Chambers of Commerce" rather than on an independent working class and "a government scheme of systematised organisation, supervision and supply, under the control of the Department of Labour". A Cape Town strike in 1901 was described as "regrettable". However, if *Izwi* was careful not to run foul of the state in this regard, it nevertheless put the strike's cause down to the "wretched housing" and "wage irregularities" of labourers.[37]

One reason for this interest was the Eastern Cape's position as a migrant labour depot. Strikes from the 1870s, including a three-day strike in Port Elizabeth in 1901 and a strike on East London docks in 1903, ensured labour issues were not far from the editor's eye. Other influences sharpening Soga's interest in labour were his brief experience in the Labour Office of the Cape Civil Service and then as a labour agent and road inspector, giving him glimpses into labourers' lives. Educated in the UK and attaining the position of Acting Resident Magistrate, Soga was shifted sideways from Native Affairs to the new Labour Office established by Cecil Rhodes. Part of Soga's job was to monitor conditions of labourers from the Cape working in the Transvaal but he soon resigned in the face of determined opposition from the Kruger government to ameliorating their conditions. Also relevant to his approach was a growing SANC concern for workers, the above-mentioned editorial contact with workers and their headmen, and the influence of socialist ideas.[38]

Soga reprinted socialist ideas apparently in accord with African realities. He quoted Keir Hardie, who received a hostile reception from white workers on his 1908 visit to South Africa, at length on socialism. In 1908, *Izwi* stated that black problems "must increase ... unless the Labouring Classes in England and South Africa unite and extend a helping hand to their more ignorant black ... brethren". Black and and white people "will come to recognise that their economic salvation rests with socialism". Soga even denounced white civilisation "for its history is laid in a trail of blood and savagery".[39]

There are contradictions in Soga's "socialism". In 1902 he donated to the Rhodes Memorial fund to mark "all that this great Englishman has done" for black people. In 1909 he complained that the "educated and cultured few" would be "forced back ... on the mass" by inclusion of a colour bar in the Act of Union. He often prefaced his exposures of labour conditions by phrases respectful of the state. In 1901, he called on black people to respect their "superiors". Yet the same article also urged the "importance ... of safeguarding the health and comfort of our labouring classes". Such contradictory tones do not simply indicate the vacillation of a *petit bourgeois* but also betray a tactical decision to survive in a hostile milieu. *Izwi* ceased in 1909. Soga took part in the SANNC's formation. By 1920, he had abandoned his "socialist" and ANC leanings, as well as journalism, to join the Bantu Union and work as a civil servant.[40] Nevertheless, *Izwi* helped form a bedrock of sympathy for black workers in Congress, as did other pro-Congress newspapers.

Not all black newspapers felt such kinship with Congress. J. T. Jabavu's moderate *Imvo Zabantsundu* kept its distance, as did *The South African Spectator*, founded by Francis Zaccheus Santiago Peregrino. A Ghanaian educated in Britain, where he worked as a warehouse clerk and ironworker, Peregrino also laboured in the US before turning to journalism. In 1900, he settled in Cape Town where he represented the Pan African Association. His Pan-Africanism reflected broad black demands for civil rights but he also reported a range of issues affecting workers: agitation of Ndabeni resident workers around rents and housing, forced labour, discriminatory wage rates and white union racism. He gave prominence to, and supported, the Anti-Slavery Society's objections to forced labour practices in the Transvaal. He opposed the forced labour and exploitation of the Kimberley compound system, and exposed the "perpetuation of race prejudice and the debasement of the black or coloured artisan" in policies of the white Plasterer's Union. Equally scathingly, he denounced a white correspondent to the *Cape Times* for "gratuitous and indiscriminate abuse of a people who after all form the workers". He reminded white people of their "insane policy of exacting from [the black labourer] the maximum of labour for the minimum of wages and without regard to his material or moral well-being". Yet the limitations of Peregrino's blind faith in Empire were evident when he dismissed any criticism of Cecil Rhodes. Like other African people, he bristled at the racism of organised white labour, in 1909 reminding readers of *Voice of Labour* that there was nothing in socialist doctrine even hinting at racism. Gradually his radicalism withered away. Divorced from radical political currents, Peregrino in 1910 lavished praise on mine owners in an obsequious pamphlet penned following a government-sponsored tour of the mines; he later encouraged African enlistment for World War I and ran a domestic workers' agency.[41]

If lacking such a seemingly quasi-solid proletarian background as Peregrino, then many editors of Congress-aligned newspapers rather consistently reported black labour. Congress figure Silas Molema owned *Koranta ea Becoana* ("Bechuana's Gazette", 1901-8), edited by Sol Plaatje in Mafeking, whose national role in the SANNC is discussed in the next chapter. Historians of Plaatje hitherto have downplayed his commitment to labour. However, *Koranta* often highlighted miners' low wages and mistreatment. When the state relied only on the views of magnates to investigate such mistreatment, *Koranta* took up the issue, supplying its own evidence on harsh conditions. It linked plans by "insatiable Rand ... capitalists" to indenture Chinese labour directly to moves to lower black wages. Plaatje attacked "the greed" of Rand mine magnates for "wrongfully and illegally withholding the just wages of their labourers". He stated: "We are willing to labour but for a living wage."[42]

Koranta urged Africans to do more to redress the wrongs suffered by black workers. It accused Marshall Maxeke of "callous indifference" in failing personally to expose their exploitation. It interviewed chiefs on labour issues. Chief Sekgoma protested the harsh labour conditions on the Rand where "our people … suffer to enrich the mine owners". Chief Linchwe stated that his people on the Rand had been victims of forced labour contracts at low wages. Plaatje printed the Barolong Paramount Chief's appeal urging "mining employers to increase the … scarcely … living wage".[43]

Plaatje frequently denounced the harsh and discriminatory treatment of African labourers: exploitation of unpaid apprentices; refusal to employ certain ethnic groups; high accident rates. The latter was a "butchery" occurring "with terrible frequency", even at De Beers. It pricked Plaatje's conscience, causing him to reflect: "We have at times used our columns for the cause of [De Beers] mines." However, he was more especially concerned over questions of justice: that the mines could escape liability for such events. *Koranta* reported a strike of labourers at De Beers, but was more concerned with what it saw as the underlying issue: justice for a victim of an assault by a white employee. Plaatje, whilst observing that unfortunate accidents did occur at De Beers due to mud rushes, urged Rand magnates to "take a leaf out of the Kimberley book".[44]

Plaatje here undoubtedly gave vent to a parochialism that exaggerated De Beers' concern for its African employees. Yet, he often worked into his columns comments about labourers. Noting De Beers' huge 1903 profits, he stressed: "Our people may pride themselves … that their black muscles are [its] pillar." He denounced Kimberley capitalists whom he considered exploited Africans: Walter Whitworth's "business motives … were no reason for him to reduce "the hard-working wage earner's pay". De Beers's "promiscuous distribution of monetary gifts [dividends] … very often overlooked the interest of the most loyal and harmless (though important) section among its labourers". This characterisation sums up Plaatje's attitude to black workers. He recognised them as vital to the economy. *Koranta* was their defender: "the organ of the majority of [De Beers] employees" and "representing the labouring classes", whose role it frequently sought to explain and defend. African labourers failed to renew contracts not because they bought wives, as mine officials claimed, but due to harsh conditions. Plaatje exposed a "crank who threatened some Native labourers with the 'sack'." Yet, if happy to pose as defender of such workers, Plaatje revealed his own distaste for their involvement in class struggle and satisfaction with their political impotence. He wrote: "The rowd[y]ism of the white miners last week has demonstrated the peaceable harmlessness of black labour." He added: "Unlike any class of labourers the world over, [black labour] can produce a spotless record of years of loyal and faithful service."[45]

This attitude was due to the importance Plaatje attached to ethnicity and liberalism. He saw Africans as a "race-class". *Koranta* was "mouthpiece of the Natives" as much as organ of De Beers' employees. It proudly claimed to have been "the first native organ that held up the personality of Booker Washington", an advocate of black capitalism, "as an emblem of emulation by the Native youth". Yet *Koranta* also groped towards an awareness of wider labour interests: it noted a decrease in wages of Durban labourers and printed the appeal by Soga Mapkela, Ndabeni Location Secretary, to prevent forced labour. *Koranta's* circulation of only 1,000-2,000 copies limited its readership by workers; but it was able to publicise burning issues affecting them. A few years later, as we shall see, Plaatje returned to journalism, this time in Kimberley, where with a relatively high ratio of workers, this attention to labour issues made even more obvious sense.[46] The labour reporting of *Koranta* and *Izwi* helped keep workers before the eyes of black people.

Natal

The Natal Native Congress (NNC), formed in 1900, focused at first chiefly on land and the franchise. Its members consisted mainly of *kholwa*. Some NNC leaders were prominent landowners or peasant-farmers, including chiefs at relatively prosperous mission stations such as Edendale, who had begun to accumulate capital—if unevenly and with limitations imposed by pass laws. Class stratification increasingly was evident in struggles between landowners and tenants in Edendale in the early 1890s. The tense political and precarious economic environment of Natal inclined *kholwa* to combine—in land purchasing, occupations, and organising. Depression, rising demands of creditors and land-hungry farmers, relative stagnation of African enterprise in the face of a fast-capitalising white economy, calamitous effects of the 1896 rinderpest epidemic, war in 1899, declining job opportunities for youth, and steady erosion of already limited African rights drove downwardly mobile *kholwa* to realise the need for political organisation.[47]

Congress did not emerge out of a political vacuum. An aspirant stratum of property owners constructed loose but wide-ranging networks of African solidarity through earlier political battles and, as Khumalo observes, via a sphere based on exchanging letters and reading newspapers and books, a domain allowing us to transcend the "teleology of the nationalist narrative" and see the convoluted nature of African politics at local levels. Peasant-farmers at mission stations such as Groutville, Edendale, and Ekukhanyeni deployed these new media to help build economic resources and assert political rights.[48] However, *kholwa* status was fragile; many were obliged to work for a living and some became prominent in Congress and its predecessors.

By the early 1890s, the Pietermaritzburg newspaper *Inkanyiso yase Natal* ("Light of Natal" 1889-1896) began—gently at first, then more stridently— to criticise pass laws, the tenuous status of Africans granted exemption from Native Law, and lack of *kholwa* employment opportunities. It exposed the failure of employers to provide medical aid for sick workers and their prejudices against black workers, and reported grievances of farm workers forced to work for 10 shillings a month, yet facing demands to give up two months wages just to purchase a pass. The editor, Solomon Kumalo, dismissed fears by white artisans of black competition. In 1894, *Inkanyiso* highlighted a bitter dispute between the Durban Corporation and Daniel Lutuli, arrested under curfew regulations despite his exempt status. The paper, strongly criticising the arrest, summoned a mass protest meeting. *Inkanyiso*, with its aim "to enlighten and improve", became the organ of the *kholwa*.[49]

Letters from young *kholwa* soon to dominate African politics—John Dube and Josiah Gumede—graced *Inkanyinso's* pages. In 1894, Dube signalled his panacea for the "labour problem"—industrial training, in which he would develop strong pecuniary interest. He challenged the logic of white racists who claimed Africans were too lazy to work, yet refused to encourage apprenticeships for fear of competition. There was sound race logic in his plea to readers to patronise services employing black labour such as Inanda Seminary laundry and printers/carpenters at St. Alban's College, printer of *Inkanyiso*.[50]

Inkanyiso reported closely the activities of *Funamalungelo* ("Society of Exempted Natives"), established in 1887. The Society attracted members across a wide geographic base, including John Kumalo (Estcourt), Daniel and Martin Lutuli (Groutville, Durban), Sol Kumalo, Sikweleti Nyongwana, Stephen Mini, J. Tshange and S. Msimang (Edendale), Isaiah Mgadi (Georgedale), Isaac Mkize (Cedera) and James Majozi and Philip Mtembu (Indaleni). By 1895, *Inkanyiso* editors, increasingly aware of the frustration of black economic and political aims by white power structures, spoke openly of their lack of political status and the remedy: "steady organisation" towards "political freedom". *Funamalungelo* was an important step on the road to African unity, but neither it nor *Inkanyiso* survived; the latter folded in 1896 under government pressure, the former limped along until about 1908, yielding in importance to Congress. Despite its demise, *Inkanyiso* had, argues Jabulani Magagula, widened criticism of government and, after a reader accused it of neglecting the masses ("*Labo abafundile abasizi ngani labo betu abanga fundile?*" = "Why do those of us with education not help our people who are not educated?)", narrowed the gap between *kholwa* and uneducated classes.[51]

Of all these early African political bodies and their members in Natal, NNC activists would most consistently champion African interests. They did so via newspapers, *Ipepa lo Hlanga* ("Paper of the [African] Nation", Pietermaritzburg 1898-1904), edited, published and printed by Mark Radebe, and *Ilanga lase Natal* ("Natal Sun", 1903-) edited by John Dube. These media reflected the broad socio-political concerns of *kholwa*, including Christian values and exemption, but also articulated Congress views and raised labour issues. In 1900, *Ipepa* urged readers to "proclaim the Congress so that it may belong to all natives". During the South African War, *Ipepa* was alert to the duplicity of settler designs. It predicted post-war efforts to cut black wages: "whites will all unite to formulate some schemes by which they may make the Native industrious … The truth is that it will be fortunate for us if for three years we obtain the same wages." *Ipepa* challenged the widespread notion that a black worker "has no right to choose his own master, and to sell his labour at the best possible market". The editor conceded unskilled labourers had "to do all the rough work" but protested that Africans "are looked upon by many as camels or any other beaste of burden". In 1901-1902, *Ipepa* reported—without a hint of pro-capitalist bias—a series of strikes. *Ilanga*, if more inclined to subscribe to capitalist tenets, in 1903 nevertheless warned of attacks on black jobs, pointing out the best way to improve alleged labour shortages was to "give higher wages to those working underground". Dube noted the imposition of onerous new poll taxes in 1905-1906 placed added burdens on young black workers. In doing so, he distanced *Ilanga*—and the NNC—from the state.[52]

Martin Lutuli (1847-1921) of Groutville, a farmer with 300 acres and previously a wagon maker, was first NNC chairperson (1900-1903). He told the Native Affairs Commission in 1904 that Congress was "the voice of the Natives" with representatives across the province; it aimed to defend the welfare and "represent the whole" of black society. NNC meetings he attended as Chairman for its first three years attracted from 50 to 100 people. Earlier, in 1894, Lutuli had attacked police extortion rackets directed at the "beer-making class". Chief Stephen Mini of Edendale was another Congress chief to invest in and encourage artisan trades. Both Mini and Lutuli were wagon makers, a business providing capital accumulation, but also perhaps bonding them in some ways to the workers who practised their craft alongside them. Mini, appointed Edendale Headman in 1893 after an acrimonious tussle, told the Natal Native Affairs Commission in 1906 that white farmers should not hold black farm labourers to ransom by using passes to force down wages. Just as we saw in the Cape, where African property-owners "needed" workers, so a complex relationship developed between these two strata in Edendale. Sheila Meintjes observes that, at a time in the 1890s of increasing class stratification—even *between* African landlords—among those dependent on wage labour or salaries, and with rental income an increasingly attractive option, Mini gained legal charge over workers renting in Edendale, some of whom complained of his exploitative money-lending practices. By 1909, Mini was the second largest African landowner in Edendale, holding 125 acres. That the above-mentioned African political activists were all male reflected continuing legal and economic marginalisation of black women in the province; indeed, by 1919, only 11 of 205 Edendale landowners were African women.[53]

The "rise and fall" of this black peasantry was swift, but the presence of such people in Congress ensured a complex approach to labour. From its earliest days, its leaders expressed more than passing interest in labour matters. This was, in part, due to intricate kin and spatial ties across a society dominated by working peoples facing ever-increasing exploitation, but also in part to the way wider social lobbying was inherent in the nature of an organisation formed to present "any matters of grievances or complaints, or requests" that "Africans had to make to government".[54]

John Langalibalele Dube came from a *kholwa* family. Educated in the United States, where at times he had to undertake manual labour to pay for his studies, he was thoroughly committed to the Protestant work ethic. In 1891, he wrote that, given that many Zulu youths at mission schools were obliged to work at trades to pay their expenses it was important to "teach them to work" to civilise them. Dube sought to "elevate" his people. In 1908, he spoke disparagingly of Africans' "indolence and uselessness in the labour market" and before the 1906 Natal Native Commission, he emphasised African children should be "compelled to go and learn" industrial training, his panacea for a rapidly shrinking job market in the wake of Indian indentured labour. Yet, as Shula Marks argues, such statements could be "very carefully contrived for maximum effect" on white readers.[55]

Despite his moderation (and later he strongly opposed radicals), Dube, as Muzi Hadebe makes clear, strongly defended Zulu culture and King Dinuzulu during the latter's trial. Dube also harshly criticised state repression of Bhambatha's anti-poll tax resistance of 1906; in doing so, he carved out space to defend African interests, earning a popular name among the Zulu as *uMafukuzela*, rendered by Hadebe as "the one who works tirelessly".[56]

The rebellion, through a mixture of socio-economic, cultural, and political forces, induced many urban workers to return to Zululand to join what was largely a peasant revolt. If appreciative of the unjustness of underlying causes (higher taxes), *kholwa* such as Dube were hesitant to join such a one-sided battle and, publicly at least, pledged loyalty to the Crown. Yet, as Shula Marks observes, the revolt became a major symbol of African nationalist resistance. Swirling about were other protests from British socialists to Congress leaders in other colonies such as Alfred Mangena and A. K. Soga. If Dube was cautious in his criticism of repression then these diverse protests formed an important base for the later unity represented in a national African Congress.[57]

Hauled before the Natal Governor, who on behalf of the "ruling race" warned of sedition, Dube argued that innumerable contributors to *Ilanga* had convinced him the government was guilty of injustice. Dube also was clearly in favour of better conditions for African workers. In contradiction of his earlier missionary-influenced views, he later made it clear that African reluctance to undertake wage labour was due not to any alleged laziness but rather lack of industrial habits. He rejected forced labour and called for cessation of labour touting whereby workers were "systematically deceived both as to their wages and the class of work" they undertook. Dube related cases where ricksha workers suffered work injuries and advocated discontinuation of the trade. He urged sugar and tea plantations to employ black workers and provide proper worker housing.[58]

Cleopas Kunene, *Ipepa lo Hlanga* editor in 1903, adopted the same sort of commonsense approach to labour issues. He complained of frustrated career paths of African clerks who, despite their education and hard work in lawyer's offices, had "neither [decent] pay nor honour", received "paltry salaries" barely covering expenses, and had "no prospects whatsoever" of promotion. Kunene supported better housing and feeding of mine labourers, wondering why their conditions had been so bad for so long. Instead of relying on imported labour, employers should pay them better wages. Kunene had worked as a teacher at Edendale, where he closely followed the careers of apprenticed workers and teachers, then as a clerk, and even for the Swazi Queen and Transvaal Secret Service.[59]

Ipepa supported moves by the Natal Native Teachers' Association for higher salaries and expressed solidarity with Basutoland chiefs uniting to oppose negative effects on their economies of the Rand Native Labour Association's rapacious labour recruiting. *Ipepa* argued that instead of ruminating about "lazy" African workers, public opinion should address more serious issues such as white strikes, entirely explainable by inadequate pay but a principle equally applicable to the black worker whose tactic of "returning to the kraal" instead of striking caused "no pain either to himself or would-be employer". *Ipepa* expressed outrage at the injustice and racism inherent in disregard of African evidence in the case of a farm worker fined in the Pinetown magistrate's court for "desertion", but who had merely—and patiently— sought a wage increase. This benevolent concern for African workers was of a national, not class, nature. *Ipepa's* editors fear of class struggle was clear in their loathing of (white, racist) labour organisation—personified by the rise of the Australian Labor Party—and its ability via strikes to cripple industry, and their fervent hope it would never spread to black people. When, soon after, a strike by African workers broke out at Durban Point, *Ipepa* hastened to welcome its quick resolution.[60]

Such comments on strikes appeared with a nod to the close state scrutiny of the black press. This inclined *Ipepa* to over-emphasise loyalty—even to the point of condemning Plaatje's *Koranta* for daring to criticise Milner's Transvaal policy. Yet a few months later, in the face of imported Asian labour—which in January 1904 it condemned as affecting the earnings and marring the chances of gaining a "decent livelihood" of Natal black people—and plummeting black mine wages, *Ipepa* reproduced interviews with Tswana chiefs condemning the horrors of Rand mine labour. That contact with workers was taking place is evident from the fact that in February 1904 the editor interviewed an African carpenter denied work on the Rand by the racism of white artisans. *Ipepa* was now firm in its advocacy of the need for improved and stable mine wages and its explicit criticism of the Chamber of Mines and implicit criticism of government grew louder, even suggesting Africans may soon have to act independently, in competition with white people. Such candid reporting and views induced pressure by government that probably hastened its demise.[61]

Mark Radebe, publisher of *Ipepa*, had worked in a wagon-maker's workshop for five years. He then was educated for four years at Lovedale and, after 1892, became a licensed storekeeper. Radebe was twice elected NNC Secretary. Giving evidence to the Lagden Commission in Pietermaritzburg in 1904, he promptly drew attention to black worker complaints about forced labour (for both chiefs and white farmers) and to pass laws that interfered with worker freedom of movement. Many Africans were forced into low-paying farm work on farms but, argued Radebe, the farmer "has to pay them what they will get anywhere else". He raised problems faced by African artisans in sustaining their craft in impoverished communities and given lack of certification. Radebe complained that the African worker "never gets the same wages" as white or Indian people. These issues he also addressed in the pages of *Ipepa*, which he described as "a paper speaking for the nation—that is to say, for the black people".[62]

NNC leaders attempted to represent African workers' interests in other ways. Martin Lutuli, like Radebe, protested to the Lagden Commission against that "which I hear most from the Natives ... *isibahlo*, the compulsory labour". He claimed to have heard "many people talking and crying" about forced labour. Africans, he argued, needed to be free to choose their place of work and needed education that was more industrially oriented, so they could earn good wages. Other NNC leaders also raised labour questions with the Commission. Petros Maling, a NNC co-founder, stated that a 14-shilling tax was too onerous for Africans "in receipt of very small wages" of around £2 a month. Poverty wages were not just a proletarian matter. "All natives, even those with whom I am living on the farms ... receive very small wages, and are not able to purchase food and clothing for themselves owing to these wages being so small." All Africans, he added, should be paid alike according to the quality of services, from £4 to £6 a month. There were contradictions, typical of *kholwa* larger-landowners, in Maling's relations with Africans: tenants on his Newcastle farm paid him £2 a month rent. Yet he felt satisfied they were better off as they were "free to go out to work" and not forced to perform obligatory roadwork. Sikweleti Nyongwana, NNC Chairman (1906-7), later *Ilanga* editor, had similar views. He told the 1906 Natal Commission that forced labour should be "done away with"; Africans should get civil service jobs, and fair wages would solve labour shortages.[63]

Josiah Gumede, another NNC co-founder, had worked as a teacher in the Cape, and on the Rand making mattresses, as a way to accumulate capital. Born in 1867 in Healdtown, of Zulu ancestry, his father owned a transport business in Grahamstown. Gumede worked as a solicitor's land agent for Africans seeking redress over land rights, and became a farmer with substantial land holdings. He became prominent in African politics in the 1890s, writing letters to *Inkanyiso* protesting "inexpressibly weighty" laws. He testified to the Lagden Commission: "Natives are very fond of work ... all they want is an incentive ... to work by being paid a higher wage."[64]

Gumede was emerging as a leading player in African politics not only in Natal, but also in the Orange River Colony, where he joined a delegation of chiefs to England (see below). The deputation was a failure, but Gumede made contact with Pan African Henry Sylvester Williams and British socialist Keir Hardie. The latter contact was useful for Gumede when convicted for leaving Natal without a pass in 1907; he sent a telegram to Hardie, and in the same year wrote to the British Labour Party asking it to champion justice for black people. Gumede's lawyer had the conviction quashed.[65]

Around this time, Congress leaders also came in touch with left-leaning Labour Party politician Ralph Tatham—as Marks muses, perhaps another early social democratic influence on Gumede to explain his later pro-socialist radicalism. Tatham proposed an abortive co-operative scheme, using Congress as a vehicle, to improve black access to land, trade, and representation. He attended NNC meetings and had close ties with its leaders, including Gumede, Dube and Saul Msane.[66]

When a NNC delegation met with the Natal Prime Minister F. R. Moor in June 1907, Tatham's good offices facilitated the meeting. NNC leaders—Nyongwana (chair), Lutuli (deputy-chair), Radebe (assistant secretary) and Chief James Majozi—asserted their Empire loyalty and supported Moor's role as Secretary of Native Affairs. They also raised the question of re-appointing J. S. Marwick as Transvaal Agent; he had proven his concern for migrant labourers during the South African War but his position had since been eliminated. NNC leaders expressed their concern for the interests of such migrant workers. Nyongwana noted members of "our Congress and our people in the Transvaal" had raised the issue and the NNC executive felt it "a serious and important affair". It is interesting that the only substantive issue raised at this meeting was to do with black labour.[67]

Even before formation of the SANNC in 1912, the NNC had begun to gain support across Natal. Besides the urban centres of Durban and Pietermaritzburg, Congress meetings took place in regional towns. In 1903, a meeting of the *Iso Lomuzi* ('Eye of the Village') vigilance association under NNC auspices occurred at Gardens Ville for *kholwa* of Newcastle and Dundee Districts, at which a report of a NNC deputation to meet Joseph Chamberlain was read. In northern Natal, pockets of more settled black wage earners began to develop, notably in colliery towns such as Dundee. There is little extant evidence of direct Congress contact with such workers, but the growth of its branches suggests there may have been some.[68]

These testimonies indicate early attempts by NNC leaders to speak on behalf of workers by advocating wage rises and freedom of movement for labourers. Of the views of workers themselves, except in the guise of *kholwa* who assumed wage labour for a period, we unfortunately know little. Yet it is reasonable to suggest that the excursions of some Congress leaders into the work force, if only temporary, may have influenced the ways in which they viewed labour. Similar trends are apparent in the history of the Orange Free State.

The Orange River Colony

By the first decade of the century, African political organisations had formed in the Orange River Colony (ORC). The Native Committee of Bloemfontein, established in 1902, grew into the ORC Native Vigilance Association in 1903. Its scope widened on 16 June 1906 when delegates from across the colony met at Waaihoek Location to create the ORC Native Association, which soon became the ORC Native Congress. Executive members were Reverend B. Kumalo (AME Church, President), Thomas Mtobi Mapikela (Treasurer), S. Chaka, S. Tshongwane, Henry Reed Ngcayiya, Joseph Twayi, Mahoholi John Mocher, Peter Phatlane, and J. Labers. According to John Mancoe, who in the 1930s wrote a biographical directory of Bloemfontein Africans, the Association's articles stipulated that its aims were to "watch, safeguard and further" the material, social, political, and religious interests of Africans. Odendaal further notes that it campaigned on issues of political representation and harsh anti-black municipal regulations, and had close ties with the ORC Native Teachers' Association.[69]

If teachers were "respectable", their professional association nevertheless represented wage earners (many of whom received low wages) and their interests, and comprised a thread attaching Congress to employees. If the public viewed preachers in general as similarly respectable, then the state viewed AME church leaders such as Ngcayiya and Tantsi, who cut their organisational "teeth" in the 1890s when they engaged in a vigorous correspondence of protest with government, with great suspicion.[70]

African leaders faced a brick wall of indifference from authorities. Typical of this indifference was the 1909 recommendation by the ORC Prime Minister urging the Governor not to accede to a Congress petition seeking political rights on the basis that such rights were not warranted because, aside from a small number of Africans in Witsieshoek and Thaba 'Nchu, "all other natives are scattered as labourers all over the colony".[71] Ironically, stereotyping all Africans as labourers spurred an interest in labour in African political circles.

Giving evidence before SANAC in September 1904, ORC NVA leaders not only presented land and political grievances but also put forward views on work and workers widespread among *kholwa*. Africans must be able to learn all branches of work so they could become "skilled workmen", stated Reverend Kumalo. Now, those at school did not learn "real" trades and did not become skilled workers. Similarly, the Reverend E. T. Mpela advocated that Africans should find good positions such as in the Public Service, but it was difficult for them to find work. Joseph Twayi emphasised the common grievances of land and passes.[72]

Their comments reflected the class composition of African political bodies. The NVA speakers before the SANAC included ministers of religion, contractors, a mason (Mocher), brick-maker and dray cart driver (Twayi). John Sello Mocher, later President of the Orange Free State ANC, had a mixed class background. He received a basic education, in 1899 receiving third-class teachers' and woodwork certificates from Healdtown Institution and then worked as a constable, bricklayer, and mason, though, as we shall see later, such a working background was no guarantee of class-conscious politics. Other local black political leaders who were wage earners included Peter Phatlane, who from about 1911 worked for the Town Council for a relatively small wage. In contrast, Reverend Joel Goronyane, close to but standing outside Congress, was a landowner in Thaba 'Nchu, with many farm hands who gave him free labour.[73] As in other parts of South Africa, these leaders held a variety of social occupations.

In this period, Mapikela and Mocher emerged as ORC Congress leaders. They submitted petitions to colonial authorities on a range of issues affecting Africans. Mapikela also began to assume a national role, joining the 1909 African protest delegation to Britain. In 1907, Mapikela petitioned the Governor with Congress resolutions thanking Britain for its concern for Africans but expressing regret at government's failure to meet black demands for representation. In 1906, as leader of the Native Vigilance Committee, precursor of Congress, he petitioned King Edward VII chiefly on matters of representation, but lamented the passing of *togt* legislation that would amount to "nothing short of enforced labour". In these petitions, we glimpse contradictions in his approach to workers. As an aspirant local entrepreneur who became a successful building contractor, Mapikela epitomised the apparently sycophantic attitudes of some early Congressmen to imperial rule and the concern for profits of nascent African *petit bourgeois*. Yet even before SANNC formation, Mapikela declared his interest in not only political but also economic justice.[74]

Mapikela's career illustrates the complex class forces among ANC members. He was born in Lesotho in 1869 and educated in the Cape, but moved to Bloemfontein in 1892. In the words of Mancoe, Mapikela "made himself a hard-working man". He began his working life as a carpenter. In 1886, he undertook an apprenticeship in cabinet-making in Grahamstown, and from 1890-1892 worked as a tradesman in Queenstown. Moving to Waaihoek in Bloemfontein in 1892, colour-bar restrictions forced him to abandon his trade and he worked for some years as a storeman for an ironmonger. In 1903, Mapikela established himself as an independent building contractor but this business continually faced impediments of discriminatory administrative regulations. In 1909, he successfully lobbied the Bloemfontein Town Council for permission to open a lodging house to serve Africans. Selby Msimang, who knew Mapikela, recalled him as a "first-class carpenter" who later became a contractor and insurance agent. By 1903-1904, Mapikela was involved in the Bloemfontein and then ORC NVA and thereafter remained active in Congress.[75]

Beyond Bloemfontein, agriculture was the main base of the colony's economy, but small industries were developing and some 4,000 black people worked on the Jagersfontein diamond mines in 1907. Employers in 1902 complained of labour shortages and the rising cost of black labour. The African professional strata, even smaller here than in Natal, comprised only 0.2 per cent of the male population. In contrast to Natal and the Transvaal, at the turn of the century women, not men, dominated domestic work. Africans could only purchase or lease land in reserves at Witzieshoek and Moroka. These restrictions fragmented their settlement patterns, which centred in towns or on white farms. In the ORC, stated the South African Native Races Committee in 1908, the African "cannot buy or lease land; he has no political rights". Africans in the ORC had lost substantial land in earlier decades. In Witzieshoek and Harrismith, white settlers had taken much black land from the 1880s. Efforts to reclaim the land brought African traditional leaders into contact with Congress. In 1906, Chiefs Moloi, Lesisa and Lequila drew up petitions and employed Josiah Gumede, then active in the Natal Native Congress but with wide contacts, to investigate their claims. In 1907, Gumede, as interpreter and counsellor, joined their unsuccessful delegation to England to petition the right to purchase land. The ORC Native Congress also asked Gumede to raise the general condition of black people in the colony with the Secretary of State.[76]

In 1909, the ORC Native Congress played a central role in bringing together black opposition to the racist clauses of the draft Act of Union, first at its annual Congress in Winburg, involving delegates from between 11 to 15 towns, and then in calling a national convention of African leaders. Twayi, Mapikela and Mocher all were prominent. The ORC Congress also condemned the harsh treatment of African farm workers under the Masters and Servants Act. In general, therefore, the urban base of the ORC Congress and the difficult economic conditions of Africans in the Colony provided the organisation with members who had some experience of and sympathy with workers. It contained less of the more-affluent African landowner seen in the NNC, though both bodies attracted *kholwa* who used wage labour as a base for business.[77]

Leaders of all these provincial Congresses came together in March 1909 in the South African Native Convention to protest discriminatory aspects of the Draft Act of Union. Presided over by Rubusana, they protested the restricted franchise and "oppressive pass laws" of northern colonies that served to "limit in a grievous manner the right of natives to earn their living by the labour of head or hand". These were leaders cautious not to offend authorities, but determined to draw attention, in the first place to lack of political representation of Africans, and also to their economic injustices.[78]

The propensity of the Congresses to seek to represent *all* black strata, and their developing tendency to include workers in their ambit claims for black rights, was indirectly encouraged by state policies characterising every African as suited only to menial work. Just as the state and its bureaucracy began to evolve an official discourse imposing the notion of a "native problem", so then ANC leaders engaged in their own discourse with state officials. The hearings of commissions that became contested terrain as Congress challenged the right of the state to "represent" Africans revealed this; in 1903, the SANC sent an urgent telegram to the Prime Minister stating its "disfavour" with his summoning of witnesses. In future, it stated, selection of "representative" black witnesses should rest with the Congress executive.[79] As later chapters will show, representation of the interests of all Africans would be a recurring theme in the ANC's on-going engagement with the state.

Localised pressure groups now gave way to African national unity in the face of the 1910 Union of South Africa. The South African Native Convention met in March 1910 and passed resolutions, including one on the rights of black labour.[80] Thus, the groups out of which the ANC emerged took some interest in labour. Political Union also stimulated standardisation of labour laws and intensification of black exploitation, which helped make the plight of black labour more visible to ANC members.

Conclusion

The leadership and membership of African political organisations preceding the formation of the ANC was dominated by educated, Christianised, representatives of a social stratum that, relative to the great mass of Africans, was well to do. Yet neither this "elite", nor the majority of Africans at this time can be regarded as constituting well-formed classes; migrant workers maintained ties with the land, peasants often needed to engage in wage labour, *kholwa* needed to supplement their incomes with artisanship or arrangements with artisans or tenants, and also preferred to acquire land. Moreover, state intrusions, natural disasters, and periodic economic crises constantly impeded smooth class formation.

Early African political associations represented or included those with experience of the modern labour market or with ties to labour. Increasingly, as a sense of a wider African nation developed, working people came to be seen as a natural component of those represented, though this was still complicated by elite notions that insisted on promotion of sectional interests giving African politics a contradictory tension that would be exploited constantly in the twentieth century by white power structures.

Africans were not passive in the face of this ongoing pressure. The conscious political activities and choices of both *kholwa* and working people inserted black labour issues into the political discourses of the day. There was nothing accidental about this. If a good percentage of *kholwa* kept a keen eye on capital accumulation for their benefit, then they also began to see the value of broader political support (that could include working peoples) as a new political culture of newspapers and public meetings emerged. Ties of kin, culture, nation and space—common location residence—enmeshed *kholwa* with their worker compatriots. Repeatedly, to government commissions, or in public meetings or in the pages of the black press, African political leaders began to comment upon and champion labour issues. Weak and temporary, yet meaningful bridges between African labour and African political movements began to appear.

There is considerable continuity here—later concerns of the ANC for the fate of African workers had their precedent in these earlier decades of petitions and more polite protests over wages, conditions and political representation. Moreover, these essentially provincial-based political movements continued, sometimes as we shall see, in tandem with but at other times in defiance of central structures, tendencies that offered space for tactical alliances or divisions between African political and labour forces. However, the formation of the ANC in 1912 was to insert these issues onto a nation-wide canvas, providing opportunities both for Congress and for workers to cement a fragile working alliance.

Notes

1   D. Williams, "African Nationalism in South Africa: Origins and Problems", *JAH* v. 11 1970, pp. 371-384; Etherington, *Preachers,* p. 169; N. Etherington, "Mission Station

Melting Pots as a Factor in the Rise of South African Black Nationalism", *IJAHS* v. 9 (1976), pp. 592-605; *The Journal & Selected Writings of the Rev. Tiyo Soga,* ed. D. Williams (Cape Town: Balkema, 1983), pp. 39, 178-182, 151; L. de Kock, *Civilising Barbarians: Missionary Narrative and African Textual Response in 19th Century South Africa* (Johannesburg: Wits UP, 1996), pp. 179-184; *Report of the Select Committee Relative to the Native Question* (1869), pp. 52-53.

2 V. Khumalo, "Political Rights, Land Ownership and Contending Forms of Representation in Colonial Natal 1860-1900", *JNZH* v. 22 (2004), pp. 109-148, p. 110.

3 C. Crais, *White Supremacy and Black Resistance* (Cambridge: CUP. 1992), p. 220; *Imvo Zabantsundu* [hereafter *Imvo*] 19 Jul. 1888.

4 Odendaal, *Vukani Bantu,* pp. 23-29, 83-85; Kennedy, "Missionaries"; "Native Separatist Churches," A.W. Roberts Papers, Cory Library, *passim.*

5 C. Page, "Black America in White South Africa: Church and State Reaction to the A.M.E. Church in Cape Colony and Transvaal, 1896-1910", Ph.D. thesis, University of Edinburgh, 1978; J. Campbell, *Songs of Zion: The African Methodist Episcopal Church in the United States and South Africa* (Oxford: OUP, 1995), pp. 147-152; L. Coppin, *Observations of Persons and Things in South Africa, 1900-1904* (Philadelphia, [1905]), pp. 11, 15, 55; A. Cobley, "'The African National Church': Determination and Political Struggle among Black Christians in South Africa to 1948", *Church History* 60 (1991), pp. 356-371, p. 356.

6 J. Stuart, *A History of the Zulu Rebellion* (London: Macmillan, 1913), pp. 97-98.

7 C. Bundy, *The Rise and Fall of the South African Peasantry* (London: Heinemann, 1979); Etherington, *Preachers,* Chapter 8; N. Etherington, "African Economic Experiments in Colonial Natal 1845-1880", *African Economic History* (1978), pp. 1-15, p. 9; La Hausse, *Restless Identities.*

8 A. Odendaal, "African Political Mobilisation in the Eastern Cape, 1880-1910", Ph.D. thesis, University of Cambridge, 1983, pp. 122, 210; Odendaal, "White Boys", pp. 13-15, Odendaal, *Vukani Bantu,* pp. 8-21, 61; Kirk, *Making a Voice,* Chapter 4; L. Ntsebeza, "Divisions and Unity in Struggle: The ANC, ISL and CP, 1910-28", B.A. (Hons.) thesis, University of Cape Town, 1988, pp. 13, 60, argues the early ANC was a prisoner of liberalism, blind to opportunities to mobilise workers.

9 *The Friend* cited in editorial of *Koranta ea Becoana,* 4 Jul. 1903.

10 SANAC, v. 1, (Report), pp. 66, 80-83.

11 "South African Native Affairs Commission", *Ipepa lo Hlanga,* 27 Nov. 1903. Denoon (*A Grand Illusion* [London: Longman, 1973] p. 106) notes SANAC rejected the representativeness of bodies like SANC.

12 W. Rubusana, J. Mocher, T. Mapikela to Colonial Secretary 29 Nov. 1909, VAB G[overnor's] 110 file 444/9, ORC Native Congress Executive Committee. Petition to the King 14 Sep. 1908, G91 file 292/1. In 1903 there were 8,000 African voters in the Cape (1,114 in Port Elizabeth) but only two in Natal and none in either the Transvaal or OFS: SANAC v. 1 p. 94; S. Trapido, "White Conflict and Non-White Participation in the Politics of the Cape of Good Hope 1853-1910", Ph.D. thesis, University of London, 1970.

13 Ginwala, "Women and the ANC", citing Odendaal, "Mobilisation".

14 Annual Report Transvaal Northern Division 1904, *Correspondence Relating to Conditions of Native Labour Employed in Transvaal Mines,* p. 123; Odendaal, *Vukani Bantu,* pp. 50-54, 74-75; SANAC v. 4, pp. 853-855 (Molatje). Native United Political Association's London representative, H. Sylvester Williams, in March 1905 presented a petition for African rights to King Edward VII: "A Native Petition," *Imvo* [Apr. 1905], in S. Johns, *Small Collection of Anti-Apartheid Material Issued by Various Groups* (CAMP).

15 Odendaal, *Vukani Bantu*, pp. 53-54; he notes Tsewu's later friction with Congress; Denoon, *Illusion*, p. 110 (Tsewu); "Natives & Land" *Imvo* [Apr. 1905], *Small Collection*; Kumalo and Germiston NVA to J. Chamberlain 8 Jan. 1903, Secretary Native Affairs [SNA] 21/191/1903, SOU/1/6; *Mining Industry Commission Evidence* (TG2-08), p. 1452. The Pietersburg area, and its Mphahlele and Matlala chiefs, as Bonner ("Kgatla Conspiracies, Pedi Plots") shows, was a real stronghold of Congress and its predecessors.

16 "The Native Question", *Ipepa lo Hlanga*, 9 Oct. 1903; SANAC, v. 4, pp. 790-794, 805.

17 *Mining Industry Commission Evidence*, pp. 1082-1085, 1445.

18 *Mining Industry Commission Evidence*, pp. 1446-1448. Makhothe claimed he had been a contractor since 1903 and worked at Wits Deep Mine (p. 1452), but mine manager Henry Hay alleged he never worked there. Hay's evidence was coloured by wild claims and when Makhothe was recalled, whilst inaccuracies in his evidence were uncovered by the Commission, they saw no grounds for perjury (p. 1502).

19 *Mining Industry Commission Evidence*, pp. 1445, 1442.

20 *Mining Industry Commission Evidence*, pp. 1442, 1449.

21 *Mining Industry Commission Evidence*, p. 1443. Labour Bureau Director Taberer (p. 1309ff) rejected Phooko's complaints but conceded whipping was illegal and agreed with Makhothe that educated Africans should be employed. He admitted he had seen some Africans "rather badly knocked about underground".

22 Bickford-Smith, "Black Labour at the Docks".

23 Mangena to *South African Spectator* 10 Aug. 1901; Z.K. Matthews, "Advocate Alfred Mangena", *Imvo* Jun. 1961; Headmen to Table Bay Harbour Board, 10 Oct. 1901 cited in Dubow, "African Labour", p. 123; Bickford-Smith, "Protest", p. 91, Bickford-Smith, "Black Labour", p. 97; M. Skota, *The African Who's Who* (Johannesburg, 1966), p. 9; La Hausse, *Restless Identities*, p. 167. On wage demands, see J. Watson to SANAC v. 2 p. 231.

24 Page, "Black America", p. 244; *Report of the Select Committee on the Native Locations Act (No. 40 of 1902)*, pp. 40-55 (Mdolomba), pp. 67-72 (Makwena). In World War I, Mdolomba was Chaplain to the Native Labour Contingent: Skota, *African Who's Who*, p. 119.

25 SANAC v. 2, pp. 285-288, 372, 386-391, 414-415, 448. Ndabeni had 7,500 occupants, "most of them labourers": Ndabeni Supervisor, p. 419. In 1906, Mdolomba argued for higher African wages and against forced labour: Natal Native Affairs Commission, *Evidence*, p. 911. He had worked as a teacher for nine years before being ordained: *A Brief Account of the Jubilee Celebrations in connection with the Normal Training Institution, Healdtown* (1906), p. 33.

26 *Report of Labour Commission*, p. 21.

27 SANAC v. 2 pp. 501-504, 514-515 (Mhala), 563-567 (Seti). Jabavu (p. 727), although not aligned with Congress, also detailed labourer complaints about wages, but his main concerns lay elsewhere; *Reports of the Transvaal Labour Commission. Minutes of Proceedings & Evidence* (Cd. 1897, 1904), pp. 599-601.

28 *Correspondence Relating to Conditions of Native Labour Employed in Transvaal Mines* (Cd. 2025, 1904), pp. 2-37: also in *Reports of Delegates, together with Correspondence relating to Visit of Native Representatives from the Colony Proper and the Transkeian Territories to Johannesburg to Enquire into the Conditions of Labour & the Treatment Accorded to Native Labourers* (G4-1904); *Report of Proceedings Annual Meeting of the Transkeian Territories General Council, 1904* (East London), p. 4.

29   SANAC v. 5, pp. 63-65 (Mti), v. 2, pp. 1032-1047 (Mamba); Odendaal, *Vukani Bantu,* pp. 44-45; C. Bundy, "A Voice in the Big House: The Career of Headman Enoch Mamba", in Beinart and Bundy, *Hidden Struggles,* pp. 78-105, who notes Mamba's populist and almost "Africanist" approach; *Report of the Select Committee on the Native Labour Regulation Bill* (SC3-11), pp. 307-321.

30   "Rules of the Native Congress", *Izwi LaBantu,* 16 Jun. 1903, translation, Cape Archives Depot [CAD] Natives Affairs [NA] 544/579; CAD GH 23/58 file 252 1/307, Tunyiswa to Governor, enclosing SANC King William's Town resolution 27 June 1902; GH 23/58 to Chamberlain, 30 Jul. 1902; SANC telegram 3 Jul. 1903, NA 544/579; GH 1/496 1906; GH 23/58 1902 1/307, GH 23/93 1906, 139; CC King William's Town to SNA, 24 Jul. 1902, SNA "Memorandum on SANC", 28 Apr. 1906, "Memorandum: SANC", 25 Jul. 1902, NA 544/579, Resolutions of SANC Meetings, 19 Apr. 1906, East London, 10 Apr. 1906, Queenstown, GH 23/93 1906, 139; *Izwi Labantu,* 14 Apr. 1906; GH 23/94, 165, 139.

31   GH 23/58 1902 1/307, GH 23/93 1906, 139; Civil Comm. King William's Town to SNA 24 Jul. 1902, SNA. "Memorandum on SANC", 28 Apr. 1906, SNA. "Memorandum: SANC", 25 Jul. 1902, NA 544/579; GH 23/94 1906, files 165, 139; L.S. Jameson, Minute 1/363 31 May 1906, NA 544/579.

32   S. Ngqongolo, "Mpilo Walter Benson Rubusana 1858-1910: The Making of the New African Elite in the Eastern Cape", MA thesis, University of Fort Hare, 1996, p. 169; "Names of Natives Who Met ... under the Designation of 'The Native Congress'", SNA "Memorandum: SANC" 25 Jul. 1902, NA 544/579 (also in GH 23/58 1902, 2); Resolutions of SANC Meeting 10 Apr. 1906, Queenstown, GH 23/93 1906, 139.

33   Soga to Civil Commissioner East London, 25 Apr. 1906; SNA "Memorandum: S. African Native Congress", 25 July 1902, SNA 1/237 4 Jul. 1903 "Native Congress, Indwe and Dordrecht"; "Meeting at King William's Town," [1902]: CAD NA 544/579; I. Bud-M'belle, *Kafir Scholar's Companion* (Alice: Lovedale Missionary Press, 1903), p. 11; Odendaal, "Mobilisation", pp. 170-171, 196.

34   Odendaal, *Vukani Bantu,* pp. 21, 41, 69, 95 (citing *Izwi Labantu,* 1 May 1906); *Izwi LaBantu,* 23 Feb. 1909. Soga had worked as a clerk for the Native Location Inspector, King William's Town: SANAC v. 2, p. 583.

35   Articles from *Izwi Labantu:* 8 Feb., 16 Mar. 1909, 6 May 1902; "The Rand and Labour", 4 Nov. 1902; "Native Labour", 29 Sep. 1908; "Native Labour", 8 Feb. 1909, 13 Oct. 1908; 9 July, 6 Aug., 3 Sep., 3 Dec. 1901, 19, 26 May, 21 Jul., 24 Nov. 1908, 13 Jan. 1909, 13, 20 Feb. 1906.

36   *Izwi Labantu* 4 Nov. 1902, 29 Sep., 13 Oct., 19, 26 May, 21 Jul. 1908, 16 Mar. 1909.

37   *Izwi Labantu,* 16 Mar., 8, 23 Feb. 1909; 13 Oct., 29 Sep., 20 Oct. 1908; 9 Jul., 6 Aug., 3 Sep., 26 Nov. 1901.

38   G. Minkley, "'I Shall Die Married to the Beer'", *Kronos* 23 (1996), pp. 135-157, p. 138; Baines, "Disturbances," pp. 11-19; Mabin, "Strikes"; S. Allen, "Mr. Alan Kirkland Soga", *Colored American Magazine* Feb. 1904, pp. 114-116; KC v. 4, p. 149. On Soga's enforced move from Native Affairs to Labour Office, which may have stimulated a bitterness manifest in his radical period, see Allen, "Mr Soga" and C. Saunders, "Ngcongco, Jabavu, and the South African War", *Pula* v. 11 (1997), pp. 63-69.

39   *Izwi Labantu* 6 Oct., 7 July, 10 Mar., 29 Sep., 19, 26 May, 21 Jul., 27 Oct. 1908.

40   Odendaal, "Mobilisation", pp. 199, 218; *Izwi Labantu* 6, 27 May 1902, 21 July, 3 Nov. 1908, 3 Dec. 1901, 4 Feb., 16 Apr. 1909; Soga to Governor ORC 27 Mar. 1909, VAB G113 461/6; *Black Man* Nov. 1920. Rhodes recruited Soga to edit *Izwi* after Jabavu supported rivals: Allen, "Soga", p. 116.

41 *South African Spectator,* 6 Apr. 1901 ("Deputation of Coloured People"), 8 Mar. 1902 ("A Real Grievance"), 14 Jan., 23 Mar. ("Mr. Moffat Defends the Compound System," "Colour Discrimination in Labour") 1901, 22 Mar. 1920 ("Native Labour in the Compound"), 13 Jul. ("Industrial Discrimination") 1901, 22 Feb. 1902 ("The Labour Question"), 8 Mar. 1902 ("The Coloured Man as a Labourer"), 18 May 1901 (Rhodes); Peregrino to *Voice of Labour* 14 Aug. 1909, *Life among the Native and Coloured Miners in the Transvaal* (Cape Town, 1910), *His Majesty's Black Labourers* (Cape Town, 1918); *SA Spectator* 5 Oct. 1901, C. Saunders, "F.Z.S. Peregrino and the *South African Spectator*", *Quarterly Bulletin of the South African Library* v. 32 no. 3 (1978), pp. 82-87, N. Parsons, "F.Z.S. Peregrino 1851-1919: An Early Pan-Africanist", *Tinabantu* v. 1 no. 1 (2002), pp. 104-115; Page, "Black America," p. 232.

42 *Koranta ea Becoana,* 13 Sep., 11 Oct. 15 Nov. 1902; "Scholar & Patriot", *Umteteli wa Bantu* 6 Aug. 1932; Willan, *Plaatje,* Chapters 5-6. Plaatje, *Selected Writings* ed. B. Willan (Braamfontein: Ravan Press, 1996) continues the tendency yet a different selection of texts can demonstrate a *more* labour-conscious Plaatje; *Koranta:* editorials 20 Jun., 25 Jul. 1903, "Asiatic Labour," 29 Aug. 1903; "Native Labour," "Natives in Transvaal", 31 Dec. 1902; 11 Apr., 23 Sep., 7 Feb., 2, 9 Dec., 4 Nov. 1903; "Native Labour", 17 Jan. 1903; "Hats Off for the Colonial Secretary", 24 Jan. 1903; "Labour", *Koranta* 4 Nov. 1903.

43 "Labour Commission", *Koranta ea Becoana,* 23 Sept. 1903; "Chief Sekgoma" and "Chief Linchwe of Mochudi", *Koranta,* 4 Nov. 1903 (also reported in *Imvo* and *Ipepa*); "Native Petition", *Koranta,* 7 Feb. 1903.

44 *Koranta ea Becoana,* 20 Jun., 23 Sep. 1903; "Native Miners' Mortality", *Koranta* 30 Sep. 1903; *Koranta,* 11 Jul., 2 May 1903; "De Beers", *Koranta,* 9 May 1903; "De Beers Compound", *Koranta,* 20 Jun. 1903.

45 *Koranta ea Becoana,* 2 Dec., 28 Oct., 25 Jul., 2 Dec., 18 Apr., 24 Jan., 29 Aug., 28 Oct., 18, 11 Nov. 1903.

46 *Koranta ea Becoana,* 4 Apr., 27 Jun., 18 Apr., 14, 7 Mar. 1903; Willan, *Plaatje,* pp. 109, 125.

47 Marks, *Reluctant Rebellion,* pp. 68-69, S. Meintjes, "Edendale 1850-1906: A Case Study of Rural Transformation and Class Formation in an African Mission in Natal" Ph.D. thesis, University of London, 1988, pp. 208, 308-311, 320-328 (uneven accumulation); La Hausse, *Restless Identities,* pp. 157-165.

48 Khumalo, "Epistolary Networks" pp. 18, 28, 57; S. Khumalo, "Ekukhanyeni Letter Writers: A Historical Enquiry into Epistolary Network(s) and Political Imagination in KwaZulu-Natal, South Africa", in K. Barber (ed.), *Africa's Hidden Histories* (Bloomington: Indiana University Press, 2006), pp. 113-142, p. 115.

49 *Inkanyiso yase Natal* 26 Mar. 1891, 25 May, 31 Oct. 1894 (employers), 9 Apr. 1891, 1 Jun. 1894 (farm workers), 21 May 1891, 16 Feb. 1894 (pass), 7 Sep., 21 Dec. 1894 (artisans), 26 Jan. 1894 (Lutuli). The paper's critical tone increased after founding editor Reverend F. J. Green left in 1891: J. Magagula, "*Inkanyiso yase Natal* as an Outlet of Political Opinion in Natal, 1889-1896", BA (Hons.) thesis, University of Natal, 1996, p. 21, who notes circulation climbed to 2,500 by 1891.

50 *Inkanyiso yase Natal,* Gumede and Dube letters 16 Feb., 11, 18 May 1894; Dube, "Native Labour Question," 22 Jun. 1894; Dube, "Mr Tatham's Pamphlet Criticised," 13 Jul. 1894. St. Alban's printed *Inkanyiso.*

51 *Inkanyiso yase Natal,* 28 Feb., 5, 26 Jan., 25 May, 1 Jun. 1894; Odendaal, *Vukani Bantu,* p. 19; S. Meintjes, "The Early African Press in Natal: *Inkanyiso yase Natal,* Apr. 1889-

Jun. 1896", *Natalia* 16 (1986), pp. 5-11; Meintjes, "Edendale" p. 265; "Organisation", *Inkanyiso*, 16 Aug. 1895; Magagula, *"Inkanyiso"*, pp. 47-64.

52 Khumalo, "Epistolary Networks" pp. 292, 66; *Ipepa,* 14 Dec. 1900, 14 Jun. 1901, 17 Jul. 1902, 11 Dec. 1903, *Ilanga* 10 Apr., 9 May 1903 in Warwick, *Black People,* pp. 163, 171, 144; Marks, *Reluctant Rebellion,* p. 73; Odendaal, *Vukani Bantu,* p. 61; H. Davis, "'Qude Maniki!': John L. Dube, Pioneer Editor of *Ilanga Lase Natal*", in Switzer, *South Africa's Press*, pp. 83-98, p. 87; Meintjes, "Edendale", pp. 385-386.

53 *SANAC* v. 3 p. 860; *Inkanyiso*, 22 Jun. 1894; *Natal Native Commission*, 1881-1882, p. 135; Native Affairs Commission. *Evidence* (1906), p. 910; Meintjes, "Edendale", pp. 308-313, 446-466; S. Meintjes, "Family and Gender in the Christian Community at Edendale, Natal in Colonial times", in Walker, *Women and Gender*, pp. 125-145, p. 130: other major landholders in 1909 were Simeon Kambule (149 acres) and Daniel Msimang (98). Saul Msane held 36, Joel Msimang 0.5. In 1919, Msane still had 36, Msimang only one.

54 Evidence of P. Maling to SANAC, v. 3, p. 495.

55 J. Dube, *A Talk upon My Native Land* (Rochester, 1892), pp. 28, 33; J. Dube, *The Zulu's Appeal for Light & England's Duty* (London: Unwin, 1908), p. 6; Natal Native Affairs Commission, *Evidence* (1906), pp. 961ff; Marks, *Ambiguities*, pp. 54-55.

56 M. Hadebe, "A Contextualisation and Examination of the *Impi Yamakhanda* (1906 Uprising) as Reported by J. L. Dube in *Ilanga Lase Natal*, with Special Focus on Dube's Attitude to Dinuzulu as Indicated in His Reportage on the Treason Trial of Dinuzulu", MA thesis, University of Natal, 2003, pp. 17, 59, 83, 144, 183; M. Hadebe, "Pleading for Clemency through Poetry: Discursive Issues in the 1906 Poll Tax Rebellion", paper to UKZN History Dept. seminar, May 2007 and Graduate African Studies Conference, East Lansing, Sept. 2007.

57 S. Marks, "Class, Ideology and the Bambatha Rebellion" in D. Crummey (ed.) *Banditry, Rebellion and Social Protest in Africa* (London: Currey, 1986), pp. 351-369, pp. 355-357, 364-365; J. Guy, *Remembering the Rebellion: The Zulu Uprising of 1906* (Scottsville: UKZN Press, 2006), pp. 160-161.

58 "Notes on an Interview between ... the Governor ... and John Dube May 17 1906" *British Documents on Foreign Affairs* v. 3, pp. 291-297; Gebuza [pseud.], *The Peril in Natal* (London: Unwin, 1906), pp. 24-25. Dube had been outspoken even earlier: *Inkanyiso,* 11, 18 May 1894; M. Marable, "African Nationalist: John Langalibalele Dube", Ph.D. thesis, Maryland University, 1976.

59 "Natives as Clerks", *Ipepa lo Hlanga,* 5 Jun. 1903; *Ipepa* 5, 17 Jun. (wages), 26 Jun. 1903; "Should South Africa Import Labour or Not?". *Ipepa,* 20 Nov. 1903, "The Labour Question", *Ipepa,* 4 Dec. 1903; *Evidence* (1906), p. 915; *A Brief Account* (1906), p. 33. Cf. Kunene's evidence to SANAC, v. 3 p. 974, v. 5 p. 137ff.

60 *Ipepa lo Hlanga,* 7 Aug, 9 Oct., 10 Jul., "Strikes and Effects", 12 Jun, 17 Jun, "The Labour Commission", 27 Nov. 1903. *Ipepa* applauded the ideas of Booker T. Washington, but (26 Jun. 1903) but debunked a notion that a tour by him addressing the "dignity of labour" would solve the "Labour Problem".

61 "Natives and the New Colonies", *Ipepa lo Hlanga*, 28 Aug. 1903, "Transvaal Labour", *Ipepa,* 8 Jan. 1904; "Natives & Professions", *Ipepa,* 26 Feb. 1904; "Native Opinion on Labour", *Ipepa,* 11 Dec. 1903.

62 SANAC v. 3, pp. 521-522, 528, 532, 537-538, 544.

63 SANAC v. 3, pp. 864-865, 492-591 esp. p. 493ff. Micah Kunene, Chief Gule's represent-ative, accompanied Maling and also complained that African wages were too low: pp. 512-

513; Marks, *Rebellion*, p. 359; *Evidence* (1906), p. 914. *Isibalo* had long been a *kholwa* grievance: Meintjes, "Edendale", p. 260.

64   SANAC v. 3, pp. 461-467, 513; R. van Diemel, *"In Search of Freedom, Fair Play and Justice": Josiah Tshangana Gumede 1867-1947: A Biography* (Cape Town, 2001) who notes (p. 8) Gumede's 1886 stint as Dinuzulu's *induna* aroused his suspicion of British imperialism; letter of Gumede, *Inkanyiso,* 16 Feb. 1894; Verwey, *New Dictionary*, p. 86; Marks, *Reluctant Rebellion*, pp. 68, 360.

65   SNA 1/1/369 1907/1420 SNA Natal, "Cablegram ... by Josiah Gumede to Mr. Keir Hardie"; Gumede to Labour Party (Colenso Papers, KCM), cited in Khumalo, "Epistolary Networks", p. 192; Magistrate Bergville to USNA, 28 Dec. 1906, SNA C250/1906, SNA 1/1/369 1469/07, 1/1/367 1420/07, R2/1907.

66   Marks, *Reluctant Rebellion*, pp. 359-360; Cobley, *Class and Consciousness*, p. 163.

67   NNC Address of Welcome to PM, mimeo, "Transcript of Notes ... between the PM ... and Certain Members of the Natal Native Congress ... 22.6.1907" and other papers in NAD SNA 1/1/369 1561/07.

68   "Iso lo Muzi ... Congress" and brief report in English, *Ipepa lo Hlanga*, 2 Oct. 1903; Edgecombe and Guest, "Labour Conditions".

69   J. Mancoe, *The Bloemfontein Bantu and Coloured People's Directory* (Bloemfontein: White, 1934), p. 33; Odendaal, *Vukani Bantu*, p. 58. Odendaal uses "Phatlane", Mancoe uses "Phahlane"; K. Schoeman, *Bloemfontein: Die Ontstaan van 'n Stad 1846-1946* (Cape Town: Human & Rousseau, 1980), pp. 223-226. Before preaching, Ngcayiya worked as a teacher for eight, and a clerk for six years: *A Brief Account*, p. 33.

70   Page, "Black America", pp. 135, 216, 229 ff.

71   Minister's Minute 993/6 25 Jun. 1909, VAB Governor (G) 91 292/1. On white indifference see J. Haasbroek, "Die Verhouding tussen die Swart Inwoners en die Stadsraad van Bloemfontein gedurende die Oranjerivierkolonie-Tydperk, 1902-1910" *Navorsinge van die Nasionale Museum* v. 15 (1999) pp. 1-28.

72   SANAC, v. 4, pp. 373-374 (Kumalo, Mpela), 368 (Twayi).

73   Odendaal, *Vukani Bantu*, p. 57; SANAC v. 4, pp. 292, 368; *A Brief Account of the Jubilee Celebrations in Connection with the Normal Training Institution* (Healdtown, 1906), p. 35. Goronyane in 1910 helped underwrite *Tsala ea Becoana*; Mancoe, *Directory,* p. 75; Mweli Skota, *The African Yearly Register* (Johannesburg: Esson, 1932), p. 241. If focused on administration see also C.J.P. le Roux, *Die Verhouding tussen Blank en Nie-Blank in die Oranjerivierkolonie, 1900-1910* (Pretoria, 1986), pp. 174-188 on Thaba 'Nchu.

74   Mocher to Governor Goold-Adams 21 Jun. 1909, VAB G113 461/6; Mocher and Mapikela to P.M. 2 Mar. 1909, C.O.572 1193/1; Mapikela to Goold-Adams 8 Aug. 1907, VAB G51 103: Native Congress ORC file; "Responsible Government" 1906, p. 3, VAB Native Affairs Branch 3 180/06; S. Belot, "The Life History of Thomas Mapikela 1869-1945 and his Role in the ANC", Mayibuye Centre, MCH133hf.

75   Mancoe, *Directory,* p. 72; KC v. 4, p. 74; C. Twala, "'Ulundi-Kaya': The Dwelling of Thomas Mtobi Mapikela in Bloemfontein (Mangaung): Its Historical Significance", *South African Journal of Cultural History* v. 18 (2004), pp. 63-79, p. 66; "Native Rest House and Minutes of a Meeting of Executive Committee, Municipal Association Bloemfontein", 11 Aug. 1908, VAB MBL 4/1/1/16 file 193/09: Mapikela file; Matthews, "Mapikela"; Msimang, "Autobiography", p. 77, Aitchison Papers, PC 14/1/1/1-3, Paton Centre and Struggle Archives; C.J.P. Le Roux, "The Role of T.M. Mapikela in the Municipal Administration of Black Affairs in Bloemfontein 1902-1945", *Historia* v. 42 (1997), pp. 67-79.

76   *South African Natives* pp. 9, 35, 69, 104, 230; *Report of the General Trades of South Africa* (London: King, 1902), p. 115; Diemel, *In Search of Freedom,* pp. 25-32; *South Africa*, 12 Jan. 1907.

77   Odendaal, *Vukani Bantu*, p. 157, citing *The Friend*, 27 Feb., 2, 5 Mar. 1909; "The Act of Union: Report of Native Delegates," *Imvo Zabantsundu,* 2 Nov. 1909.

78   [South African Native Convention] "Natives and Union: Text of Resolutions Adopted" attached to letter of A.K. Soga to Orange River Colony Governor, 27 Mar. 1909, in VAB G113 file 461/6.

79   A. Ashforth, *The Politics of Official Discourse in Twentieth Century South Africa* (Oxford: Clarendon, 1990); Rich, *State Power*, pp. 9-10; SANC telegram to PM 2 Jul. 1903, CAD Native Affairs [NA] 544 file 579; Minister's Minute 993/6 of 25 Jun. 1909, VAB G 91, file 292/1.

80   "Resolutions Passed at SA Native Convention ... 24th Mar. 1910", Native Affairs Dept. [NAD] 1118/F.374, Silas T. Molema and Solomon T. Plaatje Papers, University of the Witwatersrand Library.

Part 2

The ANC and Labour, the First Decade

5

The SANNC and African Working People

This chapter outlines the emergence of the South African Native National Congress (SANNC) and its complex and contradictory relations with African working peoples in the second decade of the twentieth century. It does so from the perspective of *national* African politics (provincial and local politics are discussed in the next two chapters). It addresses themes essential to any potential Congress liaison with workers: SANNC national organisation and its policies and attitudes towards labour. It argues that members paid considerable attention to labour and it will become evident that some leaders at an early stage in their careers expressed sympathetic sentiments towards black workers. Thinly documented, yet tangible, ties between certain politicised workers and Congress emerged from these early contacts. Commitment to the alleviation of the plight of black labour followed from the logic of Congress's basic policies.

To draw public attention to conditions of Africans, Congress used various avenues, including government commissions, the press, mass meetings, and other political or industrial organisations. An examination of instances of these relations demonstrates that definite trends began to emerge in the orientation of Congress policy toward labour—a policy clearly marked by great concern for the welfare of exploited black workers. This concern Congress couched in *national*, not class, terms, but it underpinned this approach with some knowledge of labour conditions and sympathy for workers' predicament.

In this period, the SANNC made very limited headway among most workers. Its bonds with black labour tended to be uneven, characterised by brief, shifting alliances. Yet these contacts were recurrent and some workers joined or interacted with Congress, which became aware of their difficult conditions. In theory, the inferior social status of African leaders vis-à-vis white people brought them common interests with black workers; they all faced discrimination. Residential near-proximity heightened this commonality. If there was just enough social mobility for educated Africans to rise above labourers in lifestyle, then political powerlessness and impediments to *continued* social mobility tended to keep many of this elite within the same broad social orbit as workers. Before black workers formed their own class organisations in the 1920s, they protested in *political* arenas, including Congress. This does not mean workers eschewed independent action—but they found allies necessary.

This period was notable for diverse ideological and intellectual currents, including devout but variegated versions of Christianity and Empire loyalism, liberalism, nascent African proto-nationalism, and the first seeds of socialism in South Africa. However, Africans used liberalism and loyalism as an ideological weapon against further erosion of their already truncated rights. African leaders' professions of loyalty, of being "your Excellency's humble and obedient servant",[1] can be interpreted to mean not blind faith in ruling ideology but an implicit statement of defiance; that the African is a *better* servant than others or that the African literally is a servant, trapped. It is necessary to consider carefully the meanings of African texts. The need for textual interpretation does not mean that we must read every statement about workers by an SANNC leader as a cynical appeal to garner political support. The extent to which Congress expressed genuine sympathy for workers is difficult to establish. However, it is important to remember this was a formative period when African workers and political leaders struggled not only politically against the state but also intellectually to come to grips with these ideologies. Finally, it should not be imagined that SANNC involvement with workers was purely rhetorical, confined to the realm of speeches. Below I present evidence of the physical commitment of some members to struggles involving workers.

Localised African political pressure groups (discussed in Chapter 3) gave way to African national unity in the face of the 1910 Union of South Africa. The South African Native Convention met in March 1910 and passed resolutions, including one on the rights of black labour.[2] Thus, the groups out of which the ANC emerged took some interest in labour. Political Union stimulated standardisation of labour laws and intensification of exploitation that helped make the predicament of labour more visible to ANC members.

The SANNC: Membership and Class Composition

One to two hundred delegates, characterised by Mary Benson as including not only "the sprinkling of educated men and representatives of political associations" but also "clerks and messengers and servants, members of the new African urban proletariat", descended on the Wesleyan School, Waaihoek, Bloemfontein, on 8 January 1912 and founded the SANNC. Journalist F. Z. S. Peregrino wrote at the time that the gathering was "nothing less than a Native Parliament". It was "the real voice of the people."[3] In keeping with such ambitious claims, Congress began to develop nation-wide contacts and attract support from diverse African social strata.

SANNC founders were, Walshe writes, "ministers, teachers, clerks, interpreters, a few successful farmers, builders, small-scale traders, compound managers, estate and labour agents. They were not trade unionists, nor were they socially radical." Yet in 1912, there were *no* African unions. African moderates such as J. T. Jabavu attacked SANNC leaders for their "radicalism" and "revolutionary" opposition to "slow evolution". The driving force was indeed professionals and the intelligentsia. However, members also included wage earners such as "teachers, clerks, interpreters". The 80 delegates to the 1914 SANNC conference included "several ... kicked out of Government service to make room for the white man". Their career-paths blocked by discrimination, some turned to politics. Some industrial workers, with little education, also joined. Thomas Zini, a migrant worker from Queenstown who represented the Cape Peninsula Native Association (CPNA) of which he was President, took part in the founding. Alfred Cetyiwe, S. B. Macheng and T. Tladi joined provincial ANC bodies. In addition, vigorous SANNC protests against the 1913 Natives' Land Act led to some rural working people joining.[4]

The influx of these diverse strata into Congress helped broaden its class base. One report on the March 1913 SANNC conference in Johannesburg tallied some 106 delegates: 60 from the Transvaal, 25 from Natal, 12 from the Orange Free State, eight from Bechuanaland and (oddly) only one, from Kimberley, representing the Cape.[5]

Concern for workers came from other quarters. Chiefs were involved in the SANNC: eight sat in its upper House of Chiefs. However, this number was not many, and over time chiefs increasingly found themselves in an ambiguous position as the state sought to integrate them into ruling structures, leading many to disengage from Congress. However, some chiefs were prepared to speak out on behalf of their subjects, which included workers. This tendency was apparent even before the SANNC formed. Chiefs had complained to

SANAC in 1903 about the whole process of proletarianisation and treatment of labourers. Chief August Mokgatle of Phokeng complained that due to limited land, his people now lived entirely by labour, "all over the towns, wherever we can obtain work". Chief Jonathan Molapo (Maseru) expressed complaints on behalf of workers: "The grievances they bring to us are these: they say the work in the gold mines is not like the work in Kimberley." He and Chief Lerothodi had worked in Kimberley, where they were well paid; but now, he complained, the worker "does not get his wages properly. And they are complaining of us, their Chiefs, selling them."[6]

The 1919 SANNC constitution stated Congress would include chiefs representing "their districts and places under their rule or control". It imagined chiefly representation implied affiliation to the SANNC of those people, including migrant and farm workers, under their "jurisdiction". Concern of *inkhosi* (chiefs or kings) for workers was more hegemonic than disinterested, but as outlined below, many chiefs associated with Congress tended to identify more closely with problems of labour than those who became mere state functionaries. Some chiefs visited "their" labourers on the mines. Sotho Chief Letsie told labourers to guard "against their tribal animosities". In 1919, police suspected Chief Mabandla of secretly plotting mine strikes in conjunction with Congress. Swazi royalty were closely involved in Congress: Queen Labotsibeni was a major underwriter of the Congress organ *Abantu-Batho*, and Prince Malunge Dlamini solicited funds from migrant workers for SANNC land-fund campaigns at least up until 1921. In Kimberley, chiefs spoke out in the Congress-aligned black press in defence of rights of "their" labourers.[7] A good many SANNC leaders thus had some experience of, or knowledge about, working life though this rarely extended to working lives underground, on farms, or as domestic workers. More significantly, Congress remained weak.

Congress grew slowly. In its first years, wrote R. W. Msimang in 1919, "[t]here was no co-ordination ... Branches everywhere acted almost independently." One reason for this was the newness of the organisation[8]. In his first "annual report" in late December 1912, John Dube reported to members and chiefs that Congress surely was "one of the most interesting movements in the history of the Black race". He felt it would be not only a political, but also a "progressive movement along all lines of modern progress", thus requiring standing committees on such matters as industrial education, agriculture and "pure home-life" to enable the uplifting of "the masses of our people". Dube sensed organisational problems: he suggested annual conferences shift to Johannesburg, and warned of "firebrands" or "dangerous or suspicious tendencies". This did not happen. "What is wanted," reported *Abantu-Batho* in 1917 in the light of problems such as members having to pay their own expenses to conferences invariably held in Bloemfontein, which was becoming a "dumping ground" for meetings, "is organisation".[9]

Another reason for weakness was ethnic differentiation, long encouraged by the state and reflected in factionalism. Congress also faced financial limitations, an oppressive state, and limited communication channels. These weaknesses made it incapable of reaching many workers or winning concessions for them. SANNC regulations restricted its ability to mobilise fully all sections of the population.

The SANNC did not permit direct female membership. This limited both its community links and the potential involvement of women workers in Congress. This is the major reason that women's voices appear only fleetingly in the pages to follow; another is the fact that African politics in general, and not just Congress politics, was masculine-led and oriented, even if at times such leaders made due deference in their statements to the struggles of African women. [10]

In general, men marginalised both white and black women from "high politics" in this whole period. White women only got the franchise in 1930 and even then only because of a calculated move by white politicians to limit the power of the "coloured" vote. However, in this period African women did form various kinds of clubs and self-help organisations. Initially some of these had a regional base, such as the Bantu Purity League, formed in 1919 by Sibusisiwe Makhanya and aimed at protecting young women. Others became more broad-based, in terms of both geography and class. Church-based prayer-unions grew in popularity in the 1910s and continued to expand by the 1920s, when women came to call them *manyano* ("union"). *Stokvels* (mutual-aid credit unions often formed by a *manyano*) or sewing clubs were economic in function. Whilst initiated from within *kholwa* circles, some female wage earners joined *manyanos*. Factory worker Ester Mqhayi saw them being for "ordinary women". The practice of holding *manyano* meetings on Thursday afternoons related to the rhythm of washerwomen, observes Deborah Gaitskell.[11]

These organisations were not directly engaged in politics but through them, as Helen Bradford argues, women could "express protonationalist" protests. *Manyanos*, argues Fatima Meer, were "the most authentic African women's organisation", supporting female roles in the "overtly political" sphere; their "potential for quick politicisation" seen in 1913 anti-pass protests. Women also used culture in political ways and developed women's cultures of resistance.[12]

This raises the question of women's indirect support of African politics in general, or of the Congress edifice in particular. Some Congressmen may have tended to regard women as "tea and cake ladies" when it came to the *formal* political sphere. Women were involved in catering, accommodation, and other supportive acts of Congress meetings. We know little for this early period about whether women were involved in raising funds for Congress. However, in the first decade of ANC history, the determined anti-pass actions of women, including workers, at least situated them in wider political discourse. Their political protests are very likely to have influenced (male) Congress members; their incomplete recognition generated differences with some Congressmen during protests.

Charlotte Manye Maxeke

Charlotte Manye Maxeke (1871 [or 1874]-1939) was the most prominent African female political activist of the day. She attended the founding conference of the SANNC. Her father was a worker, later a road-gang supervisor, her mother a teacher. Educated in Port Elizabeth, she became a teacher in industrial Kimberley where labour issues could not but help influence nascent black communities. As part of a choir, Maxeke toured England where she met suffragist Emmeline Pankhurst. Continuing her education at the AME Wilberforce University in Ohio, she obtained a Bachelor of Science degree and imbued black advancement ideas. Returning to South Africa, she taught in the Cape and then Pietersburg, where the active Transvaal Native Vigilance Association may have inclined her towards politics. In 1903, with her husband Marshall Maxeke, who was active in the AME and against forced removals, she founded the AME Wilberforce Institute at Evaton.[13]

The mere fact (as Phyllis Ntantla observes) that Maxeke absorbed moderate ideas did not stop her joining militant protests such those in 1913 in Bloemfontein organised by the Native and Coloured Women's Association. When the state threatened to force African women in the Transvaal to carry passes, she helped found the Bantu Women's National League. Full details of its founding are obscure; most sources date it to 1918, though *Abantu-Batho* reported a meeting of National League of Bantu Women (Transvaal Province) in Nancefield on 9 December 1917 "under the presidency of Mrs Maxeke of Kliptown". I discuss these events in the next chapter, but it seems probable that the Transvaal Bantu Women's League branches merged with surviving branches of the Native and Coloured Women's Association that still existed in 1917, for example in Winburg.[14]

The consummating conference came at an all-day, all-night meeting in Ebenezer Hall, Johannesburg on 18 January 1918. Police spies reported that among the 300 women and 100 African men present, delegates came from different parts of the country, especially the Orange Free State and Kliptown, and that most women gave short speeches "expressing their warm hearts against these pass laws". One declared they preferred to "die out in the street fighting against" passes. Others related stories of recent anti-pass struggles. The meeting elected Maxeke president, Mrs C. Mallela of Winburg and Mrs More vice-presidents, Mrs Nonjekwa secretary and Mrs Mohan treasurer. Also elected was a delegation, including Maxeke, to meet with government. Maxeke clashed with SANNC President Makgatho at the meeting. He was perturbed women chose to act independently of Congress. Maxeke disagreed—and received support from Transvaal Congress leaders. The League appears to have remained active for at least three years, bombarding government with petitions against pass laws and sexist inspections of domestic workers.[15]

Maxeke also became involved in support for protests of workers on the Rand and raised the troubles of women workers (see Chapter 5). Part of this interest in subaltern classes may have been rooted in her family background and, as James Campbell suggests, her view of African culture as not inherently "pagan" marked her off from other *kholwa* and was seen in her willingness to ride on railway cars with migrant labourers.[16] In such ways, some women associated with Congress found ways around restrictive policy.

The SANNC, according to many historians, was a middle-class elite construct dominated by ideologies of European-derived liberalism and nationalism, and detached from the masses. Contemporary socialists had a similar view. David Ivon Jones in 1919 characterised "Victorian liberalism" as the "sheet anchor" of the "Native Congresses' political faith".[17] These views accord with accepted images and documented practices of SANNC leaders. Whilst there is nothing inherently repellent to workers in liberalism or nationalism, the elitist presentation of these ideas did not necessarily strike a familiar chord with workers if they heard it at all, given SANNC weaknesses. Africans remained divided by class, ethnicity, ideology and region. The proletariat was numerically small and fragmented. Workers confined in compounds were difficult to access by political groups. Black workers were still in the process of forging their own working-class cultures. In smaller towns, where industrialisation had barely begun, SANNC members would have had difficulty in clearly identifying a distinct working class.

SANNC Policies and Actions towards Labour

There was little specific identification of workers as such in SANNC policies but the inclusive nature of the "nationalism" it espoused did not exclude workers. Domination of Congress by liberalism was far from universal, making any simple equation of Congress with liberalism too narrow a view of the organisation. At first sight, the policies of SANNC leaders towards the state may appear conformist, even obsequious. However, I shall demonstrate that its actions often accorded with wider black, including labour, interests.

The inclusion of "National" in its name signified the adoption by the SANNC of the trappings of modern nationalism. Nevertheless, whilst tempered by the demand of its members for incorporation into South African public life, Congress objectively presented an anti-colonial variety of nationalism. Colonial-settler capitalism imparted such an orientation to all black, subordinated classes. Moreover, this variety of nationalism was neither totally separate from, nor uninfluenced by black workers. African middle strata had to return repeatedly to the need for cross-class unity to survive. Still, it was necessary for workers and their allies in Congress to advance consciously and strenuously the claims of labour for a place in the nascent African political opposition.

The fact that Congress drew from its early days support from various black social strata related to its emphasis on African national unity. The objects of the new body declared in 1912 (as paraphrased by ANC member Selope Thema in 1928) were:

> (1) To effect unity ... (2) to educate public opinion on matters affecting the political, land and economic conditions of the people; (3) to encourage the spread of knowledge; (4) to be the channel of communication between the government and the people; and (5) to cooperate with all ... interested in the welfare of the Bantu people.

SANNC convenor Pixley Seme repeatedly called for a Congress in which "every section of our great people should be more than fairly represented". In public pronouncements, he stated that African "everywhere ... know that a ... Congress ... will give them the only effective means ... to make their grievances properly known". In his call for African Union in October 1911, Seme emphasised the need for national organisation and unity; on his proposed agenda for the first Congress, labour was the last item, but it was there.[18]

The first SANNC constitution, adopted in 1919, listed several aims that either related to black worker interests, or were inclusive enough to incorporate trends among workers, such as combination. One aim was "to agitate and advocate by just means for the removal of the 'Colour Bar' in political, education and industrial fields"—of vital importance to black workers because the industrial colour bar meant for them low wages and restricted job opportunities and job mobility. Another aim was to "propagate the gospel of the dignity of labour"—a rather vague commitment to worker rights. Other aims compatible with black workers' interests included the need for "elimination of racialism and tribal feuds ... by economic combination", the desirability of "mutual help", and the need to "record all grievances and wants of native people and to seek by constitutional means the redress thereof". Such clauses may have owed their existence to the presence on the committee that drew up the constitution of more radical members such as Daniel Letanka and Josiah Gumede, but they also represented a continuation of the tradition of articulating popular grievances established by the colonial Congresses.[19]

SANNC leaders favoured constitutional tactics of petition and polite protest. Many historians have looked down their noses at such *politesse* as supposedly an indication of elitist isolation from workers. Such tactics are not inherently anti-worker; indeed, social democratic/labour parties with worker support in places such as Western Europe adopted them. In both working-class and colonial situations, petitions have been prominent tactics of the disenfranchised and powerless. For example, Chartist petitions in the England of 1839 and 1848 had over a million signatures affixed, and waves of petitioning sometimes accompanied revolutionary situations.[20] Workers themselves made use of petitions, especially before they developed strong unions.

Deference to established social procedures did not stop Congress adopting resolutions in keeping with worker aspirations. "Native labour" was on the agenda of its first meeting. Resolutions of its founding conference included increased compensation for injured miners, reduction of mine deaths and "promotion of the educational, social, economical, and political elevation" of Africans. Inaugural SANNC committees included an "Education and Labour Board" that oversaw "contracts, wages and fair treatment" of workers. Congress appointed a "Minister for Labour" and "Secretary for Mines". From the start, it addressed labour issues, an approach influenced by the recent passage of the discriminatory Mines and Works and Native Labour Regulation Acts.[21]

In its first three months, SANNC leaders held meetings with state ministers on job discrimination on the railways, the draconian Squatters' Bill, imposition of passes on women, and the need to extend workers' compensation to mine labourers. Delegation members included inaugural SANNC president John Dube, Solomon Plaatje, Thomas Mapikela, S. M. Makgatho and Edward Tsewu. Plaatje, commented Dube, "made a good stand" against location laws.[22]

Such meetings continued in 1914-1915. SANNC leaders Saul Msane and Richard Msimang met government ministers and labour officials. They prefaced their remarks with professions of Congress loyalty to government, but emphasised their concerns for the need for protection of migrant labourers—and also of rural Africans—against wanton acts by white people commandeering their property. They paid close attention to the wages, conditions of service, and compensation offered labourers in a government scheme to satisfy its requirements for a "reliable supply of native labour" in Namibia.[23]

Mass support for Congress began to grow, especially after it led protests against the Land Act. Examples of this included large attendance at meetings in 1913 and collection of relatively large sums of money to support protests.

Saul Msane raised £100.9s in one afternoon in the rural town of Bethal. Dube received £266 in the Northern Transvaal. A social evening held in conjunction with a 1914 SANNC special conference, attracted a capacity crowd of over 1,000 people. A measure of Congress's growing mass support was the state's use of martial law to stop its 1914 convention. One effect of this protest movement was that some leaders, such as Plaatje and Gumede, travelled widely and saw first-hand evidence of mass poverty and suffering. Reminiscing nearly 60 years later, Selby Msimang, involved in the campaign, noted it "helped us to spread the principles of the ANC and to invite others to join", but he felt it was a serious distraction for Congress, which thereby neglected important work of organisational consolidation.[24]

SANNC 1914 UK delegation: from left, Walter Rubusana, Thomas Mapikela, John Dube, Sol Plaatje, Saul Msane

Congress protested against the Land Act's denial of African land owning and purchasing rights and unequal land apportionments. Many writers argue that ANC contact with peasants and workers was incidental, that its protests against the Land Act fizzled out as its leaders put all their faith in the imperial petitions and delegations to England of 1914 and 1919. Some argue that the Act enabled Congress *petit bourgeois kholwa* to project their own interests as the general interest and thus claim to represent all African people, whilst reinforcing resentment of Congress landowners by the proletariat.[25]

There are weaknesses in these arguments. Firstly, they tend to take an *ex post facto* view of ANC history. At this time, *no* organisation, white or black, union or political, was capable of mobilising the mass of black workers. Congress in any case had no structures with which to organise them. Secondly, Congress did organise numerous protests. The SANNC constitution spelt out clearly its role as including protest and even "passive action". Thirdly, with respect to SANNC attitudes to Empire, some leaders viewed petitions as a limited *tactic* with only a possibility, rather than probability, of success. Moreover, as Christopher Saunders argues, we can interpret Empire loyalty as "a kind of anti-colonialism" and, as Andrew Thompson reminds us, such loyalism related both to perceptions of a valuable alliance and ideological influences. Fourthly, whilst early SANNC delegations were failures, the 1919 delegation at least succeeded in gaining the sympathy of British Prime Minister Lloyd George who communicated his sentiments to Jan Smuts. Such "success" served to perpetuate the illusion of the tactic held by some leaders. Finally, the land-owning, *petit-bourgeois* nature of some Congress leaders did not preclude class unity on political matters. If anything, moderates moved closer to "the masses" during the protests. A resolution of a Congress meeting at New Marabastad attacked the "iniquitous Act ... aiming by despotic legislation to reduce the aboriginal inhabitants ... to a condition of servility and helotage". In 1916, the draconian provisions of the Native Affairs Administration Bill led Plaatje to denounce the Bill, the government, and segregation.[26]

Congress linked the Land Act with labour exploitation. The SANNC petition presented to the British government in 1914 referred to the aims of the Land Act as including "the forcing of the native to labour by making it the only condition of his living on a white man's farm; that they are to bargain with the owner ... on the sole condition of supplying three months labour". A SANNC delegation meeting with the Secretary of Native Affairs in Thaba 'Nchu in 1913 stressed provisions of the Act that would have a "disturbing effect upon" the "means of livelihood ... [of] many of the natives working in the towns [who] supplemented their earnings by running stock". A special SANNC conference of 1916 stated that the aim of the Act was not only to deprive Africans of land but also to "reduce ... by artificial means the Bantu people as a race to a status of permanent labourers ... with little or no freedom to sell their labour by bargaining on even terms with employers in the open markets of labour".[27]

In July 1913, a SANNC delegation consisting of Plaatje, Makgatho, Msane, J. Nyokong and Enoch Mamba met Acting Native Affairs Minister F. S. Malan. Plaatje and Makgatho detailed African hardships due to the Land Act. Plaatje also raised the fate of black mineworkers imprisoned for their part in the 1913 white-led strike. He argued these workers "were only doing what their white overseers told them to do ... Six months hard labour was rather long, and there was room for ... clemency." Makgatho contrasted state assurances to the delegation that Africans on the Rand were content, with a report by the British Secretary of State for Colonies that the government had deployed troops during the strike "owing to the serious unrest". Mamba added that migrant workers needed protection if repatriated due to the strike. Their unexpired labour contracts required "some compensation, seeing that it was not their fault that the contracts were broken. The journeys being long, some were bound to get sick on the road and Congress was anxious for their protection." Mamba criticised the way illicit liquor led workers to squander their wages and stated that doctors who were "servants of the mining companies" distorted the severity of phthisis among mineworkers and their right to compensation. Concerning white strikes, he feared the impending visit of socialist Tom Mann. Mamba expressed concern for workers at a 1914 meeting of the Transkeian Territories General Council where he moved the appointment of a select committee on black labour questions. Africans objected to being "practically sold to the mines at so much a head, like pigs and goats". He strongly criticised the system of labour advances and the Chamber of Commerce's lack of consultation with Africans. His rationale was not working-class solidarity but a sense of fair play. "By their loyalty during the recent industrial crisis natives had earned the right to be consulted in matters which concerned them." Yet he was concerned "skilled and educated [black] men were not wanted [and that] ... shareholders of mining companies were losing money by the rejection of skilled native labour". If Mamba's rationale that black workers' loyalty could somehow be bargained industrially for consultation over working conditions was naive, and if his argument on skilled labour centred on profitability rather than higher wages, he nevertheless addressed migrant worker concerns about conditions and dignity. What is clear from these statements is the concern of SANNC leaders for the conditions and welfare of workers, even if this concern stemmed from their blackness rather than their class, and even if they feared strikes *per se*.[28]

A special SANNC meeting of July 1913 resolved to disassociate Congress "entirely from the rumours tending to aggravate the situation arising out of the recent strike" on the Rand. Writers present this as proof of Congress's lack of worker ties but the situation was more complex. Firstly, whilst the SANNC expressed distaste for radical actions in general, their main opposition here was to white (often racist) unionists whom they regarded as inimical to black interests. Secondly, Congress did express concern for the fate of black workers affected by the strike; there was no guarantee from the Government, it argued, that black workers "being deported to their homes" would be "protected from violence and robbery". Thirdly, the unplanned nature of the action of some black workers, who became involved in the strike only after white people went on strike, and their lack of organisation, did not lend itself to liaison with Congress. Fourthly, delegates did debate whether Congress should express solidarity, but Plaatje succeeded in defeating the proposition. Many leaders undoubtedly felt uneasy about strikes. In 1913, Plaatje clashed with Transvaal Congressmen who proposed to use strike action to seek redress over the Land Act. Willan argues that the SANNC did not contemplate industrial action, but this does not mean that some members (see below) did not consider striking.[29]

SANNC leaders also refused to support the 1914 white workers' strike. Dube told Director of Native Labour, Colonel Pritchard, that Congress "would do all in their power to induce" Africans on the mines to "not mix themselves up in the trouble". Yet he also urged adequate food be supplied to black workers, who also should be protected against possible striker intimidation. "Ostentatious display of force" in compounds should be avoided, as it would suggest to Africans the government "distrusted their intentions". The delegation even assumed the mantle of the workers' moral guardian, supporting precautions taken to protect workers "against themselves", namely "prohibition of the sale of pearl barley, golden syrup, and similar ingredients ... used in the manufacture of intoxicating drinks in the compounds".[30]

Despite its refusal to support white strikes (and given the attitude of white labour to black people there is little reason to suppose it should have), Congress continued to be concerned with interests of black labour as an integral part of their constituency. This interest was not mercenary. As Hofmeyr argues, the "very logic of a mass [oriented] organisation" required moderates to give some support to mass struggles.[31] An established tradition of broad support for black labour in Congress's antecedents (as seen in earlier chapters) and its existing contacts with workers, a degree of shared ideology and suffering influenced Congress-worker reciprocal relationships. Changes in the class composition and policies of Congress reinforced these more long-term factors.

These attitudes were evident in Congress attitudes to World War I and black labourers involved in the war. The period 1917-1920, when strikes and protests erupted on the Rand, was a time of militancy in ANC history when Empire began to be criticised. The war generated an expanded domestic and military need for labour. Many Africans were deployed as labourers in South West Africa (where strikes erupted), East Africa, and France, where South African officials insisted on keeping "tribes" in the non-combative Native Labour Contingent together to avoid contact with socialist ideas, for "trade unionism is not indulged in by the Natives at present". Africans' enthusiasm for the war effort appears to have been stronger among "elite" strata, and there is evidence, including intercepted letters, of anti-Empire sentiment among black workers on the Rand. A mine strike in October 1914 perhaps related to workers' perception of a crisis of colonial rule. Increased African recruitment required pressure, but some workers enrolled. Stimela Jingoes, who had worked underground on the mines and then as a compound salesperson, served in France, where he spoke out against racism among white South African soldiers.[32]

The SANNC gave official support to the war effort. In December, 1918, a SANNC memorial to the King spoke of loyalty and sacrifice of extensive "manual labour work in the French docks, and behind the trenches in Flanders", just as black miners for four years "steadfastly maintained the supply of labour" to the gold mines.[33] "We felt as a Congress," recalled Selby Msimang, "that we should not disturb the Government machinery" in wartime, yet because Congress "kept quiet" it was powerless to stem rising prices and wage stagnation. Even among Congress leaders committed to this policy, loyalty was blended with anticipation of a resumption of political campaigning. Loyalty had its limits. In 1916, Seme was severely cautioned by the government for writing an uncensored press report (in Zulu) on war events. He reported the "bravery" of the German King and army who had driven "our people (the English) from all places". The British had "had enough" of the War; their government was "in a state of chaos"; Africans should "expect any day that [King] George will ask you to go and assist"—in which case they should, intimated Seme, be led by Zulu King Solomon Dinuzulu.[34] Seme was reporting the news but he also probably thought that he could more safely speak his mind in the vernacular press. The invocation of the Zulu monarchy, part of a movement to have him officially recognised by the state, was a way of asserting African identity.

The previous year Seme had agreed not to speak of grievances until the war's end, but he added: "As soon as the war is over, Congress will press forward until our inalienable rights be attained—liberty, unity and equal opportunity." Other leaders expressed misgivings. Saul Msane told the Natives' Law Commission in 1917, with regard to Congress protests over the Land Act: "We suspended our agitation, but we have not dropped it." A meeting of over 1,000 people convened by Dube in Johannesburg in May 1915 unanimously supported a policy of not debating at Congress meetings any contentious matter, but also resolved to alert the Municipal Council to "the extremely unhealthy condition under which many Natives are at present residing".[35]

Others expressed a more qualified "loyalty". "Owasekaya" opposed the view that in wartime they should fight shy of discussing "questions of immediate interest". Some Congress leaders in Natal were forthright. Chief Stephen Mini adroitly combined professions of loyalty to the front with complete rejection of the Native Affairs Bill of 1917. Josiah Gumede argued that black rights were more important than Empire loyalty. The Natal Native Congress combined "unswerving loyalty" with a plea for the pardon of deposed chiefs. In 1918, SANNC Chaplain the Reverend Henry Reed Ngcayiya, part of an SANNC delegation, told the Prime Minister that in the face of severe economic hardship "when people are starving they will stand against the Government. No people can be expected to be loyal under such difficulties."[36]

After the war, this measured scepticism towards the Crown was evident in Congress attitudes that took an "upward tendency" of militancy likened by Congress President Makgatho to the "rising of the sun", a comment not unnoticed by Native Affairs. In December 1918, SANNC held a special session that sent a memorial to King George V professing its loyalty but reminding London that Africans had "steadfastly maintained the supply of labour" during the war but still "lived under a veiled form of slavery". Africans could not "bargain ... [their] labour" and received "extremely inadequate" compensation for injury or death during wartime employment.[37]

In 1919, another SANNC overseas delegation including Gumede urged Britain to intervene against "serious injustice and cruel oppression" inflicted on Africans by discriminatory laws. In a joint letter with Henry Ngcayiya from Britain, Gumede stated: "We ask for freedom, liberty, justice and fair play." The deputation's failure, lack of war compensation, and the impact of protests in 1918-1920 helped rupture this belief in "fair play", for soon Gumede was to become a leading radical opponent of the government.[38]

Despite such radical rhetorical flourishes, white socialists viewed the SANNC as largely unrepresentative of black workers. Nevertheless, these socialists saw Congress as offering an avenue of contact with these workers. In 1916, the International Socialist League (ISL) derided SANNC policies as "pro-native-landlord protests against the Land Acts, old-fashioned bookish aspirations for the vote as the be-all and end-all, and snobbish cravings by an educated few for social recognition as whites". Two years later, they saw Congress as not "satisfactorily representative; built from above". The ISL suggested the SANNC should "replace itself" with more representative councils "embracing the whole working ... population". Yet it agreed to accept an invitation to send a delegation to the 1918 SANNC conference at Village Deep—itself an indication of SANNC willingness to challenge the Establishment. The ISL argued that any such meeting was an opportunity to increase intercourse between white and black workers and that an "understanding of the range of ideas prevailing at such a congress is very necessary to white Socialists". The conference met "not as a democratic working class body [but] as a nationalist group of chiefs and leaders". The "audience, though many of them were proletarians, were drawn away from a realisation of their economic status into the whirl of rudderless opportunism inseparable from racial or patriotic movements". Congress, it concluded, was "an admirable buffer enabling the ruling class to stave off the real emancipation of the natives". The ISL organ *The International* commented ironically, that meetings of the SANNC and the white Trade Union Congress "revealed both as equally steeped in capitalist ideology". The ISL's Bill Andrews noted that in Congress, "racial appeal is the strongest" but when he addressed it his reception, if not enthusiastic, "was not hostile". There was similar scepticism of SANNC ideology from black socialists. Two delegates of the Industrial Workers of Africa addressed the January 1919 ISL conference: one denounced the SANNC as a "capitalist gang" for claiming that socialism was "Germanism" and for fearing the organising work done by the ISL among black workers; the other dissented from such a characterisation of Congress. Yet at times Congress could be ahead of the ISL, as when it opposed the transfer of ex-German occupied South West Africa (Namibia) to South Africa.[39] Its leaders put SANNC policies forward in complex and at times contradictory ways. They did so in a variety of arenas: in the press, at mass meetings, and before state commissions.

"Educating These Large Masses to Peaceful Methods": Leaders and Labour

Before considering in more detail the attitudes to workers of SANNC leaders, it is useful to grasp the intellectual background in which they developed. One of the most effective tools Congress could employ to get across its policies was the press. Early newspapers such as *Imvo Zabantsundu* ("Native Opinion", 1884), *Koranta ea Becoana* ("Bechuana Gazette" 1901-8) and *Ilanga lase Natal* ("Natal Sun", 1903) were commercial ventures, modest in size, and generally moderate. However, they operated in the midst of a society that discriminated harshly against black people. Hence, they often articulated black protests. Most of these papers also printed, from time to time, reports on black labour. Government publicly stated its preference for African political groups conducting their deliberations constitutionally and through the press rather than by "secret plotting". Nevertheless, privately it objected to press criticism. In 1906, the Native Affairs Minister attempted to deny Dube permission to establish a "larger scale" Natal Congress "until the native press ... adopt[s] a more respectful and proper tone towards the Government and the white race". In the face of this close state scrutiny, African journalists made use of techniques such as irony and appeals to "fair play" to pursue their aims. Many early black newspapers were linked to the wider process of political mobilisation, and thus to Congress.[40]

A marginalised black "elite" certainly controlled black newspapers, but these journals tried to represent Africans as a whole. Black workers shared with the black middle class a membership of churches and some other bodies, including Congress, and thus were potentially receptive to political messages of this press, which frequently was a conduit for Congress policy. The circulation of the early black press was slight and could have reached only a small fraction of workers, whose literacy levels were low. Even by 1934, the black press directly reached only 25,000, with only 850,000 Africans literate. Yet they influenced those more politically instrumental groups and there was a mushrooming effect as people passed issues from hand to hand or recounted aloud stories from their pages.[41]

The black press in general was sympathetic to the plight of black workers, but it was newspapers associated with Congress that more consistently championed black labour rights (if in terms of the African nation) in the period before the emergence of black unions. Jabavu's *Imvo Zabantsundu* did raise labour issues from time to time: for instance, on 22 May 1890, it bemoaned the replacement of black interpreters by white people. However, Jabavu's cautious moderation meant *Imvo Zabantsundu* rarely made the sort of challenges to white exploitation that we will see reflected in Congress newspapers in the coming chapters.[42]

Congress and its presses publicised the low wages, harsh lives and protests of black labour. In doing so, they claimed to be entitled to speak on behalf of workers. One can argue that this was a presumptuous claim, that rather the proletariat can represent itself.[43] However, in this period the African proletariat was too fragmented and poorly resourced to secure self-representation, both because of lack of black unions and the limitation of their journalistic organs. Hence, the representation of workers by Congress had a measure of functionality for black workers. Conversely, ANC leaders, in speaking with the "masses" through the pages of the press, absorbed and then transmitted some worker demands.

Contemporary African writers, some of who were Congress members, also influenced Congress leaders in their pronouncements. Sol Plaatje (see below), S. E. K. Mqhayi and S. M. Molema and others helped conceptualise, if often indirectly, ANC attitudes to black and labour rights. Mqhayi, who worked as a journalist and teacher, wrote satiric verse pointing to the ambiguity of choices faced by African leaders and was active in the SANNC. Colonial authorities censored his trenchant criticisms of white people "preparing for war ... against innocent people". Molema, later an ANC leader, in a book published in 1920, expressed views common among Congress leaders of the day about the central role of black labour. He argued that the mines "depend entirely on this lazy kaffir. The labyrinth of railways throughout South Africa is constructed by him." The myth of a "labour shortage" emanated from "capitalists [who] want cheap labour and will have it at any price". He pointed to how the process of working side by side in mining compounds cemented feelings of African unity. Africans resented low wages and the forced nature of work. He believed that African workers were "forcing back the pendulum".[44]

Many early ANC leaders had a contradictory attitude to labour. The fact that they did not themselves work in industry tended to distance them from the lives of workers. At the same time, the common socio-economic and political oppression of all black strata inclined them towards profound feelings of sympathy for black toilers, and some became involved in labour issues. Among those to hold the position of ANC President-General between 1912 and 1940, only Gumede (1927-1930), who worked as an artisan, teacher and legal advocate before becoming a landowner, generally is regarded as a radical. However, Mahabane (1924-1927, 1937-1940), Makgatho (1917-1924) and Xuma (1940-1949) openly supported black worker rights, whilst Dube (1912-1917) did so more discretely and equivocally. Many of those who held the position of ANC Secretary-General had labour contacts. Sol Plaatje (1912-1916) worked as a courier, interpreter, and editor, in which role he took a close interest in labour. Isaiah Bud-M'belle (1917-1919), and Saul Msane (1919-1923), whilst opposed to strikes, attended meetings in 1917-1918 to consider worker demands. Msane, as noted in the previous chapter, worked as a compound manager and labour recruiting agent. T. D. Mweli Skota (1923-1927) worked as a mine clerk in 1910-1911 and 1920, and interpreter from 1913 to 1919. E. J. Khaile (1927-1930) was a teacher and communist. Executive member Elka Cele, a prominent fundraiser for SANNC overseas delegations, was educated at Adams College but worked on the mines in Kimberley and in Johannesburg as *induna* at Simmer and Jack mine and Assistant Compound Manager at Robinson Deep. Despite his later land purchases in Natal, he died poor. Cele was originally from Inanda and related to John Dube by marriage, but Selby Msimang, who was his secretary in 1913, recalls that it was while at Robinson Deep that he began to identify with the ANC. Marshall Maxeke, SANNC vice-president, once worked as an apprentice harness-maker. In 1920, he became editor of *Umteteli wa Bantu,* a Chamber of Mines paper that, whilst pro-capitalist, addressed issues of concern to miners. SANNC Treasurer Thomas Mapikela was a building contractor, but began his working life as a carpenter.[45]

Too much should not be read into these cases, for occupations such as compound manager, whilst providing some knowledge of worker conditions, involved the exercise of limited control *over* workers. This was quite different to *experience* of labour exploitation, something more apparent in ANC leaders of later decades, such as Walter Sisulu (Secretary, 1949-1955), who experienced working life as a mine labourer. The incomplete induction of most SANNC leaders into proletarian life and their divided class loyalties is evident in their words and actions. Nevertheless, as long as national oppression remained, ANC leaders could be expected to sympathise with fellow black people and identify with mass discontent. Formulation of ANC policies somehow had to include demands of the majority of the population—rural toilers and urban workers.[46] That leaders who were not workers largely decided ANC policies helps account for many of the inconsistencies of its approach to workers, such as apprehension of class struggle. However, a more detailed examination of the attitudes to labour of its leaders reveals a complex web of class influences and experiences through which many of them acquired long-lasting insights into labour issues and a commitment to the rights of black workers.

The Secretary for Native Affairs and Cabinet in 1919 conceded that the SANNC claim to represent "the various tribes" was "a bold one", and that it "can speak for its members and has no doubt considerable following".[47] Whilst mass support for Congress was a matter of concern for the state, on labour matters it was more comfortable with a small group of SANNC leaders who tended to keep their distance from workers.

Pixley Seme, SANNC convenor and Treasurer, developed few ties with workers. He earned a comfortable living as an attorney from 1911 and in 1913 acquired extensive lands. Even so, whenever he attempted to enter the ranks of the "bourgeoisie" he was frustrated—in 1916, his landlordship of Mooifontein, a farm southeast of Middelburg in the Eastern Transvaal, lapsed because of the Land Act. Seme had sought to settle Africans on the farm, but charged tenants the high rent of £12 a year, evicting those who could not pay.

His primary concern here, argues Robert Morrell, was to profit from the Act's effects. Nevertheless, Seme's broad political work—in convening the SANNC, arguing for an inclusive "nationalism" (not excluding black workers), and establishing a national Congress newspaper, *Abantu-Batho*, later supportive of worker rights—indirectly helped open avenues whereby workers could join or be represented in the Congress movement.[48]

The contradictory approaches of moderation and resistance are apparent in the politics of John Dube (see also Chapter 3). Dube saw it as his duty to "keep in check" ANC radicalism. Behind this stance was his class position: as owner of Ohlange Institute and minor sugar plantations, he had all the trappings of a small-scale capitalist. However, Dube's commitment to African unity and liberal ideals often clashed with increasingly repressive state policies and white prejudices, on occasions propelling him into the unlikely role of a champion of black labour. In 1912, he gave his views on labour. "To the white people the natives represented merely 'labour'—a very defective labour ... [Africans] were willing to be the white man's 'faithful servants,' but they deserved from their masters the same sort of care bestowed upon his dumb servants his horses." In a 1912 letter, Dube warned racist segregation would founder on white need for black labour and rounded against white labour that complained against black labour earning only £2 a month. At a 1913 public meeting, he said; "It was time that a strong protest was entered" against the Land Act. Later in 1913, he drew attention to farm workers "unwilling to become slaves at 10s a month". Nevertheless, he adhered to both capitalist and imperial causes.[49]

In 1912, Dube told SANNC members that, "for my patron saint, I select that great and edifying man, Booker Washington"—a champion of black capitalism. Congress, to Dube, represented "the whole body of educated Nativedom", a view betraying his elitism. Black people, "as citizens of the glorious British Empire", were "just awakening into political life". Hence Congress policy should be one of "treading softly, ploddingly", of "deep and dutiful respect for the rulers God has placed over us; a policy of hopeful reliance in that sense of common justice and love of freedom so innate in the British character, that these will ultimately triumph over all other baser tendencies". Dube in 1918 unsuccessfully urged striking workers in Durban to return to work; nonetheless, he did not hesitate to speak on their behalf, signing a petition outlining their grievances of low wages and rising prices with his name followed by "for the native workers".[50]

If most of its leaders had secure incomes, legal campaigns often depleted SANNC finances. In July 1913, it could boast a credit balance of only £11.[51] Even if Congress could throw off the stultifying influence of leader individualism, it was thus in no position to be able to effectively mobilise workers. Yet in a sense, this very weakness, a reflection of the generally restricted financial resources within the black community, helped Congress appear to be closer to ordinary black people. This closeness to the people began to bear fruit when in 1917 Dube made way as SANNC President for the more radical Sefako Mapoch Makgatho (1861-1951), who served from 1917 to 1924.

The son of a chief, Makgatho was educated in England and later became a real estate agent. Nonetheless, he had ties to wage earners. From 1895 to 1906, he worked as a teacher and founded the Transvaal African Teachers' Association; one writer suggests socialist Keir Hardie influenced him at this time. Later he established its journal, *The Good Shepherd*. As president of the TNC (1912-1930) and its predecessors the African Political Union (1906-1908) and Transvaal Native Organisation (1908-1912), Makgatho was exposed to the needs of the nascent black proletariat on the Rand. His obituary refers to him as a leader who was active in the 1911 "African higher wages strike." A "life-long friend" of the radical Levi Mvabaza, Makgatho supported the radical *Abantu-Batho* (discussed in detail in the next chapter). His successful legal defence, on behalf of Congress, of black peoples' rights to use trains and pavements, and on women's passes and taxes, helped form a bridge to ordinary workers, as they shared an interest in these issues. During his presidency, there was the first direct case of ANC-worker solidarity: open support by Congress for black strikers in 1918. Labour issues were a key element in his 1919 SANNC Presidential address: white people received higher pay for their strikes, but "our first strike for 6 pennies a day over 2 shillings ... was met on the part of the Government by violence, arrests, heavy fines and imprisonment". His characterisation of black workers' action as *our* strike illustrates the close race bond felt by ANC members with black workers. During his presidency, according to Mweli Skota, the ANC "made wonderful progress" and, adds Z. K. Matthews, "attracted a lot of attention and added many members to its roll because of his militancy in fighting against the ill-treatment of Africans". Makgatho was later strongly opposed to anti-communism in the ANC, perhaps due to his militant policies in the ANC's first decade. David Bopape, a communist and a teacher active in the ANC in the 1940s, stated; "Under Makgatho, the Congress was in fact a mass organisation."[52]

The career of Saul Msane, elected SANNC General Secretary in 1919, combined contact with, and sympathy for, black workers, and apprehension at their more radical actions. Msane's occupation and ideology influenced this approach. He worked from the early 1890s as a compound manager and later as a labour recruiting agent. As a supervisor of black workers, Msane was unlikely to support their independent organisation.

When Msane gave evidence to the SANAC in 1904, he had been Compound Manager at Jubilee Mine since 1895. He had started on £8 and by 1904 was earning £26.10 shillings a month. He owned land and was in favour of the franchise for "the educated and well-conducted people", but was *against* mass franchise. Similarly, "with the masses it is quite necessary that we should have a pass law", yet he objected to forcible application of pass laws. He emphasised this again in 1907 to the Mining Industry Commission, singling out pass laws as the *only* complaint of his compound workers, who objected to the way passes restricted their liberty and movement. Msane also objected to the high rate of imprisonment of pass defaulters. Henry Taberer, Government Native Labour Bureau Director, could not help but remark that Msane's only apparent objection to the difficulty of black labour was pass law administration. In the same year, TNC Secretary Makhothe observed that, as compound manager of Jubilee Mine, Msane was "very popular amongst his boys" and that his compound was clean and the diet adequate. Hence there is probably some truth in the matter, but not to have raised the question of the need for higher wages, when so many other black speakers did so, suggests Msane increasingly was prepared to compromise with the system.[53]

Msane's liberal ideas stressed measured resistance to injustice. In a speech to a SANNC meeting protesting the Land Act in 1913, Msane began by drawing attention to the British flag "floating over them [that] was an emblem of liberty". Africans had not been consulted in recent legislation. "What they wanted was fair play … Before the Europeans … there were no paupers … Ultimately … they would all be paupers." Implicit in the speech is a fear of proletarianisation and a respect for the Crown and "fair play". Yet a realisation that polite protest had little chance of success tempered his respect. In 1913, he bluntly characterised General Botha as ruling in a "spirit of tyranny" and "ready to shoot the natives down for selling their labour to the best market". Msane linked the Land Act to attempts to arrest black "advancement … by reducing them to poverty, so that their services can be easily obtained at any mean rate of wages". Msane did not however identify with workers at all. He told the Natives' Land Commission in 1917 he was worried Africans "had lost all their property" and was particularly perturbed the Commission was meeting with "this class of people everywhere—the most primitive". Msane was pushed in different directions by his position as an African leader and his prior experience as a controller of black workers. He was willing to attend, even during the World War, radical socialist meetings, and for a period was editor of *Abantu-Batho*, but not prepared to support strikes in 1918, a decision which contributed to his marginalisation from the TNC (see Chapter 5).[54]

Isaiah Budlwana [Bud-] M'belle's labour attitudes were similarly complex. His work as a teacher, insurance agent, and interpreter meant he was aware of the work stresses of black clerical workers. From his first appointment to the Cape Civil Service in 1894, white officials refused him normal clerical allowances. He was obliged to work not only in his appointed position as an interpreter in the High Court of Griqualand and the Northern Circuit Court, which often occasioned long hours of overtime, but also as a clerk in the Kimberley Magistrate's office. Bud-M'belle was regarded by officials as a "most efficient and useful officer". They also viewed him as "very highly paid", earning (in 1903-1905) £375 per annum, £25 more than the Assistant Magistrate. However, when he passed the Civil Service examination in 1906 he did not receive the normal salary increment. In the same year, three English fitters in Kimberley assaulted him, inflicting severe head injuries: an experience that would not have endeared him to the cause of white Labour.[55]

In 1916, Bud-M'belle wrote that life in the Civil Service "was not a bed of roses". Only after strenuous representations did white officials award him at first half, and finally the whole, clerical rate due him. Nevertheless, for over a decade he received no wage increase whilst white civil servants did. In the same year, he lost the interpreting job he had held for 20 years. Frustration inclined him to accept the post of SANNC Secretary in 1917 and to get nominally involved in labour protests in 1918. Like Saul Msane, he opposed strikes and refused to support the full shilling a week wage rise demanded by the TNC and workers. This was, according to Bennett Ncwana, "received with great alarm and anxiety" by Africans, and led to his expulsion from the elite Johannesburg African Club. In 1919, he resigned as SANNC Secretary after regaining a civil service position.[56]

Richard Msimang, a lawyer entrusted with formulating the first ANC constitution, became active in agitation against the Land Act. Together with Plaatje, he toured rural areas and gathered testimonies from tenant farmers, sharecroppers, and labourers on evictions, forced labour and cases of unpaid wages. The SANNC then published the evidence. Msimang saw a clear labour dimension to state motives. *"These evictions are being deliberately made with the sole intention of getting forced labour."* In 1914 he characterised SANNC leadership of protests against the Act as a

> Difficult and responsible task in leading a large mass of people whose methods of resisting or displaying dissatisfaction is and was to resort to arms. The

leaders have done great service to the Union in educating these large masses to peaceful constitutional methods; the people's patience is exhausted ... They ask ... when [will] the grand old days of the late Mother-Queen Victoria the Good return again? ... We cannot conceive the people of England tolerating any law for forced labour.[57]

These statements display a trust in moderation and belief (or tactical hope) in the "fair play" of the "grand old days" typical of many African political leaders with an ambiguous social status. Msimang and Saul Msane address themselves primarily to "civilised and respectable" Africans. In other statements, such as their concern for rural Africans expressed at a 1914 meeting with the Director of Native Labour, there is an implicit undercurrent of concern with broader labour matters that any leader seeking to represent a constituency consisting largely of "toilers" needed to confront.[58]

Benjamin Phooko, a member of the SANNC Land Act Emergency Committee, expressed a more radical viewpoint. In 1916, he addressed an open letter to the Director of Native Labour. He warned that if black labourers, the linchpin of South African financial prosperity who had been "unearthing the gold that fills the Capitalist's coffers at very little or no consideration of their services", should "down tools one day, the whole superstructure of beautiful White South Africa would come down in a terrible crash". Phooko argued that the "Director" of Native Labour should rather be a "Protector" who consulted with black labour, and that the entire black labour system required a "complete overhauling" to "check the economic exploitation".[59]

In keeping with the times, SANNC leaders expressed liberal ideas, but they also expressed growing frustration with political developments and shared a concern for the fate of black workers. They were not a monolithic block: Makgatho had closer ties with workers than Seme; Phooko was more prepared to criticise capitalism than Dube. Nevertheless, they confronted a common dilemma of how best to act in the interests of workers, a dilemma epitomised in the career of Solomon Plaatje.

"Friend of the People" and Friend of the Workers? The Case of Sol Plaatje

In this period, Sol Plaatje worked primarily at a national level; as SANNC General Secretary, he was prominent in opposition to the Land Act and took part in overseas delegations. His journalism and some of his work centred on Kimberley but even here, his reporting ranged across the country. For convenience, I deal with him here, rather than Chapter 6, which focuses on

Cape provincial politics. In Chapter 3, I discussed his earlier journalism in Mafeking.

Plaatje's general concern, as SANNC leader, for exploited black workers I have already noted. It is important to distinguish three aspects of this stance. Firstly, behind his "defence" of black labour rights lay his identification with the role of black wage earners, influenced by his own working days. He started work as a letter courier on £72 a year in 1894, later working as an interpreter and editor. This identification decreased in later years as his memories of his own wage-earning days receded, and as his apprehensions of gathering trends towards the foreclosing of non-manual employment options for black people increased. Aged 26, he boldly told Sir Godfrey Lagden at the SANAC Commission that there were indeed African grievances. He detailed how in *Koranta* he had reported loss of moneys to labour agents by Transvaal African miners visiting Mafeking and how a reader had provided details, then investigated and the labourers' monies eventually were returned. Plaatje later gained an external perspective of the tribulations of migrant labourers when in 1909 insolvency forced him to work briefly as a labour recruiter. His lack of higher education set him apart from most other SANNC leaders. In 1903, he reminded a *Friend* correspondent, who had dubbed him a [well-educated] "Lovedale beauty", that not only had he received little English education until the age of 14 but had walked barefoot to a labour centre with only 15 pence in his pocket. Now, he proudly retorted, he owned a property and bank account. By the time he became SANNC Secretary he remained of limited means. In 1912, John Dube had to pay Plaatje's expenses for a Congress delegation to Cape Town.[60]

Secondly, Plaatje had undoubted sympathy for exploited black workers, expressed in SANNC meetings and deputations and in his writings. *Native Life in South Africa*, his major polemical work on the devastation caused by the Land Act, raised questions about the predicament of black labour. In it, referring to state policies on African women, he also committed Congress to refusing "to protect the comfort of black men by degrading black women". He wrote an historical epic novel, *Mhudi*, which ends with reference to the notion that white people see Africans purely as labourers. In *The Mote and the Beam,* his sensitivity to the hypocrisy of white miscegenation is even more interesting as he chooses to illustrate his argument with reference to the dilemmas of a domestic worker. Plaatje, if a devout British Empire loyalist, used the prevailing discourses of the day and irony to re-create, in the coloniser's language, African dignity.[61]

Thirdly, Plaatje was deeply suspicious of radicals and found white Labour racism intolerable. This influenced his acceptance in 1918 of De Beers support for his opposition to "socialists" in Congress. Whilst he succeeded in blocking leftist influence in the SANNC at its 1918 conference, the fact he used the gift of a tram shed from De Beers not for Congress, but for the Brotherhood Movement, indicates not only his acceptance of class collaborationist ideas underlying that movement but also that his interest in Congress was shifting into other areas. De Beers and state officials courted Plaatje as an antidote to rising socialist agitation but had earlier begun to perceive the relationship of Congress to black workers. The company booked 100 seats at the 1914 SANNC Kimberley conference's public reception and offered delegates a free train excursion to their mines. By his acceptance of De Beers' support, the status quo effectively co-opted Plaatje. Yet despite his acceptance of aid, too much can be made of Plaatje's alleged pro-capitalist views. He remained sceptical that white capitalists cared for the black poor. Mine magnates, who generously endowed white schools, "never think of the children of their docile mining labourers."[62]

Moreover, Plaatje was somewhat aware of the burgeoning power of the socialist movement. Interviewed by *Labour Leader* in 1919, he conceded, "the only people from whom we have any sympathy and support are the International Socialists, and, unfortunately, they are an insignificant minority". In all his writings, there is evidence of what Njabulo Ndebele calls Plaatje's implicit awareness of class conflict and his commitment "on the side of a large economic group against another economic group". This does not mean Plaatje elevated labour over political issues; he always gave priority to land and franchise. Yet even in his political pamphlets, he incorporated demands of wage earners; of 11 grievances raised in a 1918 London pamphlet, four dealt with black workers: lack of pensions for miners; dismissal of black interpreters; exclusion of black mechanics from skilled work; exclusion of Africans from the civil service "except as 'casual' menial labourers".[63]

All these influences are evident in Plaatje's journalism, in which he paid considerable attention to labour. In 1910, he became editor of the self-styled "independent race newspaper" *Tsala ea Becoana* (later *Tsala ea Batho*, "Friend of the People"). After he became SANNC Secretary in 1912, readers increasingly viewed *Tsala* (whose circulation rose from 1,700 in 1910 to 4,000 in 1913) as a de facto Congress organ. Edited in Kimberley but published simultaneously also in Johannesburg, Pretoria, Bloemfontein, Thaba 'Nchu and Potchefstroom, *Tsala* was, according to Z. K. Matthews, "widely read" by Tswana in the western Transvaal, north west Cape, Orange Free State, and on the

Kimberley mines. It also attracted a much wider ethnic readership. Plaatje in 1913 claimed Africans in the Orange Free State and Transvaal took "great interest" in the paper, in the pages of which writers discussed industrial and political issues of national importance for Africans. Prompted by *Tsala's* mining city base, it regularly carried strike reports, letters from mine employees, and expressions of concern for the welfare of black wage earners. Plaatje, as editor (and who wrote his own leaders), criticised the retrenchment of black interpreters and post office workers in favour of less skilled white employees. He attacked the meagre pensions accorded to Africans and their "niggardly wage".[64]

Sol Plaatje, investigating the effects of the Natives' Land Act on bicycle, ca. 1917–1919

Workers responded to this attention. Richard Jordaan worked in Winburg, Orange Free State, for £1 per month. He wrote to *Tsala* complaining that he had been fined £1.10 shillings or 14 days' hard labour merely because officials refused to accept his registration. E. Monye of Dutoitspan Mine wrote on behalf of himself and other workers about unfair dismissals. Other letters received from the mines discussed mortality rates and high prices. Labourers at Dutoitspan formed a "benefit society" and requested *Tsala* to print its regulations. "Native Sufferer" described the harsh conditions of the Orange Free State farm labourers and domestic workers. *Tsala* regularly carried mining company advertisements, as well as Native Recruiting Corporation policies, suggesting that at least some mineworkers read it.[65]

In 1913-1914, strikes and job colour bars often featured in *Tsala*. In 1913, Plaatje contrasted the "dignified manner" of striking Durban *togt* labourers with "the ugly spectacle" of a fight between Basotho and Shangaan labourers on Premier Mine. During the Rand strike of 1913, he detailed the "dissatisfaction" of labourers following cessation of their pay and their statements that white people had made them "familiar with the meaning and effect of a strike". Following the "pillage, sabotage and bloodshed" of the strike, he contrasted the withdrawal of charges against white strikers with the harsh sentences given to "native accomplices". He urged clemency but indicative of a greater interest in race justice than worker solidarity, added that "just grounds" existed to imprison them if "white agitators" also went to jail. In the face of intense state intimidation of black people, *Tsala* urged Africans not to participate in the 1914 white strike.[66]

However, *Tsala's* editorials originated not solely in ideas of race. Commenting favourably on "an interesting sketch of moderate Trade Union views", *Tsala* affirmed: "To deny to the working man or to his Union the right to bargain ... is to show a lack of the most elementary rudiments of common justice."[67] Whilst notions of justice are explicit here, such opinion also is as much in keeping with the tenets of social democracy as the sort of *petit bourgeois* stance usually ascribed to Plaatje.

Tsala reported in some detail political and social struggles of interest to all Africans, including workers, including news of SANNC deputations concerning such issues as the Land Act, workers' compensation, and passes. Its staff closely followed demonstrations against passes by Bloemfontein women (see Chapter 6). The root cause of the "black peril" scare (alleged assaults by black men on white women) was analysed by Plaatje as partly due to the "houseboy" system of domestic labour on the Rand and partly due to the liquor traffic that "makes devils out of good black labourers". [68]

Tsala detailed the proceedings of meetings of government and SANNC leaders in 1914-1915 on the protection for migrant workers. There were stories on Natal Agricultural Union resolutions that objected to wage advances to migrant labourers, and prominent accounts of Parliamentary debates about payment of black workers on Durban railways. *Tsala* reproduced reports on migrant labour, the colour bar in industry, and digger insistence on expulsion of Xhosa labourers from Kimberley. It reported on matters of everyday interest to black workers, such as living conditions and assaults committed by white Labour against black labourers. The latter increasingly preoccupied the editors. A 1914 editorial gave "a thousand apologies" to the Chamber of Mines, which it had "always accused ... of deliberately shutting out Natives and Coloured labourers from skilled work". Now, it stated, it "seems clear that our limitation is the result of a conspiracy between the Union Government and the Labour Party".[69]

This was a time of intense black suspicion of the white labour movement. That Plaatje lacked a commitment to "socialism", as seen in his opposition to leftwing activists in the Transvaal Congress, was due to a large extent to the hostility engendered at the time by the racist policies of the Labour Party. In 1910, *Tsala* urged black voters to vote for H. A. Oliver, since the creed of the alternative, Labour candidate, was "White, White, White!" Labour Party officials were "requesting employers to sack their native servants". Whilst this reporting indicates a concern for welfare of black workers, the paper's rationale for Oliver's election more dubiously linked to labour interests: it would provide "a proper link between the lofty and the lowly". *Tsala* did reproduce a speech of the radical Labourite Robert Waterston explaining why white people had encouraged black people to strike, but in general remained hostile to Labour, which it accused of conspiring with the state to reserve jobs for white people.[70]

Plaatje helped forge closer relations between the SANNC and African Political Organisation (APO, later African People's Organisation), which claimed influence among "coloured" workers. *Tsala* warned these workers against joining strikes by "our arch-enemy, the lily-white Labourite". It urged them (despite the contradiction in supporting its other "arch-enemy") to "stick to the Government might and main!" In all these labour-related matters, Plaatje opposed strikes. Some Africans, notably "women and some of the chiefs", favoured "a general strike among the native labourers". However "when the strike is declared and those women begin to jeer at the pusillanimous labourers who hesitate to join, we will have the whole quarter million out on strike ... Many ... will be shot". Here he was concerned as much with preventing violence and exhausting constitutional protest as opposing radicalism *per se*. Despite his distaste for strikes, Plaatje continually re-affirmed the central role of black labour: Kimberley was "supported by 15,000 [worker] pillars".[71]

These extracts indicate openness to dialogue with labour by an ANC figure often portrayed as hostile to left movements. If Plaatje was a moderate then he nevertheless was sympathetic about the harsh conditions of black workers and protested their mistreatment. Whilst he generally opposed strikes or other radical actions, he could often understand their causes. This "Friend of the People" may have been firstly a friend of black people as a race and educated black people in particular, rather than proletarians, but he recognised black workers' interests. Moreover he was, as *Bantu World* eulogised in 1932, "a thorn in the flesh of the oppressors and exploiters".[72]

Various factors explain Plaatje's willingness to publicise black labour's lot. In Kimberley, with its heavy preponderance of mine labourers, one could hardly avoid labour issues. His sympathetic labour reporting probably also linked up with his need for readers. Part of the paradox—that he appears both pro- and anti-worker[73]—lies in his own experience of the labour market, and in the position of Africans in society. White people generally treated black people as a servile mass pre-destined for labouring lives. It was impossible for Plaatje to escape this notion: either in his own past, or in the present of his compatriots. Nevertheless, he viewed black workers not primarily as workers, *sui generis*, but as Africans. He couched reports on workers in terms of the interests of Africans as a whole. Nothing in his columns suggests that he favoured an *independent* role of labour.

Plaatje tried to articulate the views of "voiceless" Africans, including workers, in his Congress activities and writings, which reflect not only his opinions but also the undercurrent of movements and ideas that were part of Congress and the diverse social classes supporting it. "Middle-class" movements influenced Plaatje, but they in turn were responding to other influences, such as the immiseration and frustration of black middle classes under white domination and a growing social presence of workers. Plaatje combined black protest against national domination with glimpses of the class-consciousness of Africans expressed both collectively as an underclass and separately as working and middle classes. He mixed heterogeneous elements: commitment to African emancipation, the influence of liberalism, opposition to radicalism, and sympathy for black workers. Taken alone, each could "prove" his class identification but we cannot ignore the presence of workers in the writings of the first ANC General-Secretary.

Conclusion

Many commentators claim that the early Congress was nothing more than an annual confabulation. There is some truth in this assertion. Z. K. Matthews heard stories that "people thought of the ANC in terms of the Annual Conference" and there was no real branch structure until the 1940s (when he became active); that the practice of membership tickets and branches came later with the ICU. However, lack of a written history at this level has allowed rumour to dominate. In fact, as the following chapters will show, Congress branches at provincial and local levels were quite active, had membership lists and their own regional conferences and campaigns despite their paucity of funds.

Steadily increasing black urbanisation and proletarianisation meant that Congress had to come to terms with black workers as a significant, and growing, part of its constituency. The failure of ANC land protests, as Chris Lowe notes, moved the centre of its attention towards "city-based professionals and workers".[74] Yet if black workers were gaining in numbers, they lacked industrial representation. Congress partly filled a vacuum caused by the absence of African unions and lack of a social democratic party that could claim to represent African workers practically and genuinely in labour and political structures. Congress leaders experienced direct and indirect contacts with black workers. Whether their concerns for labour signalled merely a desire for moral uplifting of workers, a more general empathy for black people as a race, or genuine concern for workers, is not always clear. Probably their sympathy was a combination of all these themes and varied from leader to leader depending on their own lives and objective conditions. We can understand better the extent and consistency of such contacts by a closer examination of the history of early relations between the grassroots branches of Congress and the labour movement.

Notes

1   This particular obeisance, typical of contemporary correspondence, is in a letter of A.K. Soga to the Orange River Colony Governor 27 Mar. 1909, OFS Archives (VAB) Governor's Office G113 file 461/6.

2   E. Dower (SNA) "Resolutions Passed at SA Native Convention … Bloemfontein 24th Mar. 1910", in Native Affairs Dept. [NAD] 1118/F.374 in Silas T. Molema and Solomon T. Plaatje Papers, University of the Witwatersrand, William Cullen Library, Historical Papers.

3   Walshe, *Rise of African Nationalism,* pp. 10, 15, 32; Benson, *Struggle for a Birthright,* p. 24; F.Z.S. Peregrino, "The SA Native National Congress: What It Is", *Tsala* 30 Mar. 1912 (also in *Imvo* 19 Mar. 1912: but compare *Imvo* 26 Mar. 1913).

4   Walshe, *Rise of African Nationalism*, p. 34; *Imvo* 10 Jun., 15 Jul. 1913, 9, 16 Jul., 17 Sep., 19, 27 Nov., 3, 24 Dec. 1918, 27 May, 26 Aug. 1919; *Tsala* 14 Mar. 1914; Odendaal, *Vukani Bantu* pp. 272-278; Kinkead-Weekes, "Africans", p. 205; Skota, *African Yearly Register*, pp. 137, 175, 273. The CPNA continued to function—at a meeting soon after, Zini condemned the Squatters' Bill as oppressive to Africans; other speakers saw the Bill as serving only the interests of capitalists: "The Squatters' Bill", *Imvo* 19 Mar. 1912. See also "Our People in the Cape", *Imvo* 24 Oct. 1911 for earlier meetings.

5   "Imbizo yaBantu Ejozi (The South African National Congress)", *Izwe la Kiti* 2 Apr. 1913.

6   Odendaal, *Vukani Bantu*, pp. 277-281; SANAC v. 4, pp. 650 (Mohatle), 393 (Molapo). In 1913, the Zulu king stayed with Seme in Sophiatown: "Dinizulu's Visit to the Rand", *Izwe la Kiti* 26 Mar. 1913.

7   "SANNC Constitution", 1919 ts. (also KC v. 1, pp. 76-82); Walshe, *Rise of African Nationalism*, p. 241; *Tsala* 17 Feb. 1912; South African Police (SAP) "Unrest amongst Natives at Springs Mines", 1 Apr. 1919, Dept. of Justice [JUS] v. 255 file 3/527/17, Reports on Activities of ISL, Native Congress, IWA, Industrial Unrest); C. Lowe, "'The Tragedy of Malunge,' or, the Fall of the House of Chiefs: *Abantu-Batho*, the Swazi Royalty, and Nationalist Politics in Southern Africa, 1894-1927", African Studies Association paper, 1993, pp. 11, 75; C. Lowe "Swaziland's Colonial Politics: The Decline of Progressivist South African Nationalism and the Emergence of Swazi Political Traditionalism, 1910-1939", Ph. D. Yale University, 1998.

8   R.W. Msimang, "Introductory Note" to SANNC Constitution (1919) in Xuma Papers (XP), ABX 1919 reel 2; "Preamble" [Constitution], Molema-Plaatje Papers.

9   [Dube], "South African Native Congress", *Izwe la Kiti* 1 Jan. 1913; "Notes and Comments" *Abantu-Batho* 20 Dec. 1917, JUS 3/527/17; such reports show how the paper was becoming an organ of Congress.

10 Ginwala, "Women and the ANC"; Erlank, "Gender and Masculinity in Nationalist Discourse".

11 S. Marks, *Not Either an Experimental Doll* (London: Women's Press, 1987), p. 23; D. Mindry, "'Good Women': Philanthropy, Power, and the Politics of Femininity in Contemporary South Africa", Ph.D. University of California, 1999, pp. 85, 191, 220-268, 328-332; D. Gaitskell, "Devout Domesticity? A Century of African Women's Christianity in South Africa", in Walker, *Women & Gender*, pp. 251-272, p. 257.

12 H. Bradford, "'We Are Now the Men': Women's Beer Protests in the Natal Countryside, 1929", in Bozzoli, *Class & Conflict*, pp. 292-323, p. 308; F. Meer, *Women in the Apartheid Society* (New York: UN, 1985); M. Kuumba, "African Women, Resistance Cultures and Cultural Resistances" *Agenda* 68 (2006), pp. 112-121. In the 1950s, *manyano* were seen as respectable, middle-class institutions, though domestic workers still joined: M. Brandel-Syrier, *Black Woman in Search of God* (London: Lutterworth, 1962), p. 46.

13 A.B. Xuma, *Charlotte Manye (Mrs. Maxeke): "What an Educated African Girl Can Do"* (Nashville: Women's Mite Missionary Society, 1930); [Z.K. Matthews] "Defender of Women's Rights" *Imvo* 9 Sept. 1961; J. Millard, "Charlotte Manye Maxeke: Agent for Change", in J. Malherbe, M. Kleijwegt and E. Koen (eds.) *Women, Society & Constraints* (Pretoria: Institute for Gender Studies, 2000), pp, 167-176; Campbell, *Songs of Zion*; C. Page, "Charlotte Manye Maxeke", in R. Keller, L. Queen and H. Thomas (eds.), *Women in New Worlds: Historical Perspectives on the Wesleyan Tradition* (Nashville: Abingdon, 1982), pp. 281-289; M. McCord, *The Calling of Katie Makanya* (Cape Town: David Philip, 1995), pp. 10-11.

14 P. Ntantala, "Black Women Intellectuals and the Struggle for Liberation", seminar paper, Wits University 8 Aug. 2006; "The National League of Bantu Women (Transvaal Province)", *Abantu-Batho* 20 Dec. 1917 (copy, JUS 3/527/17).

15 "Bantu: Women [sic] National League", police report on meeting 18 Jan. 1918, JUS 3/527/7; Page "Maxeke", p. 286. Ginwala ("Women"), argues that Walshe, who gives both 1913 (p. 80) and 1918 as founding dates, conflated the League with the Native and Coloured Women's Association. The press reported League branches in 1917, for example in Winburg, unless this was a similar conflation. It seems probable that the January 1918 meeting formalised matters.

16 Campbell, *Songs of Zion,* p. 285.

17 Trapido, "African Opinion"; Ntsebeza, "Divisions", p. 19; Lowe, "Swaziland's Politics", characterises Congress of this decade as an "alliance of modern and traditional elites"; *International* 4 Jul. 1919.

18 R.S. Thema and J. Jones, "In South Africa", in M. Stauffer (ed.), *Thinking with Africa: Chapters by a Group of Nationals Interpreting the Christian Movement* (London: SCM, 1928), pp. 36-65, p. 60; P. Seme, "The Native National Congress", *Tsala* 17 Jul. 1915; Seme, "Native Union". *Imvo* 24 Oct. 1911.

19 Msimang, "Note"; SANNC Constitution 1919 s.12-7/9/15; Meli, *South Africa Belongs to Us,* p. 54.

20 See L. Heerma van Ross (ed.), *Petitions in Social History* (Cambridge: CUP 2001), esp. pp. 3-5.

21 "S.A. Native Congress," *Tsala ea Batho* 17 Feb. 1912; Odendaal, *Vukani Bantu,* p. 277; P. Walshe, "The Origins of African Political Consciousness in South Africa", *Journal of Modern African Studies* v. 7 (1969), pp. 583-610, p. 601; Trapido, "African Opinion", pp. 27-28.

22 *Tsala ea Batho* 6 Apr. 1912; "Native Affairs", *Imvo* 2 Apr. 1912; J. Dube to Chief Lekoko 13 Apr. 1912, Molema-Plaatje Papers.

23 *Tsala ea Batho* 14, 28 Nov. 1914, 23 Jan. 1915. The government in return requested of Congress their co-operation with control of African labour, "particularly on the Rand".

24 *Tsala* 15 Nov. 1913, 10 Feb., 31 Jan., 14 Mar. 1914; SANNC 1914 conference flyer, CKC 2:DS7:30/1; *Minutes of Evidence before Select Committee on Native Affairs* (SC6A-17) p. 629; Msimang interview by D. Hemson 1971, PC14/1 Aitchison Papers, Paton & Struggle Archives UKZN. In 1915 the SANNC equated labour tenancy with slavery: *Ilanga* 13 August 1915 cited in H. Feinberg, "Protest in South Africa: Prominent Black Leaders' Commentary on the Natives Land Act, 1913-1936", *Historia* 51 (2006), pp. 119-144.

25 Trapido, "African Opinion"; Lodge, *Black Politics,* p. 3; Walshe, *Rise of African Nationalism,* Chapter 3; J. Lambert and R. Morrell, "Domination and Subordination in Natal, 1890-1920", in Morrell, *Political Economy,* pp. 63-95, p. 91.

26 C. Saunders, "African Attitudes to Britain and the Empire before and after the South African War", in D. Lowry (ed.), *The South African War Reappraised* (Manchester: Manchester University Press, 2000), pp.140-149; A. Thompson, "The Languages of Loyalism in Southern Africa c. 1870-1939", *English Historical Review* 117 (2003) pp. 617-650, p. 637; Willan, *Plaatje,* p. 244; Police report on TNC meeting Vrededorp 14 Sept. 1919, JUS 3/527/17; "Public Meeting, Transvaal Congress 31 May 1913, New Marabastad", in *Schreiner Papers* 2182, SOU/1 file 6, University of York; "Sol Plaatje's Outburst", *International* 8 Jun. 1917.

27 "Native Land Act: Full Text of Petition", *Imvo* 20 Jul. 1914; *Tsala* 27 Sep., 9 Aug. 1913; SANNC. "Resolutions against the Natives Land Act 1913", Pietermaritzburg 2 Oct. 1916,

with letter of Selope Thema, SANNC, to T. Buxton, Anti-Slavery & Aborigines' Protection Society, 1917, CKC 2:DS7:41/8.

28 "Govt. Memo. of Meeting of Delegation of SANNC ... 30 Jul. 1913" NA 315 2972/13/1 814, SOU/1 6, University of York; S. Plaatje, *Native Life in South Africa* (London: King, 1916), p. 203; Walshe, *Rise of African Nationalism,* p. 49; "Industrial Crisis", *Tsala* 26 Jul. 1913; *Tsala* 21 Mar. 1914.

29 *Tsala* 9 Aug. 1913; Walshe, *Rise of African Nationalism* pp. 46-49, Ntsebeza, "Divisions", p. 19; Simons, *Class & Colour* p. 160; B. Willan, "Sol Plaatje, De Beers and an Old Tram Shed: Class Relations and Social Control in a South African Town, 1918-9", *JSAS* v. 4 (1978), pp. 195-215; W. Hofmeyr, "Agricultural Crisis & Rural Organisation in the Cape, 1929-1933", M.A. UCT, 1985, p. 8; Willan, *Plaatje,* pp. 155, 163, 222; H. Feinberg, "The 1913 Natives' Land Act in South Africa", *IJAHS* v. 26 1993, pp. 65-109, pp. 83-94.

30 "'Mafukuzela' at the Storm Centre: The Mine Natives" *Tsala ea Batho* 17 Jan. 1914; "Loyal Assurances Given", *Transvaal Leader* 15 Jan. 1914 (in *Correspondence Relating to the Recent Strike in South Africa),* p. 87. Dube, noted J. X, Merriman, was "on the horns of a dilemma," having taken 'a prominent part in the agitation" but now apprehensive: Merriman to Prime Minister, 8 May 1914, PM 1/1/474, SOU/I.

31 Hofmeyr, "Crisis and Rural Organisation", pp. 3-6.

32 PRO W.O. 107/37 "Report of the Work of Labour with the BEF during the War", pp. 25-28; B. Willan, "The South African Native Labour Contingent, 1916-1918" *JAH* v. 19 (1978), pp. 61-86; A. Grundlingh, *Fighting Their Own War: South African Blacks and the First World War* (Johannesburg: Ravan Press, 1987), pp. 15-16, 59, 130-131; S. Jingoes, *A Chief is a Chief by the People: The Autobiography of Stimela Jason Jingoes.* Ed. J. and C. Perry (Oxford: OUP, 1975), Chapter 3.

33 SANNC, Memorial to H M King George V, 16 Dec. 1918, Molema-Plaatje Papers, Cc9.

34 Msimang interview with Hemson, p. 4; State Archives, Pretoria, Director of Native Labour (GNLB) 192: "Anglo German War: Native Newspapers: *Abantu Batho*" and clippings of *Abantu Batho* 6 Jan. 1916. Seme was invoking Solomon because of the struggle to have him officially recognized as Zulu king; I thank Paul La Hausse for this insight.

35 "The Natives & the War", *Tsala* 29 Aug. 1914; Transvaal National Council Resolution 11 Dec. 1916, NTS 7204 17/326; Seme, "Native National Congress", *Tsala* 17 Jul. 1915; *Minutes of Evidence Eastern Transvaal Native Land Committee, Natives Land Commission 1916-1918* (UG32-18); B. Nasson, "A Great Divide: Popular Responses to the Great War in South Africa", *War & Society* v. 12 (1994), pp. 47-64.

36 "Owasekaya" to *Tsala* 29 May 1915; SC6A-17, p. 647; Resolutions NNC May 1915, J.S. Gumede to CNC 3 Jun. 1915, CNC 236, 701/15; NTS 214, 737/18/F473: "Notes of a Meeting 9th Jul. 1918 ..."

37 *Dept. of Native Affairs Report* 1913-1918, p. 34; SANNC "Memorial to ... King George V", Molema-Plaatje Papers Cc9. On the state's dismissive reply see *Imvo* 26 Aug. 1919 and official correspondence in CO 551/111, copy in CKC 2:DS7:92/3; *Imvo* 31 Dec. 1918.

38 SANNC resolution and Gumede letter, *Imvo* 14 Oct. 1919, J.T. Gumede and H.R. Ngcayiya, "A Cry for Freedom, Liberty, Justice and Fair Play", Sep. 1919, ms. letter copy, Hoover Institution; Simons, *Class & Colour,* pp. 214-219. Failure of their appeals made Congress more amenable to joint action with socialists: Mbeki, *Struggle,* p. 27.

39 *International* 1 Dec. 1916, 13 Dec., 21 Dec. ("Nationalism, Freedom's Foe") 1918, 10 Jan. 1919; Andrews to D. Jones, cited in R. Cope, *Comrade Bill: The Life and Times of W.H. Andrews, Workers' Leader* (Cape Town, [1943]). p. 212; *International* 10 Jan. 1919.

40   L. Switzer, "The Beginnings of African Protest Journalism at the Cape", in L. Switzer (ed.), *South Africa's Alternative Press* (Cambridge, 1997), pp. 57-82; Natal Archives Depot [NAD] SNA 991/1906, J. Dube to Native Affairs (NA) 29 March 1906 and replies citing *SA Native Affairs Commission Report 1903-1905* s.324-5; Switzer "The African Christian Community and its Press in Victorian South Africa", *Cahiers d'études africaines* v. 96 (1984), pp. 455-476, p. 464; Odendaal "Mobilisation", pp. 122, 210.

41   E. Rosenthal, *Bantu Journalism in South Africa* (Johannesburg: Society of Friends of Africa, 1949), pp. 13-14; A. Friedgut, "The Non-European Press", in E. Hellmann (ed.), *Handbook on Race Relations in South Africa* (Cape Town: OUP, 1949), pp. 484-510; Odendaal, *Vukani Bantu*, p. 63; A. Bird, "The Adult Night School Movements for Blacks on the Witwatersrand 1920-1980", in P. Kallaway (ed.), *Apartheid and Education* (Johannesburg: Ravan Press, 1984), pp. 192-221; Roux, *Time Longer than Rope*, p. 343; "The Bantu Press and Race Relations", *Race Relations* v. 2 no. 1 (1934), pp, 129-130.

42   *Imvo* 22 May 1890, "Native Labour Crisis", *Imvo* 1 Oct. 1896, *Imvo* 13, 6 Apr. 1891; W. Mills, "Intra-African Hostilities among Educated Africans in the Cape Colony, 1890-1915", paper to Canadian Association of African Studies conference, 1975, p. 20-21.

43   See Dunn, "Politics of Representation", pp. 162-164, on self-representation.

44   Peires, *House of Phalo*, pp. 176-7; E. Mphahlele, "Landmarks", in Mutloatse, *Umhlaba*, pp. 1-20, p. 7; S.M. Molema, *The Bantu, Past and Present* (Edinburgh: Green, 1920), pp. 253-258, 275, 302-306. J. Starfield, "A Dance with the Empire: Modiri Molema's Glasgow Years, 1914–1921", *JSAS* v. 27 (2001), pp. 479–504, p. 503 characterises Molema's "petty bourgeois" position, as the son of a well-to-do chief whose fortunes were now under attack, as "dancing towards and away from Empire".

45   Meli, *South Africa Belongs to Us*, p. 38 notes that the first SANNC executive included "ministers of religion, lawyers, an editor, a building contractor, a teacher and estate agent, an interpreter and Native Labour Agent"; Skota, *African Yearly Register*, pp. 70-71, 137, 175, 257, 277; Willan, *Plaatje* Chapter 2; S. Plaatje, "Native National Congress", *Tsala* 28 Feb. 1914 and U17-11 p. 334 [Cele]; Khumalo, "Epistolary Networks", p. 182; S. Msimang, "The Emakhosini Mission Station", p. 22, Aitchison Papers, PC 14/1/1/1-3; Msimang, "50 Years on the Road to Liberty", *Contact* 2 Apr. 1960, pp. 9; Cele obituary, *Ilanga* 17 Aug. 1923; Marks, *Rebellion*, pp. 69, 360; Z.K. Matthews "Thomas M. Mapikela", *Imvo* 2 Sept. 1961; Campbell, *Songs of Zion*, p. 147; Walshe, *Rise of African Nationalism*, p. 227; KC v. 4, p. 74.

46   Govan Mbeki (*Learning from Robben Island* p. 127) argues, "before 1920 ... the working class took an active part" in Congress and cites Letanka, "arrested in a workers' strike in 1917, in the executive" as proof.

47   "An Important Document", *Imvo* 26 Aug. 1919; CO 551/111 225 15 Feb. 1919 reply to SANNC Secretary I. Bud-M'Belle to Governor General, enclosing memorial to King, 25 Jan. 1919, CKC 2:DS7:92/3.

48   R. Morrell, "Rural Transformation in the Transvaal: The Middelburg District, 1919 to 1930", MA Wits, 1983, pp. 139-140 citing NTS 299/308; Morrell, "African Land Purchase & the 1913 Natives Land Act in the Eastern Transvaal". *SAHJ* v. 21 (1989), pp. 1-18; R. Rive and T. Couzens, (eds.) *Seme: The Founder of the ANC* (Johannesburg: Skotaville, 1991); C. Saunders, "Pixley Seme: Towards a Biography", *SAHJ* v. 25 (1991), pp. 196-217. On the politics of *Abantu-Batho* see the very insightful: C. Lowe, "*Abantu-Batho* and the South African Native National Congress in the 1910s", paper to CRCSA, May 1998.

49   "John Dube's Work", *Tsala* 30 Mar. 1912; [Dube] "Segregation: The Native View," *Izwe la Kiti* 4 Dec. 1912; S. Plaatje, "Native National Congress", *Tsala* 28 Feb. 1914; *Tsala* 10

May 1913; "Mr. Dube on the Situation", *Tsala* 1 Nov. 1913. By 1910, Dube had received £3,000 from the U.S. for Ohlange where he charged boarders £6 per year: *Voice of Labour* 7 Jan. 1910.

50 NAD CNC Natal 214/1912, Dube address to "Chiefs & Gentlemen of the SANC" Phoenix 2 Feb. 1912; R.H. Davis, "John L. Dube: A South African Exponent of Booker T. Washington", *J. African Studies* v. 2 (1975), pp. 497-528; petition 11 Aug. 1918, NTS 214, 658/18/F473; Cope, *To Bind the Nation*, p. 98. Msimang recalled: "almost his whole outlook on political questions was influenced by Booker T. Washington": *Biography* p. 78, PC14/1/3/1. Khumalo, "Epistolary Networks", p. 73 notes that Dube forwarded to government some radical letters sent to *Ilanga*.

51 *Tsala ea Batho* 29 Nov. 1913.

52 *Bantu World* 2 Jun. 1951; KC v. 4, p. 68; Skota, *African Who's Who*, p. 70; L. and D. Switzer, *The Black Press in South Africa & Lesotho* (Boston: Hall, 1979), p. 28; Africanus, "Sefako Mapogo Makgatho", *Sechaba* Jun. 1985; C. Haines, "A Political History of the Congress Alliance in South Africa, 1947-1956", Ph.D. SOAS 1981, p. 34; Makgatho, Presidential Address 6 May 1919, KC v. 1, p. 107; Z.K. Matthews, "Great Teacher-Politician", *Imvo* 28 Oct. 1961; [Biographical notes, S.M. Makgatho] Unpublished ts. CKC 2:XM22:96.

53 SANAC, v. 4, pp. 856-858; Transvaal. *Mining Industry Commission 1907-1908*, Evidence pp. 1309 (Taberer), 1444-1446 (Msane), 1442. On Msane's family background, see Meintjes, "Edendale", Moreover, as La Hausse, *Restless Identities*, p. 167 notes, Msane in 1912 was charged over misappropriation of worker funds.

54 *Tsala* 10 May, 18 Oct. 1913, 8 Jun. 1912; UG32-18, pp. 34, 171 (also in CKC 2:DS7:30/2). Joseph Hlubi, another SANNC leader, expressed similar thoughts: black people wanted benefits of civilisation but opposed "the shackles of the white man" imposed on those working on white farms. Msane's conservatism was perhaps typical of what Khumalo ("Epistolary Networks" p. 241, referring to Msane's view in *Inkanyiso yase Natal* 19 Sep. 1891 that African women should obey their husbands) sees as evidence of how African patriarchs were pushed by government to accept the status quo.

55 *Brief Account*, p. 34; Magistrate Kimberley to Sec. Law Dept., 18 Jan. 1908; Memo. of Magistrate Kimberley, 15 May 1908; Leave applications, 1904-1911; Bud-M'Belle to Magistrate Kimberley, 21 Jan. 1908; Minute of 13 Nov. 1903; letter of Bud-M'Belle (London) to Sir John Graham, 23 May 1908; Court record 204 1906, Magistrate Kimberley 19 Jan. 1906: CAD JUS 2 2562/04, "Papers I. B. M'belle".

56 "A Bantu Benefactor" *Imvo* 22, 29 Aug. 1916; "A Short Review of Bud Mbelle's Life Story", *Imvo* 16, 23 Aug. 1947; "Mr Bud-M'belle Retires", *Umteteli wa Bantu* 5 Jul. 1930; B. Ncwana, "Kadalie's 'Political Renegade,'" *Izindaba Zabantu* 8 Jul. 1927; Willan, *Plaatje*, p. 252; KC v. 4, p. 104; N. Sonderling (ed.), *New Dictionary of South African Biography* (Pretoria: Vista, 1995), p. 170.

57 R.W. Msimang (ed.), *Natives Land Act 1913: Specific Cases of Evictions and Hardships etc.* (Cape Town: Friends of the South African Library, 1996, repr. 1914), p. [ii] (emphasis in original), passim; Msimang, "Native Lands Act: an Appeal to the People of England", *Tsala* 13 Jun. 1914; "Funeral of R.W. Msimang: Tributes to an African Leader", *Umteteli wa Bantu* 16 Dec. 1933.

58 *Tsala ea Batho* 14, 28 Nov. 1914.

59 [Phooko] "Firm & Just: or, Just & Firm", *International* 15 Dec. 1916; Simons, *Class & Colour*, p. 196.

60 Willan, *Plaatje,* Chapter 2; SANAC v. 4, p. 268; Z.K. Matthews, "Solomon T. Plaatje 1877-1932", *Imvo* 24 Jun. 1961; "Passing of Sol T. Plaatje", *Umteteli wa Bantu* 21 May 1932; *Koranta* 21 Mar. 1903.

61 Plaatje, *Native Life,* p. 99, *Mhudi* (1930), *The Mote & the Beam* (New York: Youngs, 1921), pp. 86-91. L. Chrisman, "Fathering the Black Nation of South Africa: Gender and Generation in Sol Plaatje's *Native Life in South Africa* and *Mhudi*", *Social Dynamics* v. 23 (1997) pp. 59–73 and *Rereading the Imperial Romance: British Imperialism and South African Resistance in Haggard, Schreiner and Plaatje* (Oxford: Clarendon, 2000) sensitively reappraises Plaatje's attitude to gender. P. Mpe, "Orality, Mediation and Subversion in Sol Plaatje's *Mhudi*", *African Studies* v. 57 (1998), pp. 79–91 focuses on the politics of the oral in Plaatje's fiction. Limb, "Sol Plaatje Reconsidered: Rethinking Plaatje's Attitudes to Class, Nation, Gender, and Empire", *African Studies* v. 62 (2003), pp. 33-52 brings together these and other new interpretations.

62 Bantu Brotherhood flyer, Xuma Papers; Willan, "Gift"; Willan, "Sol Plaatje, De Beers and an Old Tram Shed: Class Relations and Social Control in a South African Town 1918-1919", *JSAS* v. 4 (1978), pp. 195-215; Willan, *Plaatje,* pp. 218-224; Plaatje, "Along the Colour Line", *Tsala ea Batho* 10 Jan. 1914; "The Recent Congress", *Tsala* 14 Mar. 1914; Letter of J.S. Kokozela and T.G. Diniso [Kimberley Congress leaders] *Tsala* 14 Mar. 1914. Plaatje linked De Beers' interest to the presence of delegates from areas where the "industry draws its labour supply": Plaatje, "Native National Congress", *Tsala* 28 Feb. 1914; Plaatje, *Native Life,* p. 183.

63 "Homeless! Landless! Outlawed!", *Labour Leader* 1919 reprinted in *Plaatje 1876-1932,* pp. 59-63; KC v.4, p. 127; N. Ndebele "Actors and Interpreters", in *Plaatje Lectures,* pp. 51-71, 57-60; S. Plaatje, *Some of the Legal Disabilities Suffered by the Native Population of the Union of South Africa and Imperial Responsibility* (London: The African Telegraph, [1918]), pp. 2-3.

64 Switzer, *Black Press,* p. 61; Matthews "Plaatje"; *Tsala ea Batho* 2 Dec. 1911, 17 Feb. 1912, 2 Aug. 1913, 17 Oct. 1914, 17 Jul. 1915, 10 May 1913, 2 Dec. 1911, 17 Feb. 1912; *Report of the Natives Land Commission* v. 2, Evidence, (UG22-16), pp. 92-94 (Plaatje); Starfield, "Lore", p. 20.

65 *Tsala ea Batho* 17 Jul. 1915; letters to *Tsala* of E. Monye (10 May 1913), G. Matlhako (Bultfontein Compound; 5 Jul. 1913), A. Kipalisa (Nourse Mine, 19 Jul. 1913); "Benefit' Societies", *Tsala* 30 Aug. 1913; "Native Sufferer" to *Tsala* 25 Oct. 1913; "Native Wages on Their Mine", *Tsala* 18 Apr. 1914.

66 *Tsala* 18 Oct. 1913; "Trouble at the Premier Mine", *Tsala* 29 Nov. 1913; *Tsala* 23 May 1914, 12, 26 Jul. 1913, 17, 24 Jan. 1914; Johnstone, *Race, Class & Gold,* p. 170. Plaatje's 1913 letter to Molema also shows the former's general distaste for strikes: Molema-Plaatje Papers, Da23. See Starfield, "Lore", p. 22 on Plaatje's aim to use *Tsala* to generate a Tswana-Pedi response to "Zulu dominance" in African politics.

67 *Tsala ea Batho* 23 May 1914.

68 *Tsala ea Batho* 17 Feb. 1912, 2 Aug. 1913, 17 Oct. 1914, 6 Apr. 1912, 10 May, 26 Jul.1913; letters of J. Tulwana *Tsala* 2 Aug. 1913, M.W. Sadusadu, *Tsala* 3 Sept. 1910; *Tsala* 1 Jun., 18 May 1912.

69 *Tsala ea Batho* 14, 28 Nov. 1914, 23 Jan., 15, 22, 29 May 1915, 3, 17 Sep. 1910; "The APO" and "'Industrialising' the Native", *Tsala* 24 Dec. 1910; *Tsala* 30 Aug. 1913, 21 Feb. 1914; "The Passing of the Colour Bar", *Tsala* 7 Mar. 1914; "Mr. Kotze and Miner's Contract System", *Tsala* 4 Apr. 1914.

70   "The White Labour Party" *Tsala* 1 Oct. 1910; editorial *Tsala* 10 Sep. 1910; "Syndicalism",
     Tsala 18 Apr. 1914; "The Rand Colour Bar" *Tsala* 23, 30 May, 13 Jun. 1914 (from *Pretoria News*); *Tsala* 9 May 1914, 9 May, 17 Oct. 1914, 12 Jun. 1915, 4 Apr., 14 Mar. 1914.
71   Plaatje, "Along the Colour Line", *Tsala* 3 Jan. 1914; *Tsala* 17 Jan. 1914.
72   *Bantu World* 25 Jun. 1932.
73   This ambiguity confused state officials who were undecided whether he should be seen as an agitator or an ally against radicalism. Police closely monitored his movements for years: see SAP to SJ re Movements of Plaatje, 1923, JUS J269 3/1064/18 C.2 59/20, 22/12/23, and Starfield, "Lore", p. 11.
74   Lowe, "The Tragedy of Malunge", pp. 3-10, 77-79

To "Heartily ... Assist the Working Movement as Best They Can": Congress and Black Labour in the Transvaal, 1912-1919

In its first decade, Congress essentially was a decentralised "confederation of provincial organisations". It "remained a political association of 'leading' Africans".[1] This limited both its ability to speak with one voice to workers and its resources to reach out to and recruit them. At times deep divisions arose over provincial powers.

Yet relative independence from the strictures of centralised control by moderate SANNC leaders could aid closer labour ties by some more radical regional leaders. Transvaal Congress support for labour protests in the period 1918-1920 and less dramatic forms of sympathy for black workers from ANC bodies in other regions vividly demonstrated this. This chapter focuses on the Rand, the area of most rapid industrialisation, objectively positioning the TNC closer to the emergent black proletariat than any other provincial body of Congress.

Industrial growth after the 1880s was more heavily concentrated in southern Transvaal than any other region. It was not accidental that it was here the ANC took its first, hesitant, steps to engage with black industrial and mine workers. Such industrialisation also occurred in the Pretoria District; by 1910, there were 15 000 urban workers with another 14 000 at the Premier Diamond Mine.[2]

As black militancy grew in this region in the latter part of the decade so white authorities groped about seeking explanations. Some felt militancy was due to "detribalised" Africans starting to live nearer their work and lamented that such agitation was likely to increase "with so many masterless men and unrestrained women floating about". However, the transformation of underlying socio-

155

economic causes into action requires very real and very purposeful politics, and this is where Congress came in.[3]

In the period from 1912 to 1920, the Transvaal Native Congress (TNC) developed a number of viable branches and a wide range of contacts. Membership figures are sketchy, and there may have been overlap between TNC and SANNC members. Of some 106 delegates to the March 1913 SANNC conference in Johannesburg, over half, 60, hailed from the Transvaal. They represented a broad range of places, from urban Johannesburg, Kliptown, Sophiatown, Evaton, Vereeniging, Pretoria and Alexandra to rural Phokeng, Lydenburg, Spelonken, Volksrust, Heidelberg, Waterberg and Bethal. Five delegates came from the Rand mines: P. J. Mapela, H. M. Napo, D. S. Mohale, Ben Sekuane and T. W. M. Kunene, about whom we know little.[4]

The TNC tried to forge ties with workers in town and country. Agitation against the 1913 Land Act, which it viewed as reducing Africans to "penury and want", helped some branches broaden their contacts. The Vereeniging branch called a meeting in August 1913, attended by "over 100" farm toilers. However, the TNC's chief support came from the Rand. Here, as outlined in the previous chapter, its predecessors had set a precedent by supporting black workers.[5]

The TNC Constitution was more "class conscious" than that of the SANNC. It aimed not only "to protect the economic and material interests of [Africans] by constitutional means", but also "to protest against and strive for the removal of all oppressive class laws". A small measure of the TNC's orientation was that its membership card presented information about a member's employment and wages.[6] The TNC also got closer to workers through its supportive attitude to labour struggles, as seen in its support of black strikers, women workers, and army labourers.

The mine strikes of 1913 and 1914, described in Chapter 2, alerted employers and the state to the gradual erosion of their control. In 1913, Governor General Gladstone, doubtless giving vent to class and racial prejudice and keen to justify his deployment of 1,419 imperial troops, worried about "terrible" consequences if the 250,000 African Rand workers, with an attitude "full of peril", joined white strikers. We know very little of the "ringleaders" among striking African workers in 1913, later jailed, except that they stated that white strikers had told them to strike for higher pay, but their harsh treatment by the authorities may have influenced radical TNC attitudes articulated in 1918-1920.[7]

During the 1914 General Strike by white workers, government went to great lengths to shore up the loyalty of black workers and, as noted in Chapter 4, SANNC leaders. The Government Native Labour Bureau made elaborate arrangements for repatriation of miners and hinted at conciliatory measures in an enquiry headed by Commissioner H. O. Buckle, Chief Magistrate of Johannesburg.[8]

Commissioner Buckle reported in 1914 that black miner respect for compound managers and police, as well as inter-tribal rivalries, were tending to break down. He painted a dramatic stereotype of a black proletariat able to "mobilise themselves in a few minutes", all wanting more pay, with most of them "savages, whose only idea of reform is violence", which after recent strikes they now saw as an effective tactic. This was wartime, with black people urged by both white and black political leaders to be patriotic, yet Buckle made a clear connection between the labour unrest and growing African political unity as evident in the "native press, the proceedings of native political unions"—a clear allusion to Congress. There were, he firmly stated, "deliberate attempts" to unite and educate Africans to fight for better conditions, bringing "in its train agitation and organisation". A clear instance of this movement, he added, was the strike of African women in Bloemfontein, underlining that the Africans "with whom we have now to deal is a very different person from the native of a generation back".[9]

The number of African women workers on the Rand was small but growing: only 214 African women lived on work premises in 1915 compared to 4,279 men, though 766 women as opposed to 1,065 men lived in self-hired premises. Their position was harsh. There was little family housing for Africans, many of whom lived illegally on the fringes of the city, as in Klipspruit, 20 kilometres to the south, adjoining mines on sewage land. Further north, in Pretoria, a 1910 report pointed to high rates of diseases among female workers. Women faced strong competition for domestic work from black men, though by 1912 this began to change. Often forced into low-paying occupations such as laundering, or riskier beer brewing or prostitution, they were excluded from the formal capitalist economy and became the target of moralising stereotypes about their sexuality, just as missions strongly encouraged their "proper" place in household and domesticity rather than on the factory floor or in politics.[10] However, African women were far from passive.

Characterised by outsiders as "slums", these settlements were nevertheless the site of vibrant survival and resistance tactics that, if rarely aligning directly with the Congress sphere of official politics, sometimes used similar methods. In 1910, 17 Klipspruit women formed a deputation to the Johannesburg Mayor to complain of expensive travel costs to work in the city. In the same year, Ellen Leeuw and 122 black women from the same location presented another petition in which they complained that work opportunities for women were "unsympathetically locked up".[11]

There was interest in women's conditions by men who had just formed Congress. In 1912, before the Commission Appointed to Enquire into Assaults on Women several gave evidence—as did, interestingly, some labourers, including W. Mohlaodi of Premier Mine. Walter Rubusana (of the Cape Congress) warned about sexual exploitation of black domestic workers on the Rand. The Transvaal Native Council complained to this commission of the "injustice to our females" of domination of domestic work by "great hulking Zulus and other males" that "exposes the black females to poverty". The Council's J. S. Noah rejected passes for women and the sexual molestation by police that this could involve.[12]

Further north, African women rather than men spent more time in the nascent black freehold township of Alexandra, working at washing and illegal beer brewing (which attracted not just police but also workers from Johannesburg). In addition, African women rather than men, as John Nauright shows, formed the backbone of numerous boycotts of buses and shops in Alexandra from the 1910s until the 1940s. Out of these complex interactions social and political networks formed in which local or ethnic based associations rather than specifically political movements appear to have predominated in protests against police raids and prices. However, a Vigilance Committee formed there in 1919 and there is evidence of an active ANC branch by 1923 (see Chapter 9). E. P. (Emmanuel Peter) Mart Zulu, involved in the Vigilance Committee, which he chaired, local residents (and liquor) groups, and later the ANC branch, seems to have acted as a bridge between formal and informal politics. Black women too may have played a part in this bridging process. Although women's participation in formal politics in general was very limited at this time, there had been several women's petitions and Charlotte Maxeke's National Bantu Women's League had many branches, including perhaps members in Alexandra. African women from Alexandra were involved in a 1919 protest delegation.[13]

These trends suggest other reasons besides undoubted patriarchal attitudes within Congress and its lack of wider community reach for the disjuncture between Congress politics and women's protests. Exclusion of black women from the formal capitalist economy made them less exposed to new ideas circulating on the Rand about political organisation, whilst the low social prestige engendered by negative stereotypes of urban African women would have done little to encourage men to mobilise them directly.

Moreover, African politics did not operate in a vacuum. Not only were African women strongly discouraged from even coming to the urban centres where black politics was developing but other forces competed for their time and loyalty. In 1911 alone, just one Christian denomination made over 1,000 sorties onto the Rand, a good number of them to proselytise among African women.[14] Churches also could be a base for politicisation, but the impression of "apolitical" (in a formal sense) attitudes predominating among black women of the day we can partly explain by such competition for souls.

Nevertheless, it was none other than the TNC that first highlighted African women's activism within Congress. The Transvaal Congress exposed their exploitation as workers. It did so in 1916, and again in November 1917 in Pretoria, when it "lodged a strong protest" before the Secretary for Native Affairs against attempts to impose passes and medical examinations on women. Passes cost valuable money and thus affected workers. The TNC organ *Abantu-Batho* ("People") challenged men to act: "Shall we stand [by] whilst our women should be troubled by other men? No!" Passes for women, wrote the TNC's Dan Motuba, constituted "an indirect declaration of war" about which African men from the Rand to Rustenburg "were simply raging mad".[15]

It is worth looking at some of these reports in more detail. *Abantu-Batho* in 1916 took up the cause of working women. They were "extremely overworked". Employers were "so inconsiderate and almost brutal that they do not care even for their female native servants to be housed properly". Laundry workers— expected to wash "bundles of washing of extraordinary quantities ... at quite a low wage", often without breaks—endured a "sweating-system of a most shameful character". Specific working hours and wage rates evidenced harsh conditions. Workers were warned "against collaboration" with white Labour following refusal of craft unions to support black labour. The paper urged the TNC to "inquire into the question of how natives are employed ... In the absence of organised labour among natives it is suggested that the inquiry should be directed to hours of work, rate of pay, and general treatment, particularly of women and girls". In December 1917, the paper re-iterated its opposition to passes for women, relating the issue to existing written work contracts for men; it would become the same for women doing kitchen work.[16]

When women began to organise, the TNC expressed support. In December 1917, *Abantu-Batho* welcomed "meetings formed by women from different places". This referred to a Winburg Native Women's League gathering (with C. Mallela as Chair and A. Serrero Secretary) that urged formation of women's leagues to fight "these brutal laws ... with unrelenting vigour", and to another by the "National League of Bantu Women (Transvaal Province)" in Nancefield on 9 December 1917 (see Chapter 4) "under the presidency of Mrs Maxeke of Kliptown". *Abantu-Batho* noted, "The first organization of women has started, there is no other. Women and girls read the paper. You will find life and betterness and understand about your rights, your men's and children's. Read this paper."[17]

Africans *did* read the paper. In December 1917 at Ermelo A.M.E. Church, a meeting of 150 people, mainly women, heard the contents of an *Abantu-Batho* article attacking passes read out to them. The women unanimously agreed to oppose the pass laws, collected funds for a deputation to link up with SANNC Chaplain Reverend Ngcayiya, and promptly formed their own committee, possibly a branch of the Bantu Women's League.[18]

Charlotte Maxeke proposed independent action by women. In 1917 she had linked anti-pass struggles of both genders; the impact of "iniquitous Pass Laws which have turned thousands of [our] beloved sons into criminals" now sought "to degrade the honour" of women, hence it was "high time the voice of Bantu women was heard. They must get themselves ready for the struggle". After all, she argued at the Nancefield meeting after listening to speeches of men, "How can men liberate women from the Pass laws when they themselves are subjected to them?" Maxeke concluded, "Let men and women cooperate against these pernicious Laws and then we shall be free (cheers) ... In this building up of the nation, women must lead. 'Dux femina facto' (cheers)." By 1919, she complained of how men took jobs away from women domestic workers.[19]

Such audacity prompted SANNC criticism but she received some support from the TNC, whose Vice-President Daniel Letanka addressed the founding meeting of the National League of Bantu Women in January 1918, described in the last chapter. He conceded, "Women are organizing themselves without the aid of the Congress because [it] has failed to do its duty." TNC Chairman C. S. Mabaso agreed with Mrs Mallela that in 1913 "our men did not help us in our distress". Other TNC members also expressed solidarity. These protests were not limited to elite women. Police gathering data from shebeens and on the streets reported "tons of women" across the Rand expressing opposition to passes and they met many women apparently coming from Women's League anti-pass meetings in Randfontein and Krugersdorp. Maxeke, who raised the plight of women workers forced to submit to contracts that "bind the native woman servant to … her employer till the time of contract expires", even if subjected to inhumane treatment, began to work more closely with the TNC.[20]

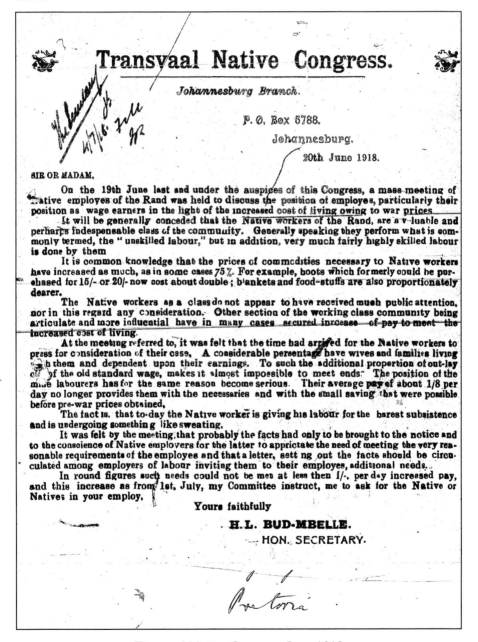

Transvaal Native Congress flyer, 1918

In June 1918, Maxeke took part in protests called by the TNC to protest the gaoling of black strikers. She told a crowd of 1,000-2,000 on 19 June that Africans "receive low wages and yet have to pay heavy taxes". She added the woman worker's dimension to harsh working conditions. A woman in Nancefield must leave the township early in the morning, work the whole day washing for only 2 shillings and yet pay 7d for fares, leaving her inadequate means to maintain her family. "Kitchen girls" who received £2 month in 1913 now got only 30 shillings a month. Maxeke sympathised with, and protested the arrest of strikers: "A native is handcuffed for asking for bread." At another large meeting on 29 June, she reported that employers were underpaying kitchen workers on the excuse that they had to donate to the war effort. She called for men to show sympathy as best they could with the arrested strikers and with women.[21] In fact, the TNC provided the avenue through which Maxeke could publicly articulate demands of women workers.

The TNC expressed concern for labourers involved in World War I and, as we shall see below, after the war its support for striking workers would increase. It adopted a more critical position to the war than the SANNC. TNC President Sefako Mapoch Makgatho questioned whether government was more interested in repressing black people than sending troops to Europe. Another TNC leader asked what the state was doing about black unemployment during the war. The qualified "loyalty" of TNC radicals resonates in a strongly worded resolution carried at a TNC mass meeting in 1916. Signed by Letanka and TNC Secretary Herbert Msane, it viewed "with a deep sense of horror" the failure of government to publicise statistics concerned with black war involvement. It demanded "fair and legitimate consideration" of compensation for dependants of war labourers. At a June 1916 ISL meeting, black people present were "very much alive to the irony" of a proposal put by the TNC's Robert Grendon to mark the death of Lord Kitchener. In December, the TNC's Benjamin Phooko drew attention to the contradiction between calls for African people to support the war and government's denial of full black war involvement.[22]

It was during the War and its aftermath that the TNC became involved in direct support for strikers, a fact related to declining black conditions generally. Prices rose by an average 31-39 per cent from 1914 to 1918. A particular burden on black budgets was an increase of five shillings per 100 pounds of mealies from 1919 to 1920. Persistent drought, and debilitating influenza pandemic, exacerbated black budgets. African wages remained stationary and the real value of African mineworkers' wages fell by about 25 per cent between 1910 and 1919. Not surprisingly, black miner strikes erupted: in 1915, 1916, 1918, 1919 and 1920. Journalists linked this upsurge to "deep-lying grievances" fuelled by rapid inflation that "prompted African workers ... to organise and to strike for the first time on a significant scale". Between 1918 and 1920, black worker militancy reached a peak, attracting strong support from the TNC. In early 1918, black miners launched store boycotts. A government report noted they used pickets and were more aware of the much lower purchasing power (21 shillings to 10 shillings before the war) of their wages. Officials worried this could lead to strikes that could spread more widely given another perceived feature of the boycott: Africans from different ethnic groups combined.[23]

In February 1918, police reported acute unrest among Benoni workers. Workers picketed Kleinfontein mine, to be met by mounted police; those at Brakpan compound faced motorised police. There were strikes by sanitary workers in June and by gold miners in July. The harsh repression of the former strikers sparked strong TNC solidarity. In the war's wake came more inflation, food shortages and retrenchments, mixed with disappointment at continued denial of black rights. The Chamber of Mines noted the well-organised nature of a mine strike of February 1919. In November, miners at Rose Deep mine compound held protest marches over food and dismissal of a worker. A huge mine strike erupted in 1920 (see Chapter 9), also supported by the TNC. To understand better the TNC role in these events it is necessary to examine these protests in more detail, though I omit some description due to the prior work of Bonner and Johnstone.[24]

Following a successful strike by white workers in March 1918 about 50 Johannesburg black municipal sanitary workers struck on 6 June for an extra 6d a day. Two days later 4,000 black municipal workers echoed the demand. The "bucket strike" faced harsh state repression with over 150 Africans sentenced to two months' hard labour. Magistrate T. G. Macfie stated: "If they attempted to escape ... they would be shot down. If they refused to obey orders, they would receive lashes." This severe treatment, noted *Round Table*, "created a tremendous stir in native circles". TNC leaders, including Makgatho and Horatio Bud-M'belle, later testified that they new nothing of the strike until after it erupted. Yet, it was the TNC that mobilised black resentment in a series of public protests.[25] In calling meetings over the treatment of strikers and calling for a general strike, it was identifying with worker struggles, and benevolently presuming to lead it. They also worked with radical socialists on this issue.

The first ISL-Congress joint meeting had taken place in February 1916 in protest over the Land Act. Saul Msane attended but declined to speak, even in the ISL's "upper room", invoking a SANNC pledge of wartime loyalty. Socialist arguments presented at a meeting in April reportedly impressed Levi

Mvabaza of the TNC. *Abantu-Batho* editor Robert Grendon "expressed a keen interest" in the ISL in June when he addressed an ISL meeting on "the race problem of Africa and its connection with the working class movement"—though his talk dealt chiefly with the "better" rights Africans held under Queen Victoria. Saul Msane drew strong support from the audience by calling for white unions, "formed to fight the natives", to remove restrictions on black membership.[26]

In 1917, the ISL joined Congress leaders in loudly protesting the harsh effects of the Native Affairs Administration Bill. ISL protests included Congress speakers: Saul and Herbert Msane, Richard Selope Thema, and Horatio Bud-M'belle addressed meetings at the Johannesburg Trades and Labour Council. On 11 March, Saul Msane greeted a packed hall with the words: "I hail you as the conquerors of colour prejudice." Bud-M'belle's speech made a "good impression" on the ISL who saw his outlook as "distinctly nearer to that of the landless industrial [sic]" than other black leaders. The ISL published his report of the meeting (that he characterised as a "revelation of sincere [ISL] sympathy" with Africans) and invited him to address the next May Day rally.[27]

Few Africans were associated with the ISL, but most were TNC members. T. W. Thibedi joined the ISL in 1916. He addressed its May Day Rally in 1918, urging black workers present to join "the native organisation in existence". Mvabaza became active in 1916. Letanka (TNC Chairman, 1916), Jeremiah Dunjwa (TNC Secretary, 1919), Herbert Msane and Mabaso were also involved. The TNC shared platforms with the ISL and organised joint meetings to discuss labour issues. Out of these meetings emerged the first documented African labour organisation: the Industrial Workers of Africa (IWA).[28]

Police files reveal the level of enthusiasm for class struggle and contradictions in thinking of TNC "socialists". In July 1917 the first IWA meetings occurred, under ISL auspices. Herbert Msane and Horatio Bud-M'belle of the TNC participated. The former took a leading role; the latter served as secretary but his attendance was irregular. Msane in July 1916 had penned an article on Ethiopianism for *The International*. By July 1917 he was "keenly interested" in the ISL and spoke at their meetings. At an IWA meeting in November, Msane compared the IWA and Congress: he was a member of both, but to his mind, the union was stronger. He hoped more TNC members would "attend our meetings". As *Abantu-Batho* editor, he made clear his support for unions.

Africans worked in the ... bowels of the earth digging gold ... yet only get three pounds a month. These men have found ... it is necessary to start the ... IWA [in which] ways will be found of making the capitalists learn when the workers want higher wages, and to arrange hours of work, and all the rights of workers. This seems a good thing, and if our people were ... developed they would support this organisation and make it strong.

The IWA constitution referred to the inevitability of class struggle "until the workers of the world organise as a class ... and abolish the wage system". It is doubtful to what extent members shared this Marxism. One IWA member, interviewed by the white press, saw the IWA object as "purely to obtain for the native a fair rise in pay".[29]

The IWA faced severe problems, including police infiltration and small numbers. Wilfred Jali, a spy, even became acting secretary. In July 1918, it "only embrace[d] a few hundred". Alfred Cetyiwe, a worker and IWA leader, later active in Congress, explained to an IWA meeting "We are treated by sjambok and gaol; that is why you see this hall is not full up." There are no detailed membership records beyond sketchy police files and efforts to expand to other towns do not seem to have been successful, but some members were industrial workers. A list compiled by Jali identified Herbert Msane and Bud-M'belle as "chief mischief makers". Others included Hosea Phooko, James D. Ngojo, and Reuben Kapan who carried out propaganda among miners. Ngojo, also a Congress activist, addressed an anti-pass meeting in November 1917 on behalf of the IWA. In January 1918, he chaired an IWA meeting and introduced its aims to the Bantu Women's League's founding conference, reporting: "The women were very pleased to hear about our meeting and they agreed to assist us in every way and at the same time we will assist them." He tried to set up an IWA branch in Benoni, and in October spoke to a black people's social evening, where he related the harsh experiences of imprisoned workers.[30]

The IWA's more proletarian nature produced scepticism about Congress credentials to represent workers. In August 1917, ISL leader S. P. Bunting asked IWA members their opinion of Congress. One replied it "was composed of well-known men who owned lands ... [and] had nothing to say as regards the bad treatment" of Africans. When TNC leaders joined IWA delegates at joint meetings on labour unity in December 1917, the ISL drew attention to the "class division between ... horny-handed" IWA members and TNC "respectables". Some IWA members present expressed opposition to joint action with Congress "men who organise rich and high people". Nevertheless, some "respectables" favoured unity. Letanka saw the TNC and SANNC as independent of the labour movement but the TNC would "heartily ... join and assist the working movement as best they can". They thrashed out an agreement to form a joint labour committee.[31]

In the face of heightened black anger at the harsh treatment of the municipal strikers, some workers and the TNC forged a closer alliance in a series of meetings in June 1918. I quote extensively from the meetings as they illustrate the strength, if also the ambiguity of TNC attitudes to workers. In early June, a joint TNC-IWA meeting unanimously protested the use of riot laws against "an innocent demand for an increase of wages". It resolved to support "a general demand for increased wages to all native labourers" and requested the SANNC to *demand* the strikers' immediate release. At a meeting of 250 black people held under TNC auspices on 10 June, TNC Chairman Mabaso attacked the gaoling of strikers merely for "demanding more money", whereas white strikers "were given what they wanted". Mabaso supported a strike: "If you can just fold up your hands and stop work you will surely hurt the whiteman." The meeting, police noted, "seemed to agree to make a general strike".[32]

At a follow-up TNC meeting on 12 June, Mabaso detailed workers' poor living quarters in Nancefield. Plaatje spoke on the death of four Orange Free State Africans, relating how a white man had killed one of them for his horse. He compared this to the "bucket" strike. "That shows that we will be shot down as dogs, as the ... magistrate said to the natives arrested while demanding an increase to their wages." Plaatje, not normally associated by historians with strikes, was prepared to address a strike meeting and express a form of solidarity with workers. Subsequently, Herbert Msane proposed a secret committee of TNC and ISL leaders to plan a proposed July general strike. Co-operation became a reality as a steering committee of five delegates from the IWA, ISL and TNC met.[33]

A meeting attended by 1,000-2,000 black people from many Reef towns occurred on 19 June. Mabaso urged solidarity with gaoled workers. He signalled an emerging alliance with the ISL who he saw as "friends of the black races". Nevertheless, Makgatho viewed the ISL with suspicion. They were akin to the Labour Party; they were just like "all white people"; and they would shoot black strikers. He was "absolutely opposed to [a] strike", and asked all Africans to "follow him as their father". Selope Thema identified the strikers as "my brothers guarded with rifles ... for asking for bread". Mvabaza, representing the steering committee, proposed a strategy: all workers should demand a shilling a day increase, but negotiations with employers would occur through the committee. If employers rejected the rise, then workers would strike. He juxtaposed Marxist and African village conceptions of class.

He harked back to a golden age of "classless" society in which there had "never been blood shed between poor and rich". He contrasted this with the present regime under whose "flag, the poor is poor; let him die in his poverty oppressed by the capitalist". Letanka recounted how, when he had tried to see the gaoled strikers, officials had demanded "what right the Congress [had] to defend" them when Native Affairs was "representing the natives". White people, he added, are "made richer and richer by the labour of black people". All reported Congress speakers expressed solidarity with strikers.[34]

The TNC drew up a letter to employers. It illustrates the effect of working class influences on its thinking. Signed by Horatio Bud-M'belle, it stated that black workers were "indispensable" to the community but gave their labour "for the barest subsistence". They had been unable to secure wage rises despite steep price rises on basics such as boots, blankets and food. The letter spoke in clear class terms. Whilst "other section[s] of the working class community being more articulate and more influential" had "secured increases of pay", the black workers "as a class" had not "received much public attention". They then presented the demand for the shilling rise.[35]

TNC activists were prominent at IWA and ISL meetings on these issues. At an IWA meeting of 27 June 1918, Horatio Bud-M'belle, Letanka, Mvabaza and Herbert Msane attended. Thibedi, in the chair, called on Msane to speak: "Are you ready to strike? 'Yes' the whole hall answered … Have you organised all the g[i]rls working in kitchens?" Msane sought to broaden the issue beyond wage demands. Rather than simply striking for an increase it was better, he argued, to get fellow workers "to join your movement as industrial workers". Mvabaza urged secrecy of their strike plans.[36]

At this meeting, IWA, ISL and TNC speakers expressed scepticism that the strike could succeed with so little planning. Hamilton Kraai, a warehouse supervisor who became active in Congress, doubted whether the shilling rise would "ever be granted". Elected to the IWA Executive in January 1918, Kraai emerged as a leading black proponent of socialism. He and another speaker, Sibigo, tried to explain exploitation. Sibigo called for abolition of wage-labour. Kraai, revealing his intimate knowledge of working life, detailed the gold production process and roles of white and black employees. White people got "full wages but the native gets nothing but Maheu for all the hard work". Black people, "especially those working in the mines, do not get the product of their labour … Even if your wages are increased you will not be emancipated from slavery." Kraai interweaved Congress and IWA histories to stress unity in action:

> My fellow workers, how long has the Congress been calling you? It is ... over 10 years. How long has the IWA been calling you? ... You said, when you heard the Congress calling to you—they only want money ... Who wants money today? ... [We will be free] ... by organising ourselves and [by] Unionism ... We are slaves under the Union Jack ... we must not forget to return our Africa ... This gold is also ours. It was placed by God for us ... If a bull of another herd comes to another kraal, the strange bull is bound to be beaten ... It does not matter how strong the strange bull might be.

This was a speech full of symbolism and mixed ideologies. It linked the historic struggles of Congress with the new venture of the IWA. It alluded to the state not being omnipotent and saw unionism as a weapon to return black lands. It rejected British patriotism yet invoked God, perhaps because religious metaphors were likely to appeal to an audience including Christians. At an earlier meeting, Kraai had stated that the IWA aimed to abolish the capitalist class by organising on a mass scale. God created the Earth for all, not just the capitalists, but ministers of religion were "press[ing] us under the capitalist class". Black workers already lived in Hell so "we better unite comrades and abolish the capitalist classes that we can be safe in burning in the other hell".[37]

On 25 June, Cetyiwe told an ISL meeting of 76 Africans and one white person (T.P. Tinker) that Mabaso had ruled there was no need to strike as gaoled workers were now free. Tinker then gave his opinion of Congress: it "belongs to the Native Capitalists ... [Congress] were against the strike from the very start." He lumped together Congress leaders and ascribed to all of them the views of a few, such as Saul Msane, ignoring that Mvabaza, who had proposed the strike, was a Congress figure. White socialists did admit in June that the "close coincidence of native and working-class interests" might yet see a role for Congress. Police were concerned that, whilst "leaders of the Native Congress ... do not favour" contact with socialists, "ultimately ... by force of circumstances they must fall into line" with the ISL. Thibedi already was exchanging ideas with Bunting. A leaflet, signed by Thibedi, informed workers about the IWA: "Black Africans open your eyes ... Workers come together and be united and join your own Native Council."[38]

Three more joint TNC-IWA protest meetings took place from the 28 to 30 June. At the first, 1,000 African people heard Letanka report that TNC material support for strikers, including funds for a solicitor, had led to the quashing of convictions. All black workers on the Rand had now agreed to support the wage demand. They should demand the increase peacefully and collectively. Again, the TNC would lead: "We shall form [the strike] on ourselves as your leaders, and we shall tell you what to do after we have heard from you that your bosses [will] not give you the increase." The TNC, like a union, would protect strikers: "Remember that we are here and will assist you in every way by organising and tak[ing you] out of gaol." Mvabaza also spoke. He combined national and class issues. Pointing to the example of decrepit "rooms of the domestic servants", he alleged that white people had the "aim of killing us" to seize black lands. However, "we are a strong nation and can fight ... If you ... workers listen to what we say as your leaders, you will surely succeed ... and the whole of South Africa in one day will go on strike".[39]

Nine hundred attended the second joint meeting. Mvabaza, who recognised miners and "bucket" strikers in the crowd, continued to urge central leadership: "if you carry out this strike as you are told by your Leaders, you are sure to win". When Isaiah Bud-M'belle and Saul Msane opposed striking, Mvabaza objected, stating, "I am out for a strike." He castigated Msane for "trying to sell his own people, while he is a member of the Congress". Msane, added R. W. Msimang, wanted miners to "take no part in the matter", yet knew little of their lives. Msimang, a lawyer, tried to bridge the class gap between his own middle strata and workers present, a gap probably felt by workers in the presence of the highly educated (though there is not much evidence of just what workers thought of Congress). He was, he told workers, "your friend up to the last day of our life ... I think that as I am an educated man I am a good help to those who are not educated (loud cheers) because I do not think it is any good for any black ... to have ... rights while others are suffering." Msimang backed this up by acting as a legal advisor to the strikers. Letanka criticised Saul Msane's negative attitude to the strike. He claimed if they had not acted in unison strikers would still be in prison. He thereby sought to tap workers' sense of solidarity with comrades. Selope Thema reminded workers: "Today [the authorities] are telling you that if you want to be a rich man you must wait until you die." Makgatho, who earlier that day had argued in favour of a wage rise to Prime Minister Louis Botha, stated that all Africans now realised "their power" and demanded more money. They were no longer "afraid to do so. They know today that by organising they can make their voice heard."[40]

A third joint meeting occurred on 30 June. A rowdy crowd of "thousands" burnt a Union Jack. Makgatho assured workers that Congress would make the white people grant the increase "in any way". He again assumed the mantle of workers' "father", urging them not to strike until so advised by Congress. Continuing the paternalistic metaphor, he likened strikers to children simply asking for bread, who parents should not smack.[41]

A propaganda war ensued. Radicals led by Horatio Bud-M'belle drew up leaflets for distribution to workplaces. Moderates hit back with "statements in the English papers". *Cape Times* was relieved to report that the "older natives" did "everything in their power to instil common sense in the native mind". The "older natives" were leaders such as Saul Msane and Makgatho who opposed strikes. Makgatho certainly spoke against striking. However, he expressed sympathy for the strikers—and there is circumstantial evidence from a "boss boy" that a "'Makato' from Pretoria" spoke to workers at the Felber and Jucken yard two weeks earlier and "advocated striking for more pay". Msane was less equivocal but forced to walk a tightrope between black public opinion and his beliefs. He issued a leaflet in the vernacular stating: "It is only right that we should ask for an increase in money because things are dear ... [but] a strike will only hurt you and we shall lose all, because a strike ... can only be successful when there is a union which is known, and a strong one too, and if you have a strong purse." He urged workers to "elect good men who know how to manage an affair like this ... I am against a strike". In urging them not to strike, Msane nevertheless expresses strong sympathy for their cause whilst being careful not to say anything that the authorities could misconstrue as inflammatory. He urges use of elected worker representatives and suggests the need to form unions. His advice about requirements for successful strikes would not be out of place in the language of social democracy; but his main intention was to stop strikes.[42]

The chorus of protests forced the release of the sentenced strikers on 25 June. The seriousness with which the state regarded events was evident in the personal intervention of Botha. He sent a message to a Congress-led meeting on 30 June urging loyalty and declaring the establishment of the Moffat Commission to investigate causes of the strikes. Botha also agreed to meet black representatives to discuss grievances. Negotiations resulted in Congress calling off the proposed general strike.[43]

However, some workers still went on strike, including those at the Palace Steam Laundry, a flourmill and small chemical factory, boarding-house domestic workers, hospital staff, and municipal compound employees. Following a display of force by mounted police, they changed their minds. Also on strike were 6,000-15,000 mineworkers at the Ferreira, Robinson Deep and Crown mines. They took up arms in the face of armed repression. There were reports of youths stoning trams and police after meetings at Newclare and Vrededorp at which "the usual Socialistic" speeches were made.[44]

The 1918 strikes were defeated. State repression and lack of support by white unions restricted the birth of black unions and the failure of the strikes

Copy. JB/   *Benoni* 7.7.18.

NATIVE WOMEN'S LEAGUE.

The Mass Meeting was opened with Hymn 30 in kaffir and prayer by the Reverend Mtshula. After the prayer Mrs. Malelia introduced the President and Nombard of the Native Congress.

Mr. Lettanka Ladies and Gentlemen I am sorry that the white people who have got nothing to do with this meeting are also present. I shall be glad if they would be told. I can only say this as regards the trouble in Johannesburg of the Sanitary Boys re the increase of 6d a day. They appealed to the Chief Magistrate and were taken to the Jesses Police Station and charged for refusing to work. I was then informed that they were all arrested.

I then engaged a Mr. Ritch. Mr. Ritch took the case. One Pass Office Official asked me why I stood for these people. I then made arrangements to tell them that they were being defended. There would have been no trouble had the Municipality people have heard the grievances of the natives. I also blame the N.A.D. who was called and had he been a wise man he would have come forward and spoke to the natives. What the white people want is that natives should be sjambokked.

A Mass Meeting held that an increase of 1/- should be made on the 1st July. Not a strike but a request. A meeting was called, the Manager prevented all the boys from attending. People were miss told that there was going to be a strike.

They took it that there was going to be a strike on the 1st July. The Government knows it too. General Botha and his Ministry. We will meet him on Tuesday.

The strike in Johannesburg is caused by the European. They are to blame who prevented boys from coming to the meeting. There is no strike which will take place. We only want 1/-. If there would be a strike we shall call upon our Chiefs.

Mrs. Maxeke in a very brief speech preached unity amongst natives. We are no more afraid of Gaol. This is high time may they be more strict (Nation before church). Government seeing that there is a lot of money gained with passes from native men. He now suggested that women should carry passes too. We are only upon this that this money increase has been postponed. What we want is unity. We must all wake up.

The Bishop said in the meeting held by the Women's Association as regards to doings in Johannesburg. Strikes are all over. Even today white people were mourning for the July Strike, but if natives begin to ask more wages they think that they are going against the Government. The Bishop's address was that natives were children, but they are now old and can walk, what we want is only 1/- a day in addition. Ask your request through the Congress.
As you are afraid of a small Dutchman; we are not even afraid of a big one as we are going to see him on Tuesday.

Mrs. Mallela. Mr. Thema - Chairman Ladies and Gentlemen. I am glad to be here. You have heard from all speakers. You will remember that we are two nations. Some are white people, who come from Europe. We are the aboriginals. Instead of that they broke the law and came to South Africa our land.

Police report on Native Women's League, 1918

foundered on this strategic weakness. This lacuna also thrust the TNC into the position of a de facto representative of black labour. This elicited an interesting comment from Bunting. He generally viewed Congress as *petit bourgeois*. Yet, by his admission that "if any public organisation called a strike it was not the I.S.L. but the Native Congress", he conceded a degree of Congress influence among workers.[45]

Congress interest in workers continued. On 6 July, Mabaso, Letanka and Mvabaza spoke about the strike to an evening meeting of eight-five in Boksburg New Location that delegated local residents Schreiner Baduza and Masbiqa to join protest delegations. A meeting of the Native Women's League the next day in Benoni attracted 250 people, with TNC leaders again present and Mrs C. Mallela in the chair. Letanka outlined the demands for wage rises. He noted that after he engaged a lawyer to defend the workers, white officials repeatedly quizzed him on why he stood for black workers, reminding us that official discourse always sought to divide Congress and workers. Selope Thema added that the rise should apply to all black workers. He mixed black nationalism with appeals to fair play and Empire loyalty. White people had driven black people into barren places yet they remained loyal. "What we demand is only a sixpence. Why should we be shot for our demand? ... We are only fighting against the Kaiser ... People who arrest us are against King George." Charlotte Maxeke, urging unity above all, pointed out that government sought to squeeze more money from Africans by imposing passes on women but Africans were no longer afraid of gaol. Maxeke also testified to the Moffat Commission on the strikes, pointing out many African women resorted to liquor selling due to lack of alternatives.[46]

On 9 July, a joint delegation of African political and religious leaders and Rand workers met Botha. Delegation members included SANNC leaders Saul Msane and Isaiah Bud-M'belle. TNC leaders protested at their virtual exclusion from the meeting; they declined to nominate only two representatives to meet Botha and instead attempted to join the meeting *en masse*. In doing so, they sought to oppose the elitist nature of state attempts to co-opt black leaders. The Native Affairs Department conceded that the Director of Native Labour and compound managers had selected the delegation, with preference given "to men of good standing—such as sons of chiefs". It described TNC leaders as "some of the more turbulent and less desirable of the 'Young Turks' being desirous of bringing their organisation into prominence as representative of and spokesman for the Native people whether industrial or other". The delegation, the press noted, was representative of *indunas*, ministers, police overseers, clerks and interpreters, and some compound workers. Twenty of

(121)

TRANSVAAL NATIVE NATIONAL CONGRESS

The meeting was held at the Ebenezer Hall, Johannesburg on Monday the 10th. June 1918, and consisted of about 250 natives and about 12 whitemen. The Chairman of the Congress - Mabaso presided.

He told the meeting that this meeting was called on behalf of the Municipal natives who were arrested while asking for a 6d per day increase to their wages. 49 of them were arrested and tried outside the Court yard by a Johannesburg magistrate. After these natives were arrested, Mbele, Mbaso, Lentaka and Mr Ritch, the Solicitor went to Gaol to speak to the arrested natives, but they were refused to, but on asking them, they atlast allowed them. He said it was shameful for these natives to be put in Gaol whilst demanding more money, as the whitemen who went on strike and stopped all the work whilst demanding £8/2/- per week, they were given whatthey wanted, while these natives were sent to Gaol. The magistrate said any of th them who shall attempt to escape or who wont obey the orders of the Gaol will be shot down dead. Mabaso then addressed the meeting and said he knows that there are some detectives who write down everything said in the meeting but they can do as they like. He said it was now your chance to take and follow the steps of the action taken by the Municipal boys to better your conditions. He said last month these natives first asked for some more money from their boss and he told them that he will see at the end of the month. At the end of the month when they wnet for their pay and expecting more money they were paid just the same, so they outspanned and demanded more money. Then the manager without asking them anything, called for the Police and arrested them. The same night when they were arrested the closets were cleaned by the Police boys. It is because these natives united that they went on strike. He said the main cause were the Pass Law that they were arrested. When the whitemen went on strike they were not arrested be-cause they carried no passes with them, and nobody could find them anywhere If this is not a good step for you to follow, you will understand nothing. If you can just fold up your hands and stop work you will surely hurt the whitemen, so you must do so. He said another 150 natives have been arrested for the same thing, and for these a solicitor has been engaged, and he wants £5/5/-. Another native seconded the above lecture. Mbele, Ritchie's Clerk then said - Why do the whitemen open their eyes so much towards money when it is against natives? He suggested that we should make a reso-lution and send a petition to the Governor General of the Union to decrease the penalty of these natives from two months. To that another native re-fused for a petition to be sent, but that we should ask them to release our friends, if not so, we tell them that we shall all stop work and strike if they did not let them out. Another native said we should not go on strike because we are young, and we cannot take out the burning fat from the fire, and this strike has been started by law Sanitary natives. He agreed sending a petition to the Governor General and stop the strike. The meeting shouted -"Let the fire burn as much as it likes, and you are a coward". Then Tinker of Neppes'Buildings was asked to say a few words, on which he fully explained to the meeting that we should all unite into thousands and go on strike, first for the release of our friends, and secondly for our rights. If we organise into a 100 or 200, the Government will put us in Gaol, but in 1000's he's got no place to put us, and even in Gaol we shall refuse to do any work. He called his meeting on Saturday evening and asked each one to bring 20 or 30 of his friends, and they all agreed. In this meeting they all seemed to agree to make a general strike, after they have organised into a big number.

The meeting closed at 12 midnight.

TRANSVAAL NATIVE NATIONAL CRONGRESS

The meeting was held at the Ebenezer Hall, Johannesburg on Wednesday the 12th. June 1918, and consisted of about 200 natives and 3 whitemen - Tinker, Hanscombe and another. The chair was occupied by Mabaso. He said he was sorry that we have waited so long for the President Mr Makgatho, who was to address this meeting, but shortly afterwards he came in. The Chair-man said, we shall then hear the president's address, and afterwards the Secretary will read the letter from Pretoria, and then Plaatje will address the meeting and give his reports from the Freestate of the 4 natives shot dead there. Then the president said, he was very glad to attend this meeting today and find such a big number of natives. He said he sent Plaatje to the Freestate to see about the 4 natives shot there. He said the whitemen want to make this country their own by shooting and killing the natives for nothing.

CONTINUED

Police report on TNC meeting, 1918

them spoke, raising the need for increased wages, and improved living and working conditions. The next week, Mvabaza reported back to a TNC meeting of 2,000 at Vrededorp. He urged non-violence to prevent possible banning of their meetings, claimed Botha conceded Africans now formed a nation, and advised that all workers could visit Moffat to present grievances.[47]

Such negotiations, together with state promises of reforms and the decision of the SANNC to seek redress at the Paris Peace Conference temporarily diverted TNC interest from wages struggles. Nevertheless, the events had a powerful symbolic effect. The joint arrest of ISL, IWA and TNC leaders after the strike was described by Skota as the "first time in South Africa [that] members of the European and Native races, in common cause united, were arrested and charged together".[48] In terms of ANC-worker relations, the events had an even greater effect. In the course of defending strikers and agitating for wage rises, the TNC temporarily cast aside the class barrier that previously had quarantined political groups from workers. TNC leaders displayed a blend of elitism and empathy when trying to lead workers. There is no denying their sympathy, even Makgatho, who opposed striking. This sympathy was rooted in race, class, or a combination of both. TNC attitudes were a mixture of populism, growing black consciousness and nascent African nationalism, inherited liberal and occasionally more radical, even socialist, ideas held by some members. However, the political and economic causes of the protests continued, and so did TNC solidarity with workers.

The TNC and Anti-Pass Protests of 1919

Ongoing strikes by African workers in 1919 continued to fuel Congress interest in workers. Springs miners downed tools in March. In April, a strike by Burnside coal miners saw "a considerable amount of dissatisfaction and unrest". Workers at Rustenburg Tabak Ko-Operatie threatened to strike. In addition, a Tweefontein colliery strike in May involved 600 workers, some armed.[49] What comes out of these, and similar, reports is the militant nature of worker struggles. The intensive anti-pass campaigning at this time by the TNC, who linked passes directly to workers' wage demands, helped encourage a mood of resistance by black workers.

In the period 1918-1920, the TNC co-ordinated anti-pass protests across the Transvaal. It appealed to a wide audience. A TNC protest card, "The Anti-Pass Cry", drew on diverse, but moderate symbols: a Union Jack, a declaration that "We are fighting against tyranny and oppression," and a plea "for justice. We are loyal." (See illustration page 179) Notwithstanding this broad approach, the TNC made a direct connection between passes and wage demands. In late 1918, its Johannesburg meetings focused on work contracts. Mvabaza told a meeting "Congress is against the Pass Law, and the Contracts under which the natives work." TNC leaders argued that since contracts and passes caused the failure of the 1918 strikes, they should be abolished. Only Congress, with "branches all over the union", could mobilise black people Africans to reject labour contracts. They even suggested, somewhat naively, that it might reach some arrangement with mine owners if Congress collected money to replace recruitment and pass office fees.[50]

There was a growing perception by Africans that passes adversely affected their working conditions by denying freedom of movement. The TNC declared before the 1919 Low Grade Mines Commission that the entire coercive system comprising contract labour, compounds and job colour bars existed to "obtain cheap and enforced labour". Therefore, it must be abolished. The TNC presented a comprehensive indictment of the system addressing worker grievances. Employer claims that African workers could survive on "traditional" needs were false. Recruitment fees and wage advances ensnared workers in debt. The mines did not inform newly recruited mineworkers about compulsory unpaid labour. TNC leaders raised in considerable detail the problems faced by black workers dealing with white foremen. They explained such exploitation in class terms, as due to the tendency of "capitalists and others" to "adopt unsavoury methods in the acquirement and mobilisation of labour", to secure cheap labour. Capital made "excess profits, to exploit the labour of others". TNC leaders vigorously raised labour issues at a meeting with the Minister of Justice in April. Makgatho stated, "The pass system is a form of slavery." Letanka argued that "forced labour" and passes compelled Africans to accept low wages. Herbert Msane charged that Native Affairs was "more concerned with protecting the interests of the employers" than Africans. J. T. Matshige (Matshiqi) stated that Africans felt a "grievance" that they could not freely leave employers.[51]

The TNC thus saw anti-pass agitation as very much part of the whole struggle for better working conditions. Government took careful note: the 1920 Inter-Departmental Committee on the Native Pass Laws floridly stressed that ever since the 1918 bucket strike, the aims of Congress had been to "abolish passes and [labour] contracts" to give Africans "freedom of action to paralyse the industrial world by strikes".[52] This was clearly an exaggeration, but reflected the intense involvement of Congress in the strikes.

In 1919, the TNC launched a co-ordinated campaign of passive resistance and pass destruction, tying this to wage demands. A TNC leader, Ntintili, speaking to a mass meeting on 12 January, linked the need to abolish passes to wage rises. At TNC meetings in Vrededorp on 26 January and 9 February, Mvabaza stated Africans should seek pay rises through industrial action. At a meeting on 23 February, Mabaso explained that the existence of short labour contracts and passes militated against effective worker action. After destroying passes, "we can easily see to the 1 shilling increase" and have freedom to leave employment, he argued. This view was echoed at many meetings called by the TNC in April, some of them attended by 2,000-4,000 people, and in a TNC leaflet circulated in the same month. The fact that TNC leaders stressed a close connection between struggles for wages and removal of passes was partly the result of pressure from below indicated by such large numbers. At a Vrededorp meeting on 1 April, passes were collected and it was agreed to urge workers to strike, to picket city workers, to concentrate on municipal compounds, and to mobilise mine clerks to involve the mineworkers. At several of these gatherings, speakers made a direct connection between abolishing passes and the success of wage demands. A young worker, recently released from gaol for protesting, declared at a TNC meeting in Vrededorp that his wage was merely £2 a week but he cared only for liberty. Ngojo spoke to the same meeting, arguing that if unity was achieved then "surely all the mine boys and everybody can rise up" and join their protests. However, fierce state repression largely quarantined mineworkers from the agitation.[53]

Immediately before these events, there had been a strike by miners at Springs. Police saw this as evidence of "propaganda work". A Wesleyan minister, Hlabangwane, told Native Affairs the TNC was "entirely responsible" for unrest in Pretoria. When police arrested ten Africans carrying a bag of passes, they all gave their name simply as "Congress". The courts convicted three of "inciting and inducing" after they had "held out sacks and invited natives to put their passports [passes] therein".[54]

Some of these protests incorporated aspects of unionism. *The Star* reported that in Johannesburg "several thousand" Africans marched to the Pass Office, where speakers explained the tactics: "strike and decline to carry passes", whilst "pickets ... entered shops and demanded the passes of the Native employees". Both employer and employee testimonies confirm penetration of workshops by TNC activists. Manager Oswald Field stated they "molested" his employees. Another manager, Seider, saw a large crowd of 500 Africans threaten "to pull out all the boys who were working". Worker "Japie" recounted how TNC leaders entered his workshop and told all Africans "to stop work and join them (the Congress)" and "to strike at once". Workers immediately joined the crowd. Police reported that many black workers were "accosted" and "told to strike for an advance of pay". Rolling demonstrations swept across the Rand. There were hundreds of arrests.[55]

Awareness of connections between wages and passes was apparent in other arenas. Evidence to a commission into allegations of police brutality pointed to such a connection. Commissioner George Boyes concluded, that "a large section of the natives were very upset" by pass laws. A February 1919 meeting of the Boksburg TNC heard speeches from workers who complained laws "did not give them a chance to travel about freely and get work". A detective observed that ever since, local Africans had been complaining about passes and low wages. He attributed the radical mood to Josiah Matshiqi, Boksburg TNC Secretary, employed on the mines as a clerk, who had issued leaflets aimed at workers, calling a meeting to discuss "native wages ... pass laws ... illtreatment of natives underground and [their] being compelled to work at lashing without adequate pay". About 200 people subsequently attended a meeting in April at which passes were collected. Police were concerned that agitation would spread to the mine compounds due to Matshiqi's mine contacts. The TNC attempted to penetrate other compounds. In 1919, Pretoria Secretary T. D. Ditshego requested permission to hold TNC meetings inside railway and cement company compounds. The government denied the request.[56]

The situation in Pretoria summed up the bonds Congress was developing with workers. Some 1,000 Africans attended an April TNC 1919 anti-pass meeting. Organisers hoped to raise a levy of 2/6 on every African for Congress funds to fight the pass laws. Press reports noted many attending were workers from the central and eastern parts of the city, who afterwards marched back to their workplaces in formation, closely followed by mounted police. There had been several such meetings in Pretoria around the time, one of which saw 16 protestors, including one woman, arrested.[57]

Mabaso and Bud-M'belle co-authored a Johannesburg TNC leaflet addressed "To our people in Town and in the Compound," which bluntly stated: "We want rights. We want living. We want money." They explained the rejection of wage demands as due to passes and informed compound workers that on May Day African workers would "hold their own meeting where they will discuss grievances". Police reported that the leaflet "freely circulated" among workers in E.R.P. mines compound—indicating a successful, if temporary, TNC penetration of closed compounds. Bud-M'belle, Dunjwa and P. J. Motsoake disclosed further TNC attempts to reach workers. In a *Star* interview, they revealed the TNC intended to use passive resistance and had invited all Africans, whether working in stores, houses or mines, to strike. Bud-M'belle was less restrained by fear of social ostracism than SANNC leaders. He put his position as a clerk in jeopardy when convicted in 1919 during what he later termed the anti-pass "upheaval". After release from gaol, he did not hesitate to address a TNC May Day meeting, calling on those present to heed a call from an earlier meeting to strike. After the meeting, he travelled to Bloemfontein and Queenstown to consult with chiefs on passes, and continued to associate with the IWA and Thibedi, indicating his socialist commitment.[58]

Speakers raised the necessity to strike at other TNC meetings. At Vrededorp in May, branch chairman "Moshoeshoe" told a crowd of 200 people that the TNC would soon call "a general strike" to demand government "destroy passes, tax[es] and increase wages". It had decided that those who continued to work and carry passes would not be victimised, but would be levied to support those gaoled. Mr. Tsitsi stated that Africans had "opened a new Congress there on the hill", referring to the gaol. TNC meetings at the end of June heard Mabaso, Tsitsi, Selby Msimang and Dunjwa argue "that all the wealth of the Europeans … was derived … from … native labour, and that if all native labourers would unite and stop working … it would bring the white man to a realisation of the value of native labour". There were more anti-pass mass meetings from September to December in Johannesburg, Vrededorp and Pretoria. A TNC meeting in December was addressed by Mabaso, Z. P. Ramailane, and James Ngojo (who acted as TNC Secretary during Bud-M'belle's gaoling), and passed resolutions against passes and high prices. Ngojo, with his Ethiopianist background, probably elicited active support for the anti-pass campaign among Ethiopianists such as G. G. H. Makunga, expelled from the National Catholic Episcopal Church for preaching "sedition against the Government" during the campaign.[59]

The TNC endorsed typically working-class tactics such as picketing. At a meeting on 3 April 1919, groups of 20-30 people were "chosen to go in the town and stop the other boys from working". It promptly replaced—in ways reminiscent of the UDF in the 1980s—the arrested leaders. A speaker stated: "When your leaders are arrested you must be leaders yourself." Women were mobilised to penetrate the mines and raise funds. Mvabaza advised workers at a TNC meeting in January that if employers refused to let the women "enter compounds you must strike, strike, and stop the work". A woman, Miss Kekane, threatened to kill any man she knew with a pass.[60]

By mid-1919, arrests and disunity slowed the campaign's momentum. Divisions arose at TNC gatherings in June and July. At a meeting in July, only a small group led by Horatio Bud-M'belle and Thibedi dissented from a decision that passes would have to be accepted. Moderate leaders convinced

TRANSVAAL
NATIVE
CONGRESS.
(JOHANNESBURG BRANCH.)

THE ANTI-PASS CRY.

WE are fighting against tyranny and oppression. We refuse to be any longer degraded and enslaved here in the land of our birth, for the mere reason that we happen to be black (natives). We claim liberty. We plead for justice. · We are loyal. · We appeal for co-operation and monetary armaments. **GOD IS OUR HELPER.**

Transvaal Native Congress card, ca. 1919

workers to refrain from striking. Chief Solomon told workers at a social function on 5 July to eschew anti-pass agitation. He criticised the TNC as "a body which had acted without the authority of the Chiefs". When Lydenburg workers favoured striking in April, Chief Manok advised them against it, as did Sol Plaatje, who warned them not to "quarrel with your Masters". Not all accepted this. Worker Jacobus Ditabeni retorted: "it is all very well [what] Plaatje spoke about, but … we must strike". Not all chiefs were so moderate. At a TNC meeting in July, Chief Pilane declared Africans should pursue strikes and must unite. Despite differences over tactics, anti-pass actions continued. Talk of a "general native strike" continued at meetings in July. Radicals Horatio Bud-M'belle, Dunjwa, Mabaso, and Ngojo were re-elected at TNC elections in August. The TNC agreed the campaign had paid scant attention to areas outside Johannesburg and held meetings from Benoni and Hammanskraal to Koefontein farm in Springs, Pietersburg and Lydenburg. Its message now had more potential of filtering down to other industrial, and farm workers. In Benoni, TNC agitation led to 231 people being arrested. Such intimidation drove many to seek new passes from "their employers", indicating the presence of workers among the protesters.[61]

There also was solid support for Congress around Waterberg. The district had sent the largest number of delegates to the 1913 SANNC conference, suggesting multiple branches. Activists included Saak Mabalane, Paulus Mogale, Enoch Maloa, Jeremiah Makgatlhe, and Skoto Mamba. A TNC Waterberg East branch, founded in 1918 and claiming 800 "members" by 1919, protested about aged people "still pressed and forced to farm work", forced youth labour and eviction of labourers for insubordination. TNC meetings in Doornkop in 1919 discussed matters that affected workers—such as taxes, passes, beer, and location conditions. A mass meeting in Potchefstroom addressed by Makgatho passed resolutions against taxes and passes. A memorandum of the Bethal magistrate warning that African tax receipts for 1919 amounted to only 50 per cent of the 1918 total showed the effectiveness of TNC calls for a moratorium on taxes. [62]

The Pietersburg Congress branch, as Bonner shows, meshed its policies nicely with chieftainship politics, particularly in the Matlala chiefdom. In August 1919, a mass meeting called by the branch demanded the removal of the Sub-Native Commissioner or else they would launch a general strike. The following year it launched a vigorous campaign against greatly increased poll taxes. Over 100 local people were arrested but they were subsequently acquitted, and the Poll Tax overturned. [63]

The TNC also drew big crowds in Doornkop, Middleburg and Potchefstroom. In Doornkop, Makgatho and Horatio Bud-M'belle raised the prospect of a general strike. At Wakkerstroom, a meeting of 600 people in October demanded abolition of passes. In November, a similar number heard Mabaso present a report prepared by "the Committee of the Congress" detailing cost of living figures on food, fuel and rent. The report demonstrated many workers could not survive honestly. Indicating a broad conception of the constituency of Congress, he claimed "the whole of the natives of South Africa" as members. He disclosed it had 677 members "out of the thousands of natives employed in Johannesburg" and hoped "the whole of the native workers on the Rand should enrol"—symptomatic of the outreach of TNC leaders and their apparent lack of fear of workers. The meeting passed a motion moved by Ramailane that all workers should ask for a wage increase and, if unsuccessful, should strike and bring their employer's address to Congress for "suitable action". The meeting agreed to raise a £1000 strike fund in case of scabbing by workers from other provinces, suggesting the TNC was learning from white union tactics. TNC leaders consequently met twice with employers in January 1920, securing a vague commitment of wage increases for some, but not mineworkers. This was communicated to a meeting of 3,000 that included many miners. Two weeks later, a strike of 71,000 black mineworkers erupted, a momentous event discussed in detail in Chapter 9.[64]

Bonner ascribes Congress involvement in the protests and strikes of 1918-1920 to the pressure of crises on a wavering middle class, influenced by reduced wages. Worker demands found some support among a "stunted" black "petty bourgeoisie" more likely to contemplate "downward identification" with workers with its upward mobility blocked by the state. Wage differentials between black strata were small and the rise of relatively more radical Congress leaders met the objective political conditions for cross-class alliance. Simultaneously, a degree of class stratification and residential polarisation, and strong state pressure on African civil servants not to engage in politics inclined propertied black people, exemplified by Saul Msane and Isaiah Bud-M'belle, towards moderation.[65]

This is a compelling argument. Nevertheless, what were the origins of TNC sympathies with workers that saw it distance itself so quickly from the SANNC and openly defend worker rights? I argue such ties were not a momentary impulse. Historians often view the 1918-1920 protests as a deviation from a normally moderate ANC path. Yet TNC sympathy for workers was more long-term. Whilst economic crisis thrust its leaders into a position of solidarity, it was the interplay of political factors—policies of already-established TNC branches, initiatives of new political and industrial bodies, and actions of individuals—that focused discontent. The common socio-economic position of Africans, exacerbated by political discrimination more acute in the Transvaal, was a constant factor inclining TNC leaders to view workers as allies. Though their prior protests against labour conditions were less intense than in 1918-1920, TNC attitudes expressed in this period were in keeping with its earlier declarations. By articulating earlier opposition to the colour bar, which in turn was a major cause of worker discontent, it indirectly contributed to the cohesion of strikers. Moreover, the very formation of the TNC and its ability to monitor conditions of workers through *Abantu-Batho* and obtain feedback from workers through mass meetings strengthened African urban political organisation. In other words, viable methods of propaganda and structures of organisation already existed in the TNC.

If the TNC was to take up labour demands seriously then actions of individual members had to make these background forces explicit. Particular leaders did take up these demands. They did so for different reasons. Some had contact with socialists or workers. Other keenly felt the crisis of imperial and state hegemony when the War's end failed to solve black problems. The involvement of radical socialists in African protests helped keep agitation focused on labour issues. Socialism provided coherent explanations for labour exploitation though it did not yet convincingly explain national oppression. The vigorous involvement of workers in the events fed the growing TNC concern for wages. Socialist ideas sharpened by economic crisis and state and employer intransigence at times inspired the attitudes of TNC members to workers. It also was a further development of a longer period of TNC interest in and sympathy for black workers. A closer focus on individual leaders and their organ *Abantu-Batho* makes this clearer.

"Fight This Control and Abolish It": The Congress Press

Whereas SANNC leaders tended to shy away from direct support of workers, their TNC counterparts more strongly identified with black labour struggles. The role of these leaders in labour protests has been outlined, but it is useful to focus on a common thread in their political careers, *Abantu-Batho*, in which they articulated their radicalism.

Congress supporters financed and launched *Abantu-Batho*, which the TNC declared its organ in 1918. Promoters of a linked £5,000 capital float for the African Trading Company included Dunjwa, Letanka, Kapan, Mvabaza, Mabaso and Selope Thema. Members were urged to read "their press". At a TNC meeting in Doornkop in 1919 Ngojo urged those present to read it to "know Congress news" and be aware of threats "imposed by the white people". At a Vrededorp meeting, TNC leader Ntintili stated: "Buy the *Abantu-Batho* paper which will open your brain to understand how things are going on … Do not say you cannot read, someone will read for you."[66]

Abantu-Batho editors and staff included Cleopas Kunene, Letanka, Mvabaza, Dunjwa, Mabaso, Grendon, Saul Msane, Herbert Msane, Horatio Bud-M'belle, Skota, Selope Thema and Ben Phooko. Many became interested in labour issues. Mvabaza, a SANNC founder, worked as a location wardsman in Port Elizabeth before becoming *Abantu-Batho* editor in 1913, in which role he championed the cause of black labour and urged Congress to demand higher wages. Letanka worked as a musician, interpreter, and then as journalist and poorly paid secretary-bookkeeper of *Abantu-Batho*. Dunjwa was an interpreter and teacher before joining *Abantu-Batho* in 1913 as Xhosa editor, in which role, after visiting the mines, he exposed the harsh conditions of miners. He earned as little as £5 a month. In July 1919, he took up the case of a young African worker dismissed from work. Phooko, a clerk on City Deep mine, expressed solidarity with strikers in 1918.[67]

Mabaso worked as a teacher, clerk, shopkeeper, and on the mines. He served as *Abantu-Batho* secretary-bookkeeper. An indication of his identification with workers was his 1919 speech as TNC chairman welcoming home South African war leader (and Director of Native Labour) Colonel Pritchard. "We know ... that you have got to please the Government and the Mining Magnates, but we hope that you will not be the first to forget us, the native labourers, and how we are affected by the high cost of living."[68]

Grendon, a "coloured" teacher and poet educated at Zonnebloem, had been a supporter of the black franchise since the 1890s. He worked as a printer (on *Inkanysio yase Natal*), as a teacher at Edendale (1900-1903), Ohlange (1904), Swaziland (as tutor for Queen Labotsibeni) and Johannesburg, and as a journalist, periodically editing *Abantu-Batho*. In a 1977 interview with Couzens, Selby Msimang recalled Grendon as "'very radical' and 'inclined to be leftist'". Grendon strongly sympathised with black workers. In 1918, referring to successful struggles of white workers and Indian passive resisters, he wrote that the black person "has learnt two important lessons ... It is now his turn to question the laws laid down for the control of his industry and toil, which he—educated, as well as raw—perceives are producing wealth, and ease, and luxury for others". He not only drew attention to this rising class-consciousness but also pointed to political solidarity, arguing that: "The White Socialist is in principle a brother to the Black Socialist."[69]

Horatio Bud-M'belle and Herbert Msane both wrote for *Abantu-Batho*. Bud-M'belle matriculated from Lovedale, entered the civil service and worked as an articled clerk for Seme. His radicalism did not end with the June strikes. In July 1918, he was on a "committee dealing with the Native Wages' movement". In 1919 and 1921, he took a leading role in pass protests. Skota called him "one of the foremost leaders of his people". Herbert Msane played a major role injecting socialist ideas into the TNC. He printed socialist leaflets in Zulu in October 1917; in November, he gave one of the earliest arguments by an African in favour of radical unionism: workers were organising for their rights; the idea of industrial organisation was valid; therefore, they should join the IWA.[70]

Abantu-Batho sympathetically reported labour over a long period. In 1916 it bewailed the wretchedness of "unskilled labour and all kinds of drudgery, both in the mines and in urban areas ... by [Africans who] ... belong to the working class, are the mainstay of the country's industries ... the most worked and the least paid". As already noted this report took up the cause of working women and, "in the absence of organised labour", urged the TNC to intervene on labour matters.[71]

A number of themes emerge from this report: a clear recognition of black labour's central economic role; close attention to conditions of, not elite, but low-paid, female workers; appeal to the TNC to seek state intervention for labour protection—indicating that Congress was seen as a capable and legitimate body to address labour matters.

The ISL perceived that this report "sounds at last the initial rumblings of a spontaneous, indigenous class-conscious industrial movement", but caricatured *Abantu-Batho* as a "humble henchman" of the capitalist press. Despite this criticism from the white left, it continued to protest passes and spoke in similar terms against contracts imposed on domestic workers. Against a backdrop of rising oppression, the TNC organ saw a cause and a clear political solution: "oppressing laws ... [are] our fault because we do not report our grievances ... Congress ... can accept our grievances, but [we] do not want to make them known. There are bad times coming, my friends, so we must be on the look-out."[72]

Abantu-Batho was "on the look-out" during rising labour agitation in 1918, reporting workers' meetings and describing miner response in ways suggesting first-hand contact. It attacked the contract system itself, revealing a strong commitment to change industrial relations. Using the gaoling of strikers as an example, it argued that Africans "cannot go on strike like the white people" because of contracts; hence it was necessary to "fight this control and abolish it". It called on Africans to emulate Gandhi's passive resistance and the 1914 white strikers, concluding, "Under the British Empire you shall never get anything if you do not go on strike." It urged black people to "go up to the fort [gaol] for the [purpose of challenging the labour] contract". They must fight for shorter contracts that would not hamstring their ability to take industrial action. Readers were invited to send in ideas on how to abolish contracts.[73] *Abantu-Batho* thus advocated to workers an alternative strategy of resistance to exploitation with clear demands that, if implemented, would have extended their industrial rights.

In 1918, *Abantu-Batho* criticised job colour bars. It described strikes and explained their causes. It pointed out that since many of those who struck were refused permission to attend a Congress meeting that decided against industrial action, and hence believed others were on strike, it was publishing the decision that "every worker must read so that he may know". The implicit suggestion that many workers read the paper was dreaming, but it indicates the claim of ties with black labour. *Abantu-Batho* warned readers not to be "misled by statements ... written in the name of ... [Saul] Msane" who uses a silk hat … He is the one who now says the Compound natives must not ask for the increase of their wages … He is the Vice-President of the Congress … [but] never attended any of the meetings held about the sanitary boys … but he is seen standing in the Whiteman's Office alone … Every man must understand that he is not talking for the Congress … He must go, there is no hope for him to natives.[74]

The findings of the Moffat Commission and the court case of ISL, IWA and TNC leaders were closely reported. *Abantu-Batho*, in detailing the comments of J. B. Moffat (Chief Magistrate, Transkeian Territories), drew attention to inadequate compensation for injured mine labourers, passes, low wages and poor housing of workers. In outlining the arguments of the protagonists in the court case, the Congress newspaper helped popularise among Africans such ideas as the need for industrial organisation of black people, and that "the reward of the workers should have no distinction of colour".[75]

Abantu-Batho's reporting was not restricted to the Rand. It reported protests over high prices by black people in Durban, and demands by 2,000 black workers in East London for a shilling increase. It called attention to struggles by African workers for higher wages in goods sheds and railway workshops in Pietermaritzburg. Their wages, it stated, should be increased. Black workers were urged to maintain their agitation for a wage increase every time that they were paid, even if threatened with dismissal.[76]

Abantu-Batho kept its readers informed about the progress of black negotiations with government over wages. In 1919, it continued to report anti-pass protests as the TNC extended the campaign across the Rand and into the countryside. However, the role of the paper was not limited to reporting: the TNC viewed it as an organising tool. Africans were directed to make campaign donations via *Abantu-Batho* offices, which would then publish lists of donors. Mvabaza warned that he did not want to see chiefs relying on Native Recruiting Corporation hospitality when visiting the Rand. Instead, "they must go to the Bantu Batho" for all their needs. Chiefs should collect "money from their people and send that to the Bantu Batho". At a TNC meeting in Vrededorp in February 1919, Mabaso urged workers willing to throw away their work passes to send their names to *Abantu-Batho* so that "we can print them [and] when any trouble comes we can then call them".[77]

The 1920 mine strike was very sympathetically covered by the Congress press. Its attitude to the king, who had consented to turning black rights "upside down" at Union, mirrored this radicalism. Congress deputations were "ignored with the usual hypocritical" stance he protected all his subjects. This was the case, *Abantu-Batho* noted, only in war, not peace, adding irreverently, "It is nonsense for any king to speak like that."[78]

This militancy had its price. By 1919, powerful state and business interests, supported by Saul Msane, determined that a counter was needed to marginalise the TNC. In the early 1920s TNC communication lines with black workers were choked off by company-funded newspapers and state initiatives. Self Mampuru of the Transvaal Congress, in a 1943 pamphlet, gave three reasons for the decline of a militant TNC: "police terrorism and offers of good posts in government departments to the leaders of Congress"; lack of TNC "administrative experience"; and leadership friction: the 1918-1920 strikes "did not succeed because there were many Moses in the Congress".[79]

"You Europeans Do Not Work, We Are the People Who Work."

Mampuru had his roots in rural Transvaal, in what is today Limpopo Province. Many Africans working on the Rand returned to rural areas when they could, and Congress had wide support across these lands. After all, the TNC, as noted in Chapter 3, had its origins in African political organisations in the Northern Transvaal where the predecessors of the ANC had strong support among both commoners and chiefs, and in cities like Pretoria and Pietersburg. Congress did form branches in other parts of rural Transvaal, though it is not always clear whether they paid allegiance to the TNC or SANNC. The ripples caused by the 1913 Land Act aroused many rural peoples. Congress leaders and local Congress branches protested the attack on black rights.

Makgatho, representing both the Transvaal Native Council (Congress) as President, and the SANNC, as Vice-President, boldly presented black grievances over the Land Act to Sir William Beaumont of the Natives Land Commission in Pretoria in April 1914. He complained about loss of lands, lack of consultation, and evictions of farm tenants and farm workers who must now face the prospect of being forced to contract the labour of their entire family, including wives and children. Africans were likely to get the worst farms, and be forced to live in climates they were not used to that would be injurious to their health. Segregation was a "painful thing". Unlike subservient chiefs, who often used (though perhaps with a touch of irony) the phrase "we are your dogs", Makgatho asserted African dignity and spoke plainly: "We look upon this [Act] as slavery, nothing else." TNC General-Secretary, E. H. Chake, an interpreter based in Pretoria and SANNC founder, followed Makgatho, showing that African land holdings whether in urban or rural areas were under threat.[80]

In both Eastern and Western Transvaal, shrinking access to land and advancing (partial) proletarianisation intensified class stratification and political divisions within many chieftaincies, which in turn could influence Congress politics (see Chapters 9 and 12). These processes intensified in the next two decades but even in the 1910s, the land situation was to become acute.

In October 1917 at Pokwani, the Pedi Chief told government officials his lands were "too small ... old and useless. The location is overcrowded." The following month at Schoonoord, Stephanus Isesane (a counsellor to Chief Gelukwe, away in France with the Native Regiment) remarked that many of their people worked on farms but "don't care to be farm labourers because they don't get a chance of ploughing their own land". It was the same story everywhere.[81]

In the Western Transvaal, challenges from below to the authority of chiefs were particularly pronounced among smaller Tswana chiefdoms around Rustenburg. At first Congress courted local chiefs. Based on archival rather than oral sources, Graeme Simpson estimates TNC influence in Rustenburg "at best sporadic and haphazard". His evidence shows local chiefs in regular contact with Congress only in 1917, when the TNC held meetings on the Land Act in Phokeng and Leeuwkraal attended by Sol Plaatje and SANNC President Makgatho at which police spies claimed there was radical talk. Simpson argues the Land Act forged "a tenuous and short-lived alliance between the T.N.C. leaders and land-hungry chiefs". He ascribes the decline in TNC activity to a combination of Congress support for pro-democracy elements opposed to chiefly autocracy and to radicalisation of Congress on the Rand that alienated traditional leaders; for example, Chiefs Mamogale and Mokgatle *supported* pass enforcement and arrests against the TNC "Young Turks" leading the 1919 protests. Earlier, in 1918, Councillor Ramochane from Saulspoort had derided moderate chiefs. Others, such as Isang Pilane, son of Linchwe, were under police suspicion of linking up with Congress or even rebellion. In other areas of Western and Northern Transvaal, as Bradford notes for the 1920s, Congress had much stronger local support than the radical ICU, a support that had first arisen in the 1910s.[82]

The state used the large number of farm and migrant labourers in the Boshof and Hoopstad districts to deny black land claims. Andreas Mokoele, Boshof Branch Secretary of Congress and a teacher, in 1918 presented a petition of some 500 "men and women spent with toil" from the region, complaining of land dispossession and high taxes, warning of future labour supply scarcity and proposing land grants under "self-government".[83]

Turning to the Eastern Transvaal, Morrell found little evidence of TNC activity of Middelburg, except in 1919. In a later study he did remark on TNC campaigns there of the mid-1920s (see Chapter 9). Congress leaders such as Seme and Msimang had however toured Transvaal rural areas, especially in the north and east, since the time of the Land Act, collecting funds. In June 1914, Chief Jafita of the Middleburg district spoke wearily of his people "driven from the land" and "working on the farms without pay—for nothing; every member of the family has to work and we receive no remuneration". In 1917, Dirk Kana of Berlin Mission Station, Lydenburg recalled speaking with a member of the Congress British delegation (probably Saul Msane).[84]

Evidence to the Beaumont Commission from South-Eastern Transvaal gives an inkling of Congress' connection with labourers. In 1914, labourers and chiefs from Heidelberg and Standerton expressed their opposition to the Land Act. Farm labourers Jabob Maloie and "Jhlameni" both made a plea for land. In April 1914, numerous Congress-backed meetings had been held around Heidelberg and a document under the name of the SANNC was drawn up articulating grievances of "delegates and branches". T. M. Dambuza read it to the Commission: it spoke bluntly of the "uneasiness and alarm" and ruination caused by the Act, that "causes our people to be derelicts and helpless", rejected segregation, and called for a form of self-government for black townships or reserves. The petition drew attention to old workers being evicted as they lacked children of working age "worn out faithful servants who have served most of their life time on farms and who would be quite paralysed by this Act". The petition used the metaphor of winter to characterise the Land Act: "In winter the trees are stripped and leafless." Dambuza also raised the question of working hours, objecting to tenant labourers having to work for white farmers for nine months, arguing it was unfair. What black people wanted from government, he added, was clear work contracts "so that if there is any unfairness we may know where to run to and complain".[85]

Black commoners and chiefs from other areas echoed Makgatho's sentiments, not only on rural land issues but also concerning urban workers. "The white man is suppressing us … [and] will suppress us under his foot … We have no representation in the Union Parliament," stated Reverend G. W. Nkosi of Ermelo. Johan Msimang, a farm tenant of Ermelo, opposed dispossession from lands where they had laboured and for which they had paid. Jeremiah Ngwenya, a Bethal farm tenant, worried that African people would be left only with land consisting of "stone kopjes"; Makomane Ntsweni also of Bethal, a squatter, complained he would have to split up his family and sell cattle before he could squat. Stanton Nzoyi, of Leslie township, Bethal district, presented a statement signed by himself and 34 others. Congress possibly influenced matters, as there were branches in the area that petitioned "for the establishment of a farm labourers' office to regulate the written agreements of wages and time of service, and to facilitate the engagement of farm labourers", one of the earliest attempts to protect farm labourers.[86]

In Pietersburg, it was the same story of land hunger and labour exploitation. The district was overwhelmingly African, comprising some 215,335 black people to only 10,908 white people in this period. In May 1914, Chief Zebediela urged more land for his people, many of whom worked on the farms and especially the mines. Headmen Cornelius Makapan and Aaron Nawa, whose people supplied farm labour, echoed the call for more land, as did Chief Mphahlele, an original member of Makgatho's African National Political Union. Other chiefs deployed biting metaphors to show their exasperation with white rule: Chief Mamaboel snorted: "I scarcely know whether I am a human being or not." Chief Kibi said government "just seem to throw us away ... Bicycles and motor cars ... just run over us; they cut our legs off, and also our arms." In Louis Trichardt, Zoutpansberg traditional leaders expressed similar frustration. Headman Piet Booi lamented, "our children ... go out to work, and they return with probably an arm lost or a foot cut of due to accidents"—and they were forced out to work to pay unjust taxes. Chief Senthimula remarked African child labourers on white farms stood little chance of impartial justice if charged with an offence. Chief Shikunda similarly grieved that "our children have returned from the towns, where they have been working, without a penny, because they have been fined right and left, and for no offence at all". Moreover, he added, "you Europeans do not work, we are the people who work. The train was brought here by us; we laid the track out."[87]

The Ermelo District Branch held meetings in January 1918, which rejected the Native Affairs Administration Bill, called for the shelving of such legislation until after the War, and urged consultation with Africans. Branch leaders Solomon Tutu, Simon Siluma, Joseph Msimang, and Joseph Hlubi found segregation repugnant and asserted their rights to land. Hlubi complained of the lack of freedom for black workers on white farms. He told the Eastern Transvaal Natives Land Committee acerbically that, if the English had been segregated from the Romans, they would not be what they were today. The government, he declared, "Want to keep us underfoot"; the Bill "is killing us".[88]

Other Congress leaders addressed the Eastern Transvaal Land Committee. Selope Thema, then working as a solicitor's clerk, addressed issues of land

and representation but he was willing to adopt a reformist approach to try to increase African land holdings even though he made it clear that he opposed the Act. Makgatho, representing the SANNC, spoke of the difficult lives of African people both in rural areas and in Riverside, Pretoria, where he lived and where most residents were domestic workers and, even after 11 years, lacked sanitation services. In the countryside, farm-worker families, with males away at the War, had been dismissed from farms with government making no provision. Filipus Bopape of Leshoane Mission wrote to the Sub-Native Commissioner in Pietersburg condemning the forced labour—"working for nothing 'Boroko'"—on white farms.[89]

Saul Msane was strident in his opposition to the Land Act at Graskop in October 1917. He bluntly told state officials that Africans had fought against the Act that "took away rights that we formerly possessed. We were astonished that such a thing should happen under the British flag." The moral economy of British justice had clearly been broken. There was no justice in the chronic inequality of the Act; "You want to destroy us". The law "is unjust to us, it destroys us". Because of the war "we suspended our agitation, but we have not dropped it". He emphasised conditions appeared to indicate slavery and prayed that the Act would be repealed. The other speakers, David Mokuena and Jonas Mapope, supported Msane. Mokuena stated: "We sent our people to England to fight this Act."[90]

The ability of the young Congress movement to recruit or mobilise in these rural towns, farms, and mines must have been very limited. Workers themselves had even less resources with which to build their own protective structures. To take one example, in the isolated mines around Sabie, plague devastated 20 per cent of the mine workforce in 1918 and in the following year, many workers did not return to work, the mine operating at only 30-50 percent strength. The situation, wrote a local settler, merely underlined that "We are dependent on the native labourer". [91] The question was whether black workers could form unions or, in their absences, whether Congress could step into the breach.

The evidence presented above points to an organisation well informed about the detail and problems of black rural and working lives and capable of boldly conceptualising and challenging the entire fabric of specific forms of capitalist exploitation. The TNC, whilst it included leaders with socialist leanings, had a less "pure" working-class ideology than the IWA. However, although IWA meetings continued to occur for some time, it failed to become a national movement, and dissolved into the ICU in 1919. The IWA, as Johnstone argues, probably pushed TNC politics "to more working class concerns". Nevertheless, he adds, Congress also shared "leadership roles among African workers".[92] Historians have not highlighted the Congress impact on the IWA. The TNC provided central IWA activists, who had gained their initial political tutoring in the TNC, and, in *Abantu-Batho*, an organisational tool and focus for mobilisation during protests. The IWA disappeared. Congress remained intact.

The TNC established a reputation among Africans, including workers, as a defender of their interests. The presence of its leaders in strikes suggests a commitment of a section of Congress to the well-being of workers and their willingness to speak out on this matter, even at a time of war when their loyalty could be questioned. The TNC came in touch with workers and seriously, if unsuccessfully, attempted to address their demands. This contact increased under the impact of economic crises. However, there were more constant factors: the more-or-less unbroken TNC record of sympathy for black workers; the influence of *Abantu-Batho*, which regularly drew attention to labour issues; the levelling effects of white repression on diverse black strata; and the creation of political bodies that facilitated unity in action. A window of contact between Congress and workers was opened. Moffat, reporting on the strikes, perspicaciously observed that the only place where black people "have a voice is in their meeting[s] of the Congress".[93]

Conclusion

Significant developments and events across its first decades exposed Congress in the Transvaal to both working-class as well as "petty bourgeois" influences. Proletarian influences, whilst not at all predominant in the organisation, helped incline Transvaal Congress members towards a more sympathetic understanding of worker needs. By 1920, it remained numerically small. Nevertheless, in two decades of lobbying, organising, and publicising the lot of black people under increasingly repressive white rule, they took up many matters vitally affecting the well-being of black workers and forged a reputation as defenders of all Africans. Congress achieved this partly through involvement in and support for protests against the Land Act and passes, and for better worker conditions. It also was due partly to activities of its own "organic" intellectuals who spread information about Congress activities and protested exploitation of black workers in meetings and in the press. Congress had contact with a wide range of black social strata, from chiefs to teachers and other urban wage earners. Much of this contact was occasional. The SANNC avoided directly organising workers but the Transvaal Congress was able to reach out more effectively than the SANNC to the "masses" and articulate broad national, political opposition to oppressive practices. It did this in a manner that made use of not just petitions but also mass meetings and public pronouncements, and was *inclusive* of, and often sympathetic to, black workers, if not specifically claiming to represent their *class* interests. Moreover, whereas in countries such as England and Australia, trade unions preceded and influenced formation of Labour parties, in South Africa Congress preceded the first African labour unions. It was thus in a position to influence them and act as a mentor.

The African proletariat in this period was small, divided and dispersed. It was only beginning to evolve new cultural formations and encounter socialism. It lacked its own unions, media, and recognised spokespersons. Hence, it was difficult either for Congress to establish firm and meaningful ties with workers, or for workers to appreciate ANC policies. Deep economic crises influenced the swing of radical Congressites to workers in 1918-1920. Both the consistent and broad ANC policies to unite and represent *all* Africans and some degree of personal interaction of its leaders with workers aided this orientation. Moreover, the construction by Congress of a definite if fragile political machine that included newspapers, annual conventions, and mass meetings aided these processes. Congress, some might still validly argue, eschewed working class forms of resistance. However, a tendency to romanticise strikes can make it too easy to paint Congress as aloof from labour. Workers had been involved in industrial action for decades but strikes were only one tactic in their arsenal. The peaceful presentation of demands, normally associated with Congress, was not alien to workers who undertook strikes only after exhaustion of appeals. Rejection by employers and governments of moderate appeals by workers and Congress inclined both to more radical steps. They learned from each other and from socialists: Congress learnt about strikes and mass action; workers learnt about propaganda and organisation. Under favourable circumstances, some ANC branches in closer proximity to workers supported strikes. That Congress was able to call so many large-scale protests and become (partly) involved in strikes indicated its growth and widening social base. The growing urban presence of workers increasingly made them more effective constituents of Congress. African politicians could not ignore them.

Whilst the engine of South African industrialisation was the Transvaal, less spectacular, but steady, involvement of Africans in the labour market in other provinces required the regional branches of a political organisation claiming to represent all Africans also to take cognisance of African workers in these areas, which we will now explore.

Notes

1   Walshe, *Rise of African Nationalism,* p. 223; R.V. Selope Thema, "The African National Congress: Its Achievements and Failures", *Umteteli wa Bantu* 14 and 21 Sep. 1929.
2   *Blue Book on Native Affairs 1910* (U17-11), p. 250.
3   "Reef Natives Quiet", *Rand Daily Mail* 13 May 1919.
4   "Imbizo yaBantu Ejozi (The South African National Congress)", *Izwe la Kiti* 2 Apr. 1913.
5   *International* 15 Dec. 1916 citing *Abantu-Batho* 30 Nov. 1916; *Tsala ea Batho* 16 Aug. 1913.
6   "Constitution SANNC", s.9 15; Transvaal Archives Depot (TAD) Dept. Native Affairs (DNA) NTS 7204 17/326 "Transvaal African Congress ", TNC Constitution [1918?]; TNC membership card, JUS, 3/527.17. At the time, "class laws" could refer to race laws.
7   Gladstone to Sec. of State, 12-13 Jul. 1913, *British Documents on Foreign Affairs*, v. 10, pp. 360-371.
8   "Repatriating the Natives" *Transvaal Leader* 10 Jan. 1914, reprinted in *Correspondence Relating to the Recent General Strike*, p. 38. See also Chapter 4 on John Dube's profession of SANNC loyalty.
9   *Report of Native Grievances Inquiry 1913-1914* (U.G.37-14) p. 64. Characterisation of worker resistance as inevitably "violent" emerged in other colonial situations: see Chandavarkar, *Imperial Power*, pp. 156-157.
10 S. Parnell, "Race, Power and Urban Control: Johannesburg's Inner City Slum-Yards, 1910-1923", *JSAS* v. 29 (2003), pp. 615-623, pp. 620-621; U17-11, p. 349; D. Gaitskell, "'Christian Compounds for Girls': Church Hostels for African Women in Johannesburg, 1907-1970" , *JSAS* v. 6 (1979), pp. 44-69: D. Gaitskell "Female Mission Initiatives: Black and White Women in Three Witwatersrand Churches, 1903-1939", Ph.D., University of London, 1981, pp. 118, 201. For domesticity in an earlier period see J. and J.L. Comaroff, "Home-Made Hegemony: Domesticity, Modernity, and. Colonialism in South Africa", in K. Hansen (ed). *African Encounters with Domesticity* (New Brunswick: Rutgers University Press, 1992), pp. 37-74.
11 K. Eales, "'Jezebels': Good Girls and Mine Married Quarters, Johannesburg, 1912", African Studies seminar Wits, Oct. 1988, and "'Good Girls' vs 'Bad Girls'", *Agenda* 4 (1989), pp. 1-22, p. 17.
12 Eales, "'Jezebels'", pp. 18-20 citing NTS 86 3338/19/F164 and TNC evidence to Commission. Others to give evidence included S. M. Makgatho, Stephen Mini, and Levi Mvabasa, editor of *Moloma oa Batho*: *Report of the Commission Appointed to Enquire into Assaults on Women, 1913* (UG39-13), pp. v-ix. Rubusana was both paternalistic and modernist: in 1913, he supported increased African women's legal rights and opposed their minority status in Natal: *Report from the Select Committee on Native Custom & Marriage Laws* (SC6-1913), p. 15.
13 J. Nauright, "'Black Island in a White Sea': Black and White in the Making of Alexandra Township, South Africa, 1912-1948", Queens University, 1992, Chapter 1, especially pp. 52-61, citing JUS 234 3/460/16, letter of E. P. Mart Zulu 20 Dec. 1919.
14 Gaitskell, "Female Mission Initiatives", p. 162.
15 "Native Drudgery" *Abantu-Batho* Nov. 1916 in *International* 1 Dec. 1916; "Passes for Women," (original) and "Women and Pass Law" (translated) *Abantu-Batho* 20 Dec. 1917; M. Poseka, "About Native Women's Passes", *Abantu-Batho* 13 Dec. 1917 (translation);

"A Resolution: Native Women Pass Law," *Abantu-Batho* 6 Dec. 1917 (attached to SAP Ermelo to SAP Pretoria 12 Dec. 1917), JUS 3/527/17.

16 "Native Drudgery", *Abantu-Batho* Nov. 1916 cited in *International* 1 Dec. 1916; "Women and Pass Law", *Abantu-Batho* 20 Dec. 1917, translation, JUS 3/527/17.

17 *Abantu-Batho* 6, 12, 20 Dec. 1917 clippings and translations, JUS 3/527/17, "The National League of Bantu Women (Transvaal Province)", *Abantu-Batho* 20 Dec. 1917 (copy of entire issue), JUS 3/527/17.

18 Report of Native Corporal S. Mofokeng, Ermelo, 18 Dec. 1917, JUS 3/527/17.

19 "National League of Bantu Women", *Abantu-Batho* 20 Dec. 1917; *Rand Daily Mail* 19 May 1919; K. Eales, "Patriarchs, Passes and Privilege: Johannesburg's African Middle Classes and the Question of Night Passes for African Women, 1920-31" in P. Bonner, *Holding their Ground,* pp. 105-140.

20 Police reports on meetings 18, 21, 31 Jan., [11 Feb.] 1918, JUS 3/527/17.

21 "Native Unrest", *International* 21 Jun. 1918; GNLB 281 446/17/D48: "TNNC & IWA" 19 Jun. 1918; "Details of Mass Meeting of ... Natives 19.6.[1]8"; police reports attached to CID to DNL 21-22 Jun. 1918; "TNNC & IWA" 29 Jun. 1918 and report of Moorosi 30 Jun. 1918, GNLB 281 446/17/D48; report of Jali 29 Jun. 1918, "The Workers' Indaba", *Abantu-Batho* Jul. 1918 [translated], JUS 3/527/17.

22 *Tsala ea Batho* 29 Aug. 1914; Transvaal National Council "Resolution" 11 Dec. 1916, NTS 7204 17/326; *International* 16 Jun., 15 Dec. 1916 ([Phooko] "Firm and Just: Or, Just and Firm".

23 Johnstone, *Class, Race & Gold*, pp. 173, 181; Grundlingh, *Fighting Their Own War*, p. 148; Simons, *Class & Colour*, p. 220; W. Andrews, *Class Struggles in South Africa* (Cape Town, 1941), p. 49; *Union Statistics* p. H-5, 23; *Natal Advertiser* 4 Apr. 1919; *Reports of the Special Commissioner appointed to Enquire into the Boycotting of Rand Storekeepers by Natives* (UG.4-19), pp. 1-2, 6-8. Prices of boots before the war were 10 shillings; now they were 17 shillings and blankets had skyrocketed from 6 shillings to 12/6d.

24 SAP. "Unrest amongst Natives in Benoni Area", 18 Feb. 1918, ER19/4/3/4, JUS; Baker, "Crisis", pp. 216-217, 248; "Comrade Bill Notebooks" v. 1, p. 67, *Cope Papers*, University of York; D.D.T. Jabavu ("Native Unrest in South Africa" *International Review of Missions* v. 11 1922, pp. 248-259) saw the war's effects as causing "growing tendencies for organisation on trade-union lines"; SAP Germiston to SAP Pretoria 11 Nov. 1919, JUS G.4/86/19. See also Breckenridge, "Speak for Ourselves", p. 78.

25 *International* 7 Jun. 1918; Bonner, "Transvaal Congress", p. 274; "Unrest in South Africa", *Round Table* v. 9 Dec. 1918, pp. 194-200, p. 198; *International* 2 Aug. 1918; *International*, 14 Jun. 1918.

26 *International* 18 Feb., 7 Apr., 2, 9 Jun. 1916; Meli, *South Africa Belongs to Us*, p. 59. Msane, to the ISL, was "the veteran spokesman of the industrialised native": *International* 9 Jun. 1916.

27 *International* 8 Jun., 9, 16 Mar. 1917; H. Bud-M'belle, "From the Native Standpoint", *International* 16 Mar. 1917; *International* 5 May 1917; R. Goode, "May Day: International Labour Day" *SALB* 9 (1984), pp. 58-76.

28 Thibedi to L. Trotsky, 10 Aug. 1932 in A. Drew (ed.) *South Africa's Radical Tradition* (Cape Town: UCT Press, 1996), v. 1, p. 130; *International* 3 May 1918; *Abantu-Batho* 18 Jul. 1918; KC v. 4, p. 107; Cope, *Comrade Bill*, p. 197; J. King to SAP 12 May 1919 (list of members appended), JUS 3/527/17; Odendaal, "African Political Mobilisation", p. 263; *Abantu-Batho* 15 May 1919 copy in TAD 7204 17/326; *Imvo Zabantsundu*, 16 Jul. 1918; Skota, *African Yearly Register*, p. 147.

29   F. Johnstone, "The IWA on the Rand: Socialist Organising among Black Workers on the Rand 1917-1918" in Bozzoli, *Labour & Protest*, pp. 248-272; Msane, "The Ethiopian Movement" *International* 21 Jul. 1916; "Internationalist Socialistic Meeting" 19 Jul., 15, 22 Nov. 1917, Msane, "White Natives", *Abantu-Batho* 22 Nov. 1917 (translated): JUS 3/527/17, *International* 30 Nov. 1917; *Sunday Times* 28, 7 Jul. 1918.

30   Police reports 15 Nov., 14 Sep. 1917, 21 Jan., 20 Feb. 1918, JUS 3/527/17; Simons, *Class & Colour*, p. 204; *Sunday Times* 7 Jul. 1918; *Cape Times* 8 Jul. 1918; police reports 4 Jul. 1918, "IWA enrolled," [Nov. 1917], SNA letter [Oct. 1917] and police reports 7, 24 Oct. 1917, 14, 17 Jan. 1918, in JUS 3/527/17.

31   SAP report of 16 Aug. 1917, JUS 3/527/17; *International* 4 Jan. 1918; Johnstone, "IWA," p. 259. B. Lahouel, "The Origins of Nationalism in Algeria, the Gold Coast and South Africa", Ph.D. Aberdeen University, 1984, pp. 471-473, 497, 548 argues that some ANC leaders had "direct knowledge of [labour] conditions", and were closer to black workers than "ISL fully privileged whites".

32   *Cape Times* 8, 10-11, 13, 15 Jun. 1918; "Transvaal Native National Congress" [TNNC] meeting report 10 Jun. 1918, TAD Director of Native Labour (GNLB) 281 446/17/D48. At a TNC meeting in Doornfontein on 30 Dec. 1919, and after *Nkosi Sikelel' iAfrika* was sung, Mabaso urged members to stop singing Rule Britannica and pray to a pre-colonial African God: report, 3 Jan. 1920, JUS 3/527/17.

33   "Transvaal Native National Congress" [report of meeting 12 Jun. 1918] in GNLB 281 446/17/D48; "Industrial Workers of Africa" 13 Jun. 1918, GNLB 281 446/17/D48; *International* 5 Jul. 1918.

34   *International* 21 Jun. 1918; "TNNC & IWA" [19 Jun. 1918]; "Details of Mass Meeting of...Natives 19.6.[1]8"; police reports attached to CID to DNL 21 and 22 Jun. 1918, all in GNLB 281 446/17/D48.

35   TNC letter [to employers] 20 Jun. 1918, JUS 3/527/17; *International* 30 Aug. 1918.

36   "Industrial Workers of Africa" [27 Jun. 1918 meeting], in GNLB 281 446/17/D48; Rex v. Msane 2 Jun. 1919, in *South African Law Reports (Transvaal Division)*, p. 197.

37   "Industrial Workers of Africa", report of Moorosi [27 Jun. 1918], "IWA"[13 Jun. 1918], GNLB 281 446/17/D48; CKC 2: XK20:96 (Kraai). On Kraai's election see: Report of Jali 17 Jan. 1918, JUS 3/54/l.

38   "ISL" [25 Jun. 1918 report] and Report of Moorosi 30 Jun. 1918, both in GNLB 281 446/17/D48; *International* 14 Mar. 1919; *International* 21 Jun. 1918; Deputy Commissioner CID to Secretary SAP, 3 Jul. 1919, and leaflet "Industrial Workers of Africa" signed by Thibedi [1919?], in JUS, 26/379.

39   "The TNNC Meeting..." and [Report of Detective Moorosi], 29 Jun. 1918, GNLB 281 446/17/D48.

40   "TNNC & IWA" 29 Jun. 1918 and Report of Moorosi 30 Jun. 1918, GNLB 281 446/17/D48; J.E.H. Grobler, "Msimang", in Sonderling, *New Dictionary*, p. 141; report of Jali 29 Jun. 1918, translation of "The Workers' Indaba", *Abantu-Batho* Jul. [4?] 1918 JUS 3/527/17.

41   "TNNC & Industrial Workers of Africa", 30 June 1918, GNLB 446/17/D48; *Abantu-Batho* 4 Jul. 1918.

42   Moorosi report, 29 Jun. 1918, GNLB 281; *Abantu-Batho* 4, 18 Jul. 1918; *Cape Times* 1 Jul. 1918; Statement of Major Bell ("boss boy") attached to SAP to DNL 26 Jun. 1918, JD 4/538, GNLB 281; *Sunday Times* 20 Jun. 1918. By opposing the strike Msane was "rewarded with the epithet ...'Enemy of the People': it was the end of his political career":

Willan, "De Beers", p. 208, Willan, *Plaatje*, p. 222. The TNC continued to see him as "a great danger": "Native National Congress" 16 Dec. 1918 3/527/17.

43   *Cape Times* 13 Jun. 1918.

44   *Cape Times* 26 Jun., 1-5, 8-9, 11 Jul. 1918.

45   *International* 6 Sep. 1918.

46   Police reports, Boksburg 6 Jul. 1918 and "Native Women's League" Benoni 7 Jul. 1918, JUS 3/527/17; Eales, "Jezebels" p. 19, Campbell, *Songs of Zion*, p. 288, Gaitskell, "Female Initiatives", p. 130.

47   Thema to SNA 3 Sept. 1918, C. Barrett [NA] to Mr Brebner 17 Jul. 1918: NTS 7204 17/326; *Cape Times* 11 Jul. 1918; "Transvaal Native National Congress" SAP report, 16 Jul. 1918, JUS 3/527/17.

48   *International* 26 Jul. 1918; *Imvo* 16 Jul. 1918; Skota, *African Yearly Register*, p. 171.

49   M. Arkin, "Strikes, Boycotts and the History of their Impact on South Africa", *SAJE* v. 28 (1960), pp. 303-318, p. 312; SAP Minaar and Witbank to SAP Pretoria 12 May 1919, JUS 3/527/17; *Natal Advertiser* 28 Apr., 24 Oct. 1919; Sub-Inspector Rustenburg to SAP Pretoria, 26, 29 Apr. 1919, JUS 3/527/17.

50   TNC anti-pass card, JUS 3/527/17; "Native National Congress", police reports on TNC meetings 1, 17 Dec. 1918 attached to SAP to SJ 4, 23 Dec. 1918, JUS 3/527/17.

51   Johnstone, *Class, Race & Gold*, pp. 176-177, 190-199. Msane told the Commission that gaoling of strikers had aroused resentment against the whole contract system; "The Pass Laws", NA 658/18/F473.

52   *Report of the Inter-Departmental Committee on the Native Pass Laws, 1920* (UG41-22) p. 5.

53   Police reports of TNC meetings of 12, 26 Jan., 9, 23 Feb., 3, 4, 11, 13, 14, 20, 21, 27 Apr. 1919, TNC leaflet Apr. 1919, "Native Unrest 1919", report of SAP 10 Apr. 1919: JUS 3/527/17.

54   SAP Witbank to SAP Pretoria 29 Jan. 1919, "Diary: Re Tramway Strike & Native Unrest" CID, 7 Apr. 1919, "Unrest amongst Natives at the Springs Mines", SAP Springs to SAP Benoni 1 Apr. 1919, JUS 3/527/17; "Native Unrest: Pretoria" 5 May 1919, TAD 7204 17/326; *Rand Daily Mail* 9 May 1919.

55   *Star* 3, 21 Mar. 1919; affidavits of O. Field, S.H. Seider and "Japie", 12, 14 Apr. 1919, JUS 3/527/17; "Native Unrest 1919."

56   *Report of Commission of Enquiry into Native Unrest, Johannesburg, May 1919* p. 1, SAP report of Boksburg TNC meeting, 27 Apr. 1919, Detective Brandon to SAP Boksburg 30 Apr. 1919, Head Const. Boksburg to Comm. Boksburg, 29 Apr. 1919 (citing TNC leaflets), SAP Boksburg to SAP Pretoria 1 May 1919, JUS 3/527/17; *Rand Daily Mail* 28 Apr. 1919; T.D. Ditshego to H. Thipe, 25 Apr. 1919, H.D. Hemsworth, DNA to SNA, 30 Apr. 1919, 481/141/19, in TAD 7204 17/326.

57   "Amendment of the Pass Laws: Natives' Wishes in Pretoria", *Rand Daily Mail* 10 April 1919. Another "largely attended" TNC meeting occurred in Vrededorp a few days later: "Native Meeting at Vrededorp", *Rand Daily Mail* 14 April 1919.

58   Translation of leaflet, CID to SAP 22 May 1919, JUS 3/527/17; *Star* 1 Apr. 1919; M'belle to NEC, Evidence, 25 Mar. 1931, p. 5953. He was first appointed as a clerk in 1908: Sec. Law Dept to Attorney-General 20 Mar. 1908, CAD JUS 2 2562/04; Report attached to SAP to SJ 8 May 1919, CID to SAP 8 July 1919, reporting on Thibedi and Bud-M'belle at TNC meeting, 6 July 1919, JUS 3/527/17.

59   Police reports, TNC meetings 18 May, 28-9 Jun., 16, 20 Sep., 5 Dec. 1919, JUS 3/527/17. Ramailane was a TNC leader until 1921. He worked in the OFS and as a clerk on the

Rand: Skota, *African Yearly Register* p. 252; H.C. Moloatsi to Native Separatist Churches Commissioner 18 Jan. 1922, "Native Separatist Churches".

60 N. Sibisi Report, TNC Vrededorp meeting 3 Apr. 1919, M. Ngwenya report TNC meetings 5 Jan. 1919: JUS 3/527/17; B. Hirson, "The General Strike of 1922", *Searchlight South Africa* 11 (1993), pp. 63-93.

61 SAP reports on TNC meetings 15, 22 Jun., 6 Jul. 1919, 5 Jul. 1919, 23 Apr. 1919 (Lydenburg), 7, 10, 13, 15 Jul., 6 Aug. 1919, JUS 3/527/17; NTS 7204 17/326: TNC to SNA 30 Dec. 1916, 17 Jan., 28 July 1917, 20 May 1918; SAP Benoni to SAP Boksburg, 4 Apr. 1919, JUS 3/527/17. Pilane continued to attend TNC meetings, such as a December 1919 gathering in the African Catholic Church, Doornfontein, to hear a report on the SANNC British delegation: police report 3 Jan. 1920, JUS 3/527/17.

62 "Imbizo yaBantu Ejozi", *Izwe la Kiti* 2 Apr. 1913; NTS 7204 17/326: TNC Waterberg East to Sub-Native Comm. Nylstroom 26 Jan., 21 Feb. 1919; TNC notice, *Abantu-Batho* 15 May 1919, translated in NA 1217/14/D.110: see also comments on the SANNC and TNC in Waterberg by J. J. Kekana, "Pitso ea morena Dower", *Abantu-Batho* 20 Dec, 1917, copy in JUS 3/527/17; memo. of Magistrate Bethal, 21 May 1919; Dunjwa to Magistrate Potchefstroom, 7 Aug. 1919, and Magistrate's notes, 11 Aug. 1919.

63 Bonner, "Kgatla Conspiracies, Pedi Plots".

64 *Abantu-Batho* 15 May 1919, NTS 7204; Dunjwa to Magistrate Potchefstroom 7 Aug. 1919, SAP on TNC meetings June, 30 Oct., 27 Nov, 5 Dec. 1919, JUS 26/351; Johnstone, *Class, Race & Gold*, p. 179.

65 Bonner, "Transvaal Congress," pp. 298, 289. Cf. Johnstone, *Class, Race & Gold*, p. 172.

66 TNC Constitution s.19, copy in TAD NTS 17/326; "Masizake! Lituba! Eli! African Trading Coy. Ltd." Supplement, *Abantu-Batho* 20 Dec. 1917, in JUS 3/527/17; Switzer, *Black Press*, p. 25; CKC 2:Xl13:96/1; Detective S. Mgedeza on TNC meetings June 1919, Detective M. Ngwneya on TNC meeting, 12 Jan.1919, JUS 3/527/17. *Abantu-Batho* soon incorporated other early papers: *Motsoalle=Moromioa* ("Friend"), edited by Letanka, and *Umlomo wa Bantu=Molomo oa Batho* ("Mouthpiece of the People") of Mvabaza.

67 *Abantu-Batho* 18 Jul. 1918, 15 May 1919, TAD 7204 17/326; Odendaal, "African Political Mobilisation", p. 263; *Imvo* 16 Jul. 1918; CKC 2:XL13:91/2; Sonderling, *New Dictionary*, pp. 61, 137-139; Skota, *African Yearly Register*, p. 147; SAP report on TNC meeting 22 Jul. 1919, JUS 3/527/17; Bonner, "Transvaal Congress", pp. 276-279. Lowe ("Abantu-Batho" and "Swaziland's Colonial Politics", p. 265ff) gives the most nuanced account of the organ's internal politics. Dunjwa later was sentence to five years jail because of a Klipspruit location riot, but released in late 1920: *Umteteli* 7 Aug. 1920.

68 S. Msimang, "Great Loss to Bantudom" *Bantu World* 31 Aug. 1935; Skota, *African Yearly Register*, 3rd. ed. p. 114; "Meeting called by Johannesburg TNC 11 June 1919," NTS 7204 17/326; *Rand Daily Mail* 15 Jun. 1919.

69 R. Msimang, "The Late Chief Josiah Vilakazi", *Umteteli* 27 Jun. 1931; *Ilanga* 11, 18-19 Oct. 1918, T. Couzens, "Robert Grendon: Iris Traders, Cricket Scores & Paul Kruger's Dreams" *English in Africa* 15 (1988), pp. 49-91; T. Couzens "The 'New African': Herbert Dhlomo and Black South African Literature in English 1857-1956", PhD Wits, 1980 Chapter 5: Grendon in 1903 published poems glorifying the dignity of labour.

70 J. Mancoe, *First Edition of the Bloemfontein Bantu and Coloured People's Directory* (Bloemfontein: White, 1934), p. 74; *Abantu-Batho* 18 Jul. 1918, 13 Jan. 1921; Skota, *African Yearly Register*, p. 196. Bud-M'belle was *Abantu-Batho* editor when arrested in

1919: report of M. Gallagher 12 Apr. 1919 and "Internationalist Socialistic Meeting", 19 Jul., 15, 22 Nov. 1917, H. Msane, "IWA": JUS 3/527/17

71   "Native Drudgery", *Abantu-Batho* Nov. 1916 cited in *International* 1 Dec. 1916; "Women and Pass Law," *Abantu-Batho* 20 Dec. 1917, translation, JUS 3/527/17.

72   *International* 1 Dec. 1916; "'Beware of Labour Cranks'", *International* 19 Oct. 1917, citing *Abantu-Batho*; *Abantu-Batho* 13, 20 Dec. 1917 translated in JUS 3/527/7; *Abantu-Batho* May 1918 cited in *International* 10 May 1918; "Hard Times", *Abantu-Batho* 13 Dec. 1917, translation, JUS 3/527/17.

73   *Abantu-Batho* Nov. 1917, translated in *International* 30 Nov. 1917; *Abantu-Batho* 22 Nov. 1917, 4, 18 Jul. 1918, translated in SAP report of TNC meeting, 29 June 1918, "Contract" *Abantu-Batho* 24 Oct. 1918, translated in SAP to SJ, 1 Nov. 1918, JUS 3/527/7.

74   "Rights of Small Nations", *Abantu-Batho* Apr. 1918, reprinted in F. Wilson and D. Perrot (eds.), *Outlook on a Century: South Africa 1870-1970* (Lovedale: Lovedale Press, 1972), pp. 231-233; *Abantu-Batho* 4 Jul. 1918 (translation), JUS file 3/527/17; *Sunday Times* 7 Jul. 1918.

75   "About the Case", *Abantu-Batho* 29 Aug., 5 Sept.1918 (translation), JUS 3/527/7.

76   "Money Complaints", *Abantu-Batho* 29 Aug., 5, 12 Sep. 1918, (translation), JUS 3/527/7.

77   *Abantu-Batho* 24 Oct. 1918, JUS 3/527/7; NTS 7204 17/326, TNC notice *Abantu-Batho* 15 May 1919, NA 1217/14/D110; *Abantu-Batho* 3 Apr. 1919, TAD DNL309 125/19048 cited in Bonner, "Transvaal Congress", p. 300; Police reports of TNC meetings 1, 17 Dec. 1918, 23 Feb. 1919, JUS 3/527/17.

78   *Abantu-Batho* Feb. 1920; "Are We the King's Subjects?" *Abantu-Batho* Aug. 1919, in *International* 8 Aug. 1919. In contrast, *Imvo* (9, 16 Jul., 17 Sept., 19, 27 Nov. 1918) saw strikes as a "bad example".

79   Bonner, "Transvaal Congress", pp. 298, 289; Willan, *Plaatje,* p. 252; S. Mampuru, "Transvaal African Congress: Presidential Election, Feb. 1943", election flyer, in XP reel 2, ABX 430225.

80   *Report of the Natives Land Commission* v. 2, Evidence (UG.22-16: includes UG.22-14), pp. 284-285. Makgatho gave his occupation as "general dealer" but it is also recorded as "lawyer" in other evidence.

81   *Minutes of Evidence of the Eastern Transvaal Natives Land Committee* (UG32-18), pp. 14, 21.

82   G. Simpson, "Peasants and Politics in the Western Transvaal, 1920-1940", MA Wits, 1986, pp. 100-108, 177-183; SAP Rustenburg reports 14, 27 Feb., 7 Mar. 1918, JUS 3/527/17; H. Bradford, "'A Taste of Freedom': Capitalist Development and Response to the ICU in the Transvaal Countryside", in Bozzoli (ed.) *Town and Countryside*, pp. 128-150, p. 144. On Pilane, see F. Morton, "Fenders of Space: Kgatla Territorial Expansion under Boer and British Rule, 1840-1920", in P. Limb, N. Etherington and P. Midgley (eds.) *Indigenous South(ern) African Responses to Colonialism* (Leiden: Brill, forthcoming).

83   *Report of the Natives' Land Committee, Western Transvaal* (UG23-18), p. 10, Mokoele petition of 7 Nov. 1918, pp. 58-59 and evidence p. 34.

84   *Minutes of Evidence of the Eastern Transvaal Natives Land Committee* (UG32-18), pp. 14, 21; Morrell, "Rural Transformation"; UG32-18, p. 29; UG22-16, p. 410 (Jafita). Cf. Morrell, "African Land Purchase".

85   UG.22-16, pp. 291-294.

86 UG.22-16, pp. 324 (Nkosi, Msimang, Ngwenya 325), 326 (Nzoyi). Johannes Sechel was a delegate from Bethal to the 1913 SANNC conference: "Imbizo yaBantu Ejozi", *Izwe la Kiti* 2 Apr. 1913.

87 W.M. Macmillan, *The Land, the Native, & Unemployment* (Johannesburg: Council of Education, 1924), endpapers: figures for Zoutpansberg were 134,053 to 4,455; UG.22-16 pp. 349 (Zebediela, Makapan, Nawa), 362-363 (Mphahlele, Kibi, Mamaboel), 379-380.

88 Submission of Ermelo Branch, UG-32-18, p. 205; UG32-18, p. 171.

89 *Minutes of Evidence of the Eastern Transvaal Natives Land* Committee (UG32-18), pp. 95, 112, 210.

90 UG.32-18, pp. 34-35.

91 John W. Giles, Spitzkop, to Secretary of Justice 18 Jan. 1919, JUS 3/48/19: "Goring of Son of Native Umkovu-Mapoisa on Government Farm Zwarfontein, Barberton District".

92 *Abantu-Batho* 4 Jul. 1918, JUS 3/527/17; *International* 10 Oct. 1919; Johnstone, "IWA", pp. 263-4.

93 "About the Case", *Abantu-Batho* 5 and 12 Sep. 1918, translated by W. Jali, JUS 3/527/17.

7

"Join Our Union—You Will Find Good Result": Congress and Labour in the Cape, Natal and Orange Free State, 1912-1919

In the 1910s, the most pronounced class and political contradictions existed in the Transvaal, and steady, if gradual, industrialisation and urbanisation proceeded in other major cities. This, combined with increasingly repressive legislation and the post-war economic crisis, influenced the whole country. The 1913 Natives' Land Act had particularly deleterious effects on farm tenants and labourers in the Orange Free State. Municipal restrictions on Africans in Durban spurred worker protests. In the Cape, the 1920 Port Elizabeth strike mirrored the dramatic events on the Rand in 1918-1919. During this decade, Congress responded to these and other events affecting labour, not always with great impact or consistency, but always with a measure of concern for their working-class compatriots.

The Cape

Congress had various regional strengths. The Cape Native Congress and Bechuanaland-Griqualand West Congress were particularly active, with strong branches in Ndabeni, Cape Town, Port Elizabeth, East London, Kimberly, and Queenstown; the first three places were also notable for strikes by black workers. By 1910, some 9,800 Africans lived in Cape Town. In Ndabeni dissatisfaction continued among labourers compelled to live there whilst another 350 inhabited the Docks Location, where many were labourers contracted for South West Africa. Other wage earners, such as, warehouse workers and messengers, included registered voters able to live elsewhere in the city. There also were other pockets of wage earners in the area, such as vineyard labourers and, across False Bay, workers in the De Beer's explosives

201

factory at Somerset West. The latter lived in compounds and were largely poorly paid migrant labourers from the Transkei. They were far from passive and, following fatal explosions, went on strike in 1920. They protested at the paltry £20 death compensation and demanded an increase of their daily wage from 4 shillings to 6 shillings a day. These labourers were probably influenced by the strikes in Cape Town and showed signs of organisation by forming pickets.[1]

Against a background of limited proletarianisation and limited political experience, some people with working-class experience nevertheless joined Congress. These included a migrant worker, Thomas Zini, and S. B. Macheng, who was once a mine labourer. Some wage-earners with radical ideas, such as James Ngojo, a court interpreter from Paarl, with IWA and TNC experience, also joined the movement. The background of such activists was diverse. For instance, before 1917, Ngojo was active in the Ethiopian Catholic Church.[2]

The point here is, that given the very incomplete and shifting nature of the black working class, points of entry into black politics "from below" were diverse. African independent churches, for example, sometimes provided a link between Congress and subaltern peoples. In 1919, for example, Dora Tamana, much later to be a powerhouse in the ANC Women's League, joined her father at a meeting of Enoch Mgijima's Israelite church at Bulhoek. Not involved directly in politics until the 1940s, she recalled in a 1977 interview that in 1919, at the age of 18, she saw Mgijima's church as involving "a sort of change in the mind that the people must fight for themselves". Tamana added: "Mgijima told us about the African National Congress which will bring freedom for us, so we had a hope that these things can come." Such indirect introductions to politics were common in the rural areas: Tamana hailed from Nqamakwe in the Transkei, from a *kholwa* family.[3]

In contrast, the Cape Peninsula African population was rather more proletarian than *petit bourgeois* and became increasingly so as migrant workers largely contributed to its growth. Hence, as Congress leaders began to mobilise in Cape Town, labour issues often stared them in the face. The Cape Congress took up the cause of the "bucket" strikers described in the previous chapter. It called a protest meeting at Ndabeni on 17 June 1918. Present were Reverend Zaccheus Mahabane, R. M. Tunzi, James Moleboloa, J. Fuku and others. Speakers expressed "continued devotion" to government but viewed the sentences imposed on strikers "with alarm". White strikers did not face similar prosecution and such discrimination would "perpetuate discontentment, suspicion and unrest". They emphasised not the right to strike but the danger of the sowing of the "undesirable seeds of separation", as Mahabane put it.

Moleboloa wrote to the *Cape Times* that whilst "natives did wrong in going out on strike" their sentences were "unduly harsh".[4]

Mahabane (1881-1970) had joined the Cape Congress in July 1917 (and became its president in 1919). Mahabane claimed to be "voicing the feelings of a large number" of Africans when he protested the treatment of the strikers. Whilst careful to profess his loyalty, by acknowledging Prime Minister Botha's conciliatory moves to resolve the strike, he drew attention to the immediate issue: saying that, "Feeling is growing among all the native workers ... that they are being underpaid and that the remuneration generally offered them is altogether not commensurate with the amount and difficulty of the work they, as a class, have to perform". He added ominously "this feeling, like a gathering cloud, is sure to break out". To prevent such an outbreak he urged formation of a commission to investigate wages, or a conference of employers and black representatives. He made clear "the supreme advisability" of increasing black wages. Part of his empathy for labour relates to his work experiences. Born into a Thaba 'Nchu *kholwa* family, he worked as teacher and court interpreter before turning to religion in 1908. In addition he emphasised the need for ANC cohesion. When black public opinion regarded white people as pillorying black workers, events compelled an organisation that gave priority to black unity not to strand aloof.[5]

The Cape Congress also organised a delegation to the mayor to urge a minimum wage for Africans. The Ndabeni branch held a "largely attended meeting" in November 1918 at which it appealed for black representation at the Paris Peace Conference. These events took place against a backdrop of growing propaganda work by socialists. After 1918, IWA leaders Cetyiwe, Kraai and Ngojo gravitated to Cape Town. The black unions formed here were, notably, the Industrial Workers Union in 1918, and the Industrial & Commercial Workers Union (ICU) in November 1919. These unions, together with groups such as the African Political Organisation (APO) and the Industrial Socialist League, began to spread socialist ideas among Africans on the docks and among "considerable numbers of coloured and native people ... in District Six".[6]

ANC concern for black labour continued. During a black dockworkers' strike organised by the ICU in Cape Town in 1919, a joint ANC-IWA-ICU meeting in Ndabeni, presided over by Kraai, heard Mahabane back their demands. Speaking to a Cape Congress meeting at Ndabeni on 5 March 1919, Mahabane stressed that black people were "absolutely defenceless and helpless ... Even the weapon of the strike they are absolutely incapable of employing to any serviceable degree for the lack both of organisation and of the funds necessary to save them and their families from starvation". His comments suggest ANC reluctance to support strikes may have had much to do with *realpolitik*. This reluctance evaporated in December 1919 when Congress supported the first major ICU-led strike.[7]

There was contact between the ANC and the first black labour unions in the Eastern Cape. In Port Elizabeth, Samuel Masabalala sat on the Congress Executive in Port Elizabeth from 1919 and on the SANNC Executive. He had ample working-class experience, having worked as a driver, miner, fitter, electrician, teacher, and as a pharmacist's clerk and insurance agent. He helped form the Industrial and Commercial Coloured and Native Workingmen's Union in 1919. The foundation of this organisational growth was the growing proletariat of the city: the Africans of New Brighton, numbering some 5,600 people in 1914, constituted in the words of the Location Superintendent, "a labouring class". The East London Native Employees' Association, claiming a membership of some 2,000-4,000 workers by 1921, also linked up with Congress leaders—Gary Minkley sees it as "a pressure group of location elite". In 1903, 1911, and 1918, there were major dock strikes in the river port.[8]

Some Eastern Cape ANC leaders supported, if inconsistently, better conditions for black workers. Rubusana, a leading SANC figure until 1919, stood for the Cape Provincial Council in 1912 on a programme of less tax for the poor and a solution to the labour question that would satisfy both black people and mine owners. As SANNC vice-president, he actively opposed the effects on rural workers and peasants of the Land Act and represented Africans' land claims to government. Based in the working-class city of East London for many years, he was aware of labour's plight. As Songezo Ngqongqo notes, Rubusana "did not forget the overtly political and economic aspirations", but he feared class struggle. He saw passes as "savouring of class distinction … [that] will be the cause of much unrest". In August 1918, when 2,000 East London dock-, rail- and store-workers threatened to strike over high prices and to "fetch … out of town" any scabs, he tried to dissuade them. Aligning himself with the mayor, he urged workers to consider that monthly-paid Africans might lose wages if there was a strike. Most workers would not listen to him, most probably because he proposed a wage increase of only sixpence a day at a time of soaring inflation. In 1919, he negotiated a successful, but very meagre, pay rise for Africans. By 1920, Rubusana had switched his allegiance from Congress to the far more moderate Bantu Union. He was involved in a desperate attempt to stem the rising tide of militant worker anger in Port Elizabeth.[9]

Elsewhere in the Eastern Cape, Congress had less-pronounced contact with workers reflecting lower levels of proletarianisation and obstacles to its growth. In the Cradock Location protest meetings on December 1912 supported employment of black interpreters and teachers over white counterparts. However it is unclear if Congress was involved. The Bantu Women's League in Queenstown told Ngojo in 1919 that the state had bribed chiefs not to attend Congress meetings. Conservatives compelled organisers of a meeting in honour of SANNC President Makgatho to hold it in a "white people's hall", discouraging attendance. Congress leaders, noted Ngojo, "were not known by the Queenstown people." Queenstown was a major centre for Congress, especially before the Transkei railway line opened, as people would congregate there whilst travelling.[10]

Isolation lead to different attitudes about significant contemporary issues. In December 1913, the "Native Congress" met in Qumbu, representing Oxkraal, Kamastone and Hackney (Queenstown district) villages. It delegated Ema Makalima (Hackney) and Reverend B. S. Mazwi to address the Beaumont Commission; both supported the Land Act in the (vain) hope that segregation would solve their land problems. Mazwi distanced himself from those electing to appeal to the Imperial government, a clear reference to the SANNC. In Cala, Xalanga region, Africans determinedly resisted land alienation and imposition of District Councils. To this end in 1911 they engaged the support of Congress co-founder Walter Rubusana. Solomon Kalipa and Duncan Makohliso, referred to by government as "agitators", asserted Africans' land rights before the Beaumont Commission, where they read the resolutions of a public meeting in Cala held on 8 January 1914 that called for land and franchise rights. Similarly, in the Ciskei region, Congress figures spoke out for Africans' rights. George Kama (in later decades ANC national "Governor") of Middledrift told the Natives Land Commission in 1914 that the Land Act had harmed Africans, and drew attention to unjust removals. State repression of cultural practices offered other possibilities to build support. In 1918 in King William's Town, a meeting of 1,000 people heard chiefs from Alice and Peddie demand "hands off" beer brewing and initiation ceremonies, and call for a single nation. They were possibly echoing SANNC policy.[11]

Other Congress leaders were active in the region. Alfred Mangena had fought for black workers' rights in the previous decade (see Chapter 3). In 1912, he had been a founder of the SANNC, which elected him a vice-president; he also helped Makgatho establish the short-lived *Native Advocate* in Pretoria. In 1913 he joined a Congress deputation to protest the Land Act. Local bodies in rural East Griqualand and Transkei engaged Mangena to challenge highly unpopular dipping taxes. It is unclear to what extent he represented Congress, but in 1914 he helped local people establish action committees that took part in vigorous anti-dipping protests. The link to workers here are the thousands of Transkeian migrant labourers who, suggests Bundy, imbibed the lessons of covert organisation and direct action from the 1913-1914 Rand strikes. Whilst evidence of direct ties to Congress is thin, the SANNC and TNC were active in 1913-1914 around the Land Act and spoke up in support of black mine workers' rights. Hence, it is conceivable that the general notions of Congress as the people's representative were emerging among some migrant workers.[12] Little is known of Congress organisation in the Transkei region during this decade although it is likely that Enoch Mamba continued to promote Congress. The evidence adduced above seems to indicate that some Congress figures were active in several areas. Whilst urbanisation across the entire Eastern Cape was slight, migrant labour issues were part of Congress concerns.

In the Northern Cape the Bechuanaland-Griqualand West Congress was more structured. With the mining town of Kimberley in its midst, labour issues were always before its eyes. In Chapter 4, I demonstrated how Sol Plaatje's *Koranta ea Becoana* and *Tsala ea Batho* newspapers frequently exposed the exploitation of, and prejudices against, black labour. I also explained the complexity of Plaatje's approaches to labour questions. Plaatje was also the head of the Congress branch in Kimberley. In December 1913 he told the Beaumont Commission that scarce land was driving Africans from the Transkei and elsewhere, to towns such as Kimberley in search of work.[13]

In Kimberley, black communities that had emerged from the closed mine-compound system in locations such as the Malay Camp gradually began to exhibit class stratification, although there also was a commonality of life, as explained in Chapter 2. The ugliness and poverty of the Kimberley location had struck Katie Makhanya in the 1890s: "only row upon row of corrugated iron buildings". The young teenager Z. K. Matthews, studying in Kimberley, already knew of Congress, even though his father was a miner and the body was only a few years old. That local black people knew of Congress related to the work of prominent local activists such as Plaatje and their Congress-aligned press in which, as noted in Chapter 4, even chiefs spoke out in defence of rights of "their" labourers. Whilst Plaatje's press articles would have had a rather limited effect among the multi-national mine labourers, some of whom hailed from as far away as Mozambique, by the 1910s the basis of the town's economy had broadened. Families had settled, and African urban culture was developing. It was in this context that Congress's name became commonplace. The only delegate from Cape Province to attend the 1913 SANNC conference was from Kimberley.[14]

An important reason behind Cape Congress support for workers was a developing interest in labour issues by its founder members. Another reason was the intensification of economic crisis, seen in protests both against the Land Act and by early black unions. In the Cape, Congress statements and actions in support of the rights of black labour, and the involvement of some of its members in early black unions, helped to establish the ANC as a force sympathetic to the broad aspirations of black workers.

Natal

Building on the earlier work of the Natal Native Congress NNC, outlined in Chapter 3, and continuing with the formation of the South African Native National Congress (SANNC), the Congress's prestige grew in Natal. At a meeting in Durban on 23 February 1912, the NNC agreed to affiliate to the SANNC and harmonise its constitution with that of the national body. John Dube led the NNC during this decade. He was highly considered among many Africans in Natal, especially during the term of his SANNC presidency from 1912 to 1917. Against a backdrop of white suspicions of black loyalty, heightened by the 1906 Bhambatha Revolt, Congress repeatedly declared its loyalty to the *British,* not the *Settler* state. In 1911 the NNC gained an audience with Governor General Gladstone, but only on his condition that their address be of a "purely complimentary nature and contain no reference to political topics".[15]

Protestations of NNC loyalty increased during World War I. Dube constantly petitioned the Chief Native Commissioner (CNC) in late 1914 to call joint Congress-government meetings to combat pro-German war rumours. Dube argued such meetings would purely express loyalty. The NNC backed its words with relatively substantial material contributions, resolving to contribute to the War Relief Fund and asking that their donations be "devoted towards the relief of distress among the relatives" of troops. Congress stalwarts were generous in raising personal or clan donations.[16]

On the other hand, the irony of the War coinciding with the prosecution by the state of the Land Act was not lost on prominent NNC leaders. Many of them spoke out strongly against the Act's effects at the 1917 hearings of the Natal Natives Land Committee. Reverend Alfred Kumalo of Bergville and Philip Mtembu and C. P. Dlamini of Newcastle drew attention to the injustice of loyal Africans losing land rights during the War. Mtembu, Chairman of the NNC Newcastle Branch, remarked "we do not like the idea, while some of our members are fighting [in the War], that such laws should be made which would scatter them like goats". He relayed the hostile views against the Act coming from a recent meeting of the Newcastle Branch. Other Newcastle NNC leaders, Isaac Mabaso, Irvine Matshobongwana, and George Ncamu, echoed these views. Ncamu pointed to growing race solidarity when he observed Africans across Natal "feel for each other". Vryheid NNC leader William Washington Ndhlovu, lawyers' clerk and emergent local landowner, opposed the loss of *kholwa* lands under the Act, just as he had two years earlier before the Beaumont Commission when he remarked Africans "could not help sympathising" with their "own flesh and blood" evicted from farms. Ndhlovu was no radical. He underlined landowner respectability but also noted that in Vryheid most Africans were town workers. Mtembu addressed the Beaumont Commission in May 1915, when he led an "SANNC" Newcastle Branch delegation, which also included Elijah Xala and Isaac Mabaso. Mtembu opposed segregation and called for special provision for chiefs living on private lands. Mabaso objected to the prospect of forced proletarianisation which ensured "that we should not be allowed to buy or hire land but only to give labour". In northern Natal, as noted in Chapter 3, colliery towns had more settled black wage earners, some living on nearby black-owned farms, suggesting possible Congress contact with such workers.[17]

John Dube was diplomatic; in May 1915 in Pietermaritzburg, he told the Beaumont Commission that in extensive tours by Congress leaders around Natal to gauge Africans' feelings about the Land Act, they had not claimed the legislation was unfair. Whether out of naiveté or class interest, or seduced by the prospect of a kind of "Transkeian option" of eventual "self-government", Dube was almost obsequious in his denial of the injustice of the Act, and spoke of land sales around Inanda, in which he had an interest. Only when pressed by Commissioners—after all, Dube's condemnation of the Act was public knowledge—did he relay the widespread opposition of Africans to the loss of land rights and labour obligations. Farmers, he said, "want our labour, but we cannot stay as rent-paying tenants".[18]

Dube (SANNC President) and Chief Mini (NNC President), speaking in Durban before the Natal Natives Land Committee in 1917, attacked the Act. Mini criticised its deleterious effects on Africans' land and labour rights. The Act aimed to secure (cheap) labour. Instead, Mini argued for the right to free labour movement. Black labour, he intimated, should be quite free to leave employers unable to cater to their labour rights. Africans and their Chiefs, Mini added, viewed the Act as slavery legislation that would force women and children to work as labour tenants. The Land Act's provision denying Africans the right to form land companies of more than five people was preposterous, "seeing that ordinary natives get such poor pay when working for the white man". There were, however, internal class contradictions beginning to emerge around the Act. "Mpofu" Ogle of Umzinto noted landless Africans hated those of their number who had acquired land through the Act. Mabaso made clear that one of his major objections to the Act was its denial of (rather lucrative) farm and labour tenants to black landholders such as himself.[19]

Government did not relish providing opportunities for Congress to gain further legitimacy among Africans. NNC efforts often included subtle attempts to assert such legitimacy. However, a government determined to paint black political organisations critical of government, such as Congress, as "not entitled to express the views of the Native population", rebuffed them.[20]

Nevertheless, express the views of the black population they did, for there was a wider dimension to Congress in Natal. The NNC claimed 23 branches within a few months of its founding and its conferences attracted delegates from many centres of the colony. Some leaders spoke of the centrality of labour in African lives. Moreover, the main branches were in more industrialised towns, not just Durban and Pietermaritzburg but also rural towns with sizeable worker populations such as Vryheid. By 1910 the nearby Hlobane colliery employed 600 Africans, whilst Newcastle collieries employed 1,700 black workers and where, as noted above, Phillip Mtembu had established a branch. Such a peri-urban focus made labour issues more visible to some NNC leaders.[21]

In nearby Dundee, the Lutheran Mission/Natal Missionary Conference in September 1912 launched a Zulu newspaper, *Izwe la Kiti*. Despite its spiritual tone and that the missionary H. J. K. Rössler did the editing, its columns soon reflected rising interest in Congress by its African correspondents. Members Mark Radebe in Pietermaritzburg, J. Ray Msimang in Howick and Reverend Abner Mtimkulu in Dundee became agents, and the paper circulated as far as the Rand, Kimberley and Jagersfontein Floor Compound, suggesting it reached some workers. *Izwe la Kiti* reprinted a letter on segregation sent by John Dube, as SANNC President, to the *Mercury*. Over the next few months, further Dube missives and reports on Congress meetings were printed. In this way too, Congress was publicised.[22]

Attendance at the 1915 SANNC conference reflected the broadening geographic reach of Congress. Delegates arrived from various Natal towns. Chief Mini from Edendale, Dyer Nxaba (Stanger), J. T. Gumede (Bergville), Reverend C. N. Sibisi, J. Ngwenya and Nath Mbongwe (Estcourt), Reverend W. J. Makanya (Durban), A. Sibiya and Reverend Daniel Zama (Noodsberg),

Charles Barlen-Dhlamini (Vryheid), S. Kambule, S. Xaba, L. Mndaweni and William Tshabalala (Driefontein), Luke Khumalo and M. Malinga (New Hanover), Chief J. M. Majozi, J. Mcunu, and P. Mntaka (Indaleni), Chief Theo Ntombela and Paul Africa (Ladysmith), and S. Bavenda, Reverend S. Mndaweni and Isaac Mabaso (Newcastle).[23] On the other hand, such a group was hardly proletarian in character and most of the above-mentioned places typified the *kholwa* spirit.

The NNC's approach was more pecuniary than that of the TNC. The 1915 NNC constitution included the aim of assisting Africans "to seek and learn trades", as well as promoting "commercial undertakings" and "positions for educated persons". It stipulated a Committee of Works to help Africans find work in trades or establish businesses. Head office in Pietermaritzburg "would seek work for the Natives and notify the branches of available situations", charging the fee of one shilling if successful.[24]

NNC policies were not as straight-laced as one might suppose of a body led by *kholwa* imbued with western notions of respectability. They were not averse to championing such plebeian pastimes as beer brewing or selling, as occurred in a NNC Executive "prayer" to government composed during its 1916 Congress. The prayer also called for repeal of pass laws (seen as bonding an African "like a slave to his employer or his landlord"), mining laws and sections of the Native Code. The petitioners raised other grievances such as access to the civil service, re-appointment of African waiters on trains, and waiving of rent for widows and the aged on mission reserves. In 1916, Josiah Gumede also championed rights of widows. Nevertheless, Congress did not become a mass organisation. If it did start to gain influence beyond *kholwa* strata, it did not allow direct female membership and there would have been very few, if any, peasant or labourer members. African women in Natal remained legal minors. We know little of their role in politics at this time, though Adelaide Dube, sister in law of *uMafukuzela*, published a political poem in 1913 painting Africans: as "outcasts in their country" and pledging, "Struggle I must for freedom."[25]

Despite Dube's moderation, radical issues occasionally filtered through the pages of *Ilanga,* which had several different editors in its first two decades: there were many sympathetic references to the Bhambhatha Revolt. In 1916, the state accused Dube of supporting a movement for pardoning convicted "rebels". In the same year, *Ilanga* printed a speech on evolution and socialism and the next year it reproduced an article by S. P. Bunting depicting the white ruling class as enemies, both of Africans and of workers.[26]

Dube had to confront the contradictions inherent in the position of Africans in the colonialist economy of South Africa. By 1910, government magistrates complained of increased "insolence" by labourers and ricksha-pullers in Durban, and across the province, land hunger and residential instability were common.[27]

Dube's rhetoric echoed the growing disempowerment and impoverishment of Africans: no amount of imperial loyalty could disguise the naked self-interest of white settler rulers. Dube's ambiguous rhetoric was evident in his 1912 speech to a gathering in Eshowe of over 300 "kraal and Kolwa" Africans, state officials, chiefs, *indunas* and African police. He spoke of Zululand as "our England", emphasising "this is our country". Nevertheless, his intention was to emphasise unity and avoid violence:

> you are not like a people; you have no voice—you cannot speak for yourselves ... We want the South African Native subjects of his Majesty, the King, both within the Union and beyond it, to unite ... No, we do not want to fight, we cannot fight. The very idea is ridiculous ... All we desire, all we want, is to find grace, favour, with the white people, that we, too, like them, might have our voice.

Dube wanted Africans to find their "voice" through Congress and "let the authorities know your real, true feelings". He proceeded to tell the crowd about Congress, whose aim was "to unite, to form an organised body to represent the voice of the native people" and urged them: "Join our union—you will find good result". Dube went to great pains to emphasise his moderation: "we want to gain the goodwill of the Government, to crawl on our knees before" them. Labour was the other main theme. He sarcastically reminded his audience, pointing to the carefully tended sugar fields stretching between Durban and Gingindhlovu, that they lacked the European work ethic. The themes of work and the need for education recurred in many of his addresses. He urged Africans to learn trades and warned of the social evils awaiting young workers on the Rand. Instead of sending young men to the Rand mines, Dube argued, send them instead to local cane-fields "where you can take their earnings". When challenged by Chief Sikonyana's representative Nkomidhli Mlongo that he was merely repeating the words of government, Dube spoke more directly to workers: "I say let's unite and get the money 'opened' (wages increased) here close at hand." Dube saw a close interconnection between labour and the economy. The segregation announced by the Minister of Native Affairs, Albert Hertzog, meant that Africans had nowhere to go. In any case, so many Africans now worked for white people in Durban, "how could the white people live if all these Natives were taken away?" In these ways, Dube invoked African workers even if his class position was now securely in the middle class.[28]

Government authorities thwarted other Congress attempts to formalise its legitimacy. During 1916-1917, Dube and the NNC Durban branch began to organise. They sought to use the Location Hall for SANNC meetings, causing government officials to worry whether the Scylla of granting legitimacy was much better than the Charybdis of an even-larger mass meeting in the open air away from "proper control".[29]

Dube and the NNC Durban branch led opposition to the harsh Native Registration by-laws. These imposed compulsory vaccinations of all African workers and tough work contracts and night curfews. In 1916, the newly founded Municipal Native Affairs Department (MNAD) of the Durban Corporation established the Durban Native Committee as a purely consultative body through which it hoped to facilitate control over Africans. However, NNC leaders, many of whom, as La Hausse observes, had become successful small entrepreneurs, soon gained control of the Committee. That they probably sympathised with the onerous conditions imposed on African labourers by the new regulations was due not just to their pecuniary interest as traders—operating within the "interstices of the labour-coercive economy" (La Hausse)—in retaining black customers. For some of them, it also had to do with their own working-class experiences. Charles Msomi (Chairman) had been a carpenter in Edendale, William Bhulose (Vice-Secretary) began his working life as a municipal employee, and A. T. Mtetwa worked as a gardener.[30]

At an African meeting in Location Hall on 7 August 1916, Dube argued that the introduction of the Native Committee was a positive step in that, for the first time, white people had asked for a Committee of Africans. Yet, Dube conceded, it was "only a bridge between white and black—nothing more" and its members must bravely "ask for all" demands raised by Africans "even though they knew it was unfavourable to the Europeans". The following week Dube spoke to a mass meeting of about 800 Africans on the Western Vlei or Racecourse Flats. He alleged they had to meet "in the open in the long grass" as the municipal council refused Congress the use of the Town Hall because Africans, allegedly, "were not clean enough". Dube could not fathom this decision. After all, he argued, invoking the central economic role of black labour, "it is you people who helped to build the Town Hall, every bit of it. You carried the bricks and the stones, and mixed the cement. We are the people of the land, we were born here, and yet we have been refused." The next month, a NNC Durban branch meeting discussed its relations with the Native Committee. The branch elected three more of its members to serve on it, a move viewed by the MNAD as "a determined effort to capture the control" of the Committee.[31]

J. S. Marwick, MNAD Manager, asserted his authority, claiming the Committee of Natives must operate under his leadership. Marwick was fiercely against the independent organisation of black labour. He had long experience as a labour recruiter and probably resented the intrusion of Congress, whose politics had "done a good deal to unsettle the minds of the more ignorant natives in Durban", into "his" realm of paternalistic labour control. Marwick was well aware that most leaders of the Native Committee were NNC members and were "anxious to secure a semi-official status" for the Committee to facilitate mass meetings. He was particularly piqued at committee secretary Philemon Lutuli's characterisation of Marwick's role as purely a "connecting link" between Africans and the Town Council. Marwick claimed he was "credibly informed" that Congress had "declared itself opposed in every way" to the MNAD. Hence, he argued, it was "dangerous to allow the Native Committee (on which the Native Congress is strongly represented)" any recognition that would enhance the influence of Congress.[32]

The Native Committee, which in September had sought "properly constituted" and clearly defined powers, soon rejected Marwick's *diktat* that their role was to be purely consultative. The Committee forcefully advised the mayor that they would resign *en masse* unless he revoked Marwick's interpretation.[33]

Dube retreated into narrow NNC politics after his defeat as SANNC President by Makgatho in 1917. Strong parochialism marked NNC politics and resentment at Dube's defeat caused it to withhold monies from the SANNC until Dube returned to the National Executive in 1919. Dube did retain a commitment to broad national struggle. At the October 1919 SANNC executive meeting he was glad that agitation for Africans rights was continuing. The "only thing to do was to continue fighting". In January 1918, Dube spoke in Roodepoort at a concert by his Ohlange singers, held ostensibly to raise funds for the school, but also to call for donations to meet costs of a libel case won by Marwick after Dube denounced him in *Ilanga*. Dube called for national African unity, said he was prepared to die in the struggle, and commended African women for their struggle against pass laws.[34]

The displacement of moderate NNC leaders did not occur until 1924. Yet the radicalisation of black working and middle strata that took place on the Rand had its parallel in Natal. There were strikes by Durban's African workers in 1918. African labour, writes Cope, "became radicalised and was represented in the NNC's body politic". In 1919, rising prices forced a NNC response. A meeting chaired by Dube addressed inflation and resolved to send a petition to government asking for relief through reduced prices. Dube argued that inflation was especially severe on farm workers, as prices of staples such as mealies were much higher. The meeting "dispersed" after a "quarrel" between Dube and the rather more radical NNC President, Stephen Mini—though both were men of property. This lack of unity, combined with Dube's reluctance to transcend the tactics of petition, made the NNC less inclined to achieve any concrete relief for workers.[35]

Dube favoured property, rather than labour, rights and adopted consistently moderate policies. Other NNC leaders, sharing Dube's concerns about attacks on African land rights, began to challenge more seriously the right of state departments to "represent" Africans. In doing so, they raised the question of treatment of workers.

Many Congress activists gave evidence on behalf of Congress to the 1915 Beaumont Natives Land Commission and 1917 Select Committee on Native Affairs. Josiah Gumede, representing the NNC Pietermaritzburg, told the Beaumont Commission in May 1915 that government must extend, not reduce, African landholdings. He claimed to know personally of at least 40 cases of landless Africans in Pietermaritzburg. This showed that Congress was not isolated from ordinary people. Indeed, Congress often was in the public eye, holding frequent meetings in places such as Market Square, Pietermaritzburg.[36]

Chief Cristian Lutayi, another NNC leader to address Beaumont, detailed the injustice of a £6 annual tax imposed on farm workers who earned as little as £1 per annum. Stephen Mini, Josiah Gumede and Abner Mtimkulu affirmed to Beaumont that Congress represented Africans of both Natal and Zululand. They also expressed concern about the situation of Africans in other provinces. Such claims to representativeness ensured that, notwithstanding any elitist tendencies, Congress kept the affairs of all Africans within its wide ambit. Mini stated bluntly that Congress viewed the Native Affairs Administration Bill as discriminatory. Mtimkulu urged that future commissioners be "appointed by the people themselves". Jerishem Gumede, NNC General Secretary in 1916, totally rejected the Bill as "taking away my freedom and liberty".[37]

By 1915, in Dube's temporary absence and with divisions emerging between the Durban and Pietermaritzburg camps of Congress, Josiah Gumede was general secretary and Mini, president. Gumede had some prior experience of wage labour and he had glimpsed mass suffering whilst taking part in protests against the Land Act. But from 1916 to 1918, he acquired considerable private property, probably several hundred acres, largely transacted under the same Act, but he had difficulty servicing the many mortgages incurred, forcing him back to work as a lawyer's clerk and broker. This ambiguity may help explain Gumede's initial reluctance to condemn the Land Act and his subsequent antagonism toward Dube when he was critical of the SANNC British deputation. However, Gumede was radicalised by the publication of the Beaumont Report and its rejection of the land claims of Gumede's Sotho clients.[38]

Gumede's emphasis on land rights was in line with the concerns of many African workers in Natal who retained some access to land or who aspired to land ownership. He was concerned not only for the rights of big landowners but also for the fate of "thousands" of squatters. Gumede addressed the Select Committee on Native Affairs at length on labour issues, indicating he knew a good deal about the working lives of Africans. He spoke of sharecroppers who laboured on white peoples' farms in conditions based only on verbal agreements, and of the many obliged to work on mines or sugar fields for six months a year. Gumede revealed a detailed knowledge of provisions of the Masters and Servants Act. In essence, he agreed with them, due in part to their facilitation, in theory, of African workers' right to complain to magistrates over employer mistreatment. Nevertheless, he condemned the fact that white farmers forced workers to labour for 12 months of a year as "serfs". Simultaneously, he indicated his attachment to tradition by objecting to any changes in industrial laws diminishing paternal control over sons until they were able to pay taxes. However, Gumede rejected elitism. In response to a question from the Minister of Native Affairs about whether government should invite only "the educated class or the Chiefs" to a convention (proposed by the NNC), Gumede replied: "All the classes concerned."[39]

In the next few years, Gumede became more radical. At the end of June 1918 he attended meetings of the TNC and militant workers on the Rand. He promoted Congress ties with the grassroots through his establishment in Pietermaritzburg of *Iso Lesizwe Esimnyama* ("Eye of the Black Nation", 1918) as a NNC organ. His disillusionment with the Empire grew but he also expressed anti-Communist sentiment. In 1919, at the trial of communist David Ivon Jones (for writing a pamphlet *The Bolsheviks Are Coming*), Gumede claimed, "We, as natives, don't like this circular, it frightens us." He feared that Bolsheviks would kill chiefs and enslave Africans; views influenced by the white Establishment. The magistrate viewed such a pamphlet directed at white workers as criminal, but "diabolical to appeal to hordes of natives, scarcely yet removed from barbarism". Gumede's notions also perhaps reflected his equation of communist plans with Afrikaner republicans and a fear that his by now considerable land holdings might be at risk under communism. Yet, as discussed in Chapter 4, in connection with his role in the SANNC delegation to Britain, his belief in "British fair play" had been breached. A few years later he was to show strong solidarity with black workers and even with communists.[40]

Away from the big cities such as Durban and Pietermaritzburg and its Midlands heartland, Congress often had less direct contacts. In Southern Natal, activists from across the Umtamvuna River in the Eastern Cape, influenced the growth of black political organisation. Natal Native Congress influence appears to have been weak in Southern Natal but regular cultural, labour, and political links across the river brought some contact with Eastern Cape forces. Reverend E. B. Koti of the Native Baptist Association helped draft the first SANNC constitution (completed in 1919). He moved from Queenstown to Harding in Alfred County in 1917, although little is known of his political activities in Harding.[41]

During World War I, the government suspected many Africans in Natal and Zululand of "disloyalty". Police reports confirmed African antagonism to war recruiting. There was a labour dimension to these protests: in 1915, chiefs and commoners alike refused to enrol in government schemes to send African labourers to build railways for the war effort in South West Africa (Namibia). In February, at public meetings in Harding, Alfred County, neither Congress leader John Dube nor labour-recruiter Taberer could convince the men. The men demanded more money and derided Dube and Taberer as they "did not know them". Dube was "severely heckled" by the meeting.[42]

This was a time of tension and rumours. Police reported widespread cases of alleged German sympathies among Africans from Zululand to the South Coast, often encouraged by local German traders. Rumours were rife of German submarines off the coast magically transforming sunken ships into gunboats; of Germans marching on Durban and sequestering cattle; even of Dinuzulu fighting in Germany. Police blamed ex-Bhambatha Rebellion (1906-1908) rebels for one rumour envisaging Bhambatha and John Dube landing with imperial German troops at St. Lucia Bay. They would land to punish white people "for maladministration" and "all Natives who supported Govt. during [Bhambatha] Rebellion will be exterminated". Another wild rumour, circulating in Zululand, claimed a gunboat had stopped the ship on which Dube was travelling forcing him to return to England. The British feared he "would unsettle Natives after having been [to] Germany and received sympathy there regarding the Lands Act". The Chief Native Commissioner reported the Machi people were "undoubtedly disloyal". Police accused KwaMachi Chief Jolwayo of active disloyalty when he and supporters, fearing arrest and confiscation of their cattle armed themselves and briefly crossed to Pondoland. Behind the actions, however, was militant opposition by Pondo and Machi chiefs and followers to forced war labour and proposed hut tax rises.[43]

These examples shows that even under moderate leadership, individual NNC members were prepared to challenge the white community's hegemony and, in so doing, draw attention to harsh conditions of workers. The role of chiefs, both in Congress politics and representing black worker interests, was more complicated. Both *kholwa* and chiefs tended to either employ labour or receive rent from tenants. However, as noted above, *kholwa* active in Congress were quick to tell government commissions of widespread complaints about forced labour for chiefs. Congress drew its main strength from *kholwa*. In its early years, before 1912 in particular, Congress only occasionally attracted chiefs, but had more success with appointed and Christianised chiefs such as Mini. Yet, the recent history of the province included resistance by some chiefs to colonialism. Whilst this abated as the century advanced, some chiefs still endeavoured to cling to power and to do so they expressed the interests of their subjects. In general, however, the locus of power within Congress was swinging more and more towards urban Africans, as seen in the Orange Free State.

The Orange Free State

Interest in labour matters within Congress was due partly to the general predicament of Africans and partly to the presence of wage earners in the organisation. The Orange Free State lacked the intense industrialisation and concomitant development of a black working class like the Transvaal; a 1904 industrial commission remarked on the lack of manufacturing, with farming as the economic base and thus a desperate need to attract *any* kind of industry.[44] Yet, as in other provinces, socio-economic and political forces were driving political organisations to a growing awareness of their shared interests with black labour.

Throughout the province, black workers' wages were low. A relatively low proportion of labourers went to the Rand. Farm labourers in Kroonstad and Harrismith districts earned between 10 and 20 shillings a month; in Rouxville and Jacobsdal between 10 and 15 shillings; women in Bethulie only between 5 and 10 shillings. In many districts they were paid only in kind. In Thaba 'Nchu, where Africans predominantly farmed or sharecropped, there was little wage labour, but chronic overcrowding. The African population of the district rose from 7,280 in 1884 to 24,716 in 1911 as land loss and (by 1916) irredeemable mortgages saw African land ownership drop from 95 to 11 farms. The resultant "crushing of the poor" increasingly drove Africans to wage labour.[45]

By 1916, the estimated provincial African population was 351,790 (compressed into only 244 square miles of African-owned land) with only 48,751 in urban or mining areas. However, urbanisation was on the rise in Bloemfontein. All over the province, after 1904, Africans outnumbered white people in cities. Here poor sanitation and overcrowding brought chronic health problems and dissatisfaction over regulations fanned discontent that found an outlet in Congress. In 1910, an estimated 18,382 Africans lived in the Bloemfontein municipal area with a further 12,063 on private land.[46]

Mining spurred on urbanisation and wage labour. By 1910 mining was increasingly the principal employer of black labour, employing an average of 8,000-9,000 people in four diamond mines and collieries. At the Voorspoed diamond mine near Kroonstad, labour contract disturbances occurred in 1910.[47]

By 1913, underground mining began at the previously alluvial diamond mine of Jagersfontein (employing 4,000-5,000 workers). In January 1914, 14 workers, mainly Sotho, were killed by armed white people because of what authorities described as a "formidable outbreak" from the compound. The outbreak happened because of a strike over the death of a co-worker beaten by a white miner. Back home in Maseru, workers Joe Letsie and Sepinare Phahlahla, in solidarity with fellow workers, expressed their outrage. However, the fact that they felt only able to speak freely of these matters outside of South Africa indicates how difficult it would have been for African workers to organise. Industries also began to develop round about this time. In 1917, at the Portland Cement Works on Winburg, strikers assaulted the manager. This required police from two districts to quell the action. More generally in the Orange Free State, white farmers and the state ruthlessly enforced the 1913 Natives' Land Act against African sharecroppers and landholders, to "subvert a semi-independent black peasantry" and help spawn a rising rural and urban proletariat.[48]

The foundation meeting of the SANNC held in Bloemfontein, at the Wesleyan School, Waaihoek, gave a boost to local Congress organising. In 1915, the Orange Free State (OFS) Native Congress claimed to represent Africans of the entire province. In 1912, it held a special general meeting that reported, inter alia, on proposals that black mine workers should receive the same rate of compensation paid to the white employees. By the March 1913 SANNC conference, OFS delegates included three delegates from Bloemfontein (John Mocher, Thomas Mapikela and B. King), four from Bethlehem, and one each from Senekal, Thaba 'Nchu, Vrede, Viljoen's Drift, and Chief Ntsane from Witsie's Hoek. In 1915, the Thaba 'Nchu Branch conference discussed the Land Act, passes for women, education, hostels for domestic workers, and state replacement of black rail workers and interpreters by "poor whites". Thaba 'Nchu offered a fertile zone for Congress penetration. As African property-owners and farm workers or sharecroppers alike lost out to white expansionism, support for Congress rose. Z. K. Matthews, whose childhood was spent in Kimberley, recalls stories that Thaba 'Nchu residents strongly supported Congress fund raising.[49]

The Land Act preoccupied Congress. Many of its leading figures raised land and labour issues before the Beaumont Commission as it toured the OFS in 1913. President W. Z. Fenyang and supporter Joel Goronyane submitted a statement of a Barolong deputation to the Commission that Thaba 'Nchu should be set aside as an African residential area. Goronyane testified about disruption caused by the Act. Mapikela, representing the OFS Native Congress as its General Secretary (and still then working as a carpenter), told the commission in Bloemfontein that Congress had received many complaints about the effects of the Act from the whole Province. He recalled that in 1908 Congress succeeded in opposing the Coloured Persons Property Bill, whose effect would have been, similarly to the Land Act, to "compel people to be forced labourers". Mapikela and fellow Congressman Peter Phahlane criticised the Act's sudden impact and lack of consultation.[50]

In the town of Thaba 'Nchu itself, on 12 September 1913, farm tenants turned out along with Congress stalwarts such as farmer and ex-teacher Jeremiah Makgothi. Sol Plaatje graphically described the scene:

> A thousand Natives came from the surrounding farms, some on horseback, others on bicycles, and other conveyances such as carts, wagons, etc.; they included evicted wanderers and native tenants under notice to leave their farms, with letters of eviction and other evidence in their pockets; they included some refugees, who had likewise been evicted from other districts.[51]

A few weeks later, Abram Mofulu and 50 other residents of Bethlehem district submitted a petition on behalf of the Eastern Native Vigilance Committee, calling not only for land rights and the franchise but also for legal protection for farm workers and due payment for child farm workers. Mofulu explained that white farmers had driven his people from the land, often for trifling reasons, and now they "get very small wages in the towns". Obed Mokhosi explained that children over 14 years had to do forced labour. When the commission moved on to Harrismith, they faced yet another Congress activist, Josiah Gumede, who as noted above, was employed to fight for the rights of the Bakhulukwe people, and who spoke of their "great hardship" under the Land Act. Retired Witsieshoek farm worker Tsolo Mopeli told the commission: "Our children are out working. It is not right to say that we have not worked, for all the roads and bridges, railways and different works … in the State have been helped by our hands."[52]

If Congress activists did not always get their hands dirty, then at least they sometimes listened to workers. Richard Msimang wrote down the testimonies of farm labourers and squatters such as Simon Teatea. In 1914, he published them in the ANC's agitational pamphlet, *Natives Land Act 1913: Specific Cases of Evictions and Hardships*. Teatea, of Senekal District, spoke of how he and his sons had worked for no wages and been forced to move from farm to farm.[53]

Behind this intense interest in land and rural labour lay the worsening conditions of many Africans. In 1910 government officials reported dissent in Reitz and Edenburg. Even a government report of 1918, that sought to gloss over Africans' grievances, imagining instead "unanimous satisfaction" with state efforts at consultation, conceded widespread overcrowding, loss of movable and landed property, and (forced) migration. Some 1,300 people had moved across the border from Seliba Reserve to Bechuanaland. In Thaba 'Nchu Reserve, at least 1,050 sharecropping households had been driven off white farms by the Land Act, with livestock numbers of Africans plummeting three to six times in four years in the face of severe drought and the Act's enforcement.[54]

Despite these economic difficulties and legal provocations, OFS Congress leaders generally emphasised moderate tactics. The years John Mocher spent as a worker did not automatically incline him to radicalism. In May 1912, he told an OFS Congress conference: Africans should "set aside any ideas of division" that would bring "distress and misery" and "allow ourselves to be guided by [white] men of moderate views". Such moderation was partly the result of outside influences. The conference was opened by Wesleyan minister J. W. Housscham, who urged Africans to confine themselves to "constitutional methods and never to resort to strikes or armed protests". The lack of a history of industrial disputation or black unionism in the lightly industrialised OFS contributed to moderate policies.[55]

The attitudes to labour of Thomas Mapikela, an aspirant black businessperson but with an artisan background, were contradictory. Mapikela served as ORC Congress General Secretary and, from 1912 to 1915, as OFS Congress President. In 1914, he became SANNC Junior Treasurer. He epitomised continuity in Congress, serving continually as ANC speaker in the first two decades of its existence. Mapikela's career illustrates the complex class forces among ANC members. In a 1913 letter to *Imvo,* on behalf of the ANC, he not only complained of restrictions on land acquisitions placed on Africans but also argued that the overall aim of the Land Act was to impoverish them "so that their services can be easily obtained at any mean rate of wages".[56]

The prospect of lower wages would normally please an aspirant entrepreneur, given the likelihood of higher rates of profit. Yet, in his public pronouncements, Mapikela stressed the central role of black people, not business, in the economy. Far from being a burden on taxpayers, Africans contributed "in direct poll tax four times as much" as the white populace. He combined criticism of colonial and racial exploitation: "If the white man were to work himself the natives would have no grudge against him. But [he] wishes the natives to work for him, while he stands and looks on putting all the profit in his pocket."[57]

Mapikela's commercial survival indicates that room remained for small black business to manoeuvre. He was vitally concerned for the fate of black business and, undoubtedly, afraid of being driven back into the ranks of the proletariat. However, Mapikela's attitude to workers was more complex. Experience of wage labour and of national oppression made him sensitive to worker conditions. His Congress role sharpened his understanding of, and focused his attention on "solutions" to, their general predicament. This was a recurring feature of his political career—he later presented the "odd" picture of a black businessperson championing the rights of black trade unions.

The protests of African women concerning growing restrictions on women, including employees, soon extended to Congress. This related to the growth of the African female workforce in the province, where their labour was in high demand, especially for domestic work. This fact compelled white people to demand control over their labour by means of passes. Such rigid control also restricted women's mobility and disrupted family life. Congress interest also related to the activity of women around Congress. During 1912, African women, assisted by SANNC leader Walter Rubusana, collected 5,000 signatures on an anti-pass petition that a delegation took to Cape Town and which not only attacked the indignity and inferiority that pass laws created but also exposed how they were "an effective means of enforcing labour" of African women. During May 1912, at a special meeting of the OFS Congress,

Mesdames Pitso, Mashukela, Ndebele, Mokhele, Prince, Lecohenyo and Forster were all delegates. This occurred at a time when elsewhere female participation in Congress was limited. One reason for greater male solidarity in the Orange Free State may have been a sharp decline in the economic fortunes of the black elite.[58]

Women wage earners, such as laundry workers in Winburg and Jagersfontein, also spoke out and demanded better conditions. When women organised themselves into the OFS Native and Coloured Women's Association, they became active in the 1913 anti-pass passive resistance which also involved women workers. Unless one takes a very narrow and unrealistic view of "working class" to include *only* labourers, the presence among 80 women arrested in May 1913 in Waaihoek of the wives of skilled workers (carpenters, brick-makers, plumbers, and shoemakers) indicates the varied class composition of the protesters. Whilst some of these women, such as Liza Japhtu, wife of a cab owner, can be characterised as more "elite", three of the Association's executive members, Rachel Talka, Mietha Kotsi, and Helen Louw were illiterate, suggesting the subaltern nature of some activists. The protests were large-scale and took place over several months: 800 marched in Winburg and 600 in Bloemfontein, carrying sacks of passes. In June women physically fought police. Many marched in the mining town of Jagersfontein, led by a Mozambican woman, Aploon Vorster. Prisons filled up with demonstrators sentenced to forced labour.[59]

The women had led. They also moved African men to act. Now the OFS Congress vigorously took up the issue. It arranged for women protesters to join its meeting with the Secretary of Native Affairs in Thaba 'Nchu in September 1913. A delegation from the OFS Native Women's Association addressed delegates to the 1914 SANNC conference. Sol Plaatje and Abdurahman solicited donations to aid the resisters through their newspapers. Plaatje visited 34 of the women in gaol. Denied their own boots, and forced to carry out forced labour, "some of the most refined … women of Bloemfontein are negotiating the pebbles and the cement floor with the bare skins of their feet". When in Waaihoek, he "found that the passive resisters *included* members of the most respectable coloured families, and sisters and daughters of ministers and teachers".[60]

However, the issue affected women workers as well. Passes cost workers valuable money. Given the tiny size of black "respectable" social strata, it is unlikely that all 1,400 marchers were uniform of class. Police arrested women workers during the course of their work. *Tsala ea Batho* noted, about the arrests in Bloemfontein, that "40 working women are kept away from their work". Dozens of domestic workers, Plaatje stated, "failed to take up their positions beside the kitchen stoves ... [as] on their way to town they had been accosted by the police, arrested, and locked up for not having passes". At the Wesleyan Mission School in the Vredefort location, police arrested Urbaniah Motshumi, a teacher living with her parents, for failing to produce a pass. A similar fate befell Ruth Pululu in Winburg.[61]

Some Congress members even related passes to mine workers' grievances. At a meeting in Waaihoek in 1914, Joseph Twayi of the OFS Congress pointed out that mine owners were retrenching black workers. Rejecting the reply of the Waaihoek location superintendent not to "cry before you are bitten", Twayi insisted than an African had

> ... every right to inquire about what work he was to do. Neither was it fair to ask a native to go and work for 1s.6d. or 1s. a day (Applause). What was especially required was for the Town Council to prevent natives who were not in possession of passes being run in by the police ... [that is], the natives who had come into the town from the mines quite recently and could not find work.[62]

As the women's civil disobedience rolled on, men began to act in earnest. The Winburg Native Vigilance Association warned of a general strike by working men. Propertied male members of the black community sought compromise and convinced the Bloemfontein Town Council to concede an elected African Advisory Board. However, as Julia Wells shows, they could not control the women "who refused to be divided along class lines" and continued their actions until the onset of the World War brought a lull in protests. Women, although largely excluded from political bodies, had launched the largest, most militant campaign against race oppression of the period. Men in Congress were visibly impressed, or shocked. A pyrrhic victory came when the 1923 Native Urban Areas Act exempted women from passes but shifted the burden to other areas of urban life such as rents.[63]

By 1917, there were changes in the OFS Congress leadership. Fenyang remained president, but the December annual general meeting elected Robert Setlogelo secretary and J. M. Nyokong treasurer. The press reported a "heated dispute" about branch credentials but this was "finally amicably settled". Shortly afterwards government officials forced TNC executive members arriving for the SANNC conference to strip and be dipped in sheep wash, thus ramming home the indignities faced by Africans in the province. [64]

In this period, other Congress leaders gained insight into worker demands. Selby Msimang (born 1886), better known for his later work in Natal, was an important activist in black worker organisations in Bloemfontein from 1917 to 1922. He came from an Edendale *kholwa* family but whilst his brother Richard was educated in Britain, his father could not afford the same for Selby, educated at Edendale and Kilnerton Institute. Selby Msimang did not undertake industrial work but became involved in a wide range of occupations. He worked in Johannesburg as an interpreter for Native Affairs Labour Inspection and for a labour agent, thereby gaining some knowledge of workers' problems. He worked then in a magistrate's court where he experienced "the painful experience of a conscientious interpreter". During his youth, Msimang awakened to the injustices of workers when he discovered black miners were forced to "work 30 days without pay" if sick. He worked for the Post Office and as a law clerk for Seme. Thereafter he worked in Vrede until he resigned on principle when his wife was obliged to get a permit. He later assisted his brother, Richard Msimang, and Elka Cele, to raise funds to protest the 1913 Land Act when he travelled to Sekhukhuneland, Pondoland, and Kimberley. In 1915, he opened a small grocery shop in Sophiatown, which failed. He worked on a mine in a job negotiated by some Transkei mine workers he had met. After two weeks he returned to work briefly for Seme and then for a solicitor in Verulam, but for only a small wage, which led him to take on a matchwood contract. He had sufficient capital to go into small business with Selope Thema and in 1917 applied to lease 100 acres of land in Mtunzini to grow sugar. These diverse occupations provided him with insight into working lives but when he moved to Bloemfontein, he was attracted to the radicalism that swept up sections of Congress and brought him in close contact with workers. He recalled that after 1913 he "developed a strong conviction that our salvation as a race lay in the mobilisation of our prowess as workers. I felt that we could so organise our people as to be ready and willing to withhold their labour."[65]

Msimang agitated for higher wages and better conditions for African council workers from 1917 to 1920. In 1917 he drew attention to the harsh daily lives of Africans. He argued successfully that the municipality should allocate more money to the black, rather than white, council workers. Location residents, who received very few amenities, should not have to pay the same as white people for the same services. He viewed low wages as a major contributor to high African mortality in Waaihoek during the 1918 influenza epidemic. After the War, despite a tripling of living costs, African wages remained stagnant. Msimang organised protest meetings, addressing three or four meetings a day as he traversed the urban sprawl. Workers wanting to strike for higher wages approached him. He took up their cause. In an interesting statement on the levelling of social strata, he noted all African workers in Bloemfontein earned only 2 shillings a day irrespective of work. In February 1919, he led agitation for a wage rise to 4 shillings and sixpence only just covering food needs. The thrust of the campaign was to convince authorities diplomatically, but instead it stimulated a backlash from the white community. The army was deployed and martial law declared. To police, Msimang was a "noted Native Agitator". The Cape Congress strongly protested his subsequent arrest, allegedly for "wrongfully, wickedly and maliciously" inciting a meeting of "1000 or thereabouts" of African "labourers and residents" to "obtain an increase in their wages". Police were confident the "better class native [was] not affected", but Msimang effectively had bridged the worlds of African politics and labour.[66]

Over the next few months, he helped Bloemfontein workers form the Native and Coloured Workers' Union, which soon merged with Kadalie's ICU. In August, Msimang gave a public lecture, under ICU auspices, in Cape Town. He condemned abuses of the labour recruitment system and lack of African freedom in the OFS and warned of impending intensification of job colour bars in industry He called on Africans to organise industrially, "failing which their cause was lost".[67]

Msimang chose to become active in Congress and joined the Bloemfontein branch led by Peter Phahlane. Here he exposed the corruption of African "block men" (later Advisory Board) secretly paid by the Municipality, which then levied extra taxes on working people to pay for the payments. In 1919, block men had been willing to accept much lower wages for workers than Msimang had recommended. He noted the resentment, by block men, of Congress "intrusion" in municipal matters. This spurred the ANC on to work harder among workers. Msimang worked in rural towns, opposing child labour and female passes, helping to improve the water supply of black residents of Brandfort, and opposing exploitation in Ficksburg of workers from across the Caledon River.[68]

In an interview late in life, Msimang captured an important reason underpinning ANC support. The "rigid enforcement of pass laws served to disillusion many urban Africans" and "succeeded exceedingly well in bringing about demoralisation of the African people" but they sought "ways of extricating themselves from these entanglements" and one day will be "like an erupted volcano" and "became aware of political freedom they should strive for. There lay the strength of the ANC". He spoke of his experimentation in organising the ordinary African worker who observed there was a spark of self-realisation and silent protest against conditions thrust upon him. ... I have attempted an experiment on raising a solid organisation among farm labourers. I selected a district in the Orange Free State of Kopjes. The idea was to raise cells scattered all over the district ... [and] indoctrinate members and each cell and establish communication between the cells. If the cells system could spread throughout the province, a date could be fixed for simultaneous action by all the cells ... But unfortunately several of the members were dismissed ... The other misfortune was lack of funds and illiteracy.[69]

Selby Msimang was the quintessential "two caps" leader, able to bestride ANC and black union movements. He took "much of the initiative on labour matters" in Congress (Walshe) and was "one of the few" ANC members "actively interested in labor organisation" (Karis). He helped form the Bloemfontein ICWU in 1919-1920, which elected him President. He wrote in his diary on 11 May 1919: "The first African workers meeting was held in Bloemfontein." In the face of what, in 1921, he would term a cruel police "war of extermination against us", he saw the need to build both political and industrial organisation. As Wickins observes, leaders of the ANC elite such as Msimang were "imbued with the ideals of western social democracy". But whereas Wickins contrasts the ICU (and Msimang's) astute grasp of African economic grievances with the failure of the OFS Congress to see this, Msimang remained committed to Congress.[70]

In the OFS, as in the other provinces, Congress leaders and members had some knowledge of and experience of the working lives of Africans. In the face of economic crises, the intensified land dispossession that hit Africans particularly hard in the province, and continued denial of African political rights, Congress in the Orange Free State reached out to urban Africans and sought to articulate their demands.

Conclusion

The conclusions made in the previous chapter about the uneven if intensifying relations between Congress and workers largely hold for the other provinces where, however, less concentrated industrialisation and urbanisation resulted in less contact. Nevertheless, in the Cape, Natal and the OFS at this time, there was much experimentation with new forms of alliances or representations of workers by Congress activists. At times, there were sharp differences between more moderate and more radical Congress leaders over what this relationship should be. Yet all ANC leaders felt obliged—perhaps by the very force of numbers of black workers or by feelings of common interests between different black social strata, or through experience of working lives—to (at least rhetorically) stand up for a better life for black workers. However, the next decade was to see intensified government repression and economic crises that would sorely test the level of commitment of Congress to the cause of labour.

Notes

1   Kinkead-Weekes, "Africans in Cape Town", p. 205; *Blue Book on Native Affairs 1910*, p. 299; Z.K. Matthews interview with G. Carter and T. Karis, 19 Mar. 1964, CKC 2:XM66:94; police report, 20-21 Dec. 1920, JUS file 2/950/19 "Unrest in Cape Peninsula".

2   Mweli Skota, *African Yearly Register*, pp. 137, 175; *Imvo Zabantsundu* 17 Jun. 1913; KC v. 4, p. 113; K. Rasimeni and Ngojo statement to Native Separatist Churches Commission, 28 [Dec. (?)] 1921, in "Native Separatist Churches", *Papers of A. W. Roberts*.

3   H. Scanlon, *Representation & Reality: Portraits of Women's Lives in the Western Cape, 1948-1976* (Cape Town: HSRC Press, 2007), pp. 170-1.

4   R. Kingwill, "The African National Congress in the Western Cape: A Preliminary Study", B.A. (Hons.), UCT, 1977, Chapter 2; Hofmeyr, "Crisis", p. 74; *Cape Times* 21, 14 Jun. 1918.

5   Mahabane questionnaire reply 1959, CKC 2:XM10:91/2; Skota, *African Yearly Register*, errata; Mahabane, "Premier and Rand Natives" *Cape Times* 13 Jul. 1918 and "The Industrial Situation on the Rand and Natives", *Imvo* 30 July 1918; T. Matshikiza, "Long Life, Great Times", [Mahabane] *Drum* May 1957.

6   P. Wickins, "General Labour Unions in Cape Town 1918-1920", *SAJE* v. 40 (1972), pp. 275-301; *Imvo* 31 Dec. 1918; police reports 10 Jul. 1919, JUS 3/527/17 (a meeting of 200 black workers discussed formation of a union quite separate from Congress): B. Hirson, *Frank Glass: The Restless Revolutionary* (London: Porcupine, 2003), p. 20; E. Mantzaris, "The Promise of the Impossible Revolution: The Cape Town ISL 1918-1921", *Studies in the History of Cape Town* v. 4 (1984), pp. 145-173, p. 148; Hirson, *A History of the Left in South Africa* (London: Tauris, 2005), Chapter 2.

7   Bonner "Transvaal Congress", p. 54; *Natal Advertiser* 10 Mar. 1919; *International* 19 Dec. 1919; *APO* 30 Dec. 1919.

8   Baines, "Disturbances", pp. 45, 78-79, 103-34, 184; KC v.4, p. 76; G. Baines, "Masabalala, Samuel Makama Martin", in Verwey, *New Dictionary of South African Biography* v. 2, pp. 95-96; Wickins, *The ICU*, pp. 51-55; Mancoe, *Directory*, p. 73; Walshe, *Rise of African Nationalism*, pp. 74, 240; Baines, "From Populism to Unionism: the Emergence and Nature of Port Elizabeth's ICWU 1918-1920", *JSAS* v. 17 (1991), pp. 679-716; Skota, *African Yearly Register*, p. 187; UG22-16, p. 249; G. Minkley, "'Did Not Come to Work on Monday': The East London Waterfront in Comparative Perspective, c.1930-1963", in P. Alexander and R. Halpern (eds.), *Racializing Class, Classifying Race* (New York: St. Martin's Press, 2000), pp. 193-212, pp. 196.

9   Odendaal, *Vukani Bantu*, p. 248; S. Lusipo, "U-Boni Dr Walter Benson Rubusana: Intshayebelo", SOAS, 1969, Ms. 380263 citing Rhodes letter 12 May 1900; Rubusana to J. Harris 17 Jan. 1917, "Letters of W.B. Rubusana 1910-1922", SOAS Ms. 380264; Ngqongolo, "Rubusana"; *Natives of South Africa*, p. 297; "Dr. Walter B. Rubusana", *Imvo* 26 Aug. 1961; Native Affairs. *Report*, 1911, p. 30; "Native Unrest at East London", report by SAP Grahamstown, 29 Aug. 1918 on meeting of 23 Aug. 1918, and "Money Complaints", *Abantu-Batho* 29 Aug., 5 Sep. 1918, translated, JUS 3/527/17; Wickins, *The ICU*, p. 51.

10 "Oppression of the Native and Coloured Races", *Izwe la Kiti* 24 Dec. 1912; S. Mgedeza to CID on Congress meetings Jun. 1919, JUS 3/527/17; Matthews interview with Carter and Karis, 1964, p. 7: he recalls stories of Congress activity in the Transkei led by Mdolomba and chiefs.

11 UG22-16, pp. 118-119; 135 (Kalipa, Makohliso), and annexure 6; Ntsebeza, *Democracy Compromised*, pp. 83-89; UG22-16, p. 154 (Kama); *Native Affairs Report, 1911* (UG10-13), pp. 24, 27; "Native Unrest" report, SAP Grahamstown, 26 Aug. 1918, JUS 3/524/17.

12 Verwey, *New Dictionary*, p. 154; C. Bundy, "'We Don't Want Your Rain, We Won't Dip': Popular Opposition, Collaboration and Social Control in the Anti-Dipping Movement, 1908-16", in Beinart and Bundy, *Hidden Struggles*, pp. 191-221, p. 202.

13 UG22-16, pp. 92-93 (Plaatje evidence, Kimberley Dec. 1913).

14 E.J. Africa, *The Kimberley Malay Camp, 1882 to 1957* (Kimberley: Sol Plaatje Educational Trust, 2006); McCord, *Calling of Katie Makanya*, p. 23; Z.K. Matthews, *Freedom for My People: The Autobiography of Z.K. Matthews* (London: Collings, 1981), p. 20; "Imbizo yaBantu Ejozi (The South African National Congress)", *Izwe la Kiti* 2 Apr. 1913; curiously, eight attended from Bechuanaland.

15 NNC. *Constitution* (1915), p. 12, copy in Natal Archives Depot (NAD), Chief Native Commissioner (CNC) 642/2 and 2316/20l; Telegram NA (Pretoria) to NA (PMB) 28 Jun. 1911, and related correspondence, CNC 16, CNC 691/1911.

16 John Dube ms. letter, Sep. 1914 and typed letter of 26 Sep. 1914 to CNC Natal and reply of CNC 23 Sep. 1914, NAD CNC 1302/14; CNC Natal Circular no. 20 to all magistrates, Natal, 17 Sep. 1914; CNC 183, War: Relief Fund: Contributions by Natal Native Congress, file 1466/1914, NAD, which includes a large receipt book of donations channelled through the NCN. Chief Stephen Mini donated £11 in Jan. 1915; Chiefs Laduma and Mgqomo raised £73 and £40 respectively.

17 *Minutes of Evidence of the Natal Natives Land Committee* (UG35-18), pp. 38 (Kumalo), 51, 203 (Dlamini, Mtembu), 52-53, 204-205 (Mabaso, Ncamu, Matshobongwana), 235 (Ndhlovu); UG22-16, pp. 636, 630 (Ndhlovu), 595 (Ntmebbu, Mabaso); Edgecombe, "Labour Conditions". Matshobongwana, a Xhosa, was "SANC Newcastle Secretary", whether of the NNC or the Cape SANC is unclear. On Ndhlovu, see La Hausse, *Restless Identities*, p. 205, who notes (p. 183) the ruthless advance of capitalism in Vryheid, a point also made by Marks, "Bambatha Rebellion". p. 359.

18 UG22-16 (including UG22-14), p. 555ff.

19 *Evidence, Natal Natives Committee*, pp. 99 (Dube, Mini), 2 (Ogle). Kumalo noted (p. 39) that whilst in his district "we are not opposed to the Congress in any way ... we are insufficient in numbers to belong to it". On Mabaso, see La Hausse, *Restless Identities*, p. 168. In 1914, authorities criticised Mini as too involved in political matters beyond his region of Edendale, of seeking to "play the part of an agitator": Assistant Magistrate, Umgeni Court to Chief Magistrate PMB, 4 Jun. 1914, NAD 1/PMB 3/1/1/2/1 86/14: "Pietermaritzburg Magistrate. Native Congress Meetings 1914-1918".

20 CNC to SNA, Letter Addressed to His Excellency the Governor General by Certain Members of the Natal Native Congress, 15 Jul. 1915, NAD CNC 918. CNC (Addison) "thanked the signatories for their expression of confidence but informed them that they could only express the views of their Congress".

21 Odendaal, *Vukani Bantu*, p. 69; Trapido, "African Opinion", p. 7; Walshe, *Rise of African Nationalism*, p. 228; Magistrate Newcastle to CNC 14 Oct. 1914, NAD CNC 918, 38/13/14/32: under martial law, Mtembu felt it necessary to seek permission to hold NNC

meetings; U17-11, pp. 238, 241. By 1911, 5,439 Africans worked on the collieries, where poor conditions engendered discontent: UG10-13, pp. 38, 41.

22 "UMafukuzela eTembalihle" 9 Oct. 1912, "Natal Native Congress", 23 Oct. 1912, [Dube] "Segregation: The Native View" 4 Dec. 1912, "Ezas'Eshowe," "Imihlaba yaBantu", 11 Dec. 1912, "The Native Congress" 2 Apr. 1913, letter of "Nyamazane ka Mtobela", Jagersfontein, 22 Jan. 1913, "Intshumayelo ka Mafukuzela ku Congress", 9 Apr. 1913, *Izwe la Kiti*. An editorial ("The New Cabinet") of 24 Dec. 1912 supported black representation in Parliament. Contributors included Magema Fuze and Petros Lamula.

23 "Imbizo ya Bantu Ejozi", *Izwe la Kiti* 2 Apr. 1913.

24 NNC *Constitution*, 1915, pp. 2, 9. Dube initiated meetings to explain SANNC aims: March 1914 correspondence on his New Hanover "emissary" P. Dhladhla, NAD 1/KRK 3/1/14, 174/1914, CNC 338.

25 "The Prayer of the Natal Native Congress ..." Apr. 1916, letter of Mini and Gumede, NAD CNC 236, 550/16, also in P. La Hausse, "Drink and Cultural Innovation in Durban: The Origins of the Beerhall in South Africa, 1902-1916", in Crush and Ambler, *Liquor and Labor*, pp. 78-114, p. 103; Gumede in UG22-16, p. 533; A. Dube, "Africa: My Native Land" in M. Daymond et al (eds.) *Women Writing Africa: The Southern Region* (New York: Feminist Press, 2003), p. 158; Couzens, "New African," p. 204.

26 Hadebe, *"Impi"*; CNC 226B 23/1916, SNA 7 Jan. 1916; *International* 21 Jul. 1916, 20 Apr. 1917.

27 UG17-11, p. 310 ff.

28 "Notes of Meeting of John L. Dube with Natives in the Court Room of the Magistrate, Eshowe ... 30 November 1912", translated by Carl Faye, Zulu Interpreter, Campbell Collections, ms. 1093. Some chiefly representatives dismissed Dube's appeal for unity, but half the audience indicated they would "enter our union". Dube appointed a local man, Diki Zibisi to represent Congress in the area.

29 J.S. Marwick, Manager, Municipal Native Affairs Department to CNC Natal, 28 Jul. 1916 and CNC to Marwick 8 Aug. 1916, CNC 247, 1179/1916 (file entitled "The South African Native National Congress wish to hold meetings in Durban"). The best analysis of these and most other NNC-related events of the period is La Hausse, *Restless Identities*, pp. 54-55ff.

30 La Hausse, *Restless Identities*, pp. 54-55, 64-65.

31 Acting Manager MNAD to CNC Natal, 21 Aug. 1916 with attached report of African meeting of 7 Aug. (others to address the meeting included Chief Martin Lutuli), Manager MNAD to CNC Natal 1 Nov. 1916, with Report on African meeting of 12 Aug. by Inspector A.W. Hines of 15 Aug. 1916 attached, and Marwick (MNAD) to Town Clerk Durban, 31 Oct. 1916, all in CNC 247 1179/1916.

32 Marwick to Secretary, Committee of Natives, 14 Nov., CNC to MNAD (Marwick) 17 Jan. 1917, and Marwick to Town Clerk, Durban, 31 Oct. 1916, all in CNC 247, 1179/1916.

33 Durban Native Committee to Manager MNAD 14 Sep. 1916, and Durban Native Committee (signed Philemon Lutuli, Secretary, and F. Xulu, Henry Mkwanyana, F. Caluza, C. Msomi) to Mayor and Town Council, 8 Dec. 1916, in CNC 247, 1179/1916.

34 CID to SAP 9 Oct. 1919, report on SANNC Executive meeting of 6 Oct. 1919, and police report on Dube speech at Roodepoort 9 Jan. 1918, JUS 3/527/17.

35 Cope, *To Bind the Nation*, p. 99; "Meeting of Natal Native Congress at Pietermaritzburg 7 Nov. 1919", CID to Sec. SAP 13 Nov. 1919, JUS 3/527/17.

36   UG22-16, p. 533; *Minutes of Evidence, Select Committee on Native Affairs* (SC6A-17), p. 629; Magistrate to Town Clerk PMB 22 May 1918, NAD 1/PMB 86/14: "Pietermaritzburg Magistrate. Native Congress Meetings 1914-1918".

37   UG22-16, pp. 531-3; SC6A-17, pp. 618-626, 638; J.S. Gumede, General Secretary NNC to CNC Natal, 5 Apr. 1916, CNC 505/16. Colonial officials sometimes conflated J. T. and J. S. Gumede: it appears J. T. Gumede served briefly as General Secretary in 1915 until replaced by J. S. Gumede.

38   NNC *Constitution*; On Gumede's land deals see: CNC 226B 1916/29: "Natives Land Act" 224 1915/1359, 253 1916/1464, 326 1752/18; van Diemel, *In Search of Freedom*, pp. 40-50. La Hausse, *Restless Identities*, p. 77 infers part of the inspiration for Gumede's land acquisitions was Garveyism.

39   SC6A-17, pp. 626-645.

40   "'Workers' Indaba", *Abantu-Batho* Jul. [4?] 1918 translation, JUS 3/527/17; NAD 1/PMB 3/1/1/2/3. 234/14, "Registration … *Iso Lesizwe Esimnyama*"; *International* 25 Apr., 16, 2 May 1919 (cf. *South African Socialist Review* March 1958, p. 10); "Maritzburg Bolshevik Case", *Rand Daily Mail* 9 May 1919. Gumede (in "A Cry for Freedom, Liberty, Justice and Fair Play," ms. 1919, Hoover Institution) refers to how Africans were "unmercifully disenfranchised" in Natal where they were also taxed without representation and lost access to previously rent-free mission reserves.

41   There is scholarly neglect of this region but see N. Cele, "Between AmaZulu and AmaMpondo: Community Building at KwaMachi, Harding, 1820s-1948", Ph.D. Michigan State University, 2006. Cele interviewed the Koti family but (wrongly) his son denied any political activity by his father.

42   "Native Unrest: Harding Division", SAP PMB to CNC 26 Apr. 1915 and 11 Feb. 1915, enclosing report by Detective F.G. Tranchell of 8 Feb. 1915, CNC 1302/14, "European War: Arming of Jolwayo's People". Police also blamed the pecuniary interests of Labour Agents for hindering war labour enrolment.

43   SAP Natal to CNC 26 Apr. 1915, SAP Harding to SAP PMB 11, 13 Feb. 1915, Magistrate Alfred to CNC Natal 11 Feb., 21 Apr. 1915, SA Police PMB to CNC 11 Feb. 1915, enclosing detective report 8 Feb. 1915: CNC 1302/14. For rumours see daily wires from CNC Natal to SNA Pretoria Feb. to Nov. 1914; on Dube see confidential wire 627 (Bhambhatha) and wire 926 5 Sep. 1914 (Germany). Cf. NAD CNC 1196/16 CNC "Rex vs. Sandile Nkabinde" 1, 10 Aug. 1916, Attorney General to CNC 9 Aug. 1916 accusing Nkabinde of stating African prisoners would be "set free" by an Army "coming to this country."

44   T. Keegan, "The Restructuring of Agrarian Class Relations in a Colonial Economy: The Orange River Colony 1902-1910", *JSAS* v. 5 (1979), pp. 234-254; ORC, *Report of Industrial Commission 1904* p. 65.

45   *Blue Book on Native Affairs 1910* (UG17-11), pp. 251-257; "The Thaba 'Nchu Division" in *Natives Land Commission: Minute … by … W. H. Beaumont* (UG25-16), p. 28; UG10-13, p. 11.

46   *Report of the Natives Land Commission* v. 1 (UG19-16), IV-8; UG17-11, pp. 52, 341, 355-357, 364; W.M. Macmillan, *The Land, the Native, & Unemployment* (Johannesburg: Council of Education, 1924).

47   UG17-11, pp. 53, 252-253.

48   Report of Commissioner SAP, 1917, p. 65; "Native Rising at Jagersfontein," *Transvaal Leader* 12 Jan. 1914 (in *Correspondence Relating to the Recent Strike in South Africa*, p. 167); Gladstone to Sec. of State, 10, 15, 20 Jan. 1914 (in *British Documents on Foreign*

Affairs 10, pp. 402-411); Ranger, "Fighting", pp. 70-71; Simons, *Class & Colour*, p. 168; C. Murray, *Black Mountain: Land, Class and Power in the Eastern Orange Free State, 1880s-1980s* (Edinburgh: Edinburgh University Press, 1992), p. 5, and Chapter 2.

49 J. Haasbroek, "Founding Venue of the African National Congress (1912): Wesleyan School, Fort Street, Waaihoek, Bloemfontein", *Navorsinge van die Nasionale Museum* v. 18 no. 7 (2002), pp. 125-160; *Tsala ea Batho* 8 Jun. 1912, 24 Jul. 1915; "Imbizo yaBantu Ejozi," *Izwe la Kiti* 2 Apr. 1913; Z.K. Matthews interview with G. Carter and T. Karis, 19 Mar. 1964, CKC 2:XM66:94.

50 UG22-16 pp. 23-26, Annexure 1 (Goronyane), pp. 45-46 (Mapikela, Phahlane).

51 Plaatje, *Native Life*, p. 132; E. Kuzwayo, *Call Me Woman* (London: Women's Press, 1985), p. 61.

52 UG22-16, pp. 57-58 (Mofulu, Mokhosi) and Annexure 2 p. 66 (Mopeli) and p. 61 (Gumede). Gumede also refers to the failure of Bakhulukwe claims in his 1919 letter "A Cry for Freedom".

53 R.W. Msimang, *Natives Land Act 1913* (1914, reprinted 1996), pp. 27-32.

54 UG17-11 p. 342; *Report of Orange Free State Local Natives Land Committee 1918* (UG22-18) pp. 1-4.

55 *Tsala ea Batho* 8 June 1912; Mancoe, *Directory*, p. 75.

56 Mancoe, *Directory,* p. 72; J. Mocher and T. Mapikela [OFS Congress], "Free State Natives," *Imvo* 10 Jun. 1913; KC v. 4, p. 74; Verwey, *New Dictionary*, p. 155; AB MBL 4/1/1/16 file 193/09: Mapikela file.

57 Letter of T. Mapikela to *The Friend*, reproduced in *Tsala ea Batho* 14 Mar. 1914.

58 J. Wells, "The History of Black Women's Struggle against Pass Laws in South Africa 1900-1960", Ph.D. Columbia University" 1982, p. 71; J. Wells, "The War of Degradation: Black Women's Struggle against Orange Free State Pass Laws, 1913" in Crummey, *Banditry*, pp. 253-270, p. 255, J. Wells, "Why Women Rebel: A Comparative Study of South African Women's Resistance in Bloemfontein (1913) and Johannesburg (1958)", *JSAS* 10 (1983), pp. 55-70; "Petition of the Native & Coloured Women of the Province of the Orange Free State", in Daymond, *Women Writing Africa*, pp. 158-161.

59 Wells, "War of Degradation," passim; Ginwala, "Women and the ANC"; Odendaal, *Vukani Bantu*, p. 87; Plaatje, *Native Life*, pp. 94-95.

60 *Tsala ea Batho* 14, 21 Jun., 12, 19 Jul., 16 Aug. 1913, 22 Aug. 1914; Plaatje, *Native Life*, p. 115; Mancoe, *Directory*, p. 73; Plaatje, "Women's Passes in the Free State", *Tsala ea Batho* 15 Nov. 1913.

61 Plaatje, *Native Life,* p. 115; Plaatje, "Women's Passes in the Free State." Women's refusal to pay for passes continued to worry the Bloemfontein Council: "The Municipal Budget" *The Friend* 23 Apr. 1918.

62 *Tsala ea Batho* 5 Sep. 1914. On Twayi see Mancoe, *Directory*, pp. 83-84.

63 Wells, "War of Degradation", pp. 261-266, upon which this section is based.

64 "Orange Free State News" and "Dipping Regulations", *Abantu-Batho* 20 Dec. 1917.

65 Msimang, "Autobiography", SOAS, pp. 66, 98-139; Msimang Autobiography, Aitchison Collection, Paton and Struggle Archives UKZN, PC14/1/3/1, pp. 3-5, 11; KC v. 4, p. 105; Msimang, "The Emakhosini Mission Station", in "Early Autobiographical Writings Pre-1972", PC 14/1/1/1-3; D.S. Deane, *Black South Africans: A Who's Who* (Cape Town: OUP, 1978), p. 118.

66 *The Friend* 27 Aug. 1917 in J. Haasbroek, "Die Rol van Henry Selby Msimang in Bloemfontein, 1917-1922", *Navorsinge Nasionale Museum* v. 16 no. 3 (2000), pp. 33-66, p. 39; Msimang, "Autobiography", SOAS, pp. 98-139; "Autobiography", PC14/1/3/1,

pp.11a-11d; interview with D. Hemson, 1971, pp. 1-4 in PC14/1: these manuscripts have slightly different content; NAD CNC 291 1917/2352; Msimang to Influenza Epidemic Commission cited in H. Phillips, "'Black October': The Impact of the Spanish Influenza Epidemic of 1918 on South Africa" Ph.D. UCT. 1984, p. 77; PC14/1/3/1; "Rex vs. Msimang" Decisions of Supreme Court (OFS), Jan-Sep. 1919, p. 39, VAB HG 4/1/2/1/171 Crown vs. Msimang 12 May 1919, cited in Haasbroek, "Msimang", p. 58; police telegram, 3 Mar. 1919, 6/661/19/3, JUS.

67   *Cape Argus* 20 Jan. 1920; Wickins, *ICU*, pp. 43-51; Starfield, "History"; SAP Cape Town "Notes on Local Agitators", 23 Jun. 1919, Detective Evans to SAP 11 Aug. 1919, SAP Bloemfontein to Pretoria 2 Mar. 1919: JUS 3/527/17; *Cape Times* 9 Aug. 1919. See also Schoeman, *Bloemfontein*, pp. 280-282. According to Henry Daniel Tyamzashe, Maben Mocher was first OFS ICU secretary: "Summary History of the ICU", (East London, 1941), p. 4, transcript in Saffery Papers, B5.

68   "Autobiography", PC14/1/3/1, pp. 11-12, 11a-b; interview with Hemson, pp. 1, 16. The "block" system worked in ways analogous to black councils operating under apartheid.

69   Msimang, "The Emakhosini Mission Station", pp. 12-13.

70   Walshe, *Rise of African Nationalism* p. 247; Msimang, Biography, PC14/1/3/1; *The Friend* 7 Jun. 1921, cited in Haasbroek, "Msimang in Bloemfontein", p. 48; Wickins, *The ICU*, p. 43. Wickins interviewed Msimang in 1971.

Part 3
The Second Decade

"A Strong Seed in a Stony Bed": The 1920s

The 1920s were a tempestuous decade that saw the largest pre-war black labour strike, formation of the Communist Party of South Africa (CPSA) and branches of Marcus Garvey's Universal Negro Improvement Association (UNIA), as well as the mercurial rise and fall of the ICU. In addition, it saw an armed revolt by white employees literally bombed into submission and the subsequent Pact government between white labour and Afrikaner Nationalists. The decade closed with the rise of a pro-communist president of a moderate ANC. Historians have neglected 1920s ANC history, although important and enduring contacts involving Congress began to form in this decade.

During the 1920s, in the eyes of some workers, other groups overshadowed the ANC. Nevertheless, labour continued, if spasmodically, to influence a Congress that would become receptive to working-class ideas. It remained a relevant organisation for some politicised workers. In different ways, Congress presented itself to all Africans, including workers, as their organisation. Membership was compatible with their status as workers. Most ANC leaders continued to express sympathetic, if ambiguous, attitudes to workers. Their predicament was rooted in their conflicting social roles where they regarded themselves as leaders of a vast mass of oppressed people and simultaneously as leaders of a tiny "elite". However as discrimination intensified, they sought allies amongst the workers.

Behind these developments in African politics lay substantial socio-economic and wider political developments at national and provincial levels. The 1920s, as explained in Chapter 2, saw partial industrial take-off.[1] Based largely on the Rand, there was solid if much slower economic growth in provincial capitals. The resultant steady, if still limited and uneven, growth of the black industrial workforce offered the ANC opportunities for building support. If the general impression is that it failed to secure this support then that does not mean there

235

was no activity within the ANC to this end, particularly at provincial level. I discuss regional events in the following pair of chapters.

African mineworkers on strike, City Deep Mine, 1920

Important changes were occurring in the cultural sphere: for instance, newspapers began to mushroom, and sports such as soccer grew in popularity. Urbanites formed social clubs. Expansion of newspapers, experimentation with public meetings, and a more closely-knit social life offered opportunities to political groups to network. Furthermore, there were provocative state policies exemplified by legislation such as the 1927 Native Administration Act and the brutal repression of African protestors as vividly seen at Bulhoek in 1921. The climate of the 1920s can indeed be summarised as turbulent. The characterisation by historians of the decade as one of quiescence by the (national) ANC therefore needs explaining.

The early 1920s were a watershed in African politics. The vigorous and large-scale strikes and anti-pass protests from 1918 to 1920, led variously by black workers, early socialists, and Transvaal Congress radicals, scared the state and mine employers. In 1920, a state committee was aghast at the militant stance on passes of the SANNC and TNC who were "uncompromising" and refused to condone pass laws in industrial or urban areas. The Chamber of Mines promptly founded the pro-Mines newspaper *Umteteli wa Bantu* to blunt the appeal of the TNC's *Abantu-Batho*. In 1920, the mines and missionaries launched weekly film showings to African workers, "every foot of film being carefully censored". If worker audiences at times responded sceptically to propaganda films that simplistically or insensitively portrayed their own working lives, in general the effect of all these cultural sorties was to dampen down militancy, as was their intention.[2]

The Joint Councils, inspired by American missionaries, funded by corporate tycoons, and aided by African conservatives such as Aggrey, took off successfully and siphoned Congress intellectuals. It would take the ANC another 30 years, to the 1950s Defiance Campaigns led by Nelson Mandela and Walter Sisulu, to recapture the scale of a mass movement; unsurprisingly, over the same period, mine wages remained largely static.

As more Africans gradually settled in urban areas and gained shop-floor experience, new labour movements emerged; the ICU (1919), CPSA (1921) and industrial unions (late 1920s) captured the loyalty of some workers. It was a time of ideological experimentation and short-lived, shifting co-operation or rivalry between the ANC and these bodies, which historians have perceived as more worker-based than Congress, whose alleged *petit bourgeois* character they adduce mainly by analysing the class origins of its leadership. At first, this appears a truism, for both ICU and CPSA *claimed* to speak directly for workers. But it is also necessary to prove to what extent *their* leaders were *more* working class than the ANC. Membership is one guide to this question; the class nature of members another.

The ANC in the 1920s: Membership and Structure

The end of the period of TNC radicalism and the simultaneous formation of potent rivals make the start of the 1920s a useful marker for periodising the history of the ANC. A supporter, briefly surveying ANC history and lamenting divisions in the organisation, wrote in 1933: "All went smoothly until 1920, but from that time there has been trouble."[3]

The 1920s saw many changes in the ANC. Its May 1923 conference adopted the name "African National Congress". Behind the change was the influence of new leaders, recent events, and new ideas. Delegates assembled at Bloemfontein clearly were furious at the 1923 Native (Urban Areas) Bill. Referring to Parliament's ruling that "the black man ... has no right of ownership of land in this, an African land" as "injustice of the grossest magnitude", Congress passed a resolution of Pan-African and cross-class unity aimed at:

> ...all peoples of African descent domiciled within the borders of the Union of South Africa and in other parts of the continent of Africa, and whereas it is in

the best interests of the African people that all existing Bantu organisations such as the Interdenominational Native Ministers' Association, the Native Teachers' Association, the Native Farmers' Association, Workers' Union, Bantu Women's League, Vigilance Committees ... shall be affiliated with this Native National Association, it is resolved that the [SANNC] shall henceforth be known and described for all intents and purposes as "The African National Congress".

A shift in political thinking sought to articulate a wider African nationalism and appeal to a broader mass of people. In ANC circles, there was a gathering interest in Pan-Africanism, Garveyism, and events elsewhere in Africa. Radicals increasingly used the term "African": as noted in Chapter 5, a 1919 leaflet signed by communist T. W. Thibedi began: "Black Africans open your eyes." *Abantu-Batho* editors urged the ICU's *Workers' Herald* to join it in a "Conference of the African Press". Sol Plaatje attended the Pan-African Congress in 1919.[4]

Most historians see the 1920s as a time of ANC decline. Estimates of membership vary from 1,000-4,000 during the inter-war years. Yet there is no doubt Congress was now well established. The 1920 Inter-Departmental Committee on the Native Pass Laws and the 1925 Native Churches Commission pointed to increasing ANC influence. The former spoke of Congress wielding "an increasing influence in formulating" African opinion across the whole country, even if "numerically small". The latter called it "the strongest" African political organisation with membership "on the increase". In 1928, visiting American scholar Raymond Buell saw Congress as the *major* African political body.[5]

Press and state estimates of membership and attendance at ANC mass meetings suggest a total of 3,000-4,000 people in the early 1920s in the Cape and Transvaal. S. H. Thema, organiser in Pietersburg, Waterburg, Lydenburg and Zoutpansberg, Districts claimed in 1933 that, according to his books, membership had been 3,000 in 1920 and 2,000 in 1921. Z. R. Mahabane in 1920 gave Cape Congress membership as 1,200. In 1926, and again in 1927, he gave "membership" as 100,000. This was no doubt an exaggeration, but he probably meant to suggest supporters rather than members. He told a state committee it was "upwards of 100,000 ... I cannot tell you how many members have paid". In fact: "At present we have no paying members, for the last two years no subscriptions have been paid." John Dube retorted that despite this purported figure, Congress had "but little influence", although he still was optimistic it could prosper.[6]

ANC influence was actually much wider. D. D. T. Jabavu, a rival, conceded that in 1920 Congress articulated "the strongest single volume of native feeling" in South Africa. There was an interlocking of membership, or cordial relations, between it and Advisory Boards, Vigilance Associations, the 20,000 strong Ethiopian Church of South Africa (Henry Reed Ngcayiya of the ANC was its leader, having left the AME), and the Cape Native Voters' Convention. There were joint meetings between the ANC, ICU and CPSA and overlapping membership. Thus, one must qualify assessments of ANC influence by distinguishing paid membership from indirect membership of affiliated organisations and supporters.[7]

Despite this wider influence, the ANC did not have a mass membership, making its ability to make contact with and represent workers largely symbolic. Govan Mbeki asserts it was "top-heavy with very little support amongst the masses". The class structure of membership remained largely non-proletarian. The 1920 Committee on the Native Pass Laws saw "a large majority" of Congress members having a "certain amount of education only to find the professional clerical and skilled avenues of employment practically closed to them", resulting, it opined, in some members "reduced to living on their wits". It drew, states Walshe, its leadership "essentially from ministers, small-scale entrepreneurs, clerks ... journalists, lawyers ... and ... artisans".[8] The African proletariat was too fragmented and unorganised to impact heavily on the ANC but, as already outlined, there were workers in the ANC and several of its "middle class" figures had experienced wage-labour.

Yet neither the ICU, nor CPSA, nor black industrial unions succeeded in attracting many African industrial workers. In 1924, police claimed ICU membership to be 11,734, including 3,859 semi-skilled and only 97 skilled workers. By mid-1925, the ICU claimed 30,000, but only half were financial. It was weak in some cities: only 600 in Durban and 300 in Kimberley. A massive growth in ICU numbers took place in 1927-1928, especially in rural Natal. Membership was estimated to be from between 100,000 to 250,000. The bulk were peasants with only fleeting membership. By 1929-1930, the ICU had declined. The CPSA and FNETU attracted some industrial workers, but remained small. The CPSA claimed to have 1,600 Africans out of 1,750 members in 1928, but declined markedly by the early 1930s. FNETU in 1928 claimed 10,000-15,000 affiliated members (an exaggeration), but disappeared in 1931. Whilst these groups appear on the surface to have temporarily eclipsed the ANC, the latter's 1,000-4,000 paid-up members were roughly comparable with CPSA figures. A similar position existed in some churches. In 1921, Transvaal Methodist *manyano* membership was only 3,330. By the mid-1920s, the Congress at least had a central office at 134 Anderson Street, Johannesburg.[9]

Several factors suggest genuine, if episodic, relations between the ANC and working peoples. It is necessary to have a broad conception of both to understand the precise nature of the relationship. The ANC made occasional forays into radicalism, which at times included direct support for African workers, who in turn had socio-political and cultural ties with other black strata; there were many bridges between classes. Part of the source of the political culture they began to develop was the ANC itself. National ANC leaders were not proletarians, but the ANC's appeal transcended class divisions and appealed to Africans on a national basis. The appeal of nationalist politics could be strong where ties between urban and rural dwellers remained intact, and where a sort of camaraderie existed between Africans of different social strata. It was in this milieu that a political culture, and the ANC, developed.

However, organisational inefficiency limited the ANC's outreach and Congress lacked money. In June 1922, Josiah Gumede told an NNC meeting in Pietermaritzburg that the SANNC had authorised a five-shilling levy on all members as debt had climbed to such an extent that "Congress found it very difficult to carry on the work". Exacerbating a tenuous general financial position was the calling in of loans from government and the Aborigines Protection Society for £237 and £400 respectively to pay expenses of SANNC delegates to Britain.[10]

The ANC secretary-general wrote of 1924 being "perhaps [its] worse year". Western Cape and Transvaal branches ignored ANC resolutions, did not remit dues, and violated the ANC constitution. They ignored presidential orders and "open rebellion was manifested". In 1928, the ANC Transkeian Territories lamented that Congress lacked co-ordination: "each officer practically acted as his own master … branches everywhere acted almost independently; Provincial Congresses … exercised a defiant influence towards the Mother National Congress."[11]

Other barriers to reaching workers were repressive industrial laws, restrictive compounds and isolated farms. These served to cut off the ANC from farm workers and mine workers. The vast distances involved in trying to reach them, and the general poverty of black workers, made contacting them difficult.

"Stars of Africa, Even for Generations to Come": Women, Youth, and Congress

The ANC continued to keep in place self-made barriers to mobilise large sections of the population. As it began its second decade, members' realisation that the organisation had come to stay did not include awareness that this would require attention to youth and women.

There had been prior occasional protests by branches (such as the TNC Waterberg East branch in 1919) against forced youth labour. In the 1920s, as we shall see, Africans associated with Congress protested youth exploitation. Charlotte Maxeke attacked their criminalisation; the ANC-Transkeian Territories exposed their exploitation by labour recruiters; Selope Thema defended their right not to undertake forced labour. Yet ANC leaders did not realise the need to nurture and socialise them in a Youth League.

Women still had no right to full ANC membership, which was not conceded until the 1940s. Female auxiliary members, expected to succour convention delegates, could not vote unless by proxy. They were excluded from polite ANC "gentlemanly" lobbying. Women from different social strata nevertheless took part in ANC campaigns, organised functions to raise funds, and were included in branch membership lists. In 1925, seven women were among 37 Vredenburg members. Frene Ginwala argues that women's struggles often were more mass-based than men's struggles, reflecting their closer experience of daily struggles. Some of these more politically active women were in touch with workers.[12]

Congress continued to reflect wider social attitudes to women; as Florence Jabavu noted in 1927, in rural areas the man remained "absolute head of the family" whereas in towns working women faced squalid conditions, often becoming "narrow in vision and interest" due to lack of relevant training and suffering an inferiority complex. This was not an ideal social context to encourage women's direct involvement in politics.[13]

What was new was the emergence of self-help groups, some involving urban and rural workers. In rural Eastern Cape, *zenzele* ("We do it ourselves") home-improvement or self-help clubs emerged from the 1920s, encouraged to some extent by men in the advisory council, or Bhunga. In Alice, Florence Jabavu established the African Women's Self-Improvement Association in 1927. Angeline Dube, wife of inaugural SANNC president-general John Dube, appears to have founded another body, the Daughters of Africa. Whilst *zenzele* were party to the cultivation of a cult of mission-inspired domesticity, there is evidence of their assertion of cultural nationalism through, for example, encouragement of African over Western dress. Moreover, as Catherine Higgs argues, they helped forge greater economic independence. If such bodies did not directly engage in formal politics—as Charlotte Maxeke noted in 1927, women remained the backbone of churches, probably distracting them from politics—the act of bringing them together facilitated communication and (hypothetically) allowed them an avenue of protest.[14]

In this regard, women's organisations had the potential to form a link to Congress and its campaigns, and vice versa. More research can determine the mutual interaction between women and Congress, though in the next two chapters we will glimpse instances of women taking vigorous action at local levels and of their support of Congress.

Charlotte Maxeke initially continued to associate with the ANC and with organised black labour, attending ANC meetings and actively participating in the ICU founding conference in 1920. In 1923, she was still identified as Bantu Women's League president. ANC activist Mweli Skota recalled many years later to Mary Benson that Maxeke had "remarkable abilities". To ICU co-founder Selby Msimang, Maxeke was "a real leader ... able to meet women of every level in life", but Kadalie's sometimes-harsh anti-Christian rhetoric surely alienated her from the ICU. Maxeke was probably behind a successful resolution at the 1924 ANC national conference supporting capital punishment on men convicted of assaulting women. Moreover, as Campbell observes, she deeply resented women's exclusion from the 1919 SANNC Constitution. This gave her little choice but to try instead to develop the Bantu Women's League.[15]

The League struggled on for a few more years in several provinces. Together with Daisy Nogakwa and Grace Letanka, Maxeke testified before the 1920 Inter-Departmental Pass Committee on behalf of the national body of the League. M. Manana and A. Sishuba spoke on behalf of the Port Elizabeth Branch, and C. Moloi, A. Mebalo, N. Dhlamini, and M. Pitso represented the Orange Free State. In 1928, the League's officers were summoned to a special meeting of ANC executives and in 1929 it was still meeting as a separate section of the annual Congress. In April of that year, in Bloemfontein, the League carried a resolution supporting tough legal action against white people who had killed an African farm labourer, Sixpence Temba. Historians, however, know even less about the role and fate of the Women's League at this time than about the complex work of the pivotal Maxeke.[16]

Maxeke gave perhaps her most eloquent address at the 1920 Bantu Women's League meeting in Queenstown. It was later printed (in Southern Sotho) under the somewhat disapproving notice of a moderate Congressman and teacher, C. R. Moikangoa, in the Chamber of Mines "mouthpiece", *Umteteli wa Bantu*, edited (until 1922) by none other than her husband. She made an impassioned appeal for grassroots leadership. The *League ea Mafumahadi*

(League of Women), she reported, was doing well in Queenstown and the Orange Free State. In Gauteng, it drew support in Marabastad and Pietersburg, but branches were languorous. The problem, she argued, was a crisis of leadership "cliques" in Gauteng. To achieve prosperity Africans needed "clean", truthful and knowledgeable leaders who loved Africa, loved being African, and loved their fellow Africans, who liked togetherness and peace, not conflict. Africans did not want tokenistic, window-dressed leaders that paid lip service to the people but rather those "who are lifted up by us (the people), not self-lifted" ("Re batla banna ba ikokobeditseng ba tla ba phahamisoe ke sechaba ..."), who must be stars of Africa, even for generations to come.[17]

Although increasingly drawn away from Congress into missionary and Joint Council arenas, in 1927 Maxeke was still League president, but its activities now appear minimal. From 1922 she became a "welfare" and probation officer in the Johannesburg Magistrate's court. Maxeke served as chaplain for African women prisoners, and worked on various charitable projects. In all these situations, she often met with young workers.[18]

This intimacy with working lives encouraged Maxeke to speak out against poverty and destitution and to assert the dignity of labour, as at the Sixth General Missionary Conference. In 1929, radical lawyer Hyman Basner came to know her. Indeed, he "entered into African politics" through Maxeke, particularly through her ANC connections. He later wrote that the fact that she was one of the few African women intellectuals meant that Congress leaders requiring action regarding African women invariably turned to her for help. Basner noted the influence on her thought of W. E. B. Du Bois. She formed a short-lived employment bureau to help women find domestic work. Despite her moderation—the CPSA derided her plan to fight the "black peril" by substituting female for male domestic workers as betraying "little more than partial assimilation of the ideology of the exploiting class"—she kept ties with workers. Her personal income remained modest. At first, she worked gratis, later earning £12 a month as welfare officer. In 1926, she worked as a head teacher in Lotha, Idutywa, where her husband died two years later. When she died in 1939, she was poverty-stricken.[19]

Maxeke's work as a probation officer brought her in touch with prisoners, a group by definition not easy to organise politically or industrially. Here Maxeke may well have sensitised ANC men to the fate of prison workers. Many prisoners had been either urban or rural workers. Farm and mine employers made use of Jan Davis, a plumber, between 1919 and 1929; Jini

Selani, a farmer, was sent to the mines; Johannes Booysen, a mason, was deemed unsuitable for farm labour as he had five stock-theft convictions.[20]

There were other "ANC" women at this time who were denied full membership but who continued at the provincial level. These women included A. Temba, Women's League president (who was arrested in pass protests), Mrs Nuku and Mrs Phala (Kimberley), M. Bobojane and M. Kondile (Boksburg), Minnie Bhola, H. Oliphant, S. Grootboem (Cape), and Ethel Humphrey (Durban). Some women's groups worked with the ANC, notably the Bantu Women's League. The Pietersburg branch of the League raised farm-worker grievances in 1921, and in 1920, the Zoutpansberg branch protested about exploitation of rural women workers (see Chapter 7). Both the Daughters of Africa and Zenzele became affiliated to Congress.[21]

Not all women endorsed Congress. Emblematic of growing public disdain of Congress's ineffectiveness was the poetry of self-styled *imbongikhazi* Nontsizi Mgqwetho. Moving to the Rand, at the instigation of *Abantu-Batho* editor Levi Mvabaza, she published a long set of poems in the rival *Umteteli wa Bantu*, edited by her mentor Marshall Maxeke. In some poems, she trenchantly criticises Congress and its Transvaal organ, aiming, it seems, at Transvaal Congress radicals for its growing disunity.

> ...Kuba o Funz'eweni
> > Bashumayela
> > Abangakwamkeli ku Congress
> > Bakwenze indaba ze sizwe.
>
> Imkile i Natal Congress
> > Ngenxa yabo
> > Imkile kwane Free State
> > Nantsiya ne Koloni izintlantlu ngentlantlu.
>
> [For rabble rousers,
> > Without leave from Congress
> > Sermonise
> > And hit the headlines.
>
> And as a result
> > Natal's Congress walks out,
> > The Free State's walks out,
> > The Cape's splinters splinter].

("Yimbongikazi Nontsizi u Chizama", *Umteteli wa Bantu*, 27 Nov. 1920)

On the other hand, Mgqwetho was close to SANNC stalwarts Charlotte and Marshall Maxeke. Notwithstanding the contradiction in her support for a white-owned newspaper and its anti-strike editor, she expressed solidarity with workers ("Unity, black workers … We must stand as one/to face the bosses"). Jeff Opland explains her views in terms of urban alienation and the inseparability of her politics and religion. Congress condescension to women in politics and Transvaal Congress militancy (sometimes accompanied by anti-mission clericalism) possibly fuelled her anti-Congress angst. Ironically, the stagnation in Congress she so aptly characterised in 1924 ("has anyone seen where it's gone") largely flowed from the departure of its leaders to the Joint Councils, and to the *Umteteli* that she so passionately defended. Besides her poetic allusion to being arrested and prosaic mention of taking part in 1919 anti-pass actions (where, facing a huge police presence, "Our leaders took to their heels"), we have scant biographical data to suggest wider involvement in either workforce or politics. Instead she appears to have found a home in *manyano*, which in a 1924 poetic expression of solidarity, she linked with protesting women in Herschel. Here was a woman prepared to attack repression but presented with nowhere to go in Congress. There are other isolated, documented cases of action. In 1925 a mine nurse, apparently an ICU organiser, was sacked for protesting conditions at Modder B mine. Here the ICU represented a step forward in giving women a direct role, and even claimed in 1925 that one third of its members were women. However, the organisation would not last long.[22] Structural inefficiencies thus limited ANC penetration of communities, but it kept in touch with labour issues through actions of supporters. ANC policies and actions reflected this.

ANC Policies and Practices in the 1920s

The harsh state repression of the 1918-1920 strikes played a part in the waning of ANC radicalism. Leading ANC figures turned to moderate institutions. Yet, Congress continued to address labour-related issues. Policies and leaders' attitudes illustrate this, though we should not extrapolate too much from statements alone. Party policies rarely fully reflect long-term goals of leaders, or class influences on them. ANC policies before 1927 did not accord much direct attention to workers, thus reflecting its own class composition. It was more prepared to state its concern for African interests, though these policies at times accorded with labour interests. In times of labour crisis, it often spoke in support of black workers. When the ANC spoke on behalf of workers, it was usually from the point of view that workers were Africans. Nevertheless, some forms of political struggle that the ANC employed—mass meetings and protests—continued to facilitate links to black workers.

Contemporary writers, from the left and right, tended to stress ANC moderation. Nevertheless, they detected a deeper potential for change rooted in its predicament. Basner likened its growth to "that of a strong seed in a stony bed, with long years of dormancy". In 1928, liberal J.D. Rheinallt Jones noted that it was "not as vocal or as powerful as it was ten years ago, but if the proposals ... for a separate Native franchise become law the Congress is bound to acquire a new importance". During 1921, communist David Jones saw it as loosely organised, "satisfied with agitation for civil equality and political rights", but he perceived that to obtain these demands "the mass cannot be moved without this moving in a revolutionary manner ... The national and class interests of [Africans] cannot be distinguished ... Here is a revolutionary nationalist movement in the fullest meaning of Lenin's term."[23] At that time many would have been aghast at the notion of a revolutionary ANC. However, its supporters, and a good few of its members, must have seen it as potentially delivering some form of national salvation, justice and re-distribution. Moreover, the very looseness of organisation to which Jones refers was to facilitate penetration of radical ideas.

Despite its reputation for moderation, the ANC continued to make immoderate statements by prevailing standards, for several reasons. Firstly, there was some continuity of personnel with the radical 1918-1920 period. An element of discontinuity saw some moderate leaders, such as Isaiah Bud-M'belle, effectively retire from ANC politics. Others, such as Plaatje and Selope Thema, sought greener pastures in the Joint Councils, but most did not entirely abandon Congress, which continued to protest black inequality. In 1927, Selope Thema simultaneously held a salaried post as Johannesburg Joint Council Assistant Secretary and sat on the ANC executive. Mabaso served as ANC treasurer-general under Mahabane from 1924 to 1927. Mahabane and Makgatho remained ANC leaders and continued to express concern for workers' welfare, as did Letanka and Josiah Gumede. At the ANC's 1929 conference, Mahabane moved a declaration on rights referring to the "class incongruities" of South Africa. As ANC Chaplain-in-Chief, he delivered an Easter address on "The Resurrection of a Nation", lamenting: "We are a race of servants, hewers of wood and drawers of water for the white man." Nevertheless, he saw signs of black revival.[24]

Secondly, legislation reinforced the ANC tendency to resort to militant resolutions reflecting its concern with overall conditions of Africans. In 1923, an ANC delegation met with the Prime Minister to protest exclusion of African freehold title in the Urban Areas Bill. At the meeting Gumede not only demanded the Bill be withdrawn but also, with an appreciation of the largely proletarian nature of the black community argued: "Some of us took part in the construction of these towns ... We feel that we are being put in an impossible position." Selope Thema supported him: "we have sacrificed many lives in the mines, we have built the cities." Revealing his own class position, he added that government was ignoring the rights of "professional men" and "little businesses". Rebuffed, Congress passed radical resolutions at its June 1923 conference. One indicated similar awareness of the centrality of labour: "We have sacrificed many lives in the mines, we have built this city." Another called on "all existing Bantu Organisations", including teachers and farmers associations and "Workers Union[s]" to affiliate to the ANC and invited representatives to join its meetings. Other resolutions radically departed from earlier positions of deference; disillusioned with Britain, Congress called for a republic. Following massacres at Bulhoek and Bondelswarts, the ANC declared no confidence in Smuts as Native Affairs Minister.[25]

James La Guma

This militant stance continued in 1924, when the ANC affiliated to a new, short-lived body, the United Non-European Congress, with communist worker James La Guma as secretary, which included the ICU, APO, and UNIA. However, Congress still had inconsistent approaches to events. Although in 1924 it condemned Smuts and called for equal pay for equal work, the Cape ANC welcomed Hertzog's segregation policy.[26]

Thus, while historians paint the early 1920s as a moderate period in ANC history, its leaders actually expressed quite radical ideas, even though organisational fragility meant they rarely reached a wide audience. In the second half of the decade, influenced by growing ICU and CPSA activism, but also by its own members' initiatives, the ANC swung even further to the left under the leadership of Gumede. It established much closer ties with a range of bodies claiming to represent black workers. The ANC called upon the leading labour union of the day, the ICU, to join it in fighting the government's "class legislation". ANC members were active in all the main streams of black unions—industrial unions, teachers' associations and the ICU. The closer relations of unions with the ANC that this implied was limited by workers' lack of viable means of independently communicating with the ANC, by ANC leaders' inability to exploit these contacts to forge stronger ties, and sectarianism. FNETU aligned itself too closely to the CPSA to enable it to become a seedbed of ANC-worker contact, whilst the ICU pursued its own political agenda.[27]

ANC leaders Makgatho and Selope Thema were chairpersons, respectively, of the Northern and Southern Transvaal Native Teachers' Associations. This merged in 1926 to become the Transvaal African Teachers' Association. In 1929, it succeeded in gaining sick-leave benefits and a definite scale of salaries for members. These experiences provided an avenue to help ANC members understand industrial issues, and partly explain the interest of such leaders in labour issues. Nevertheless, teacher union concern with conditions of workers generally, or of Africans as a whole, did not emerge spontaneously. Albert Luthuli, who in 1928 became secretary of the Natal African Teachers' Association, recalled how the union's main concern was simply "agitating for better wages", and that, "like most young teachers at the time, I did not think of a social and political situation".[28]

These contacts gave ANC leaders some insights into the emergent black labour movement. The political careers of ANC leaders vividly demonstrate both the impact of diverse ANC ties to workers, and the contradictions in ANC labour policy.

ANC Leaders and Black Labour in the 1920s

Some prominent ANC leaders of the previous decade, such as Dube and Plaatje, increased their remoteness from workers in the 1920s and largely withdrew from national politics. Yet even Dube and Plaatje retained broad sympathy for the African nation, which included workers. This remoteness was a tendency reinforced by state attitudes that increasingly disadvantaged workers.

Despite Plaatje's rejection of radical socialism, the state continued to regard him with suspicion; as noted above, police monitored his movements for years. His graphic description of the wretched conditions of Lichtenburg miners in 1927 shows that he continued to witness and commiserate with the plight of workers. Yet, a fear of proletarianisation haunted many leaders. When Mahabane (ANC president, 1924-1927) led an ANC delegation to give evidence to a state committee in 1927, he lamented that the Land Act had fuelled the ejection of "respectable, well-to-do men" who could not live "as mere labourers".[29]

The denial of black political rights and the considerable restrictions on black capital accumulation inclined many, more prosperous political leaders towards the alternative of a broad alliance with other social strata, including workers. That they often rejected radical solutions does not lessen their basic concern for the future of black labour. This mixture of fear of radicalism and concern for workers was evident in Mahabane's 1927 comment that if Africans were granted equal citizenship rights then African "industrial workers will enjoy the same rights as the European workers. They will get satisfactory wages and conditions of labour, and that spells peace. At present they do not get satisfactory wages or satisfactory conditions of labour and there is unrest in their minds." That, he feared, would "create a fertile mind" for "the doctrines of the Communists". Mahabane chose to illustrate his dream of the future with reference to contented black workers, and his nightmare with reference to black workers in revolution. This typified the dilemma of many moderate leaders who dreaded transformation into workers, yet needed the masses, if not yet for direct support, then to champion their rights; but they needed them to be pliant. Notwithstanding his rejection of revolution, Mahabane significantly used the occasion to urge better wages. He claimed some intimacy with workers' conditions. He had lived in Vrede for the past six years and knew labour conditions in the district. He was well aware of spiralling black urbanisation in Bloemfontein and Kroonstad, and the situation of unemployed Africans in Waaihoek.[30]

Many ANC leaders often did little effectively to translate their ideas into practice. Yet, frequently in their declarations, there was a continuing concern that workers receive just treatment. Under the influence of the ICU, CPSA, and Garveyism, ANC leaders moved beyond the confines of restricted electoral politics (voters numbered less than one per cent of the African population) and interacted with the wider community. Although the mid-1920s saw little apparent open ANC support for, or from, workers, there were indications of significant changes in the air. This was particularly apparent in the rise of Josiah Gumede to become president of the NNC in 1924 (see Chapter 8), and then the ANC in 1927. Earlier, I outlined the complex class influences on Gumede's early career; here I focus on his attitude to workers whilst ANC president.

J. T. Gumede described himself to a state commission in 1929 as "a landowner. … I am living in Johannesburg, but I have a farm of my own in Natal." However, the volley of anti-black laws enacted after 1910 and his visit to England in 1919 as part of an unsuccessful SANNC delegation helped shift his belief in the hegemony of capitalism and imperialism. Selby Msimang later claimed it was in 1919 that Gumede "lost his faith in British justice". Gumede became full-time SANNC General Organiser in 1921, a position bringing him into greater contact with suffering black social strata. He began to express open support for the ICU and CPSA and took an increasingly critical view of society. In 1924 he wrote to his friend Reginald Slade that Africans "are still suffering from injustices … are evicted from farms … [and] thrown out of work". He held no illusions about salvation from white people: "You can hardly expect land grabbers with the rifle and machine guns in hand to honour … promises." His son Archie remembers him relate that the ANC was "learning the lesson when the ICU was established … [of] the need for a mass base, a mass organisation". If accurate, and not telescoping history, it shows Gumede saw need of a "new type" of organisation.[31]

Gumede spearheaded a modification of ANC labour attitudes. A Catholic, and previously hostile to Bolshevism, he was deputed by the ANC to participate in an anti-imperialist conference in Brussels in 1927, together with James La Guma, a seasoned industrial worker and communist. It is likely that La Guma helped uncork Gumede's latent radicalism. In Brussels, Gumede met other anti-colonial leaders, such as Nehru, who encouraged his growing anti-imperialism. Gumede stated that he thought South Africa was still a colony where Africans lived as slaves. He noted the poor wages and long working hours of miners and farm workers, and condemned the "abominable" labour recruitment system, deaths on the mines, and job colour bars. He used terms such as "proletariat" and "capitalist", indicating his growing familiarity with Marxist concepts. He concluded: "I am not a Communist, but we find that the Communist Party are [sic] the only people who are with us in spirit." He saw imperialism and the "Workers' Republic" as the two effective forces in the world. The conference adopted a resolution on South Africa, signed by Gumede, demanding, "on behalf of all workers and oppressed people", not only "the right to self-determination through the complete overthrow of the capitalistic and imperialist domination", but also "abolition of all contract labour; the right of all categories of workers to organise themselves ... for their ... emancipation; unrestricted freedom of speech and assembly for all workers".[32]

Gumede then visited the USSR. Upon his return, he argued the need for radical change. He addressed well-attended ANC meetings and shared a platform with CPSA leaders in April 1927. A large crowd at the TAC hall heard Gumede say: "For my part, though not a Communist, I am a 'Bad Boy', and I want you to be 'Bad Boys', and I don't mind asking the Communists to help us." Linking up struggles of "colonial toilers", he said "the greatest enemy of the working classes the world over was the capitalist class", a statement that shocked the pro-business *Star*. At the June 1927 ANC conference, which elected him president-general, Gumede declared: "Of all political parties the Communist Party is the only one that honestly and sincerely fights for the oppressed." Referring to the USSR, he declared: "I have seen the new world to come, where it has already begun." At a meeting in March 1928, he stated that, "the Bantu has been a Communist from time immemorial" (a common notion at the time, even among moderates, but here given a different twist). In 1929, he told a conference of the newly founded united-front League of African Rights that the African is "underpaid and exploited ... Give [him] his rights viz. 'freedom', 'liberty', 'justice' and fairplay?" Today "leaders of native thought" must "combine and organise ... strongly in order to save the people from oppression, repression, exploitation and slavery".[33] This speech illustrates not just Gumede's heightened anti-imperialism but also his continued public articulation of ideological trends apparent in ANC history since 1912: a liberal demand for equality of opportunity; a national(ist) call to unity, and, less acknowledged by historians, a denunciation of exploitation.

His audacious actions in visiting the USSR and working with the CPSA testify to new ways of thinking by an ANC leader. In 1929 he told a state commission he was not a communist, but an anti-imperialist; "a freeman, and if I want to become a Communist I shall do so ... I am against imperialism because it took our land ... I know that Communism is a different thing altogether, because I have had to study it." Yet he did not speak for the CPSA, which he termed "a new party [which] we still want to find out about". Rather he spoke on behalf of the ANC and the League against Imperialism.[34]

Gumede mixed radicalism with an awareness of the need for unity. In a letter to African leaders in 1927, he urged them to sink their differences by saying: "There are two wings to [the] Bantu movement for political and economic emancipation ... the conservative and the radical. These wings are absolutely necessary for our progress ... Just as a bird must have both wings for successful flight."[35]

This approach was evident in his relations with the ICU. Gumede's Natal African Congress in 1927 held a joint mass meeting, "composed of all classes", with the ICU to protest the colour bar. It wrote to Smuts about how colour bar laws had led to the dismissal of boot workers. In June 1929, during

Josiah Gumede

a boycott that merged into a strike, a meeting of 5,000 people at Cartwright Flats presided over by Champion heard Gumede urge workers to "combine and take our freedom, and if the other fellow doesn't want to give it, let us take it. The black man must be directly represented in Parliament. We shall go into a big strike if we do not get into Parliament." He challenged the right of Dube's moderate NNC to speak on behalf of workers: "The ICU has taken the place of the [NNC] absolutely in Natal". All these radical actions were remarkable given his 1919 evidence against the communists. Some later radicals, such as Stephen Dlamini, saw Gumede as "very good. He was conscious of the workers."[36]

Conservative forces within Congress bitterly opposed Gumede's new perspectives. Chief Joseph told the Second Annual Convention of the ANC Upper House in 1928 that the CPSA was "the most dangerous party in the world". He moved opposition to any ANC-CPSA co-operation. Gumede defended the CPSA as the "only Party that worked for the oppressed". The chiefs repudiated any such alliance, urging instead ANC-ICU unity.[37]

Gumede's *realpolitik* helped the ANC develop a more critical, yet flexible, response to state policies. The ANC attacked the Urban Areas Bill, but once it was law Gumede switched to demand Congress should scrupulously implement and monitor sections favourable to Africans—such as "native villages"— in order to turn it to their advantage. At a conference at the Johannesburg Workers Hall against tightening of pass laws, Gumede called for repeal of the entire pass system. His popularity saw a temporary swelling of ANC ranks. His speech in Ndabeni in March 1928 "was attended by almost the entire community". Activists re-established a formerly militant ANC branch in Dasenburg following Gumede's address there. In Springs, a crowd of 500 heard him "with enthusiasm at a very high level".[38] Gumede's radicalism was more the exception than the rule in Congress of the 1920s, although he did have allies and supporters.

Other "ministers" in Gumede's "cabinet" expressed an eclectic mix of radicalism, moderation, and nationalism. I discuss Champion in the following chapter. Selope Thema and Selby Msimang were moving away from radicalism. They stressed the commonality of employer-employee interests but the unrewarded travail of workers appalled them. They both signed a submission to government by prominent Africans protesting the 1926 Mines and Works Act Amendment Bill, noting that despite their education and urbanisation, they "are yet in touch with the feelings and thoughts of their countrymen, not only those in the mines and towns but even those in the territories". No doubt such claims carried an element of exaggeration, but they affirm the significance attached to such contact.[39]

Historians generally regard Richard Victor Selope Thema as a moderate. In the 1920s, partly under the influence of liberals (see below), he often adopted an elitist approach. In 1928, he argued that radicals preaching "Africa for the Africans" had a large following as their programme "appeals to the ignorant masses". He advocated racial co-operation, as Africans "need the guidance and leadership of the white race".[40] Moderates such as he were moving further away from any real intimacy with the "ignorant masses". However, the "white race" increasingly was imposing its "guidance" through diktat, reminding such leaders of the broad contours of repressive black labour conditions.

Selope Thema was not lacking in loose ties with workers in either his personal life or ANC work. He was born into a squatter family in Haernertsburg in 1886 and lived as a squatter before the South African War. Events forced him to work as a labourer during the war and as a domestic worker in Pretoria in 1902. At the age of 20, he went to Lovedale, after which he worked first as a clerk with the Native Recruiting Corporation and from 1915 for lawyer Richard Msimang. During this time, he became active in Congress and acquired the trappings of a liberal thinker.[41]

Selope Thema made numerous public statements on the wretchedness of black workers. His close knowledge of the difficult position of farm workers underlines the accessibility of ANC leaders to workers. At the 1924 Governor-General's Native Conference, he condemned replacement of black by white labour. He gave detailed evidence to the 1925 Select Committee on the Masters and Servants Law in which he defended the rights of farm labourers. He called for an enquiry into their conditions. Black workers, including youths, on farms should receive payment for their work, and work under the same conditions as white, urban workers. He cited specific cases of hardship, such as the killing of a young girl who ran away from a white farmer in Standerton. During his term as SANNC Secretary (1915-1917), he had had personal dealings with farm squatters and their grievances. In 1921, he was concerned with farm workers' grievances about unpaid and forced labour in Lydenburg and Pietersburg. He visited women farm workers—some pregnant—who police had arrested in Sabie. One had given birth whilst loading heavy goods. Under intense and persistent questioning by Committee members, he refused to concede their claim that farm workers were adequately "paid", or accept their notion that parents desired legal power to force children to work for farmers. Selope Thema defended the right of African youth not to undertake heavy forced labour. Labour conditions were so bad that "today the people are forced by conditions to say 'I will enslave myself'".[42]

This broad commitment to justice for African workers continued. In 1926 Selope Thema wrote, "conditions under which natives live and work on the farms are intolerable". He criticised the Land Act Amendment Bill as a device to enable farmers to obtain cheap or "free labour from landless and homeless Natives". In 1927, he explained the causes of "native unrest" in harsh legislation making farm labour intolerable. In the same year, he cited views he had heard of African women living on the Rand among mine workers that "things are very bad nowadays". State officials regarded these declarations in support of workers as "rather strange sentiment from an educated native".[43]

This raises a crucial point in understanding the labour views of ANC leaders. Such comments would have been unusual coming from conservative leaders *not* associated with the ANC (such as J. T. Jabavu). However, they were quite *typical* of ANC policy. Therein lies the key to their attitudes: association with the ANC helped give empathy for workers by the established precedent of earlier, and contemporary, ANC policies. Selope Thema did not accept that the practice of hiring farm labourers to the detriment of squatters (in other words, their proletarianisation) was "progressive". Would acceptance of such "progress" in a Marxist sense have made him a faithful representative of workers' wishes? Because most farm workers were in the ambiguous position of being incorporated into capitalist wage labour yet at the same time restrained by pre-capitalist social relations, leaders attempting to articulate their interests were placed in a difficult position.

Selope Thema served as chairman of the ANC Committee of Commerce and Industry under Gumede. Together with communist Eddie Khaile, he edited the ANC's *National Gazette*, which included contributions by Gumede and Msimang. Selope Thema's support for demands of the black *petit bourgeoisie* was clear. Municipal authorities should allow black businesses in townships. The incoming ANC Executive should "assist and help in every possible way" black business. He believed in the powerful goals of modernity—progress and development. Black commercial expansion would "secure for us a place in the affairs of civilised mankind". He closely linked economic and political goals: "Economic and commercial independence of the race" implied "political and social emancipation from the thraldom of race hatred". Congress, he asserted, aimed to promote its own business enterprises, organise all African business people into a mutual-aid societies as well as to assist African business. Gumede's more moderate successor Seme also promoted these ideas of co-operation and African development—another example of continuity in ANC policies.[44]

Such ideas, argues Cobley, constituted an ANC move towards a "fully articulated economic strategy" influenced by the ICU, by the presence of traders in Congress, and especially by Garveyites and communists in Gumede's executive. He cites a 1927 ANC programme (similar to Selope Thema's aforementioned ideas) that emphasises the ANC should promote and assist African business and organise sick and burial societies. The latter would involve workers. Moreover, in 1929 the ANC annual conference resolved to encourage "industrial and commercial organisations, and syndicates".[45]

The emphasis here is on business rather than unions. Garveyite or ICU inspiration may have stimulated ANC attempts to set out a more detailed blueprint of African economic renaissance. Yet both Gumede and Selope Thema had long been interested in African economic advancement and industrial rights. The evolution of their political ideas contributed to development of a more coherent ANC economic policy. Neither should it be lost sight of that in this period, the ANC issued a declaration that under the Conciliation Act the African worker was "paid the lowest possible rate. As a pass-bearing labourer he is precluded from making use of the strike weapon ... All avenues of skilled employment ... are closed ... and hundreds of Native labourers ... thrown out of employment."[46] One can just as easily imagine such a declaration issuing from the ICU or CPSA.

Selope Thema became closely involved with the Joint Councils and wrote for *Umteteli wa Bantu*, articulating a growing anti-communism. In 1924, he made his politics clear when he sought "means whereby the dissemination of Bolshevism among the Bantu people could be combated". This does not mean he stopped writing about workers. In an essay in 1928, he contrasted the well-developed political, mining and Zimbabwe-like architectural structures of pre-colonial African people with the "dependent and servile" nature of contemporary black labour in South Africa. Patronisingly he stated that "nowhere in the world are to be found more docile workers if they are treated justly". However, he emphasised their poor conditions saying "their wage is not large, about two shillings a day, while the wage of the white skilled worker is from 10 to 15 times as large". Farm workers were "as near as can be to serfdom". However, he revealed his predilection for *petit bourgeois* solutions, "Not until they are free to contract for their own labour will it be possible to raise these unfortunate people to the status of a self-respecting, industrious, progressive and prosperous peasantry." His penchant for peasant, rather than proletarian, development was in keeping with his own growing involvement with business – and his rural origins.[47]

Despite his liberal proclivities, Selope Thema remained committed to the ANC. In 1928, he described it as "the most powerful of Bantu political organisations". He defended the role of educated Africans typical of an ANC leadership that white people often claimed were "out of touch with their uneducated brethren". Whilst constituting "a minority", they had "not lost touch with the people ... [and were] the spokesmen of their inarticulate people". He captured here the ambiguity of ANC relations with workers. He clearly saw its leaders as speaking on behalf of Africans in general, including "inarticulate" workers, a phrase suggestive of paternalism. His reference to the primary position of the ANC flew in the face of the ICU at that time, but he may have regarded the ICU as an economic, rather than political body. For all his *petit bourgeois* accoutrements, he remained conscious of the central position of the black worker. "On the docks ... he has no equal as a winch-winder, while in the mines he has shown himself as skilful as ... the semi-skilled white worker."[48]

Selby Msimang was well aware of the strategic significance of black labour. As noted above, he received insights into worker lives in his early career. In the early 1920s, he at first deepened this awareness by personal contacts but then lost touch with labour movements. Msimang forged close ties with workers such as Samuel Masabalala in Bloemfontein and when, in 1920, the latter was literally put under siege by vigilantes and police during a strike in Port Elizabeth, the ICU asked Msimang to intervene. He described the tense situation as one in which the "least mistake could lead to a bloodbath". His tactics in Port Elizabeth were to restrain militancy. In itself, this hardly implies alienation from the broad labour movement. Restraint of strikes is a common tactic globally of reformist social democrats and moderate unions. Despite his moderate politics, police continued to regard him as a labour "agitator" and monitor his movements, closely watching his visits to Port Elizabeth and Queenstown in 1921-1922. They also perpetuated the belief that he wished to visit Moscow. Police reported, in Queenstown, that he told a poorly attended location meeting that mine recruiting was a "crime" and that the 1922 white miners' strike was a dispute among white people over the share of profits won by black workers. During the strike, he kept in touch with the mood of workers, reporting (an initial) lack of violence "against the African miners" and touring the Rand to promote a united labour union. The killings of Africans during the 1922 strike, however, served to divide further white and black labour, making young activists such as Msimang more wary of the broad labour movement.[49]

In 1923, Msimang boldly called for Africans to deploy the "weapon of organised labour". He stated: "As workers we have to find emancipation by our own efforts." In the same year, he told a state committee that Africans were "forced into ... towns somehow or other by bare necessity" to form a class who "have nowhere else to go". Yet at the same time he strongly supported growth of black business, "interpret[ing] segregation [to mean] ... we will be in a position to improve and to develop on our own lines ... by establishing our own industries". These ideas did not represent any sudden abandonment of labour principles as they were typical of his earlier views. He believed in compromise in the class struggle stating that "workers and capitalists must respect each others' interests"—but so did many social democrats. Like many of the generation of ANC members who fought against the Land Act, he continued to emphasise Africans' land scarcity. The mines would receive a "regular class of worker and a better class of worker" if Africans "have their own area". The "class of natives" born in the cities deserved the right of "permanent homes". Such attitudes may appear to indicate his *petit bourgeois* nature but the demand for better urban housing for black people accorded with worker interests. Msimang's interest in black business mixed with continuing concern for labour's lot. In 1924, as the threat of white-imposed segregation increased, he called for a conference of leaders to discuss industrial and agricultural growth in African areas in order to counter segregation and tackle unemployment.[50]

There was profound ambiguity in Msimang's allegiance to labour. S. P. Bunting stated, in reference to Msimang's role as a writer for *Umteteli*, that he could not serve both labour and the Chamber of Mines. This ambiguity was rooted in a split labour market, endemic racism of white labour, and Msimang's own move away from unions to journalism. In 1924 he sent a message to the ICU conference warning workers that any suggestion of growing support for their cause among white labour was an illusion. He felt overwhelmed by the task facing the ICU, saying "to organise non-European workers in this country is not an easy or a pleasant task". Nevertheless, he clearly felt some continuing attachment to the cause of black labour, proudly telling ICU members that he stood "ready to offer you my co-operation, or if need be to stand aside" for other leaders.[51]

Msimang was chairman of the ANC Labour Committee under Gumede. In *National Gazette,* he asserted ANC awareness of black labour issues indicating that the ANC "is fully conversant with the plight of all African workers who are hard put and how difficult for many homes to make both ends meet on the low scale of wages they are paid and the unusually long hours they do". His efforts to set in motion a new black labour organisation were less realistic. He urged all ANC branches to help organise labour. He continued to support moderate unionism believing that they could overcome class conflict through conciliation. This, however, required black labour to be organised. Thus, Msimang conjured up a non-existent labour federation, "the African Trade Union Congress", to be an ANC-aligned federation to ensure conditions of all workers, "whether domestics, farm labourers, transport workers, m[otor] drivers ... shop assistants and parcel deliver[er]s". This proposal, he argued, should be thoroughly investigated by a commission and, in conjunction with "its political wing" (the ANC), be implemented. Msimang triumphantly announced workers had only "to group themselves" into 12 occupational categories. Under his programme, any racial hostility among workers did "not arise". This utopian scheme was not backed by action but he was grappling with industrial unionism, something the CPSA was about to implement.[52]

Msimang, like Selope Thema, was aware of the growing power of nationalism. During the 1918-1920 protests, simply to "voice our protests was found good enough to command the rallying point of every African". Congress "was completely put out of gear" when the ICU "captured much support" by tapping national feelings. However, he closely linked labour and national struggles. Msimang, whilst aware that "sporadic upheavals", such as the wage demands he had led at Bloemfontein, reflected Africans' "colossal frustration", felt organised labour, in the form of the ICU, should work hand-in-hand with Congress. "I had always felt that we could not afford to exist apart from the main body of our political influence [Congress]", with the ICU playing more the role of a pressure group, as the "militant wing of the national movement". Msimang warned the ANC Old Guard, fearful of a "dual loyalty", that failure to "identify themselves with the workers movement" would endanger Congress.[53] Both Msimang and Selope Thema sought to combine and canalise national and labour demands in a moderate manner whilst openly opposing exploitation.

T. D. Mweli Skota was ANC Secretary-General from 1923 to 1927, and again in 1930. His ties with workers in this period are obscure. He was, claims ANC veteran A. Kgokong, organiser of an "African Workers Organisation". This claim and the body remain unverified. In 1928, as editor of *Abantu-Batho,* he encountered Gumede's radical espousal of black labour, but Skota generally was less concerned with labour than commercial ventures. He promoted a co-operative trading company in 1927 as well as various other business schemes. In his ANC role, he was chiefly concerned with internal matters as indicated by his 1925 secretary's report, which dwelt on administrative weaknesses. Despite the organisational chaos surrounding him, he believed that the ANC was "serving ... the rights and interests of the Black masses" who faced "perpetual slavery". He later characterised the ANC as uniting "all small political unions, associations and societies".[54] Thus despite, or because of, his focus on business, he sought to convey a wider African nationalism, and to appeal to the masses. In the 1930s, he raised labour issues in his role in the ANC press.

Nimrod Tantsi personified an African nationalist willing to engage with workers. He was, at various times, ICU and ANC organiser, League of African Rights vice-chairman, and CPSA member. In 1925, he rubbed shoulders with workers such as Moses Kotane and Gana Makabeni at the CPSA's Ferreirastown night school. Tantsi appears to have joined the ANC before the CPSA. He worked as a paid ANC organiser in eastern Transvaal. Before entering the AME ministry in 1930, the year he helped organise an ICU-led strike, he worked as an insurance agent and teacher. In the 1930s he was TAC chaplain. His political career is further proof that the ANC did not discourage involvement with working class movements. Many ANC leaders, including Tantsi, Marshall Maxeke, Henry Ngcayiya and S. P. Matseke were active in politicised, independent churches, which included workers. Close ANC ties with such churches were just as much a link with such workers as proof of the leaders' *petit bourgeois* nature.[55]

ANC leaders in the 1920s shared a commitment to improving labour conditions. The means of achieving this varied from helping workers to form unions to helping them to become *petit bourgeois*. The attitudes to labour expressed by its leaders, though far from consistently radical, were instrumental in maintaining the ANC as an *inclusive* organisation, one that continued to view workers as part of its constituency and deserving of sympathy. These attitudes developed in a complex political situation that sometimes inclined ANC leaders to seek solutions in outside bodies. External forces of both right and left influenced ANC policies. This illustrates both the depth of, and limitations to, ANC contacts with the labour movement, as well as contradictions in its claim to represent black workers.

State Policies and the ANC

State strategy in the 1920s had a particularly devastating effect on the ANC. This took several forms. Firstly, the law barred state-employed teachers and civil servants from office in political groups, denying the ANC an important section of "white-collar" workers. A government committee estimated the majority of ANC members had acquired education, but lack of access to skilled jobs frustrated many of them. The state viewed any kind of government workers as bound by this rule. As a witness to this, consider the case of Hartswater construction worker David Fundisi, an ANC member, who was hounded by officials.[56]

Secondly, a vortex of state-sponsored palavers sucked in ANC leaders. The ANC participated in Native Conferences held under the 1920 Native Affairs Act. Congress leaders may have seen these forums as an opportunity to influence state policy but at a time when their energies could have been used to combat ANC decline, many, including Dube, Molema, Makgatho, Msimang, Selope Thema, Charlotte Maxeke, Mapikela, Mahabane and Plaatje, took an active part in purely advisory meetings closely regulated by state officials. Yet they managed to raise political issues concerning working-class conditions. Maxeke attacked criminalisation of African youth and urged all Africans to "fight their grievances together". In 1925, an ANC deputation met with the Native Affairs Commission to discuss the election of not only political, but also labour, representatives to these conferences. Msimang noted African "working class from the Cape" working in the Transvaal lost all rights enjoyed in the Cape. Selope Thema told the 1924 Native Conference Africans "felt very keenly" efforts to replace their labour by white employees.[57]

Thirdly, the state undermined a pillar of ANC support by moving to integrate traditional rulers into its machinery. Yet if the state co-opted many chiefs into segregationist structures then the ANC maintained ties with some. The 1927 ANC Chiefs Convention attracted 22 chiefs and helped maintain their support. In the same year, Chief Walter Kumalo related the lack of land made available to Africans to their low wages when giving evidence as part of an ANC delegation to a state committee. Chief Kgori Pilane was TNC Treasurer, and Chief Mini was NNC President. When the ANC, in response to shootings of Africans in 1925, declared a boycott of a Royal visit, Chiefs Sol Motaung and Mandeselo supported them. From 1927, radicals led the ANC Council of Chiefs Department: Gumede was chairperson, Letanka secretary. In 1928, Letanka, in this capacity, wrote letters of protest about the South African jury system. Whilst the 1928 ANC Chiefs Convention adopted an anti-radical stance, Letanka issued a pamphlet rejecting the wider powers over Africans outlined in the 1927 Native Administration Act.[58]

Selope Thema's description, in 1928, of the attitude of chiefs to the ANC shows the ambiguity of ANC relations with chiefs, as well as revealing much about his own conception of the role of the intelligentsia. "Although most of the chiefs are not active [ANC] members ... nevertheless they are in sympathy with its objects ... [They] are bound to acknowledge sooner or later the leadership of the intellectuals." Following a conference of chiefs under ANC auspices, he claimed, "it cannot be denied that [ANC] influence ... is penetrating the backveld". Whilst the continued attendance of chiefs at ANC conferences indicated an ANC rural presence, these instances of ANC ties with chiefs were limited. By the late 1920s, the state had succeeded in co-opting many traditional rulers. This re-alignment was to provide a barrier to easy contact of the ANC with migrant workers based in areas still under the nominal control of the chiefs.[59]

The ANC did not simply succumb to state manoeuvres. As the bureaucracy moved further along the road to fashioning a "grand tradition" of official discourse on the "native problem" in response to post-war crises of hegemony, so ANC leaders engaged in a rival discourse with officials at hearings of official committees.[60] The aims of engaging in this discourse chiefly were to reiterate concerns over loss of land and political rights since the Act of Union, but in doing so, they also incorporated protest over labour issues.

Evidence given by ANC leaders to state committees illustrates the contradictory position they found themselves in when defining their attitudes to the state. A committee on the 1920 Native Affairs Act heard their submissions. Walton Fenyang, OFS ANC, challenged the selection process for commissioners and the lack of avenues of appeal to their findings. Selope Thema and Dube placed exaggerated faith in provisions for consultation by the state with African representatives enacted by the Act, which the former viewed as the "Magna Charta of the native people", whilst the latter praised it as the "best attempt yet" to meet African needs. Dube saw a role for the local councils established by the Act in canalising radicalism. Mahabane objected to the Act's incorporation of the principle of segregation and denial of direct African political representation. Contrary to Dube he saw the proposed (purely advisory) councils as too parochial, divisive, and powerless. He had witnessed strong opposition to the local council system during the six years he lived in Herschel. Mahabane regarded the creation of a Native Affairs Commission as superfluous; if established it should comprise three Africans and only two white people.[61]

It was in the interests of the state to depict the ANC as unrepresentative. Mahabane countered it was "already ... able to influence native opinion ... outside the Congress. In the Transvaal the Congress is stronger than in any other part of the country." He claimed mass support: the "larger mass of uneducated thought and opinion clamours for direct representation in Parliament ... When we hold meetings with them or speak with them that is what they say"; direct representation was in accord with African traditional *kgotla*. He maintained this position before a state committee in 1927 saying Congress "was largely representative of the Transvaal, but we had representatives from all the provinces".[62]

ANC leaders keenly monitored the economic condition of African workers and presented this data to state bodies. The 1923 Select Committee on Native Affairs heard evidence from ANC members H. R. Ngcayiya, Abner Mtimkulu and Selby Msimang. Ngcayiya drew attention to farm labourers who "barely make sufficient to feed and clothe themselves ... The result is that many of them go into the towns ... [but] can get no work ... They have no place where they can wait until they get work." Workers in town often purchased stands but when work ran out were unable to keep up payments on the stands, which they then sold to the municipality for a much lower price than what they had paid for them. Africans, he argued, could solve these problems if they owned the ground on which they built and if workers had more time to look for work.[63] Such solutions were hardly radical, but were a practical attempt to protect workers from exploitation.

S. M. Makgatho, in his 1923 ANC presidential speech, viewed the Native Urban Areas Act as "rendering [Africans] homeless and landless". Behind the Act was white workers' fear of job competition. He told ANC delegates: "we have built the railways and the cities, and have sacrificed precious lives in the gold, diamond, and coal mines ... [Hence] we feel justified in demanding the enjoyment of the fruits of our labour." Earlier, *Umteteli wa Bantu*, financed by the Chamber of Mines, had derided his 1920 presidential address as "truculent" and "inflammatory" when he raised the need for direct action.[64]

Despite their exaggerated faith in opportunities to change state policy, many ANC leaders had sufficient knowledge of workers to raise their rights *within* liberal, constitutional limits. Makgatho's use of "we" to refer to African labour indicates how ANC leaders saw workers as part of a race-class. The ANC faced intense competition for workers' support from left and right, but learned important lessons from these rivals.

The ICU and the ANC

The meteoric rise and fall, from 1919 to 1929, of the first successful black labour union, the ICU, is well chronicled and repeated here only in relation to ANC history. In the face of state repression, the ICU established a tradition of combining mass political agitation for black rights with industrial demands. "Events ... soon imparted to it the character of a nationalistic awakening", wrote Jordan Ngubane. The ICU thus shared common ground with the ANC in the sense that it was compelled to maintain a political profile. This politicisation brought contact and competition with the ANC. Selby Msimang, associated with both, felt "the ICU captured much support and weakened the ANC". The anti-union and anti-communist drive of the state encouraged ANC distrust of unions. Yet if the ICU outstripped Congress in mass appeal, then there is nevertheless good reason to concur with Walshe who judges the ICU "dependent in large part on the prior political awakening for which Congress was largely responsible".[65] A close examination of relations suggests that the prevailing impression of an ANC passively submerged beneath a vibrant ICU needs revising.

The period of ICU formation evinced ANC support for the union, and the efforts of radicals, some of whom were ANC members, to mobilise workers. Fred Cetyiwe and Hamilton Kraai of the IWA joined the Cape Province Congress, which in May 1920 concluded a formal alliance with remnants of the IWA. Cetyiwe led the Cape Town Central branch. The ISL had schooled Cetyiwe but he tended to use national metaphors. Addressing a meeting, he depicted the ICU's 1920 conference as "the beginning of the Song of Emancipation". In March 1920, an Ndabeni branch meeting expressed solidarity with striking Rand miners. It condemned the methods of "Government and the employing classes ... of settling labourers' strikes by victimisation of the leaders, [and] threatening repatriation". However, it viewed such methods through the prism of fear of revolution, as likely "ultimately to ... foster Bolshevism". ANC members in Ndabeni (where Impey Nyombolo led a rival IWA branch) may also have helped spread radical syndicalist ideas among dockers. Worker actions thus had reverberations in Congress. Historians have tended to assume few ANC links with workers at this time. Wickins expresses surprise that a "conservative and moderate" Congress joined with the IWA. Yet he concedes that, before the ICU, Congress "seems to have been the chief channel for the communication of Black grievances".[66]

With regard to ICU history in Port Elizabeth, Gary Baines who "ironically" observes that Congress made *more* class-based and strident denunciations of killings of workers when the ICU suffered violent repression in 1920, expresses similar surprise. Mahabane led a mass meeting in Cape Town condemning the shootings, calling them "a direct result of the short-sighted policy of capitalism". He urged basic change of the "whole social, economic and political system". A stereotyped vision of Congress held by historians explains why they view ANC militancy ironically. If ANC branches made more class-based and strident protests than the ICU, then this should be a starting point of analyses of the ANC, not just class-origins of leaders. Baines adds: "The common perception that the ... Cape Native Congress was rather insular and distrustful of working class mobilisation, needs qualification." His need to re-assess the nature of Congress accords with my view we cannot automatically assume Congress represented *purely petit bourgeois* interests. His observation that the Port Elizabeth ICWU mobilised workers through "a radicalised *petite bourgeois* leadership", implying that not only Congress but also unions used such leadership, suggests another similarity between Congress and early unions.[67]

There were other ties. Some veterans of 1919 Congress anti-pass protests, such as Mtshoakae, became ICU activists. Congress formally convened the first national ICWU conference in Bloemfontein in July 1920. SANNC representatives attended. According to Cape Native National Congress general secretary E. B. Mkumatela, Kraai, Nyombolo and Msimang had proposed the meeting to the SANNC Queenstown conference. Also present was Congress radical Cetyiwe, representing the IWA Cape Town Central Branch. Selby Msimang chaired the ICWU conference and made a forthright statement of problems: "The white worker has only the capitalist as his foe, while we have the capitalist and the [white] Trade Unions." Delegate Impey Nyombolo stated whilst the ICWU was "the only body that will authoritatively ... represent the masses" of Africans "industrially", Congress remained their *political* leader. The conference selected the pro-ANC *Morumioa* ("Messenger"), founded by Msimang in 1918, to be an ICU organ, later superseded by *The Black Man*, and then *Workers' Herald*. The latter gave prominence to ideas of worker and African solidarity. It looked to the ANC, seeing the ICU as the labour arm of the "only political body [the ANC] we recognise".[68]

The complexity of ANC-ICU ties is evident in the career of *The Black Man's* editor, Samuel Michael Bennett Ncwana, a World War I veteran who moved to Cape Town in 1919 after his Johannesburg business failed. ICU secretary Kadalie had recruited Ncwana and, as ICU chairman of propaganda, Ncwana may have helped formulate wage demands of dockers. He was sporadically active in the ANC. In 1923 he attended the ANC convention and joined an ANC delegation to the Prime Minister. Ncwana had an eclectic philosophy. In 1920, he spoke favourably at Garveyite meetings and supported socialists Cetyiwe and Kraai at an Ndabeni ICU meeting. He launched various abortive Garvey-inspired enterprises "to induce the various battalions of workless Natives ... to settle on land", revealing more *petit bourgeois* inclinations. He served on the ICU Executive until expelled, apparently on the insistence of Isaiah Bud-M'belle who saw him as a "dangerous character". He then moved his allegiances erratically between ICU splinter groups. He was involved in a failed Burial Society in Cape Town and, briefly, in a venture with Josiah Gumede. In 1926, the ICU denounced him for abandoning unionism and being a "dupe of the capitalists". In 1928, he worked as a journalist in Aliwal North, by which time he was implacably opposed to Garveyism. He briefly assisted the Independent ICU in 1929.[69]

The Black Man was devoted to "organisation of industrial workers throughout the African continent". It attacked the labour recruiting system as "pernicious to the working classes". It demanded "free labour throughout the continent … more money … new conditions for farm labourers, a reasonable minimum wage for our women … reconsideration of salaries of ministers and teachers of our race". It thus had a broad, national, conception of workers. It attacked De Beers' "vicious" closed compounds, strongly advocated unionisation of black women workers, and endorsed some strikes.[70]

The Black Man adopted a critical attitude to Congress. It attacked "interference" by Cape Congress leaders like H. R. Ngcayiya and Simon Jordan in an ICU strike, opposing their tendency "to co-operate with the oppressors when Unions are involved in an industrial dispute". Ngcayiya "conferred with the employers to frustrate the demands of the workers". It obliquely referred to ANC prevarication during strikes on the Rand, warning of Transvaal leaders who "allow themselves to be tantalised by fertilised flattery purposely invented to divert their plans from pure industrial to political camouflage". This was an ICU declaration of independence from Congress. The events also show continued Congress interest—if of an anti-radical kind—in the direction of worker movements.[71]

Whilst *The Black Man* called on Jordan to resign, harsher criticism was kept for others. It denounced *Umteteli wa Bantu* as "organ of the Transvaal slave owners". Editor Marshall Maxeke was a "jackal … leading [workers] to the trap laid for them by the capitalist" and "making another attempt at breaking the forces of … Congress". Bantu Union leaders Rubusana and A. K. Soga were "out to reinforce the enemies of the working class" with their rejection of strikes and divisiveness in forming a body "totally opposed to the principles" of Congress. *The Black Man* contested the conservative nature of ANC leadership, not its *status* as national black political vanguard, stating: "Our people will do well to stick to the National Congress." It noted that if TNC affairs "are not conducted on practical lines, yet we cannot overlook the efforts and energies of those composing it, for the protection of our people.

We trust the workers in the Transvaal will respond effectively to the appeal made by the leaders" for funds. This was a clear statement by a black union organ in support of the political role of Congress, which it realised could give "a helping hand" to unite disparate union groups. The journal ceased in 1921. Police noted it had been "suspected of favouring the capitalists and discarded" by workers.[72] Its failure to survive or offer workers practical support was encapsulated in a contradiction: commitment to labour, but a largely rhetorical stance rooted in the class position of the editor.

Some women associated with the ANC supported the ICU. In October 1920, the ICU convened a meeting to organise women factory workers at which was formed an ICU women's branch. Charlotte Maxeke was instrumental in moving successful resolutions to admit women as full members and for equal pay at the first ICWU conference. Maxeke also encouraged women workers to be active in Congress. Ida Mntwana, a dressmaker who joined the ICU in 1927, was first president of the Transvaal ANC Women's League. Bertha Mkhize (1889-1981) was active in both ICU and ANC in Natal, where she became a tailor in the ICU clothing factory, Vuka Afrika, managed by Champion's wife, until it closed in 1929. In a 1979 interview, Mkhize recalled she, and many other women, joined the ICU because its leaders spoke about problems "happening every day".[73]

Closer ANC-ICU relations were checked when moderation became the keynote of ANC policy. Msimang tried in vain to obtain official ANC backing for the ICU in 1920. Still, relations were not hostile. At a mass meeting in Cape Town in 1925, Kadalie claimed Africans "must keep the white man trembling by speaking with one voice through" the ANC. When the ANC invited ICU delegates to attend a special ANC conference at the end of 1925, Kadalie remarked that ICU "proletarian delegates" had "gingered" the ANC "into action". In 1925, he visited the Rand to link up with the ANC's anti-pass campaign. Disappointed by "a certain amount of selfishness" by some ANC leaders, he was "grateful" to the TAC who "drove the [anti-pass] matter into the Courts and thereby won victory". In the mid-1920s, the ANC even appointed (on paper) Kadalie as "Minister of Labour". Fraternal relations also were evident when ANC president Mahabane sent a telegram to the 1926 ICU conference urging it success in organising black workers.[74]

There are many other examples of interaction. In Cape Town, initial rivalry faded when James Thaele, Western Province ANC president, joined the ICU in 1923. Vice-president of the Cape Congress, William Kutu, a transport contractor, moved a vote of thanks to Kadalie at a meeting in Green Point in 1926. OFS ICU secretary Thabo Wilfred Keable 'Mote was active in the

ANC. He organised a strike in 1925, and at the 1926 ICU congress called for mass passive resistance; in January 1929 he called on a meeting in Heilbron to embrace "the revolution of the proletariat". He was not always so radical: in 1928, he had cautioned labourers against striking. Another ICU official in the OFS with ANC connections was Simon Elias. Robert Dumah was a teacher who became ICU Herschel secretary. He was active in the ANC. Over two-thirds of delegates at the 1927 ICU conference were Congress members. This working relationship stood in sharp contrast to the ICU's poor contacts with other bodies such as the Bantu Union, which rebuffed attempts at co-operation. If the ICU claimed to represent workers in particular, then it nevertheless continued to recognise the prestige and central position the ANC held among Africans. The union did not regard the ANC as completely aloof from workers. Kotane noted Kadalie's attendance at ANC conferences and that many saw the ICU as "the trade union wing of the organisation".[75]

Closer relations developed for various reasons. Firstly, the ICU never really became an *industrial* union. Instead, as Kroonstad ICU leader Robert Sello observed, many of its officials "treated it as a pseudo-political body". It assumed nationalistic pretensions and as such was either a natural ANC ally or rival. Secondly, repression prompted ANC-ICU solidarity. Thirdly, some individual ANC leaders proved sympathetic to the ICU. The advent to the ANC presidency of Mahabane, who had earlier expressed broad solidarity with the ICU, and later the leftist Gumede, favoured co-operation. At the 1926 All-African Convention, dominated by the ANC but with ICU delegates, there was talk of a broad alliance. This did not fully materialise, but the ICU made use of ANC support. This support was uneven. In 1924 a Johannesburg ICU branch formed with the aid of CPSA members when ANC leaders in the Transvaal, Makgatho and Selope Thema, proved unsympathetic. On the other hand, the ICU spread to Natal with the assistance of Gumede. Kadalie recalled that when he first visited Durban in 1924, "my only acquaintance there" was Gumede, and it was Gumede and Mini who facilitated formation of an ICU branch. Frustrated by repeated failure of ANC deputations, Gumede moved further to the left and invited Kadalie to recruit in Natal. In August 1924, Gumede became NNC president. In his presidential address, he saw the NNC's "bounden duty" was "to help the ICU organise Native Labour in Natal and Zululand". In the same year, he became head of the ANC's Commerce and Industry "shadow-cabinet" portfolio, serving to focus his interest on industrial matters. Dube challenged Gumede's election as ANC president but Gumede received support from ICU circles. G. M. Kuzwayo told *Workers' Herald* readers the split induced confusion among the rank-and-file. He appealed to the ANC and ICU to resolve the conflict. A degree of collegiate feeling in ANC politics aided unity. ANC past-president, Makgatho, gave Gumede "cooperative support".[76]

Fourthly, interaction was encouraged by shared ideologies. At first, there were quite close ties between radicals in the ICU, ANC, and CPSA, based upon interlocking membership, shared socialist ideas and joint meetings. Communists John Gomas, James La Guma and Eddie Khaile were ICU leaders. Because they were active in the ANC, the linkage opened up avenues for contact between the ANC and workers. In addition, rising mass support for the ICU tended to boost temporarily their prestige in the ANC. The communist link injected socialist ideas into the ICU and the ANC. In 1925 and 1926, Kadalie, who espoused an eclectic philosophy that included a vague socialism, called at one stage to "overthrow the capitalist system". He stated in 1928: "We have no intention of copying the stupid and futile 'Non-Political' attitude of our white contemporaries." This political approach to unions opened the door to co-operation with the ANC.[77]

The communist connection aroused the hostility of conservative and liberal[78] forces, some within the ANC. Closer ties between ICU and ANC moderates received a boost as a result. Kadalie successfully moved expulsion of communists from the ICU in late 1926. The ICU invited the Durban Native Welfare Officer to address its meetings "to keep ... their members from going across the Railway line where the Communists were holding their meeting". The anti-communist onslaught was not entirely successful. In 1928 there were again joint ICU-CPSA rallies in Cape Town and Durban. However, one effect of these moves may have been less ANC contact with militant workers. Because ICU growth indirectly offered the prospect of a bridge to the ANC for workers, any reduction in ICU-worker ties also served to reduce the likelihood of ANC-worker contact. Yet ICU leaders now began to see ICU-ANC co-operation as more important than CPSA ties.[79]

This strategy culminated in 1928 when the ICU approved formal co-operation with Congress. Both groups met separately at Easter for their annual meetings. When the ICU lost its venue, the ANC allowed the Union use of their hall. The ANC Council of Chiefs delivered a letter to the ICU declaring closer cooperation a "long-felt want". A joint meeting of executives ensued, agreeing in principle to co-operate on national issues, provided the ANC renounce communism. There were some definite, if transitory, results. A joint ICU-ANC meeting in Waaihoek in June 1928 denounced "all legislation which aims at discrimination between different sections of the working class on racial grounds". A conference at Johannesburg Workers' Hall against passes attracted delegates from the ANC, ICU and other unions. Such co-operation could attract workers to the national movement. Naboth Mokgatle, a labourer in the 1920s, recalls in his autobiography that his first political meeting was a joint open-air gathering of ANC and ICU radicals.[80]

In 1929, after the ICU ousted Kadalie, he formed his own Independent ICU (IICU) with remnants of the original union, including H. D. Tyamzashe and Alexander Maduna. In the IICU organ *New Africa*, edited by Tyamzashe, Kadalie called for a united "army of organised African labour". Desperate to deliver land to members, he announced the union had formed a company to this end that "with the assistance of the African Congress ... will restore the confidence of the masses". He called on the Chambers of Industry and Commerce to summon a conference that would include groups representing Africans, the "industrial-political sections" of which included not only unions but also the "African Transvaal Congress". Whilst, pointedly, no mention was made of the national ANC, IICU leaders viewed the TAC as a major group representing African industrial interests.[81]

Which (if any) of these groups legitimately spoke for workers? ICU leaders claimed to speak on behalf of labour, but their credentials in some respects were no more impressive than ANC leaders. Kadalie had worked only briefly, as a teacher and clerk. Champion was an ex-mine clerk who increasingly combined business with union work. ICU leaders were loath to support strikes. At the 1927 ICU congress, a vote on supporting strikes was decisively defeated. Kadalie gave them little encouragement. In 1927, he declared strikes "wicked, useless and obsolete". His lieutenant, Henry Tyamzashe, in 1928 boasted that the ICU had used strike action only thrice since 1919. Strikes in 1928 by 35,000 Lichtenburg miners and 100 Onderstepoort ICU members received only nominal ICU support. Hence too much should not be made of ICU leaders' proletarian credentials. Claims, such as those by John Daniel, who accused the "middle class" ANC of only supporting strikes on "rare occasions", need measuring against a similar ICU example.[82]

Behind the reluctance to strike was the fierce arsenal of repressive laws (see Chapter 2) that would swing into action to crush any black strike. Strengthened by the 1927 Native Administration Act criminalising incitement to "racial hostility" and making it a trespass offence for unions to enter work areas, the Chamber of Mines and government, as Keith Breckenridge shows, wasted no time in intensifying strict policing of the mines to smash an incipient ICU "threat". From 1923, the union had tried without success to penetrate compounds. By 1925, it had made some contacts. By 1927, it was able to sign up some miners from Randfontein Estates, but police surveillance intensified. In 1925, Kadalie shifted the arena to the reserves, forming branches in rural towns where the ICU gained support of some migrant workers. However, the state sent its officials through rural areas to combat the union and companies shut the ICU out of industrial relations.[83]

Mid- to lower-level ICU officials included wage-earners such as teachers 'Mote, Dumah, John Mancoe, Gilbert Coka and Walter Makgothi, and artisans such as carpenter James Ngcobo, printer Tyamzashe, compositor Jim London, and contractor Doyle Modiakgotla. There was quite a difference between such artisans and the more professional, peak ANC leaders. Yet teachers and artisans also held local ANC posts.[84]

ICU "rank and file" were an amorphous group, including farm labourers and tenants and urban workers. Waschbank, Volksrust, and Wakkerstroom members were largely farm labourers. The ANC could not match the huge spurt in ICU membership in 1927-1928 that attracted many such workers, yet most of these ICU recruits had only a fleeting membership. Moreover, the ICU's lack of a systematic approach to mine recruitment and the action of ICU leaders in declaring a 1927 Natal coal strike illegal did not help long-term recruitment of mine workers, also largely absent from the ANC.[85]

Both organisations had intellectuals, professionals and wage earners involved at national and local levels. Historians contrast upper-strata ANC leadership with lower-strata ICU leaders. The differences were not basic but more a gradation within repressed social strata. Both bodies, as Neame argues, had "revolutionary-democratic" and "bourgeois-nationalist" wings representing complex interaction between national and social forces.[86]

Leaders with worker contacts retaining ANC ties tended to continue to support labour. This included leftists and those, such as Msimang and Bennett Ncwana, who progressively became more moderate. By 1927, the latter had distanced himself from the ICU and viewed the ANC as led by "a typical communist propagandist" in Gumede. Nevertheless, he continued to be active in the Cape Congress and took part in the 1927 Natal ANC special convention. Some other veterans of the Congress-led protests of 1918-1920 also joined the ICU. Herbert Msane became a leader of the Greytown ICU. At the 1928 ICU conference, he spoke in favour of a uniform national approach to improving wages of farm labourers. The Johannesburg storeman William Selebogo was active in both bodies.[87]

In contrast, those leaders who severed ties with the ANC often ceased to address labour issues. Allan Soga, who championed labour rights in the first decade of the century, now worked as a road overseer for Kentani Council, trapped in the public service "no-politics" rule. His membership of the Bantu Union brought few contacts with workers. He opposed ICU influence in Kentani: "their propaganda ... is inclined to divide the ignorant masses from the more intelligent law-abiding classes."[88]

If relations were cordial, the ICU criticised ANC prevarication. In 1926, *Workers' Herald* accused Plaatje of "plaintive thanksgiving" in failing to confront government at a conference. Tyamzashe admonished Selope Thema for lacking "the pluck" to attack the "scandalous wage paid by the Chamber of Mines". Thomas Mbeki told the 1927 ICU conference the ANC's "failure ... is due to too much prayer and no direct action". Mancoe told the 1928 conference the ANC had effectively failed to combat passes. The conference, however, agreed the ICU should still consult with the ANC on national action.[89]

The ANC, for its part, had not yet developed a consistent policy towards unions, beyond a vague notion they were a good thing. It was willing to form a united front on an African Nationalist platform, but did not yet have a coherent ideology of nationalism. Nevertheless, the experience of shared oppression began to form a medium across which a dialogue between workers and leaders could develop, which also facilitated the development of loose ties between the ANC and communists.

CPSA-ANC Relations

Writers have well documented CPSA history.[90] I focus here on its African members and attitudes to the ANC. A comparison of respective leaderships places ANC approaches to workers in clearer perspective. Africanisation of the CPSA in the late 1920s involved it more closely with black workers. As we have seen, the ANC also had black labour contacts, but these were more indirect. CPSA growth formed a bridge to enable workers and ANC to interact but some ANC leaders perceived CPSA influence as a threat and the effects of this tension created obstacles to free interaction of workers and the ANC.

The CPSA, formed in 1921, at first was a white party. T. William Thibedi, a teacher, was for some years the only black member. However, in 1923-1924 it gained labourer Thomas Mbeki and teacher Stanley Silwana. Others, such as leather worker James La Guma, factory worker Gana Makabeni, labourer Johannes Nkosi, and tailor Johnny Gomas, followed. In 1926-1927, the CPSA elected La Guma, Makabeni, and Thibedi to its Central Committee (CC) as Africanisation saw more attention devoted to African issues and languages in party propaganda. More black teachers, some dismissed from their jobs for their politics joined, including Edwin Mofutsanyana (who also worked on the mines), Albert Nzula, S. M. Kotu (who also worked in industry), and J.

B. Marks. Nzula in 1929 became the first African CPSA General Secretary. When Moses Kotane joined in February 1929 he observed: "Africans were the overwhelming majority at every meeting."[91]

Moses Kotane, son of poor working peasants, worked as a farm labourer, photographer's assistant, domestic, semi-skilled surface mineworker (for six months), and from 1928 as a bakery packer. In that year he joined both the leftist African Bakers' Union and TAC. By 1929 he was active in the CPSA and FNETU. He recalls, without distinguishing between ANC and TAC that contemporary ANC leaders were "middle class or intellectual"; "you went to meetings and you protested but you learned nothing". However, his emphasis on unity and national identity helped maintain his commitment to the ANC. In the black townships there was "nothing like a bourgeoisie ... All these little African businessmen also have to carry passes ... and the Government was always trying to close them down and force them into the factories. The same applied to doctors and teachers and priests."[92]

Most of these black communists were associated with the ANC. Silwana was listed as a potential ANC executive member in 1926; later he was an organiser for the ANC Western Province. Mofutsanyana joined the TAC as early as 1921 or 1923, five years before he joined the CPSA in 1928. He worked on Rand mines as a clerk and checker to pay his way through teacher's college. In 1981, he told Robert Edgar he joined the ANC in Johannesburg "when I left school. It was then that the ANC was fighting a number of cases" such as passes, "defending the women, travelling second-class on trains, walking on sidewalks". His aim in joining "was to fight for people to have equal rights in their own country". Makabeni and Marks also joined the ANC. Gomas, La Guma, Thomas Mbeki and Khaile combined ICU and ANC roles; Thibedi worked in the CPSA and ICU and was active in Congress in the 1930s. The ANC in 1927 elected Khaile its general secretary. He brought considerable ICU experience, and some class analysis. In 1925, he had served as ICU branch secretary in Port Elizabeth, where he had worked for two years as a bookkeeper, which trade served him well when elected ICU financial secretary. In August 1927, he addressed a Congress public meeting in Senekal, OFS, denouncing "class legislation". Not all these communists were consistent Marxists. Khaile's commitment to class struggle was short-lived. Trained as a theologian in 1916, he used Biblical metaphors in political speeches, and in 1930 joined his father as an ordained AME minister. He appears to have had little further involvement in the ANC. Thomas Mbeki was probably a police spy.[93]

The mobilisation of workers that communists achieved was in some, though by no means all ways, related to ANC spadework. Nkosi, first a farm and then domestic labourer, born in 1905 into a poor peasant family, took part in ANC anti-pass campaigns in 1919. He joined the CPSA in 1926 and worked to build the Durban CPSA. His success in building mass support related to his use of symbols of Zulu nationalism and the accord felt by Africans for the anti-pass campaign initiated at the time by the party. Such accord, however, was in part the result of over a decade of anti-pass protests led mainly by the ANC.[94]

An infusion of Africans into the CPSA thus took place in the later part of the decade. However, one should not exaggerate the CPSA's proletarian nature any more than the ICU's. As Bradford and La Hausse show, we can distinguish between some ICU/CPSA leaders and the ANC. We may characterise the former as somewhat more "proletarian"—yet even the likes of Champion (clerk, then businessman), Kadalie (intellectual) and the host of teachers and other "white collar" employees in the ICU were no more "blue collar" than ANC leaders. On the other hand, there was overlap. The "two hats" phenomenon of activists active in both (or all three) bodies is seen in people like Gomas and La Guma, Kotane and Mofutsanyana. After the demise of the ICU some ex-activists moved to (or returned to) the ANC fold. One should not romanticise any of these organisations.

Like Congress, the CPSA made use of intellectuals and professionals. In 1929, the CPSA-CC included not only black workers such as Nkosi and Kotane, and the teacher Nzula, but also lawyer Bunting and journalist Douglas Wolton. A leading communist, Eddie Roux, wrote that the black labour movement was "organisationally weak". Cobley stresses *petit bourgeois* influences in the CPSA. Kelley claims "mission-educated Christians" such as Thibedi, Kotane and Nzula "brought to the Party all the frustrations and securities of their own religious world". Africanisation of CPSA leadership smacked of tokenism. Like the ICU, by the early 1930s the CPSA experienced a meteoric decline.[95]

The CPSA lacked a comprehensive approach to the ANC. In 1922, Bunting claimed "national liberation movements [were] only stepping stones at best". In 1924, the CPSA saw the ANC as "dominated by instruments, conscious or unconscious ... of the ruling class". It used the example of Plaatje who, "expected to figure as a leader of the blacks to emancipation", repudiated the idea of a reprieve for an African sentenced to death. It accused Msimang, Selope Thema and Charlotte Maxeke of cajoling ANC delegates to the 1923, Native Conference into accepting pass laws at the workers' expense. In 1923 Bunting editorialised that "every intelligent worker, whether of European or

African descent, must associate himself with the demands of ... Congress" for equal political/economic rights. In 1924, *International* stated the ANC "might have functioned" to mobilise workers, but for its moderate leaders. The CPSA hoped Congress might convert to a more radical policy.[96]

The ANC did convert to a more radical policy. Gumede's rise to lead the ANC in 1927 coincided with a dramatic shift in communist policy aiding ANC-CPSA co-operation. ANC communist La Guma played a key role in this shift. The theses on a Black ("Native") Republic, adopted in 1928 by the Comintern and subsequently by the CPSA, first appeared publicly at the International Congress of the League against Imperialism in Brussels in 1927, attended by La Guma and Gumede. La Guma was involved in discussions before the Comintern adopted the theses, stressing the struggle in South Africa should firstly be for majority rule. The Comintern ruled that South Africa was a "British dominion of a colonial type". It laid out concrete policies: assistance to African agriculture, increased land, abolition of all forced labour, and autonomy to Africans. The Party should

> pay particular attention to the embryonic national organisations among the natives, such as the African National Congress. The party should participate in these organisations, should seek to broaden and extend their activity. Our aim should be to transform the African National Congress into a nationalist revolutionary bloc against the white bourgeoisie and the British imperialists.

The party should launch a special newspaper in African languages and intensify efforts to forge a South African branch of the League against Colonial Oppression.[97]

Some communists resisted this course. In 1928, Bunting still regarded the ANC as "a moribund body ... inclined to ignore ... the native proletarian movement". Yet, in perceiving that ANC "demands ... reflect[ed] the poverty stricken conditions of the native masses", he was alert to ways it might address labour concerns. Roux argued against the Comintern line. Conditions in South Africa mean that development of a "Native bourgeoisie" was "almost impossible". Roux's alternative slogan of "An Independent Workers' and Peasants' South African Republic" was defeated. The logic that "practically all natives are workers and peasants" was enticing; and it encouraged co-operation with the ANC.[98]

Communists began to court the ANC. Charles Baker of the CPSA told Africans at a meeting at Vereeniging in March 1928 that "you must unite, join us and link up with the African National Congress". In Johannesburg a Defence Committee of the ANC, CPSA, APO and black unions formed. *South African*

Worker devoted a regular column to ANC news. In 1929 the CPSA saw its work increasingly centred on "extension of the party's influence wherever possible in native bodies like the ANC or ICU".[99]

Comintern instructions to "pay particular attention" to the ANC prompted formation, in 1929, of a short-lived united-front body, the League of African Rights. It included ANC members. Gumede was president; ANC chaplain Nimrod Tantsi, deputy chair; ICU and ANC activist Modiakgotla, vice president. The League did not specifically refer to worker demands, but adopted policies akin to ANC policies, such as abolition of passes. It launched an anti-pass campaign and a mass petition, and held mass meetings.[100]

At the same time, the Gumede-Khaile leadership sought to transform the old ANC. The CPSA observed that the 1927 ANC convention had abandoned the previous "rather loose type of organisation". It now aimed to "build up the Congress on the basis of a duly registered individual membership" and paid "closer attention to the conditions of the workers". The new approach was reflected in a resolution on labour, which stated class unity had been "lacking owing to the fact that Congress has not in the past delved deeply into the question of the conditions of the working class". It also called for formation of an African Labour Congress within the ANC. There followed occasional joint meetings of the ANC, CPSA and ICU, such as a mass meeting of 500 Africans in Pretoria in September 1928.[101]

The election of Gumede, and the fact that ANC leaders could express such sentiments, signified a closeness of ANC members to labour, even in the face of concerted anti-communism. It was during the Gumede presidency that the CPSA attracted wide support on the Rand, in Durban and Bloemfontein and began publishing in African languages. Generally writers ascribe this growth to CPSA actions but, as with ICU growth, it was aided to some extent by bedrock ANC support and spadework. The ANC lent the CPSA some "legitimacy" in the sense that many new African communists had ties with or sympathies for the broad national struggle epitomised by Congress. Kotane, when asked to join the CPSA in 1929, replied: "Look, I … already … have my trade union … [and] I belong to my national organisation the ANC which fights for the liberation of the African people."[102]

Hence, the ANC gained legitimacy in the eyes of some politicised black workers. The success of leftists dedicated to working-class solutions within the ANC signified to them they could win over the ANC to support the demands of the proletariat, whilst the adoption of the Black Republic strategy focused them for years to come on the ANC. Such theoretical developments affected little the lives of the great mass of workers. Those who did have their hopes raised by the ANC's sudden turn to the masses were soon sorely disappointed as its leadership retreated into passivity in 1930. Still, these advances were important. Influential people such as Kotane, La Guma, Marks, and Mofutsanyana felt ideologically comfortable in their twin homes of the CPSA and ANC. Even if at times they despaired of its effectiveness, politicised black workers continued to view the ANC as an important part of any political solutions to national oppression.

This was possible for three reasons. Firstly, there was not a total gulf between leaderships in terms of class origins or sympathies. The ANC had local leaders who were workers, or had ties with workers. Class differences were most apparent at the national level. However, in 1927 even the national leadership included radicals with worker contacts. Secondly, the ANC had always supported, in general terms, amelioration of the harsh conditions of black labour. Adoption of specifically labour-oriented resolutions in 1927 therefore was not a departure from tradition. Thirdly, the very looseness of ANC structures meant individuals such as Gumede could capture the leadership with a handful of votes. This worked the other way in the 1930s, when Seme stacked meetings to secure re-election. Nevertheless, fluidity of ANC procedures made it possible for radicals temporarily to bypass entrenched *petit bourgeois* forces. In general, despite definite social distinctions between many ANC, ICU, and CPSA leaders, there also was overlap and continuity, particularly at local levels. This is apparent in joint memberships and the fact that some leaders moved from one organisation to the other. The contrast seems apposite when made between, say, rural ICU branches and the national ANC. However, when we consider local urban or rural ANC branches, then distinctions are rather less sharp.

Consequently, in the 1920s the ANC found both competition and common ground with the ICU and CPSA. Whilst the ICU briefly eclipsed the ANC in numbers and worker members, Congress continued to be receptive to radical working-class ideas. The CPSA was more worker-oriented in its policies than the ANC, but it remained small in numbers. Both the ICU and CPSA had an overlap in membership with the ANC. The ANC under Gumede briefly embraced both bodies and swung sharply to the left. Other political forces also were to provide both challenges and inspiration to the ANC.

Garveyism, the Joint Councils, and Congress

Another ideological influence that complicated ANC contact with workers was Garveyism. Marcus Garvey's ideas of race pride, black business, and solidarity spread from about 1920, disseminated by dockers and Pan-Africanists. Some workers welcomed it. Selby Msimang writes that when he visited Tsetsikamas Hoek, workers asked him when ships would come with Garvey. Kadalie stated: "My essential object is to be the great African Marcus Garvey." ICU activists Moses Itholing and Ben Majafi embraced it. By 1926, the Garveyite Universal Negro Improvement Society (UNIA) had eight South African divisions.[103]

Garveyism influenced ANC leaders such as James Thaele, Josiah Gumede, Selope Thema, Mweli Skota, Bennett Ncwana and Joel Mnyimba and, briefly, Plaatje and Dube. In 1920, *Abantu-Batho* had published letters from Garvey, and throughout the 1920s reflected Garveyist ideas. In 1922, Congress received a UNIA invitation to attend a race conference in New York. In 1925, Skota urged the ANC to organise a Pan-African congress. Garveyist influence increased—there were some joint UNIA-ANC protests, for instance in 1924—but it was uneven. The ANC in 1925 marked Garvey Day and protested Garvey's arrest. The lure of Garveyism offered an opportunity to ANC leaders to help attract workers, if they could relate it to their plight. Leftists such as Gumede fused Garveyism with communism. Moderates such as Thaele and Bennett Ncwana combined Garveyism with their own eclectic philosophies of nationalism and economic self-help.[104]

Garveyism also presented problems to the ANC. The delineation between ANC, UNIA, and ICU groups was not always clear. In some rural areas, people identified the ICU as Garveyist; some UNIA activists posed as ANC leaders. The ANC letterhead carried a UNIA motto. These diverse influences tended to make the specific work of the ANC confused in some minds. Garveyist support indicated the persistence of competing loyalties. Loyalty to Empire, nation, government, church, and ethnic group could compete with loyalty to Congress or labour union. The inculcation by the state of respect for "law and order" made some people suspicious of opposition groups. Herbalist Louisa Mvemve freely informed on Garveyist and ICU activist Ben Majafi of Evaton.[105] Divided loyalties also were apparent in the impact of the Joint Councils on Congress.

The CPSA, ICU, and UNIA siphoned off members from the left of the ANC. An analogous process took place on the right. Increased state, employer, and liberal pressure drove a fall in ANC radicalism. The Chamber of Mines, Basner argued, felt the way to deal with the ANC in the 1920s was "to cut off its head". If they could "divorce the educated Africans from ... Congress" this would render them "non-political". With the average Congress branch, in his opinion, consisting of local clergy, teachers, and a few shopkeepers, some members fell for the gambit of the Chamber of Mines and white philanthropists and "left the Congress at a time when there was no hope except for a life of poverty and a life of militant struggle". At the same time, it was "child's play" for the Chamber to buy off ANC journalists. There is a contradiction here between Basner's simple characterisation of a timid, middle-class Congress and its "militant struggle", but he evokes its decline.[106]

The Establishment enmeshed ANC leaders in these plans, using a visit to South Africa by James Aggrey in 1921 to promote moderation. Chairing a meeting in his honour in Pretoria, Makgatho claimed that, despite global unrest, Africans were "loyal". A meeting attended by, among others, Selope Thema and Letanka, resolved to join white liberals to form the Joint Council of Europeans and Natives. Councils formed across the country, succeeding in diverting some moderates such as Isaiah Bud-M'belle from the ANC. They attracted some labour leaders, such as Champion, leader of the Native Mine Clerks' Association, who might otherwise have then embraced the ANC. The 18 black members of the Johannesburg Joint Council (JJC) included five drawn from the TNC, three from the Mine Clerks. The Council was not a rival to Congress in seeking to *mobilise* Africans; rather it sought co-option of leaders. Members who were more radical had to struggle to assert black labour interests. Early JJC meetings broke up in disarray when white members refused to accept statements on the inadequacy of black wages by Champion. ANC members supported him. By 1926, only one JJC office-holder, Selope Thema, was black.[107]

Nevertheless, together with the Institute of Race Relations, formed in 1929, the Joint Councils established impressive credentials in researching workers' conditions and discretely lobbying government on their behalf. In 1924, the JJC submitted critical reports on Labour Bills. Secretary J. D. Rheinallt Jones in 1929 outlined a policy for "an intelligent, industrious, Christian Native working class". The Council invited ICU and ANC leaders to address its meetings. In 1929 the white chairman of Pretoria's Joint Council opened a TAC meeting. These factors account for the Councils' recruitment of moderate ANC leaders, including those with labour interests. In 1926 Msimang was a JJC committee member, and in 1928 addressed its meetings. Councils were "warmly embraced" by Dube's NNC.[108] The Councils virtually took over the ANC labour agenda. Their claim to speak on behalf of workers was a serious challenge to ANC legitimacy among Africans.

Despite the competition of all these rivals and its weak organisation, the ANC continued to address issues of concern to black workers, and to attract some of them. This was due to two underlying causes: continuing harsh political, social, and economic conditions that oppressed Africans, and the conscious actions of ANC members.

Conclusion

The 1920s did see a retreat from the militancy associated with Congress in the period 1913-1919. The use of the heavy artillery of the police, press, and clergy against Congress radicals in the early 1920s certainly dampened their militancy. However, it did not entirely sever the ties between Congress activists and ordinary workers.

Congress, if haphazardly, co-operated with movements claiming to speak on behalf of workers. This was a fundamental difference between it and most other black bodies. It got involved in the maelstrom of national and class struggles even if it soon retreated from the latter. Labour could thus view it as either part of the solution, or the problem, to oppression. Notwithstanding awareness of labour matters by its leaders, one cannot deny that an image of the ANC as conservative grew and contributed to membership decline.

These leaders, Cobley argues, were part of a nascent middle class using the ANC to create an economic base. There is no denying moderateness or growing business interests. Nevertheless, to suggest the ANC was *specific* to the interests of these strata[109] is to over-simplify its nature, for at local levels it engaged quite vigorously with labour issues. Individual leaders could be more, or less, committed to labour but the ANC remained consistently committed, largely due to its claimed position as representative of all oppressed, Africans.

Profound paradoxes marked the actions of major national ANC leaders. They empathised with the plight of black workers and were prepared to represent labour interests, as *they* saw it, in whatever avenues were open to them, yet they were attracted to ideologies that sought to minimise the power of an independent black working class. Similarly, they continued to recognise the importance of the ANC and yet rushed to join its rivals. There also was a basic contradiction in the nature of the ANC which was small, with a bare handful of paid officers, and influenced by liberal ideologies. Nonetheless, it was willing to work with radical labour groups to achieve its ends. It was in the policies and actions of ANC branches that this tension was most sharply experienced.

Notes

1   Marais, "Structural Changes in Manufacturing"; Freund, "Social Character of Secondary Industry".

2   UG41-22, pp. 7, 11; R. Phillips, "Social Work in South Africa" in D. Taylor (ed.), *Christianity and the Natives of South Africa: A Year-Book of South African Missions* (Lovedale: Lovedale Press, 1927), pp. 145-151, p. 148; G. Reynolds, "'From Red Blanket to Civilization': Propaganda and Recruitment Films for South Africa's Gold Mines, 1920-1940", *JSAS* v. 33 no. 1 (2007), pp. 133-152, p. 146.

3   Letter of M.W. Somntunzi in *Umteteli wa Bantu* 8 Jul. 1933.

4   "ANC", *Umteteli wa Bantu* 2, 9 Jun. 1923; *Abantu-Batho* [Apr.?] 1924, reprinted in *International* 4 Apr. 1924; "African Journalist Conference", *International* 4 Jan. 1924; reports on Kenya, Swaziland in *Abantu-Batho* 14 Jun. 1923 (copy in Swaziland Archives, Resident Commissioner's Secretariat, 486/23: I thank Chris Lowe for this copy.

5   Walshe, *Rise of African Nationalism* pp. 65, 239-244; UG41-22, p. 5; *Report of Native Churches Commission*, p. 5; R. Buell, *The Native Problem in Africa* (New York: Macmillan, 1928), p. 122.

6   Selope Thema in *Umteteli wa Bantu* 18 Feb. 1933; *Minutes of Evidence: Select Committee on Native Affairs* (SC10A-20) p. 27, *Minutes of Evidence: Select Committee on the Subject of the Native Bills* (SC10-27), p. 299; J. Dube, "Native Political and Industrial Organizations in South Africa", in Taylor, *Christianity and the Natives*, pp. 53-59, p. 55.

7   Walshe, *Rise of African Nationalism* pp. 239-244; Pampalis, *Foundations*, pp. 30, 69, 78; H.R. Ngcayia to Native Separatist Churches Commission, 16 Nov. 1921, in "Native Separatist Churches".

8   Mbeki, *Struggle for Liberation,* pp. 37, 43; UG41-22, p. 5; Walshe, *Rise of African Nationalism*, pp. 239-244.

9   Bradford, *Taste of Freedom*, pp. 2, 112, 282, 148; *Evidence to Economic and Wages Commission* ... September 19th, 1925 (Johannesburg: ICWU, 1925), pp. 2, 19. Police claimed Natal ICU membership was 2,842 in 1929: *Natal Mercury* 10 Jul. 1929; S. Johns, "The Birth of the CPSA", *IJAHS* v. 9 (1976) pp. 371-400; Bunting, *Kotane* pp. 44-46; Roux, *Bunting* pp. 104, 82-3; J. Ford, "Affiliation of FNETU to RILU" 1928, *SAIRR Collection* ICS; [S.P. Bunting] "Statistics of SA Labour: Report to RILU," [1929], JUS reel 5; Gaitskell, "Female Mission Initiatives", p. 360.

10 CID to SAP 12 Jun. 1922, and SNA to CNC Natal 26 Apr. 1920, NAD CNC 2316/20.

11 T.D. Mweli Skota, "ANC. Secretary General's Report" [1925], CKC 2:DA14:30/65, 30/8; ANC-TT to Minister of Justice 20 Feb. 1928, CAD CMT 3/1471 file 42/C, pt. 1, "ANC" 1924-.

12 Ginwala, "Women"; Kimble, "We Opened the Road" p. 19; *African World* 19 Sep. 1925.

13 [F.] Jabavu, "Bantu Home Life", in Taylor, *Christianity and the Natives*, pp. 164-176, p. 166.

14 C. Higgs, "Zenzele: African Women's Self-Help Organizations in South Africa 1927-1998", *African Studies Review* 47 (2004), pp. 119-141; Bradford, "We Are Now the Men"; Maxeke, "The Progress of Native Womanhood in South Africa", in Taylor, *Christianity & the Natives*, pp. 177-182.

15 "Ixwili na Manina e Monti" [R. Godlo], *Umteteli wa Bantu* 31 Mar. 1923; *Native Affairs Commission Report* UG40-25, p. 17; *Friend* 14 Jul. 1920; M. Benson, *A Far Cry* (London: Viking, 1989), p. 136; Msimang, *Autobiography*, p. 82; Taylor, *Christianity*, p. 195; Skota *Register*, p. 195; *Imvo* 3 Sep. 1961.

16 UG41-22, pp. 23, 26; "Notice" and "Congress Notes," *Umteteli wa Bantu* 16 Sep. 1928, 13 Apr. 1929.

17 "Ho Utsuoa ha League ke Congress Queenstown", *Umteteli wa Bantu* 12 Jun. 1920. Page ("Maxeke") points to a "solid union" but marital tensions with Marshall may have arisen given Charlotte's radical tendencies.

18 C. Maxeke, "Social Conditions among Bantu Women and Girls" in *Christian Students & Modern South Africa* (Fort Hare, 1930); D. Gaitskell, "Housewives, Maids or Mothers: Some Contradictions of Domesticity for Christian Women in Johannesburg, 1903-1939", *JAH* 24 (1983), pp. 241-256, p. 242; Maxeke, "Inkedama Zetu" and "Native Orphans Hostel Building Fund", *Umteteli wa Bantu* 7, 14 Oct. 1922.

19 Maxeke, "The Native Christian Mother", *The Evangelisation of South Africa, being the Report of the Sixth General Missionary Conference 1925* (Cape Town: Nasionale Pers, 1925), pp. 127-134; H. Basner, "Interview Transcript" *Basner Papers*; *International* 7 Sept. 1923; "Native Girl Servants to Oust the Boy", *Star* 17 Oct. 1923; "Ruin of Native Girls" *Rand Daily Mail* 14 Jul. 1924; Skota, *Register* p. 195; *Imvo* 3 Sep. 1961; Verwey, *New Dictionary*, p. 168; Campbell, *Songs of Zion*, p. 284; *International* 7 Sep. 1923. She was active in promoting "social hygiene" and in 1928 joined the Board of the Bridgman Memorial maternity hospital and encouraged poor women to use the hospital: C. Burns, "Reproductive Labors: The Politics of Women's Health in South Africa, 1900-1960", Ph.D. Northwestern University, 1995, pp. 36, 40, 247-8: see also *Star* 6 Jan. 1928.

20 "Particulars of Indeterminate Non-European Convicts for Release", SAIRR-B, B.24.4 reel 9.

21 Skota, *Register* pp. 95, 132-133, 230, 237; Kimble and Unterhalter, "We Opened the Road", p. 19; *African World* 11 Jul., 8 Aug., 19 Sep. 1925; Wells, *We Now Demand*, p. 152; Ginwala, "Women and the ANC".

22 N. Mgqwetto, "Yintsomi yo Nomeva!!" 13 Dec. 1924, "Yimbongikazi Nontsizi u Chizama" *Umteteli* 27 Nov. 1920; J. Opland, "Nontsizi Mgqwetho: Stranger in Town", in G. Furniss and L. Gunner (ed.), *Power, Marginality and African Oral Literature* (Johannesburg: Wits UP, 1995), pp. 162-184, p. 171, J. Opland, *The Nation's Bounty: The Xhosa Poetry of Nontsizi Mgqwetho* (Johannesburg: Wits UP, 2007); *Evidence ... 1925* (ICWU, 1925), pp. 26-27, 40.

23 H. Basner, "The Black Price of Gold in South Africa, 1870-1960", *Basner Papers*, ICS, p. 174; J.D. Rheinallt Jones, "Missionary Work Among the Bantu in South Africa", *International Review of Missions* v. 17 (1928), pp. 175-185, p. 180; D.I. Jones, "Communism in South Africa", p. 68.

24 R.V. Selope Thema, "Out of Darkness: From Cattle Herding to the Editor's Chair", 1936, SOAS MSS. 320895, pp. 70-73; Taylor, *Christianity* p. 195; CKC 2:XM1:96; Skota, *Register* 3rd ed. p. 114; "Native Unrest", *Umteteli wa Bantu* 6 Apr. 1929.

25 "ANC" and "Amalungelo Abantu", *Abantu-Batho* 14 Jun. 1923; *Cape Times* 10 Jul. 1923; Bennett Ncwana, "Kadalie's 'Political Renegade'," *Izindaba Zabantu* 26 Aug. 1927; *Friend* 10 Jul. 1923; *African World* 17 Oct. 1925 (citing 1923 ANC resolutions); *International* 13 Jul. 1923.

26 *International* 18 Apr., 11 July 1924.

27 "ICU vs Congress", *National Gazette: A Record of Congress Activities, Resolutions* v. 1 no. 2 (1927); E. Weinbren to Roux 27 Apr. 1929, *Roux Papers*, ICS; Nzula, *Forced Labour*, pp. 131-137.

28 Peteni, *Towards Tomorrow*, pp.22, 52; *Bantu World* 2 Jun. 1951 (obituary); A. Lutuli, "Let My People Go" ms., *Lutuli Papers 1948-67*; M. Benson, *Chief Albert Lutuli of South Africa* (Oxford: OUP, 1963), pp. 7-11; Luthuli, *Let My People Go* (London: Collins, 1962), p. 34;

E. Callan, *Albert John Luthuli and the South African Race Conflict* (Kalamazoo: Western Michigan University, 1965), pp. 24-29.

29   SAP to SJ re Movements of Plaatje 1 Nov. 1923 and Attendance at ANC Meetings 1923, JUS J269, SOU/1; Plaatje, "Native Life at the Alluvial Diggings", *Daily Dispatch* 7 May 1927; SC10-27 p. 294. Plaatje still attended ANC conferences: see his resolution in "African National Congress: Bill of Rights", *Umteteli wa Bantu* 6 Apr. 1929.

30   Evidence of Mahabane, 1 Jun. 1927, SC10-27, p. 299.

31   Gumede evidence, "Native Riots Commission Minutes of Evidence 1929", NAD Durban 3/DBN 14/5 pp. 419-22; H.S. Msimang, "Why Mr. Gumede Failed", *Umteteli wa Bantu* 31 May 1930; Walshe, *Rise of African Nationalism*, p. 214; Verwey, *New Dictionary*, pp. 86-88; Gumede to A. Slader 8 Sep. 1924, Pim Papers, SOU/I file 7; A. Gumede, interview transcripts, *Apartheid* (London: Granada, 1986), ICS archives.

32   Gumede, "The Congress against Colonial Oppression", *Ilanga* 25 Mar. 1927; *SA Worker* 1 Apr. 1927; "Jimmy La Guma: a Biography", (UCT Library, 1964), p. 31 (published Cape Town, 1997).

33   *SA Worker* 15 Apr. 1927, 2 Mar. 1928; Simons, *Class and Colour*, p. 217; "ANC Convention of Chiefs", *Umteteli wa Bantu* 14 Apr. 1928; *National Gazette* v. 1 no. 2 (1927); *Sechaba* Dec. 1982 pp. 20-27; *SA Worker* 30 Mar. 1928, 31 Dec. 1929. See also J.T. Gumede, "Congress and I.C.U.", *Umteteli* 2 Jun. 1928.

34   *Report of Commission of Enquiry into Native Riots at Durban* [1929] p. 2; "Riots Minutes", p. 419.

35   Letter of Gumede, 7 Sep. 1927 in *National Gazette* v. 1 no. 2 Sept (1927).

36   J.C. Smuts, *Selections from the Smuts Papers* (Cambridge: CUP, 1973), v. 5 p. 296; *Natal Mercury* 10 Jul. 1929; P. La Hausse, "The Message of the Warriors: the ICU, the Labouring Poor and the Making of a Popular Culture in Durban 1925-1930", in Bonner, *Holding their Ground*, p. 37; S. Dlamini interview with the author, Lusaka, 1989.

37   *Umteteli wa Bantu* 14 Apr. 1928; *SA Worker* 13, 27 Apr. 1928.

38   "Riots Minutes", p. 421; press fragment in *SAIRR Clippings*; *SA Worker* 2, 30 Mar. 1928

39   "Representation to the Prime Minister and Minister of Native Affairs from Certain Educated and Leading Natives in Johannesburg, in the Matter of the Mines and Works Act 1911 Amendment Bill", 28 Apr. 1926, SAIRR-B reel 22 B.72.11. Other signatories included boot-makers, teachers and clerks.

40   Selope Thema and J.D.R. Jones, "In South Africa", pp. 36-65, pp. 64-65.

41   R.V. Selope Thema, "Out of Darkness", pp. 2-4, 47-48, 67-73; KC v. 4, p. 155; Verwey, *New Dictionary*, pp. 245-246; Selope Thema evidence, *Report of the Select Committee on Subject-Matter of Masters and Servants Law (Transvaal) Amendment Bill* (SC12-25), pp. 101-102. For the "ethnic" dimensions of his politics see P. Bonner, "Kgatla Conspiracies, Pedi Plots: African Nationalist Politics in the Transvaal in the "Dead" Decade of the 1930s", UKZN History Seminar paper, 2002.

42   *Native Affairs Commission Report 1925*, KC v. 1 p. 168; SC12-25 pp. 99-107, 114-119, 120-121.

43   *Umteteli wa Bantu* 28 Aug. 1926; *Ilanga lase Natal* 8 Jul. 1927; SC12-25 pp. 120-121, 99; Selope Thema, "Social Conditions of the Africans", in D. Taylor, *Christianity and the Natives*, pp. 45-52, p. 44.

44   *National Gazette* v. 1 no. 2 Sep. 1927.

45   Cobley, *Class and Consciousness*, pp. 160-161, citing 1929 draft ANC program.

46   "Native Congress Resolution", (Reuters) newspaper clipping dated 7 Dec. (ca.1928), Bloemfontein, *African National Congress Collection*, CAMP.

47 *International* 15 Aug. 1924; Selope Thema and Jones, "In South Africa", pp. 42-50; Starfield, "History"; Selope Thema, "Out of Darkness".

48 Selope Thema and Jones, "In South Africa", pp. 60-61, 54.

49 Msimang, Biography, PC14/1/3/1; 9, 25 Report on Communism, 21 Feb. 1921, 11 Aug. 1922, JUS 3/527/17; Msimang "Autobiography" pp. 80, 115; SAP to SJ 31 Jan. 1922, JUS. For the most complete coverage of 1922, though one saying little of African political protests at the killings, see J. Krikler, *White Rising: The 1922 Insurrection and Racial Killing in South Africa* (Manchester: Manchester University Press, 2005), Chapters 1 and 5.

50 H. S. Msimang, "The Plight of Bantu Workers", *Umteteli wa Bantu* 24 Mar. 1923; SC3-23, pp. 116-119; Msimang circular 25 Sep. 1924, in Molema Papers, Cc9: "ANC 1910-1924".

51 S.P.B.[unting], "God or Mammon?" *International* 28 Mar. 1924.

52 H. S. Msimang, "African Trade Union Congress", *National Gazette* v. 1 no. 2 (1927).

53 Starfield, "History", pp. 19, 28-30; Msimang, "Autobiography", SOAS, p. 138; Msimang, *ANC: 1913 Deputation to England on the Land Act* (n.d.); Msimang, Biography in PC14/1/3/1, p. 13.

54 A. Kgokong to Ray Alexander 10 Jun. 1968, *Simons Papers* 5.5.3; Cobley, *Class and Consciousness*, pp. 153-156; Mweli Skota, "ANC Secretary General's Report" [1925], CKC 2:DA14:30/65, 30/8; Skota, *Register*, pp. 423-425.

55 Campbell, *Songs of Zion*, pp. 319-25; Simons, *Class & Colour*, pp. 376, 425; *SA Worker* 28 Feb. 1930.

56 UG41-22, p. 5; CAD PAS D59/3 Ref. 4/337: Political Activities of Government Servants: ANC.

57 M. Roth, "Black Councils, White Parliaments, 1920-87", ASI paper 29 Apr. 1991; *Report of Native Affairs Commission* UG17-23, pp. 29-38, UG40-25, pp. 17, 20-24, UG17-27, p. 14.

58 Skota, *Register*, pp. 82, 200, 427; Walshe, *Rise of African Nationalism*, p. 228; Cope, *Bind the Nation* p. 187; SC10-27 pp. 289, 292; *African World* 23, 30 May 1925; ANC Council of Chiefs Dept. *Records of Work Done* (1928), with letters of Letanka to Makgatho 2 Jul. 1928, SNA to Letanka 11 Oct. 1928, enclosing *The Powers of the Supreme Chief Under the Native Administration Act 1927* (ANC, 1928): CAD GG 1184 50/1313.

59 *Umteteli wa Bantu* 30 Apr. 1927; Selope Thema and J.D.R. Jones, "In South Africa", pp. 60-61.

60 See Ashforth, *Politics of Official Discourse* and Rich, *State Power*, pp. 9-10.

61 SC10A-20, pp. 7-13, 23-28.

62 SC10A-20, pp. 27-28; SC10-27, p. 298.

63 SC3-23, pp. 31-33.

64 "The Black Man's Viewpoint" and "The March of the Workers", *International* 15 Jun. 1923; "The Native Congress", *Umteteli wa Bantu* 5 Jun. 1920.

65 Wickins, *The ICU*; Bradford, *Taste of Freedom*; Msimang, *Autobiography*, p. 138; Walshe, *Rise of African Nationalism*, p. 248; J. Ngubane, "A.W.G. Champion", *Drum* Oct. 1952.

66 *Natal Advertiser* 10 Mar. 1919; *International* 19 Dec. 1919, 27 Feb. 1920; *A.P.O.* 30 Dec. 1919; *Cape Argus* 24 Feb. 1920; "African Miners Strike", *Christian Express* Apr. 1920; Wickins, *ICU*, p. 27.

67 Baines, "Populism"; Baines, "Disturbances", pp. 167-168; *Cape Times* 1 Nov. 1920.

68 *Friend* 14 Jul., *Cape Times* 7 Jul., 1920; *Umteteli wa Bantu* 24 Jun. 1922; police report 16 Jul. 1920, JUS 5/242/16; Wickins, *ICU*, p. 45; L. Switzer, "Moderate and Militant Voices

in the African Nationalist Press during the 1920s", in Switzer, *Alternative Press*, pp. 147-188; *Workers' Herald* 28 Apr., 15 Dec. 1926, 15 May 1925, 18 Mar. 1927.

69 Ncwana, "Kadalie's 'Political Renegade'", *Izindaba Zabantu* 17, 24 Jun., 8, 15, 22 Jul., 19, 26 Aug. 1927; *Abantu-Batho* 14 Jun. 1923; Wickins, *ICU*, pp. 66, 41; Campbell, *Songs of Zion*, p. 303; *Izwi lama Afrika* 13 Nov. 1923, *International* 11 Jan. 1924; "Non-European Political Organizations in the Union", 29 Jul. 1926, TAD NA 39/362; *Workers' Herald* 15 Dec. 1926, 17 May 1927; Ncwana statement 23 Aug. 1928, 2/SPT 16 N/1/9/2 "Native Unrest, Butler H. Wellington"; Cobley, *Class and Consciousness*, p. 215.

70 *The Black Man*, Aug. 1920; "The Recruiting System," *The Black Man* Sep., Oct. 1920.

71 "Our Demands" and "I.C.U. and Mr. Simon Jordan", *The Black Man* v. 1 no. 4 Oct. 1920.

72 *The Black Man* Oct., Nov. 1920; S. Masabalala letter and "Non-European Labour Congress", *Black Man* Dec. 1920; SAP "Bolshevism, Industrial Unrest", 31 Jan. 1922, 3/1064/18, JUS (v. 289 File 3/1064/18).

73 *A.P.O.* 2 Oct. 1920; *Friend* 14 Jul. 1920; Bradford, *Taste of Freedom*, p. 110; *Workers' Herald* 15 Dec. 1926; Champion, *Igazi ne Zinyebezi* (Durban, 1930): NAD CNC Natal to SNA 8 Nov. 1929; B. Mkhize interview transcript 4.8.1979, Unisa Library; McCord, *Calling*, pp. 214-222. Maxeke's sister, Katie Makhanya, briefly joined the ICU, leading a march of hundreds of women in Durban. See also Chapter 8.

74 *Cape Times* 26 Oct. 1925; "National Secretary's Report", *Workers' Herald* 28 Apr. 1926; Wickins, *ICU* p. 90; Trapido, "Opinion", p. 28; *Workers' Herald* 28 Apr. 1926; *National Gazette* v. 1 no. 2 1927.

75 Wickins, *ICU*, pp. 72, 85; *Workers' Herald* 15 Nov., 27 Mar., 28 Apr. 1926, 17 May 1927; "Brays by 'Mote" *Umteteli* 19 Jan. 1929; Van Onselen, *The Seed*, p. 147; Mancoe, *Directory*, p. 70; P. Rich, "Managing Black Leadership: Joint Councils, Urban Trading and Political Conflict in the Orange Free State 1925-1942", in Bonner (ed.) *Holding Their Ground*, pp. 177-200; Bradford, *Taste of Freedom*, p. 83; G. Carter, "Notes on Kotane," CKC 2:XK16:94, pp. 4-6.

76 R. Sello, "Minutes of Evidence," Feb. 1931, Native Economic Commission [NEC] 1930-1932, p. 4786; Wickins, *ICU*, p. 73; *Natal Witness* 19 Aug. 1924; T. Zania, "The ICU", *AC* 38 1969, pp. 62-79, p. 68; Kadalie, *My Life*, pp. 61-64; *Cape Times* 13 May, 26 Oct. 1925; G. Kuzwayo to *Workers' Herald* 15 Nov. 1926 [Zulu]; "Mr. S.M. Makgatho's Unselfish Support for Gumede", *National Gazette* Sept. 1927.

77 Kadalie, "My Life", ms. p. 26, CKC reel 23; 35th "Report on Communism in SA", 15 Jun. 1926, JUS reel 5; Bunting, *Kotane* p. 27; *SA Worker* 19 Jul., 3 Dec., 8 Oct. 1926; *Workers' Herald* 28 Apr., 27 Mar. 1926, 15 May 1925; Kadalie, "The African Labour Movement", *Foreign Affairs* Apr. 1928, p. 307; "Rejected Manuscript of Kadalie's Book", ICU Records, University of the Witwatersrand (ICUW).

78 On ICU anti-communism see: E. Lewis to W. Holtby, Creech-Jones to Holtby 25 May, 1 Mar. 1928, 8 Oct. 1926, ICUW; E. Parker (Scotland Yard) to High Commissioner 7 May 1928, TAD NA 40/328; W. Holtby, "Kadalie's Resignation", ts., *W. G. Ballinger Papers, 1920-1960*.

79 Thibedi to Roux 27 Jan. 1927, "Roux Papers" ICS; Roux, *Time Longer than Rope*, p. 42; *South African Worker* 24 Dec. 1926; *Cape Times* 4 Jan. 1927; J. Rawlins, Monthly Report Native Welfare Officer, Durban 13 Jan. 1931, ICUN collection; Kadalie, *The Relation Between Black and White Workers in South Africa* (ICWU, 1927), p. 6; Bradford, *Taste of Freedom*, p. 306.

80   *Workers' Herald* 12 May, 15 June 1928; "Red Money for Natives", *Star* 10 Apr. 1928, *Star* 26 Apr. 1928, "Rise of the Bantu" *Friend* 16 Apr. 1928; *SAIRR Newspaper Clippings* reel 13; Mokgatle, *Autobiography*, p. 178. ICU-ANC unity articulated "grievances of the urban African working class": L. Torr, "Lamontville: A History 1930-1960", in Maylam, *People's City*, pp. 245-273, p. 247. Kadalie made use of the CPSA Hall: E. Roux to N. Leys 16 Sep. 1928, *W.G. Ballinger Papers*.

81   C. Kadalie, "The Outlook", *New Africa* v. 1 no. 2, 29 Jun. 1929; ICWU. "Administrative Report Jun. 1929", cited in Cobley, *Class & Consciousness*, p. 160; ICU to Chambers of Industry 27 Nov. 1929 cited in W. Ballinger "Statement" to NEC, May 1931, p. 5.

82   Bradford, *Taste of Freedom*, pp. 71-73; *Workers' Herald* 17 May 1927, 30 Nov. 1928; "Coloured Labour in South Africa" *Negro Worker* v. 1 no. 1 (Jul. 1928), pp. 12-16; Daniel, "Resistance", p. 37. For an overview of the ICU from the inside see H. D. Tyamzashe, "Summary History of the ICU" (East London, 1941) ts., Saffery Papers, B5.

83   This paragraph is based on Breckenridge, "Speak for Ourselves".

84   Bradford, *Taste of Freedom* pp. 62-69, 295; Wickins, *ICU* p. 198; Skota, *Register* pp. 180-184, 277; H. Tyamzashe, "Why Have You Educated Me?" *Christian Express* Sep. 1921; Champion, *Igazi*.

85   *Workers' Herald* 31 Dec. 1928, 14 Oct. 1926; *Natal Witness* 20 Oct. 1928; Bradford, *Taste of Freedom*, pp. 164-167.

86   T. Zania [S. Neame], "70th Anniversary of ICU", *AC*, 116, 1989, pp. 33-48; Bradford, *Taste of Freedom*; S.N.[eame], "The ICU of Africa", *Sechaba* Nov. 1979, pp. 28-32.

87   B. Ncwana, "A Dangerous Attitude", *Ilanga Lase Natal* 15 Jul. 1927, Ncwana, "Wanted: New Native Leader", *Ilanga* 22 Jul. 1927; *Izindaba Zabantu* 1 Jan. 1927; Bradford, *Taste of Freedom*, p. 78; Mancoe, *Directory* p. 101; *Workers' Herald* 12 May 1928; "Will. Selebogo Agitator", TAD NA file 43/328.

88   "Council Officials: Membership of Political Organisations" Chief Magistrate Umtata to Dist. Council Kentani (KC) 3 Jan. 1930; Sec. Kentani Vigilance Association to KC 6 Feb. 1930, CAD 1/KNT 40/12.

89   *Workers' Herald* 15 Dec. 1926, 6 Apr., 17 May 1927, 12 May 1928; T. Mbeki, ICU, to G. Hardy 25 Jun. 1926 (intercepted by Scotland Yard), JUS 3/1069.

90   See S. Johns, "Marxism-Leninism in a Multi-Racial Environment: The Origins and Early History of the CPSA, 1914-1932", Ph.D. Harvard University, 1965 Chapter 11, and Simons, *Class and Colour.*

91   S. Bunting, "The Labour Movement in SA", *International Press Correspondence* 2.98 1922; B. Bunting, Memo [n.d.], CKC reel 14A; A. Kgokong to R. Alexander 10 Jun. 1968, *Simons Papers* 5.5.3; Bunting, *Moses Kotane*, pp. 27-8, 44-46; Roux, *Bunting*, pp. 79-86, 116-18; CID report 27 Apr. 1923, JUS 3/127/20; Roux, *Rebel Pity*, p. 107; CKC 2:XN63:96/2; Skota, *Register*, p. 230.

92   "Autobiography of M. Kotane", in A. Davidson, I. Filitova, V. Gorodnov, V. and S. Johns (eds.), *South Africa and the Communist International: A Documentary History* (London: Cass, 2003) v. 2, pp. 19-20; Kotane to *SA Worker* 30 Nov. 1929; Bunting, *Moses Kotane*, pp. 8-10, 41-51; Notes on Kotane, CKC 2:XK16:96/1; "Obituary of Moses Kotane", ANC press release 23 May 1978, *Simons Papers*; "Moses Monari Kotane" in *Subversive Movements in South Africa* 10 May 1963, CIA SC00591/63C, *CIA Research Reports: Africa 1946-1976,* reel 3.

93 KC v. 4, pp. 50, 67, 75-76, 63, 84, 92; *Umsebenzi* Sep. 1991; *Ilanga Lase Natal* 10 Dec. 1926; Mofutsanyana interview with Robert Edgar, Roma, Lesotho, 1981. On Silwana's activity in the 1930s see *Umteteli wa Bantu* 24 Jun. 1933; Mancoe, *Directory,* pp. 71, 36; *National Gazette* Sept. 1927; Khaile (ANC) to Joint Council 7 Mar. 1928, *African National Congress Collection* CAMP, Chicago; Campbell, *Songs of Zion*, p. 320; Personal communication, M. Roth, Oct. 1996. Marks and Mofutsanyana, claims Basner, came to the CPSA via the ANC: "Interview Transcript", p. 18.

94 *Umsebenzi* 8, 29 Aug., 19 Dec. 1930, 9 Jan., 16 Jan. 1931; *Cape Argus* 15, 17 Dec. 1930 "Johannes Nkosi", *African Communist* 60 (1975), pp. 78-84; "Phillip Thompson Native Agitator", TAD NA53/328; "Riots Minutes", p. 293; S. Ndlovo, "Johannes Nkosi and the Communist Party of South Africa: Images of 'Blood River' and King Dingane in the late 1920s-1930", *History & Theory* v. 39 (2000), pp. 111-132; La Hausse, *Restless Identities*, p. 234.

95 *SA Worker* 17 Feb. 1928, 6 May 1927, 30 Mar. 1929; *SA Worker* 31 Jan. 1929; Roux, "Subject Races Within the Empire" Oct. 1927 ms., *Roux Papers*; Cobley, *Class & Consciousness* p. 190; R. Kelley, "The Religious Odyssey of African Radicals: Notes on the CPSA 1921-1934", *Radical History Review* 51 (1991) pp. 5-24; A. Drew, "Bolshevizing Communist Parties: The Algerian & South African Experiences", *International Review of Social History* 48 (2003) pp. 167-202, and A. Drew, *Discordant Comrades: Identities and Loyalties on the South African Left* (Pretoria: Unisa, 2000).

96 S.P. Bunting, "The 'Colonial' Labour Front,"[1922] SAC 23/X/22; *International* 11 Jan. 1924; "Bluffing the Blacks", *International* 21 Mar. 1924; *International* 1, 15 Jun. 1923, 11, 4 Jan. 1924.

97 Meli, *South Africa Belongs to Us*, p. 78; *The Times* (London) 15 Nov. 1928; Comintern. *VI Congress Session* 27-28.7.28 and letter of Roux 25 Sep. 1928, in SAC; Bunting, *Imperialism,* p. 23; F. Meli, "The Comintern and Africa", *African Communist* no. 43 (1970), pp. 81-99.

98 Bunting, "Statement ... 6th Comintern Congress," in Drew, *South Africa's Radical Tradition* v. 1 p. 89; ECCI. "Resolution on South African Question" 19 Aug. 1928, H/10459/10, E.R. Roux, "Thesis on South Africa", Jul. 1928, pp. 2-6, Roux, "The Colonial Thesis on South Africa", 25 Aug. 1928, B/FS/10431/10, *Comintern Papers* 1928 Congress fond 493/ fiche 2887; "Our Annual Conference: An Inspiring Gathering", *South African Worker*, 31 January 1929. For more on these debates see Davidson, *Communist International* and Drew, *Discordant Comrades*.

99 Cobley, *Class & Consciousness*, p. 191 ff.; "Communist Meeting, Vereeniging 11 Mar. 1928," in JUS v. 267; *South African Worker* 30 Mar. 1928, 31 Jan. 1929.

100 *South African Worker* 30 Nov. 1928; Bunting, *Kotane,* p. 31; Roux, *Bunting,* p. 114; Simons, *Class and Colour,* pp. 417-425; "A League of African Rights ...," 25 Aug. 1929, SAC; SAP to Magistrate Queenstown 27 Aug. 1930, CAD 1/KNT40/12. The ANC role was not deep; the CPSA noted Gumede joined in "individual capacity. His organisation as such has held aloof": Executive Bureau CPSA to Comintern [1929], Roux to R. Bunting Aug. 1943: SAC reel 5.

101 "ANC Takes New Line", *South African Worker* 15 Jul. 1927, 19 Sept. 1928.

102 Bunting, *Moses Kotane*, p. 44.

103 Msimang, "Autobiography" p. 80; SC3-23 p. 147; Hill and Pirio, "Africa for the Africans", p. 215; SAP. "Communism in SA", 1922, JUS3/1064/18; "Moses Itholing Native Agitator", NA 39/328; "Majafi," NA 44/328.

104 "Communism in South Africa" 9th report 1921 (citing *Abantu-Batho* 27 Jan. 1920) 22nd 1922, 6th 1926 JUS 3/1064/18; ANC Report 1925; Cope, *To Bind the Nation,* p. 102; Cobley, *Class & Consciousness*, pp. 183-188; R. Vinson "'Sea Kaffirs'; 'American Negroes' and the Gospel of Garveyism in Early 20th Century Cape Town", *JAH* 47 (2006), pp. 281-303, p. 300; R. Hill (ed.), *Marcus Garvey and Universal Negro Improvement Association Papers* v. 10 (Berkeley, 2006) pp. lxxxiii, cxlix and p. 371 for a favourable reception of Garvey's writings in *Abantu-Batho* ca. 7 Aug. 1926.

105 *A.P.O.* 25 Feb. 1922, 2 Oct. 1920; Hill and Pirio, "Africa for the Africans", p. 237; E. Khaile ANC to A.W.G. Champion ICU 20 Sep. 1927, on letterhead, in Hill, *Garvey Papers* v. 10, p. 398; Coka, "Story", p. 188; L. Mvemve to Governor General 17 Jul. 1928, TAD NA 44/328. Cf. C. Burns, "Louisa Mvemve: A Woman's Advice to the Public on the Cure of Various Diseases", *Kronos* no. 23 (1996), pp. 108-134.

106 *Bantu World* 16 Apr. 1932; Basner, "Interview Transcript", pp. 16-19.

107 *Pretoria News* 20 Apr. 1921; "Minutes of a Meeting … 27 Apr. 1921"; J.D.R. Jones, "Brief Report on the Joint Councils Movement" Jun. 1933; Pretoria Native Welfare Assoc. [PNWA] Executive Report 1922/3/4; Joint Council Minutes 1 Jun., 18 May 1921; JJC Constitution, 1921 and Report, 1926: "Records Relating to the Joint Council of Europeans & Natives 1929-1940" (hereafter JCR); R. Haines, "The Politics of Philanthropy and Race Relations: The Joint Councils of South Africa, c1920-1955", Ph.D. SOAS, 1991.

108 JJC. "Memo. to Mining Industry Board," SOU/I file 7; SC3-23 p. 111; Jones, "The SA Economic Problem", 1929, JCR; B. Hirson, "Tuskegee, the Joint Councils & the All-African Convention", SSA 10 1981, pp. 65-75; JJC. Annual Report 1924-1925, JJC Minutes, Oct. 1929, PNWA Report 1928-1929, Minutes, 23 May 1929, JCR; *Rand Daily Mail* 28 Mar. 1928; Rich, "Managing"; La Hausse, "Warriors", p. 41.

109 Cobley, *Class & Consciousness*, p. 156.

"The Ruling Class is Getting Lost in the Mist and Sea of Selfishness": Natal in the 1920s

In the 1920s, ANC provincial structures continued to be loosely based and poorly financed and to suffer splits. This situation limited their potential appeal to workers as an effective organisation able to represent their rights. However, these branches were able to continue to attract some black workers to their ranks, and in general to stand up for their rights. Direct connections with labour unions and workers were often easier at the grassroots level, away from the high politics of national ANC deliberations. In the 1920s, this trend was most noticeable in Natal, which also saw the dramatic rise of worker organisation and militancy in the ICU. This chapter therefore focuses on ANC and labour history in Natal, with the following chapter picking up the same thread in the other provinces.

The 1925 *Report of Native Churches Commission* seems almost to have discovered a sort of law of African politics: "the activities of Congress vary inversely with the prosperity" of Africans; it contrasted ANC strength in the Northern provinces with its weakness in the Transkei and Natal.[1] There was good reason for this prognostication: Congress in Natal had fractured and, if black people were hardly "prosperous" under escalating white economic diktat, other movements influenced many rural Africans.

The 1920s saw substantial industrial take-off in South Africa. Although this was based largely on the Rand, Durban also witnessed considerable economic growth. Natal's growing, but largely migrant, African labour force tended to push ANC labour policy into contradictory positions, such as towards acknowledgement of the need for relief from their harsh exploitation, but away from pursuing industrial unionism to a more syncretic form of representation of workers who still had close ties to the land. The greater concentration of workers in Durban offered opportunities to political and union leaders to organise on a more industrial basis, but even here the high levels of casualisation militated against the sort of ANC-labour intimacy present on the Rand.

There was nothing moderate, however, about resolutions of a Congress meeting held in the Salvation Army Hall, Pietermaritzburg in March 1921 and chaired by Mark Radebe. Repeal the Land and Masters' and Servants' Acts that made Africans "slaves"; declare crown lands Africans' land; reduce rents; admit black people to government work; a minimum wage of four shillings and sixpence a day; government investigations into the high cost of living and dipping practices; and allowing African businesses within townships. In advance of the meeting, Dube travelled around the province and facilitated the presence there of several chiefs, including a "listener" for Zulu king Solomon ka Dinuzulu.[2]

Even those more conservative ANC leaders were not entirely divorced from worker issues. John Dube remained influential in the Natal Native Congress (NNC) until 1924 and later in the decade he made a political comeback. He cut himself adrift from the national ANC and often took a very critical attitude toward the ICU, established in Durban in 1925, claiming white farmers would use the excuse of ICU radicalism for a bloodbath. Dube's *Ilanga lase Natal* occasionally carried radical news, such as Gumede's anti-imperialist Brussels speech, but generally criticised radicals. In 1926, it warned against ICU "extremists" and lauded the union's expulsion of communists. "What is needed," Dube wrote, "is to educate the native people to regard Capitalists as their best friends." His eschewing of radical unions did not mean he was uninterested in workers. He refused to abandon concern for the general well-being of urban Africans. In July 1927 at a missionary conference, Dube chose to highlight the lot of the African at work. He spoke of the confusion felt by Zulu workers faced by uncaring employers unable to speak their language. He lamented their detention when sent on errands, of fines disproportionate to wages, of many cases in which his people were "shockingly accommodated, badly cared for, and badly paid and I plead most earnestly for better conditions"—without which labour would be "a fertile breeding ground for hot headed agitators". Writing in a missionary publication in the same year, Dube, perhaps reflecting the sudden rise of the ICU, prioritised labour issues over trading and farming. He was more conciliatory to the ICU, conceding its admirable aims of better wages and conditions and saying it served "a useful purpose in bringing to light certain very serious conditions of Native farm labour". It was right, he argued, to sympathise to some extent with African labour leaders' "first attempts" to form unions. In 1929, Dube told the Durban Riots Commission he was "interested in the material welfare" of urban Africans whose interests "must not be overlooked". For all his moderation, the state still regarded Dube with suspicion. Black detectives shadowed Dube, even reporting a fund raising concert he organised in Loskop in 1922.[3]

Dube's Ohlange Institute aimed at industrial training. As a sugar-plantation owner, he had a stake in worker productivity. His continued association with Congress obliged him occasionally to speak out against the most blatant excesses of the labour system. In 1924, addressing a state-inspired "Native Conference", Dube criticised enforced replacement of black labour by white labour. He shared a common African dislike of colour bars serving "to bar the Natives from entrance in to the ranks of skilled labour" and reduce all black labour "to one dead level of mediocrity". Dube was aware that "even among the ranks of unskilled Native labour there are divisions that call for differentiation in … wages". In the late 1920s, he even hoped to re-settle on his own lands unemployed African workers. If he represented sections of the *kholwa* (which was certainly not monolithic), then Dube was aware of the dignity of manual labour. In 1927, he urged teachers to neither "look down upon manual work" nor despise illiterate workers.[4]

Moreover, the broad influence of Dube's leadership could influence workers. In May 1921, he addressed a meeting of the NNC Howick branch, chaired by Mahlasela Kumalo. The meeting passed resolutions on farm evictions, shootings, fencing of thoroughfares, and restrictions on beer brewing. Dube then visited the local Magistrate, telling him local African people were the "unhappiest in Natal". The Magistrate confided to his superiors that since Dube's last visit "the Natives on the farms in employment have shown marked insolence and disrespect towards the whites".[5] This suggests that firstly, the ability to mobilise could be just as effective as mere radical words and, secondly that Congress, having established its "name" in a place, remained potentially a potent force.

The urban bases of the NNC remained Durban and Pietermaritzburg but it continued to recruit in rural areas, a move opposed by some local officials. In Weenen, the Magistrate boasted he would shut out Congress, "a non-entity as far as my Natives are concerned". The Howick Magistrate who sympathised with local council objections to NNC meetings echoed this view. In a racist manner, he claimed local Africans had "only their natural improvidence and laziness to thank for" their harsh conditions. Such views did not stop Congress from holding meetings in these and other areas. The Ixopo Branch, for example, joined the Durban Branch in giving evidence to the 1920 Pass Committee.[6]

In 1922, NNC chief office bearers were Dube (president), Radebe (vice-president), Lutayi (treasurer) and M. M. Gumede (general secretary). William Bhulose and Jerishem Gumede were chairperson and secretary respectively of the Organising and Finance Committee. The organisation's finances were weak; it was in debt to the sum of £600. An NNC meeting in October 1922 requested all branches to hold fund-raising concerts and mandated fund-raising tours by Josiah Gumede and Isaiah Mkize (north from Pietermaritzburg) and Bhulose (along the south coast and in Zululand). Money problems did not help Dube's prestige. In April 1924, a meeting of 60-70 people in Edendale, presided over by Stephen Mini, questioned Dube's handling of NNC finances.[7]

In any case, Dube signalled a shift in his priorities away from Congress towards a more ethnic nationalism. At a meeting of 600 people in Durban on 7 June 1922, he refused to discuss details of the 1921 Pan-African Congress in London he had attended, preferring first to meet with Zulu King Solomon kaDinuzulu. This was because Solomon, as the central figure of the Zulu nation, could to some extent help open or close doors to political movements in 1920s Natal and Zululand. Later in the decade, he was to slam the door shut on the ICU. Dube revealed that the London meeting had brought together black leaders from around the world and emphasised unity and freedom. Dube was prepared only to report one resolution, on solidarity—the oppression of any African was the concern of all Africans.[8]

The shift towards a more ethnically based nationalism was given coherent form with formation of the conservative Zulu cultural-nationalist organisation Inkatha kaZulu, which soon became a rival to Congress and especially after 1927 to the ICU. Inkatha, first formed in 1922-1923, succeeded in gaining the support of the Zulu monarchy and in distracting from Congress affairs figures such as John Dube. Another regional cultural body that, like Congress and Inkatha, vied for the allegiance of Africans was the Abaqulusi Land Union, formed in 1926 by Lymon Maling, a former mine clerk on the Rand gold mines and Hlobane coalmines. His father had been a founder of the NNC. Maling's experience at the interface between miners, employers, and Zulu royalty visiting the mines gave him some contact with workers. Through the Land Union, he claimed to speak on behalf of rural labour tenants. Like the more radical Josiah Gumede, he also sought to assert the dignity of African history. In retrospect, neither the Abaqulusi Land Union nor Inkatha made much political headway but they point to the stiff competition faced by Congress.[9]

Dube's hegemony in the NNC finally was broken in April 1924 at the organisation's Estcourt conference (held in the Showground stable). In the face of increasingly oppressive legislation and foreclosure of land rights, J. T. Gumede displaced him as president. At the meeting, Gumede vigorously denounced white rule and the deteriorating situation of Africans, stating he would bring back the laws of Mpande and Cetshwayo and sue white people to regain African rights. Dube warned against the costs of such legal action and, during the election of officers, claimed membership irregularities, but conceded. Soon after, he alleged that Gumede's election was due to lobbying by "false means" of Isaiah Mkize, NNC Organiser. Yet a clue to probable membership dissatisfaction with Dube was the rather bland (for a time of intensifying crisis) meeting agenda: the Prince of Wales's visit, greetings to a new Governor-General, land in Zululand, inheritance law, parliamentary elections, and the Native Urban Areas Act.[10]

Signs of change, and of Gumede's rising fortunes within Congress, were apparent earlier. Josiah Gumede, who boldly stated Africans would "no longer be the slaves of Europeans as many are at this moment on the farms", chaired an NNC meeting in Pietermaritzburg on 16 December 1922. He and other speakers—Dube, Mark Radebe and Chief Christian Lutayi—emphasised the need for unity. Lutayi echoed common African disdain for organised white labour when he bragged that TNC unity had succeeded in sending Rand Revolt strikers to the gallows. Radebe openly declared, for all to hear, that Africans would no longer suffer exploitation. Josiah Gumede continued to raise his profile. On 24 June 1923, he addressed a gathering of Africans on Market Square, Pietermaritzburg, reporting on the SANNC conference and condemning the harsh penal provisions of the Stock Theft Bill.[11] Also elected to the NNC executive in 1924, as assistant secretary, was Alexander Maduna, later ICU provincial secretary in Natal and OFS. Gumede and Maduna gave voice to the NNC rank-and-file. Maduna at first adopted a radical stance. In April 1924, he warned that the government was to be "attacked"—a term in marked contrast to Dube's strategy of polite petitioning. By 1929, Maduna had broken with the ICU and Champion. He joined Kadalie's Independent ICU as assistant general secretary, only for Champion to force him to close his Durban office. Now Maduna's approach was more moderate, denouncing Champion's "mob rule" during the 1929 riots.[12]

Another ally of Gumede was Chief Stephen Mini. Later in the decade, Mini served as NNC senior vice-president and then president, generally supporting Gumede's policies. The National ANC conference in Bloemfontein in March 1929 appointed Mini as Natal provincial president.

Leadership divisions persisted. In 1926 the NNC was renamed the Natal African Congress (NAC). It rivalled Dube's *hamba kahle* forces dispersed among Inkatha and in a rump body still claiming the NNC title. The latter lapsed soon after, but Dube re-established it in the late 1920s. Unlike Dube, Gumede (and Mini) maintained ties with the SANNC. Gumede vigorously supported a proposal at the SANNC 1922 convention to establish co-operatives, a precursor to schemes of his conservative opponent Seme in the 1930s.[13]

NNC expansion faced many obstacles, including official hostility, wariness of some chiefs, and limited finances and facilities. In 1924, treasurer Walter Msimang complained at a NNC meeting in the African beer canteen, Pietermaritzburg, that Durban municipality refused to allow Congress meetings. Around Pietermaritzburg, the organising base was just as difficult, as Africans lacked their own boroughs. It was not until 1925 that African pressure, led by Congress, began to tip the balance of public opinion. A meeting, of 200 residents chaired by J. T. Gumede, D. J. Sioka and Walter Msimang, called for the building of a new settlement at Mason's Mill. To this end, the Women's Section of Congress, led by president Justina Mdaka and secretary Lydia Msimang, organised a petition of "mothers and persons intimately in touch with native life and much affected socially by existing disintegrating and unwholesome conditions", and probably also a vigil by women outside local polling stations when white ratepayers voted on the matter. In Weenen, the magistrate contemptuously reported that in the district "never a chief or induna goes near their meetings, which seem to be attended by a handful of village loafers domineered over by a few congress agitators". Behind this antagonism were views already expressed in resolutions passed at the 1924 NNC annual general meeting in Pietermaritzburg, at a meeting of "Chiefs, Indunas and the Congress Branch at Weenen", in July of the same year. The motions protested the deliberate burning of one Mpini Zakwe's huts by a Weenen property owner, and requested withdrawal of municipal injunctions until local Africans gained suitable land under the Native Urban Areas Act. The racist response of the magistrate did not help—"We cannot interfere. The native tenants have themselves to blame. Most ... are of the loafer type."[14]

Nevertheless, the NNC strove to expand its influence, both among chiefs and workers. Gumede addressed an NNC meeting in Estcourt in July 1924. Chiefs Gabangane of Draycott and Mjwayile of Loskop were present. Labour issues were on the agenda: they unanimously passed resolutions for payment of farm workers, regulation of their wages, and employer-payment of dipping fees. In 1926, Durban-based NNC assistant inspector and organiser William Hlope held meetings in Nkandla, Mapumulo, Ndwedwe, Kranskop, and Dundee. His intended audience is evident in a flyer he issued, calling on those receiving it to "make it known to all and headmen, teachers, old men, and chiefs must not miss this opportunity of hearing for themselves about the formation of branches" in wards of chiefs, locations, and mission reserves.[15]

In the far south in Harding, where Dube had received short thrift in the previous decade (see Chapter 4), Gumede also sought to extend NNC influence. He received a much warmer welcome than Dube as, in December 1924, some 1,000 people gathered at Chief Jolwayo's kraal. According to official reports, Gumede "had a great reception and was cheered". His moderate message of African progress aimed at the predominantly rural audience stressed that they must "realise their position in the land" by working and improving it, planting more trees and purchasing better bulls. The early Britons were "far more ignorant and uncivilised" than Africans but had progressed by hard work. His other messages concerned black unity and an end to faction-fighting, prohibition of European liquor, and loyalty to the state. Gumede appears moderate, even naïve, as he claimed Britain's continued interest in their welfare. Finally, he warned of new segregation laws and reported that an NNC delegation in Pretoria the previous month had submitted resolutions on the Land, Native Affairs, and Native Urban Areas Acts. Here it is unclear whether the NNC was dissatisfied with ANC representation of its interests or whether it wished to amplify African concerns. Earlier that year a local NNC meeting had sought donations to cover costs of a deputation but only 13 people were present, although a few bought membership cards at two shillings and sixpence.[16]

The NNC raised issues affecting Africans throughout the province. The NNC's 1924 annual conference protested loss of lands in Zululand, shooting of Africans in Klip River, and disputed the government's method of electing delegates to government conferences. Instead, it elected its own 15 delegates, including stalwarts Dube, Josiah Gumede, Mini, Sioka, and Lamula. Congress expressed grievances of a range of society, sympathising with the need of traditional healers in Durban for space to sell medicines, calling for land for Africans who were daily ejected from white farms, and protesting cattle dipping practices that excluded African inspectors and imposed dipping fees on Africans who did not even own cattle. It urged government to ensure exemption from dipping fees of all "tenants on private farms who supply labour in lieu of rent ... as they have no means to pay such fees". Congress sought to improve its standing with lesser chiefs, supporting land grants to landless chiefs by saying "it is a disgrace to see a native Chief being driven about by farm owners and to be compelled to supply labour". The position of workers was not neglected. Congress recorded its "extreme surprise and alarm" at the retrenchment of African workers in favour of white employees by railways and Chamber of Commerce. Gumede pressed the issue in August, calling a meeting on Market Square, Pietermaritzburg, firstly to select delegates to lobby government over worker dismissals and secondly to urge the government to exempt sacked workers from taxes. Gumede added that he would defend dismissed workers from his law office.[17]

All these acts led some black CPSA members to perceive Gumede's potential. In 1926, Johannes Nkosi wrote to the *Workers' Herald* pointing out that, whilst the last ANC conference had called for unity, divisions within the Natal Congress persisted. The solution, he argued, was for people to consult Gumede.[18]

The NNC clearly carried some weight, both among some chiefs and the public. In April 1925, a meeting in the YMCA Hall, Pietermaritzburg, chaired by Josiah Gumede, saw unanimous opposition, including from Chiefs Ntombela (Ladysmith), Siyoko (New Scotland, Pietermaritzburg) and Mini (Edendale), to payment of the poll tax. Some 500 people attended an NNC special general meeting at the Estcourt African beer canteen on 16 December 1925. The mayor of Estcourt, in a comment remarkably candid for white authorities, told the gathering that Congress "filled a very important place within the Union, being the only purely native representative body to give expression to the views of the natives themselves". Josiah Gumede, speaking as NNC president and ANC vice-president, criticised the stealthy introduction of the Native Taxation and Native Administration Bills, and attacked the Natal and Transvaal Native Land Release Act for alienating African land. The policy of the Hertzog government was a return to the laws of the Boer Republics, a "nullification and destruction" of "British" policy. Gumede rejected segregation and attacks on the African franchise. Instead, he proposed a round-table conference in Egypt, with elected representatives from African countries and presided over by English judges. Gumede called for unity among Africans, for

> You people of my race to awake from the long slumber. Our valuable lands have gone away and have been cut up into European farms ... Because we are so divided the Parliament of the [whites] ... has had ample opportunity to take advantage of our weakness. Let us join hands in the constitutional defense of our interests, rights and privileges. DIVIDED WE FALL – UNITED WE STAND.

Chief Mini also spoke, emphasising African loyalty as they had given their lives in war but now had "no place to live in this country" due to segregation.[19]

The NNC quickly saw the value of allying with the ICU. In March 1926 Gumede held a mass meeting in Durban under NNC auspices at which resolutions were adopted attacking Municipal Native Affairs for refusing the NNC and ICU use of the Native Location Hall and urging Pretoria to assume control of African affairs from "high-handed despotic" municipal authorities. Other resolutions called for abolition of the pass laws, boycott of municipal beer canteens, payment of overtime wages for delivery workers, for the NNC and ICU to work to remove de-verminising procedures applying only to African workers, and for an end to racialist restrictions on which passengers ricksha workers could engage. "All men and women" were urged to join both the NNC and ICU and "empower these organisations to stand behind these resolutions". In June, another special NNC conference was called in Pietermaritzburg. The agenda included "our bounden duty to help the I.C.U. to organise native labour in Natal and Zululand". Gumede also called for the formation of a National Women's Union. He was now less conciliatory to the state, stating: "The ruling class is getting lost in the mist and sea of selfishness, obsessed with power."[20]

Gumede and Mini sought a stronger material base for the Provincial Congress (now known as NAC)—and perhaps for themselves. In 1928, they called a NAC branch meeting in rural Klipport to consider purchasing a nearby farm. The 14 Africans present were called upon to subscribe to the farm for between £1 and £10. Josiah Gumede was careful to distinguish Congress from the ICU stating there was no "relation between us and the I.C.U. The I.C.U. deals with the working class and their cases." Mini supported Gumede and displayed the blue ANC membership card (offered at six shillings), contrasting it with the red ICU card. The meeting was a failure as those present remembered the "red" tickets that had brought them nothing, and recommended that the leaders should first purchase the farm![21]

If Gumede distanced himself from the ICU then John Dube was antagonistic. The Dundee Coal Company made payments to Dube's school in the late 1920s, possibly linked to his anti-ICU views at a time when the ICU drew 4,000 to meetings in Vryheid.[22]

The state mistrusted Gumede. Upon his election as NNC president in 1924, police warned he "should be closely watched". They unfairly caricatured him as "an extremist" whose "utterances disclose a bitter hatred towards the European", with "a certain amount of popularity amongst the young native hot heads" but "little weight with the older men". In 1925, he protested "unfair" further moves to reduce African land holdings, asserting these measures showed "plainly the impotence of unrepresented classes". He demanded a popularly elected conference and that Africans have power to tax themselves. In 1925, the Chief Native Commissioner Natal viewed him as "a very different man from his predecessor" (Dube) as he did not feel compelled to "keep in touch" with government but rather was devoted to "creating sensations". He confuses

> Consulting Native opinion with the quite different question of consulting what he calls 'the leaders of Native organisations.' ... It is possible that ... [eventually Congress] may become representative of Native opinion ... but ... unfortunately Gumede is neither personally nor in the influence which he seeks to exert, a man whom it is desirable to take into one's confidence.

Dube, the CNC considered, would soon replace Gumede. Instead, Gumede was elected national ANC vice-president and, in June 1927, president-general in the wake of heightened ANC radicalism stimulated by attempts to restrict the black franchise. Such developments inclined Native Affairs to characterise Congress as having abandoned its earlier policy of righting injustices "without incurring general displeasure from the European public", and to have now "fallen into the hands of extremists". By 1928, the Criminal Investigation Department described Gumede as "an avowed Communist".[23]

A.W.G. Champion, ICU Office, Durban, late 1920s

In the context of these internal divisions, stable ANC relations with black unions were difficult. Dube and other moderates continually criticised ICU radicalism. In 1927, Gumede and NAC general secretary D. J. Sioka visited Dube to urge him to re-launch the ANC in Natal. However, when a conference was duly called in February 1928, Dube and about 200 of his followers walked out in protest at attempts by Champion and ICU officials (supported by Sioka and Mini) to gain control of the meeting. Dube's supporters appointed him president, a claim Sioka debunked as unconstitutional.[24]

George Champion was a bridge between the ANC and workers. He was a curious mixture of radical and moderate, labour activist and businessperson, ethnic nationalist and ANC figure. He was "Minister of Labour" in Gumede's ANC "cabinet", leader of the ICU *yase* Natal, and aspirant entrepreneur. Educated at Amanzimtoti School, Champion inherited his father's land (which he sold for £600 in 1927) yet was, at first, forced into wage-labour, first as policeman from 1913 to 1915, then mine clerk and union official (chiefly on Crown (six years) and Roodepoort United (two years) mines) from 1915 to 1925. He thus had considerable union experience. Until 1925, he was in close touch with Rand mine workers, who sent delegations over mine conditions to him in that year. He claimed in 1931 to possess "unchallengeable experience of the Mine Natives life". Proud of his father's work as a "boss boy", Champion purported to have been "head native boss boy" at Simmer and Jack, and Crown Mines. He claimed to have been "interested in" the TNC-led agitation of 1918-20, but there is no evidence of his participation. In 1920, he formed the Transvaal Native Mine Clerks' Association. Its aims included to "educate its members and the mine natives generally to avoid unnecessary agitation and strife". The emphasis on avoiding agitation made it no great threat to the Chamber of Mines. The Association expressed concern at the Rand Revolt of 1922. Pointing to the example of 1920 when "mine native labourers mutually agreed to ... undergo loss of life and imprisonment in support of their claims", it warned that agitators would be encouraged "if the natives are not given proper channels". Champion boasted that his group "have been able to control our native brethren". Despite its subservient tone, the Association urged recognition of African unions on the same basis as white unions. In 1925, Champion noted that whilst clerks were used as a tool of employers, the union helped forge their relationship with the mine workers.[25]

From 1925 to 1927, Champion worked as ICU organiser in the Transvaal, OFS and Natal, before becoming ICU *yase* Natal general secretary in 1928 when the section split from Kadalie. He combined ICU work, where he drew £20 a month, with reasonably successful business ventures in clothing and small publishing. Various people have stressed his *petit bourgeois* credentials. Kadalie regarded him as an intellectual, but conceded his knowledge of miners' lives. Stephen Dlamini did not remember him as a genuine advocate of worker interests. "The chap did not employ the real outlook of the working class." Moreover, "his narrow outlook was that Africans shouldn't be together with other nationalities to the extent that even in the ANC, or the ICU, he was not happy if some Africans from the Transvaal were together with some Africans from Natal". Such "tribalism" and his hostility to Indians made broader unity of the ANC with black workers difficult. Champion, as Swanson shows, was committed to establishing a black middle class and this identification was to influence his approach to class politics. Nonetheless Champion's ability to mobilise (largely Zulu) workers in the ICU *yase* Natal was rooted in his Zuluness, his ability to communicate with such workers, and his ability to relate to local grievances, such as those over beer brewing. In this regard, the ethnic dimension of ANC regional politics, and its connection to labour issues, stands revealed.[26]

Champion's ability to forge closer ANC-labour movement ties was compromised by his continued close liaison with police, and his anti-communism. Detective Inspector R. H. Arnold was "our friend all along". This made Champion an unlikely opponent of the system even if he clashed with government. Champion told the Riots Commission that "several times [he had] been deputed by the gold mining companies and the government to watch [CPSA] meetings". He opposed communists, as they desired "to change the existing system by which men like myself who hold landed properties should be dispossessed".[27]

The ICU, Champion argued in 1929, "concentrates on the improvement of wages and social conditions". At times, he successfully represented the interests of labourers in disputes over workers' compensation, helped secure wage board gains for Africans, and took up specific grievances of individual workers: for instance, he demanded wages owed to a woman worker. According to Durban municipal officer Fred Layman, Champion wrote "scores" of letters articulating pass-law grievances of labourers. He won legal challenges to discriminatory by-laws such as "dipping" or de-verminisation of Africans, curfews, and beer-halls—issues of concern to workers. Influencing this broad approach to unionism was his experience in the ANC and an eclectic philosophy. He viewed ICU "guiding principles" as both "respect for authority and the prevention of the exploitation of the native". His anti-communism was mixed with an appreciation of the need for allies saying: "I meet these people in a friendly way only."[28]

Champion was prepared to represent, and even associate with, labourers. He gave them a voice. Among his delegation to see the Durban Mayor in 1929 "were coal-heavers, dressed in their coal-heavers clothes". He stated: "In all my deputations I always include the uneducated Native." At a mass meeting of about 300 workers in June 1929, Champion, according to police interpreter David Xumalo, "wanted all the togt boys to give their grievances". But as an "exempted native" Champion was wary of entrusting his small "fortune" to the proletarians he claimed to represent. Though he took up the demands of rickshaw (or "ricksha") pullers, he ignored mine workers and plantation workers who struck in 1927. Yet some workers had hazy notions of what a strike was. *Togt* labourer Mcijelo, whose dismissal sparked the 1929 Durban riots, believed that "'strike' meant boycott'". When dockers wanted to "strike" over beer-halls in June 1929, Champion told them "please yourselves; but I do not agree with the strike" that is not against employers. Nevertheless, his populist combination of political with union issues and his role in the ICU and the Natal African Congress, where at times he joined with the more radical Gumede, made him an irritant to the government. The Natal Chief Native Commissioner claimed in 1927 that there was, "despite Gumede's reported repudiation of Bolshevik doctrines ... [an] affiliation of the ICU" and Congress. The Mayor of Durban believed that Champion was "trying to ... lead the good old native astray".[29]

This fusing of political and labour issues helped generate what ICU supporter Alfred Batty described as, Champion's "tremendous following" in Durban. This was evident in Champion's ability to attract and control large gatherings of workers and urban dwellers. At a mass meeting of several thousand people in May 1929, Champion moved a resolution, seconded by Gumede, of support for African brewers. His call "down with [municipal] beer" led to a loud roar from the crowd. In June, *togt* labourers launched a boycott, supported by the ICU, of municipal beer-halls. Such protests had precedents related to prior ANC agitation. In April 1926, an ANC-led mass meeting in Durban had similarly condemned the beer-hall system. According to Gumede, these protests had an even earlier precedent in a 1912 SANNC resolution. Champion directed his propaganda at both African workers and Africans in general. In a letter to the Sydenham Health Board protesting beer-halls, he attacked attempts to exploit "the low paid natives ... at the expense of the voiceless members of our Community who have suffered untold pains at the hands of certain people who are out to make them a football".[30]

Champion kicked a different kind of football to help build support. The ICU and Champion, much more so than either the ANC or CPSA, saw a connection between popular culture, politics, and the working class. He co-opted soccer matches and popular music into the ICU ideological arsenal. Some ANC figures, such as Richard Msimang and Richard Baloyi on the Rand, and Albert Luthuli in Natal, were active champions of African soccer. Nevertheless, there does not appear to have been any conscious use of sports by Congress as either fund-raising or membership-gaining vehicles. ANC fund-raising concerts seem to have really developed in the 1940s under A. B. Xuma and his wife, Madie Hall.[31]

It is certain that many African workers in Durban looked to the ICU, and to Champion, to resolve their grievances. When the authorities withdrew Mcijelo's *togt* badge, thus throwing him out of work, his work mates immediately told him that they would take the matter up with Champion. Whether Champion in turn passed on some of these complaints to the ANC is unclear. He would in the first instance have articulated protests through the offices of the ICU. It is also possible that he raised such labour issues in the NAC or ANC circles. Since 1927, Champion had been on the ANC national executive, but it is unclear to what extent workers would have known of this connection. Whilst ICU support was strong in Durban, police reports point also to the persistence of ANC influence. Detective Arnold, commenting on the level of African political organisation in the city, stated that ICU influence was limited to a "certain section" of Africans. Other Africans bodies were "able to formulate claims and put them forward with one voice. There is the Natal Native Congress. Their propaganda and general demeanour is totally different from the ICU. They go more on the lines of native custom. They formulate their grievances … and take them to the proper appointed authority." It was "functioning [with] a certain number of members".[32]

At the Riots Commission, the prosecution made much of ties between Champion and Gumede. Joseph Broeknsha and Mkishwa Kala, overseer and worker respectively of a Durban African eating-house, claimed that the two were present during an attack on a beer-hall. Arnold alleged that they met after the riots. He stated that they were part of a small section, five per cent, of "highly-educated" Africans. Gumede was "a friend of Champion's, socially … They are of the same clan … neighbours … both [are] political agitators … [and] belong by birth to the category of landed proprietors in Natal." Champion admitted that he came "into contact" with Gumede, saying that "I was brought up under him and I knew him long before I knew anything about public life." He denied Gumede was a communist. Gumede confirmed these statements. He knew Champion, who had married his niece, "very well". The leader of the ANC in 1929 was thus in close touch with the leading African black unionist. Gumede and Champion, and the ANC and ICU in Natal, needed each other. Champion, however, sought to separate their respective roles: Congress "is ... merely a political party and ha[s] nothing to do with the Industrial movement".[33]

Interestingly, rival Natal ANC leaders united at the Commission. Dube testified in favour of Champion. He added: "[we] look at our leadership of the natives from different standpoints. I look at it from the religious, social and political as well as the educational point of view, whereas Mr. Champion looks at the matter more from the industrial stand-point." Champion later wrote that whereas "many natives thought there was hostility" between himself and Dube, "nothing was finer than to see natives all on one side in this matter". He added that the sympathy of Dube's *Ilanga* and Dube's evidence to the Commission proved that Africans had genuine grievances.[34]

Champion viewed African workers as "somewhat advanced ... They understand Trades Unionism". Nevertheless, he viewed unionism very broadly; his "unionism" evaporated under state pressure. At the Riots Commission, he declared that he was willing to resign his union office if an Advisory Board was established, a long-standing aim of the ICU *yase* Natal and Congress. In other words, the ICU would "have no further use". He added that if white unions accepted African members there would have been no need for the ICU. The next year, in the face of state intransigence to black unions, he totally capitulated to the tactic of capital accumulation stating, "I speak as what is known as a labour leader when I say ... that the capitalist class must be created" among Africans. The only path to liberation for Africans was "working through the middle class, to the capitalist class". To all intents and purposes, his flirtation with labour was over. In 1931, he told the Prime Minister that a second reason why he wished to retire from unionism was his desire "to teach my Native people Commerce".[35] All this suggests Champion saw the ICU more as a community grievance, than labour, body. If the leading Natal unionist thought this way, were other African labour leaders very different in their thinking from ANC leaders?

The informal contacts Champion built between workers and the ANC were jeopardised by internal ANC divisions. This prompted a well-known Zulu writer to claim, in 1926, that Congress leaders were "not 'agitators' because they quarrel amongst themselves". However, disunity did not stop some ANC adherents from taking up the cause of workers. In December 1926, the NAC convention called on government, "in view of the stringent economic condition affecting the Native workers classes", to widen the provisions of the Wages Act to include African labour in the definition of workers and thus enable recognition of African labour unions. It expressed "alarm and anxiety" at proposals to restrict the employment of African labour in the liquor industry.[36]

Ethnic nationalism also came into play. The ANC had formed to combat tribalism, but different regional interests (often expressed in ethnic terms) persisted. Support for Zulu King Solomon kaDinuzulu is often seen as "backward looking" traditionalism. Yet in a broad strategic and cultural sense, it could appear to some Zulu people as both sensible and morale boosting. Solomon at various times throughout the decade both avoided and consulted with both ICU and ANC leaders. He held discreet meetings with Kadalie and Champion and in 1929, held a meeting in Bloemfontein with J. T. Gumede over the League of African Rights. State pressure led him to slam the door shut on the ICU. In general, the monarch was a conservative force. Ironically, however, appeals to Zulu tradition helped build the CPSA Durban branch among Zulu migrant workers the following year, showing that the mobilisation of ethnicity or appeal to cultural symbols was a potent tool for all.[37]

Other individuals associated with Congress took up labour issues. Rolfes Dhlomo in 1926 attacked the government for replacing African workers with white workers. He opposed communism, but declared his support for the union aims of the ICU. The African labourer in Natal, he wrote in 1927, was in a "lamentable state", faced low wages, high prices, poor rations, and thus was fully justified in seeking higher wages. Legal clerk Ray Msimang, an ANC supporter, stated it was a sacrilege still to fly the Union Jack "knowing what it stands for", when so much oppression of workers took place in its name.[38]

Yet, Congress in Natal still failed to mobilise large sections of the urban and rural population such as rural workers and women. If from time to time Congress supported anti-pass or anti-beer hall protests of African women, then it failed to enrol many women, even as auxiliaries. Nevertheless, some women joined, and the sudden rise in the numbers of African women in Durban—from only 1,511 in 1911 to 6,345 in 1921 and 14,234 by 1936—probably increased their social impact. Ethel Humphrey of the Durban ANC Women's Section in 1925 drew public attention to the dismissal of black workers. Bertha Mkhize was active in both ICU and ANC. Born in Embo, Natal and educated at Inanda, she worked as a primary school teacher until 1922 when, with her brother, a tailor, she opened a small tailoring shop in Durban, before becoming a tailor in the ICU clothing factory. In this period, a close friend was Katie Makhanya, the sister of Charlotte Maxeke. Makhanya later recalled that despite Mkhize's sneering at the *hamba kahle* moderate tactics of NNC leaders such as Dube, her reading of the ANC's radical *Abantu-Batho* inclined her towards Garveyism. Mkhize also opposed the loss of African mine workers' jobs. In a 1979 interview,

Mkhize stated that in the early years of Congress, "we did not turn to it", yet she also was "an old member of the A.N.C." and emphasised that "what the ANC really wanted was privileges for everybody". In her opinion, "men did not dominate the ANC ... because the women did just as much for the ANC": a reference to women's role in mobilising for ANC campaigns.[39]

Thus, despite pronounced in-fighting and weak organisation, the various groups claiming to represent Congress in Natal, and their supporters, opposed the harsh conditions of African workers and sought, if sporadically and largely ineffectively, to give them some kind of a voice.

Conclusion

In the 1920s in Natal, there was considerable turbulence in Congress, with splits and divisions, but also considerable experimentation with new forms of organisation and new alliances with the emergent African labour movement. Some Congress branches and individuals had more contact with labour than others did. Some leaders took the "capitalist road"; others were more directly involved in labour struggles, indicating the considerable commitment of regional ANC structures to the cause of African labour. Even "capitalist-roaders" such as John Dube felt obliged—largely, I would argue, by their continued ANC involvement—to condemn at least rhetorically the most ruthless cases of labour exploitation. The ICU, which dominated Natal African politics in the latter part of the decade when Champion marked out his own political space separately from Congress, nevertheless had some connections with the ANC in terms of both dual membership and the broad political ideology of officials, some of whom returned to the ANC fold when the ICU collapsed. If Champion, at the end of the decade, showed his distaste for both the ANC and CPSA, at other times he tolerated the CPSA, and occasionally held joint meetings with both. Later he would switch his work to the ANC entirely. It was in his interest to work with some ANC activists. When banned in the 1930s, the ANC gave him shelter and a job. During the decade, there were numerous contradictions and ambiguities in the attitudes to labour of Congress leaders but before assessing the 1920s, it is necessary also to consider the history of the ANC in the other provinces of South Africa.

Notes

1   *Report of Native Churches Commission*, p. 5.
2   "Natal Native Congress ... eMgu'ndhlovu," *Ilanga lase Natal* 1 Apr. 1921; "Resolutions Passed at Political Meeting of Natives ... 26 Mar. 1921" and Dube to CNC 4, 14 Mar. 1921, CNC 2316/20. That some workers wished to attend the meeting is suggested in a

letter of 3 Mar. 1921 of Nathaniel Mbongwe, a farm worker of Moorleigh (Estcourt), told by his Master he needed permission to attend: CNC 2316/20.

3   *Ilanga lase Natal* 26 Aug., 5, 19 Nov. 1926, 25 Mar., 18 Feb., 22 Apr., 24 Jun. 1927; Dube, *The Clash of Colour* (Durban: Natal Missionary Conference, 1926), pp. 8-11; Dube, "Native Political and Industrial Organizations", pp. 57-58; Magistrate Estcourt to CNC PMB, 2316/20

4   *Native Affairs Commission Report 1925*; R. Cloete "The Ideology of Self-Help in the National Native Congress from 1910 to the Early 20s", *Conference on History of the Opposition in South Africa* (Johannesburg: DSG, 1978), pp. 141-149; *Star* 19 Aug. 1927; J. Dube, "The Industrial Organisation of Native People", *Report of National European-Bantu Conference ... 1929* (Lovedale, n.d.), pp. 141-147; M. Marable, "John L. Dube and the Politics of Segregated Education in South Africa," in A. Mugomba (ed.), *Independence without Freedom* (Oxford: Clio, 1980), pp. 113-128, p. 125; *Ilanga lase Natal* 15 Jul. 1927.

5   NNC Howick Branch, Resolutions of meeting 20 May 1921, Magistrate Howick to CNC Natal 21, 30 May, 2 Jul. 1921 re NNC Howick, CNC 2316/20.

6   S. Mazibuko (NNC delegate) to Magistrate Weenen 28 Feb. 1923, Magistrate Weenen to CNC 3 Mar. 1923, Magistrate Howick to CNC Natal 21, 30 May, 2 Jul. 1921 re NNC Howick, CNC 2316/20; UG41-22, p. 25.

7   NNC leaflet (Zulu) in Magistrate Ixopo to CNC 19 Mar. 1923, NNC leaflet (Zulu) with translation in Magistrate Estcourt to CNC 28 Dec. 1922, CID Pietermaritzburg report 17 Apr. 1924, CNC 2316/20.

8   CID to SAP 12 Jun. 1922 attached to SNA to CNC 24 Jun. 1922, CNC 2316/20. Cope, *To Bind the Nation*, pp. 102-103 discusses Dube's flirtation with Pan-Africanism at NNC meetings in 1920-1922.

9   Cope, *To Bind the Nation*; Marks, *Ambiguities*, Chapters 1-2; La Hausse, *Restless Identities*, pp. 158 ff.

10 Police reports, "Native Unrest 1924," 19 and 23 Apr. 1924, CNC64/2: "Natal Native Congress, African National Congress" (CNC 22/20/2); "Native Congress," *Ilanga lase Natal* 25 Apr. 1924 (Zulu; translation in CNC64/2); Dube to CNC 24 Apr. 1924, CNC64/2. Gumede's son Archie (born 1914) recalled his father was elected with the help of Mini, and Dube did not take it kindly: "Interview with Archibald Gumede by Ruth Lundie, Apr. 1995," Paton & Struggle Archives, UKZN, 95APB1. As a boy Archie was not very aware of his father's politics, but recalls meeting Selope Thema.

11 Reports of CID Pietermaritzburg 21 Dec. 1922 and 27 Jun. 1923, CNC 2316/201.

12 ICU flyers signed Maduna, Marwick Papers. An ICU flyer of February 1925 urged workers to "join the Great Campaign for Emancipation of the African Workers". Like Gumede, police described Maduna as a "hot head" with a police record: Police report, "Native Unrest 1924", 19, 23 Apr. 1924, CNC64/2; A.P. Maduna, "Vivid Accounts of Durban Riots", *New Africa* 29 Jun. 1929. See Maduna's report on NNC affairs and Chief Mini: "Usubulawa kewSizwe yi Komiti yeZimali ye NNC", *Abantu-Batho* 14 Jun. 1923.

13 Cope, *To Bind the Nation*, pp. 101-109, 179, 187-189, 255; Skota, *Register* pp. 200, 427. Walshe, *Rise of Nationalism* p. 228 ascribes the shift to ICU influence; Cope argues younger *kholwa*, lacking land, were propelled into radicalism. However, Gumede already held substantial land.

14 Police report on NNC Meeting 18 Aug. 1924, Magistrate Weenen to CNC 12 Nov. 1924, Sioka to Magistrate 24 Oct. 1924, and NNC. "Resolutions Passed at the Annual General Meeting March [1924]" CNC64/2; H. Peel, "Sobantu Village: An Administrative History of a Pietermaritzburg Township 1924-1929", BA (Hons.) University of Natal, Pietermaritzburg, 1987, pp. 23, 30-1; *Times of Natal* 29 Jun. 1925.

15 Police report on NNC meeting Estcourt 15 Jul. 1924, Magistrates to CNC: Dundee 18 May, Mapumulo 7 Apr., Nkandhla 30 Apr. 1926, Hlope to Magistrate Ndwedwe 27 Nov. 1925, Magistrate to CNC 3 Dec. 1925, NNC flyer 20 Mar. 1926, signed Hlope (Zulu and translation), CNC64/2. NNC chiefs included Mini, Sioka, Walter Kumalo, Theo Ntombela, and Mbekwa Tshabalala.

16 "Meeting of Natives in Harding … 23 Dec. 1924]", and Police report on NNC Meeting, Pietermaritzburg, 18 Aug. 1924, CNC64/2 (CNC 22/20/2).

17 "Resolutions Passed at the A[GM] … March [1924]… of the Natal Native Congress," and "Report of Native Detective Betshe on Native Unrest", 26 Aug. 1924, CNC64/2 (73/7/24).

18 J. Nkosi to *Workers' Herald* 27 Mar. 1926.

19 Report of detectives Magusha and Mgende re NNC meeting 11 Apr. 1925, "Natal Native Congress" (Gumede speech 16 Dec. 1925, ts. attached to Magistrate Estcourt to CNC 18 Dec. 1925, newspaper (*Natal Witness?*) clipping, 23 Dec. 1925, CNC64/2. The Mayor was a "newcomer", which explains his openness. In this speech, Gumede still expressed some apparent hostility to communism and Russia.

20 J.T. Gumede to CNC 19 Mar. 1926, NNC. "Resolutions", signed Gumede and P. Lamula (Chairman, Durban), CNC to SNA 1 Apr. 1926, CNC64/2; "Native Congress" *Natal Witness* 23 Jun. 1926. NNC assistant secretary E. Tshabalala was based at Northfield Colliery, Glencoe Junction.

21 SAP Waschbank to SAP Dundee 9 Jul. 1928, "Meeting of the Natal Branch: African National Congress," CNC64/2, "Natal Native Congress, ANC." Police had alluded to financial irregularities in 1924.They noted (perhaps to discredit Gumede) that Gumede and Maduna's "fiery speeches" were always accompanied by appeals for money, and in 1926, previous NNC secretary J. L. Cele had engaged solicitors to unsuccessfully seek an investigation: Police report, "Native Unrest 1924," 23 Apr. 1924, and Chapman & Didcott to Inspector of Native Labour 9 Sept. 1926, CNC64/2.

22 Edgecombe and Guest, "Labour Conditions," p. 31.

23 Police report, "Native Unrest 1924," 23 Apr. 1924, CNC64/2; SNA to CNC 23 Jul. 1925, Gumede to M. Alexander n.d., CNCN to SNA 28 Jul. 1925, NA 17/328; "Non-European Political Organisations in the Union" 1926, NA 39/362; CID PMB to CNC PMB 21 Apr. 1928, CNC64/2. J. Grossman, "Class Relations and the Policies of the CPSA 1921-1950", Ph.D. Warwick University, 1985 p. 143 argues heightened ANC radicalism derived, not from the masses, but from African petit bourgeois.

24 "Undoing Themselves" *Ilanga lase Natal* 10 Feb. 1928; "ANC" *Izindaba Zabantu* 20 Jan. 1928; Sioka, provincial secretary ANC, to CNC 13 Feb. 1928, CNC64/2.

25 Champion to Hertzog 28 Sept. 1931, TAD NA49/328; "Riots Minutes" pp. 333ff., 289; CNCN to SNA 8 May 1935, NA49/328; Champion, Statement to NEC 1930; Transvaal Native Mine Clerks' Assoc. [TNMCA] "Memorandum to Mining Industry Board 1922" ICUN; *Rand Daily Mail* 21 Jul. 1922; *Evidence to Economic and Wages Commission* 19th Sept. 1925 (ICWU, 1925), pp. 22, 50, 52. In 1925, the Association addressed a memorandum to visiting Prince Edward, appealing for him to recognise black labour's plight: TNMCA to Prince Edward 23 Jun. 1925, CKC. Breckenridge ("Speak for ourselves", p. 78) notes that in 1919 hundreds of miners marched in protest over dismissal of a compound police officer "particularly active in representing" their grievances, hence Champion's police experiences may not have been entirely inimical to labour interests.

26 "Riots Minutes" pp. 289, 345, 380; Skota, *Register* p. 137; P. La Hausse, "The Dispersal of the Regiments: Radical African Opposition in Durban 1930", ASI paper 1986; Marks,

Ambiguities, pp. 86, 98; Champion, *The I.C.U.: What it is, What it is Doing & What it Wants* (Durban: African Workers' Club, 1927) p. 19; M. Swanson, "Champion of Durban: An African Politician & the ICU", ASA paper 1968 characterises him as "radical bourgeois"; *Workers' Herald* 28 Apr. 1926; S. Dlamini interview with the author, Lusaka May 1989; Swanson, "'The Fate of the Natives': Black Durban and African Ideology", *Natalia* 14 (1984) pp. 59-68, p. 65. On Champion's disagreements with Kadalie see M. Palmer to E. Lewis 28 May 1928, *Ballinger Papers* and "Blow to I.C.U. Unity", *Star* 20 Nov. 1928.

27   "Riots Minutes" pp. 333-338, 283-311, 340, 441 (Arnold). Police claimed Champion frequently was in "the company of Communists" and had not "ejected them from his association". Walton and Bunting addressed ICU meetings chaired by Champion in 1929: "Riots Minutes" p. 291 (Walton). American missionary John Reuling, who arrived to teach at Adams College two years earlier, also was unconvinced by government claims of a communist plot linked to the ICU: letter of J. Reuling to parents, 20 Nov. 1929, John and Eleanor Reuling Papers, Michigan State University Library.

28   "Riots Minutes", pp. 285, 333-341, 342c, 357, 373-374, 378, 460-461. Cf. D. Hemson, "In the Eye of the Storm: Dock-Workers in Durban", in Maylam, *The People's City*, pp. 145-173, p. 151.

29   "Riots Minutes", pp. 440, 187 (Xumalo), 316, 321, 350-354, 391, 423 (Mcijelo); Champion to Town Clerk Durban 28 Jan. 1930, ICUN; D. Posel, "The Durban Ricksha Pullers' 'Strikes' of 1918 & 1930", *JNZH* v. 8 (1985), pp. 85-106; P. La Hausse, "'The Cows of Nongoloza': Youth, Crime and Amalaita Gangs in Durban 1900-1936", *JSAS* 16 (1990), pp. 79-111, p. 86; Cope, *To Bind the Nation*, p. 186; *Report of the Commission of Enquiry, Native Riots at Durban, 1929* (Durban: Govt. Printer, 1929), p. 2.

30   "Riots Minutes", pp. 19, 146, 158, 229, 344, 348, 421-422 (Gumede), 438-450 (Batty); ICU Natal Resolution 5 May 1929, ICUN reel 4; P. La Hausse, "Drinking in a Cage: The Durban System and the 1929 Beer Hall Riots", *Africa Perspective* no. 20 1982, pp. 63-75; *Natal Mercury* 10 Jul. 1929; "Riots Minutes", p. 25 (citing Champion letter of 4 May 1929).

31   D. Coplan, *In Township Tonight! South Africa's Black City Music & Theatre* (Johannesburg: Ravan Press, 1985), pp. 134-135; P. Alegi, *Laduma! Soccer, Politics and Society in South Africa* (Scottsville: UKZN Press, 2004), pp. 34-35.

32   "Riots Minutes", p. 424 (Mcijelo), pp. 307, 288.

33   "Riots Minutes", pp. 197 (Brokensha/Kala) 294, 310-311 (Arnold) 337, 288-305, 387, 420 (Gumede)

34   "Riots Minutes", p. 407; Champion, *Igazi*, translation, CNCN to SNA 8 Nov. 1929, TAD NA49/328.

35   "Riots Minutes", pp. 353-354, 371; "Capitalism for the Natives", *Cape Times* 7 Nov. 1930; Champion to J. Hertzog 28 Sep. 1931, NA49/328.

36   "Natal African Congress" *Izindaba Zabantu* 7 Jan. 1927.

37   La Hausse, *Restless Identities*, pp. 230-234 ; Marks, *Ambiguities*, Chapter 1.

38   *Ilanga lase Natal* 19 Nov. 1926; Rollie Reggie [Dhlomo], "The Native Problem", *Ilanga* 5 Nov. 1926; Dhlomo, "Yea a Daniel!" *Ilanga* 9 Sep. 1927; J. Ray Msimang, "The Union Jack Desecrated", *Ilanga* 5 Nov. 1926. I thank Paul La Hausse for data on Ray Msimang.

39   *African World* 17 Oct. 1925; D.J. Mackenzie, "Influx Control, Health Regulation and African women in Durban c. 1917-1949", in *Natal, 1909-1961: A Collection of Papers ...* (Pietermaritzburg: Dept. of Historical & Political Studies, University of Natal, 1983), p. 1; B. Mkhize interview transcript 4. Aug.1979, University of South Africa Library; McCord, *Calling of Katie Makanya*, pp. 214-222.

"I-Kongilesi Lilizwi enzindlwini" (Congress's Name is Household): The Transvaal, Cape and Orange Free State in the 1920s

If, in the 1920s, Natal ANC provincial structures suffered splits and had limited potential appeal to workers, then the same general observations apply to other provinces. However, this is only part of the complex regional history of the ANC's mosaic of branches. As in Natal, ANC branches in the Transvaal, Cape, and Orange Free State built on contacts with organised labour made in the previous decade and continued to catch the attention of some more politicised workers. Although the overall strength of these branches remained weak, when opportunities arose from a combination of political and socio-economic causes, Congress branches were able to mount campaigns that mobilised Africans, including some workers.

With the Rand, Cape Town, and Port Elizabeth continuing to be major industrial centres these urban areas continued as the focus of such contacts. Declining real African wages, worsening working conditions and heightened legislative discrimination created a potentially favourable situation for political action. Housing was becoming particularly scarce for Africans in cities. That is not to say class differentiation did not occur. A 1920 church survey of Africans in the Ciskei indicated that clerks, interpreters, and some "skilled labourers" (artisans) were much more prosperous than unskilled urban or farm labourers, with teachers and lower-paid skilled workers forming an intermediary strata. Some farm labourers reported earning as little as £0.00 to £3.00 per annum. Similar figures emerged from another 1920 report, in Port Elizabeth, that recorded unskilled labourers receiving only three shillings and sixpence to four shillings a day, whilst African women factory workers earned as little as two shillings a day. In general, however, the margins of social difference were narrow: since the 1913 Natives' Land Act, land was now much harder to obtain by Africans, whose occupational mobility was increasingly blocked.[1]

Political factors would be the key to mobilising Africans around their grievances. There was substantial continuity in the leadership of provincial Congresses. Despite periodic declines in organisational activity, the popular perception of the ANC as a champion of black rights, earned by in its opposition to the 1913 Land Act and its vigorous 1919 protests against the pass laws, did not entirely disappear. However, an entirely new configuration of political actors emerged at this time.

Whilst established leaders helped focus some popular attention on Congress, fresh challenges also threw up new leaders and activists. The greatest of these challenges was the rivalry posed by other bodies, such as the ICU and Joint Councils. These organisations not only temporarily drew away established leaders from Congress but also often claimed to speak more specifically in the name of black workers. Yet what is particularly interesting about regional ANC history at this time, at the grassroots level, is that despite a general lull in national ANC activity, largely due to these rivalries, members continued to maintain Congress branches and even founded new ones. More to the point, when local-level labour activists who had gravitated to the ICU found its star on the wane, some of them then turned to the ANC, or to joint membership of the ANC and the Communist Party.

The Transvaal

The industrialised Rand remained a guarantee of at least some ANC contact with workers. Following the 1918-1920 strikes, however, employers and the state were well aware of the dangers to their power and control posed by organised worker direct action, particularly when it linked up with African political movements. The result was a concerted effort by employers and the state to wean workers and politicised black people away from leftist and African nationalist influences. Whilst the main vehicle of these efforts to emasculate African radicalism was the press, they also targeted the Transvaal Congress and its radical organ. The primary catalyst of this response was the 1920 mine strike.

The February 1920 mine strike was "the first general strike of natives" (*Cape Argus*). The press ascribed its outbreak to "the influence of educated native agitators", if conceding "the increased cost of commodities ... has not been without its influence". The organised and militant nature of the strike manifested in workers "drilling in companies", erecting barricades and, as state officials noted, adopting "modern methods, including ... picketing". Police claimed that the workers' attitude was the "most defiant and truculent ever experienced". The press reported, "guerrilla scrapping in the streets", as Africans responded in kind when police opened fire on a crowd of 4,000 considering strike action. Police shootings of strikers, cordoning of compounds, and lack of a black mine union ensured the strike's defeat. The TNC did not stand aloof. It vigorously condemned *sjambokking* of strikers and sent letters to government protesting police "driving natives to work by assaults". It convened solidarity meetings, some of which police attacked with bayonets. A meeting on 22 February attracted 2,500 Africans, mainly domestic workers, shop workers, and some miners. They carried resolutions of support for strikers and broadened solidarity to urge "all workers [to] ask their employers for a definite increase in wages". Some TNC organisers tried to widen the strike to include domestic workers and, at the same time, enrol participants in Congress. The TNC held several meetings to this effect but were unsuccessful. The TNC, it was reported, "formulated demands for a weekly minimum wage" for miners. The Johannesburg branch chairperson argued, in view of inflation, that employers should increase mine wages to £2.5 shillings a week. A public meeting, on 25 February, urged labourers to "hold fast until their demands were accepted", stating that we "deeply deplore the attitude of the Government in taking the side of the masters". The TNC requested a meeting with employers "to discuss the inadequate rate of pay", but one employers' representative, John Jack, retorted that he "would not meet a deputation of niggers".[2]

The precise extent of TNC contact with miners is unclear. High levels of protest indicate that forms of communication were developing. Police reported that miners were prominent in wage and anti-pass campaigns co-ordinated by the TNC and in April 1919 attended TNC meetings in large numbers. Smaller numbers attended the more secretive IWA meetings. Both groups distributed leaflets in African languages to miners. Horatio Bud-M'belle noted: "Invitations were ... sent to the natives working on the mines" to take part in anti-pass actions. A week before the 1920 strike police reported two-dozen "educated natives visiting the Reef compounds [to] deliver leaflets".[3]

Similarly, the attitude to the strike of TNC members is difficult to establish, as they had diverse class interests. In 1920 the ISL, commenting on the strike, claimed that Congress "had little to do with the movement other than to hold a watching brief". Bonner presents the most detailed analysis of the strike's level of support in Congress and the class nature of its leaders. The TNC was polarised. A radical section continued to back worker actions, but in the face of repression and state offers to abolish some passes, members who were more conservative ceased supporting strikes.[4]

TNC leaders certainly were eager to resolve the strike, proposing a permanent conciliation-arbitration board to handle labour disputes. The press quoted one leader, part of a deputation to meet the Director of Native Labour, that if a board was granted, the TNC "will be in a position to quell a strike. But if we cannot submit a satisfactory report at tomorrow's meeting there will be [a] strike." At the end of February, the TNC resolved to defer any talk of a further strike until the outcome of representations to government for appointment of a Wages Board. Despite this studied moderation, state officials detected TNC influence in the burgeoning protests. A Native Affairs official pointed out that, whilst Congress previously focused on rural matters, "it has now got its eyes turned on the Rand, which is a good hunting ground for it ... It has a huge membership in Johannesburg ... It was well organised and knew in half an hour what was happening." In contrast, the ISL conceded that it "had no means of getting the workers' version".[5] With other bodies unwilling or incapable of assuming leadership of black labour, only the TNC effectively attempted to help the workers realise their aims.

During the remainder of this decade, the Transvaal African Congress (TAC, previously TNC) did not reach the level of involvement with strikes or socialists it had achieved in 1918-1920. It resisted involvement in the all-white 1922 mine strike, yet still worked to ensure safety of black workers threatened by white vigilantes. Breckenridge recently has shown that deadly white pogroms aimed at black workers had occurred in Vrededorp after the TNC's 1919 anti-pass actions. In 1922, at least three TNC branches existed in Johannesburg, whose meetings discussed such matters as passes, the Land Act, and the poll tax, and heard D. D. T. Jabavu speak against Garveyism. In 1923, prominent members included TNC Johannesburg secretary R. H. Map Raphela, as well as C. S. Mabaso and Chief Pilane. Some members continued to oppose conservative forces in Congress. For instance, in 1926 the TAC called for a democratic approach to ANC elections, suggesting that national elections should take place through the branches and not on the floor at the annual convention.[6]

Transvaal Congress attitudes to black workers remained sympathetic. In 1920, it vehemently protested police brutality in the aftermath of a strike at Rietkuil diamond mine. In the same year, a TNC delegation consisting of Makgatho, Letanka, Mabaso, Mvabasa, Horatio Bud-M'belle, R. W. Msimang, James Ngojo, Z. P. Ramailane and C. H. Chake, when testifying to the Pass Committee, firmly rejected pass laws as they applied to workers. In October 1920, Congress made representations to the Director of Native Labour about harsh treatment of workers arrested at diamond diggings along the Bamboespruit. The Sabie branch initiated protests against stagnant mine wages, and encouraged strike action and stay-aways from May-June 1920. This action successfully increased recruiting around Pilgrim's Rest, where mine worker Jubilee Kok recalled that "hundreds of residents" joined. Congress effectively played the role of a de facto mine workers' "union". It demanded ten shillings a day wages, and urged workers to return home until employers met this demand.[7]

From the end of 1920 when, as Christopher Mulaudzi and Stephan Schirmer argue, "the TAC became more directly involved in mobilising farm workers in the region", a key TAC activist in the Standerton, Witbank, and Ermelo areas was Mandhlesilo Nkosi, who built upon contacts Congress had previously gained over land claims to the Beaumont Commission. In January 1921, he enrolled members and held a meeting of 400 in Standerton, urging squatters to change to wage (and cash) labour for their own interest. A resultant strike in Standerton over the issue was a victory for Congress and Nkosi, but, after repression and internal Congress divisions, its support and activity in the region faded. Still on the cusp of the radicalism of 1918-1920, the TNC, as Bradford notes, had "attracted considerable support in the northern and eastern Transvaal countryside by focusing on rural grievances". She cites the Standerton strike, in which some strikers claimed their TNC membership card gave them exemption from rent. Even after the flame of revolt died down after 1921, Bradford points out that "a subdued TNC continued to address itself to agrarian issues in meetings held all over the countryside". Later in the decade, the ICU superseded Congress in the region, but it too soon faded away. The TAC had however demonstrated it had the potential to win over farm workers.[8]

The TAC responded to popular grievances in other ways. It won a legal challenge against the Transvaal Poll Tax Ordinance of 1921. In his study of the Eastern Transvaal Middelburg district, Robert Morrell did not find much evidence of Congress activity. However, in response to rural land-scarcity, the TNC did organise meetings there in 1923. In July 1924, tenant labourers in Phokwane and Waterberg organised themselves against high rents and refused to work. Local farmers went so far as to blame ANC activists for arson attacks and strikes related to grievances of labour-tenants and migrant labourers, but Congress involvement probably was much more limited. In Middelburg, where the TNC had held mass meetings in 1919, tenants faced heightened exploitation, increased hours of work, lower wages, and attempts by farmers to tighten Masters' and Servants' Acts and use violence to maintain child labour. All this intensified class stratification; a small stratum of richer black farmers adapted, but labour tenants could not. Ethnic differences sometimes complicated Congress efforts to mobilise. In 1920, SANNC president, Makgatho, was unable to collect monies donated by Swazi in the Eastern Transvaal but claimed by the Swazi monarchy.[9]

Class and ethnic stratification made for complex political terrain in the Western Transvaal. In Rustenburg, Graeme Simpson claims that, save for a lone TNC intervention in 1924 to oppose harsh state action against opponents of the BaFokeng Chief, by the early 1920s, Congress was "entirely peripheral" to local politics. The apolitical childhood of Naboth Mokgatle (later a labour activist in Pretoria), who grew up in Phokeng, anecdotally seems to confirm this, but here politics was intricate. Mokgatle, only born in 1911, probably was too young to be aware of a reasonably active Congress branch that in 1923 boasted committee members, including J. D. Magano (chairperson), H. J. Mokgatle (treasurer), and B. M. Mokgatle (secretary). Congress however did lose its previous sway with chiefs in the region when the TNC—along with Sol Plaatje—sided with local Africans asserting the democratic aspects of *lekgotla* against the arbitrary authority of Chief August Molotlegi (Mokgatle, ruled 1896-1938) and thereafter incurred the Chief's wrath. The Chieftainship had accumulated wealth alongside Paul Kruger in a symbiotic labour-client relationship, and royal-commoner friction may have contributed to political divisions. Thus, royals at first regarded Naboth Mokgatle's grandmother, Mathlodi Paulina Kenana-Mokgatle and her offspring as tainted by slavery and ineligible for royal descent. Additionally, some of the above-mentioned Mokgatle and ANC office-holders perhaps were related to her and therefore were excluded from official favour, thus driving them into oppositional politics via Congress. Support for the ANC did come from the local African Methodist Episcopal church, perhaps in Phokeng but more likely in nearby Luka, which offered to raise money for the ANC Phokeng branch. There may have been overlap in AME and ANC membership but the dominance in Phokeng of the Lutheran and Pentecostal Holiness Churches served to shut out the AME, and with it, the ANC.[10]

Some chiefs with more intimate knowledge of farm workers' lives expressed concern about labour conditions. From the late nineteenth century, capitalist expansion had reduced the Ndzundza Ndebele largely to the status of farm labourers, and in the 1920s around Middelburg some of these labourers became active in the ICU. Chief Mayisha (Mayitjha) Cornelius Mahlangu (Mapoch, ruled 1921-1961) of the Ndzundza Ndebele rented the farm Welgelegen in Pretoria district. In May 1925, he told the Select Committee on the Masters and Servants Law (Transvaal) Amendment Bill that farm workers seeking contracts had to pledge work of their entire family, including children, who often ran away due to bad treatment and excessive work loads. Many workers had little option but to endure such conditions, yet sometimes came to him for passes to leave a farm. The chief was in favour of laws "compelling every employer to pay the wages" due workers. He refused to speak *on behalf of* workers, instead insisting labourers should be asked their opinion on work contracts as they were the ones "competent to answer" such questions.[11]

The ICU gained considerable support from farm labourers across the Eastern Transvaal between 1926 and 1928. Strikes and other forms of worker resistance accompanied this new alliance, which however evaporated with the rapid decline of the union in 1929. In parts of Western and Northern Transvaal, as Bradford notes, Congress had much stronger local support than the radical ICU, which as a result had difficulty recruiting in these areas. Stimela Jingoes, a worker and ICU organiser in the mid 1920s in the Transvaal made this precise point. In 1927, he found that the large town of Klerksdorp was an ANC "stronghold" and Congress opposition to the ICU obliged him to move on to organise in Makwassie. It is therefore curious that whilst many historians write off Congress at this time, both Jingoes and Bradford point to strong support in rural Transvaal, suggesting that despite its uneven campaigns, weak leadership, and temporary eclipse by other bodies, Congress had put down deep roots.[12]

Jingoes, from Lesotho but working as a clerk in Bethlehem, Orange Free State, had joined the ICU in 1927 when a speech by Kadalie appealing for black unity and worker rights had impressed him. The prospect of unity appealed to Jingoes. Formerly he had worked underground on the mines where he observed conflicts among Basotho mine workers usually relating to the honour of chiefs. Visits to the mines by chiefs could reduce such conflicts, which nevertheless made development of worker solidarity difficult. The ICU's direct appeal to represent workers undoubtedly made a definite impact on wage earners such as Jingoes. Yet ironically, when in later decades Jingoes worked for chiefs in Lesotho, the radical commoner organisation *Lekhotla la Bafo*, which cooperated closely with CPSA and ANC radical Edwin Mofutsanyana, derided Jingoes and other ICU veterans as "good boys" who never really challenged capitalism.[13] This reminds us that the ICU's brief and often rhetorical radicalism, if leaving a lasting nostalgia among some, meant different things to others and that the differences between ANC and ICU were not always rigidly drawn.

One indication of how Congress survived is its attention to local issues. In 1924, the TAC Executive asked the CPSA to publish its resolution calling for a reprieve for an African condemned to death. TAC General Secretary Moses Mphahlele protested to police about the fatal whipping of children in 1928. In the same year, he bombarded government with requests for statistics, demanding to know the number of fatal shootings of Africans by white people since 1924, how many were convicted, the tax collected from Africans, and women convicted for possessing "kaffir-beer". Mphahlele protested the dismissal of worker Thomas Sibisi from the Department of Veterinary Services after 21 years' service, "on a slight flaw of having harnessed wrong mules to the wagon". TAC intervention succeeded in gaining re-consideration of Sibisi's case. Mphahlele took up with Veterinary Services "deserving cases" of Africans "involved [and] coerced into" a strike at its laboratory. The TAC again acted as a *de facto* union, claiming to represent labour although it was a moderate "union". Mphahlele felt obliged to couch his protest apologetically, asking the Director to forgive and forget "the slur your Department suffered, through the actions of these misguided Natives" who had gone on strike.[14]

The TAC protest against the conviction of African women for brewing beer was one expression of Congress concern over women's precarious predicament on the rapidly urbanising Rand. As noted in earlier chapters, Congress had limited its social base by denying direct female membership. This general policy continued during the 1920s. At times, however, women became involved in either Congress politics or over labour demands.

Congress female activists in the Transvaal at this time included Charlotte Maxeke, as well as M. Bobojane and M. Kondile in Boksburg, and members of the Bantu Women's League in Pietersburg. In 1921, they drew up a list of grievances concerning farm workers. The Zoutpansberg branch in 1920 protested about exploitation of rural women forced to load heavy timber. The latter branch, at least, appears in the historical record as a TNC affiliate.[15]

Female urban migration continued in the face of state and patriarchal approbation towards "undesirable women". Whilst the 1923 Natives (Urban Areas) Act excluded African women from influx control, patriarchal attitudes continued to restrict them from political and social arenas, especially in the domains of housing, marriage, and work. With no significant growth in the urban black female proletariat and with women probably feeling no direct stake in Congress, the TAC made little headway with either women workers or African women in general. This was a matter of concern for leaders mixed with patriarchal worries.[16]

Simon Peter Matseke, later Mphahlele's opponent, began to make a mark in Congress politics in the late 1920s. Born in 1878 of Kgatla background,

Matseke had direct working-class experience and commitment to action over local issues. He had worked as a driver and a coal miner in Middelburg before becoming an interpreter, and later a shoemaker, in Pretoria. In 1920, he had joined SANNC and Pretoria Native Location Advisory Committee delegations to the Pass Committee. In 1928, he led anti-pass campaigns in working-class Marabastad and joined Gumede's ANC "cabinet".[17]

Based in the centre of South African industrialisation, the TAC continued to attract some workers and radicals. Like some other communists, Moses Kotane and Edwin Mofutsanyana first gravitated to Congress and only later to the CPSA. Mofutsanyana worked as a mine clerk at New Modderfontein, Benoni, very briefly as a mine labourer, a teacher, and then political activist. He joined the TNC either in 1921 or a few years later, inspired by its 1918-1920 protests. An incident of racism against a friend prompted him to work full-time for Congress. However, he soon became more prominent in the CPSA, which in June 1928 sent him to organise the party in the rural town of Potchefstroom, the scene of TNC protests in 1919. Over the next two years the CPSA, led by Mofutsanyana and his wife Josie Mpama, a domestic worker, succeeded in mobilising large numbers of Potchefstroom location residents around opposition to lodger fees and passes. The party won considerable, if transitory, support from workers and other residents, many of whom saw the "lodgers' tax" as, in the words of Bunting, "most unpopular and irksome", as it could mean expulsion from the district. In March 1928 Mofutsanyana, Thibedi and Bunting challenged white mob violence and location regulations to address Africans on these issues, in the process winning the support of many local people. The ICU, in contrast, appears to have made little headway in the town. A meeting drawing some 300 Africans in May 1928 secured only three new members.[18]

Despite Mofutsanyana's new identification with the CPSA, his motivation clearly remained the need to fight national oppression. Many years later, in 1981, he told Robert Edgar that Congress's fight for equality and African nationalism inspired him. "When I joined the African National Congress, it was for the purpose of fighting the whites."[19]

Other workers were attracted to the TAC. S. M. Moema began work as a motor driver in 1923. In 1925 he joined Congress, which elected him to the executive. William Selebogo had worked for 30 years as a storeman in Johannesburg when arrested for inciting "hostility among the races" at an ICU meeting in 1928. He protested that he was only an "honorary" ICU member, but police alleged that he was a TAC agitator. Beecham Mpu, Klipspruit ANC chairman, received only a home education and worked as a factory tinsmith before becoming a shop owner. B. Mkasibe, Johannesburg ANC chairman, worked as a caretaker. Members also included Mozambican migrant workers Raoul Honwana and D. P. Dulelea, who worked in a cement factory.[20]

The TAC connected with African national and labour struggles through *Abantu-Batho*. Since 1917, the paper had identified as a TAC organ, though in the 1920s it also declared itself "Principal Organ of the South African Native National Congress", claiming the "largest circulation of any Native Paper in South Africa". *Abantu-Batho* sympathetically covered the 1920 mine strike. Mine conditions were so harsh that workers "were not going to put up with this any more". Being intelligent "enough to know which side [their] bread is buttered on", workers were "beginning to wake up ... [that] they are slaves to the big capitalist". In 1922, the Congress newspaper urged Africans "to organise strongly their national lines" in defence of the black franchise.[21]

In 1923 *Abantu-Batho* gave unequivocal support to African struggles, not only in South Africa, but also in Kenya and (in keeping with its financing by the Swazi monarchy) Swaziland. It published letters from Zimbabwean supporters of Congress opposing passes. In 1928, when Mweli Skota became editor, it drew attention to struggles of workers in Java and India. In 1927, it favourably reported the internationalist views of Gumede and La Guma. It derided "good boys" who supported the Joint Councils. *Abantu-Batho* greeted Garvey's *Negro World* as a fraternal publication (Henry Tyamzashe of the TAC and ICU wrote for both) and carried pro-Garvey articles. *Abantu-Batho's* language challenged state legitimacy, considering the Department of Native Affairs as the "principal offender" in failing to consult with Africans. The "oppressive and repressive" Native Urban Areas Act had driven Africans out of locations "through revolting high rent". In addition, the "autocratic provisions" of municipal regulations were "an engine of tyranny". Government officials were ready to obstruct "accredited leader[s] of the Native people in the locations".[22]

The TAC used *Abantu-Batho* to condemn the "Draconian" Land Act producing "economic strangulation of our race" and the 1923 Native Urban Areas Bill. Commenting on government-controlled Native Conferences, the editor stated that, while white public opinion had reacted with "alarm and uneasiness" at resolutions of the ANC's 1923 conference it was "hardly cognisant of the real feelings and aspirations" of Africans. The paper emphasised close connections between rural evictions and oppression of urban Africans: the "cry of the urban areas is the cry of the rural districts". The editors called for action saying: "Let the hills and valleys of this sunny land of ancestors resound with the song of protest against this cruel inhumanity." Africans should "dedicate their lives and fortunes for the economic and political emancipation of our race". *Abantu-Batho* here adopted a national, rather than a class, approach. But behind this lay opposition to national or class oppression. In 1923, it argued, "autocracy, BE IT OF EUROPEANS OR AFRICANS, is intolerable in this age of light. The new African is determined to be free in order to enjoy the FRUITS OF HIS LABOUR and equality of opportunities."[23]

The editors understood the significance of labour politics. They reported opposition to the Urban Areas Bill by an ANC delegation to the Prime Minister. The Bill sought to provide white farmers with "cheap labour" and keep Africans "In a State of Industrial Helotry". There was an organised campaign "against our economic and industrial freedom. Without our cheap labour, white men cannot maintain their position ... Today we are the victims of three capitalist forms of injustice—industrial helotry, insecurity of land tenure, and political ostracism." This was, as the CPSA fully realised, virtually a paraphrase of the Communist Manifesto. It also was evidence of a continuing deeply radical, almost socialist, tendency in the TAC. *Abantu-Batho* advocated a radical response to the barrage of anti-black laws. In 1925, it declared, "the root of the evil must be struck at rather than its branches ... If there is any genuine intention at reform 'Colour Bar must go'."[24]

Based in working-class Jeppe, black labour was never far from the gaze of *Abantu-Batho's* editors. In 1924, it reported the proceedings of the OFS ANC, which discussed the murder of farm workers. It reached out to the black labour movement, urging the ICU's *Workers' Herald* to join it in a "Conference of the African Press" with a view to present a united front in matters pertaining to the "welfare of the African race". The ICU organ was supportive, but little came of the move.[25]

Despite being surrounded by workers, evidence of *Abantu-Batho's* influence on wage earners is anecdotal. Barney Ngakane, whose parents were active in Congress in the Western Transvaal, taught at an isolated school near Piet Retief. He became active in the TNC in 1921. "I got most of my inspiration" from *Abantu-Batho* and "encouraged the people at the Driefontein holdings to take an interest in the ANC", he recalls. A circulation estimated at only 1,000 in the late 1920s is still comparable with other black political papers, in contrast with which it was in the forefront of support for black workers. Even the more class-oriented *Workers' Herald*, according to the CPSA, had a contradictory attitude to political unionism and could not fully justify its claim to be the "mouthpiece of the African worker". The CPSA press, which increasingly carried articles by black workers, occasionally exchanged articles with *Abantu-Batho*.[26]

Whilst there were these various connections with workers, it was not possible for an organisation with such limited resources to reach all parts of the province. In the 1920s, there was a TAC tendency to focus more on central Johannesburg than the growing urban townships of Alexandra or Western Areas. Yet, as David Goodhew observes, by the end of the decade it stepped up campaigning against passes in Sophiatown. A branch did emerge in the densely populated, chaotic, and proletarian Alexandra Township six miles north of Johannesburg. This square mile of a "black island in a white sea" had survived as a place where Africans could buy freehold-title to land. Despite its poverty and clutter of winding streets, Alexandra was home to a pulsating urban culture that later gave birth to *kwela* jazz, and to urban self-help associations such as the Daughters of Africa. In the early 1940s, Nelson Mandela would find "life in Alexandra was exhilarating and precarious". In 1923, the TNC formed a branch there, presided over by John L. Mophosho (or Mposho) with T. S. Mngadi as general secretary. E. P. Mart Zulu served on the committee. We know little of its fate but at this time, police identified Mart Zulu and Mposho as leaders of local protests. The colourful Mart Zulu organised many public meetings. In 1924, he even joined Umpini ka Zulu, the Transvaal branch of Inkatha.[27]

One thing in particular served to mobilise and unify these disparate TAC members: repression. When the draconian Native Service Contract Registration Bill was proposed, a TAC meeting of some 100 members condemned it. Sefako Mapoch Makgatho and Selby Msimang spoke out strongly. Resolutions attacked government treatment of rural labour as akin to economic slavery and called for standard wages for farm labourers and squatters as well as apprenticeships for their children to create "scientifically trained rural labour".[28]

Poor outreach, indicated by the low circulation of its organ, involvement of some leaders in rival organisations, and disunity all reflected the TAC's limited ability to contact workers. In 1926, bitter divisions rooted in politics and ethnicity linked to land disputes forced Makgatho to resign as TAC president. However, the TAC was able to keep in touch with labour through several long-term factors. These were its base on the industrialised Rand, the longevity of *Abantu-Batho*, the only ANC paper in the country to survive the decade, a degree of continuity with the radical 1918-1920 period, and its policies of support for the amelioration of conditions of Africans. Such policies would have generated a favourable reputation that easily spread by word of mouth in cramped locations. Leadership reflected continuity. Mabaso, prominent in the strikes of those years, served as Johannesburg ANC chairman, and Makgatho and Letanka continued to be active.[29]

By 1928, Makgatho had returned to lead the body, calling for a province-wide anti-pass campaign as well as government aid for schools for farm workers. He also condemned high black urban mortality rates. Another means of contact with the conditions of workers was through branch delegates. The 1929 TAC annual conference heard "vigorous speeches" from rural delegates who spoke of the harsh treatment by white employers of farm labourers. Finally, state policies continually provoked the TAC to action. As the government moved to replace black with white workers in 1929, the TAC Executive in October condemned "victimisation" that "tends to encourage slave labour and unemployment" and called for a state investigation into the urban and rural wages of Africans. Two months later, another executive meeting, reportedly attended by as many as 100 members, similarly slammed the Native Service Contract Registration Bill as veiled slave labour. Instead, TAC leaders put forward labour-friendly alternatives, such as, a standard wage, apprentices for children of black farm labourers and squatters, and a contract with white farmers. Makgatho added that it was necessary for Congress to "keep on agitating".[30]

The TAC received a fillip during Gumede's national leadership. For his 1928 tour, it organised a flurry of well-attended meetings in Marabastad, Johannesburg, and Springs. In Johannesburg, under its aegis, a meeting of Africans "working on the Witwatersrand" heard speeches from Selope Thema, Gumede, Matseke, and Letanka, and agreed to form an anti-pass committee. There was continuity of leadership—Selope Thema was vice-president, Mabaso was treasurer—and some efforts to improve organisation. The 1928 TAC convention agreed to bank all monies centrally and not allow branches to retain dues.[31]

By 1929, the conservative *Umteteli wa Bantu* editor was congratulating both the national ANC and Makgatho's TAC for adopting sound economic policies after the annual TAC conference proposed settlement of Africans on Crown lands, re-introduction of sharecropping arrangements, and action to reduce high rents. The honeymoon did not last long, as *Umteteli* soon raised an anti-communist scare campaign against Gumede. Radical winds also began to blow at the Cape.[32]

The Cape

In the 1920s, the main Cape provincial structures were the Cape African Congress (CAC) and ANC Western Province (ANC (WP)), which split in 1926, plus the Transkeian African Congress and the Bechuanaland and Griqualand West Congress.[33] Through these branches, the ANC sought to speak on behalf of Africans as a whole. At times, this extended to workers, with these bodies even mounting small-scale protests to protest attacks on black labour.

ANC activists with strong labour contacts included Hamilton Kraai, James Ngojo and Samuel Masabalala. Their presence not only ensured that Congress discussed labour issues but also was a reminder of radical alternatives. Kraai was part of a Cape Provincial Congress delegation that included Z. R. Mahabane and William Oliphant, Cape Town secretary, to address the 1920 Pass Laws Committee (a separate delegation of the "Cape Provincial National Congress" included Masabalala and Frank Mokwena). Within Congress there was substantial agreement between moderates and radicals on defending the rights of black labour. All "agreed that the pass system tended to keep down wages".[34]

A measure of the commitment of ANC leaders to black labour was evident when in 1920 James Ngojo travelled to the Tlaping and Taung diamond diggings, where he gained popularity among labourers for demanding higher wages and abolition of passes. By 1922, Ngojo was Cape Native Congress Chief Organiser. He ranged across the countryside, using the slogan "*Mayibuye i Afrika*", (or "*Mayibuy 'iAfrika*") increasingly popular in Congress circles, and invigorating sizeable branches in places such as Burghersdorp (which hosted Executive meetings in 1921) and Sterkstroom, probably with from 50-100 members. Ngojo affirmed: "People may have the right to withhold their labour", but condemned the shooting of black workers on the Rand by white commandos.[35]

In the early 1920s, there is evidence of old and new branches in many towns. Reverend Elijah Mdolomba, now based in Cala, remained active serving as president and senior vice president. Alfred Tshiwula, later to link the ANC with unions in Port Elizabeth, was chief organiser in Queenstown and Glen Grey, and in 1923 briefly CAC general secretary. Ngojo had a roving commission as chief organiser throughout the Cape. Other organisers in 1923 included H. Mxalisa in Nqamakwe, John James Gcingca in Tsomo, J. Zililo, M. Mbata in Mount Fletcher, and C. Mateb in Aliwal North. There also were active branches in Queenstown, Colesberg, and Indwe, where officials included chairperson Prince Ntilashe, vice-chair July Mvimbi and secretary Jeremiah Nkuzo. There even was a branch in tiny Cyphergat, a colliery in the Stormberg Mountains between Sterkstroom and Molteno, where H. Kama, D. Ndika, and H. T. Mvalo were active. We know little of this history but some leaders such as Ngojo remained active; in 1925, he was Cape ANC president and in 1927, part of an ANC delegation to a state committee.[36]

ANC ties with blue-collar workers, if still slight, tended to be closer in more industrialised towns. Besides Cape Town, this included East London, Port Elizabeth, and Kimberley. The East London East and West Bank locations, if containing middle strata and lacking heavy industry, had a predominantly working-class base. Dock and rail workers went on strike in 1921. The year before, the East London Native Employees' Association sought Congress support. Moderates Walter Rubusana and Richard Godlo dominated the Location Advisory Board, to a lesser extent the Vigilance Association and, claims Switzer, local ANC and ICU branches. The ICU East London branch, formed by Kadalie and T. B. Lujiza in 1922, adopted a cautious approach to industrial relations but after 1929 Kadalie's Independent ICU, if displaying an admixture of union with "Africanist and separatist" influences, began to address directly working-class grievances.[37] Here Congress seems largely eclipsed by the ICU, yet we know little of ANC branch organisation then.

In Port Elizabeth, closer ties developed with worker organisations. ICWU leader Samuel Masabalala, as noted above, sat on the Cape Congress and SANNC executives. He gained strong rank-and-file worker support for a strike in 1920 caused by inadequate black wages, but faced fierce state opposition. The authorities invited Rubusana, who had defected from Congress to the conservative Bantu Union, to stem the rising tide of militant black labour; some strikers derided him as "a traitor". Masabalala's arrest prompted independent worker action by 2,000-4,000 people. Police and white vigilantes opened fire, killing at least 23 black people.[38]

Only several months later in 1921 did James La Guma resuscitate the Port Elizabeth ICU. There is no evidence he was able to re-establish Masabalala's close ties between Congress and labour. In 1923, the chief officers of the Port Elizabeth ANC branch were J. Mavavana, Felton Mokwena, J. Mkosi and Thomas Mateza, about whom we know little. However, memories of events lingered in popular consciousness and help explain the continued cooperation between workers and ANC. Masabalala continued to agitate for the ICU in other towns, including Cape Town, Paarl, and Somerset West.[39]

The Reverend Z. R. Mahabane used his position as Cape Congress president to support the rights of workers. Addressing the Pass Laws Commission, he argued that passes underpinned the whole system of cheap black labour in industry and agriculture. "More attractive conditions of work and better wages would automatically solve the problem of native labour. Force was unnecessary to induce natives to work." He objected to the Masters and Servants Acts "which rendered the servant liable to criminal prosecution for absence from or desertion from work". Instead, he urged state intervention to resolve labour disputes.[40]

Mahabane was a principled supporter of the view that "trade unionism [for Africans] must be given statutory recognition". His presidential address to the 1920 Cape Congress annual conference was on the theme of the colour bar, urging "restoration of our National solidarity and identity as a distinct people in the political economy of South Africa". He drew attention to the "glaring disparity in the relative rate of pay" of black and white workers. He even urged Africans to "agitate". Mahabane's 1921 presidential address highlighted "the manly and heroic proletariat of the non-European labourers of Port Elizabeth" who protested the arrest of labour leader Masabalala. He stated that the "poor black man is ... reduced to ... utter voicelessness ... votelessness, hopelessness, powerlessness, defencelessness, homelessness, landlessness". This sort of talk was as radical as any other black political statements in the country at the time. Mahabane's 1922 Cape Congress conference address commented on the crisis at Bulhoek, where government had slaughtered adherents of a millenarian sect, and the Rand Revolt in which white miners had deployed racist slogans. Race discrimination, he stated, was "deeply rooted and embedded in the inner man of the white man". In the same year, he called not just for better market and education facilities but also for "better wages for our labourers".[41]

In 1925, Mahabane criticised the "Civilised Labour" policy "whereby Bantu labourers ... have been replaced by poor whites ... after African workers have done pioneer work in the field of labour and helped to lay the foundations of the industrial system". Despite this *rhetoric* of solidarity, it is unclear to what extent black workers actually supported Mahabane. Police reported that his speeches to African meetings in 1921, which highlighted the role of Congress, were "met with a fair amount of opposition". Mahabane was no communist. When defending the Cape African franchise against the Hertzog Bills, he spoke of the "benign reign of Queen Victoria of revered memory". However, he continued to speak of labour matters. In 1928, he stressed bitterness among Africans had intensified under a policy predicated on "dismissing of the Africans from all skilled or semi-skilled employment to make room for 'poor whites.'" The "differential treatment" by employers of black labourer wages "awakens and constantly fosters deep resentment". Whilst characterised by historians as a moderate, these examples demonstrate Mahabane's concern for labour. In part, this may have been due to his formative years—he worked as a poorly paid teacher and court interpreter before becoming a minister—but it also derived from ongoing official Congress policy.[42]

The Cape ANC at times expressed radical opposition to oppression by the white community. In early 1924, it held a mass meeting in Wynberg, characterising state legislation as aiming "to reduce the social, political and economic status of the aboriginal races to that of a slave, if not below" and adopting a policy of "passive resistance". Government-inspired "Native conferences" did not reflect black majority opinion in the Cape, which instead the ANC represented.[43] Congress never carried out consistently such resistance, but the sentiments indicate the presence of thinking in accord with radical views.

The general tendency among historians is to view the 1920s as a period of declining ANC, and rising ICU, influence. Yet, in the Western Cape, it was rather the opposite, with the ANC moving markedly to the left and gaining a substantial increase in membership among workers. This phenomenon is viewed by most historians as a brief (1929-1931) flirtation with proletarian ideas and as essentially a contest between moderates and militants. However, if this history is seen as not just a question of radicals versus moderates but of the duration of broader ties with workers and sympathy for their demands, then the period of contact becomes somewhat longer, and can be seen to last from about 1925 until about 1933.[44]

The ANC Western Province (ANC (WP)), under James Thaele, took the initiative in attempting some practical solutions to worker problems after the ICU lost ground in Cape Town. In 1925, it decided to establish a labour bureau to give "the very best advice and assistance towards placing every member of Congress (male or female), who may be out of work, in employment". However, the scheme was restricted to ANC members, which made this an impractical solution to general unemployment.[45]

Other forces militated against easy contact between ANC and workers. In Cape Town of the 1920s, most black workers were not unionised or politicised, with the workforce also divided on ethnic lines. Coloured washerwomen, for example, had no formal unions, only informal structures. Since the 1840s, they had petitioned municipal authorities. In 1920, a petition drawn up by 15 largely illiterate washerwomen protested closure of a washhouse. In such cases, however, the APO, not ANC, often claimed to represent "coloured" workers. In 1925, for example, APO leader Abdullah Abdurahman protested the injury of a washwoman.[46]

Nevertheless, the Cape Town-based ANC (WP) began to organise mass protests against political repression and exploitation of black workers. Several factors facilitated contact with workers. Firstly, Thaele had been active in the ICU from 1923 and helped edit its paper, *Workers' Herald*. Secondly,

May 23rd, 1925   THE AFRICAN WORLD.   3

the natives, so far as the Prince's visit was concerned.

"There is," he continued, "no question as to our loyalty. We are as loyal, if not more so, having regard to the conditions in which we live as any other people in the great British Empire, but my people feel piqued over the treatment they have had and they manifest that by declining to participate en masse in any demonstration of welcome. Personally, we welcome the Prince with open arms, and if His Royal Highness comes my way I, as a loyal subject, will greet him."

Mendeselo, another chief from Wakkerstroom, said he and his people were only too anxious to pay allegiance to the Prince, but since Congress decided to abstain from whatever Royal celebrations which might be arranged, he had no option but to agree in that connection. Personally, he was ready to do homage to the Prince, as his people would in a private capacity, but beyond that he would abide by the Congress mandate.

SWAZILAND'S POSITION.

Mtemba, secretary to Sabhuza II., paramount chief of the Swazis, said that arrangements were to be made by his chief to celebrate the coming of His Royal Highness, but he did not know how Sabhuza would regard the decision of Congress.

In any event, whether the Swazis participated or otherwise in the celebrations, it was an undoubted fact that their loyalty to the British Throne was intact and unalterable.

A number of headmen who were also interviewed stated that native loyalty was as strong and forceful as ever, it had been, and because the people were loyal they were content to plead their cause on constitutional principles.

AFRICAN NATIONAL CONGRESS

(CENTRAL BRANCH) *The Founders of the Head Office, W.P.*

Standing— F. R. Cetyiwe, B. R. Kukama, W. J. Godinho, W. L. Tekwe, M. Matlabe, M. Matlabe, H. P. Temba.
Sitting— C. J. Nabe, D. J. Madumo, A. D. Sulele, S. P. Mohapi, D. A. Magane.
Ass. Secretary.   Hon. Secretary.   Chairman.   Treasurer.   Ass. Chairman.

ANC Western Province leaders, 1925

he popularised, through his paper *The African World*, a form of Garveyism initially friendly to socialism and he addressed, if idiosyncratically, labour issues. Thirdly, cooperation between the ANC and CPSA was aided by the CPSA's Africanisation and, after 1927, Gumede's radical national leadership. Communists such as La Guma and Gomas, who, after their 1926 expulsion from the ICU, increasingly devoted their energies to black liberation, formed a socialist ginger force in the ANC to assist this united action. Capetonian communists strongly advocated the CPSA's "Black Republic" slogan that had some analogy with Garveyism, facilitating alliance with the ANC (WP), which adopted the slogan's broad contours. Cooperation with the CPSA included unrestricted sale of *Umsebenzi* at ANC meetings. Fourthly, the ANC (WP) became more attractive to radicals by splitting from the Cape Congress in 1926, thereby removing a moderating influence. Simultaneously, another moderating force, the Joint Council, lacked strong support among Africans in Cape Town, whilst the APO moved to the right. Fifthly, the ANC had branches in areas inhabited chiefly by African workers, such as Ndabeni, Elsies River, and Wynberg. Moreover, the Cape Peninsula's African population was more proletarian than *petit bourgeois*, and increasingly so as migrant workers formed the bulk of its continuing growth. Hence, it was logical that the ANC should address worker issues to reflect its immediate constituency. Sixthly, the activities of black unions, such as the ICU, and political groups, such as the CPSA, meant socialist ideas began to filter down to African workers, notably among the many such workers who laboured on the docks. Finally, some black workers actually joined the ANC (WP).[47]

These closer relations are evident in the reporting and editorialising of *African World*, founded in 1925 with the Garveyist slogan "Africa for Africans". This weekly attempted to articulate labour demands, or at least to subsume such demands under a black nationalist agenda. In true Garveyist style, it looked forward to a near future in which "large businesses [were] owned by blacks" as in the United States. If Garveyism underpinned *African World's* philosophy, then the ANC was its *raison d'être*. Congress had, stated the editors, "championed a fearless aggressive fight for the inherent rights of the African race". They gave critical support to ANC national policy, endorsing 1926 ANC conference resolutions but warning, "our leaders ... should not permit themselves to be classified with the pliable"; a reference to ANC participation in state-sponsored Natives Conferences. By the end of June 1925, the masthead carried the sub-title: "The Mouthpiece of the Cape African Congress". *African World* often commented on ANC affairs. Staff included sub-editor Arthur Ndollo (ANC (WP) choir conductor) and assistant-editor Johnson Dlwati (ANC assistant-secretary).[48]

African World combined Garveyist and anti-capitalist rhetoric. It predicted the "political combination of the bourgeoisie into monopolistic organisations … will be read by future historians … in the language of the fall of Rome". It saw "constitutional agitation and the cultivation of race-pride" as necessary to free Africa "from the incubus of European capitalistic control". Here "capitalist" appears to be synonymous with white domination. The ANC, it noted, "does not encourage or discourage Capitalism". But *African World* advocated a general strike—at least in theory. It urged the ANC, "as a government in embryo" of all African people, to combine with the ICU to adopt a two-stream policy of "'**Passive** Resistance' and a **Strike** …. with a view to bring to a standstill … within 24 hours the Mining Industry".[49]

African World was much less supportive of actual strikes. Commenting on the 1925 British seamen's strike that affected South Africa, it stated, "a struggle of this kind at all times is a thing to be deplored". Sympathy with strikers was possible, as black people had "no appeal from the civil and economic tyranny", but Thaele argued against being "drawn into the quarrel". Reform of industrial systems was possible, although he specifically rejected communists "who would destroy" these systems. Yet, *African World* did not exclude leftist contributions. It published radicals or communists such as Bransby Ndobe, Thomas Mbeki, Josiah Ngedlane, and Stanley Silwana, and reproduced CPSA press articles.[50]

In the pages of *African World,* workers often figured in conjunction with broader political issues. Correspondent Joel Nduma, later chair of the Congress Cape Town branch, combined belief in the dignity of labour with faith in the ANC's historic role: "through labour may our comrades subdue their difficulties and redeem their lives from barbarism … The ANC, with its well advised leaders and comrades stands [as] a bright star to the thinking man". The ANC (WP) organ was committed to wage equality: "equal pay for equal work—is it asking too much?" Attacking the creation of a South African Fascist Movement, it rejected the very idea of "one class being exploited by another". Correspondent R. J. Ndimande attacked the refusal of a white church congregation to admit relatives of a deceased African worker.[51]

African World, like *Abantu-Batho,* is proof of the commitment of ANC regional leaders to black labour. Yet its closure in July 1926 not only denied black workers an ally, but also pointed to the often-unreliable nature of ANC support for such workers.

Black workers of the 1920s left few direct, primary accounts detailing their attitudes to the ANC. However, existing biographical sketches provide insights into their views. Johnny Gomas began work as an apprentice tailor in Kimberley during World War I and experienced the rigours of working life. He was secretary of the ICU Western Cape branch before Kadalie expelled him. He joined the CPSA in January 1925 and in December, the CPSA elected him its Cape branch secretary. Gomas became vice-president of the ANC (WP) in the late 1920s, influenced by its radical and pro-labour stance, and by his own strong commitment to black liberation.[52]

James La Guma was born into a life of poverty in 1894. He worked in a bakery from the age of eight, took part in riots by unemployed workers in 1906, and at 13 became an apprentice leather worker. Despite only a few years formal schooling, he was an avid reader, and influenced by socialist literature. He worked as a contract labourer on farms, railways and in mines around Luderitz, Namibia, where his class-consciousness prompted him to lead a mine strike in 1918 and, in 1920, to found an ICU branch. In 1921, he became Port Elizabeth ICU secretary, then ICU national secretary. He felt national oppression keenly. In 1927 he became ANC Cape Town branch secretary and, in 1928, ANC (WP) secretary. At this time, according to a 1964 biography by his son, he "devoted a lot of his energy" to the ANC. He joined the CPSA in 1925, and served as secretary of the leftist Federation of Non-European Trade Unions. Other militant black workers joined the ANC (WP). Stanley Silwana and Josiah Ngedlane (who in 1929 led an Ndabeni CPSA branch of 100 members) were members of both the CPSA and ANC.[53]

Such members provided the ANC with direct labour contacts. They also put pressure on ANC leaders to adopt policies that would be more militant. Thaele responded not only to the imperatives of black politics but also to associated indirect pressure of black workers and militants. He confronted problems similar to those facing communists: how to combine black liberation with worker demands. Replying to criticism by communist W. Green (who shared the platform with Thaele during the latter's 1926 Natal tour) that the "Africa for the Africans" slogan failed to address grievances common to all workers, Thaele agreed with much of Green's class-oriented approach, particularly as the "native of South Africa is confined to the working class". But, Thaele concluded, "unfortunately, the white man, whether he be capitalist or white worker ... is at one in keeping the black down ... [Hence] the black man must think and act 'black'."[54]

Thaele at times openly supported the CPSA. This was due to his anti-capitalist, rather than Marxist, views. Addressing the "CPSA School" in 1929, he declared his "sympathies were entirely with the CPSA ... the only party that has preached real Christianity". He was adroit at adopting communist rhetoric believing that the remedy to African "economic slavery" was "preaching of the Communist doctrines". In return, the CPSA described Thaele as "one of the most prominent intellectuals" in Congress. Earlier, in May 1928, the ANC Cape Town branch adopted a resolution (confirmed by another meeting two weeks later) of "full and unqualified confidence in the CPSA" and called on ANC leaders to explore cooperation with the communists. By 1929, the ANC (WP) had developed contact with militant communists and some workers, and there was a joint ANC-CPSA rally against oppressive laws in Cape Town in December 1929.[55]

Bransby Ndobe and Elliot Tonjeni were central activists forming a bridge between the ANC and CPSA. Ndobe became ANC Herschel (Eastern Cape) organiser in 1927 and then ANC (WP) provincial secretary. He also was active in the ICU. Tonjeni was ANC provincial assistant secretary in 1929. Native Affairs claimed their "teachings gave rise to the general disrespect of authority" among Africans. Ndobe worked as a domestic helper in Cape Town for some years after 1922. In a 1925 Sotho article in *African World*, he combined religious and political metaphors, urging readers to turn away from white churches and towards Congress and black churches: "God says you must reap what you sow. The congress is calling you." As ANC (WP) secretary, he "attracted the attention of the authorities by his fiery speeches". Tonjeni, who worked in Cape Town, joined the CPSA and ICU. He left the CPSA in 1929, but still contributed articles to *Umsebenzi*. Another radical socialist, Cetyiwe was still active in the ANC (WP) Cape Town Central Branch (see photo) from at least 1925 and, together with Ndobe and Wilson Tsekwe, was charged by police with inciting "race hostility" after a June 1929 ANC meeting.[56]

These working-class radicals helped mobilise rural labourers around Congress. In 1927, the ANC (WP) began mass organising in areas populated by farm labourers. A Huguenot branch already existed in Paarl, and a new branch formed at Worcester in 1929. It soon claimed 800 members, mainly workers. A building worker, Adam Paul, was secretary. By May 1929, branches formed in other Boland towns, and ANC (WP) membership reached 2,000 most consisting of farm labourers who faced declining wages, or workers in rural towns, many of whom faced unemployment.[57]

These branches took up labour issues such as wages and unemployment. Whilst centred on rural towns, rather than on tightly controlled white-owned farms, they addressed grievances of farm workers such as the "tot" system. They paid great attention to passes inconveniencing all black workers. Both African and "coloured" workers were enrolled, many of them women. These initiatives cemented ties between workers and the ANC. The ability of the Worcester branch to recruit workers rapidly suggests there was nothing inherent in ANC policies that prevented it from establishing close labour ties. Other black political groups in rural towns, such as Vigilance Associations, agitated for franchise and trading rights, but hardly concerned themselves with the largely voteless migrant or farm labourers.[58] By way of contrast, it is when the ANC became more active that rural workers drifted into politics, however briefly.

Because of its audacious challenge to the regimented industrial relations system, Congress faced increased repression. In 1929, Kennon Thaele, ANC (WP) secretary (and brother of James Thaele), was charged under the Native Unrest Act of 1927 with inciting public violence, after telling a crowd of 200 people in Cape Town to follow the example of Ethiopia who defeated Italy in battle.[59] The Crown withdrew the case, but repression escalated sharply in 1930-1931, contributing to the decline of the branch.

Conditions in the Western Cape in the late 1920s—changes in the CPSA, economic immiseration, and radicalisation of ANC leaders—favoured a strengthening of ANC ties with workers. The situation in the Eastern Cape was somewhat different. There is no comprehensive history of the ANC in the Eastern Cape. There are some studies of important events involving urban and rural-based Eastern Cape ANC leaders. Beinart and Bundy, in a wide-ranging survey of popular movements before 1930, have uncovered the history of the temporary, if fraught, alliances between urban-based ANC leaders such as Thaele and various rural millenarian, women's, and Garveyist groups. These alliances failed to survive due to both local parochialism and the failure of outsiders to understand rural-based idioms or the "class solidarities of rural radicalism".[60] However, historians imperfectly understand ANC-labour relations in the region, and they have largely ignored the detailed history of ANC branches within the region.

The Cradock-based Cape Congress steadfastly clung to a moderate policy. Its leaders were concerned at growing African proletarianisation. CAC president, Reverend Elijah Mdolomba, told a state committee in 1927 that the number of rich Africans in his region had declined. Many Africans now left their "lands and go to the mines for employment". In areas where there was insufficient land, Africans should "be allowed to lease land and allowed, not forced, to work for Europeans".[61]

The CAC faced rivalry not only from Thaele's ANC (WP), but also from the Bantu Union (formed in Queenstown in 1919), Cape Native Voters' Convention (1924) and ICU. The Bantu Union siphoned off ex-Congress figures such as Meshach Pelem (at one time a clerk and digger in Kimberley, and labour agent), Rubusana and Soga. The Bantu Union was to the right of Congress: in 1920, it declared an "abhorrence" of how black strikes were dealt with but "firmly object[ed] to all strike agitation". The ICU incorporated black labour demands such as abolition of job colour bars and higher wages in their policies, making it difficult for the ANC to pose as *the* singular representative of black workers. Yet these other organisations soon established working relations with Congress. Many leaders of the Cape Native Voters' Convention also were, or became, involved in the ANC, including Bennett Ncwana, Frank Pendla, Richard Godlo, and Mdolomba.[62]

Other ANC branches adopted a more militant stance than the CAC. I have already mentioned ANC contacts with unions in Port Elizabeth and East London. The isolated Herschel district was ripe for "agitators". W. M. Macmillan's survey of Herschel found that in 1924 high inflation and land dispossession were "fast sweeping the natives out of their Reserves to become a landless proletariat".[63] However, lack of industry in the area inclined leaders to emphasise land and taxation rather than industrial issues. This was contested terrain between different people claiming to speak on behalf of the ANC and black workers.

James Thaele made a bid for the allegiance of local people in 1928. He told a crowd of people in Sterkspruit in March they were all under the "supervision" of the national ANC. Congress was working with the ICU— "the two parties working as one body". Thaele was careful to work within realistic limits, saying: "We [the] Congress are not going to do things you are not going to approve of". In a letter to the Herschel magistrate, he wrote, "the policy of Congress is to assist the government". He made radical demands. In April, accompanied by Minnie Bhola, Cape ANC women's leader, he called for removal from office of the local Superintendent of Natives for disregarding African rights. Addressing a Sterkspruit meeting in Xhosa, Bhola took up labour issues. She condemned state policy for denying Africans work on the railways and that African women had to work for white women for £1 a month—"only enough to pay our dog tax". Pointing to shootings in Bulhoek, Cape Town and Herschel, she called on all Africans, women and men, to "stand shoulder to shoulder against the Europeans", "amalgamate" and "fight". In August, Thaele led a delegation of local ANC figures to Native Affairs to present grievances about the non-election of headmen, land allocation, and municipal maladministration.[64]

The ANC branch in Sterkspruit took up local grievances. In July 1929, it held a mass meeting (5,000 according to the ANC; 200 according to police). It passed a motion of no confidence in the Transkeian General Council (Bhunga) and local state officials. A letter followed to the Prime Minister, signed by Templin Jabane, branch secretary and other ANC officials, including William Sefako and Micha Shotsoane, protesting unjust taxes on widows and married men. Referring to the Bible and history, Jabane also captures some of the grassroots conception of African nationalism, as it may have existed among rural working peoples. He employed alliteration to stress that discriminatory legislation, especially the colour bar, was sowing the seeds of "disaffection, discontentment, discord, disunion, disruption and disintegration". Continuation of the "iniquitous bar in the political and economic and industrial machinery of the land" was "an offence to the sense of manhood and nationhood" of Africans. Moreover, it was creating agitators. The language of this discourse suggests a strong use of irony. The reference to racial hostility probably refers to provisions of the 1927 Native Administration Act; government referred to black radical leaders as "agitators". Jabane, in words reminiscent of the French revolutionary, Danton, accepted the term with glee: "Let us agitate, agitate and agitate now and again, and rest not until this stigma has been entirely blotted out." Jabane worked with Thaele and another ANC figure, Theodore Mvalo, to oppose extension of white-owned farms at Africans' expense. These protests emphasised land and taxes but the issues were highly relevant to local working peoples as many of them were only partly proletarianised, and still clung to land holdings.[65]

Jabane and Thaele challenged white hegemony in highly individualistic, ambiguous language. However, ANC leaders—like those of the ICU—gained a measure of temporary support among rural-based working peoples by using such idioms. They interacted with ordinary people. Addressing a 900-strong ANC meeting at Sterkspruit in November 1928, they rejected criticism that Congress was "controlled by the whiteman". Thaele stated Africans must "organise themselves politically, economically, religiously and educationally" to "free themselves from the incubus of European control"—a colourful phrase which, as noted, he had used in 1925 but then with the adjective "capitalist" appended. He now changed tack and derided ANC leftists as amounting to "nothing". Drawing upon the ANC tradition of delegations, he argued that in "places like Herschel their business as officials of Congress was to consult and interview the Magistrate". If "he proves autocratic", they must then "see the High Commissioner [and] if he became [a] dictator they would pass on to Pretoria; if then, the Union government is not going to listen, they would proceed to England". Independent action was emphasised. Jabane told a Sterkspruit gathering of 500 people the month before that the state was likely to grant Africans a form of self-rule if they could unite. At a meeting at Ndofela location in February 1929, he declared that Africans should deal with problems themselves. At an ANC meeting of 600 at Sterkspruit in April of the same year, he and Thaele argued that ANC use of the courts would solve grievances such as cattle dipping and prohibitions on gathering wood. They admonished the audience for failing to haul stones to build a local ANC hall; Thaele insulted them by calling them "Bushmen and Hottentots". He mixed class and nationalist metaphors inconsistently. Smuts was denounced as "controlled by [British] financial interests, such as De Beers", whereas Hertzog was "the [best] man ... to commercially develop South Africa". Thaele (like some other ANC leaders) supported Hertzog's thinly veiled segregation proposals as an opportunity for territorial independence. Such admixture of opportunism, nationalism, and concern for industrial growth relates in part to Thaele's Garveyist ideas.[66]

Theodore Mvalo had similarly contradictory ideas. Expelled from the ANC in 1924 but later reinstated, he often campaigned as an ANC leader, yet at times, this was pure masquerade. In 1925, G. G. Tantsi of the Transkeian Congress complained about Mvalo's activities in Mqanduli, alleging he had solicited money in the name of Congress without authority. In the late 1920s Mvalo was active in Herschel. At a meeting of 100 people in August 1929, he pledged to rectify their tax grievances. His speech was a mixture of ANC, Garveyist, class and religious metaphors. The government

> ... is satan ... The English nation is a very dirty nation. South Africa is not for Europeans, it is ours ... Herschel should be full of agitators in order that matters may be put right ... The reason why you are poor is because you are being oppressed by the N.A. Dept .... I am not a Christian but I am fighting against these thieves. It is for this purpose that I have been sent here by the Native Congress ... to carry on the work ... commenced by Mvabaza, Thaele and others. Mice have their own conference because they are being killed by cats. Why should we not have one? I am speaking advanced politics which cannot be digested by children.

Mvalo spoke "down" to the audience. Yet he also used familiar images to appeal to a shared sense of poverty and oppression. He appealed to a wide range of interests. Advertising a meeting on 11 July 1929, Jabane instructed Headman George Mhlomakulu to advise all local people that he and Mvalo would address issues of rebuilding the nation; land settlement; education; "unnecessary" poll taxes; black trading; and religion. Mvalo does not accord with the stereotype Congressite. In 1930, Queenstown police viewed him as "very dangerous" and an "active agitator", not only of the ANC, but also of the League against Imperialism. Banned from Bloemfontein for five years in 1929, officials regarded Mvalo as "particularly vituperative towards those in authority" and he had 21 criminal convictions for stock theft and other felonies.[67]

Some other Garveyists, such as "Dr. Wellington" (alias of Elias Butelezi), opposed the ANC. In 1928, at a meeting of 400-500 Africans on the border of Herschel and Lady Grey, he stated that he wanted to "do away with the European Government", and keep "Africa for the Africans". He wanted "nothing to do" with the ANC or ICU as they co-operated with white people and had "registered themselves" with Native Affairs. An ANC supporter in the crowd challenged this. In 1929, the Sterkspruit ANC queried the reasons for Wellington's bannings, though it is unclear whether this was out of sympathy for him. In the Transkei, some ANC branches registered complaints against Garveyist activities. CAC president Mdolomba also attacked Wellington, though a writer to *Umteteli wa Bantu* in 1928 noted Mahabane and Thaele had spoken on the same platform as Wellington.[68]

Hitherto historians largely have ignored the role of the ANC in the Transkei in the 1920s. Walshe simply suggests it "appears to have languished". Ntsebeza's study of Xhalanga discusses complexities of local politics and the role of chiefs, yet ignores the Transkeian ANC in the 1920s.[69] Given the paucity of integrated regional political histories, this neglect is unsurprising and a detailed examination of Congress in the Transkei is long overdue.

As noted above, there were several, if disunited, local branches of Congress throughout the Transkei. In 1923, the Reverend Mazwi had represented the Transkei on an official ANC delegation to meet with the Prime Minister. In May 1924, after formal application by Transkei representatives, the ANC annual convention formally recognised Transkei as a province under the ANC Constitution. The 1925 *Report of Native Churches Commission*, although noting ANC weakness in the Transkei, detected attempts to establish a viable branch there. Govan Mbeki recalls that in 1923-1924 he attended ANC "meetings and concerts ... among peasants" at Nqamakwe. His "interest in politics was first aroused around 1925", when an AME minister "held concerts in his church to raise funds for the ANC". From 1925 to 1930, the Transkeian Territories African Congress (ANC-TT), based in Tsomo and Cofimvaba, actively engaged the state in a vigorous correspondence to gain official recognition of its role, and bombarded officials and ministers with petitions for the relief of African grievances, many of which accorded with the needs of rural working peoples.[70]

The ANC-TT raised a wide range of popular demands. In early 1924, it took up several cases of Africans sentenced in the courts. ANC-TT assistant general secretary John James Gcingca, who already in 1923 had been recognised by the Cape Congress as their organiser in Tsomo, urged clemency on "the old man" Haza Bono, a worker sentenced to prison for contempt of court. Gcingca claimed that Bono had not in fact treated the court with contempt and had promised to pay his fine quarterly when he received his pay. ANC members attended the trial with Bono and claimed that court officials had not even called his name. Gcingca also called for a pardon for the farm tenant Ngonyama Makapela, sentenced for ploughing offences whilst working on a nearby farm. James Ngojo in Johannesburg joined in, accusing magistrates of being "against native progress". These audacious demands aroused the ire of government. The Idutywa Magistrate warned the ANC it "had no right to interfere" in courts.[71]

The ANC-TT in August 1925 sent a delegation to try to interview the Prime Minister, then visiting Butterworth. In December 1926, it resolved to seek redress over the lack of land available for Africans. Gcingca, now general secretary, subsequently wrote several letters to the Prime Minister. In one letter, he sought to make mining in the region conditional upon acceptability of mining projects by two-thirds of the ANC, and to have all local mine revenue paid into a fund for the benefit of Africans. The ANC, he asserted, was the "only mouthpiece" of Africans. This was another audacious attempt to wrest legitimacy from government. In a second letter, he articulated popular scepticism about the Bhunga, which he characterised as "a futile debating society". The solution was to leave "Native Affairs" to the ANC. He proposed a national scheme to introduce "direct self-control" for Africans, whereby all Bills introduced would be put to the "Blackman's African National Parliament" that could "become a most powerful and influential [vehicle of] public opinion". His scheme included elements of internationalism, reflecting possible Garveyist or Gumede influence. Gcingca called for people "to be taught to think internationally". He envisaged a future in which "for the first time in history people will hear great subjects discussed on an international platform". In a third letter, he protested the unseemly haste in issuing of writs against African tax defaulters. This affected workers. Officials refused passes to "People going to work" before tax was paid. A fourth letter attacked Headmen who did not reside in districts they represented. A fifth letter objected to discriminatory employment practices. Firms and government employed white people exclusively as dipping supervisors and road overseers despite the presence of "suitable" African people. A final letter complained of the undue length of time served by magistrates, a practice encouraging favouritism. Magistrates did not pay heed to African needs but instead went to "cricket matches and the like leaving the people hovering without satisfaction". The ANC-TT regularly repeated these grievances over the next few years.[72]

The ANC-TT drew up a list of 28 grievances, many of which impinged on the lives of working people. Congress looked back nostalgically to a time when "people used to go to work in the fields and where they were ... honestly employed and paid according to the amount of work each man had done". This Golden Age contrasted with the unsatisfactory system of labour migration, involving child labour and exploitative recruitment practices. The Native Recruiting Corporation must go. Showing some familiarity with working lives, it enumerated discriminatory employment practices and average wages in the Transkei. Another ANC-TT petition attacked the lack of local knowledge by stock and sheep inspectors, invariably white people, calling instead for Africans to hold these jobs. Congress called for more work opportunities for black interpreters and for the employment of Africans to eradicate noxious weeds. It drew attention to the economic plight of African women. Their frequent arrest for tax defaulting meant they could not afford to maintain their families; this was "nothing else but slavery". On the other hand, the employment of white women as court clerks denied such jobs to black males and forced them to leave the Transkei in search of work. Such work should, claimed the ANC-TT in rather sexist fashion, be "for males only". It complained that mission-school domination forced African teachers to conform to religious standards or face dismissal, "compelling teachers to be preachers and to pay Church contributions".[73] Many of these petitions raised the need to employ Africans. In calling for more jobs for Africans, Congress was championing the interests of black workers, even if it said little about their wage rates or their right to organise independently.

These petitions rejected rule by proclamation indicating that "Congress, on behalf of the Territories, want our laws passed through Parliament not Proclamations framed by the [Magistrate]". It called for abolition of the Conference of Magistrates and Bhunga that ignored people's grievances. The ANC should take their place. "We think Congress is the best ... The Transkeian Congress would answer better to take the place of [the Bhunga]." ANC-TT petitions often concluded with an appeal to the Prime Minister. One urged him to "release his poor Native people and set them at liberty ... just like the other nations".[74]

In 1927, the ANC-TT acting general secretary, Abner Cetywayo Madalane, based in Cofimvaba, lobbied government over popular grievances. To the Prime Minister he enumerated manifold "grievances suffocating the Territories". Firstly, he pointed to lack of democracy or popular legitimacy of an unelected

Bhunga whose Councillors were "entirely against the Congress" and viewed their jobs as a "simple means of getting money". In writing direct to the Prime Minister, Madalane rejected official attempts to divert ANC protests into local channels. He argued from precedent; the Prime Minister himself had sanctioned them to write directly. A leader should rule "for rich and poor". In October, the ANC-TT instructed Madalane to write to the Tsomo Magistrate to complain over the too early collection of quitrents and rates. The ANC here responded to popular demands for time extensions raised at a "Headmen and peoples meeting" in June 1927.[75]

As well as general political grievances, the ANC-TT tackled labour exploitation. In May 1927, it met and carried resolutions against the entire labour recruitment system. Subsequently Madalane wrote to the Secretary of Justice urging that the Native Recruiting Corporation "be abandoned altogether" because it was "nothing but slavery and injustice". He cited cases of African youths, recruited in rural areas for mine labour, but forced to return home after proving unfit, after which labour recruiters sued them for their cash advances, with local magistrates ruling against the workers. In addition, he noted, some recruited labourers deserted after labour recruiters sent them to workplaces not stipulated in their contracts where they were "bitterly treated". As a result, "these poor people" were "arrested and sent back". Madalane cited a case from that month in which two Queenstown youths recruited supposedly for work in Swaziland finished up in Natal. They subsequently absconded due to harsh treatment, were arrested, sent to gaol in Cofimvaba, and thence back to undertake forced labour in Natal. The only way "to avoid this system of slavery", to provide "Justice", and to enable "better control and management of the Natives" was abolition of the Recruiting Corporation.[76]

These protests combined elements of both resistance to proletarianisation and attempts to ameliorate the plight of rural toilers. Although many rural migrant workers continued to have, and to desire, close ties with the land, the ANC could not realistically have expected to see its demands met. The reference to control over labour suggests that Madalane was less interested in the independent organisation of labour than its regulation by fair means. Nevertheless, the ANC-TT strongly opposed harsh labour exploitation, and sympathised with the victims of the recruitment system.

Madalane repeated complaints made in 1926 by Gcingca against discriminatory labour practices. Dipping supervisors and road overseers were all white people on high wages, whereas Africans were "suitable for the work". The entire St. Marks district suffered from a lack of justice. "Poor litigants" had to travel many miles to attend civil cases, often losing cases when "deserted by their witnesses for work, [after having become] tired of waiting". The ANC demanded that the people must elect local Headmen who were not mere magisterial appointments. "Kongresi" protested the increasing number of shootings of Africans by forest guards, alluding to sexual harassment of African women by police.[77]

Following popular complaints in Tsomo, Willowvale, and Nqamakwe, the ANC-TT in November 1927 resolved to protest high local taxes. Madalane wrote to the Chief Magistrate, complaining of bureaucratic delays preventing "poor people" from paying their taxes on time, but the magistrate rejected the ANC's claim to represent the people. Madalane then wrote to the Secretary for Native Affairs, protesting issuing of writs for failing to pay hut taxes, quitrents and road and dipping rates. The "aggrieved, sorrowful Native subjects" must be given more time to pay these onerous taxes, "for the sake of Justice and liberty for immediate relief from this unjust seizure done by Magistrates".[78]

Taken together, all these protests and petitions constitute a quite comprehensive indictment of the whole system of "native administration" and labour relations in the Transkei. They suggest that the ANC was in touch with, and well aware of, the harsh lives of grassroots Africans. The frequent recourse to "justice" by local ANC leaders suggests they retained some faith in liberal values, although we also can interpret this as a purposeful tactic.

In 1928, the ANC-TT claimed that Congress had left behind its previous inaction and had embarked upon a serious re-organisation. An ANC meeting at Chief David Sikweza's kraal at Nqamakwe, in February 1928, aimed at "representing the whole public national problems". Present were, among others, Gcingca, Madalane, Meshack Bobi Mgidlana, Enoch Malunga, Daniel Nonkeneza, German Madotyeni, and William Sabata. They discussed "the sunset in the Transkeian Territories ANC" and pretentiously linked the "prosperity and corresponding improvement in the standard of living of the population" with "the restoration of the National Congress". Gcingca later reported that, despite their loyalty to state and the Empire, police assisted by thugs linked to local headmen broke up this ANC meeting. This "cold bloodshed ... without any reason" led him to question the legitimacy of government: "Our Congress [believes] that we have been putting too much confidence" in the Minister of Justice and the Empire.[79]

Invariably the state continued to reject the ANC's own claims of legitimacy among Africans. In 1927, the Chief Magistrate in Umtata told Gcingca that in his opinion the ANC-TT "does not represent any large section of the people". He accused it of submitting grievances that "bristle with exaggeration". The

Tsomo Magistrate told the ANC in Cofimvaba that complaints of local government maladministration and taxes "do not concern your organisation". The Secretary of Native Affairs ruled that individuals should take up grievances through "recognised channels". Native Affairs viewed the ANC as "the society which has in the past given considerable trouble by interfering in judicial and administrative matters". However, Gcingca received official recognition as ANC-TT provincial president by the national ANC convention in March 1929.[80]

The extent of popular support for the ANC-TT is unclear. It managed to call meetings of quite large numbers of Africans, articulate their grievances, and maintain branch structures in different places, such as Tsomo and Cofimvaba. Its tactics consisted largely of protest letters and delegations. Yet the organisation of more radical, proletarian forms of protest was much more limited in the rural areas of the Transkei than in the towns of the Western Cape, where a rural proletariat was more established. Nevertheless, the ANC in the Transkei strove to represent in the ways it knew the demands of all Africans, including workers.

In the Northern Cape, the ANC continued to maintain the interest in workers that Plaatje and others had developed. ANC influence remained strong in the mining town of Kimberley. ANC president, Zaccheus Mahabane, lived there in the late 1920s. Leaders of the Bechuanaland and Griqualand West ANC included ex-labourer S. B. Macheng, founder and organiser, and general secretary R. Sol Sidzumo, both in Barkley West, as well as chairperson Mweli Skota, who had worked as a clerk and interpreter, and Enoch Jacobs in Griquatown. Henry Matyalana, CAC executive member, worked as a caretaker. Working-class experience did not necessarily guarantee a "radical" stance: Macheng, previously a mine worker, later opposed Gumede's ANC presidency. Yet militancy was one thing, national identity another. John Gaetsewe worked as a messenger in Kuruman in the North-West Cape in the 1920s. He recalled that he "became a member of the ANC long before my trade union", suggesting either that national oppression was uppermost in the minds of some workers, or that they saw the ANC as supportive of their demands.[81]

Some Garveyites and women were active around the Bechuanaland and Griqualand West ANC. Garveyism attracted some local Congressmen, including Joseph Masogha and Moses Itholing. The ubiquitous Bennett Ncwana lived for a while in Kimberley and identified with Congress, being part of its 1923 delegation to meet the Prime Minister, but he also founded the Griqualand West Native Voters Association. There was a Congress branch at the old diamond town of Windsorton, north of Kimberley, where in 1923 J. K.

Lekoma and a Mr Mokguthu, who served as secretary, were active members. Some Kimberley women, such as Mrs Nuku, a social worker and Women's League chairperson, and Mrs Phala, became active in Congress.[82]

Elsewhere in the Cape, other women became active around Congress—I have already mentioned Minnie Bhola; Mrs H. Oliphant and Mrs S. Grootboem also were prominent. Press reports refer to other women associated with Congress, including, for example, "Mesdames Katty, Mgobo, Mynanda" in Indwe, Mesdames E. Mnyanda, M. Kalipa and M. Mabina in Dordrecht, "Misses" Victoria and Mary Dans and Mrs Kate Dungu in Qumbu, and Mesdames E. M. Mtyekwana and J. August in Sterkstroom. In records of the early 1920s, there are still quite regular mentions of the Bantu Women's League although these fall away later in the decade. Women were fund-raisers. In 1923, the Tsomo branch of the League raised £1.7.6 for the Cape Congress, and the Dordrecht branch £6.1.3, whilst there was mention of the work of Miss Radebe and Ms Magidane in fund-raising "Busy Bees".[83] In general, however, Congress did not draw women into its leadership inner sanctum and women were not prominent writing about Congress in the press.

In overview, ANC members in the Cape were a remarkable group. They challenged state legitimacy and championed, if inconsistently, and in often-magniloquent language, the rights of poor black workers. ANC involvement in worker struggles prompts Willie Hofmeyr to argue cogently that it is not valid to characterise it as purely "middle class". Nothing more challenges orthodox vistas of the ANC than his claim that "outside Cape Town itself, the organisation itself was almost entirely working class in character. There simply was no African petty bourgeoisie in the rural areas."[84]

The Orange Free State

Urbanisation and industrialisation developed apace in Bloemfontein in the 1920s, with large-scale electricity works, extensions to abattoirs, and new factories including a municipal steam laundry. By 1922, the African population reached some 23,000, a growth of 3,000 in only two years. By 1927, there were four black locations with 4,000 houses, Africans outnumbering whites by 24,197 to 22,597 people. The condition of most African workers was harsh, notably in rural areas, whilst in Bloemfontein the overall dearth of industries pushed unemployment up and wages down. In such conditions, Africans continued to resist oppression, which at the start of the decade women and rural workers led.[85]

In November 1920, police arrested 162 women in Marquard for protesting pass laws. In July 1921, farm workers gathered at the rural town of Cornelia, heard Koos Mataung, their leader, complain of unpaid farm wages and workers forced to labour in rags. In the same year, Preacher Ngobeza in Standerton advocated a general strike by Congress. In 1923, government efforts to strengthen pass legislation, coupled with the unwillingness of local white municipalities to relax pass restrictions on women led to vigorous and large-scale anti-pass protests in the small rural towns of Bethulie and Springfontein. Selby Msimang, then active in both the ICU and Congress, probably connected both bodies to the women, through publicity or logistical support. In the following year, he helped co-ordinate yet another anti-pass protest by women, this time in Brandfort. These protests drew into the ICU a number of women, including Eva Kubedi, Magdalene Mashalane, and Emely Machoba in Kroonstad as well as A. J. Lepotane and Mabel Klassen in Bloemfontein.[86]

Msimang in 1919 had helped Bloemfontein workers form the ICWU, which elected him chairperson at the inaugural national conference in Bloemfontein in July 1920. He continued in the early 1920s to protest the poor conditions of labourers. Together with other ANC activists, he raised the ire of OFS farmers by investigating farm worker wages. Msimang developed a cheap and ingenious method of getting around the province to organise workers, issuing ICU membership cards at the cost of printing, enabling him to "reach every town". He recalled that Sol Plaatje, on his second SANNC tour of Britain, wrote to the OFS ICU and received £100—an interesting form of ICU-Congress solidarity. In June 1922, in Queenstown, Msimang chaired the third conference of the ICWU, which resolved to recognise the SANNC and APO as the official black political bodies. In his address, he prioritised the building of "one big industrial movement" among black workers and educational work to overcome ignorance about trade unionism. Whilst favouring peaceful labour relations, he foresaw little industrial peace given the selfishness of employers and the effect of racism on white workers. Later that year, Msimang moved to the Rand where after trying to build the ICU he largely withdrew from union work. He formed a short-lived company with Selope Thema, worked as a clerk from 1924 to 1928, then as a labour adviser. He remained active in Congress. In June 1922, he chaired a Pietermaritzburg Congress report-back from Dube on the London Pan-African Congress.[87]

The combined pressure of women's and ICU protests and Congress petitioning inclined Pretoria to maintain the status quo concerning pass laws and, as a result, rural protests died down for a while. Formal ANC politics, however, increasingly centred on urban areas. The same political trends confronting other provincial branches influenced the OFS ANC. Leaders often gravitated to other bodies, either more moderate or more radical. Thomas Mapikela served as vice-president of the Bloemfontein Joint Council but remained committed to the ANC. In 1928, he even chaired, in Gumede's absence, an extraordinary meeting of the ANC called to discuss the Hertzog Bills. But he did rather little to raise labour issues in the OFS. Mapikela's steady accumulation of capital, and a more moderate approach to local politics, enabled him to build a rather ostentatious double storey house in Batho Township. Nevertheless, he continued to organise for the ANC and did so also through the formation of street committees. Mapikela's daughter, A. M. Jacobs, recalled that her father made good use of his church connections to build support for the ANC, even holding ANC meetings disguised as sermons. She also recollected meetings held in Mapikela's house, in the late 1920s, where strikes over better wages and conditions were discussed.[88]

ANC OFS general secretary, Robert Setlogelo (1888-1963), organised protests against a spate of violence against rural workers in the early 1920s and protested to Native Affairs about forced removals. Impey Nyombolo, general secretary of the ICU (Amalgamated), a splinter group, and an OFS ANC member, was involved in trying to organise farm labourers. Conan Doyle Modiakgotla was secretary of both the OFS ANC and ICU Griqualand West. Wearing his ICU cap, he addressed meetings in Bloemfontein in April 1927, when he called for Africans to abandon the old cap-in-hand *hamba kahle* policy of resolutions, and instead "sit down, throw away their passes and refuse to pay taxes". The Congress continued to oppose the carrying of passes by African women. In 1924, the general secretary corresponded with the Secretary of Native Affairs on the issue.[89]

Carl Joseph Libate exemplified the complex intermeshing of African political and labour forces. Born in 1868, he was, according to John Mancoe, the "first Bantu pioneer labourer" to enter the Rand goldfields. He settled in Bloemfontein in 1890 and worked for the railways from 1897 until he retired on a pension in 1929. In 1908, he was the first African to obtain a café license in Waaihoek. He served as chairperson of the Bethlehem branch of the National Union of Railway and Harbour Servants in 1921. At the same time, he was active in the ANC, taking part in annual ANC conferences in Bloemfontein and meetings of the ANC Executive Committee in Johannesburg.[90]

Following 1925 agitation in Bloemfontein, a Municipal Wages Committee was formed, comprising representatives of white-owned business, the Town Council, Advisory Board, and the ICU. Most black committee members were ANC figures. Peter Phahlane (Phatlane) and Joel Goronyane represented the

Advisory Board. Phahlane had served as SANNC sergeant-at-arms since 1912. Simon Elias and Keable 'Mote (ICU provincial secretary), who represented the ICU, also were ANC members. In February 1926, the committee debated the merits of a minimum wage. ICU and Board delegates agreed on the urgent need for wages rises, but differed on the extent of the rise. 'Mote and Elias held out for three shillings and sixpence per day minimum. Board delegates succumbed to an employers' offer of three shillings. When employers refused to budge, the ICU demanded to report to members who had demanded six shillings and sixpence. 'Mote claimed that three shillings and sixpence was "not enough for a man to lead a decent life". He stressed the central role of black labour in the economy, arguing that without "the unskilled man we would not have had these cities and these roads".[91]

Nevertheless, board members associated with the ANC took a stance in favour of black worker rights. Peter Phahlane, elected to Gumede's ANC National Executive in 1927, referred to the suffering of low-paid workers and demanded that any wage increases be legally binding to protect workers. He favoured securing popular approval of any measures agreed to by the committee. Goronyane made a clear case for a minimum wage irrespective of whether black workers were skilled or unskilled. Current wage rates were too low, and for this, "the fault still remains with the employers". He referred to the tenuous position of all black workers, including his colleague Phahlane, who had worked for the Town Council for 15 years. Such workers received no wage increases. Employers could dismiss them merely for requesting a wage rise. A three-shilling minimum wage would not assist workers already on, or above, this amount. Even six shillings and sixpence a day was below the cost of living. Divisions between groups were not always clear-cut. ANC and ICU leaders could agree. When talks became deadlocked, 'Mote and Goronyane found common ground and the three-shilling increase was agreed upon. Both ICU and Advisory Board representatives expressed concern that workers earning above three shillings would receive no increase.[92]

'Mote was a major player in the ICU in the mid- to late 1920s. At a Johannesburg May Day ICU rally in May 1928, he derided passes as "dog licenses". He and Elias also were active in OFS rural towns. In January 1927, they addressed a large open-air meeting of about 2,000 people in the Frankfort location. Elias called for better wages for Africans and demanded: "The exploitation of native workers must cease." 'Mote also called for higher wages for African labourers. Against this militant background, the CPSA also gained ground among Africans in Bloemfontein, forming an active branch in the late 1920s and recruiting at least four ANC members, Eddie Dambuza,

Ndudula, Ntlonze and Mtyhala. The ANC expelled them in October 1929 after concerted opposition by ANC and Independent ICU leaders to the CPSA and League of African Rights in the city.[93]

The limited industrialisation in the province meant black industrial unions failed to develop, denying Congress the opportunity to forge stronger ties with urban workers. However, ANC members spoke out in favour of worker needs and repression; some even combined membership of the ANC and ICU. The above examples show both weakness and strength in local ANC commitment. Organisational divisions and inefficiencies would have made the ANC appear, in the eyes of those workers aware of their policies, less able to deliver tangible relief from either race or class repression. Nevertheless, at times ANC grass-roots branches were able to articulate labour demands.

Conclusion

In the 1920s, the weak national ANC machine failed to build substantially upon labour contacts tentatively established in the radical days of 1918-1920. Neither the ICU nor CPSA could establish extensive, permanent, ties with black workers. By 1929, the ICU was in terminal decline. The CPSA faced increasing external repression and internecine disputes that would soon decimate its membership. In contrast, the less spectacular ANC at least maintained its slim structures, and marched forward past the ruins of the ICU.

Viewed from a different perspective, the colourful and sometimes millenarian elements of ideology of the rural ICU (and Garveyites) are a curious blend of "tradition" and modernity that did not sit easily with ANC urban leaders. Sean Redding, in response to critics of the short-lived nature of the ICU, argues that such elements were an enduring part of rural people's consciousness.[94] Yet, the ANC too was by now an enduring feature of African life. As we shall see, in following chapters, at grassroots some ANC activists made use of rural metaphors to build the organisation. In terms of formal politics revolving around the contestation of political power, ICU displacement of the ANC in the mid- to late-1920s was a temporary phenomenon, graphically illustrated by the subsequent return to, or embracing of, ANC politics by a good number of ex-ICU activists.

Could the ANC have absorbed the ICU? Congress was a broad church and the ICU increasingly a nationalist body. Without the communist bogey to distract it, the ICU may well have pursued its earlier informal affiliation to Congress. The ANC could well have accommodated ICU tactics. As Hawley argues, ANC leaders tried every tactic to oppose discrimination and they did so, not out of class interest, but because they believed in a liberal society, supporting mass action to make the state listen.[95]

By showing the more persistent nature of ANC ties with workers and calling attention to its broad nature of support, I make a closer analysis necessary. Regional variations in ANC militancy suggest a most complex organisation. As noted previously, some branches had more contact with labour than others did, often due to greater local concentration of workers and more labour-oriented approaches of particular leaders. Whether leaders urged moderation or supported radical struggles, there generally was an ANC commitment to ameliorating the harsh conditions of black labour. By the 1920s, mere rhetoric[96] was increasingly losing its appeal to workers. Their passionate, if fleeting, support for the ICU was because it spoke in their *name* and offered direct improvements to their situation. When the ICU delivered nothing, workers deserted it in their thousands.

The ANC operated in a complex milieu. Class struggle and national liberation increasingly entwined in the 1920s. An irregular sort of dialogue opened between the ANC and ICU, and between ANC and CPSA, out of which they formulated and tested strategic questions about the nature of alliance. Intensified exploitation of workers, combined with growing political consciousness and denial of black political rights, continued to push Africans living conditions down and throw together disparate social strata in a national(ist) coalition that was rarely explicit but always implicit. A government report spoke of the "growth of a Native nationalism ... which must be kept clearly in view when questions affecting the Natives' social and economic position are being considered".[97] This "Native nationalism" was manifest in labour organisations such as the ICU, not just in the ANC as was the case in 1912-1919. When external and internal influences coincided, and subjective and objective conditions were ripe, alliances emerged which drew upon the common suffering of black people, but which were short-lived due to organisational weaknesses and ideological differences.

The ANC underwent a particularly radical infusion under Gumede. Historians have chosen to view this as a mere radical interlude, a brief flirtation with labour militants.[98] However, Gumede's radical role in the ANC we can date much earlier to 1921 when he became a national organiser, or 1924 when he assumed NNC leadership, and it continued in the 1930s. So the traditional way of periodising Congress of the 1920s as simply a decade of moderation does not stand up to close scrutiny at a regional level. When we take the history of all branches into account, the history of radicalism assumes somewhat broader dimensions. Neither can we see the shift to the left in 1927 as purely ideological in cause. Firstly, the ANC's loose and small nature left it open to influence of individuals and thus someone with labour leanings could catapult to its head. Secondly, the constant levelling process imposed by white society on different black social strata encouraged unity. The nature of society necessitated symbiotic ANC-labour relations. The small size of both the black working class and ANC imposed parameters on their contact. But with weak black unions, the demise of the ICU, and few effective, permanent, nationalist rivals, only the ANC continued to stand between black labour and government. It was this position of the ANC vis-à-vis workers that offered the likelihood that, eventually, forces would push it into a closer relationship. The CPSA was alert to this probability when it prophetically perceived "the exploiting class ... know that however moderate the aims and servile the language used by [ANC] leaders ... the march of events and the economic environment ... will ... drive them increasingly to recognise" the class nature of their struggle.[99]

The ANC often took a principled, if contradictory, stance towards labour. At times it participated, if erratically and ineffectively, in organising workers against attacks of the state and employers. It called for workers to support the ICU. At other times, it distanced itself from workers. Workers responded with ambivalent attitudes to Congress. The ANC never condoned attacks on workers. It did little to positively alienate them and sought redress of the worst features of their exploitation. The evidence outlined above shows Congress considered workers as part of their constituency, primarily as Africans, secondly as workers. It maintained direct and indirect labour ties through its policies and actions. It faced intense competition from both the left and right to gain worker support.

If, as Basner recalled, Congress in this period foundered in the big city among intellectuals and politicians and in the face of stiff competition from Chamber of Mines-funded newspapers, Joint Councils, and social centres, it "remained strong" in "certain country districts". The provinces managed to keep before the people the notion of an ANC interested in, and capable of, representing all Africans, including workers. There was some justification then, for the claim, in 1925, by *The African World* that "I-Kongilesi *Lilizwi ezindi ezindlwini* (Congress' Name is Household)".[100]

Notes

1   "Report of Commission of Inquiry (Ciskeian Section) into the Social and Economic Conditions of the Native People" and "Report of the Social and Economic Conditions of the Natives in Natal ..." in *Report of the Proceedings of the Fifth General Missionary*

Conference of South Africa 1921 (1922), and evidence to the *Commission into the Causes of Native Disturbances at Port Elizabeth,* cited in *ibid,* p. 52.

2   *International* 27 Feb. 1920; *Star* 18-19 Feb. 1920; *Cape Times* 20 Feb. 1920 *Rand Daily Mail* 20, 24-27 Feb. 1920; *Cape Argus* 23, 26 Feb. 1 Mar. 1920; "Native Unrest" SAP Western Area to SAP Fordsburg 1 Mar. 1920, JUS 4/719/A; Diamond, "Labour", pp. 42-57; *Rand Daily Mail* 27 Feb. 1920; "Ukudutyulwa kwa Bantu e Johannesburg", *Abantu-Batho* 26 Feb. 1920, reprinted *Umteteli wa Bantu* 26 June 1920; Breckenridge ("Speak for Ourselves", p. 79) notes that 1919 protests laid the basis for the 1920 strike.

3   Police reports in Johnstone, *Class, Race & Gold,* p. 180; Bud-M'belle interview *Star* 1 Apr. 1919. TNC contacts may have been limited by ethnic divisions. Beinart (*The Political Economy of Pondoland,* p. 159) observes that one group of Mpondo workers did not join the strike. P. Bonner, "Decompartmentalizing South African History", WISER paper, February 2007, p. 4, suggests the strike set in motion the later "moral economy" between miners and management.

4   *International* 27 Feb. 1920; Bonner, "Transvaal Congress", pp. 274, 300-304, Bonner, "The 1920s Black Mineworkers' Strike: A Preliminary Account", in Bozzoli, *Labour, Townships and Protest,* pp. 273-297.

5   *Cape Argus* 25-26 Feb. 1920; "Statement by Native Congress", *Rand Daily Mail* 1 Mar. 1920; "Natives Want a Board" , *Rand Daily Mail* 25 Feb. 1920; "The Great Native Strike", *International* 27 Feb. 1920.

6   Walshe, *Rise of African Nationalism,* p. 76; SAP. "Communism and Unrest in the Union of South Africa", 11 Aug. 1922, JUS 3/1064/18; R.H. Raphela, "Mangolo: Transvaal Native Congress", *Abantu-Batho* 14 Jun. 1923; K Breckenridge, "Fighting for a White South Africa: White Working Class Racism and the 1922 Rand Revolt", UKZN History seminar paper, 2007 citing GNLB 312, 125/19 Newspapers: Cuttings, Native Strike, 1920, Nxumalo, William Charles to *Abantu Batho,* 1920/03/18 and GNLB 310, 1215/19/48, Director for Native Labour to TNC, 1920/11/08; *Ilanga lase Natal,* 10 Dec. 1926.

7   Van Onselen, *Seed is Mine,* p. 151; UG41-22, pp. 5, 11, 23; DNL to Secretary Native Affairs 14 Oct. 1920, TAD JUS 3/1007/20 "Arrest of Natives on Alluvial Diamond Diggings"; P. Bonner and K. Shapiro, "Company Town, Company Estate: Pilgrim's Rest, 1910-32" *JSAS* v. 19 (1993), pp. 171-201, p. 196.

8   H. Bradford, "'A Taste of Freedom': Capitalist Development and Response to the ICU in the Transvaal Countryside", in Bozzoli (ed.), *Town and Countryside,* pp. 128-150, pp. 132-133; C. Mulaudzi and S. Schirmer, "Land Struggles in the 20th Century", in P. Delius, *Mpumalanga: History and Heritage* (Scottsville: UKZN Press, 2007), pp. 351-391, pp. 359-360, citing SAP report on 'Rumours of Native Unrest at Platrand Patrol Area...", NTS 6661/23/332.

9   *Abantu-Batho* 23 Nov. 1922 cited in Walshe, *Rise of African Nationalism,* p. 212; Morrell, "Rural Transformation", pp. 146-197: the ICU's Mbeki visited Middelburg in 1926 but was soon expelled; Morrell, "African Land Purchase" p. 15; Murray, "Burning the Stacks,", p. 78; H Macmillan, "A Nation Divided? The Swazi in Swaziland and the Transvaal, 1865–1986" in L. Vail (ed.) *The Creation of Tribalism in Southern Africa* (Berkeley: University of California Press, 1989), pp. 289-323, citing, SNA RCS 202/20.

10   Simpson, "Peasants and Politics", pp. 184, 248, 226; N. Mokgatle, *The Autobiography of an Unknown South African* (Berkeley: University of California Press, 1971); P. Magano, "Tsa Congress" *Abantu-Batho* 14 Jun. 1923; Morton, "Female *Inboekelinge*", pp. 203-206; Bozzoli, *Women of Phokeng,* pp. 66-68. Phokeng had not been an "ANC town" until the growing unpopularity of Mangope: Discussion with Nomalanga Grootboom, East

Lansing, 16 Feb. 2007. Chiefs' unpopularity among the not so distant Bakwena-ba-Magoba was in part due to levies (largely on workers) to finance land: H. Venable, "Orthodoxy and Counter-Orthodoxy in the Bethanie Anti-Levy Riot of 1940", Wits seminar, Mar. 1989.

11   P. Delius, "The Ndzundza Ndebele: Indenture and the Making of Ethnic Identity, 1883-1914" in P. Bonner et al, *Holding Their Own* (Johannesburg: Ravan Press, 1989), pp. 227-258; SC12-25, pp. 92-94, 98.

12   Bradford, "Taste of Freedom", pp. 140-144; Jingoes, *A Chief is a Chief by the People*, p. 107. Jingoes' reference to Congress opposition may reflect organisational rivalry, as they did unite in campaigns.

13   Jingoes, *A Chief is a Chief by the People*, Chapter 3, and p. 203.

14   *International* 11 Jan. 1924; Mphahlele to SAP 12, 14 Sep. 1928, to DNA 14, 17 Sep. 1928, to Director, Veterinary Services 26 Sep. 1928: ANC. Council of Chiefs Dept. *Records of Work Done* (Johannesburg, 1928). Earlier Mphahlele had been TAC District Secretary: Skota, *African Yearly Register*, p. 216. Bonner ("Pedi Plots") notes he "first surfaces on the historical record in 1920 at a political meeting in Pietersburg". In this period, Garveyism influenced Mphahlele: Hill, *Garvey Papers*, v. 10, pp. 358, 428.

15   Ginwala, "Women and the ANC"; Wells, *We Now Demand*, p. 152, citing a letter of 17 Jul. 1920 of what Wells terms a Zoutpansberg branch of the Transvaal Native Congress.

16   P. Bonner, "Desirable or Undesirable Basotho Women? Liquor, Prostitution and the Migration of Basotho Women to the Rand, 1920; 45", in C. Walker (ed.) *Women & Gender in Southern Africa* pp. 221-250; Eales, "Patriarchs"; D. Posel, "Marriage at the Drop of a Hat: Housing and Partnership in South Africa's Urban African Townships, 1920s–1960s", *History Workshop*, 61 (2006), pp. 57-76.

17   KC v. 4, p. 78; Skota, *African Yearly Register,* p. 427; Walshe, *Rise of African Nationalism*, p. 176; Bonner, "Pedi Plots"; UG41-22, p. 24. *Abantu-Batho's* prospectus listed him as a director: *Abantu-Batho* 1 May 1930. He was active on the Marabastad Advisory Board.

18   R. Edgar, *The Making of an African Communist: Edwin Mofutsanyana & the CPSA 1927-1939* (Pretoria: Unisa, 2005); KC v. 4, p. 92; Hirson, *Yours for the Union*, p. 170; Balabushevich, "Coloured Labour in SA" *Negro Worker* 15 Jul. 1928, pp. 12-16; *Umsebenzi* Sep. 1991; S.P. Bunting to E. Lewis 21 Jan. 1930, *Ballinger Papers*; "Potchefstroom Fracas", *Star* 28 Mar. 1928; "Communist Activity in Potchefstroom", *Star* 7 May 1928; "Communists versus I.C.U.", *Rand Daily Mail* 8 May 1928. On Potchefstroom, see also Wells, *We Now Demand*. See also J. Mpama, "The Weeks case" *Umsebenzi* 4 Jul. 1930.

19   Edgar, *African Communist*, p. 3, who notes that, like fellow communist Nzula, Mofutsanyana was educated at Bensonvale and appears to date his membership of ANC from about 1923.

20   "Orlando Advisory Board Elections", CPSA flyer [194?], *ICS 20th Century Political Ephemera*; "W. Selebogo Agitator" TAD NA43/328; Skota, *African Yearly Register*, pp. 200, 216; R. Honwana, *The Life History of Raul Honwana* (Boulder: Rienner, 1988), p. 22.

21   *Abantu-Batho* 14 Jun. 1923; *Abantu-Batho* Feb. 1920 and translation of 9 [Feb?] 1922, JUS 3/1064/18.

22   *International* 29 Jun. 1923; *Abantu-Batho* 14 Jun. 1923; J. Sinenke and D. Ngwenya to *Abantu-Batho* [ca. Jun. 1923] in Hill, *Garvey Papers* v. 10, p. 106; "Uvile uGumede" , *Abantu-Batho* 1927, reproduced in *Izindaba Zabantu* 4 Nov. 1927; *Abantu-Batho* 26 Jan. 1928; Skota, *African Yearly Register*, p. 257.

23   *Abantu-Batho* May, Jun., Jul. 1923, extracts in *International* 18 May, 1, 15 Jun., 6, 13 Jul. 1923.

24 *International* 1 Jun. 1923; *Abantu-Batho* 14 Jun. 1923, and cited in *African World* 22 Aug. 1925.

25 E. Roux, "Thinking Back over 70 Years", *Fighting Talk* Oct. 1956; *Abantu-Batho* [Apr.?] 1924, reprinted in *International* 4 Apr. 1924; "African Journalist Conference", *International* 4 Jan. 1924.

26 M. Mutloatse, *Umhlaba Wethu: A Historical Indictment* (Johannesburg: Skotaville, 1989), p. 33; *International* 18 May 1923. "Free Primary Education" (from the Young Communist League's *Young Worker*) was printed in *Abantu-Batho* Feb. 1924 (*International* 29 Feb. 1924); *International* (4 Apr. 1924) reciprocated by reprinting "White SA" from *Abantu-Batho*. On black writers in the red press, see *International* 25 Jan., 7 Mar. 1924, *SA Worker* 9, 23-30 Jul. 1926.

27 D. Goodhew, *Respectability and Resistance: A History of Sophiatown* (Westport: Praeger, 2004) p. 48; Mandela, *Long Walk*, p. 66; E. P. Mart Zulu, "Mhleli waBantu Batho", *Abantu-Batho* 14 Jun. 1923: Nauright ("Black Island" p. 91) did not consult this obscure issue of the newspaper (in the Swazi Archives RCS 486/23) and concluded there was no evidence of an ANC role; Nauright "Black Island", pp. 94-97, 122, 191.

28 "Transvaal A.N.C.", *Umteteli wa Bantu* 14 Dec. 1929.

29 "IBM" [M'belle] to Native Affairs 27 Jun. 1926 and Makgatho memo: TAD NA39/362; CKC 2:XM1:96; Skota, *African Yearly Register* 3rd. ed., p. 114; A TAC resolution against Malawi migrants reflected ethnic tensions: R.W. Msimang, "Congress Supports Deportation" *Umteteli wa Bantu* 11 Feb. 1928. R.V. Selope Thema ("The African National Congress: Its Achievements and Failures III", *Umteteli* 2 Nov. 1929) accused Letanka and Makgatho of provincialism or ethnic bias, though without much evidence adduced.

30 "TAC Executive", *Umteteli wa Bantu* 29 Dec. 1928; "Transvaal African Congress" *Umteteli wa Bantu* 15 Jun. 1929; "Transvaal African Congress" *Umteteli wa Bantu* 19 Oct. 1929, "Transvaal A.N.C." *Umteteli wa Bantu* 14 Dec. 1929.

31 *South African Worker* 30 Mar. 1928; "Agitation against the Pass Laws", *Umteteli wa Bantu* 4 Aug. 1928, "Transvaal African Congress", *Umteteli wa Bantu* 2 Jun. 1928.

32 "Hamba Kahle!" and "An Improved Outlook", *Umteteli wa Bantu* 27 Apr., 11 May 1929 respectively.

33 There were ties between branches: the Griqualand West branch was discussed at CAC meetings: see meeting agenda "Intlanganiso Yonyaka ye Cape Native Congress", *Umteteli wa Bantu* 31 Mar. 1923

34 *Cape Argus* 25 Feb. 1920; UG41-22, pp. 25-26.

35 "Shooting of Natives", *Imvo Zabantszundu* 31 Mar. 1922; T. Clynick, "Chiefs, Diggers and African Labour: The Tlaping Diamond Rush, 1920-1", *African Studies* 54 (1995), pp. 73-93, p. 91; "Burghersdorp-Sterkstroom (Cape Native Congress)", *Umteteli wa Bantu* 9 Sep. 1922 (in Xhosa). The term may originate in independent churches or (personal communication, Peter Midgley 5 May 2007) in Xhosa poetry, and (Friedgut, "Non-European Press", p. 491) thence to *Abantu-Batho* readers.

36 From *Umteteli wa Bantu*: Z.R. Mahabane, "Cape Province Native Congress" (9 Sep. 1922), "Eze Cape Native Congress e Batengini e Cala", J. Ngojo, "Malunga ne Cape Native Congress e Monti" (7 Apr. 1923); "Umhlangano Wonyaka" (30 Jun. 1923), J. Nkuzo, "Inkongolo e Mhlanga" (24 Mar. 1923), "Eze Cape Native Congress" (17 Mar. 1923); Simons, *Class and Colour* p. 343; SC10-27, p. 289.

37 Wickins, *ICU*, p. 51; Kadalie, *My Life*, p. 53; Minkley, "Did Not Come to Work", p. 197; L. Switzer, *Power and Resistance in an African Society* (Madison: University of Wisconsin Press, 1993), p. 251; W. Beinart and C. Bundy, "The Union, the Nation and

the Talking Crow: The Ideology and Tactics of the Independent ICU in East London", in Beinart, *Hidden Struggles*, pp. 270-320, p. 275. On Godlo's view of CAC politics and leaders see R.H. Godlo, "Eze Cape Native Congress", *Umteteli wa Bantu* 24 Mar. 1923.

38 Baines, "Populism"; Skota, *Register*, p. 187; Magistrate to Rubusana 17 Oct. 1921 enclosing £10 for injuries suffered at a meeting "attended at the request of the Supt. of Natives": "Letters of W.B. Rubusana 1910-22," SOAS ms. 380264; *Report of Commissioners to Enquire into the Causes of Native Disturbances at Port Elizabeth*; *Black Man*, Nov. 1920; evidence of Rubusana, cited in "Native Riots, Port Elizabeth 23 Oct. 1920", report of District Commandant, SAP, 6 Apr. 1921, JUS 2/950/19: "Inquest re Shooting of People during Native Riots, Port Elizabeth"; *Eastern Province Herald* 25 Oct. 1920.

39 S. Msimang, "Black Labour and the Facts of South African History", *Natal Witness* 3 Jul. 1975; J.J. Mkosi and T.M. Mateza, "Eze Congress e Bhai", *Umteteli wa Bantu* 14 Jul. 1923; JUS 3/1064/18.

40 *Cape Argus* 25 Feb. 1920.

41 G. Carter and S. Johns (eds.), *The Good Fight: Selected Speeches of Rev. Zaccheus R. Mahabane* (Evanston: Northwestern University, 1965), pp. 1, 10, 13-28; Mahabane, *The Colour Bar: Three Presidential Addresses* (Lovedale, 1922); SAP to SJ 1921, JUS 3/1064/18; Mahabane, "Cape Province Native Congress", *Umteteli wa Bantu* 9 Sep. 1922.

42 Mahabane to *African World* 24 Oct. 1925; Mahabane, "Problems of the African Church", in Stauffer, *Thinking with Africa*, pp. 135-146, p. 143; KC v. 4, p. 65; VAB CO394 2042/1/06.

43 "More 'Native Bolshevism'", *International* 11 Jan. 1924.

44 Hofmeyr, "Crisis", Chapter 3. Hofmeyr argues that before 1930 "the conservative petty bourgeoisie" dominated the ANC but a shaky alliance formed between Garveyists and communists.

45 "Progressive Move of Congress", *African World* 10 Oct. 1925. Thaele took on the ICU at meetings in Pietermaritzburg and Johannesburg; at the latter he was obliged to tone down his rhetoric to allow a joint meeting of TAC and ICU executives to discuss the rivalry between he and Kadalie: "Kadalie and Thaele", *The Star* 12 Apr. 1926, clipping in Marwick Papers, UKZN Campbell Collections.

46 E. Jordan, "From Time Immemorial: Washerwomen, Culture and Community in Cape Town, South Africa", Ph.D. Rutgers University, 2006, pp. 155-60.

47 Hofmeyr, "Crisis", pp. 74-79; Mahabane, "Western District Branch", *Ilanga lase Natal* 26 Nov. 1926; R. Kingwill, "The ANC in the Western Cape: A Preliminary Study", B,A. (Hons) thesis UCT, 1977, p. 14, Chapters 2-3.

48 *African World* 23, 30 May, 13, 27 Jun. 11, 25 Jul. 8, 22 Aug. 1925, 9 Jan. 1926. The ANC had its own brass band: "Report of Cape Town Political Rally", *Negro World* [ca. 16 Dec. 1929], in Hill, *Garvey Papers* v. 10, p. 532.

49 *African World* 12 Sep., 23 May 1925, 9 Jan. 1926; 4 Jul., 22 Aug., 27 Jun., 30 May 1925.

50 "The Shipping Strike", *African World*, 12 Sept. 1925; *African World* 26 Sep. 1925; Ngedlane to *African World* 3 Oct. 1925; *African World* 13 Jun. 1925; B. Ndobe, "Lefatse le Tsietsing", *African World* 8 Aug. 1925; T. Mbeki, "The Spirit of Self-Determination", *African World* 4 Jul. 1925; S. Silwana, "The Iniquities of Legislators", *African World* 26 Sept. 1925.

51 J. Nduma, "The Onlooker", *African World* 23 May 1925, Hill, *Garvey Papers* v. 10, p. 341; *African World* 10 Oct. 1925; Ndimande to *African World* 27 Jun. 1925.

52 Musson, *Gomas*, pp. 16-18, 32: Gomas chose to join the ANC due to the militancy of part of the ANC in 1918-1920; Musson, *Gomas*, p. 33 citing 1976 Gomas interview; Verwey, *New Dictionary*, pp. 80-83.

53 "Jimmy La Guma: A Biography", ms. UCT Library, 1964: he saw the black "liberatory movement [as] an essential component in the struggle against capitalist exploitation", p. 17; Wickins, *The ICU*, pp. 43-51; KC v. 4 p. 53; CKC 2:XL2:96/1; Verwey, *New Dictionary*, p. 124; Bunting, *Moses Kotane*, p. 66, Simons, *Class and Colour*, p. 426. Silwana had UNIA ties: see "Big Black Problem", *Umteteli wa Bantu*, 19 Aug. 1922.

54 *African World* 1 Aug. 1925; 35th report on "Communism in South Africa", 15 Jun. 1926, JUS 3/1064/18.

55 *African World* 23 May 1925; *SA Worker* 25 May 1928, 21 Jul. 1929. In 1930 Thaele changed direction and actively opposed the communists: *Cape Argus* 7, 12 Feb. 1930; "Jimmy La Guma", p. 68.

56 "Native Agitator Bransby Ndobe", NA 87/326(3) "Independent ANC"; CKC reel 14A:2:XT14:56/2; Skota, *African Yearly Register*, pp. 234, 137; *African World* 23, 30 May, 13, 27 Jun., 11, 25 Jul., 8, 22 Aug. 1925, 9 Jan. 1926; Ndobe, "A Troubled Nation", *African World* 8 Aug. 1925, translated in Hill, *Garvey Papers* v. 10, p. 330; *Umsebenzi* 6 Jun., 4, 11 Jul., 5 Sep., 28 Nov., 8 Jan., 19 Feb. 1930.

57 Hofmeyr, "Crisis", pp. 80-87; W. Hofmeyr, "Rural Popular Organisation and its Problems: Struggles in the Western Cape 1929-1930", *Africa Perspective*, no. 22 1983, pp. 26-49; A.B.S. Ngaleca, "Isebe (Branch) lase-Huguenot and Norder Paarl", *African World* 4 July 1925.

58 Hofmeyr, "Crisis", p. 86; Roux, *Time Longer than Rope*, pp. 159-180; Roux, *Rebel Pity*, pp. 102-105; *Worcester Standard & Advertiser* 12 Oct. 1929 in Hofmeyr, "Crisis" cited p. 94; Redding, "Making of a South African Town", pp. 87ff.

59 CAD, Chief of Supreme Court (CSC) 1/1/1/157 ref. 23, Record of Proceedings, Kenneth [sic] Thaele.

60 Beinart and Bundy, *Hidden Struggles in Rural South Africa*, p. 39.

61 SC10-27, pp. 305-306.

62 Switzer, *Power and Resistance*; *Cape Times* 4 Aug. 1920.

63 W. M. Macmillan, *Complex South Africa* (London: Faber, 1930), pp. 39, 109-121, 144-152, 177-182; W. M. Macmillan "'Export' of Native Labour," *Cape Times* Apr. 1926.

64 Police reports on ANC meetings 10 Mar., 21 Apr. 1928, Thaele to Magistrate Herschel 5 Nov. 1928, NAD to Thaele 13 Sept. 1928, all in 2/SPT N/1/9/2 "Native Unrest, Prof. Thaele". At this time, perhaps encouraged by Thaele's rapprochement with the CPSA, Bhola attended a "women's meeting in Potchefstroom" with Rebecca Bunting of the CPSA: see A. Drew, *Between Empire and Revolution: A Life of Sidney Bunting, 1873-1936* (London: Pickering, 2007), p. 162.

65 CAD Magistrate Sterkspruit 2/SPT 16 N1/9/3: "Native Unrest: ANC": Native Commissioner [NC] Herschel to SNA Cape Town, 30 Jan. 1929, NC to CNC King William's Town 17 Aug. 1929; NA213/293 SNA to B. Sisusa, ANC Sterkspruit 6 Sep. 1929, Sisusa to Assistant NC Sterkspruit 7 Aug. 1929; ANC Sterkspruit to PM 20 Jul. 1929. Jabane had been arrested in Herschel in Mar. 1928 on what he saw as trumped-up theft charges: police record of his speech at Sterkspruit 10 Mar. 1928, 2/SPT N/1/9/2.

66 Police reports on: "Native Meeting Held at Sterkspruit" 17 Nov. 1928, 27 Oct. 1928; "Native Corporal O. Sigenu to NC Herschel, 22 Feb. 1929; SA Police Sterkspruit to Magistrate Herschel 13 May 1929; "Native Meeting Held at Sterkspruit on 27/4/1929": all in 2/SPT 16, N1/9/3.

67 Skota, "ANC Report", 1925; Tantsi to Chief Magistrate Transkeian Territories (CMTT) 22 Apr. 1925, CMTT to Tantsi Apr. 1925: CMT 3/1471 42/C pt. 1; NC Herschel to CNC King William's Town 17 Aug. 1929; "Meeting Held by ... Agitator T. Mvalo", 12 Aug. 1929; flyer signed Jabane, ANC Sterkspruit, 7 Jul. 1929: 2/SPT 16 N1/9/3; DC to Magistrate Queenstown, 27 Aug. 1930, 1/KNT 40/12. Arrested for entering Germiston location without a permit in 1928, Mvalo was described as a labourer and leader of the self-styled Native Tenants' Vigilance League: "A Lawless Leader", *Umteteli wa Bantu* 18 Feb. 1928.

68 Report, Native Constable Sigenu 15 Aug. 1928; Chief Clerk ANC Sterkspruit to Assistant NC Herschel 18 Jul. 1929; Tandinyaniso [pseud.], "Concerning Herschel", translated *Umteteli wa Bantu* 21 Apr. 1928: 2/SPT 16 N/1/9/2 "Native Unrest, Butler Hansford Wellington"; W. Beinart, 'Amafelandawonye (the Die-hards)': Popular Protest and Women's Movements in Herschel District in the 1920s", in Beinart & Bundy, *Hidden Struggles* pp. 222-269, Beinart, "Women in Rural Politics"; Hill, *Garvey Papers*, v. 10, pp. 415, 430, 511. On Wellington and taxes, see S. Redding, *Sorcery and Sovereignty: Taxation, Power, and Rebellion in South Africa, 1880-1963* (Athens: Ohio University Press, 2006), Chapter 5.

69 Walshe, *Rise of African Nationalism*, pp. 224, 226; L. Ntsebeza, *Democracy Compromised*.

70 *Umteteli wa Bantu* 9 Jun. 1923; *Report of Native Churches Commission*, p. 5; leaflet signed R. Sol. Sidzumo, H.R. Ngcayiya, SANNC, 28 May 1924, and copy in letter of J.J.P. Gcingca, President ANC-TT to Magistrate Nqamakwe 28 Jun. 1930, CAD CMT 3/1471 file 42/C pt. 1 "ANC" 1924-; J. Kantor, *A Healthy Grave* (Berlin: Seven Seas, 1967), p. 202; Mbeki, *Struggle,* pp. x-xvi, 127. Cofimvaba was later to produce radical ANC/SACP leaders such as Chris Hani and Nomboniso Gasa.

71 "Umhlangano Wonyaka: We Cape African Congress", *Umteteli wa Bantu* 30 Jun. 1923; Gcingca to Magistrate Tsomo, 27 Feb., 22 Apr. 1924, Magistrate Idutywa to ANC 30 Apr. 1924, J.D. Ngojo to Magistrate Idutywa [Apr. 1925], Magistrate Idutywa to CMTT 11 Apr. 1925, Magistrate Tsomo to Magistrate Idutywa 20 Mar. 1925, Gcingca to CMTT 14 Apr. 1924: CMT 3/1471 42/C.

72 Gcingca to Prime Minister 23 Nov. 1925, 19 Dec. 1926 [7 letters of same date], CMT 3/1471 42/C.

73 Gcingca to PM, enclosing 28 petitions [ca. Dec. 1926], CAD CMT 3/1471 42/C.

74 CAD CMT 3/1471 42/C.

75 A.C. Madalane, ANC Cofimvaba, to Magistrate Tsomo 15 Oct. 1927, Magistrate Tsomo to Chief Magistrate of the Transkeian Territories (CMTT), 20 Oct. 1927, CAD CMT 3/1471 42/C.

76 A. C. Madalane, ANC Cofimvaba, to SJ 20 May 1927, CAD CMT 3/1471 42/C.

77 A. C. Madalane, ANC Cofimvaba, to SJ 20 May 1927, CAD CMT 3/1471 42/C.

78 Madalane, ANC Cofimvaba, to CMTT 8 Nov. 1927, CMTT to ANC Cofimvaba 12 Nov. 1927, and Madalane to SNA Pretoria, Dec. 1927, CAD CMT 3/1471 42/C.

79 Gcingca, Gen. Sec. ANC-TT to Minister of Justice 20 Feb. 1928, CAD CMT 3/1471 42/C.

80 W.T. Welsh, CMTT Umtata to Gcingca 27 Jan., 4 Feb. 1927, rejecting 6 petitions, CMTT to Magistrate Tsomo 24 Oct. 1927, Magistrate Tsomo to ANC Cofimvaba, 17, 27 Oct. 1927, SNA to CMTT 24 Jan., 20 Oct. 1927 CMT 3/1471 42/C; Gcingca to Hertzog 15 Apr. 1930: CMT 3/1471 42/C.

81 Skota, *African Yearly Register*, pp. 175, 193, 230, 237; Walshe, *Rise of African Nationalism*, p. 227; *Abantu-Batho* 11 Sep. 1930; B. Turok, "A Peasant's Son Turned Trade Unionist", *Sechaba* v. 5 no. 4 (1971), p. 16; "Umhlangano Wonyaka: We Cape African Congress", *Umteteli wa Bantu* 30 Jun. 1923. Dr. Molema also was active there.

82 Hill, *Garvey Papers* v. 10, p. 427; "African National Congress", *Abantu-Batho* 14 Jun. 1923; S.M. Bennett Ncwana, " A Call for Unity", *Umteteli wa Bantu* 26 May 1923; J.K. Lekoma, "British Bechuanaland & Griqualand West Native Congress: Windsorian Branch", *Umteteli wa Bantu* 24 Mar. 1923.

83 "Eze Cape Native Congress", *Umteteli wa Bantu* 17 Mar. 1923; "Intlanganiso Yonyaka: Cape Native Congress", *Umteteli wa Bantu* 16 Jun. 1923; "Umhlangano Wonyaka: We Cape African Congress", *Umteteli wa Bantu* 30 Jun. 1923.

84 Hofmeyr, "Rural Popular Organisation 1929-1930".

85 "ICWU..." *Umteteli wa Bantu* 15 Jul. 1922; *South African Municipal Year Book 1926-1927*, p. 271.

86 "Native Women Terrorized", *Umteteli wa Bantu* 20 Nov. 1920; police reports of 13 Jul. 1921, JUS 5/242/16; Hirson, "General Strike"; Wells, *We Now Demand*, pp. 60-62; Mancoe, *Directory*, p. 102.

87 Murray, "Natives", p. 109; Msimang, "Autobiography", p. 12, PC 14/1/1/1-3; La Hausse, *Restless Identities*, p. 73; "ICWU Delegates Assembly", *Umteteli wa Bantu* 15 Jul. 1922; CID to SAP 12 Jun. 1922, CNC 2316/20; JUS 3/1064/18; "Conference of the I.C.W.U.", *Umteteli wa Bantu* 7 Apr. 1923; D.S. Deane, *Black South Africans: A Who's Who* (Cape Town: OUP, 1978), p. 117.

88 Mancoe, *Bloemfontein Bantu Directory*, p. 73; "ANC", *Ilanga lase Natal* 20 Jan. 1928; Haasbroek, "Venue of ANC", p. 134; Twala, "Ulundi-Kaya", p. 71ff who notes that due to Mapikela's many building contracts the house resembled a "workshop" and was a "public" and "ANC" building; Twala (p. 78) interview with A. Jacobs, Jul. 1997.

89 C. Murray, *Black Mountain,* p. 198. W.Z. Fenyang remained ANC OFS president: Murray p. 191; SNA to OFS ANC 23 Apr. 1924, in CKC 2:AK2:47; *Report of Select Committee on Suppression of Stock Thefts* (SC4-23) pp. 193, 204-8; Skota, *African Yearly Register*, p. 203; KC v. 4, p. 91; "Away with Pass Laws", *Star* 8 Apr. 1927; SNA to General Secretary OFSNC, Thaba 'Nchu, 23 Apr. 1924, JSA/TG, in CKC 2:AK2:47

90 Mancoe, *Bloemfontein Bantu Directory*, pp. 71-72.

91 Municipal Wages Committee Minutes 22 Feb. 1926, Correspondence of Town Clerk/ Minutes of Town Council, Bloemfontein, VAB MBL 4/8/1/81; Skota, *African Yearly Register*, p. 241; Willan, *Sol Plaatje*, pp. 143, 149; Murray, *Black Mountain*, p. 43; Odendaal, *Vukani Bantu*, p. 265; Walshe, *Rise of African Nationalism*, p. 176. Mancoe uses "Phahlane", Odendaal and Walshe "Phatlane". 'Mote shared a CPSA platform on May Day 1928: E. Roux to N. Leys 16 Sept. 1928, *W.G. Ballinger Papers*.

92 Wages Committee Minutes 22 Feb. 1926 MBL 4/8/1/81. Phahlane later became a small businessman. Kadalie addressed ICU meetings in Bloemfontein: *The Friend* 2 Feb. 1927.

93 "Native Leaders and Pass Laws", *Star* 7 May 1928; "The Dream of the ICU", *Frankforter* 3 Feb. 1927 in *W.G. Ballinger Papers*; A. Drew, "The New Line in South Africa: Ideology and Perception in a Very Small Communist Party", in M. Worley (ed.) *In Search of Revolution: International Communist Parties in the Third Period* (London: Tauris, 2004), pp. 337-359, p. 343; Drew, *Empire and Revolution*, p. 193.

94 Redding, *Sorcery and Sovereignty*, p. 144.

95 Hawley, "African National Congress and the Urban Black South African", pp. 177-179.

96   P. Bonner, "'Home Truths' and the Political Discourse of the ICU" paper to South African Historical Society conference Cape Town, 1999 argues that part of the ICU's appeal was their lively uncompromising rhetoric. Yet, as I have shown, this also could apply to local ANC and Garveyist leaders.

97   *Report of Native Economic Commission 1930-1932,* p. 100.

98   Meier "ANC" entitles a chapter on 1917-1936 ANC history, "Flirtations with the Black Working Class".

99   "The Useful People", *International* 22 Aug. 1924.

100 Basner, "Transcript", p. 19; "Umbhaleli Wezinto Ngezinto", *The African World* 1 Aug. 1925.

Part 4
The Third Decade

11

From "Culpable Inertia" to Rebuilding: The ANC and Labour in the 1930s

With good reason, historians regard the 1930s as a decade of profound ANC inertia. Mary Benson claims that in this decade the "gulf between the desires of the ordinary people and [ANC] leadership had never been so deep". Some recent studies echo this view, variously claiming that historical conditions propelled developments beyond ANC control even as urbanisation was starting to generate new urban groups that eventually would force ANC leaders to adopt policies that were more assertive, and that, whilst the ANC supported black unions in theory, it did little practically to assist them.[1]

Whilst these interpretations capture a key theme of ANC politics (especially at the *national* level) during the decade—stagnation—they tend to neglect the more complex reality of ANC politics and its relations with labour, and do not deconstruct its multi-layered regional constituency. In the 1930s there were in fact moments of gripping engagement of African political activists with labour struggles. Less spectacular, and more constant, commitments to supporting labour demands also characterised ANC policy.

The 1930s saw world depression and growing South African industrialisation accompanied by a significant increase in the size and stability of the urban work force. This focused many organisations, including the ANC, on economic conditions such as mass lay-offs and wage cuts as well as alternative economic policies.[2] This helped ANC leaders—even if some of them remained remote from labouring lives—develop a greater awareness of the lot of black workers who, in the face of savage pay cuts, would have been on the one hand receptive to political mobilisation and on the other hand hesitant to engage in strikes given the decline in jobs. When a number of rival bodies failed to thrive or even survive, the appeal of the ANC as a lobby group for black economic demands increased by default.

These wider changes posed a challenge to the ANC if it was to gain the support of ordinary black people to build its own socio-political base. The ANC in the 1930s was no more a specifically workers' organisation than before. Often it was moderate in its policies to the extent of supporting black business. The ANC as a national African political body had little choice other than to strive to unite diverse black strata and their representatives. Yet, no less than in earlier times, Congress maintained a commitment to easing the burden on black workers. Moreover, it was no less effective, no less entwined with the lives of black workers than other black political groups. Members and activists maintained or forged anew some rickety bridges from the ANC to labour that were rooted in contacts with or sympathy for black labour *despite* leadership timidity or failings.

South African Federation of Non-European Trade Unions flyer, 1930

ANC Membership and Structure, 1930-1940

Congress in the 1930s continued to rely on the support of both paid-up members, and a network of informal influence among affiliated groups, such as the Advisory Board Congresses (ABC). ANC figures temporarily could disappear from ANC life to re-surface in other groups of the left and right. The ANC at this time was profoundly unstable. Due to incomplete ANC record keeping, it is impossible to establish its precise membership levels. Walshe suggests a "variable branch membership of 1,000 to 4,000" in the 1920s-1930s.[3] Similarly, the level of electoral support is impossible to quantify accurately given the restrictions on the African franchise. However, it is reasonable to assume that the ANC's espousal of broad political rights for Africans would have earned it a following.

Despite imprecise membership figures, it is possible to establish a definite decline in ANC activity in the early 1930s. Barely 69 delegates attended its 1933 conference. In a rather hazardous calculation based upon hypothetical branch figures according to the 1919 constitution, Walshe suggests an official membership of 1,325 in 1930, declining to 1,125 in 1937. On the other hand, Pixley Seme made the claim, defending his embattled leadership in 1933, that one province supporting his candidature, Western Cape, alone had 2,300 members. Whilst not reliable, both figures indicate the smallness of paid-up membership. Given an estimated membership in the early 1920s just for the Cape and Transvaal of 3,000-4,000, then decline seems obvious. However, its outspoken opposition to the Hertzog Bills indicates a rise in ANC activity in the later part of the decade. This greater activity generated a slight rise in membership. Western Province in 1937 received reports from branches claiming 1,650 members. Yet the Transvaal Congress, based on the densely populated Rand, in 1938 reported only 364. In 1939, Mahabane estimated a 4,000 national total.[4] Behind these meagre figures lies the poverty of African communities as well as state restrictions on their ability to save, or to agitate. "Survival tactics" left little room to pay membership dues to a political body, even less so for workers.

As in the 1920s, the ANC had limited awareness of the need to mobilise youth, women, or rural dwellers. Occasional protests against forced youth labour and passes for women continued. Mahabane criticised high youth unemployment; John Mancoe sought to create jobs for them; James Calata in Cradock sought to mobilise them against radicals. Voices in the press accused the ANC of neglecting youth. Ephemeral bodies rose and fell: John Dube sat on the board of the Bantu Youth League; Eddie Roux published a newssheet aimed at youth that attracted activists such as Gilbert Coka but fizzled out.[5]

By the late 1930s, a new generation of youth had passed through educational institutions. They heard whispers or more about Congress, just as some of their teachers, such as Z. K. Matthews, gradually entered politics via a revitalising Congress and government obstinacy. Matthews had known about Congress from his childhood in Kimberley—Sol Plaatje was a relative—but academic work and teaching at Adams College tended to insulate him from politics, though like Albert Luthuli he became a leader of the Natal African Teachers' Association. He recalls joining Congress around 1936. By the time Nelson Mandela got to Fort Hare in February 1939, the ANC, particularly in the Cape, had begun to revive under its energetic Secretary Calata, contributing to a subtle but significant general rise of confidence and hope among some more politically conscious black people.[6]

AFRICAN NATIONAL CONGRESS, BLOEMFONTEIN, 1930. *First row, seated on ground, left to right:* Albert Nzula, John Gomas, next two unidentified, Elliot Tonjeni. *Second row:* first six unidentified, J. T. Gumede, Chief Mandlesilo Nkosi, Z. R. Mahabane, Chief Stephen Mini, next two unidentified, Pixley Seme. *Third row:* Edwin Mofutsanyana (?), next four unidentified, S. M. Masa-balala, Thomas Mapikela, L. T. Mvabaza, S. M. Makgatho, unidentified, Mazingi, unidentified. *Back row:* P. Phatlane, Dave Mark, unidentified, R. V. Selope Thema, C. D. Modiakgotla, A. W. G. Champion, Bhulose, Theodore Lujiza, A. M. Rakaoane (?), T. D. Mweli Skota, unidentified, Morris Somtunzi, H. S. Msimang, unidentified.

ANC national conference, 1930

The ANC's gender imbalance is one indication of lost recruitment opportunities. The number of African women—let alone women workers—who directly associated with Congress was low, and formal membership remained out of the question. Female participation at ANC conferences was minimal, though women proxies were instrumental in Seme's re-election as president in 1933. Charlotte Maxeke and Mrs Mahabane, active in Congress in the 1920s, from 1937 chose to devote their energies to a new National Council of African Women. The majority of members appear to have been teachers or nurses.

Maxeke was president and Mrs Mahabane declined the ANC Women's Section presidency in 1938 in favour of becoming council treasurer. Mina Soga, a teacher and member of the Joint Council in Queenstown, became national secretary. Maxeke, who addressed the 1935 All African Convention, concentrated on her role as president of the Council, meeting the Minister for Native Affairs in 1939 in that capacity; ANC president Mahabane had urged an inclusion of a Council delegate. Interestingly, nosy state officials regarded African women as key ANC supporters. Indeed, some women raised labour issues in ANC circles. Jessie Ntandatu wrote a critical column in *African Leader*. In one article she discussed the pervasive experience of labour migration, of how "almost every one of us came to town to work". Such cases, however, were the exception.[7]

Other women, not directly connected with the ANC, spoke out on socio-economic conditions. Sibusisiwe Makhanya, a social worker, gave evidence to the Native Economic Commission calling for state aid for worker recreation, for mine compounds to give way to black villages, for more evening schools, and for women's social centres. However, such pronouncements were exceptions. The limited nature of women's political involvement was not due just to attitudes of ANC men. In this decade, changing social attitudes to women's role and rights did match increased urbanisation and proletarianisation of African women. Some African women themselves, as Margaret Ballinger noted in 1938, continued to submit to male authority, while the state refused to concede to them residential rights. ANC masculinities would have been similar to those among men in rural areas or on the mines. In general, ANC patriarchalism reflected social realities.[8]

In the 1930s, writes Walshe, many ANC members and leaders came from the "middle class". Still, Congress did incorporate workers or wage earners even though legal restrictions on activity in political organisations by state employees continued to dissuade "white collar" workers such as teachers from formal membership.[9] Whilst the ANC found difficulty in attracting financial members, rising urbanisation modified the class composition of its constituency. More workers in the cities meant that industrial issues eventually would require more prominence in ANC deliberations. This did not take place all at once.

ANC Policies and Practices in the 1930s: Stagnation & Decline under Seme, 1930-1936

This section outlines the broad contours of the history of the national ANC in the first half of the 1930s and charts its labour policies. Whilst the general passivity of Congress's peak bodies in this period is not in dispute, a complex set of ideas emerges.

A legacy of ANC radicalism of the late 1920s was a lingering support among some workers. The Railways and Harbours Department told the Native Economic Commission of 1930-1932 the ANC had "gained a certain measure of support" among its African workers. The national ANC's radical orientation continued until its 1930 convention. ANC President Josiah Gumede stated prior to the meeting that, in response to repressive legislation such as the Masters and Servants Act Amendment Bill, Congress would organise "more strongly". At the conference, he condemned capitalism and imperialism: oppressed peoples everywhere, in India, China, Java, and South Africa, were rising "against their exploiters". Africans now had "to rely on our own strength" and should embrace "organised labour unions", strikes, and boycotts to promote the "Native Republic". Astonishingly, he even called on Congress to "rely on ... the strength of the revolutionary masses of white workers the world over". The presence of communist and union delegates did not save Gumede. He was defeated as president by 39 to 14 votes by Seme, who firmly rejected communist overtures.[10]

Msimang ascribed Gumede's fall to his failure to consult with his executive, which thereby withdrew its support, and by Gumede's inclination always to seek guidance from "outside people". The loss of left-wing influence in Congress represented by Gumede's fall may have stimulated rumours in the months that followed of an imminent merger of the ICU and ANC, which, however, came to nothing.[11]

Seme's victory did not radically alter all earlier leadership positions: he simply took over intact Gumede's "cabinet". This included Mweli Skota (Secretary-General), Msimang (Labour Committee Chairman), Mabaso (Assistant Finance Secretary), Letanka (Council of Chiefs Secretary), Dube, Makgatho, Matseke, Likhing, and Mvabaza. Seme's rise did not influence any of them to abandon the sympathy for black workers that all had expressed in one-way or another. Selope Thema, just after Gumede's defeat, wrote that working conditions on farms "are intolerable ... The people are seething with discontent." It was clear urban wages were insufficient and that due to "white labour" policies "hundreds" had lost their jobs. His view that the "discontent which now prevails ... is justifiable" was hardly the outlook of a completely docile government minion.[12]

Despite continuities in personnel, the rise of Seme, a champion of Booker Washington's black capitalist philosophy, ushered in what is widely regarded as a period of ANC stagnation. Seme sounded a clear warning to radicals. He condemned strikes that "never leave any pleasant impression in the public mind". The government, he argued, not want to see any ANC people "go about stirring up strife and other trouble for the authorities". The ANC "must condemn the spirit of sedition in every form". Such statements encouraged labour radicals to give the ANC a wide berth.[13]

A stifling atmosphere descended upon the ANC. Seme's "ministers" accused him of "culpable inertia" in failing to convene conventions or even attend meetings. When the National Executive finally met in February 1931, without Seme, it passed a resolution demanding his future attendance. Dube resigned in protest at Seme's lack of consultation. Mweli Skota, Selope Thema and Msimang criticised Seme's lack of opposition to the Native Service Contract Bill (which intensified repression of farm labourers) and cuts to teacher salaries. These leaders thus continued to be interested in the well-being of workers. Neither can we assume ANC conferences under Seme necessarily represented rank-and-file views. Seme postponed a 1931 conference two days before it was due. The legality of voting procedures was challenged in 1930, and again in 1933, when he was declared re-elected on votes of proxies—a result rejected by many, especially the TAC. Many ANC notables did not even bother to attend. Analysis of the class background of delegates of these meetings therefore does not indicate the true nature of branch membership.[14]

Discontent with Seme's leadership smouldered for months. At the January 1931 conference, Seme oddly claimed Prime Minister Hertzog was "a man of conviction", and he would stand by Hertzog's pledge to allow (segregated) African trading rights. This speech, reported *Umteteli wa Bantu*, was "not well received" by delegates, some of whom accused Seme of accepting Hertzog's policy without a mandate. Seme used the departure of some delegates at the end of the conference to declare vacant the positions of four of his opponents—Mweli Skota, Selope Thema, Letanka and Mabaso. This aroused more criticism. In November 1931, Selope Thema argued that at a time of mass-scale African sackings, ANC leaders were "nowhere to be found". This was, he argued, due to Seme's lack of a programme and his attempts to centralise control by stripping provincial leaders and the ANC secretary of all powers. In 1932, Selope Thema declared that, since 1912, he had "never witnessed such inactivity and apathy on the part of our leaders". He sought inspiration instead in past black leaders, such as Moshoeshoe. Radical writer Gilbert Coka also despaired of any inspiration from current leaders. Coka, with partly digested ideas on class from the ICU and CPSA, held that the "labouring classes comp[ri]se the overwhelming bulk in every community".

He attended ANC conferences of the time. In 1932, he wrote that the most important problem facing the coming ANC conference was the economic situation of Africans, especially rising unemployment. Rather than "pass futile resolutions", he urged Africans to forge a "National Spirit" and unite in a "Bantu Salvation Campaign".[15]

Nine ANC executive members, led by Msimang, signed an open letter criticizing Seme's inaction, justified as due to the impact of economic crisis on African workers. Each month more Africans lost their jobs, only for the law to treat them as vagrants, and for them to face high rents, evictions, and prosecution under pass laws. The government had exacerbated the crisis by introducing draconian legislation; it was "deliberately oblivious to the plight in which the majority of African workers find themselves". That consideration for the fate of workers had not disappeared from ANC gatherings was evident at the July 1932 ANC emergency convention held in Kimberley—without Seme. Msimang and Modiakgotla—both with an ICU background—attacked state labour policy. The convention condemned the Native Service Contract Bill, evictions, state inaction over rising black unemployment, and "arbitrary cuts in teachers' salaries". After the conference, even Seme, marginalised, sought to account for the rebellion against his authority by "the dreadful vision of chattel slavery" in the guise of the Contract Bill.[16]

Divisions continued. Seme expelled dissatisfied members, including Mahabane, Mapikela, Mvabaza, and Coka. They re-grouped and held a public meeting, prompting *African Leader* to comment wryly that Congress "is on its feet". Dissension and moderation marked the December 1933 convention under Seme's tutelage: a resolution praised government efforts to relieve black unemployment. Despite its moderation, delegates with a record of support for worker rights, including Dunjwa, Coka, Mabaso, and Mvabaza, attended the meeting. Seme announced a new "cabinet" that included James and Kennon Thaele, Makgatho, Dube, Macheng, Mweli Skota, Matseke, Chief Mini, and Likhing, most of whom could boast a similar broad sympathy for African workers.[17]

ANC inertia continued to spawn a plethora of criticism. In 1932, E. Masibe-Langa commented that in Northern Transvaal "Congress is dead where once it was strong". Coka described Congress as "near dormancy"; its 1934 conference was a "willy nilly goody giddy convention … a complete washout", with the only delegates "a handful of … opportunists [with] no mandate from their branches, which are dead". Sebotsa Mabeta complained that Congress like the ICU failed due to poor leadership. To Mancoe, ANC "constitutional and administrative strength" had declined. Ray Phillips in the mid 1930s claimed it "is dead and can never be what it was in 1913". Respondents to a survey he carried out criticised leaders for financial incompetence. Seme admitted in 1934 that the ANC treasury was bare. According to Basner, Congress "once a mighty mass movement of chiefs, urban workers and tribesmen", survived only in the provinces. Walter Nhlapo in 1935 described Congress as lacking "public support". ANC Secretary Elijah Mdolomba mused that its decline arose when leaders "were enfeebled by wealth". In 1936, police claimed that it was "virtually dead". ANC Secretary James Calata told the 1937 conference it was "insolvent". Reuben Mtirara complained Congress wasted time on "expensive lawsuits" when it should be "in the industrial streets". In 1938, Rolfes Dhlomo lampooned ANC leaders who told people to burn passes but did not burn their own.[18]

Despite this pronounced lethargy, the ANC was not totally inactive. In 1931, 1932 and 1933 it called large-scale anti-pass protests and campaigned for the right to travel on rail coaches rather than cattle trucks. Such protests brought some contact with workers disadvantaged by passes. In May 1931, the National Executive called on all Africans to prepare for passive resistance against passes for women and all branches to organise protests. In June, together with the Johannesburg branch, it held a mass meeting to protest curfews and passes imposed on women. The meeting resolved to call for passive resistance against all passes and broadened the issue to include labour: passes made it difficult for Africans "to bargain with their labour to their advantage" and excluded them from Industrial Conciliation and Wage Acts. "No race of men" could tolerate inability "to bargain with one's labour without restriction". The state had betrayed their trust; the assault on women's dignity was intolerable. The meeting urged Congress to organise a nation-wide "campaign of passive resistance against these iniquitous and barbaric laws".[19]

National and Transvaal Congress and civic leaders including Seme, Matseke, Mabaso, Letanka, Selope Thema, Selby Msimang, Mweli Skota, Champion, and A. B. Xuma came together on 21 June 1931 at the Malay Camp, Johannesburg. After warm-up songs, ANC General Secretary Mweli Skota read out the pass law and argued, somewhat paternalistically; "We men are heads of families, why should women be given passes?" Opposing municipal efforts to force all African women in locations to carry passes, the meeting urged Africans to "not let whites rule us and rule our women", and vowed to keep making noises about women's passes to protect the women.[20]

These actions, paternalist yet meant to be protective, attracted some militant women. Bertha Mkhize, a working tailor, took part in ANC pass protests in 1931 and 1936. It is unclear how she first encountered the ANC, but she was active in the Daughters of Africa, founded in 1937 by Lilian Tshabalala of Driefontein and the Durban Bantu Women's Society with the support of Angeline Dube to promote female economic uplifting.[21] Thus, activists found ways around the torpor induced by Seme. Moreover, in the early 1930s members were still able to employ its press organs to address labour issues.

Bertha Mkhize

The ANC Press and Black Labour, 1930-1933

Most black newspapers accorded some attention to the harsh realities of working lives but those more closely associated with the ANC tended to espouse greater sympathy for black workers. In 1929, Gumede had purchased a controlling share in *Abantu-Batho*, providing the national ANC with an organ to maintain his radicalism. Editors Gumede and Letanka published contributions from many sources; they referred to Garvey as "indeed a dangerous man for all the great powers that are exploiting Africa", compared him with Gandhi, and gave prominence to his speeches. Attracted by growing communist support for national liberation, articles by prominent communists Albert Nzula and Charles Baker were printed. Nzula praised *Abantu-Batho* which "often exposed" these repressive laws. The paper also published League against Imperialism articles.[22]

Abantu-Batho 1930

Abantu-Batho combined fierce criticism of the state with wide coverage of conditions of black working peoples. It reported on ricksha pullers in Durban, where "literally blood money [was] exacted from the sweating suicidal Zulus in return for the privilege of pulling white men about the streets". It forthrightly declared the depression was "manufactured" by a government that put "many black men out of work" and then arrested them for tax default. It drew attention to the torturous life of the average Lichtenburg diamond labourer who suffered from slashed wages and sjambok blows, and whose life compared unfavourably with "that of an ordinary canine Mongrel". *Abantu-Batho* saw it as its "duty as a National organ to send an experienced representative of this paper out to the diggings to investigate the position". Three months later, it followed the story up, condemning the white diggers' practice of not paying their black employees.[23]

The vast discrepancy between "tax in proportion to the wage earning facilities of white and black" was exposed and extension of age pensions to Africans, "the backbone of South African labour", urged; it was "a most wicked and criminal act to cast aside and neglect those people in the days of their infirmity". The editors gave generous publicity to ICU and CPSA. Bunting's opposition to "class laws" underpinning "native policy" was "inspiring". A feature on unionists noted: "We are the supporters" of Congress, but "if Kadalie and Champion have failed to do anything they have not failed to force the heads of the ruling class to think about the economic position" of Africans. *Abantu-Batho* condemned "disgraceful conditions" of farm labourers, forced to work from dawn to dusk for 20 shillings a month and coerced into verbal contracts; it advocated written contracts and "earnestly ask[ed] all Bantu organisations to agitate for [better] conditions" and a minimum wage.[24]

The newspaper condemned suppression of Tonjeni's efforts to organise workers. It publicised the Western Native Township Vigilance Committee's campaign against low wages and high rents. A female correspondent condemned arrests of workers on pass violations: "Is it not wicked to employ the Native in hard toil from morning till sunset, and then not allow him an evening's relax[ation] ... Why should Whites be given our jobs?" Others rued that "very low wages" meant Africans had no chance of social mobility with those convicted of pass offences debarred from the civil service. Ex-ICU leader Modiakgotla urged opposition to rising prejudice by raising *Abantu-Batho's* circulation.[25]

Abantu-Batho referred to the "industrial throttling" of the African, "kept down in the industrial world ... by the cruellest and most unjust legislation". The editor attacked Justice Minister Pirow's repressive actions as the "sort of thing the working classes of this country may expect from him". *Abantu-Batho* thus viewed some of its readers as workers. It did defend the right of African landlords to trade in the face of restrictions. It drew attention to the case of a qualified African dentist fined for practising without white supervision. A writer protested that a black employer, "required to carry ... [the] Daily Labourers Pass", had "less facilities and freedom than his employees". In general, however, *Abantu-Batho* implied radical action was needed to ameliorate conditions. Often it did this in a fashion critical of the inertia of moderates: "Let us admit the fact, that while all classes of natives hate the pass system there is in the ranks of educated and christianised natives a certain number that do not support the throwing away or burning of passes."[26]

Thus, *Abantu-Batho* did not follow Seme's conservative lead but rather continued to promote the radicalism typical of Gumede's presidency. Hence, one could argue that after April 1930 it did not reflect ANC policy. However, many ANC leaders also opposed Seme. In this sense, *Abantu-Batho* provided a forum for members' views. Its writers attacked Seme's "clique", which "excluded the masses" and editors published readers' critical views of the ANC. Champion even accused Seme of harbouring state agents. An editorial unambiguously condemned "a class of traitors among our native leadership".[27]

The editors encouraged radicalism. Gumede remained politically active after 1930. Sesotho editor Letanka, described by Skota as the TAC's "moving spirit", had been gaoled in the 1918 strikes. Reminding readers of this fact, *Abantu-Batho* contrasted this "heroic age" of ANC protests with Seme's inaction, calling for "actual deeds" by leaders. Letanka died in 1932 "penniless ... after years of supporting himself on his small income" from *Abantu-Batho*. Skota claims Letanka "never received nor demanded compensation" for his work and there was "not a candle in his house" when he died. His long-term role on the paper (1912-1932) lent its editorialising a more consistent radicalism that defended labour rights: a consistency emphasised by an editorial stating that whilst the "editorship [had] passed from hand to hand ... policy has never changed".[28]

When Champion and his ICU comrade Jim London joined its staff in 1931, they further bolstered *Abantu-Batho's* labour-orientation. Samuel Masabalala and T. W. Thibedi also were contributors. *Abantu-Batho* dared to suggest that if "the time has come to organise the secret movements we shall not be ashamed to encourage our people to do so". Repeatedly metaphors of class and struggle pointed to the plight of Africans. The Congress paper characterised the 21st anniversary of the Act of Union in terms of cheap labour: its "whole object ... was to reduce the black man to ... a reservoir of cheap labour". Repressive laws it described in terms of their impact on workers. The Service Contract Bill would grant farmers "free license to thrash all the natives".[29]

Whilst *Abantu-Batho* exhibited sensitivity to black worker conditions, it fell far short of being a consistently labour movement or socialist or social democratic newspaper. A wide range of contributors in English and vernacular languages ensured a very eclectic style. Increasingly, advertisements for patent medicines, "Singer Bantu Records" and the services of astrologers filled its pages. *Abantu-Batho* ceased in July 1931 in the face of the draining of its journalists to *Bantu World*. However, its influence helped ensure the survival of ANC radicalism. In 1934, Coka recalled a "tide of nationalism ... led by the truly national newspaper *Abantu-Batho*".[30]

Another contemporary ANC organ also addressed labour issues, if far less radically. Seme himself edited *Ikwezi Le Africa* ("Africa Morning Star", 1928-1932), with contributions from ANC figures such as Msimang, Plaatje, Selope Thema and J. B. Crutse. Seme promoted it, as the masthead read, as "official organ of the ANC". This was more stated than executed, with coverage focusing less on the ANC than on social issues and advertising. Nonetheless, *Ikwezi Le Afrika* tried to follow its motto of "justice and fair play". It complained that Africans "by sheer force of law" would "not be permitted to emerge, to progress, not even to earn a living wage". It criticised Natal Native Teachers' Union inaction in the face of retrenchments and took up the case of a teacher denied employment. Crutse criticised low wages of Vryburg domestic and store workers, accusing employers of using the onset of the depression to cut their wages by half.[31]

Ikwezi Le Afrika objected to the refusal by local governments to advance loans to some Africans merely on the basis that they were "once conspicuous luminaries of the ICU". Efforts by ANC and ICU leaders to unite rival ICU factions, and calls to unite the ANC with ICU remnants it reported favourably. In 1931, J. T. Mosime of Bethal Methodist Church in Schweizer Reneke, wrote to *Ikwezi Le Afrika* praising Henry Maleke, the ICU district secretary, for "miracles". *Ikwezi* protested the increasing sale of black houses by location authorities. Whilst it appears thus to have been concerned with rights of black property-owners, in so doing it drew attention to how the poor were penalised.[32]

In 1932, *African Leader*, established as an unofficial ANC organ, absorbed *Ikwezi Le Afrika*. *African Leader* made use of *Abantu-Batho's* printing press, with its shares sold to members. ANC Secretary Mweli Skota was editor and it attracted other ANC writers, such as Msimang and Halley Plaatje. It claimed to have "not deviated in any way" from *Abantu-Batho's* policy. To this end, it promoted ANC policies.[33]

African Leader published Seme's statements but accused him of making ANC policy "over the heads" of the Executive. It demanded an ANC programme "competent to appeal to the masses". Halley Plaatje wrote that ANC disunity was "partly responsible for our oppression". W. B. Mkasibe, president of the obscure General African Party, claimed ANC leaders neglected youth. Levi Sitebe attacked "bogus African Leaders". The leftism of Gumede conspicuously was absent from its pages but the editors, in expressing scepticism of Seme's reliance on self-help, remarked: "Not all [ANC] members ... can be traders ... Some must for all time fill the role of workers ... Workers as a class have problems peculiar to their class [and] will always need an organisation such as the African National Congress to champion ... political emancipation." They dismissed Seme's idea of worker clubs as "obscure as we think it unwise". They argued instead: "African workers have no desire to remain in the category of cheap labourers." This was, in a sense, correct. Nevertheless, it also suggests distaste for things proletarian. Despite its claim to speak on behalf of workers, *African Leader* agreed with Selope Thema "there can be no nation of workers". It sought the comfort of moderation by claiming that whilst the ANC had formed at times of mass protest, "the conditions which called for mass organisation no longer exist".[34]

Nevertheless, *African Leader* sought "to place before the public the claims of thousands of our unhappy and unfortunate compatriots employed on private farms". It condemned the Native Contract Act that intensified this oppression. The ANC should act on such matters, "otherwise any invitation to farm labourers to join the Congress which does not hold out a definite ideal for the improvement of their lot must be robbery". Thus ANC writers encouraged labourers to join Congress. The editors decried that the rural unemployed were "bundled together and marched to prison". They published the "Xosa Roadmender's Chant", a poetic tribute to worker dignity by an anonymous poet:

Xosa Roadmender's Chant

Hard are the stones on the highway–
Rough as the hide of a crocodile–
Hard but our hammers shall break them
Rough, but our manhood shall make them
Smooth as the wings of a wild dove,
Sleek as the sides of a heifer:
Yes, we shall break them and make them
Smooth for the wheels of the white-man,
Soft for the bare-footed black-man.
   Zamani, Zamani, Sigacuma!
Rough are the laws of our rulers–
Harsh as the quills of the hedgehog,
Hard as the stones on the highway–

Hard, but in patience we labour
With pickaxes moving high mountains,
With hammers crushing hard boulders:
Steadfast and hopeful we struggle
Knowing time's tools shall not falter
In moving hard mountains of hatred,
Breaking bonds more stubborn than bo[u]lders
    Zamani, Zamani, Sigucama!* [*Persevere, persevere! We agree]

Seme later in the decade did make half-hearted efforts to address farm labour, calling a meeting in Wakkerstroom, but in general, his deeds did not match his rhetoric.[35]

Unlike *Abantu-Batho*, *African Leader* gave little direct support to radicals. However, it roused the ire of *Umteteli wa Bantu* for daring to castigate mine owners for employing "the poorest paid people" and giving low compensation to injured labourers. It also published reports on labour demands. Commenting on a mass meeting in Heilbron that demanded a minimum wage, work for all, and compensation for injured workers, *African Leader* commented, "we must ... use all possible means in our power to successfully plead that Parliament should enact legislation embodying these humane demands". It urged joint policy on such issues by the ANC and ICU.[36] Editor Mweli Skota's role in raising all these labour issues in such a forthright manner suggests that characterisations of him as simply a *petit bourgeois* businessperson (see Chapter 7) are in need of revision.

African Leader raised other issues of vital interest to workers. ANC leaders used it to protest the effects of unemployment. It supported bakery workers compelled, by "want of combination", to agree to lower than award wages. It saw an ANC role in industrial organisation: "Congress should within its ambit have a number of trades unions grouped together into a federation controlled and guided by the National Executive." Yet, the ANC organ lamented, if Congress was aware of such conditions, it "allows an opportunity which would bring the workers together as nothing else would, to slip".[37] This epitomised the dilemma workers faced with a concerned, but effete, ANC. Practically, the ANC could not at this stage lead the workers. Neither could *African Leader*, which ceased in 1933. Seme was obliged to call again for the establishment of a national Congress press, but to no avail. The ANC remained without it. Dissatisfied members and workers had to turn to other papers as a source of information on African political and industrial struggles.[38]

The above evidence suggests that a one-dimensional view of the ANC from 1930-1936 as merely Seme's private domain does not tally with the broader range of opinions expressed by ANC figures. Many of these people sympathised with workers, determinedly affirmed the rights of these workers and their unions, and helped continue ANC interest in working-class issues in a period when more conservative leaders threatened to sever this link. However, they did not envisage an independent role for black workers in politics, and were not directly representative of workers. Nevertheless, the ANC and its press was a major medium through which support for black workers was publicised. The ANC sought to represent a national constituency, a growing portion of who were workers, and helped fill a vacuum caused by the weakness of African unions. ANC representations on behalf of labour indicate some ANC contact with black workers.

ANC Rivals and Black Labour

ANC contact with workers was impeded by black poverty, self-imposed barriers to mobilising groups such as women, organisational inefficiency, inept leadership, and especially the activities of rival groups which attracted key personnel away from Congress, and tended to make it less attractive, both to workers, and to radicals claiming to represent workers. Relations between workers and the ANC played out in these groups, whose fluctuating fortunes influenced the status of the ANC among Africans.

During mass campaigns or electoral contests, and in internal ANC politics, the ANC and CPSA stood in either political alliance or antagonism. There were direct ties, expressed through the work of individual communists, some of them workers, who were ANC members. Without the ANC, they may have become increasingly sectarian. Without the communists, the ANC may have failed to build a stronger worker base in the next decade. Thus, a symbiotic relationship began to grow.

ANC-CPSA relations expressed themselves in a variety of seemingly contradictory situations. The cooperation developing during Gumede's presidency turned to mutual hostility in the early 1930s. CPSA sectarianism drove its membership into sharp decline—perhaps as low as 60 in 1932, 150 in 1933 and remaining less than 300 by 1939. Despite its small membership, the CPSA exerted influence among some black workers through unions. Often this was the work of members with ANC ties. On the Rand, the party maintained tenuous links with workers through the remnants of AFTU unions, among which ANC members such as Marks were active. The CPSA appealed to black workers through campaigns. This related, indirectly, to the ANC. ANC-led anti-pass protests since 1913 had established a tradition of resistance utilised by CPSA leaders. Communists gained personal contacts and standing in the community from their ANC membership that in turn could facilitate their CPSA recruiting. For example, CPSA Cape Town Secretary Lee Leepile was active in the ANC (WP). The party aimed distribution of its press at ANC gatherings.[39]

Memberships often overlapped. Basner, a CPSA member, recalled that many black party members had been ANC members before joining. Few such members were not associated with the ANC. However, in the early 1930s, CPSA or Seme hostility imperilled these ties. Many ANC leaders whom Basner "encountered in Mrs Maxeke's [aid] office complained of being slandered ... by the Communists".[40]

Ideological tendencies within the CPSA tended to group around a weaker faction, which downplayed the existence of a "black bourgeoisie" in South Africa, and was generally in favour of united action with the ANC, and a dominant group generally hostile to Congress. *Umsebenzi* in 1930 characterised the ANC as "an 'organisation' of 'leaders'". Even Gumede was dubbed "timid", and "surrounded by 'leaders' who ... support 'gods in the sky and capitalists on earth'". At the height of this sectarianism, in 1931, a CPSA resolution labelled Congress as "a servant of the imperialist bourgeoisie ... a committee of Native petty bourgeoisie. Organisationally it has no existence, but it is still able to wield considerable influence." In 1934, the Comintern instructed the CPSA to conduct a systematic struggle against Congress; the CPSA summed up ANC policy as one of "patient submission" to oppressors. "Comrade Mbutje" denounced "racial and hypocritical attacks" by Port Elizabeth ANC "good boy" leaders "ignorant of the oppression meted out to natives". Such views made formal contact difficult.[41]

Communists emphasised the tenuous nature of the ANC commitment to workers. However, CPSA influence among workers also was limited, by its focus on doctrinaire, rather than industrial, issues. The Comintern in 1930 judged that the CPSA had "little or no contact" with miners. From 1931-1935, the party press, in Kotane's opinion, became so turgid that it was "no more sold and read by the masses". The CPSA in 1934 stated that ANC leaders "try to make out that they are the only real defenders of the toiling masses". It added "Unfortunately many people still believe them", thus conceding a residual ANC influence among many Africans who looked to it as a champion of their rights. Congress, the CPSA argued, did nothing to stop the introduction of anti-worker laws, and schemes such as Seme's African Congress Clubs served not the working people but "the Native bourgeoisie". The ANC "of 1917-1920 that organised strikes ... is no more". The ANC (and ICU) were not, argued the

CPSA's Gomas, "doing anything practical" to fight white labour favouritism. Given the relative conservatism and inactivity of the ANC under Seme, these criticisms have some validity. In spite of this, it is important to appreciate the ambiguity of leaders forced to walk a tightrope between the never-too-distant prospects of even harsher state repression and the possibility of extracting minor concessions. Thus, just as Seme was praising Hertzog for laying the "foundation of a great temple of justice ... for all peoples", his paper *Ikwezi Le Afrika* was warning Africans to expect nothing from white rule.[42]

Some black communists joined in condemnation of the ANC. J. B. Marks was particularly scathing about "corrupt leadership" of Congress, and characterised its members as "businessmen and traders". There was vitriolic labelling of leaders: Seme and Thaele were "political adventurers ... scum of the African intellectuals". However, some black communists, especially those associated with the ANC, were able to move beyond the narrow confines of sectarianism and combine criticism with support. Marks knew "thousands of workers" had "once comprised the ranks of the ICU and ANC". He admitted ANC activities proved that it existed "ideologically but also practically". He pointed to "a tremendous revival of national reformism". Albert Nzula, writing from Moscow after Gumede's defeat in 1930, criticised the elitism and "national reformism" of ANC leaders, but conceded there was still some internal pressure for change in Congress, and argued that the CPSA should still work with the ANC.[43]

So did Kotane, though he appears to have temporarily given the ANC up for dead. In 1933, he attacked "pusillanimous policies" of "Native reformist organisations". In 1934, he accused Congress of "idle debating", yet he was more and more convinced there was "no Native bourgeoisie", only a petty bourgeoisie "more oppressed and exploited than it itself oppresses and exploits". In 1937, he wrote that the ANC convention was "a flop" attended by only 27 delegates, but hastened to add that remedial measures were possible. This was partly a strategic decision. He stated in 1934 that the thrust of fascism in South Africa "will primarily be against the national liberation struggle". Kotane gave great emphasis to national liberation. He told CPSA leaders in 1938: "I am first an African and then a Communist." He viewed the ANC and CPSA as complementary. Consequently, many ANC leaders regarded him with respect: Calata thought him "very loyal to the ANC"; Z. K. Matthews felt he "never let communism stand in [the] way of nationalism".[44]

Other black communists retained ties with the ANC. Despite his sectarian utterances, Marks continued to work in Congress. Makabeni and Thibedi, expelled in CPSA purges, became more active in unions but stayed close to Congress. Ngedlane helped form an African Vigilance Association in opposition to Advisory Boards. Mofutsanyana worked for unity. At a mass protest against beer halls in Bloemfontein in 1934, held "under the auspices of the militant section" of the ANC, he called for CPSA-ANC unity. He had a broad conception of black workers, in 1937 arguing that "so-called African 'intellectuals' are definitely workers. They are only 'intellectuals' in the sense that they have a bit more formal education than the masses." In formulating class in these terms, he facilitated, in theory, ties with the ANC. This is not to say that leftists who saw the need for unity downplayed ANC weaknesses. In 1937, Mofutsanyana viewed the ANC as an "empty" shell. Another point in common was joint opposition to international repression of Africans. The 1935 Italian invasion of Ethiopia prompted large protests supported by both groups, which also denounced British deposing of Bamangwato Chief Tshekedi Khama, and attempts by South Africa to absorb the High Commission Protectorates.[45]

By 1936, the CPSA had moved away from sectarianism to a united front policy. Attitudes to Congress began to soften, influenced by Kotane's election as CPSA Secretary and a resurgence of ANC militancy in opposition to the Hertzog Bills. Party conferences now were concluded by singing not just *The Internationale* but *Nkosi Sikilel' i Afrika*. The broad-front body *Ikaka Laba Sebenzi* ("Shield of the Workers") and the monthly journal *Umvikeli-Thebe* ("African Defender") built bridges to African national movements. Gaur Radebe, an ANC activist (in the early 1940s influential with Nelson Mandela) was Secretary of *Ikaka*, which provided unemployed relief. *Umvikeli-Thebe* adopted a stridently African nationalist stance and targeted black teachers, industrial workers, and peasants.[46]

Trotskyite groups, which included the Workers Party and Communist League, recruited only a few African members, such as Thibedi and Daniel Koza. Thibedi formed a short-lived Communist League of Africa in 1932. Trotskyites also tended to denigrate the ANC. A 1934 document stated: "We must not pander to the cravings of petty bourgeois Native nationalists." They solicited a letter from Trotsky in 1935, in which he urged the defence of what he saw as a progressive ANC from white oppressors, whilst at the same time criticising ANC "inability ... to achieve ... even its own demands".[47]

The defection of discontented ANC activists to other groups, such as the Independent ANC or W. B. Mkasibe's General African Party, weakened but did not destroy Congress. Similarly, the participation of ANC members in various non-ANC conferences gave them another forum to expose harsh labour practices. At the 1930 Non-European Conference in Cape Town, congressmen Abner Mtimkulu, J. S. Likhing, and James Thaele all spoke out against oppression of workers. Champion, Selope Thema, Mahabane, Elias and 'Mote took part in the 1931 Non-European Conference which condemned the Native Service Contract Bill and called for a minimum wage. Unionists Champion, Makabeni, Kadalie, and Tyamzashe remained ANC members. In 1932, prompted by ANC leaders Likhing and Mahabane, the African Christian Ministers' Association took up the dismissal of black railway labourers.[48]

In the 1930s, liberal groups such as the Joint Councils and South African Institute of Race Relations (SAIRR) and state-appointed bodies such as Advisory Boards were, in Basner's words, responsible for "siphoning off" ANC members. Many ANC leaders were prominent in the Councils, including Mahabane in Kimberley, Abner Mtimkulu and A. J. Sililo in Durban, Calata in Cradock, Isaiah Bud-M'belle in Pretoria, Bennett Ncwana in King Williams' Town, Andrew Frank Pendla in Port Elizabeth, and Mapikela in Bloemfontein. Mapikela and Godlo were treasurer and president respectively of the Location Advisory Boards Congress (ABC). Sililo was active in both the NNC and the ABC.[49]

Some congressmen used these forums to address issues of concern to workers. Selby Msimang in 1934 presided over a Sophiatown Joint Council meeting on poor living conditions. Mtimkulu told a 1932 Joint Council conference that unemployed Africans "were afraid to ask magistrates for relief lest the police should harass them". In 1931, he told the NEC that Africans suffered under the twin rigours of "civilized labour" policy and unemployment. Speaking of the situation in Ndabeni and Langa, he was sufficiently aware of worker conditions to detail precisely their low wages and high rents. He outlined how "coloured" labour preference policies reduced African employment opportunities and how job practices discriminated against African building workers by forcing them to obtain cumbersome bureaucratic approvals before gaining work. Isaiah Bud-M'belle, still a member of the ANC Executive, in 1931 addressed a Joint Council conference in Pretoria on inadequate transport for workers, and raised the same issue before the NEC. He believed in the dignity of labour, in 1935 eulogising Jane Ntingana, "an ordinary washerwoman ... who never looked at that occupation with contempt". However, his moderate politics were apparent when he merely encouraged "other African domestic servants to try and carry on their duties to the satisfaction of their mistresses".[50]

The U.S.-funded Joint Councils had better resources than the ANC. They often discussed labour conditions and drew up detailed estimates of cost of living expenses. In 1932, the Zoutpansberg and the Kimberley Joint Councils opposed the Native Service Contract Bill. In the same year, the Pietermaritzburg Joint Council claimed credit for raising the wages of *togt* labourers. Joint Councils in Ladysmith and Potchefstroom helped raise low black wages. In East London, the Joint Council monitored unemployment and wage cuts. A delegation of black workers even attended their May 1936 meeting. In 1932, the Port Elizabeth Joint Council raised funds that created relief work for black unemployed and in 1934 black residents of Korsten addressed the Council on forced removals and wages.[51]

Given such commitment, the Joint Councils naturally attracted ANC members interested in labour matters. The Kroonstad Joint Council gained ANC-ICU veterans 'Mote and Sello, though both retained a loyalty to the ANC and ICU. Part of the attraction of the Councils to such veterans of the working-class movement was the resources that enabled them to put forward in the 1930s a large number of detailed and impressive recommendations and submissions on behalf of black workers.[52]

Involvement of ANC figures in these groups was not uncritical. In 1931, Isaiah Bud-M'belle, a Pretoria Advisory Board founder member, felt the Boards were very unpopular among Africans due to the imposition of a majority of their members by municipal officials. Others made a connection between ANC decline and the rise of Joint Councils. Archie M'belle asserted in 1930 that the Council movement had been a "calamity" for African political leadership. He blamed them for African capitulation to the Native Administration Act, and saw in Gumede's 1930 defeat a revolt, not merely against (white) communists, but against (white) Joint Council influence in Congress. In 1932, he claimed the ANC was as "dead as the dodo" due to the work of Joint Council "agents". Another writer claimed the Uitenhage Council "despise[d] ... semi-educated or totally illiterate" Africans. In 1932, *Umteteli wa Bantu* noted that Kroonstad's African community was "impressed" by attempts to resuscitate the ANC for, whereas the Council had "captured most of the Bantu intelligentsia", now the "Natives are again asking when will the I.C.U. or the National Congress start an agitation for increased wages". This evidence reveals some Africans had an expectation the ANC could take a lead on wages. The SAIRR also paid close attention to workers, but chose only one African, D. D. T. Jabavu, for its Council in 1932. African nationalists such as 'Mote found such domination stultifying.[53]

The rise of these liberal bodies coincided with Seme's inaction on labour issues but they lacked power; their main tactic was to lobby government and industry. In protest at the "civilised labour policy", the Port Elizabeth Joint Council resolved merely to consult with the Chamber of Commerce.

Effective control of Councils remained in white hands. The East London Joint Council in 1933 had no black officials; it effetely lamented: "We cannot point to any decisive improvements in the Locations." When the Joint Councils and Advisory Boards, as Rich shows, were unable to stem deterioration of workers and traders' conditions, black leaders turned to bodies such as the ANC. In 1933, Kroonstad Advisory Board leader N. M. Mtshumi called for the ANC's rebuilding. 'Mote, who earlier had forged ties with farm workers, in 1938 turned away from the Joint Council to focus on the ANC. By 1939, many activists had abandoned these bodies, increasingly seeing a revived Congress as capable of tackling African problems.[54]

The ANC faced other rivals at this time, in the form of state structures and ideologies that strove to wrest any allegiance that Africans may have had to Congress. Notions of loyalty to the white nation-state and Empire complemented liberal ideas. In the 1930s, sections of the state apparatus still quite vigorously promoted the British Empire among Africans; the 1934 visit of Prince George and tours of rural areas by the governor general and ministers helped keep alive rival sources of legitimacy.[55]

The government re-convened its Native Conferences, in abeyance since 1927, in December 1930. State officials closely controlled these meetings but ANC figures such as Mahabane used the occasion to criticise state policies and draw attention to the conditions of Africans, including workers and the unemployed. The ANC also retained an influence through other leaders. At the 1930 Native Conference, Richard Godlo attacked the Native Service Contract Bill as the introduction of "slave conditions".[56]

The onset of the Hertzog Bills, aiming to abolish the Cape African franchise, in 1936 underlined the ineffectiveness of state-supported groups. The ANC held nationwide protests. Many Africans spoke out against the Native Representation Bill. Selope Thema described it as destroying the "principle of common citizenship". A. B. Xuma declared publicly, "there can be no compromise on the people's franchise".[57]

Two important bodies resulted from these moves. Xuma, Selope Thema and Mahabane convened the black unity All-African Convention in December 1935. At the meeting, Mofutsanyana reported on farm labour. J. B. Marks urged an end to "blundering exploitation" of Africans, while normally placid Mahabane predicted revolution if the Bills proceeded. Membership overlapped. The 1937 All-African Convention elected ANC figures: Selby Msimang (secretary) and Mahabane (vice president), as well as two future ANC presidents, Xuma and James Moroka. Msimang proposed detailed recommendations for the protection of farm workers. The ANC had a supportive, but jealous stance towards the All-African Convention. However, the latter failed to gain mass following. By the late 1930s, most ANC figures had gravitated back to Congress.[58]

ANC and labour movement officials also cooperated in electoral politics. Marks campaigned for Basner, who stood unsuccessfully for the Senate in 1937 as a CPSA candidate. Mofutsanyana, who campaigned for the CPSA but also was active in the ANC, similarly worked with Basner. Both, according to Basner, felt "they might act as a spur towards reviving" Congress. 'Mote supplied Basner with lists of "teachers, self-employed artisans, clergy, general labourers, hawkers" who had been ICU and ANC office-bearers or organisers—more evidence of the breadth of ANC contacts among workers.[59]

The 1936 Native Representation Act abolished the African franchise and offered only indirect advisory rights in a new Natives' Representative Council (NRC). The ANC was ambiguous about the NRC, at times criticizing it as a powerless token, calling for its boycott, at other times supporting NRC campaigns by ANC members. Many elected to the NRC were moderate ANC members. It is apparent from the records of NRC meetings that councillors did not forget worker conditions, despite the fact that the majority of those elected in 1937 were men of some wealth. Emboldened by an apparent greater tolerance of (rhetorical) militancy within its confines, many spoke out on labour issues. Selope Thema drew attention to farm workers on "reserves ... so congested that people today are forced to go out and work". A motion supported by William Ndhlovu, a Congress founder, stated that due to low wages, Africans "are practically compelled to resort to thieving". Selope Thema urged formation of a commission into African wages with a view to their improvement. He justified wage rises by claiming: "Africans are a fertile uncultivated home market to which the eyes of the business men ... should turn." Outside NRC meetings, he also called for higher wages, as at a 1938 Bethlehem meeting.[60]

The recognition of African unions became an issue in the NRC. Public opinion regarded Godlo and Selope Thema, both ANC members, as more radical members of the First Council. Godlo successfully moved in 1939 that the proposed non-statutory recognition of African unions be only as a temporary expedient until African employees came under the Industrial Conciliation Act. He consulted with African Commercial and Distributive Workers' Union Chairman, Daniel Koza, who "feared that the Council would accept the proposed half-way recognition". Godlo "eased [Koza's] fears" by explaining that they would not countenance any move "not in accordance with the wishes of the workers themselves", and would only support "proper recognition" of unions. The NRC, like the ANC, was acting here like a social democratic reformist party in supporting labour demands, but within the bounds of the system. This was irrespective of whether or not NRC members were happy to comply with union demands, or simply eager to accommodate them for electoral support. That Godlo bothered to meet Koza indicates that some contact with workers and members occurred. He also communicated to the NRC resolutions of the conference of the Non-European Trade Union Co-ordinating Committee, which called for full union recognition and the right to strike.[61]

Even businessmen on the NRC who were also ANC members stood up for black labour rights. Richard Baloyi and Mapikela moved in the NRC that African wages in state enterprises not be less than those in private industry. This and similar motions frequently were argued on the basis of the positive spin-off such moves would have on African business in stimulating greater purchasing power. African business could not advance without exploiting African workers. However, neither could it do so with an impoverished proletariat. In this sense, it is not surprising to see African employers supporting African labour. They also had to respond to demands of their constituents. Moreover, their ANC experience sensitised them to labour issues as Congress regularly raised such matters. Mapikela, as noted, had earlier working-class influences. Baloyi began his working life as a taxi driver, before becoming a taxi owner in 1925 and then a bus owner: he was to run foul of workers in Alexandra in the 1940s over bus fare rises. In 1938, Baloyi made his stamp as a successful businessperson by jointly sponsoring the major African soccer cup, renamed the Moroka-Baloyi Cup; one social venue that united African workers and propertied strata. Mapikela stated: "Wages paid by the Railways to the Natives are a disgrace, and the Native employees in the Post Office receive the lowest wages." Even Dube in this debate stated that black people "are very poorly paid all over ... [Their] wages ... should be increased". Representations by the NRC had some effect: in 1938, Orange Free State African teachers had allowances unpaid since 1932 restored. Other NRC members with ANC links were Alexander Jabavu (an ex-ICU official) and Bertram Xiniwe, who became Cape ANC president.[62]

The most consistent champions of black workers in the NRC were ANC figures. These non-workers spoke in the name of the proletariat, but for the purpose of class reconciliation. They may have had profits in mind, but objectively placed before government the need to improve the conditions of black workers.

The appeal of rival bodies tended to limit direct ANC contact with workers, but also offered indirect opportunities for ANC figures to gain new insights into labour problems. Given that there were yet no structures in place inside the ANC to mobilise the mass of black workers, it is not surprising that rival groups made some inroads into ANC support. Nevertheless, the ANC was not, and did not seek to be, a trade union, or communist party, or a government advisory body. Its effectiveness did not revolve around its ability to mobilise workers in a trade union manner, or its ability to propagate socialism, or give advice to government. If ANC organisational weaknesses are accepted for what they were—a poorly developed and under-financed broad African political movement—then its labour ties are more clearly appreciated. None of its rivals succeeded in posing a serious long-term alternative to the ANC: the CPSA suffered extreme factionalism; the ICU crumbled; the All-African Convention failed; state-sponsored bodies increasingly lacked legitimacy among Africans. In the absence of any other effective national black political force, the ANC revived in the late 1930s out of necessity.

ANC Re-Birth, 1936-1940

In 1936, the ANC, the once "mighty mass movement of chiefs, urban workers and tribesmen", began to revive. This re-birth in large part was due to opposition aroused by the Hertzog Bills, which eliminated the Cape franchise. In attacking the Bills, Msimang declared: "We must have intense organisation and persistent education of the masses ... We may live to see, if we have the ... determination to do [so] ... the history of the overthrow of the Russian Empire by the governed repeated." These were extraordinary words, coming from an anti-communist. Nevertheless, they illustrate the depth of emotion felt against the Bills, which was to reverberate in efforts to revive the ANC.[63]

The resolutions of the 1936 ANC national conference reflected growing unease with the Hertzog Bills. Congress urged a widening of the African franchise, opposed government practice of nominating chiefs, and called for abolition of the pass laws. The conference passed a resolution from the Cradock branch favouring home brewing instead of municipal beer halls. It also passed motions requesting Parliament to introduce old-age pensions for Africans and for regulation of African wages under the Industrial and Conciliation Act and in keeping with the urbanisation of Africans. [64]

Organisational re-thinking accompanied a transitional period of leadership under Reverends Mahabane (who ousted Seme as President in 1937) and James Calata (Secretary-General 1936-1949). Calata and Mahabane toured all provinces, and discussed problems of branches and recruited members. Treasurer Richard Baloyi attended many meetings, urging "complete re-organisation". Congress "recovered a degree of organisational coherence" and stability laying the basis for future growth.[65]

From 1937-1939, there were vigorous attempts by active members to recapture the wide public support that Congress had enjoyed in earlier years. Selope Thema and Baloyi convened a Conference of African Leaders in August 1937. They formed a Reef and Pretoria Coordinating Committee charged with reviving the ANC. It represented many political trends, from moderate black thought to unionism and communism. Actively involved were communists J. B. Marks, as secretary, Mofutsanyana, Josie Mpama, and Gaur Radebe, as well as anti-communists Calata, Ramohanoe, and Reverend Samuel Tema, who acted as chairperson. Marks, presenting its report, called for Congress to become a "broad and powerful national movement of the Africans". Congress called revival meetings up and down the country and began to better co-ordinate some African protests. The collaboration on this committee and later in the ANC of labour activists such as Marks and Mofutsanyana with more moderate ANC leaders suggests they relatively quickly rebuilt bridges from the ANC to the labour movement destroyed under Seme. Mofutsanyana was "Secretary for Labour and Social Welfare" in Mahabane's "Cabinet" and Champion held the portfolio of "Lands and Locations", although these positions were largely nominal given the weaknesses of Congress.[66]

Part of this re-thinking was a more flexible tactical approach. Leaders recognised that, given ANC weakness, it would be organisational suicide to remain aloof from other groups. Mahabane urged Africans to unite not only in the ANC, but also in "our other Organisations, industrial or other". Baloyi stated: "At this stage of its struggle for resurrection [the ANC] must adopt a very pliable line that will enable it to collaborate with all the existing organisations." Calata, in a 1938 letter urging TAC unity, observed that three views prevailed in Congress: those advocating younger leaders; those in favour of experienced leaders; and those promoting localised groups, such as unions, workers' clubs and co-operatives. He suggested members "make room for all three".[67]

Delegates and visitors with known sympathy for, or experience with, workers attended the December 1937 Jubilee ANC conference. These included: Cape ANC organiser James Ngojo and TAC activist Levi Mvabaza (both arrested in 1918 strikes); S. P. Matseke; Sam Hoho (radical Independent ANC organiser); NRC Members Mapikela, Baloyi and Selope Thema; communists Radebe, Kotane, and Mofutsanyana; J. J. S. Monaheng (ICU Bloemfontein); and Senators Ballinger and Rheinallt Jones, who recently had defended black labour rights. These moderate and radical supporters of the rights of black workers continued to articulate, if unevenly, labour interests within Congress.[68]

Seme, in his 1937 presidential address, viewed the ANC as "a national movement, not an organization". The conference saw his demise but structural problems remained. African-American Ralph Bunche, who at this time believed in class solutions to social problems, attended the conference. He was critical of the timid and ineffective ANC leadership. His notes reveal some of the opinions of ANC members. The conference was "a ridiculous waste of time", sentiments echoed by a female delegate. Kotane told Bunche that many Africans were disillusioned with the ANC.[69]

Part of the reason for this continuing radical dissatisfaction with the rate of change in the ANC was a lingering hostility to radicals by its leaders. Calata was suspicious of communists, though he placed ANC unity first. He told the 1937 conference that Congress was against sectarianism and needed a "leader who will look upon Christ as the Supreme leader!" Despite radical impatience, the ANC kept intact its broadly based policies that were capable of appealing to workers holding various political opinions. Moreover, it was apparent to some radicals, such as Edwin Mofutsanyana, that a purely proletarian-based strategy faced problems; that South Africa had "no homogeneous proletariat".[70]

ANC leaders remained intent on revival. By 1938, the ANC was paying greater attention to labour issues. Its 1938 convention passed motions on wages. One resolution requested legislation for regulation of African wages and called on government to cover African workers under Wage Boards and Conciliation Acts. Another called on Congress to combat social problems such as malnutrition, high mortality, and delinquency by "improvement of the wage level of all African workers in all classes of labour and work". The ANC also requested Parliament to extend pensions to African workers. These proposals essentially were the *same* as those advanced by black unions. However, they were still, as in previous years, couched in respectful terms, *requesting* not *demanding*. There remained a hope for a more gentrified future for all "completely detribalised and industrialised and urbanised" Africans to have the right to "erect Homes". Yet, this was in accord with the needs of workers desperately short of housing. Locations should cease being reservoirs to serve white labour needs, stated the conference, which identified the proletarian, or toiling, nature of most Africans in South Africa. At the same time, members sought to escape this fate, pledging to "struggle for the elevation of the African people from the position of mere labourers … to their rightful place". Delegates also floated the idea of a cooperative bank under Congress's auspices. In general, however, conference resolutions now exuded a more militant tone. The ANC must "make a determined effort to fight for a radical change in basic government policy". To achieve its policies, the ANC actively sought co-operation of all African organisations, including unions. A resolution urging all Africans to join the ANC even incorporated the perception that workers were very much part of Congress, referring to "this conference comprising workers and intellectuals of the African Race". J. B. Marks declared: "Labour was the most important weapon of attack that the African possesses."[71]

The turn to labour was evident in the ANC National Executive's composition: of 14 members attending, two were communists with strong union links (Mofutsanyana and Marks), and another three previously had openly declared their support for worker struggles (Mvabaza, Matseke and James Mpinda). The others were of more moderate views although Mpinda, now a small businessman (like fellow executive members Mapikela and Baloyi), had been an ICU leader arrested for his role in a 1925 Bloemfontein strike, and Mweli Skota, Selope Thema, Oliphant, Mahabane, and Calata, had at one time or another supported, at least in words, ANC resolutions for better labour conditions.[72]

J. B. Marks appears to have been instrumental in successfully pushing this more militantly pro-labour stance. The fact he launched Congress proceedings with an address, that he also deftly combined labour with national issues, claiming the channelling of labour would bring African freedom nearer, and that conference resolutions reflected his arguments all attest to his rising prestige in part accrued from his organising work. Like Kotane, he was prepared to work closely with Calata, who acknowledged their dedication to the ANC. Marks also was frank about past ANC failures: they had been too abstract, unable to lead the masses, and subject to disunity and inferiority complexes. Debate on the floor of Congress after Marks's address included discussion of the low wages of Mazelspoort water industry workers; one delegate urged Congress to educate these workers.[73]

This tilt to the workers' cause bore some fruit in that organisations concerned with labour began to look to Congress. As I noted in Chapter 2, domestic workers were notoriously difficult to organise. By the 1930s, however, the expansion of the female domestic workforce prompted action. ANC activist Bransby Ndobe attempted to form such a union in 1930. In 1938, W. J. Mvula, organiser of the short-lived African Domestic Servants League, urged Congress to oppose passes for women that would see them "subjugated below the level of slaves". This eclectic "union" was re-organised by political activist Gilbert Coka in 1939, by which time it included Ms E. T. Daba as organiser and Coka and S. K. Tutu as committee members, with soccer impresario and Bantu Sports Club secretary Dan Twala as Chairman. Briefly involved were ANC/ union leaders Gana Makabeni, Dan Tloome, and Nkagaleng Nkadimeng. Little came of the body, but it is interesting that ANC figures were involved, and that it looked to the ANC for support. However, we know little of actual contacts between domestic workers and Congress.[74]

In this period, ANC women began to speak out on labour issues. Mrs Peters, a delegate to the 1937 ANC conference, moved a resolution in favour of black worker rights, as did Mrs Benjamin in 1938. Some participants, such as the communist Josie Mpama (Palmer)—active in the CPSA and until the late 1930s spouse of Mofutsanyana—called for militant action. At the 1938 conference, Lily Nikiwe of Port Elizabeth not only advanced "several interesting arguments" to plead that ANC women, who were "deeply interested" in African politics, be allowed "to come along and assist" Congressmen, but also raised working-class issues, arguing that family disintegration, crime and starvation were due to low wages. Congress, she urged, should become "acquaint[ed] with the masses". Leaders should "attract the [church] ministers into Congress for behind them strode the masses". Growing female interest in Congress is evident in a speech by National Council of African Women president Mrs G. Maseke, who urged delegates to return to their branches and build self-reliance. The Council, meeting in tandem in Bloemfontein, passed a similar motion to that of Congress supporting home brewing of beer.[75]

Mpama, previously a domestic worker, was the most prominent African woman communist leader of the period. Her ex-spouse, Edwin Mofutsanyana, in a 1981 interview, recalled Mpama had also been active in the ANC, adding there were other black women in the party. Congress "did not have many women in it. That has always been a difficult thing, even in the Party." Epainette Moerane, after studying at Lovedale and Adams Colleges, became a teacher in Durban. She joined the CPSA in 1937 and was active in anti-rent campaigns. It is unclear if she was in touch with the ANC in these early activist years.[76]

Gender imbalance therefore weakened potential ANC strength and contacts with women workers. However, some women circumvented sexist discrimination and succeeded in raising labour issues within the ANC. Yet a basic contradiction in the historical research into African women in politics remains. Mpama, in a 1977 interview, argued that African women, even from as early as her experiences in Potchefstroom in 1926, were more active than were men in organising political meetings, court defences, and arranging deputations. Greater female involvement in politics in the 1930s is possible but, as Cynthia Kros notes, the gender and ideological bias of sources such as *Bantu World* makes it harder to detect this.[77]

Bhekizizwe Peterson stresses the "fragility" of the tiny black elite that inclined it to ideological, rather than class, pursuits such as writing for *Bantu World*. Yet this shying away from class conflict was encouraged by the paper's commercial orientation and white ownership and hastened by the demise of those black-owned newspapers close to the ANC such as *Abantu-Batho* that had been willing to raise labour exploitation.[78] As the decade wore on, and into the next, ANC discourses increasingly would took place outside the realm of mass-market newspapers or cultural domains, more directly in the political sphere.

By 1939, the ANC Executive could proudly point to "more activity this year throughout the country and a clear sign of a general revival ... Congress is not going to die ... [It] is moving ahead, but ... must adjust its policy to suit the new conditions and attract the younger man." Mahabane told ANC meetings on the Rand in early 1938 that Congress policies would continue to demand extension of pensions to African workers, a living wage for Africans, and abolition of industrial colour bars. He urged unity in Congress, and "any of our other Organisations, industrial or other".[79]

One instance of this gathering unity was a joint ANC-ABC deputation to the Minister for Native Affairs in Cape Town in 1939. The inclusion of Kotane and Marks in the ANC delegation indicated a definite, if still slight, working-class influence in higher ANC circles. Neither man was part of the deputation at first. Kotane was included when ANC (WP) President Alfred Coto did not appear; Marks was co-opted. The deputation agreed to use the 1938 ANC conference resolutions (including the need for higher wages for Africans) as its terms of reference. In caucus, they debated which issues to prioritise. They resolved to raise the following, in order of importance: education (including teachers' salaries), franchise, land, wages, locations, beer, pass laws, poll tax, and pensions and social welfare, and chose Richard Godlo (ABC/ANC) to address wages. A. J. Sililo (NRC/ABC/Natal Congress) would tackle the minister on welfare. Mahabane, Matseke, Ngojo, Godlo, Mapikela, Ramohane and Sililo addressed an associated public meeting held in Langa.[80]

The issue of low wages crept into speeches of the deputation. Mahabane inferred that Congress could gain "first hand knowledge from the people themselves" of their grievances. He chose to comment firstly on wages. "Most of the ills and evils" which Africans suffered "today could be attributed to the low wages paid to them", he argued. This extended "even to the problem of excessive consumption of Kaffir-beer", which "could be solved to a great extent if Native wages were improved". Abner Mtimkulu spoke on African teachers' salaries, which he considered too low. Teachers were "discontented" and lacked wage increments and pensions. Sililo spoke of Africans "contribution" to the country. However, their low wages meant they could not aid their poor. He gave "graphic descriptions of how Africans in old age suffer through ill health caused by hard labour", and asked for the extension of aged and sick pensions to Africans, a request that was rejected by the Minister on cost. Speakers did not directly challenge wage slavery, or even low black wages as such, preferring to try to gain some moral (or indeed financial) capital by claiming a share of the economic results of low wages. However, their intervention was an indirect indictment of the system of low wages. The Minister was obliged to read a memorandum from the Department of Labour rationalising low wages and confirming steps to recognise "certain organisations of Native workers". The ANC deputation was one more form of pressure on government to recognise African unions.[81]

In rural areas, the ANC's small size and the vast numbers of unorganised working peoples limited ties to workers. State structures increasingly co-opted chiefs and their participation in Congress declined. Nevertheless, not all chiefs simply abandoned either Congress or workers. Basner saw Congress as remaining strong in rural areas where chiefs retained loyalty to Congress. Chief A. V. Coto was Cape Congress president in the 1930s. Chief George Kama (Middledrift) was national "Governor". Chief Mini retained ties to both the ICU and ANC. Sibindi Zulu, Cetshwayo's grandson, was gaoled for three months in 1939 for inciting Natal labourers to strike. Chief Ramaube stated in 1938, at a Benoni reception in his honour, that he was "a staunch supporter" of Congress. Seme was ANC Secretary of Chiefs and in 1938-1939 called meetings of Transvaal chiefs in Marabastad to discuss their rights and "economic needs" of Africans. In the 1930s, as Bonner shows, Transvaal chiefs were deeply involved in intra-Congress politics (see also Chapter 8).[82]

The proceedings of these ANC conferences and delegations reveal the rough balance of class forces in the organisation. "Middle class" figures such as Seme or Mahabane continued throughout the 1930s to monopolise peak leadership positions. However, the continued vocal presence of radicals helped keep labour issues on the agenda of Congress, and probably inclined moderates repeatedly to mention such issues at gatherings. Nevertheless, the moderates themselves, particularly those with a background of support for black labour, presented their own agenda to protect black workers from the worst excesses of white society, as can be seen from a closer analysis of their views.

ANC National Leaders and Labour Issues

Seme's conservatism and government and liberal pressures on black leaders to avoid contact with radical socialists contributed to a decline in ANC ties with politicised black workers. Yet concentration on Seme distracts attention from the views of others more sympathetic to the predicament of labour. Many national ANC leaders expressed broad empathy for black workers. *African Leader* in 1933 published selected comments of ANC leaders that encapsulate this sympathy. Selope Thema criticised the "meagre wages paid to Native men". Selby Msimang gave details of their low incomes. Even Dube stated: "On the labour field my people are shockingly accommodated, badly cared for, and badly paid, and I plead most earnestly for better conditions." That the editor chose these comments alone to illustrate African opinion suggests how prominent labour issues were.[83]

But beyond mere sympathy, many ANC leaders expressed strong support for action to alleviate the plight of workers, even if, given the decline in ANC vitality, this more often than not was in forums other than Congress, and even if they were cautious and largely unable to translate principled opposition to oppression into effective mass action.

There are no detailed studies of the ANC's reputation among Africans at this time. The lack of contemporary comprehensive opinion polls of Africans attitudes to the ANC makes it hazardous to estimate its popularity. There were no genuine free elections involving Africans whereby the ANC could test its claim to represent all Africans. The limited number of biographies of Africans, let alone African workers, of this period makes it difficult to validate ideas about the strength of the ANC image in the lives of individual workers. However, in submissions to state commissions and in the press, ANC leaders often invoked the cause of black labour. These publications and proceedings were only a limited part of the overall discourse between workers and nationalists, and between African nationalists and government. Yet in spite of these statements, and in deliberations of the ANC apparatus, there is evidence of a definite, if small, working class influence or interest, sometimes direct, more often indirect, in Congress.

Seme distanced himself from workers although, curiously, in response to his removal from the attorneys' roll, he claimed to be "a poor man". The cause of his deregistration was "excessive, unreasonable" fees charged to "uneducated" clients. He aimed to build the ANC through re-organisation and economic incentive, but saw no political role for workers. The constitutional changes he envisaged would give his own office more power, and the House of Chiefs would control ANC finance. Seme favoured relegating women to "organising the Nation and its children". Co-operatives, he argued, would enable Africans to accumulate capital and thus avoid the need for any socialist assault on the economic power of the state, such as had been suggested by Gumede.[84]

To achieve his aims, Seme in 1932 proposed "creation of large Native markets". He did not specify how to overcome resistance of the white state to such black advancement. Rather, the ANC itself was to become the engine of economic growth. Behind the ANC were "the educated classes" who, in his opinion, "must do the work of lifting up" their people. In 1933, Seme argued that ANC branches should become "the distributing centres of communication, in all our efforts to deal with the economic disabilities of the African". ANC shops and collectives would ease the economic burden on Africans, and would be aimed at ANC members "who want to get the benefit of buying the necessities of life at the prices which will suit the low wages of our people".[85]

Seme suggested the creation of the "African Congress Workmen's Club for the benefit of all African workers in the city". This was not, however, to be a trade union. The main intention, beyond rhetoric, appears to have been to provide workers with "supplies of groceries". Seme did feel obliged to mention workers, but negated the role of any unions beyond ANC control. It was "now the intention of the ANC to look after the interests of its workers and not to leave this class of work to any other organisation as we did before". Moreover, the ANC was "going to keep in close touch" with employers and "form its own expert Department of Labour in order to protect the interests of the African workers". In 1933, he suggested letting trade unions (along with prayer unions and herbalist associations) affiliate with the ANC. However, there was no place for *independent* labour unions in his master plan to revive the ANC. He criticised a government that threw "Africans out of employment in order to make room for the poor whites". However, his solution was simplistic. "Through the Congress we can … create our own markets [and] enough employment." At an ANC meeting in 1933, Seme even referred to the advantages of a golden age of "Africa's socialism which made life better than it is to-day" with unemployment. He also envisaged a wider network of Congress clubs. He told African taxi owners and mechanics to join a "Congress Automobile Club". Members would earn a comfortable living, and be assisted to buy cars through a General African Garage. Similar ANC "national association branches" would cater for carpenters, cabinetmakers, tailors, butchers and grocers. Nothing came of his ideas, but it shows that he felt it necessary to appear to be doing something to help the workers and other subaltern classes who made up the majority of the black urban population.[86]

Seme tried to focus on "bread and butter" issue in Congress through fostering African Clubs, co-operatives and credit societies in the ANC to "exert a stabilising influence" on Africans. He rejected class struggle. Defending his leadership in 1932, he stated: "We really don't need much of that common agitator, who only wants to create strife and class hatred." He claimed: "Most of the misery which our people suffer" was due, not to class oppression, but to "one factor, no confidence between the educated classes and their own people". His solution to ANC disunity was simple: obedience to the leader, himself. His solution to black economic problems such as unemployment was the growth of "race pride" and self-help; ANC Clubs would end unemployment. Seme's schemes were utopian and accompanied by a degree of passive acceptance of state domination. He reminded Africans to "always remember that it is the duty of the Congress to satisfy the Minister of Native Affairs of our good intentions".[87]

Despite the passing references to workers in his utopian schemes, Seme's focus was "the Nation". In 1934, he wanted to turn Congress "into a real Power amongst all sections of our people". He called for unity of "all Africans of whatever political school of thought". Yet even in this respect, he was obliged to mention wages. In appealing to teachers' associations to join the ANC, he added: "Congress will give the Native teacher the necessary backbone and the support ... to be paid a living wage." Later in 1937, Seme stated Africans "have to live now by earning wages every one of you". Leaders must "consider the wages and the security ... of African life in the towns as well as in the farms".[88]

Seme referred to African workers in his evidence as part of an ANC delegation to the Native Economic Commission (NEC) in 1931. He referred most Commission questions on workers to Selby Msimang, to whom the ANC had allocated responsibility for labour. When pressed to give his own opinion, Seme stated that Congress favoured a wages system agreed by contract over any state imposed system of wages. He gave priority to questions of property rights, land, and commerce, but also argued for greater involvement of African labour in the building of new housing. Asked if his proposals would relieve growing African dissatisfaction, he conceded that one contentious issue would remain—low wages: "I find that to be the general complaint; without wages [labourers] cannot make ends meet ... Congress exists in all the Provinces and the complaints that come from the rural Natives reach me—and I find that wages are at the bottom of it." However, he only was prepared to request that if the African "wants wages we should give him wages sufficient to enable him to live and maintain his family". Such a minimalist approach to wages revealed his alienation from black union policies. Yet because Seme's approach was coloured by his African nationalist orientation, his willingness to uphold the dignity of *all* Africans tempered his clear alignment with the propertied classes. Questioned on the undercutting of white wages by Africans, he replied that it was not only lower wages that enabled Africans to secure jobs ahead of white people: the African also was "a better driver of the lorry" and would "do more of the work ... than a White".[89]

In arguing for the removal of all discriminatory legislation on grounds of profit, not solidarity, Seme distanced himself from the black union movement. Discrimination to Seme was "very unprofitable; that is why I really am against it". If state policy embraced Rhodes's goal of "equal rights to all civilised men" it would undercut arguments of "native agitators". Workers should compete in "the open labour market", with employers "free to engage whoever is efficient ... irrespective of colour". "Free and open competition" would settle unskilled wages. All forms of state interference with collective bargaining should cease. Masters and Servants' Acts interfered with freedom of contract and were a hindrance as much to farmers as workers. "Progressive" farmers paid labourers "good wages"; both were "contented". Work contracts between them should be written and registered; Congress had ascertained from meetings in Seme's home base of Wakkerstroom that Africans supported written contracts. The Native Service Contract Bill would cause "endless trouble". His evidence shows his broad opposition to *black* labour super-exploitation, but not to capitalist exploitation *per se*. Rather, he saw African property-ownership as a panacea to "counteract the evils of [urban] rowdyism" and encourage black "thrift and enterprise".[90]

Hence there is evidence to justify Cobley's claim there "was little benefit to black wage labourers" in Seme's economic strategy and "consequently, no politicised wage earner was likely to support it", thus contributing to ANC political decline. Moreover, there is little evidence of Seme's direct contact with workers. Yet we should not forget that for some black leaders even the ANC was too radical. Basner, as noted above, recalled that in this period some educated Africans "left the Congress where there was no hope except a life of poverty and a life of militant struggle".[91] We should see the weak commitment to black labour of moderate ANC leaders such as Seme in this perspective.

Halley Plaatje, ANC Chief Under-Secretary, enthusiastically embraced Seme's grand strategy of jobs generated by black trade ventures. He regretted "African labourers should be so disorganised" and admitted the ANC was "partially responsible for this state of affairs", but pledged that Seme's "comprehensive scheme" would see labour conditions "improved and safeguarded". Plaatje argued that black labour was "essential" to the success of white business and attacked state labour policy. Unemployment was an issue no ANC member could avoid in the early 1930s. To Plaatje nothing brought out "real spite and hatred like being told on asking for relief work that your government provides only for … white skins". In general, his views were equally moderate but Seme's inaction soon disillusioned Plaatje—frustrated at the lack of leadership, he resigned in September 1933.[92]

As in the 1920s, Z. R. Mahabane continued to express sympathy for African workers. It is not clear whether this was an integral part of his frequently espoused Christianity, or a product of his years of service to Congress in which at times he was obliged to declare his stance on such matters as the smashing of black strikes or soaring black unemployment. At the 1930 Native Conference, he took the opportunity of a motion of support for the Native Affairs Minister to declare that black agitation would continue as long as discriminatory state policies continued. He chose to highlight, not the franchise (discussion on which the Minister had ruled out of order in any case), but concerns of black workers, many of whom were "skilled in labour" but legally excluded from skilled jobs. "Thousands had been discharged from the railway to make room for poor whites." Africans complained they "could not draw old age pensions". Later in the conference, he attacked the draconian Native Service Contract Bill as "obnoxious and pernicious". Prevailing public concern at the onset of the depression and rising unemployment no doubt influenced Mahabane's emphasis on labour issues. However, it also was in keeping with the frequent raising of labour issues by ANC leaders over the years.[93]

In 1931 Mahabane, still ANC Chaplain-in-Chief and active in the Kimberley Joint Council, in a written submission to the NEC detailed the multitude of taxes paid by Africans. He argued this expenditure was "altogether incommensurate" with the poor earning capacity of the average Kimberley African, whose mean annual income was only £42 whilst the annual cost of living expenses of an average family was £72. The labour market worked to employ the lowest bidder, and he strongly advocated that the state introduce a fixed minimum wage tied to costs. He drew attention to a decline in salaries of African teachers. Education, he argued, served to increase the purchasing and bargaining power of African labour. "As a labourer [the educated African] becomes a fair competitor with the European unskilled labourer because he will not sell his labour at a very much cheaper rate." Rather than focus on trading or land rights, issues heavily promoted by the NEC and expected of an erstwhile *petit bourgeois*, Mahabane chose to highlight wages and living costs. His prior experiences in the ANC helped sensitise him to such issues.[94]

Mahabane's oral evidence to the NEC similarly concentrated, not on business, but wages. It was necessary, he stated, to establish under the Wage Act a minimum wage for African workers of at least five shillings a day, closely tied to costs of living. "There is no minimum wage fixed and so the employers can offer any wage" that often was accepted by rural migrant workers, thus depressing urban wages. He criticised job preference given by employers to Malawian migrants but stressed he was not opposed to labour migrants as such, only their acceptance of low wages. Mahabane criticised the low level of Orange Free State African teachers' salaries and the failure of the state to implement their wage increments. He rejected government arguments that African teachers' salary increments over the decade were adequate, pointing also to the inadequacy of municipal wages. African youth, facing poverty and restricted educational opportunities, often failed to obtain employment, but paying Africans better wages could reverse this trend.[95]

In his contributions to ANC meetings under Seme, Mahabane often dwelt on labour market themes if—in his capacity as ANC Chaplain—these speeches frequently were wrapped in impassioned appeals to trust in God. At the January 1931 ANC conference, he concluded his sermon by describing the "whole trend" of state policy as based upon "exclusion of Natives from industry". He reminded listeners that "thousands of our people" had been "dismissed from railway and municipal services under the civilised labour policy". His "our people" referred to Africans, rather than fellow workers, and his "solution" was for Africans to pay no heed to "the advice of [communist] hooligans" but "rather … [to] look to God for help and deliverance in the hour of supreme crisis".[96]

In the late 1930s, Mahabane continued to highlight labour issues. However, he presented these in the context of general black oppression. His 1938 ANC presidential address stressed that Africans had "become a virtually landless and homeless community … Nothing else but labourers". At the 1939 ANC conference, he stressed that white people regarded Africans merely as a "labour class", only permitted to enter urban areas to carry out labour for their benefit. He put forward a set of demands that broadly prefigured the ANC's 1943 *Africans' Claims*. These were a direct black role in politics, a black voice in framing laws and an end to discrimination. Also in accord with contemporary black union demands, a "rightful place in the industrial organisation … not merely as a casual labourer but as an employee whose wages and conditions of labour must be regulated under the provisions of the Industrial Conciliation Acts … [and] whose trade unionism must be given statutory recognition". He had raised this demand back in 1919, and was thus consistent.[97]

This concern with the subjugation of Africans into a labouring class indicates not only Mahabane's personal and class resistance to proletarianisation, but also his awareness of the lives of black workers. Such awareness by some ANC leaders could not but influence their policies, pronouncements, and followers. There is nothing inherently "conservative" about Mahabane's dream of Africans escaping from their rigid "labour class" status. Many workers would hardly insist on a levelling process that denied them the possibility of upward social mobility and forced them forever to remain labourers.[98]

Mahabane drew attention to the oppression of black workers but ANC radicals judged other aspects of his philosophy more conservative. At the 1938 ANC conference, communist Gaur Radebe attacked what he termed Mahabane's "eulogising" of the Voortrekker Movement and his naive belief that Africans could successfully appeal to the International Court for grievances. Mofutsanyana criticised his failure to mention Hitler's African ambitions. Despite these conservative tendencies, in his personal life Mahabane was never very far from the ranks of working people. He failed to break out of the financial restrictions imposed on the growth of black *petit bourgeois*. He accumulated little property other than his Kroonstad house, worth only R900 when he died in 1971.[99]

James Calata was a central figure in ANC revival of the late 1930s. He was based in Cradock when he joined the ANC in 1930 and remained there (see Chapter 11 for his regional role) but was also active nationally, serving as ANC Secretary-General. Politically he was a liberal, working with the Joint Councils—in 1938, he told Rheinallt Jones "Congress can only work effectively by co-operation" with the Councils and Institute of Race Relations. Calata saw the solution to African problems as residing "in God Almighty". Yet he keenly felt the economic dimension of their predicament. As ANC Senior Chaplain, he addressed the 1938 ANC conference with a sermon on "our people ... without land without homes" who had "gone back to intellectual and economic slavery". Despite his anti-communism, he worked with radicals such as J. B. Marks in Congress. A glimpse of Calata's attitude to the class nature of the ANC (and his views on ethnicity) emerges in his later characterisation of the early ANC as "unpopular with the Xhosa, they thought it was a Basuto affair, connected with mines and the people working in the big towns".[100]

Calata's contradictory attitude to labour is partly attributable to his clerical role. Walshe characterises church officialdom of the day as rather indifferent to black suffering. The church also drew off his energy: Calata confided to Rheinallt Jones in 1939 he could "not give up the Church for national work".

Yet churches were not apolitical and perhaps inclined some Christian workers towards the ANC. Church influence may have alienated some ANC members from labour radicals yet, argues Walshe, Calata was "prepared to defend the legitimacy of strikes when all constitutional methods had failed".[101]

Selope Thema epitomises dilemmas faced by ANC leaders. He had divided political loyalties. In the 1930s, he served on executives of Gumede and Seme, was ANC Corresponding Secretary, and TAC Vice-President. Aware of the inadequacies of liberal alternatives, he nevertheless was active in the Joint Councils, Bantu Traders' Association, and NRC. These bodies shied away from mass agitation against the causes of oppression. So did Selope Thema, who in 1930 declared he "personally [was] one of those who do not favour 'direct action'". He told the 1932 ANC emergency convention called to revitalise the body the solution to African problems lay with more economic opportunities. If opposing Seme's political timidity then he supported Seme's economic schemes, arguing economic interests of black and white were "inseparably interwoven". He attacked ANC-ICU "propagandists" who "embarked on an anti-white policy". The ANC could overcome the crisis of leadership by cultivating "race-consciousness" and a "Bantu nationalism" of a broad nature. He counterpoised "Bantu patriotism" to class organisation. Africans "must organise as a race and not as workers ... as a nation and not as labourers ... To that end we must reorganise and strengthen the African National Congress."[102]

In 1930, Selope Thema warned that pass laws that denied African workers the benefits of the Conciliation and Wage Acts and a White Labour policy that "has taken away their employment" were driving them into the hands of agitators. He exposed the harsh conditions faced by African unemployed workers sentenced to forced labour on Leeuwkop prison farm. In addition, he rejected the conservative view of such people as idlers, instead squarely blaming state policy. Most were victims of an "incurable disease of modern society"—unemployment—and if "found idling at street corners or in the slum yards ... it is not because they are too lazy to work but because ... many avenues of employment are closed to them ... [The] White Labour policy ... has broadened the road to Leeuwkop." Those who acquired skills were "rendered unemployable" by discriminatory state policy. Even the infamous criminal Jan Note, he noted, had turned to crime after a white employer refused to pay him.[103]

Selope Thema made similar comments about unemployment in giving evidence on behalf of the ANC to the NEC in 1931. He used this forum to draw attention to low African wages: farms, mines and urban industries all should be encouraged to pay higher wages. He described how African workers resident in Bloemfontein and Kroonstad—the "real people"—had been ousted from their jobs and forced to seek work on the Rand when "outsiders" were given job preference. He warned that educated Africans were becoming déclassé. "In the slums you find … the educated natives go down." He himself clearly did not care to "go down" and urged black *petit bourgeois* not be artificially retarded from "progress". In 1937, Selope Thema and fellow ANC member Baloyi told the Enquiry on Collection of Native Taxes the crucial factor making it "difficult, if not impossible" for Africans to pay regular taxes was "inadequacy of wages paid to workers".[104]

In 1932, Selope Thema became *Bantu World* editor. He employed a militant rhetoric tempered with liberal *realpolitik* producing an impression of a class collaborationist, yet caring, interest in labour. Assistant-Editor Jordan Ngubane recalled the paper's control by the white-owned Bantu Press discouraged reporting of class conflict and made Selope Thema "little more than a glorified clerk". In editorials, Selope Thema called for expansion of African capital. He argued black people had "no desire to overthrow" white rule. Unemployment cast such a "sinister shadow" he felt obliged to demand the "state must find work for all". He condemned Rustenburg Council's replacement of black by white labour as "shortsighted, inhumane and uneconomic", and described similar moves in Brits and Natal as "'war' against Bantu workers". Later in the decade, he continued to advocate black labour rights as a member of the NRC (see below). The above evidence demonstrates not only his identification with the middle classes, but also his sympathy for fellow Africans compelled to work, or consigned to the ravages of unemployment.[105]

Selby Msimang, with his ICU background and having held the ANC labour "portfolio" for several years, raised labour issues more regularly than Selope Thema. This interest continued in the 1930s. In June 1930, he noted African organisations were "virtually without vitality or militancy". Nevertheless, their ideals "were never more alive", whilst "an association, such as the African National Congress or the I.C.U. with lofty ideals clearly defined, will live in spite of the incompetence, failings and stupidity of its leaders". There was, he argued, no inherent reason why the ANC and ICU should have been antagonistic. The ANC "stands on its own plane serving the interests of all, irrespective of their status, in the political field; while the I.C.U. stood to serve the interests of the working class". Moreover: "The worker has identical aspirations with the capitalist in so far as the enjoyment of political rights is concerned; and in his struggle for … economic status he properly needs to organise the mass of his own kind." Here Msimang was writing just before the disillusionment that he and other ANC members soon felt with Seme. Nevertheless, he maintained the views on unions that he had held since at least 1917, and clearly saw no antagonism between the aims of a working-class organisation and those of the ANC. The ANC existed for its members, not leaders, he added, confirmed the following year when he delivered, apparently with the blessings of Seme, ANC greetings to a conference that established the Federated Orange Free State ICU. He attacked the Native Service Contract Bill. Later the new union duly elected him secretary, a position he conditionally accepted.[106]

Soon after his election to the ICU body, Msimang spelt out his proposals for labour organisation. A "competent committee" in "constant consultation" with white farmers should work to improve working conditions of farm workers and labour tenants. Squatters and African farmers should be organised separately. Neither group should be organised on union lines but be "associated with the central national executive council". "General workers" should form into unions according to their trade and unite in a federation. Others including traders and clergy could then join them in a "Unity Movement". Msimang urged people to help create a spirit of unity by attending the May meeting of the ANC.[107]

In July 1930, Msimang advocated a neo-syndicalist approach as the "Ideal Industrial Organisation" for Africans. He attacked Transvaal Provincial Council proposals to exclude Africans from any mine surface work whilst at the same time increasing taxation of already over-taxed Africans. He outlined their low wages and high taxes, noting there even was "a tax on our wages by means of Pass fees", whilst "taxes already exceed the sum total of our earning power". He then detailed typical earnings of rural and urban labourers, indicating that he kept in touch with labour conditions.[108]

In his capacity as ANC Labour Committee Chairman, Msimang gave evidence on labour issues as part of an ANC delegation to the NEC in May 1931. He argued that ANC policy was in favour of a "free labour market where each worker would be free to compete to the best of his ability and not be hampered … by a certain wage fixed at a standard of living". This policy appears at variance with union aims of a minimum guaranteed wage and offered no protection to lower paid workers who, according to Msimang's logic, would face the mercy of the "market". However, he meant this policy to apply only more broadly, and only in a situation in which wages were determined on the principle of "equal pay for equal work". Removal of pass laws would protect unskilled workers. It was the denial of the freedom to bargain, implicit in the limited time allowed African workers to seek work under pass regulations, which depressed wages. If passes went, then Africans would no longer accept low wages. Msimang added he was not against the sort of wage fixing that had occurred in Bloemfontein when the Wage Board had increased black wages, and that he approved "in principle … fixing the wages at a certain wage in all trades".[109]

Msimang also made a joint submission to the NEC with Selope Thema (who stated that he represented the ANC) and Herbert Dhlomo. They criticised "civilised labour policy" practices of retrenching black labour, and of reserving certain trades for white labour. Africans were condemned to low wages and thus existence as a "poor class of people", not by market forces of supply or demand or profits, or workers' lack of skills, but by state policy that determined wage levels "by the colour of the skin". Africans had no alternative but to accept low wages due to state-imposed laws under which they could not even strike. Msimang added that labour migration to towns was forcing urban Africans out of work. Opening the July 1932 ANC convention, he emphasised the exclusion of Africans, who had "helped to build up industries", from unemployment relief. He again raised this issue in 1933, when rejecting state insinuations that Africans used their lower wages as a form of unfair competition. Government, he noted, made no efforts to find them work.[110]

Selby Msimang continued to draw attention to harsh conditions. In 1933 he stated: "Many families are leading a life very much below what is commonly known as a bread-to-mouth existence." His 1936 pamphlet, *The Crisis*, reveals how he expressed his continuing interest in the fate of black workers. He refers to the "perpetual slavery" experienced in rural areas where "families have to give labour without any pay". The Hertzog Bills aimed to subject Africans in urban areas "to the requirements of the employing class". He reminds readers of the central role played by black labour in economic development of the country, and draws attention to calls from the white population for deployment of Africans "into labour colonies", whilst "every effort is being made to narrow the field of labour" open to Africans. The Native Land and Trust Bill guaranteed white farmer free labour: thousands would face "conditions of economic slavery". In 1938, Msimang told a meeting of 150 African teachers at Ladysmith that Africans forced to work on farms for a pittance deserved better wages. In the same year, he also formed a committee to assist exploited farmers and farm labourers on the Driefontein Estate near Ladysmith. Msimang saw an economic dimension to ANC problems. In 1935, he suggested that one reason for its leadership crisis was that Africans "did not, perhaps, provide for the maintenance of … leaders … though some of them had to leave their daily employment" to carry out ANC work.[111] In all these statements, Msimang asserts the rights of black workers. In doing so, he represents an element of continuity on labour issues among ANC leaders.

Sol Plaatje was no longer prominent in Congress, noting in 1929 that he "could not possibly find the time to earn my own living while trying to lead unwieldy masses". However, he participated in the 1929 ANC congress and joined an ANC deputation protesting passes in 1930. He maintained his opposition to radicals in Kimberley, but continued until his death in 1932 to protest the poor conditions of black workers.[112]

Plaatje's 1931 NEC evidence focused on the landless and black workers. He continued to carry a cultural baggage weighed down with cultural accretions of white society, but drew attention to the interdependence of rural and urban Africans. Even urban black people in regular employment tended to have "no money at all" in times of poor harvests. This was such a problem, he lamented, that "missionaries can hardly sell any more bibles and hymnbooks". Reduced to the status of "an industrial nomad", the rural African often had to furnish the unpaid labour of his family for three to six months a year. The situation of Kimberley diamond mine labourers was precarious. Many white diggers had "turn[ed] their labourers into the open veld: these in turn flooded into town and further demoralised the labour market". Their insecurity exacerbated by the recent closure of Griqualand West asbestos mines, labourers had been driven to become "wanderers ... content to do casual jobs at odd intervals for the price of 'a bellyfull of skoff'". Plaatje supplied answers to what white people saw as the riddle of labour "shortages", pointing out that not all Africans were fit to work underground, whilst many naturally sought higher wages than those offered on farms.[113]

Plaatje contrasted unemployed Africans compelled to "pay their poll tax or go to gaol" with unemployed white people receiving benefits. However, his view of unemployment's causes betrays a limited understanding of capitalism. One cause, according to him, was that "some little girls" from outside Kimberley "are sent in here to work and earn the tax for the brother or the father, and that results in a whole lot of unemployment". Recounting his 1927 visit to Lichtenburg diggings, he argued that the African labourer, "by the exercise of his muscles ... was banishing White unemployment". He showed that closed compounds, where labourers had nowhere else to buy goods, were a lucrative source of income for mining companies. When it came to better-paid jobs, bosses simply did not consider Africans. Wage discrimination inclined some Africans to pose as "coloured" workers, which led to protests by the latter about black people taking their work. Salaries of local African teachers, he added, had fallen from £90 to £60 in only a few years. He urged a minimum wage for Africans and pointed to examples of white businesses in Kimberley that independently of government had taken the initiative in raising black wages. Finally, he made a plea for aged ex-worker and phthisis victims to get land where they could "spend the evening" of their lives under their "own vine and fig tree". Plaatje mentioned in passing the problems of African traders, but clearly chose to give priority to problems of workers and landless. He echoed these complaints in a written submission: the African was not only "the Union's cheap labourer" but also, with "his meagre wage ... chief taxpayer". In Bloemfontein, African labourers were compelled to purchase a £3 license just to work, whereas the sale of his labour did "not cost the European labourer a penny". He protested the gross inequality in forcing paupers to pay the same poll tax and pass fees as a salaried African. "No commission," he concluded sarcastically, "ever reminded the Europeans that they owe their country's solvency to the labour of 200,000 Native miners".[114]

Later in 1931, Plaatje returned to themes of unemployment and job discrimination as he addressed the Cape Native Voters' Association in Aliwal North. The African was "gaoled for being poor" whilst the remedy, work, was denied him as it was now a white prerogative; "workless" Africans subsidised white social services by paying taxes much heavier in proportion than white employees. In November he called on "white orthographic zealots" to better spend their time "in getting a living wage" for African teachers. In the last year of his life, 1932, he travelled to Cape Town to raise with the Minister of Native Affairs the suffering of unemployed workers and the harsh provisions of the Native Service Contract Bill that made farm labourers "virtually owned by the European landowner". In his last press articles, he denounced the Bill and attempts to extend the "tot" system of farmworker payment, recounted the case of a worker arrested when trying to protest about employer assault and non-payment of wages, warned that the National Party opposed any legal obligation to pay labourers, and lamented high unemployment. For all his *petit bourgeois* accretions, which earned him a reputation among historians as a study in moderation, Plaatje remained, until the end of his life, the champion of his oppressed people, of whom workers and the landless often received pride of place.[115]

Herbert Dhlomo (1903-1956), like Selope Thema, exemplified divided loyalties. An "active member of the ANC from an early age", he worked as a teacher until 1935 and then became a *Bantu World* journalist. In a series of *Umteteli wa Bantu* articles in 1930, he expressed a mixture of African nationalism and Fabian social democracy. Black unrest was caused not by "a half-dozen ... comparatively harmless" agitators but by "atrociously low wages". Elsewhere, he conceded the historical gains made by capitalism, but called for "a new system" that did not lack a "universal economic or fiscal plan". South Africa, racked with poverty, unemployment and discontent, oozed a "gulf between the poor and the rich". Low black wages limited the prospects of black people entering business, and consigned them to making their living chiefly "by selling their labour to white capitalists". Freedom of movement of black labour was impossible under Master and Servants Acts. Such a situation required firstly that black wages increase, and secondly that African unionism be fostered. Yet it was necessary to "acquaint the black proletariat with elementary economic facts," by which Dhlomo meant not a crash course in Marxism, but recognition that some, but not excessive, exploitation of its labour was necessary for profit. In 1931, he heralded the dawn of an era of propaganda based upon newspapers and books that, unlike deputations, "reach not the rich ... only, but the middle and the lower classes".[116]

Giving evidence to the NEC, Dhlomo attacked under-employment of certified teachers, arguing that lack of state funding for black education and teachers' salaries had driven some educated Africans to "lethargy, mental deterioration, apathy and moral laxity". The Commissioners remarked on these "sharp charges against men and women of the class to which you belong". Like other ANC figures, Dhlomo was, however, capable of looking beyond his class. In 1932 he argued that Africans needed a peaceful "industrial, social and intellectual revolution", achievable via education and industrial organisation. As Ntongela Masilela shows, such ideas signalled Dhlomo's advocacy of African modernity and came at a time when African nationalism began to gain the upper hand over Marxism among black intellectuals. Modernity carried a strong belief in "progress" but so did socialism. Cobley, with good reason, stresses Dhlomo's *petit bourgeois* consciousness, but these extracts indicate he also sought just solutions to the tortured position of labour in society.[117]

The emphasis of ANC leaders on the pass laws as a central cause of unrest and poverty among workers was substantially similar to priorities established by black unions. The IICU, in a NEC submission, viewed pass laws as "most provocative", with "a grave effect on the economic lives" of Africans, turning unemployed Africans into criminals. Even moderate ANC leaders were, in this sense, in accord with black union demands.[118]

Time and again ANC leaders, in speaking or writing of black grievances, found themselves dwelling on labour issues, confirming not only the centrality of black labour in South African economic life, but also the fact that ANC leaders were obliged to address the fate of such a large section of their constituency. That the above leaders were all invariably men, and not farm or mineworkers, reminds us of the limitations of African political organisations at this time. Yet, despite the gap in occupation or class, this leading African political stratum, linked by a myriad of cultural, national, and historic ties to the great mass of black labourers and continually made aware of their glaring problems, frequently highlighted these issues in a wide range of political spheres. They failed to stem the onslaught of white domination that intensified this exploitation, but the above evidence shows that they remained firmly opposed to such exploitation.

Conclusion

Poor leadership, state oppression, sectarianism among allies, rivals, and the difficult economic conditions of black people that left little room for political contributions caused ANC disunity and weakness in the first years of the decade. Many ANC leaders displayed an ambiguity about workers that was caused partly by Seme's conservatism and partly by their own class positions. Despite its problems, the ANC supported the rights of black workers and maintained some ties with them. This was due firstly to the efforts of members with closer ties to workers. Secondly, the ANC was the one African political organisation that had an unbroken tradition of interest in black workers. This was a factor of continuity in an otherwise fragmented black political and industrial landscape.

On a national level, the depth of ANC labour ties was not great. The ANC made pious declarations about the lot of workers. In the second half of the decade, the shock of intensified political oppression and vigorous efforts of a dedicated group of members turned this lethargy around, and in so doing generated greater grassroots support and with it labour contacts. The CPSA acknowledged in early 1939 that if the All-African Convention was a failure then the ANC had "made headway by taking up mass-work".[119]

Congress, despite passing through a trough of membership and influence (in quantitative terms) nevertheless survived, and kept contact with labour. The fact that this occurred in the nadir of ANC power testifies to persistence of a deeper relationship between ANC and workers. The interplay between forces of continuity and change helped lay the foundation for more rapid penetration of working-class communities in later decades. The ANC and black workers had turbulent relations, yet continued to find common ground. Continuation of the circumscribed socio-economic situation of black people and maintenance of African political structures and initiatives by individual activists enhanced their potential unity. It was at the local and provincial level that these contacts and grassroots work reached their greatest intimacy and intensity.

Notes

1 Benson, *Struggle for a Birthright*, p. 65; S. Hawley, "The ANC and the Urban Black South African 1912-30", M.A. Queens University, 1986, pp. 177-179; P. McCullough, "The Growth of Assertive Action: The ANC and Urban Issues 1930-1948", M.A. Queens, 1988, pp. 27-30, 89-93; J. Meier, "The ANC and the Black Working Class, 1937-1948", M.A. Queens, 1994, pp. 4-5, 14, 115.

2 Walshe, *Rise of African Nationalism*, p. 144 argues the Depression's mildness contributed to ANC faith in capitalism. Yet loss of jobs and wage cuts were real. Annual African wages declined markedly: in stone and clay it dropped from £39 in 1929 to £32 from 1932 to 1935, in printing from £58 to £52 in 1932-1933, textiles £56 to £52 1929-1932: W. and M. Ballinger, "Native Wages and the Cost of Living", mimeo 1938, *Ballinger Papers*.

3 Walshe, *Rise of African Nationalism*, pp. 223, 239-244.

4 Walshe, *Rise of African Nationalism*, pp. 239-263; *African Leader* 6 May 1933; ANC Western Province report 1937, TAC "Report" [to 1938 ANC conference], in CKC 2:DA:14:30/3.

5 *Indlela Yenkululeko* 13 Jun. 1934, pp. 3-6. On Dube, Mancoe and Calata see Chapters 11-12.

6 Z.K. Matthews interview with G. Carter and T. Karis, 19 Mar. 1964, CKC 2:XM66:94; P. Limb, *Nelson Mandela: A Biography* (Westport: Greenwood, 2008).

7 *Umteteli wa Bantu* 29 Apr. 1933; "African Women Meet" *Friend* 18 Dec. 1937; C. Wright, *Beneath the Southern Cross: The Story of an American Bishop's Wife in South Africa* (New York: Exposition, 1955), p. 111-115; Mindry, "Good Women", p. 85; "Report of Joint Deputation of ANC/ABC 16 May 1939" CKC 2:DA:14:30/3; Mahabane to R. Jones, 6 Mar. 1939, *ANC Collection*; *African Leader* 25 Mar. 1933; R. Seabury, *Daughter of Africa* (Boston: Pilgrim, 1945), pp. 40, 133.

8 "Native Drift to Towns" *Natal Advertiser* 4 Apr. 1931; M. Ballinger, "Native Life in South African Towns", *Journal of the Royal African Society* v. 37 no. 148 (1938), pp. 326-338.

9 Walshe, *Rise of African Nationalism* p. 243; Skota, *African Yearly Register*, pp. 70-71, 137, 175, 188-189, 257, 273-277, 283.

10 Jones and Saffery, *Social and Economic Conditions*, p. 340; *Cape Argus* 3, 22 Apr. 1930; *Umteteli wa Bantu* 3 May 1930; *Abantu-Batho* 1 May 1930; Skota, *African Yearly Register*, p. 171; *Umsebenzi* 2 May 1930.

11 H.S. Msimang, "Why Mr. Gumede Failed", *Umteteli wa Bantu* 31 May 1930; *Umteteli wa Bantu* 7 Jun. 1930.

12 *Umteteli wa Bantu* 3 May 1930, 30 Dec. 1933; S.Thema, "Native Unrest: its Causes and its Cure", *Umteteli wa Bantu* 31 May 1930.

13 Benson, *Struggle for a Birthright* p. 56; Seme, "Condemn the Spirit of Sedition", *Bantu World* 7 Apr. 1934.

14 *Abantu-Batho* 3, 19 Mar., 24 Apr., 7 May 1931; *Umsebenzi* 16 Jan. 1931; *Umteteli wa Bantu* 8 Jul. 1933; H.S. Msimang, "Big ANC Controversy", *Umteteli wa Bantu* 18 Nov. 1933. Bonner, "Kgatla Conspiracies, Pedi Plots", notes that over half the delegates were from Bloemfontein. See also *Bantu World* 22 Apr. 1933.

15 *Umteteli wa Bantu* 24 Jan., 18 Apr., 23 May 1931; S. Thema, "The ANC", *Umteteli wa Bantu* 14 Nov. 1931; S. Thema, "Bantu May Look to Their Past for Inspiration", *Bantu*

World 25 Jul. 1932; Coka in *Bantu World* 28 May 1932; Coka to *Bantu World* 9 Jul. 1932; J.G.C[oka], "Thrift among the Bantu", *Bantu World* 14 May 1932. Coka's journal strongly supported African unions: *African Liberator* Sep., Oct. 1935.

16   "African National Congress", *Umteteli wa Bantu* 21 May, 23 Jul. 1932; *Bantu World* 9, 16 Jul. 1932.

17   "Why Congress Failed", *African Leader* 6 May 1933; *Umteteli wa Bantu* 30 Dec. 1933, 6, 13, 6 Jan. 1934.

18   Masibe-Langa to *Umteteli wa Bantu* 6 Aug. 1932; Coka, "Congress Wash-Out", *Umsebenzi* 25 Aug. 1934; Mabeta to *Umteteli wa Bantu,* 26 Nov. 1932; Mancoe, *Directory*, p. 33; Phillips, *Bantu in the City*, pp. 69, 343-344; Seme in *Bantu World* 14 Apr. 1934; Banser, "Interview", p. B12, M. Basner, *Am I an African?* (Johannesburg: Wits UP, 1993), pp. 27, 237; Nhlapo to *Bantu World* 17 Aug., 14 Sep., 26 Oct. 1935, 18 Jan. 1936; Mdolomba to *Bantu World* 11 Jan., 14 Mar. 1936; A.P. Mda, "ANC", *Bantu World* 8 Jan. 1938; Mtirara to *Bantu World* 24 Apr. 1937; "R. Roamer", *Bantu World* 2 Apr. 1938.

19   *Izwi lama Afrika* 26 Jun. 1931; *Bantu World* 23 Jul. 1932; *African Leader* 10 Dec. 1932, 18 Feb. 1933; "Women and Passes,", *Umteteli wa Bantu* 27 Jun.; *Umteteli wa Bantu* 3 May 1931; *Ilanga lase Natal* 3 Jul. 1931.

20   "Umkosi we ANC Ngomteto Omtsha we Pasi zaha Fazi" (in Xhosa) *Abantu-Batho* 9 Jul. 1931.

21   Bradford, *Taste of Freedom,* p. 110; Mindry, "Good Women", p. 85; C.L. Tshabalala, "To the Daughters of Africa", *Ilanga lase Natal* 17 Dec. 1938; *Friend* 18 Dec. 1937; Transcript of Interview with Miss Bertha Mkize, Inanda, 4.8.1979, Unisa Library.

22   Skota, *African Yearly Register*, p. 439; *Abantu-Batho* 1, 15 May 5, 17 Jun. 1930; A.N[zula], "The Tyranny of the Pass Laws & Pin Pricks" *Abantu-Batho* 25 Sep. 1930, C. Baker, "Imperialism in Practice", 4, 11 (Sep. 1930).

23   *Abantu-Batho* 1, 15, 22 May, 5, 17 Jun., 18 Sep. 1930, 25 Jun. 1931, "The Plight of Native Labourers on the Diggings", *Abantu-Batho* 17 Jul., 9 Oct. 1930; *Abantu-Batho* 3, 24 Jul., 28 Aug., 18 Sep. 1930, 7 May 1931.

24   *Abantu-Batho* editorials or leaders on: "Native Hut Tax Collection by Military Force", 31 Jul. 1930; "Old Age Pension", 21 Aug. 1930; "Mr Buntings Prosecution", 4 Dec. 1930; "A Change of System", and "Heroes of Trade Unionism in South Africa", 7 May 1931; *Abantu-Batho* 28 Aug. 1930.

25   *Abantu-Batho* 8 May, 10, 17 Jul. 1930, 25 Jun. 1931, 28 Aug., 4 Sep. 1930; J. H. M., "The British White Paper", *Abantu-Batho* 27 Nov. 1930; Letter of Modiakgotla to *Abantu-Batho* 23 Jul. 1931.

26   *Abantu-Batho* 10, 17 Jul., 19, 26 Jun. 1930, 19 Feb. 1931, 28 Aug. 1930, 27 Nov. 1930.

27   *Abantu-Batho* 12, 19 Feb., 3, 19 Mar. 1931, 15 May, 5, 19 Jun., 3, 17 Jul., 4 Dec. 1930, 30, 9 Apr., 25 Jun. 1931; Champion, "Story of My Exile", *Abantu-Batho* 16 Apr. 1931, *Abantu-Batho* 25 Jun. 1931.

28   Skota, *African Yearly Register*, p. 171 (and 3rd ed. p. 65); "Lefu la D.S. Letanka", *Bantu World* 7 May 1932; "You May Not See Us Again Alive", 7 May 1931 and *Abantu-Batho* "Alive Again", *Abantu-Batho* 11 Jun. 1931; *Abantu-Batho* 25 Jun. 1931; KC v. 4, p. 58. The 1930 prospectus (1 May 1930) for *Abantu-Batho's* sale listed directors as: Gumede (farmer); S. Matseke (shoemaker); Letanka (journalist); and Masabalala (journalist).

29   *Abantu-Batho* 7 May 1931, 16 Apr. 1931; Thibedi, "Meqoqo le Basebetsi", *Abantu-Batho* 11 Jun. 1931, in which he speaks of uphill struggles ahead, and *Abantu-Batho* 9 Apr., 11 Jun. 1931; *Abantu-Batho* 19 Mar. 1931.

30 *Abantu-Batho* 21 Aug. 1930; advertisements, *Abantu-Batho* 1 May 1930; *Umsebenzi* 21 Jul. 1934.

31 Seme circular 13 Nov. 1930, "Another Colour Bar", and J. Mngoma, "Depression and Economy" *Ikwezi Le Afrika* 9 May 1931; J. Crutse "Life in Urban Areas", *Ikwezi Le Afrika* 16 May 1931.

32 "Trade Union Unity", and "Bloemfontein Meetings", *Ikwezi Le Afrika* 27 Jun. 1931; W. Vilakazi, "Leaders: Congress, CAU and ICU," and letter of T. Mosime in *Ikwezi Le Afrika* 16 May 1931; *Ikwezi Le Afrika* 27 Jun. 1931.

33 Switzer, *Black Press*, pp. 27, 38; Roux, *Time Longer than Rope,* p. 350; *African Leader* 19 Nov., 31 Dec., 19 Nov. 1932; S.H. Mbulawa, "The Native Press", *African Leader* 28 Jan. 1933.

34 *African Leader* 11 Feb., 29 Apr., 18 Mar. 1933, 19 Nov., 31 Dec. 1932; "Why Congress Failed", *African Leader* 6 May 1933; *African Leader* 25 Feb. 1933 (H. Plaatje), 4 Mar. 1933; Mkasibe and Sitebe to *African Leader* 3 Dec. 1932; *African Leader* 15 Apr., 11 Feb., 1 Apr. 1933.

35 *African Leader:* "Exit 1932", 31 Dec. 1932; "Farm Labour Conditions: Will the ANC Find a Solution?", 11 Feb. 1933; Vulpine [pseud.], "Xosa Roadmender's Chant", 6 May 1933; Seme (Volksrust) to J.D. Rheinallt Jones, S.Thema and R. Baloyi, 19 Oct. 1937, *ANC Collection.*

36 *Umteteli wa Bantu* 19 Mar. 1932; Kadalie to *African Leader* 11 Mar. 1933; *African Leader* 1 Apr. 1933.

37 H.G. Plaatje, "The Native Mind", *African Leader* 18 Feb. 1933; E. D. Taabe, "Unemployment", *African Leader* 11 Mar. 1933; "Some of the Opportunities Lost", *African Leader* 1 Apr. 1933.

38 *Umteteli wa Bantu* 1 Apr. 1933. Xuma lamented: "we have no organ … to popularise our propaganda": Xuma to Max Yergan 27 Nov. 1936, XP ABX 361127c. In 1938 there was an "urgent need for an independent Press either owned by or acting as a mouthpiece of" Congress: National Executive Report, Dec. 1938, CKC 2:DA:14:30/3.

39 Drew, "New Line", p. 356; Benson, *Struggle* p. 60; T. Lodge, "Class Conflict, Communal Struggle and Patriotic Unity: The CPSA during the Second World War", Wits ASI seminar paper, Oct. 1985; Pampalis, *Foundations*, p. 146; *Umsebenzi* 1 Apr., 27 May 1932; SAP to SNA 9 Dec. 1936, "L.T. Leepile, Agitator", TAD NA 61/328.

40 Basner, "Interview"; Bunting, *Moses Kotane*, p. 52-5; "Typescript" Basner Papers B12; Basner, *African*, p. 35.

41 *Umsebenzi* 18 Apr. 1930, 16 Jan. 1931; Bunting, *Moses Kotane*, p. 54; Drew, *Radical Tradition*, pp. 218-24, 197-211; "Resolutions of Political Commission, ECCI, 3 Jun. 1934", Davidson, *Communist International*, v. 2, pp. 94-101, p. 105; *Umsebenzi* 27 Mar., 4 Sept., 7 Aug. 1931.

42 *Umsebenzi* 12 Dec., 2 May 1930, 11 May 1935, 4 Apr. 1936; Bunting, *Moses Kotane*, p. 58; *African Voice* 1 1938; Roux, *Time Longer than Rope*, p. 353; *Umsebenzi* 7 Apr., 27, 13 Jan. 1934, 26 Jan., 16 Feb. 1935; *Ikwezi le Afrika* 9 May 1931.

43 J.B. M[arks], "Natives & Organisation", *Umsebenzi* 4 May 1935; Bunting, *Moses Kotane*, p. 58; *Umsebenzi* 20 Apr., 26 Jan. 1935; J.B. Marks, "Native Bourgeoisie as a Class", *Umsebenzi* 16 Feb. 1935; Roux to *Umsebenzi* 20 Apr. 1935; Nzula, *Forced Labour*, p. 169. For an overview, see Drew, "The New Line".

44 Bunting, *Moses Kotane*, p. 62; CKC 2:XK16:96/1; *Umsebenzi* 27, 13 Jan. 1934; Kotane to Comintern 31 Oct. 1934, Davidson, *Communist International* v. 2 p. 119, Drew, *Radical Tradition*, p. 278.

45   *Umsebenzi* 4 May, 16 Feb. 1935, 18 Aug. 1934, 6 Jun. 1936, 9 Jan. 1937; R. Bunche, *An African-American in South Africa* ed. R. Edgar (Chicago: University of Chicago Press, 1990), p. 211; *Umvikeli-Thebe* Feb., May 1936;*Umsebenzi* 20 Aug. 1932, 23 Sept., 21 Jul. 1934; A. Ntghot and S. Pulus, "ANC & Protectorates", *Mochochonono* 26 Feb. 1938; *Mochochonono* 23 Jul. 1938 citing OFS ANC resolutions.

46   *Organise a People's Front in South Africa* (CPSA, 1936), p. 17; *Umsebenzi* 16 May 1936; Bunting, *Moses Kotane* p. 73; "All-in African Peoples Defence Conference", SAIRR reel 9 B.27.3; *Umvikeli-Thebe* Mar., Apr., Jul., Jan., Feb., May 1936; 1936; *Ikaka* Jul. 1931. Kotane (to Comintern, 31 Dec. 1935) noted Ikaka gained the affiliation of only one body, the Independent ANC: Davidson, *Communist International*, v. 2 p. 156.

47   A. Drew, "Events Were Breaking Above Their Heads: Socialism in South Africa 1921-1950", *Social Dynamics* v. 17 no. 1 (1991), pp. 49-77; "Draft Thesis: The Native Question" [Lenin Club 1934], XP reel 1; Drew, *Radical Tradition*, v. 1, p. 149; *Spark* Feb. 1939; Hirson, "Reorganisation of African Trade Unions".

48   "Equal Franchise for All People", *Cape Times* 6 Jan. 1930; *Natal Advertiser* 8 Jan. 1931; *Star* 6 Jan. 1931; *Friend* 7 Jan. 1931; *Natal Mercury* 12 Jan. 1931; *Natal Witness* 9 Jan. 1931; *Umteteli wa Bantu* 10, 17 Jan. 1931; *Daily Despatch* 26 Mar. 1936; *African Leader* 3 Dec. 1932.

49   Basner, "Interview" pp. 16-19; J. Horton, "South Africa's Joint Councils: Black and White Co-operation between the Two World Wars". *SAHJ* 4 (1972), pp. 29-44; B. Hirson "Tuskegee, the Joint Councils and the All-African Convention", *SSA* 10 1981 pp. 65-75; Mancoe, *Directory*, p. 37; SAIRR "Native Service Contract Bill" 1/32, SAIRR. "Report of Joint Council Conference 27 Nov. 1932", Joint Council Port Elizabeth, "Annual Report 1932" in JCR; "Urban Native Legislation" (8 Sep. 1930), KC 1, pp. 342-346; Godlo, NEC "Minutes of Evidence", pp. 5533-5541, 5574.

50   Joint Council (JC) Sophiatown Minutes 13 Sep. 1934, JCR; NEC "Evidence" pp. 6928, 8672; *Rand Daily Mail* 21 May 1931; *Bantu World* 21 Sep. 1935.

51   SAIRR. "Report of Joint Council Conference, 1932"; Cradock JC. Minutes of Quarterly Meeting 13 Sept. 1935; "Report of Conference of Joint Councils Bloemfontein Jul. 4 1933"; Potchefstroom JC. "Report 1931-2"; East London JC. "Minutes of Meeting," 16 Mar. 1933, 28 May 1936; Port Elizabeth JC. Annual Report 1932: JCR; *Bantu World* 14 Dec. 1935; *Eastern Province Herald* 22 Nov. 1934.

52   Rich, "Managing Black Leadership", p. 184; Evidence of R. Sello Feb. 1931, "Minutes of Evidence", NEC 1930-1932, pp. 4785-4788, 4806, 4809. Sello represented the ICU, 'Mote the Independent ICU.

53   M'belle to NEC May 1931 p. 8666; "Enquirer" [M'belle] to *Umteteli wa Bantu* 13 Sep. 1930; *Umteteli wa Bantu* 10 May 1930, 27 Aug. 1932. In 1930, A. M'belle worked as a clerk and earlier as an interpreter: see CAD AG 1746 8804 for his efforts to secure pay rises; *Umteteli wa Bantu* 23 Jul. 1932; SAIRR AGM Proceedings, 25 Jan. 1937, Minutes of Executive 13 Sep. 1932, 22 Nov. 1932, JCR.

54   JC Port Elizabeth minutes 30 Apr. 1935; JC East London Report 1933, Meeting minutes 20 Apr., 30 May 1933, 19 Apr., 21 May, 20 Oct., 12 Dec. 1934, 26 Mar. 1936, 22 Jan. 1937; M. Butler to Jones 12 Feb. 1932 in JCR; Rich, "Managing Black Leadership", pp. 186-90; 'Mote to NEC "Minutes", p. 4749.

55   A. Frew, *Prince George's African Tour* (London: Blackie, 1934). In 1937 a feast in honour of George VI's coronation was held at state expense in Kentani, with labourers paid 5 shillings each for stamping mealies: CMTT to Magistrate Kentani, 19 Mar. 1937: CAD

Kentani Magistrate, 1/KNT 40 file 1/1/2: Prime Minister; Distinguished Persons; CMTT to Magistrate Kentani, 19 Mar. 1937: 1/KNT 40, file 1/1/4.

56   Willan, *Sol Plaatje*, p. 373.

57   *Rand Daily Mail* 19, 13-14 Feb. 1936; R.V. S. Thema, "The Union's Native Policy", *African Observer* 5(1) 1936, p. 32; R.V. S. Thema to Xuma 20 Jun. 1935, XP ABX 350620, Xuma, "Representation of Natives Act", (1936), XP reel 2.

58   D.D.T. Jabavu, *The Findings of the All-African Convention* (Lovedale, n.d. [1935?]) pp. 37-46; KC v. 2, pp. 48-50; C. Higgs, *The Ghost of Equality: The Public Lives of D.D.T. Jabavu of South Africa, 1885-1959* (Cape Town: D. Philip, 1996), pp. 117-130; Bunche, *An African American in South Africa*, pp. 257-258; *People's Front*, p. 14; E. Mdolomba to *Bantu World* 11 Jan. 1936; A.P. Mda, "ANC", *Bantu World* 8 Jan. 1938.

59   Basner, *Am I an African*, pp. xi-xii; pp. 81-83, 92; Rich, *White Power*, pp. 92-96, 159.

60   Roth, "Domination", pp. 147-153; Xuma ms. letter to *The Times* 3 Jan. 1938, XP ABX 38010136; M. Roth, "Black Councils, White Parliaments, 1920-1987"; Wits ASI seminar paper Apr. 1991; Roux, *Rebel Pity*, p. 164; KC v. 4, p. 92; J.B. Marks to *Bantu World* 30 Jul. 1938; *Verbatim Report (VR) of Proceedings of the Natives Representative Council* 9th Dec. 1937, pp. 178-180; *Free State Advocate* 25 Dec. 1937, 29 Oct 1938.

61   *VR* 30 Nov.-8 Dec. 1939, pp. 401-417.

62   *VR* 30 Nov.-8 Dec. 1939, pp. 401-417; Bloemfontein Location Manager to NA 28 Apr. 1934, VAB MBL 4/8/1/80:25/43; Alegi, *Laduma!*, p. 62; *Mochochonono* 23 Jul. 1938; *Free State Advocate* 5 Mar. 1938; Roth "Domination".

63   J. Matthews, "The Roaring Years", *Fighting Talk* Jun. 1961; *Umteteli wa Bantu* 23 Jul. 1932; H.S. Msimang, *The Crisis* ([Johannesburg: Express, 1936]), p. 14. On earlier opposition see: R. Haines, "The Opposition to General Hertzog's Segregation Bills 1929-1934", in *Conference on Opposition*, pp. 150-82.

64   ANC "Text of Resolutions Passed at the Annual Conference ... Dec. 1936", mimeo, *ANC Collection*.

65   *Bantu World* 29 Jan., 28 May 1938; Baloyi "The ANC", *Bantu World* 2 Apr. 1938; Basner, "Autobiographical Typescript", in Basner Papers, ICS, B12-13; J. Hendricks, "From Moderation to Militancy: A Study of African Leadership and Political Reactions in South Africa, 1936-1960", Ph.D. University of Michigan, 1983, pp. 103-114; Meli, *South Africa Belongs to Us*, p. 87.

66   "African National Congress to Be Revived", *South African Worker* 4 Sep. 1937; *Umsebenzi* 18 Nov. 1936, 6 Feb., 6 Nov. 1937; Walshe, *Rise of African Nationalism*, p. 256;

67   "Z.R. Mahabane on ANC", *Bantu World* 12 Feb. 1938; Baloyi, "The ANC" *Bantu World* 2 Apr. 1938; "Calata's Appeal", *Bantu World* 16 Jul. 1938. Some activists took Seme's advice: A Western Township Co-operative Store was formed and in Durban, ex-ICU leader A.J. Sililo established a cooperative committee: B. Huss to W. Ballinger 9 Jun. 1934, A.J. Sililo to W. Ballinger 9 Feb. 1934, *Ballinger Papers*.

68   Minutes and Roll of Delegates ANC Jubilee meeting 16-19 Dec. 1937, CKC 2:DA:14:30/3.

69   *The Friend* 16 Dec. 1937; Bunche, *An African-American in South Africa*, pp. 29-33, 65-72, 272-282.

70   A.P. Mda, "ANC: Jubilee Celebrations," *Bantu World* 8 Jan. 1938; A. Cobley, "The African National Church", *Church History* v. 60 (1991), pp. 356-371, p. 366; E. T. Mofutsanyana, "African Labour and Wages", in D.D.T. Jabavu (ed.), *Minutes of the All-African Convention* (Lovedale: Lovedale Press, 1936).

71   *The Friend* 17, 19-20 Dec. 1938; *Free State Advocate* 31 Dec. 1938; "Resolutions Passed at the Annual Conference of the ANC ... 1938," CKC 2:DA:14:30/3; J. Burger, *The Black Man's Burden* (London: Gollancz, 1943), p. 210.

72   ANC. National Executive Report" [1938], CKC 2:DA:14:30/3; Cobley, *Class & Consciousness*, pp. 207, 175.

73   "Attainment of Freedom by Natives", *The Friend* 19 Dec. 1938.

74   W. Mvula, "The Case of the Female Servants", *Bantu World* 2 Jul. 1938; Hirson, *Yours for the Union*, pp. 51-58; African Domestic Servants League flyer 1939, SAIRR-B, reel 13. Cf. Gaitskell, "Female Initiatives", pp. 124-128 on the discourse of female worker docility in *Bantu World*, and the 1939 abortive Bantu Girls Domestic Service Association.

75   Kimble and Unterhalter, "We Opened the Road", p. 20; *Eastern Province Herald* Jul. 9 1938; ANC 1938 conference minutes, CKC 2:DA:14:30/3; *The Friend* 20-21 Dec. 1938.

76   M. Roth, "Josie Mpama: The Contribution of a Largely Forgotten Figure in the South African Liberation Struggle" *Kleio* 28 (1996), pp. 120-136; I. Filatova, "Indoctrination or Scholarship? Education of Africans at the Communist University of the Toilers of the East in the Soviet Union, 1923-1937", *Paedagogica Historica* 35 (1999), pp. 41-66, p. 62; "Epainette Mbeki: Order of the Baobab in Gold": www.thepresidency.gov.za/orders/042006/part3.pdf; T. Z. Ndebula and M. Tsedu, *Epainette Nomaka Mbeki: A Humble Journey on Her Footprints* (Johanneburg: Zazi's Productions, 2008), pp. 12, 29.

77   Kros, *African Women's Organisations*, pp. 7, 15-16, citing Mpama's (Mphama) interview with Julie Wells.

78   B. Peterson, *Monarchs, Missionaries, and African Intellectuals: African Theater and the Unmaking of Colonial Marginality* (Trenton: Africa World Press, 2000), pp. 15-19, B. Peterson "*The Bantu World* and the World of the Book: Reading, Writing, and 'Enlightenment'", in K. Barber (ed.) *Africa's Hidden Histories* (Bloomington: Indiana UP, 2006), pp. 236-257, p. 239.

79   ANC "National Executive Report", 15 Dec. 1939, CKC 2:DA:14:30/3; *Bantu World* 12 Feb. 1938.

80   "Report of Joint Deputation of ANC and Advisory Boards Congress which Interviewed the Minister ... 16 May 1939", signed J. Calata, CKC 2:DA:14:30/3. On Sililo's later ANC role see: KC v. 4, p. 141.

81   "Report of Deputation"; [Rheinallt Jones] notes of meeting in D. Smit to D. Molteno, 24 May 1939, *ANC Collection*. During recess, Marks and Mapikela sharply criticised Mtimkulu's speech.

82   Basner, "Interview" pp. 16-19; Walshe, *Rise of African Nationalism*, p. 241; Delius, "*Sebatakgomo*", pp. 295-299; Burger, *Black Man's Burden*, p. 210; *Bantu World* 29 Jan. 1938; Seme to ANC President General 8 Apr. 1939, Seme to CNC Northern Areas 7 Aug. 1939, *ANC Collection*.

83   "Opinions of Leading African Thinkers", *African Leader* 25 Mar. 1933.

84   "Struck Off", *Umteteli wa Bantu* 1 Oct. 1932; *African Leader* 25 Feb. 1933; Seme, "ANC", *African Leader* 3 Dec. 1932; *African Leader* 10 Dec. 1932; Seme, "ANC" *Umteteli wa Bantu* 10 Dec. 1932; *African Leader* 14 Jan. 1933. Co-operatives were not just taken up by moderates: Govan Mbeki promoted them in keeping with traditions of *iLima* ("neighbourly assistance") and aid to poor farmers: Mbeki, *Let's Do It Together: What Co-Operative Societies Can Do* (Cape Town: African Bookman, 1944) and Z.K. Matthews and G. Mbeki, "Native Reserves, Land Tenure", mimeo, Apr. 1944.

85 P. Seme, "The African National Congress", *African Leader* 3 Dec. 1932; P. Seme, T.D. Mweli Skota and H.G. Plaatje, "Congress Branches Must Organise and Register", *African Leader* 11 Feb. 1933.

86 *African Leader* 11 Feb. 1933; Seme, "Africans Come, All to the Nation's Call", *African Leader* 31 Dec. 1932; *African Leader* 11 Feb. 1933; *Umteteli wa Bantu* 1 Apr. 1933; Seme, "Sedition".

87 Seme, "How the African National Congress Must Be Run", *Umteteli wa Bantu* 23 Dec. 1933, *The African National Congress: Is it Dead?* (Newcastle, 1932) pp. 1-16, "Support Congress Clubs and Ensure Employment", *Umteteli wa Bantu* 10 Nov. 1934, Circular to ANC officers 13 Nov. 1930, CKC 7A; *African Leader* 11 Feb. 1933. See also Rich, *White Power*, pp. 47-9, Cobley, *Class & Consciousness*, p. 163.

88 *Bantu World* 7 Apr., 17 Feb. 1934; "Dr. P. ka Seme's ANC Appeal", *Umteteli wa Bantu* 25 Nov. 1933; *African Leader* 19, 26 Nov. 1932; Seme, "Africans Come, All to the Nation's Call", *African Leader* 31 Dec. 1932; Seme, "The Crisis", *African Leader* 18 Mar. 1933; Letter of Seme to *Bantu World* 23 Oct. 1937.

89 Evidence of P. Seme (ANC) to NEC, 6 May 1931, "Minutes of Evidence", pp. 7400-7429.

90 "Minutes of Evidence", pp. 7400-74129.

91 Cobley, *Class & Consciousness*, p. 162; Basner, "Interview", pp. 16-19.

92 Plaatje, "Congress Policy", *Umteteli wa Bantu* 18 Feb. 1933; *Umteteli* 16 Sep., 5, 12 Aug., 28 Oct. 1933; Plaatje, "The Native Mind", *African Leader* 18 Feb. 1933; Plaatje, "Wanted: A Leader", *Umteteli wa Bantu* 3 Sep. 1932.

93 "The Pretoria Conference", *Umteteli wa Bantu* 13 Dec. 1930; "The Conference", *Umteteli wa Bantu* 20 Dec. 1930.

94 Z.R. Mahabane, "Native Taxation and Education", submission to NEC, "Minutes of Evidence".

95 Evidence of Z.R. Mahabane to NEC, "Minutes of Evidence", pp. 5369-5379.

96 "Non-European Conference", *Umteteli wa Bantu* 10 Jan. 1931.

97 *Free State Advocate* 31 Dec. 1938; Mahabane, *The Fight*, pp. 45, 53; speeches in CKC 2:DA:14:30/3.

98 As seen in the movement of former NUMSA shop stewards into management after 1994: K. von Holdt, *Transition from Below: Forging Trade Unionism and Workplace Change in South Africa* (Pietermaritzburg: University of Natal Press, 2003), p. 308.

99 "The ANC Presidential Address … 1938" [and discussion minutes], CKC 2:DA:14:30/3; OFS Archives (VAB) SOK 1/1/41 file N1/4/3/129/71: Z.R. Mahabane Estate.

100 Calata interview with G. Carter, Mar. 1964, CKC 2:XC3:94; Calata to Rheinallt Jones 1 Feb. 1938, *ANC Collection*; M. Goedhals, "African Nationalism and Indigenous Christianity: A Study in the Life of James Calata (1895-1983)" *Journal of Religion in Africa*, 33 (2003), pp. 63-82, pp. 66-7: his low stipend as a priest may have inclined him towards some interest in the working people; Verwey, *New Dictionary*, p. 36; *Umteteli wa Bantu* 10 Jan. 1931; ANC Conference 16 Dec. 1938 [in Calata's hand], CKC 2:DA:14:30/3.

101 P. Walshe, *Prophetic Christianity and the Liberation Movement in South Africa* (Pietermaritzburg: Cluster, 1995), pp. 16-17; Calata to Rheinallt Jones 6 Mar. 1939, *ANC Collection*.

102 "Pass Laws" *Umteteli wa Bantu* 1 Nov. 1930, *Bantu World* 9, 16 Jul. 1932; NEC p. 7987, "Native Policy", *Umteteli wa Bantu* 31 Jan. 1931, "Union's Native Policy" *African Observer* 5(1) 1936 pp. 32-34, "White & Black in South Africa", *African Observer* 6(3) 1937, "State Must Find Work for All", *Bantu World* 7 May 1932, "Duty of Bantu

Intellectuals", "Bantu Patriotism", "Bantu Nationalism", *Umteteli wa Bantu* 23 Aug., 6, 20 Sep. 1930, "Failure of Our Organisations", "A Challenge to Bantu Leadership", *Umteteli wa Bantu* 11 Apr. 1931, 9 Jan. 1932.

103 R. V. S. Thema: "Native Unrest", *Umteteli wa Bantu* 31 May 1930; "The Pass Laws", *Umteteli wa Bantu* 1 Nov. 1930; "The Road to Leeuwkop", *Umteteli wa Bantu* 15 Nov. 1930; "The Lawless Native", *Umteteli wa Bantu* 18 Oct. 1930.

104 R. V. S. Thema to NEC 15 Apr. 1931, "Evidence", pp. 7956, 7974, 7983-7984; *Bantu World* 16 Oct. 1937.

105 *Bantu World* 23 Apr., 7, 14 May 1932; Ngubane in K. Eales, "Jordan Ngubane, *Inkundla ya Bantu* and the ANC Youth League, 1944-1951", BA (Hons.) thesis, University of Natal 1984, p. 20; *Bantu World* 16, 23 Apr., 18 Jun. 1932, 4 Jun. 1935, 14 Dec. 1935.

106 H. S. Msimang, "Ideals", *Umteteli wa Bantu* 7 Jun. 1930; *Umteteli wa Bantu* 18 Apr. 1931, Letter of H. Selby Msimang to *Umteteli wa Bantu* 16 May 1931.

107 "The Unity Movement" (letter of H. S. Msimang to) *Umteteli wa Bantu* 16 May 1931.

108 Msimang paper to AME Church Education Rally, 19 Jul. 1930, cited in M. Swanson, "The Joy of Proximity", pp. 277-278; Msimang, "Provincial Shylocks", *Umteteli wa Bantu* 5 Jul. 1930.

109 Evidence of H. S. Msimang (representing ANC) to NEC, 6 May 1931, "Minutes of Evidence", pp. 7429-7431.

110 Evidence of H. S. Msimang, R. V. S. Thema, Dhlomo and S. S. Thema to NEC 6 May 1931, "Evidence", pp. 7431-7444i; *Bantu World* 9, 16 Jul. 1932: Modiakgotla concurred: see *Umteteli wa Bantu* 12 Aug. 1933.

111 *African Leader* 25 Mar. 1933; Msimang, *Crisis*; SAP Ladysmith, Reports of Jul. 1938 meetings by Msimang: "Selby Msimang Agitator", TAD NA64/328; H. S. Msimang to *Bantu World* 5 Oct. 1935.

112 KC v. 4, p. 128; Willan, *Sol Plaatje*, pp. 321-328; *Umteteli wa Bantu* 9 Nov. 1929.

113 Evidence of S. Plaatje, "Minutes of Evidence", NEC, pp. 5283-5286, 5296, 5305.

114 NEC "Minutes of Evidence", pp. 5286-5330; "Further Evidence to the NEC", Plaatje, *Selected Writings*, pp. 390-96; TAD NA 62/276(1).

115 *Ikwizi le Afrika* 9 Jan. 1932, *Midland News* 30 Dec. 1931; R.V. Selope Thema, "A Challenge to Bantu Leadership" *Umteteli wa Bantu,* 9 Jan. 1932; S. Plaatje, "A Whiteman's Language", *Umteteli wa Bantu* 5 Dec. 1931; Plaatje, "The Crime Factory", *Umteteli wa Bantu* 13 Feb. 1932; Plaatje, "Stricken Diamond City", *Umteteli wa Bantu,* 27 Feb. 1932; Willan, *Sol Plaatje*, pp. 384-386.

116 N. Visser and T. Couzens, "Introduction," *H.I.E. Dhlomo Collected Works* (Johannesburg: Ravan Press, 1985), p. x; *Umteteli wa Bantu* 3 Jan. 1931, 10, 17 May, 6 Sep. 1930, 17 Jan. 1931.

117 Dhlomo to NEC, 6 May 1931, pp. 7431-7444i; *Umteteli wa Bantu* 27 Aug. 1932; N. Masilela, *The Cultural Modernity of H.I.E. Dhlomo* (Trenton: Africa World Press, 2007); Cobley, *Class & Consciousness*, p. 86, and *passim*, and email from N. Masilela to the author, 5 June 2007.

118 Independent ICU Witwatersrand. "Statement" by H. Tyamzashe, 1931, NEC "Evidence" pp. 8060-8063.

119 "Resolutions of CC-CPSA 29 Dec. 1938 – 2 Jan. 1939" in Davidson, *Communist International* v. 2 p. 291.

Moderate Centre, Militant Province?
The Cape in the 1930s

In the 1930s, there was diversity of ANC branch attitudes to labour, and attempts to bring them together with workers. At times, there was an aloofness from radical labour struggles. At other times, there was strong ANC support for black labour rights. Just as the Transvaal in the immediate post-World War I period, and Natal in the 1920s, were the scene of radical labour protests that Congress linked up with, so the Cape witnessed concentrated labour "agitation" in the early 1930s and important unifying campaigns in the late 1930s that brought together Congress and labour movement activists. This chapter presents a case study of these themes in the Cape; the following chapter treats the other provinces.

Congress in the Western and Eastern Cape

Closer ANC-labour ties developed in the Western Cape in the 1930s for three reasons. Firstly, many local ANC leaders focused on labour issues. Secondly, the impact of economic and political events on Africans was severe, notably the harsh effects of the depression and equally harsh state measures. Thirdly, in the Cape Peninsula and Boland towns many Africans were workers.[1] ANC-worker contacts in the decade were unstable: rising at the start and end of the decade, and abating in the mid-1930s, due largely to fluctuations in ANC policies and leadership. However, at both nodes the ANC became closely involved in the sharp class struggles of black workers, whilst even in the more quiescent interregnum it still supported their rights.

As black unemployment grew during the depression, so then the organisational work of the ANC intensified. The presence of socialists Tonjeni, Ndobe and Cetyiwe gave the ANC (WP) a sharper focus on workers. Tonjeni had mixed proletarian credentials. He stated publicly at a 1931 meeting in Tarkastad that he "never had any schooling. My father was a poor man and could not afford to give me any education," yet his father had been a member of the Bhunga. Soon, the ANC in the Western Cape "emerged as a vibrant organisation".[2]

THE AFRICAN NATIONAL CONGRESS ON THE MOVE.

Purging the African National Congress of Bolshevik tendencies.

A Herculean MASS MEETING organised under the aegis of the African National Congress, will be held on the

GRAND PARADE

Sunday, 15th June, 1930, at 2 p.m.

when the emisaries of the Communist Party Mr. Thomas Faku and his ilk will be exposed and opposed. Far reaching resolutions will be passed re their expulsion from Congress.

Prof. JAS. THAELE will preside.

The race must be saved from subversive influences of Judas Iscariot.

All cordially invited to attend at 2 p.m. sharp

Published by the African National Congress, 102 Caledon St., and Printed by the Swift Press, cor. Sydney & Chapel Streets, Cape Town.

ANC Western Province flyer, 1930

Much of the reported ANC rhetoric expressed African nationalist sentiment, but there also were direct appeals to workers. Tonjeni, at the time ANC Provincial Assistant Secretary, stated in March 1930 that the ANC was preparing a "general strike of all underpaid coloured workers in the country ... to demand a minimum wage ... for coloured farm labourers". His approach differed from that of "top-down" TNC militants of 1918. He told a large gathering of workers in April "unless they fought their own battles they would remain in the mud". However, he still saw a leading role for the ANC. Workers should "be ready when the Congress gave the word to break loose from slavery". The propensity to adopt working-class tactics such as strikes was due in part to increasing direct ANC contact with farm and rural labourers, who joined the ANC (WP) in their hundreds in 1930, and in part to a close working relationship with the CPSA. Tonjeni continued to promote *Umsebenzi* within the ANC, and to use it to expose the harsh conditions of workers. In its pages, he described the living quarters of black workers in Graaff-Reinet location as "fit for rock-rabbits ... frightfully overcrowded". He saw a close connection between ANC and worker struggles and viewed the growth of the ANC (WP) as "due to the terrible conditions under which non-European farm labourers are groaning". Persistent state repression aimed, as Tonjeni argued, at "the legitimate attempts of the black labourers to organise", also stimulated ANC identification with workers.[3]

ANC (WP) support assumed mass proportions in the face of rising unemployment in rural towns and attempts to force down farm wages. In May 1930, it organised a mass march in Worcester against the Riotous Assemblies Bill. Local Chamber of Commerce president L. Goldberg stated: "Congress had such control over the meeting that the situation was very dangerous." Over 400 black workers marched in the Worcester May Day parade. The Worcester ANC regularly drew crowds of 200 at weekend worker meetings. Radicals around the country warmed to this news. In April, as the annual ANC (WP) conference met, the CPSA enthused that this radical Congress branch "sets the example". *Abantu-Batho* strongly supported the radicals. However, state and employer repression nullified these organisational advances. Workers who joined the ANC faced victimisation. Police and vigilantes assaulted ANC officials; five black workers (all ANC members, according to state reports) were killed at a rally in May 1930. Labourers who attended ANC meetings were dismissed; *Cape Argus* noted that farmers had "decided not to employ in future any new labourers" belonging to Congress; *Umteteli wa Bantu* that rail and other employers "dismissed all Native workers who are members of the African Congress". Riotous Assemblies Act amendments made it more difficult for the ANC to organise. When nine Robertson farm-workers left work and were collected by ANC "motor-lorries carrying native agitators", they were promptly dismissed. Even so, the ANC managed to organise jointly African and "coloured" workers. This perturbed the Worcester magistrate who advocated segregation to separate them and "remove them from the influence" of Congress "agitators". Tonjeni responded by threatening "an industrial and agricultural strike". He became very popular among Africans, who dubbed him "The Black Lion".[4]

Government officials banned the radicals from town after town. In January 1931, a magistrate found Tonjeni guilty of being in a prohibited area and sentenced him to a month's hard labour, yet he had merely alighted on the George railway platform. A court upheld Tonjeni's appeal, but police continually prohibited him from organising. By late 1930, there were reports that Worcester ANC leaders Arnoth Plaatjes and Peter Vumazonke were "to retire from Congress activity" and that, faced by fines, the Congress hall in Worcester would have to be sold.[5]

James Thaele briefly joined forces with the radicals when police arrested ANC organisers in Worcester. Influenced, according to police reports, by the left's defeat at the national ANC convention, he soon took exception to "Bolshevik tendencies" and suspended Tonjeni and Ndobe. In June, Thaele called a mass meeting on the Parade in Cape Town to purge "emissaries of the Communist Party" (see illustration) arguing: "The race must be saved from subversive influences of Judas Iscariot." When Thaele denied radicals access to the ANC platform on the Parade and then succeeded in barring communists from any ANC positions, a split ensued. In November, he called for a campaign against the spread of communism. In January 1931, Seme declared that Thaele was "with me".[6]

The level of support given to workers was a central issue in the split. A leaflet signed by leading leftist ANC members, including Gomas, Thomas Faku, and Josiah Ngedlane, criticised Thaele's attacks on unemployed activists and ANC radicals. They demanded that the ANC "take up officially the struggle on behalf of the hundreds of starving" Africans. Tonjeni issued a manifesto stating the present ANC leadership had "lost all fighting spirit". A vote of 200–3 at an ANC meeting supported him. ANC Montagu secretary J. Fortuin commented: "We who have to slave 14 hours a day for eight pence on the farms are waking up ... Down with the 'good boys'!" ANC Worcester branch chairperson Arnoth Plaatjes wrote letters of support to *Umsebenzi,* which some increasingly saw as a *Congress* tool, and which by the end of 1930 had agents as far apart as King William's Town, De Aar, and Port St. Johns. A joint meeting at Ndabeni in September, with Ngedlane in the chair, heard unity speeches from Gomas and the ANC's Sam Hoho, previously an ICU organiser, who had opposed Thaele's anti-communism in ANC meetings on the Parade, and now thanked the CPSA for its fight against "slave laws".[7]

The radicals then formed, in November 1930, the Independent ANC (I-ANC) with Tonjeni as president. One may argue the I-ANC was no longer the ANC. Technically this was so, yet the existence of ICU splinter groups or rival "ANC" bodies in Natal and the Cape has not prevented historians from considering them part of the history of these organisations. Similarly, I interpret the I-ANC in relation to the Congress tradition because firstly, people who until then had been prominent in Congress led it, secondly it retained "ANC" in its title, and thirdly some members after its demise either returned directly to the Congress fold or retained an identification with it. At the grassroots, it is unlikely many would have seen a clear distinction between these Congresses. In any case, Ndobe and Tonjeni had already achieved major gains in their Congress-labour organising *before* Thaele forced them out of the Western Province ANC.

Stanley Silwana, John Gomas, Bransby Ndobe

Whereas Thaele's power base was in Cape Town, the I-ANC gained strong support in Western Cape rural branches, the Southern Cape, and the Midlands. It did this by campaigning on black demands such as franchise and land, but also on issues of special concern to workers, such as unemployment and rents. The manifesto of the I-ANC laid great emphasis on national oppression: Africans were "slaves in the land of their birth"; but it also claimed to speak directly for "the suffering masses", and referred to the suffering of workers. It would co-operate with all bodies dedicated to the "liberation of the African people", and render assistance "to all African trade unions with the object of improving the conditions of the black workers". Tactics, in marked contrast to Seme's ANC, were to be "militant struggle" against government, including "agitation and mass demonstrations and organisation aimed at securing a general stoppage of work and civil disobedience". Seme's ANC was "a mere tool of the Government".[8]

At the I-ANC inaugural conference in Cape Town in December 1930, this militant concern for labour was evident. Tonjeni condemned "pitiful wages; [and] the killing of scores of miners weekly". He saw a need to "engage in active struggle". I-ANC support for the "Black Republic" slogan was the clearest expression of its demands for equality. This enabled the state to claim that it worked "in close consultation" with the CPSA.[9]

Driven by state repression from the Western Cape, the I-ANC spread rapidly in Southern Cape towns such as Swellendam, George and Oudtshoorn. It held regular, well-attended meetings of workers and unemployed. Oudtshoorn had about 200 members and Tonjeni drew big crowds there, including 650 people in November 1930. However, state repression and bitter rivalry from the ANC (WP) took their toll and I-ANC influence began to wane, though a branch in Oudtshoorn persisted into 1932.[10]

In 1931, Tonjeni and Ndobe turned east and crisscrossed the Midlands, holding meetings in Middelburg, Naauwpoort, Cradock and other towns, generating enormous worker support closely tied to economic conditions. The depression hit the Midlands economy hard. Black workers faced persistent attempts to reduce their wages and employers retrenched many of them. The I-ANC forged a close nexus with working people in Graaff-Reinet, Cradock, and Middelburg by vigorously taking up local labour grievances over unemployment, poll taxes, and passes. By August 1931, the I-ANC Middleburg had a paid-up membership of 300. Some of its leaders, such as labourer John Mana and unemployed worker John Sholoba, were clearly working class. Hofmeyr notes black unemployed "flocked to join" this "clearly mass based organisation".[11]

Behind this support for the radical ANC offshoot was depression and racism. In Cradock, rising unemployment and poverty fuelled long-term discontent over high taxes. For many years, Africans owned very little land around Cradock and the majority of the town's black population were workers, chiefly domestic workers. As the depression bit, the Town Council neglected black workers, focusing relief on white employees and dismissing Africans. At a time when the Cradock mayor went to Cape Town to plead for more relief for white workers, he bluntly told a deputation from the Joint Council seeking relief for unemployed black workers and their starving children that he could not "understand" location unemployment given shortages of farm labour.[12]

The active and creative campaigning by I-ANC leaders built on discontent. Mass meetings, some attracting 500-1,000 people, were a favoured tactic. It is clear, from reports by black moderates and white people who complained of workers "wasting their time" at ANC meetings, that workers attended. Leaders used a range of metaphors to appeal to audiences. Tonjeni and Ndobe used Biblical analogies to urge support for the I-ANC. This is not proof of any particularly strong religious current in the body: it was critical of mainstream churches and even condemned religion. The strongest current was proletarian. At a meeting of 650 people in Oudtshoorn, Tonjeni urged "downing tools". He told 1,000 Africans on a Cradock football field that black people "were sacked from the railway to give the Boers work". Ndobe told a meeting at Pacaltsdorp that society was comprised of "two classes of people ... those who toiled ... and those who lived ... by exploiting the working classes". Africans "were oppressed as a nation and as a working class". The most vivid illustration of I-ANC combination of socialist and nationalistic emblems was its unveiling of its own flag, consisting of the ANC colours, plus red.[13]

The independent ANC radicals also invoked heroes of African resistance to colonisation in ways that must have sent a feeling of pride yet simultaneously a shudder of fear along the spines of moderate ANC figures. Tonjeni told a gathering of 2,000 at Tarkastad in July 1931 that Makana and Sandile were "never satisfied with the foreign yoke". He called out: "African people, you must rise in your large numbers like Makana and fight for emancipation." Tonjeni was rash, as he clearly recognised police spies in the crowd, but this was not wild rhetoric; he mixed careful quotes of wages figures from the 1922 Chamber of Mines report. The aim was organisation. "My friends, come out of slavery and join the ranks of organisation ... African people have become outcasts. The people have left the most important weapon – the spear of organisation."[14]

Another I-ANC tactic was visiting farms, but due to farmer hostility, this was rare. Demonstrations were more effective. In February, March and August 1931 and March 1932 it led large marches to the Middelburg mayor calling for jobs and protesting high rents. I-ANC activity encouraged female membership. "Women must join ... they are as much exploited as men," stated one leader. Women were active in its campaigns against passes and rents. In Middelburg, the I-ANC supported a well-attended women's demonstration in March 1931. It initiated rent and poll tax boycotts. The latter resulted in a 50 per cent drop in poll tax collection in Middelburg between 1930 and 1931, attributed by the local magistrate to ANC agitation. Pickets took the place of arrested protesters. In October 1931 400 people blocked police seeking to deport Middelburg I-ANC Secretary William Hendricks (or Hendrik Velapi), a worker. In January 1932, the I-ANC in Cradock called a strike, and on May Day 1932 it mobilised 600 unemployed workers in a march for jobs and food.[15]

Speeches at June 1931 meetings in Cradock illustrate I-ANC tactics. At one meeting, directed at the "coloured" community, 800 people heard Tonjeni argue: "Coloured people were slaves and the only remedy was organisation." He sought to play on religious thinking. Condemning the hovels in which Cradock black people lived, he asked: "If you profess to be Christians would it be right to keep quiet?" Tonjeni employed gendered arguments. White people were "out to make your wives and girls go down on their knees to scrub the floors for their white women". To prove the breadth of I-ANC's ambitions he concluded: "We are not out to claim a district: we want the whole continent." Plaatjes spoke in Afrikaans, emphasising national oppression: "You are all aboriginals. The white people are foreign: they have only come to rob." Black and coloured people should unite behind the I-ANC.[16]

It was a potent message. Cradock police arrested the leaders for challenging regulations under the Native Administration Act that prevented entering of locations without permission of the white superintendent. Police recently had arrested them three times in Middelburg for the same offence. Passing judgement, the magistrate conceded that their aim, "to arouse the interest of the local people in the Congress and to enrol members", was laudable, but convicted Tonjeni and Plaatjes of promoting hostility between the races, imposing four months' hard labour. The local white newspaper agreed with the sentence but warned that unjust laws and inequality "play right into the hands of the agitators and swell the ranks of their unions". Less charitable was the view of E. Xholla and E. Pokomela, chairperson and secretary of the rival Cape African Congress's Women's Section, Cradock branch, who personified respectability in feeling "thoroughly ashamed" at the I-ANC speeches and wanting their meetings in the location banned.[17]

The I-ANC faced massive repression: violent attacks by farmers, deportation of leaders. By 1932, Tonjeni had retreated to New Brighton. He and Ndobe wrote for the CPSA. The state considered Velapi sufficiently dangerous to law and order to order him to leave Middelburg. The I-ANC responded by developing deeper organisation. Lower-level members sprang up to replace banned leaders—much as did the UDF in the 1980s. In August 1931, in Tonjeni's enforced absence, unemployed and starving residents angrily confronted the Middelburg Mayor, deriding his suggestion that they put their faith in a Vigilance Committee, which they said had been "bought for a shilling". Worse was to follow for the authorities in September when 80-90 determined, largely unemployed, residents in the proletarian Rooilaer section of Cradock location wielding sticks and stones drove back police checking tax receipts. A "large amount" of foot, and mounted, police overpowered the resisters, but black women "lost complete control of themselves and rained sticks, stones and tins at the police", defiantly calling out in Afrikaans: "You won't take him—he has no work. Neuk the police—beat them." The press apportioned blame to "Native Communistic propaganda", but black people resented paying taxes with so many of their number unemployed. Location authorities blamed Tonjeni's sowing of the seeds of revolt on violence in January 1932, with 56 arrested; some for assaulting domestic workers on their way to work; youths sang communist songs whilst in jail. In April 1932, 17 black workers in the location refused to undertake farm work. May Day saw 400-500 people gather in Cradock; a group of 100-150 joined the rally, singing the "Native Independent National Conference song", carrying sticks, and sporting signs "We Demand Work Immediately" and "Down with the Anti-Native Laws". A young "coloured" man, Blesmaahle, went to jail under an ordinance prohibiting singing without Council permission. When police tried to arrest rally leaders the crowd prevented them, but they managed to arrest Cradock I-ANC chairperson George Camies. Prosecutors complained that week after week there had been "unrest" in the town and location.[18]

By the end of 1932, repression had effectively silenced the Middelburg I-ANC branch, though a branch persisted in Cradock. Its legacy lived on. Kotane moved to Cradock and in 1934 wrote that the I-ANC "has deeply entrenched itself in ... Cradock and Tarkastad, and its leaders are extremely popular". Probably the experience of seeing a popular ANC in action inspired Kotane to reject his earlier disdain for the body; in 1931, he had defended the I-ANC against condemnation by the sectarian CPSA leader Douglas Wolton.

A rump I-ANC group gave a report to the ANC 1938 national conference, affirming: "Our hearts and souls are with the Congress! We are men of and for the Congress." The image of the defiant Ndobe and Tonjeni lived on among some workers across the region. In Port Elizabeth, domestic worker Veronica Kanyangwa demanded in 1932 that Ndobe "return to us and help in this big movement. The police stole him away from us."[19]

The significance of the I-ANC goes beyond a brief flirtation with workers. Hofmeyr concludes that it adopted the most militant programme and methods among African nationalist groups before 1949. It had mass support and a decidedly proletarian flavour. It mobilised black workers on working-class demands but in a local, not industrial, manner, and for a period in most cases lasting only two years. Yet, there was a measure of continuity. The later success of the Food and Canning Workers Union in the Western Cape drew upon the enduring legacy of activism generated by the I-ANC, and both the CPSA and CAC later were able to draw upon politicisation by the I-ANC to help maintain viable branches in the 1930s in places such as Worcester and Cradock.[20]

As noted above one could argue the I-ANC was not part of Congress, but virtually a CPSA branch. However, the CPSA, immersed in sectarianism, distanced itself from the organisation. Some I-ANC leaders received their political education from the CPSA. Yet, it is clear from their statements on broader national issues, from their use of the green-yellow-black (and red) flag, and by their continued use of the name of Congress, that they envisaged the I-ANC as the continuation, on more radical lines, of Congress. The I-ANC is part of ANC history. It recruited black workers, adopted working-class tactics, and advocated policies fully in keeping with workers' demands. The history of the I-ANC, like the TNC in 1918-1920, demonstrates that, given a favourable conjuncture of conditions—namely the existence of a largely proletarianised community, the onset of economic crisis, and astute political leadership by a radicalised cadre with an ideology influenced by working-class ideas and methods—Congress could be part of, or even lead, working-class struggles.

The ANC (WP), by 1930 led by moderates, nevertheless continued to protest against poor conditions of black workers, if less consistently than in 1929. It sought to expand to Cradock and Graaff-Reinet where, led by Faku, it provided strong competition to the I-ANC. In seeking to dislodge the radicals, he was obliged to support local worker grievances against unemployment and rents. Faku organised a rent strike in Aberdeen. By adopting such policies, the ANC (WP) attracted the same sort of repression directed at the I-ANC. In Cape Town, despite his anti-communism, Thaele faced bans. Consequently, he was temporarily radicalised and, seeking allies, invoked the working class in public statements. When bans on Sunday meetings impelled him to cancel a meeting scheduled for Rawsonville in March 1930, he declared that if Pirow's ban was permanent, "we shall disobey his orders ... We are a working class and that is the only day we have to discuss things." Congress, stated Thaele, wished to organise farm workers; it had established a night school in Worcester to overcome worker illiteracy and was "going to agitate until we get the Wage Board to fix a minimum rate of pay". This rhetoric may have convinced Ndobe that Thaele was worth persevering with as an ally. In 1932, Ndobe told *Umsebenzi* Xhosa readers that union members should work together with Thaele, Calata, and local elders to start a campaign in the townships to improve living conditions. However, Thaele soon succumbed to state pressure, and cancelled many ANC meetings.[21]

ANC (WP) secretary Kennon Thaele also took an interest in labour issues, and suffered bans consequently. In 1931, he aroused the ire of the Sutherland magistrate by demanding that the state exempt an aged farm worker, Klaas Danster, from taxation and refund his tax payments. The magistrate complained that Thaele visited the district regularly and was "upsetting the local order of things" by his "interference with coloured and Native labour and local addresses to them". Workers were "leaving their farms on flimsy pretences to satisfy Thaele and his society". Subsequently, the state prohibited him from the area under the Riotous Assemblies Act. In 1933, he drew attention to difficulties faced by black workers in Cape Town forced to apply for passes.[22]

The ANC (WP) continued to take up political and labour issues. It linked passes to oppression of black labour. In 1932, Chief Organiser Faku explained to readers of *Bantu World* how enforcement of pass laws on black workers in Cape Town exacerbated unemployment and made it easier to impose white labour preference policies. Congress held mass-based anti-pass protests. In November 1932, a reported capacity crowd of 1,755 attended an ANC mass meeting in Cape Town City Hall. Resolutions protested high black unemployment and job discrimination. Rents were not "proportional to the earning capacity of the working man". The abolition of labour compounds was necessary. Such actions encouraged local support for Congress in some areas. Congress held a large-scale protest estimated at over 10,000 people in Langa. Four ANC members from Worcester wrote to *African Leader* that they desired to revive the ANC there. The "majority of the people here, are all staunch supporters of the Congress but, unfortunately, they have no leaders". Thaele had "sneezed at our complaints". They naively requested personal intervention by Seme.[23]

There was, in all this activity, something rather at odds with the view of those historians who steadfastly cling to a notion of an ANC that merely met once a year and went away again. The ANC Grassy Park branch was particularly active at this time, and involved some women. Mrs Vickia Mapalam, branch assistant secretary, claimed that, "in spite of the economic recession", it had achieved "wonderful progress" by managing to build and furnish a local hall and to hold a "largely attended meeting" in March 1933. The branch met weekly, the executive committee, comprising 13 members, monthly.[24]

James Ngojo, a Congress organiser in the Cape in the 1930s, strongly defended the rights of black workers in a comprehensive submission to the NEC in 1931. In passing, he also noted his support for the rights of black traders. Nevertheless, his main contention was the need for better conditions for black workers: a fixed scale of wages for skilled and unskilled workers, linked to rents; extension of pensions to Africans; an end to the "bond of slavery" of pass laws; legalisation of African unions. African women domestic workers earned very low wages and now had an extra burden of doing the washing of an entire house, a task previously undertaken by washerwomen who in turn were "being deprived of a livelihood". Neither did he forget educated workers deprived of jobs by the "civilised labour" policy. Ngojo, who had lived in Paarl for four years, spoke in detail of the arduous working and living conditions of road and farmworkers in the region. Many of these workers previously were employed constructing mountain roads and now worked in quarries, street work, and in factories. In this period, Ngojo also led a deputation of Ndabeni residents to the Location Superintendent, protesting plans to introduce passes.[25] Ngojo's earlier involvement in ANC support for workers (in 1918 and 1921) and the prior support of working-class demands by other Western Cape ANC leaders (such as Ndobe, Tonjeni, and even Thaele) influenced his interest in workers. The ANC's pro-worker policies and organisational efforts had established the context in which people such as Ngojo operated.

Sam Hoho, ex-ICU and ANC but now I-ANC organiser, addressed the NEC. Recently, he stated, low black wages in Cape Town had declined still further. The cost of living of working-class families with whom he had spoken cancelled out their wages. Showing great familiarity with their precise daily expenses, he made a case that the state should increase black wages from 4/6d to 6/6d per day. Workers had to pay high transport fares, taxes, burial insurance, food and rent, as well as church contributions. They could not return the long distances to their homelands on weekends and, in any case, severe drought obviated their support in rural areas. He urged amendment of the Industrial Conciliation Act to end prohibition on the unionisation of black rail and farm labourers. Some of these workers, he said, clearly were not temporary migrant workers, having worked for 20 years on the railways. Often they were highly experienced, yet earned only 4/3d a day. Hoho took up other worker grievances. Dockers, he stated, had very irregular jobs, denying them a steady wage. He denounced the 1926 "Colour Bar" Act for denying work to black skilled workers. Africans could not afford to have their children undertake apprenticeships. The Native Service Contract Bill made the African virtually a slave; it must not proceed. Instead, farmers should pay higher wages and permit genuine work contracts. Government was refusing to let capable leaders of black workers represent their interests at International Labour Office (ILO) conferences.[26]

These diverse ANC actions on labour matters were poorly co-ordinated, due in part to persisting rivalries between Thaele and Calata that prevented unification of the Cape sections. Divisions continued for years. Thaele refused to acknowledge his defeat in elections at the 1936 ANC (WP) conference by a group led by Alfred Coto (a trader), Stephen Oliphant, and John Masiu, and expelled this faction. His megalomania prompted remnants of the I-ANC to declare in 1938 that the ANC should "protect genuine national movements against uns[c]rupulous crooks and sweet tongued exploiters". Thaele continued as ANC (WP) leader until 1938, when the national ANC ruled against his claim to be legitimate leader of the province. Congress was thus deeply fragmented.[27]

ANC weaknesses alienated some labour activists and drove them to form new bodies. Gomas, who had exposed exploitation of tailors in 1930 and low wages of crayfishermen in 1934, was frustrated with ANC inaction. By 1935, he also started to drift away from the CPSA due to its united front strategy that gave attention to white labour. ANC and union reformism failed to rouse black workers against the "civilised labour policy", he stated. In 1934, in his booklet on the centenary of the "end" of slavery, he pointed to recent strikes and anti-pass struggles as evidence of growth of national and class struggles. The ANC and ICU were "two mighty mass organizations" of the black masses that at their militant best had awakened mass support. They lacked leaders with "experiences and tradition of struggle of the international working class", but would be re-built. Though hostile to its reformism, he thus acknowledged the ANC as a *mass* organisation and saw it had a future. Frustration with these bodies prompted Gomas in 1935 to join La Guma to form the National Liberation League, combining black liberation with working-class ideologies and embracing a range of tactics from petitions to strikes. At first, it gained strong support, with 1,000 members in Cape Town and branches in other towns and provinces but sectarianism contributed to its decline by 1938.[28]

ANC and worker representatives also came together in the nationwide Non-European United Front, formed in 1938 with strong Western Cape involvement. Its 1939 conference involved Kotane (secretary) and Oliphant (ANC (WP)), Marks and Baloyi (ANC and Transvaal United Front), John Mtini (Non-European Railway and Harbour Workers' Union), Jeremiah Dunjwa and Hawa Ahmed (Laundry Workers' Union), and other delegates. Baloyi expressed the ambiguous views of black businesspersons, arguing: "Money makes the man, without it, nothing could be done." Marks stressed: "Our organisational work should include mines, agriculture, railways and harbour." Workers such as Mtini and Ahmed mixed with ANC members such as Hoho and Oliphant. The Front held a large rally against segregation in March 1939 in Cape Town but did not last long. Yet it is further proof of an emergent, if erratic, worker-nationalist discourse and another body in which ANC members co-operated with workers.[29]

After a period of quiescence caused by repression and internal divisions, the ANC in the Western Cape began to regain its earlier militancy. This was due to several factors: the profound shock to Africans of the Hertzog Bills; nation-wide efforts to revive the ANC; and the role of radicals, notably communists, led by Kotane. The latter helped re-focus the ANC on black workers. Kotane resided in Cape Town from 1937. In 1938, the CPSA headquarters shifted there. Kotane was CPSA General Secretary but also threw himself into ANC work, becoming chairperson of the ANC Cape Town Central branch and working to build grassroots structures. He was a strong link between the ANC and black workers, between the ANC and CPSA, and between the ANC (WP) and the national ANC. Other communist ANC (WP) activists were John Masiu (a trade unionist), Johnson Ngwevela (variously a labourer, clerk, and peddler), Joseph Nkatlo (a clerk), Stanley Silwana, and R. Ndimande. Ngojo also returned to ANC activity. With these working-class-oriented leaders, the ANC gained some support among more settled, urbanised black workers in places such as Langa. In February 1939, the ANC Cape Town branch issued a new programme. Kotane, Nkatlo and C. T. Kumalo signed the programme and called for mass action. They dedicated the branch to fighting for not only broad black emancipation but also labour demands such as a fair minimum wage and free black unions. In June 1939, the branch called a public rally over conditions in the Peninsula.[30]

In the 1930s new black unions emerged in the Cape (see Chapter 2). They were not yet strong enough to build effective bridges with the ANC, but the foundations of future close relations developed. Food and Canning Workers Union leaders of the 1940s, such as Elizabeth Mafekeng and Oscar Mpetha, were workers and ANC activists who helped popularise ANC policies among workers. Mafekeng, who worked in Paarl canning factories from 1939, later participated in ANC campaigns. However, the ANC faced enormous problems in enrolling the impoverished, temporary workers in squatter camps. Moreover, this period of radicalism was again short-lived. Moderates led by Oliphant and Bennett Ncwana displaced Cape ANC radicals in the early 1940s.[31]

The Cape African Congress (CAC) had separated from the ANC (WP) in 1927. It followed a moderate path in the 1930s. Reverend Elijah Mdolomba was re-elected president at its 1930 annual convention. His conference address highlighted the self-help theme promoted by Seme. The conference cautiously "prayed" government would "reconsider" the poll tax and criticised African exclusion from pension schemes. Conference speeches by the local magistrate, D. D. T. Jabavu, and Joint Council members "advised the convention to hasten slowly, observing moderation and constitutional methods". Jabavu remarked that Congress, previously seen as "dangerous", was now "a moderate body", obliged to "fight with its back to the wall against Bolshevism".[32]

CAC leaders such as James Calata strongly opposed I-ANC penetration of the Midlands. Calata, an Anglican minister and son of a peasant, had once been a moderate supporter of the Bantu Union but after moving from Korsten to Cradock in 1928, and witnessing the poverty of the people, he joined the Cape Congress in 1930. The CAC soon elected him president, a position he held until 1949. Calata firmly opposed local socialists such as Tonjeni, and used the local Advisory Board and Vigilance Association to warn people against radicals. Calata urged police to deny Tonjeni access to the town in March 1931, and in 1932 appeared at meetings with police to urge moderation. In October 1932, he warned Midlands' teachers against communism spreading to "the ignorant masses". This did not mean, he added, that Africans should "not agitate for our rights", but they should do so constitutionally. Calata feared "the uncivil and uneducated" workers who followed the I-ANC. Tonjeni in turn denounced moderates such as Calata as "black traitors".[33]

Calata used very different tactics than those of the I-ANC to advance black interests. He sought to sway Africans and government with polite persuasion. However, the depression drove him to confront economic issues. In October 1931, he delivered the presidential address to the Midland African Teachers Conference in Cookhouse. Having witnessed the suffering caused by unemployment and aware of the anxiety teachers felt about their salaries (£6 a month), Calata warned of imminent wage cuts. He also warned of communism, which—in clear reference to Tonjeni—in Cradock had "got hold of the ignorant masses and threatened the churches". Anti-communism so obsessed Calata he wanted every teacher to disassociate from it—a move the conference rejected as counter-productive—though he hastened to add he did "not mean that we must not agitate for our rights"; rather, agitation must be constitutional. He conceded communists were right to condemn capitalism's selfishness. Yet all Calata could suggest by way of solutions to combat the crisis was frugality and avoidance of "dazzling amenities of civilization" (such as bioscopes), measures hardly likely to appeal to workers.[34]

Instead, Calata gave credence to the Joint Councils. He served as joint secretary of the Cradock Joint Council, jointly preparing its submission to the NEC, and speaking out against efforts to try to solve unemployment by dismissing black workers. The 1931 annual report of the Council noted that communists (Tonjeni) had been effective in Cradock, holding twice-weekly meetings that were "largely attended" and "having a disturbing effect on the minds of the more ignorant". In 1932, Calata drew the attention of the East London Joint Council to the "serious hardship" of the unemployed and at the same time attacked the "disturbing effect" of communist influence "upon the minds of the more ignorant". In 1938, he was disturbed when Cradock Municipal Council sought to intensify evictions of black rent defaulters and turned to the Joint Council for support; in part, this was because Native Affairs refused officially to deal with Congress. Again, he played the anti-communist card, warning that unless the Joint Councils supported the ANC "there is no other course for Congress but to join hands with the Communists". As Tetelman argues, Calata was part of the black elite interested in uplifting these black masses, yet he did not totally isolate himself from Cradock's poorer residents.[35]

In Port Elizabeth, a growing working class began to exert pressure on a moderate ANC. In the 1930s, the ANC in New Brighton was "virtually moribund and had a distinctly middle class leadership", states Gary Baines. The ANC, led by Andrew Frank Pendla, Alfred Z. Tshiwula, and Frank Mokwena, failed to mount active campaigns against the Hertzog Bills. It was, writes Janet Cherry, "inactive and largely middle-class".[36]

Yet, these moderate ANC leaders were obliged, in one way or another, to take up labour issues. Pendla had diverse interests. In 1929-1930, he unsuccessfully stood on the ANC ticket for the Cape Provincial Council. In 1930, he was chairperson and secretary respectively of the New Brighton and Port Elizabeth Vigilance Committees, and sat on the Native Welfare Society executive. He worked as an interpreter and postmaster, but mainly as an attorney's clerk. For several years, he ran an eating-house. Despite this interest in commerce, he was conscious of the plight of labour. In a 1931 NEC submission, he agreed that employers underpaid black workers and argued for a minimum wage.

However, his views on obtaining wage justice were paternalistic. A wage determination recently had broken down, and Pendla believed "leaders of the Native people" and not agitators or unions should "approach the employers" and arrive at a "better understanding" over wages. This view was his "private personal opinion. It is not a view shared by a lot of my own people, who make it a business to study labour questions." This suggests not only aloofness from local unionists, but that individuals, and not ANC policies, were behind such aloofness. Pendla saw merit in the spirit of co-operation inherent in the "tribal system" whereby "when a worker's health breaks down, the Natives ... club together, make a collection and send him home". His elitism was apparent when he claimed to speak on behalf of workers. He expressed his distaste of "agitators". Rather than promote the ANC, he felt the Vigilance Association should continue to elect "responsible" leaders "if the masses feel that they are recognised by the authorities". Pendla often referred to such "masses" as "our weaker brethren", to be encouraged through education "to come up to us". However, he clearly was perturbed at the essential ambiguity of his position. The state invariably told black leaders, "You do not represent the masses", whilst the masses "naturally blame the leaders ... for not speaking out". Hence, Pendla was starting to feel pressure "from below". Black leaders, he claimed, derived their views from "personal experiences, through being in contact with and living among these people". This especially was the case in New Brighton, where different black social strata lived in relatively close proximity.[37]

Other ANC leaders supported, in principle, the broad rights of black labour. Tshiwula and Mokwena were active in the New Brighton Advisory Board, which occasionally addressed worker issues, such as wages. Horatio Bud-M'belle, radical TNC leader in 1917-1919, who now worked as an attorney's clerk, also sat on the Board. In 1931, he gave evidence to the NEC about discriminatory treatment of Africans under the Native Labour Regulation Act. He attacked the denial of pensions to black workers. A black person's life in Johannesburg was "not valued highly, to the maximum of £50". Under the Miners' Phthisis Act, compensation awarded to Africans was "very much lower than what a farmer would get" as stock compensation. White people could organise as workers but Africans raising "legitimate aspirations" were termed "agitators". He accused government of not wanting "our people to lead us", a curious inversion of a typical pretension of black leaders to speak on behalf of the people, perhaps a residual effect of his ISL days. When it came to solutions, however, his radicalism long since had vanished. He now viewed education and the Joint Council as the key to reduce racial ill-feeling. Yet, he still maintained contact with unions, in the early 1930s serving as president of the IICU (though it had long since lost its working-class militancy) before his death in 1933.[38]

Tshiwula had been ANC Cape Province secretary in 1919. He worked as a teacher, then sales representative. Moving to New Brighton in the 1930s, he was active in ANC and Advisory Board politics, criticising official corruption and poor housing. In the late 1930s, he organised the African General Workers Union with the aid of William Ballinger and the Eastern Province Trades Council, which opposed colour bars. According to Cherry, Tshiwula was an "aspirant petty-bourgeois ... wary of the ANC although he was a member". This inability to forge a stronger nexus with workers was not purely due to the inclinations of local ANC leaders. In the 1930s, black workers in the region were chiefly unskilled and unorganised, not well placed to initiate or maintain political alliances. It was not until the 1940s that ANC-union ties flourished. The point here is that even some "petty-bourgeois" ANC members were involved with workers.[39]

Despite the inertia of moderates, an ANC renaissance of sorts took place in the late 1930s. Dora Mbilana of New Brighton reported after Calata's visit of May 1938: "We breathe a different spirit in this city ... The reverend gentleman accomplished within his short stay what had appeared to us an impossible thing. The unity of all the Bantu leaders of New Brighton under the banner of the Cape African Congress." The 1938 CAC conference in New Brighton heard reports on "labour and commerce" by Tshiwula, "health and sanitation" by B. Makapela, and "urban areas" by Ngojo. Calata advised members that there was "no need for despair or for violent speeches". Yet Mr Nyoka and other delegates from the floor vigorously questioned guest speaker Major Stubbs, Native Recruiting Corporation controller, about wages, food, and housing of miners, indicating that moderate leaders did not prevent rank-and-file speaking on labour issues.[40]

Thus in the 1930s, the Port Elizabeth ANC had definite, if irregular, relations with workers, though small size limited growth: paid membership in 1939 was less than 100. In 1941, the CAC executive included only one worker: James Mafu, a railway employee. Nevertheless, it continued to urge recognition of black unions, greater expenditure on miners' health, higher wages, and freedom of movement for black workers. These policies helped lay the basis for stronger ANC-labour relations. In 1941, Pendla chaired a meeting of dockers that rejected attempts by employers to parry wage demands. By the late 1940s, the local working class had grown considerably but it was no coincidence that the ANC had an infusion of worker militants.[41] To have developed such a working-class base in just a few years, despite its scanty resources, points to effects of previous patient, preparatory work to build community support so that working people could start to identify with the ANC.

Kadalie's IICU, established in 1929, maintained its largest following in East London (and rural Transkei) in the early 1930s. East London's industrial workforce was concentrated on the river port docks and railways, with many workers operating through networks based in their home areas in the hinterland, features that came to influence the nature of support for IICU strikes and strategies. In early 1930, some IICU meetings were large-scale, with 6,000-8,000 attending, involving men and women workers, and rural peoples; even some chiefs spoke out in support of strikes. Supporters are likely to have included ANC supporters, but the IICU, not Congress, captured the imagination of workers in January 1930, when Kadalie launched a general strike in East London that spread across most sectors of industry in the town. He was able to capture the support of workers because the IICU squarely addressed labour grievances, proposed solutions, and met regularly with workers. Dock wages were low: wages in 1930 were not much more than they were in 1903. The strike was widely supported and women were active in it, but the depression had generated widespread unemployment, making this an inopportune time for industrial action. In the face of determined police action—they arrested Kadalie and his strike committee—and strikebreakers, the strike eventually collapsed but not before some rank-and-file, notably stevedores and domestic workers, dragged out resistance for many months. The IICU limped on, engaging with local urban and rural grievances that resonated with the many workers retaining rural ties. Beinart and Bundy show the complex and resilient "ideologies of protest" at play among the diverse classes, both rural- and urban-based, that supported the IICU, and how IICU leaders wove together African nationalist, independent Christian, and class metaphors to build a following. Yet the policies of the IICU (like that of the ICU in the late 1920s) were now in a way as broad and amorphous as those of the more moderate ANC, with whom historians have contrasted it.[42]

IICU political rhetoric was apparent in a January 1930 mass meeting of 1,500 people near East Bank location that heard radical speeches of union leaders from around the country. Tyamzashe invoked the memory—and fate—of Hintsa, as did Peter Mkwambi, Johannesburg secretary, who called for Hintsa and Shaka to "rise from the dead" and "help us". Like Tonjeni, these activists blended modern and traditional ideas. Mkwambi urged people to "go to night classes, leave the bible alone, that only teaches you to be soft … Look at East London, there is not a single business in the whole town belonging to a native … I feel that it is high time that reformation should come as in the year 1600, break down the churches and then a new God will come with a new religion." Palisane from the Orange Free State told "the Whiteman to get out of our Country".[43]

The following year a judge found the IICU guilty of loose money handling. A few months later, an IICU conference in East London stripped Kadalie of leadership. Splits occurred in rural areas as well. Kadalie unsuccessfully tried to revive the IICU in 1937, and he and Tyamzashe gave evidence to the Wage Board in East London in 1938 on wages and slums. The organisation survived into the 1940s, but only as a skeleton. Whilst the IICU engaged solidly with grievances of urban and rural workers and gained the allegiance of many, this was a transitory phenomenon eventually leaving them defenceless.[44]

The ANC was not particularly active in East London—D. H. Reader alleges they, like the ICU, had fallen into some disrepute in the 1920s—but contributed indirectly to keeping the position of black workers in the public eye. Richard Godlo, a previous Cape Congress East London secretary, also prominent in the ABC and NRC, gave evidence to the NEC in 1931. He spoke on behalf of the Advisory Board but in this city, it worked closely with the ANC. Godlo argued that labour taxes had forced Africans to migrate to towns. Greater access to land, and better trading opportunities, were keys to their economic progress. Though focusing on commerce, he was not blind to the position of workers. Wages were inadequate for African needs and had not kept pace with the cost of living, he stated. The urban African worker no longer could rely on rural succour and today "lives on a level with the unskilled European worker". A solution, he suggested, was an increased "entrance wage" of five shillings per day for new African workers.[45]

Two East London newspapers with Cape ANC connections took an interest in black workers. *Izwi Lama Afrika* ("Voice of Africa", 1931-1932) directed its editorial preferences to the Joint Council, but some articles supported the ANC. "Musa" advised "all Native town dwellers to take a little more interest in fighting organisations such as the Independent I.C.U. and the A[NC]". *Izwi Lama Afrika* writers included Bennett Ncwana and H. D. Tyamzashe of Kadalie's IICU. In July 1931, Kadalie announced that "thousands of his followers" would boycott traders not advertising in *Izwi Lama Afrika*, which in turn welcomed "this patriotic gesture", no doubt impressed by inflated claims of Cape ICU membership of 20,000. It praised Kadalie's support for moderate British-style trade unionism, which, it stated, would assure him support from not only Africans, but also employers.[46]

Izwi Lama Afrika lavished praise on a constable who "made himself popular amongst the Natives during the last Native strike". It feared a Garveyist "threat", declaring it would "endeavour to do away with ... radicalism which is the bane of this country". This conservatism did not prevent it raising problems affecting black workers. It attacked the "wretched conditions" of East Bank (East London) inhabitants. It appealed for justice for workers Thomas Lekoko, denied wages for 14 months, and Jacob Matolengwe, a worker of nine years service dismissed for arguing. It highlighted church resolutions calling for "drastic revision of the conditions of labour". It urged better roads as a means to provide jobs for Africans, attacked the harsh provisions of the Native Service Contract Bill, and protested moves to increase taxation of "the poorest class". Despite harsh laws, *Izwi Lama Afrika* was optimistic that "a nation of servants and beggars may yet rule the world".[47]

Izwi Lama Afrika accused employers of underpaying Africans, urged a minimum wage, supported local office workers denied pensions, attacked disparity between white and black Town Council wages, and condemned the permit system for African workers. One reason for this pro-labour stance was a concern that the revival of trade depended on the "increase of the Natives purchasing power". Belief in justice was another: justice should be "done to these men who have to support large families at a hand-to-mouth wage".[48]

The views of its writers also influenced *Izwi Lama Afrika's* labour reporting. Bennett Ncwana in 1930 advised Africans "to support whatever party comes into power" and chided their leaders for not welcoming "with open arms" state moves (supposedly) to extend the franchise. Such opportunism casts doubt on the sincerity of his sympathy for workers. It may have influenced *Izwi Lama Afrika* to take a more indirect approach to workers. A lead story of early 1932 stated the paper would work with the Department of Health to educate Africans on hygiene and "Purity of Life". It requested readers to circulate the paper "among Native Labourers and Domestic Servants" who apparently were seen as the chief threat to health, and were not regarded as subscribers. Yet there is no denying Bennett Ncwana's predilection to dabble in labour issues. In 1931, he rekindled his occasional relationship with the ICU. Accompanying Kadalie to give evidence for the IICU to the NEC he stated: "The ground on which we [the IICU] stand as a labour union is ... that we are totally against the recruiting system." In 1932, he argued that, due to racial discrimination, Africans suffered more from the depression. Behind these statements were conservative ideas. He claimed low black wages endangered the "money market". His solution was simplistic: "patriotism". At the time, he was secretary of the East London Non-Europeans Unemployment Committee, which sought to ameliorate the lot of the black unemployed. He also was involved with the National Helping Hand Society, and in 1933 launched the shadowy Bantu League of Economic Independence, which advocated economic racial segregation. He attended Cape ANC meetings, took part in debate, and sat on the official "platform" at the 1931 ANC convention. Later, from 1941 to 1944, Bennett Ncwana briefly served as Cape ANC Vice-President.[49]

Umlindi we Nyanga ("Monthly Watchman," 1936-1941) was edited by Godlo but controlled by white capital, which accounts for some ambiguity in its labour reporting. It displayed a commitment to black liberty and sympathy for black labour typical of a moderate, but determined, strand of ANC thinking. It swore unwavering loyalty to the crown in its lamentation on the death of King George V, yet the ANC often couched its opposition to white supremacy in pro-Empire terms. *Umlindi we Nyanga* was a strong supporter of black rights. Columnist H. D. Tyamzashe criticised the state's refusal to appoint Africans to commissions on African affairs. An article on mine labour asked when South Africa would sign ILO conventions. Workers and radicals used the letters columns to draw attention to the need for higher wages and adult education for African workers. One letter noted Umtata labourers "cannot afford to purchase food". Margaret Ballinger's maiden speech, defending black worker rights, received front-page prominence. In 1938, it reprinted articles from the radical *Guardian* in support of black union demands. A 1939 editorial called for equal wages. Infant mortality and juvenile delinquency were "inextricably interwoven with … inadequacy of wages". In 1939, the newspaper reported a miners' strike sympathetically.[50] This was not "socialist" reporting but the paper's journalists consciously or unconsciously saw some connection between labour struggles and their readers. Godlo's ANC experiences helped encourage this concern for labour interests.

The ultra-moderate role of leaders such as Calata, Pendla and Bennett Ncwana gave the Eastern Cape ANC no real appetite for any kind of direct involvement in workers' struggles. In general, however, ANC policies continued to exhibit a strong sympathy for exploited black workers. Whilst the ANC's outreach into the wider black community was limited, the fact that it continued to take a stand in favour of black labour rights must have made some impact upon politicised Africans, thus helping to lay the foundations for later much deeper, and more action-oriented, ANC-worker relations.

The Transkeian Territories African National Congress (ANC-TT) also had a moderate leadership. In 1930, this consisted of: John Gcingca, president; Meshack Bobi Mgidlana, vice-president; Enoch Malunga, treasurer; German Madotyeni, chaplain; and William Sabata. The majority had ousted as secretary Abner Madalane, accused by Gcingca of embezzlement and the "complete overthrow" of the branch, but Madalane retained a measure of support by holding "ANC" meetings in Idutywa in 1930. By 1933, Madalane, based in Idutywa, claimed to be ANC-TT general secretary. He made representations on behalf of Africans living in the neighbourhood of the villages of Tsomo, Nqamakwe, and Cofimvaba about fees for use of village commonages and the impounding by officials of their cattle, issues not unique to workers, but of considerable importance to many rural-based migrant workers. The ANC, he stated, had instructed him to write to the chief magistrate following a public meeting in April 1933. Some Africans thus looked to the ANC as an avenue to raise "bread and butter", and not just political, complaints, whilst the ANC saw its responsibility as extending to these issues. The chief magistrate, however, rejected the ANC's legitimacy to raise such matters. The impounding of cattle was "not a matter in which your organisation can be considered as having any status". Rather, he ruled, it was a Bhunga matter. The ANC-TT disputed this ruling and sought a way around it by claiming to represent not just people around Cofimvaba, but also the entire region.[51]

The view of historians that the ANC was concerned mainly with high politics thus needs to take cognisance that this role was to some extent forced on it due to the state's rejection of its right also to represent Africans on socio-economic matters. The ANC faced obstacles to raising the concerns of working peoples, as whenever it attempted to do so the state rejected its claim to represent Africans on such issues.

In seeking recognition as the legitimate representative of all Transkeian Africans, the ANC-TT sought to distance itself from radicals. In a letter to Hertzog, Gcingca conveyed "our feelings [of] loyalty to Great Britain", and indicated his willingness "to assist the authorities", a reference to ANC-TT concern at the "intolerable" and "disloyal" activities of the Transkeian Territories UNIA, led by Theodore Mvalo. Garveyism was by now a spent force. However, this body, which state officials claimed had ANC and ICU connections, gained support in Nqamakwe, where it claimed 1,800 members. Some of the members violently resisted Mvalo's arrest in 1932. Gcingca contrasted this open defiance with the ANC-TT's "frankly practical work to educate the people direct" and to ensure that they "prosper [in] their social economic and moral rights". Some local people, however, continued to confuse the two bodies, viewing, as late as 1940, the UNIA as the "UNIA African Congress League".[52]

Mvalo claimed an association with both the ANC and League of African Rights. In August 1930, he held a meeting attended by 58 Africans in Cofimvaba village. Mvalo told the audience that he was there to form an ANC branch. Mindful of his earlier arrests, he stressed that the ANC "had nothing to complain about the government", but merely wished to defend African rights. An "ANC" committee of ten formed with Stephen Ndlaleni as district chairman and Alfred Tshwula as secretary. Half the dues of six shillings went to the ANC in Pretoria, the balance retained for local work. Following the meeting, Mvalo led local people to the office of the local magistrate to complain about headmen, but failed to get an interview. It is doubtful the group was recognised as an official ANC branch, though police treated it as such. In 1936, ANC-TT organiser Meshack Bobi Mgidlana, who had conducted a separatist church in Ndakana for some years, sought the protection of local magistrates from the activities of the UNIA "of Wellington" which "is wrongly called the African National Congress" (possibly another reference to Mvalo). It suggests that in the eyes of local people there was considerable confusion about just what constituted the ANC. Local magistrates, who regarded Mgidlana as "an obstinate and ignorant old man", interpreted his request as an attempt to gain official recognition of the ANC.[53]

The ANC-TT continued to organise meetings through to the 1940s.[54] Its activities are evidence that the ANC had some standing among local peoples. There is little direct evidence of workers as members, but Govan Mbeki first became active in the ANC in the region in the 1930s. In 1933-1934 at Fort Hare, he met Eddie Roux and Max Yergan, who influenced him towards Marxism. Resistance to the Hertzog Bills firmed his radical nationalism, and he joined the ANC in 1935, perhaps due to his friendship with Mofutsanyana. Mbeki, who moved briefly to Durban to teach, quickly was baptised into worker politics. Dismissed for trying to organise a union whilst working in a newsagent, the state later removed him from his teaching position in 1939 for political activity. He published *Transkei in the Making,* in which he attacked state efforts deliberately to import capitalism "into the African territories - any attempt to destroy the people's cattle is no less than a declaration of that most iniquitous system". Mbeki, as noted in Chapter 1, perceived that the lack of a firm rural base weakened the liberation movement nationwide. This militant nationalist, with experience of industrial agitation, declined to join the CPSA until 1953, choosing instead to work in the ANC.[55]

The Northern Cape

The interest of the Bechuanaland-Griqualand West ANC in labour issues related to its base in the mining city of Kimberley and its members' backgrounds. Doyle Modiakgotla was branch chairman of Labour and Complaints. Simultaneously he served on the Orange Free State ANC and national ANC executives, and was third secretary of a disintegrating ICU. He continued his mission of fighting for black labour rights that he began in the 1920s in the ICU, but now also used the forum of Congress to promote it. At the ANC branch's 1930 conference, he attacked state duplicity in providing jobs to white people but not to Africans. He contrasted the great inequalities of wages paid to black and white workers. Branch President John Skota Likhing also spoke out on black labour rights, condemning the "unsatisfactory conditions under which non-Europeans are labouring". The violent suppression of ANC radicals in Worcester was a symptom of "unequal administration of justice, oppressive legislation and the denial of equal opportunities". The conference passed resolutions to abolish poll taxes, and to introduce old-age pensions for African workers. Any lingering faith in Britain as the defender of African rights dwindled as the conference drew attention to a new international source of support for black workers: the forthcoming Commonwealth Labour conference in London.[56]

In 1931, branch leaders gave evidence on labour conditions to the NEC. Modiakgotla, on behalf of the residents of Kimberley's Number Two Location, argued that black "wages are utterly inadequate". Efforts to secure wage determinations for Africans had foundered on state prevarication. He proposed only partial solutions. Employers should give preference to urban Africans to prevent undercutting of wages by rural black people seeking to supplement their farm income by wages. The widespread use of convict labour on the mines at a time of high unemployment "kept out 1200 free labourers from working"; free labour, he added, should not face such unfair competition. Likhing stated that Africans simply had "no facilities for earning money".[57]

The Bechuanaland-Griqualand West ANC gave support to exiled ICU leader Champion in 1931. In April, he was guest-of-honour at its meetings in Kimberley. Modiakgotla introduced him at an open-air meeting of 175 people. Two days later, Likhing told a crowd of about 100 people (referred to by police as "of the ordinary class") that Africans "will always welcome [Champion]". In reply, Champion alluded to national liberation by using an allegory of land, which, once dried-up by white people, again has water when the rain comes. He declared Africans "will be the rulers of South Africa, because God has given us this world and I am going to be Prime Minister".[58]

Black unemployment was taken up by Likhing in 1932, who warned that "the depression is hitting hard especially among the Africans who are not considered when the unemployed of the other sections are provided for". The branch declined in the late 1930s. It presented no written report to the 1938 ANC conference. Modiakgotla reported that a cell functioned in Vryburg under Chief Lethlogile, and urged Congress to approach the British Bechuanaland

Chiefs' Association to organise the ANC in the area. However, labour contacts eventually produced results. In 1941, the Kimberley ANC branch reported that it was "instrumental in founding a Workers' Union" of about 400 members, and in getting a wage commission appointed in Kimberley for the first time.[59]

ANC branches in different regions of the Cape thus protested the escalation of oppression faced by black workers in the 1930s. Whilst they did not enrol many workers, or consistently advance their specific class interests, and despite the fact that some of their leaders were ambiguous about their attitude to workers, and had vested interests in their own "middle class", these branches regularly defended the rights of black workers to equal wages and improved conditions. They met more regularly and engaged more consistently with labour grievances than the national body, and were able to help lay the groundwork for the rebuilding of the reputation and infrastructure of Congress that began in the last years of the decade. In this regard, it was no coincidence that two of the leading proponents of the renaissance of Congress—Calata and Kotane—worked in the Cape.

Notes

1   R. Kingwill, "The ANC in the Western Cape: A Preliminary Study", BA (Hons.) UCT, 1977, p. 14.

2   Tonjeni speech, Tarkastad 27 Jul. 1931, CAD 1/TAD 4/1/2, 1/9/2, "Native Politics & Unrest. Disturbances"; Skota, *African Yearly Register* p. 137. Tonjeni's "educated, yet disaffected" father Charles challenged government over location authority (W. Beinart, "Conflict in Qumbu: Rural Consciousness, Ethnicity and Violence in the Colonial Transkei", in Beinart and Bundy, *Hidden Struggles*, pp. 106-137, esp. p. 129); in 1904 he had supported moves to form a Transkei labour bureau: *Report of Proceedings Annual Meeting of the Transkeian Territories General Council, 1904*, p. 17; Lalu, *The Communist Party Press*, p. 20.

3   *Cape Argus* 15 Mar., 7 Apr. 1930; *Umsebenzi* 6 Jun., 4, 11 Jul., 5 Sep., 28 Nov., 8 Jan., 19 Feb. 1930; open letter to the government by Tonjeni, *Cape Times* 24 Oct. 1930. See also *Cape Times* 5 Dec. 1930.

4   *Cape Argus* 1-2 May, 7, 12 Feb., 19 Mar. 1930; *Umsebenzi* 16 May, 6 Jun., 18 Apr. 1930; *Abantu-Batho* 8 May, 10, 17 Jul. 1930, 25 June 1931; *Umteteli wa Bantu* 10, 17 May 1930; *Cape Times* 2 Apr. 1930; letter of Magistrate Worcester 15 May 1930, in Hofmeyr, "Agricultural Crisis and Rural Organisation", p. 141; *Cape Argus* 19 Mar. 1930.

5   NA 87/326(3) "Independent ANC"; Rex. vs. Tonjeni, George Court 34/31: evidence of Constable C. van Tonder; copy of Judgement; and Supreme Court (Cape) appeal judgement, 31 Mar. 1931: CAD Supreme Court CSC 1/3/1/17 40: "Elliot Tonjeni"; Hofmeyr, "Agricultural Crisis and Rural Organisation" p. 128; *Umteteli* 27 Dec. 1930.

6   "The African National Congress on the Move: Purging the ANC of Bolshevik Tendencies", flyer 15 Jun. 1930; Rochlin Collection of South African Political and Trade Union Organizations, Webster Library, Concordia University; *Umteteli wa Bantu* 15 Nov. 1930;

KC v.4 p. 158; Hofmeyr, "Agricultural Crisis and Rural Organisation", pp. 130-132; *Umteteli wa Bantu* 24 Jan. 1931.

7   "An Appeal to ANC Members", *Umsebenzi* 20 Jun. 1930; Tonjeni, "Chiefs in the Transkei", *Umsebenzi* 12 Sep. 1930; *Umsebenzi* 8 Aug., 26, 12 Sept. 1930; Roux, *Time Longer than Rope*, p. 232; Lalu, *The Communist Party Press*, p. 21, citing Roux to CPSA Executive 30 Nov. 1930 in *Roux Papers*. Ngedlane continued to agitate in Ndabeni: see "Impilo Nentlalo Bantsundu", *Umsebenzi* 25 Dec. 1931.

8   Hofmeyr, "Agricultural Crisis and Rural Organisation", p. 74; *Umteteli wa Bantu* 6 Dec. 1930. For the manifesto, see Hofmeyr, "Agricultural Crisis and Rural Organisation", pp. 185-186.

9   *Cape Argus* 26 Dec. 1930; *Umteteli wa Bantu* 6 Dec. 1930, 3 Jan. 1931; Hofmeyr, "Agricultural Crisis and Rural Organisation", pp. 156-158.

10   Hofmeyr, "Agricultural Crisis and Rural Organisation", pp. 164-179.

11   B. Ndobe, "Vuka wafa Mtu Ontsundu" *Umsebenzi* 8 Jan. 1932; *Umsebenzi* 11 Jul. 1930, 16 Jan. 1931, 19 Feb. 1932 6 Feb., 27 Mar. 1931; Hofmeyr, "Agricultural Crisis and Rural Organisation", pp. 167, 188, 208, 239-248, 260, 290.

12   U17-11, p. 326; Cradock. Report of Board of Works Committee 20 Feb. 1933, Minutes of Ordinary Meeting of Council, 31 Mar. 1933 and Special Meeting of Council 29 Jan. 1932, 23 Jun. 1933, Report of Location Committee Meeting, 14 Nov. 1933, in *Cradock, South Africa Collected Papers, 1929-1962*, CAMP.

13   Hofmeyr, "Agricultural Crisis and Rural Organisation", pp. 172, 174, 176, 193-202, 238, 264-269, 285. The Cradock Town Council refused to grant permission for some I-ANC meetings: Minutes of Special Council Meeting 29 Jan. 1932, Ordinary Meeting 26 Jan. 1932: *Cradock, South Africa Collected Papers*.

14   Report of Tonjeni speech at Tarkastad, 27 Jul. 1931, CAD 1/TAD 4/1/2 file 1/9/2.

15   Hofmeyr, "Agricultural Crisis and Rural Organisation", pp. 235-246, 292, 300-303; *Umsebenzi* 30 Oct. 1931, 13 May 1932. Records do not mention Bransby's wife Flora but in 1932 she won a *Bantu World* beauty competition: L. Thomas, "The Modern Girl and Racial Respectability in 1930s South Africa" *JAH* v. 47 (2006) pp. 461-490, p. 476.

16   "Tonjeni & Others Arrested," "Tonjeni before the Court", "Committed for Trial," "Tonjeni's Defence", *Midland News & Karroo Farmer* 8, 15, 18 Jun., 2-3 Jul. 1931. Police confiscated copies of *Umsebenzi* sold at the meeting, noting participants had sung a verse printed in it they termed "the National Anthem". There were 5,000 black people in Cradock at the time: "A Location Problem", *Midland News* 26 Jan. 1932.

17   "The Native Agitation", *Midland News* 4 Jul. 1931.

18   Hofmeyr, "Agricultural Crisis and Rural Organisation", pp. 191-197; Magistrate Port Elizabeth to CNC King William's Town 28 Apr. 1932, TAD NA 56/328; Tonjeni, "Imeko Zabasebenzi e Bayi zi caZwa", Ndobe, "Ubuigebenga bo Mlungu" *Umsebenzi* 19 Feb. 1932; *Friend* 23 Oct. 1931; *Midland News* 24 Aug., 9-10 Sep. 1931, 2, 26 Jan., 30 Apr. 1932, "May Day in the Location" and "Hindering the Police", *Midland News* 3, 7 May 1932.

19   *Free State Advocate* 25 Dec. 1937; Hofmeyr, "Agricultural Crisis and Rural Organisation", pp. 74, 138, 233, 303-306; *Umsebenzi* 1 Sep. 1933, 20 Jan., 5 May 1934; Kotane letter of 23 Feb. 1934 in Y. Dadoo (ed.), *South African Communists Speak* (London: Inkululeko, 1981), p. 120; Lalu, *Communist Party Press*, p. 26, citing undated Kotane interview in Bunting Papers, UWC; Bunting, *Moses Kotane*, p. 63; *Mochochonono* 4 Jun. 1938; V. Kanyangwa, "Through the Eyes of a Domestic Servant", *Umsebenzi* 22 Jan. 1932. In

sectarian CPSA debates, Kotane earlier had questioned party denunciation of the I-ANC: Drew, "New Line," p. 349.

20 Hofmeyr, "Agricultural Crisis and Rural Organisation", pp. 233, 306, and Chapter 8.

21 Hofmeyr, "Agricultural Crisis and Rural Organisation", pp. 191-197; *Umteteli* 4 Oct. 1930; *Cape Argus* 15 Mar. 1930: Thaele told a meeting "We will have a Black Republic and black government ... before long ... Continue to sing that one song and watch the ANC": Hofmeyr, "Agricultural Crisis and Rural Organisation", p. 99; Ndobe, "Ubugebenga," *Umsebenzi* 18 Mar. 1932.

22 K. Thaele to Magistrate Sutherland 18 Nov. 1931, Magistrate to DNA 18 Nov. 1931, CNC KWT to SNA 6 Sep. 1940: "Kennon Thaele Native Agitator", TAD NA 54/328; Thaele, "ANC", *African Leader* 18 Feb. 1933. In 1940, Thaele ran a café in Port Elizabeth and was refused permission to enter New Brighton due to his "agitator" past: SAP Port Elizabeth to Grahamstown 14 Oct. 1940, NA 54/328.

23 *Bantu World* 23 Jul. 1932; *African Leader* 10 Dec. 1932, 18 Feb. 1933; letter of A. Swan and A. and J. Oosthuizen to *African Leader* 25 Mar. 1933.

24 V. Mapalam, "African National Congress: Grassy Park Branch", *African Leader* 25 Mar. 1933.

25 Evidence of Ngojo to NEC 25 Apr. 1931, "Minutes of Evidence", pp. 7062-7069a.

26 Evidence of Hoho to NEC 25 and 27 Apr. 1931, pp. 70669h-7076.

27 "G.P. Cook, Supt. of Natives Cape Town", to NEC; ANCWP Executive reports, 1937-1938; I-ANC. "To the National Conference in Session in Bloemfontein, 16-19 Dec. 1938", CKC 2:DA:14:30/3. Oliphant at this time wrote a pamphlet *The Salvation of a Race* (Cape Town, 1939) which if written in a somewhat rambling style nevertheless openly refers to South Africa as "the land of oppression".

28 *Umsebenzi* May 12 1934; Gomas to *Cape Argus* 3 Apr. 1930; Musson, *Johnny Gomas*, pp. 88-94; R. Alexander, "Johnny Gomas as I Knew Him," *South African Labour Bulletin* 15, 5 (1991), pp. 80-83; *Liberator* Apr. 1937; J. Gomas, "Now How is this 'Civilised Labour Policy' to be Fought", *Umsebenzi* 16 Feb. 1935; *Umsebenzi* 25 Apr. 1936; Gomas, *100 Years*, pp. 5-16; *Liberator* Sep. 1937; "Jimmy La Guma", pp. 83-84.

29 Non-European United Front. *Minutes of the Conference ... 8-10 April 1939* (Cape Town: NEUF, 1939), pp. 8-11; "Jimmy La Guma", p. 95; *Bantu World* 23 Apr. 1938.

30 Bunting, *Moses Kotane*, pp. 84-91: revival "was almost entirely Kotane's work"; KC v.4 p. 116; Kingwill "ANC,", pp. 29-47: ANC leadership "tended to be drawn from the unskilled, though urbanised working class, the core of the ANC (WP) itself"; ANC flyer 14 Jun. 1939 in *Simons Papers* 5.26.3.

31 Ray Alexander interview with the author, Lusaka, May 1989; R. Goode, "A History of the FCWU 1941-1975", MA UCT, 1986; R. Close, *New Life* (Cape Town: FCWU, 1950); "Elizabeth Mafekeng", [n.d.] in Federation of South African Women. *Papers*, CAMP; Kingwill, "ANC", pp. 44-47.

32 *Umteteli wa Bantu* 5 Jul., 9 Aug. 1930. Jabavu was not active in Congress but attended some ANC conferences: see *Umteteli wa Bantu* 10 Jan. 1931; *Midland News* 24 Jun. 1930; Hofmeyr, "Agricultural Crisis and Rural Organisation" p. 256.

33 Calata claimed "we shut the leftist out of any office" yet acknowledged Tonjeni's meetings "were attended by all the people": interview, G. Carter, CKC 2:XC3:94; Tetelman, "We Can", pp. 45-51: Calata used songs, sport, and Scouts to mobilise youth against radicals; Hofmeyr, "Agricultural Crisis and Rural Organisation" pp. 252-269, 282ff., 302; Goedhals, "African Nationalism", p. 66.

34 Calata, "The Present Economic Situation", *Midland News* 9 Oct. 1931. Indicative of the racial dimension of the depression in South Africa was the action of the Maraisburg Council to dismiss all African labourers but only reduce the wages of white workers: *Midland News* 22 Oct. 1931.

35 *Midland News* 5 Dec 1931; *Umteteli wa Bantu* 10 Jan. 1931; *Izwi Lama Afrika* Jan. 1932; Calata interview with G. Carter, CKC 2:XC3:94; Calata to Rheinallt Jones 1 Feb. 1938, *ANC Collection*; Tetelman, "We Can", p. 32

36 G. Baines "'In the World But Not of It': 'Bishop' Limba and the Church of Christ in New Brighton, c1929-1949", *Kronos* no. 19 1992, pp. 102-134, pp. 108, 119; Cherry, "African Working Class", pp. 61-73.

37 KC v. 4 p. 126; Skota, *African Yearly Register* p. 237; NEC "Minutes" 26-27 Mar. 1931, pp. 6006-6047. G. Baines, *A History of New Brighton, Port Elizabeth, South Africa 1903-1953* (Lewiston: Mellen, 2002) p. 253 argues that in New Brighton it may be more accurate to speak of "competing cliques" rather than moderates versus radicals, and that vigilance and advisory committees could be complementary.

38 M'belle, NEC Evidence 25 Mar. 1931, p. 5949ff; *Umteteli wa Bantu* 21 Jan. 1933; Mancoe, *Directory* p. 74.

39 Skota, *African Yearly Register* p. 275; Baines, *New Brighton*, p. 250; "Formation of Native Workers' Union", clipping 9 Feb. 1938, in *Ballinger Papers*; Cherry, "African Working Class", pp. 61-73.

40 *Bantu World* 28 May, 11 Jun. 1938; "Cape Native Congress", *Eastern Province Herald* 7 July 1938.

41 Walshe, *African Nationalism*, p. 389; *Izwi lase Afrika* 14, 21, 28 Nov. 1941; *Inkokeli ya Bantu* Aug. 1941, Jul. 1942; *Midland News* 5 Jul. 1941; Cherry, "African Working Class", pp. 145-153, 185-190. Tshiwula and Xuma later corresponded on labour issues: Xuma to Tshiwula, 18 Jun., 21 Sept. 1942, XP, ABX 420618a, ABX 420921a.

42 Kadalie, *My Life*, Chapter 13; Minkley, "Did Not Come to Work", p. 195; Beinart and Bundy, "Talking Crow"; "Strike Threat Not Carried Out", *Cape Times* 11 Jul. 1930; M. Hunter, *Reaction to Conquest* (Oxford: OUP, 1936), pp. 568-570; W. Ballinger, "Native Trade Unionism", *Umteteli wa Bantu* 12 Nov. 1932.

43 Beinart and Bundy, "Talking Crow," p. 310; "Native Agitators & Native Unrest", police report East London 9 Jan. 1930, CAD ELN 86 C3: "Native Unrest 1930-1933"; Switzer, *Power & Resistance*, pp. 255-260.

44 "Independent ICU Transactions", *Daily Dispatch* 27 Apr. 1932; *Umteteli wa Bantu* 22 Oct. 1932, 1 Jul. 1933; Beinart and Bundy, "Talking Crow", p. 316; J. Ngcobo to NC Ixopo, NAD CNC 92 PMB; Ballinger, "Unionism"; "The Rise & Fall of the I.C.U.", *Umlindi we Nyanga* 5 Jun. 1937; "Distributive Trade Wages?" *Daily Dispatch* 14 Jun. 1938.

45 D. H. Reader, *The Black Man's Portion* (Cape Town: OUP, 1961), p. 17; Godlo to NEC, "Minutes of Evidence", pp. 5533-5541, 5574.

46 "Joint Council", *Izwi Lama Afrika* 27 Feb. 1932; Musa, "The Hemming-in-Process", *Izwi Lama Afrika* 14 Aug. 1931; *Umteteli wa Bantu* 24 Jan. 1931; "ICU Activities", *Izwi Lama Afrika* 12 Jun., 17, 24 Jul. 1931.

47 *Izwi Lama Afrika* 3, 10 Jul., Nov., 17 Dec., 14 Aug., 8, 15 May, 19, 5 Jun. 1931; H. D. T.[yamzashe], "Location Roads" *Izwi Lama Afrika* 3 Jul. 1931; "Native Service Contract Bill", *Izwi Lama Afrika* 12 Feb. 1932.

48 Articles in *Izwi Lama Afrika*: "Complaints Against Employers", 12 Jun. 1931, "Location Native Staff" 3 Jul. 1931, "Native Revenue Account", Jan. 1932, and "Permit System", 14 Aug. 1931.

49 *Umteteli wa Bantu* 28 Jun. 1930; S.M.B. Ncwana, "The Franchise", *Izwi Lama Afrika* 5 (v2) Jul. 1930; "Fighting Dirt" *Izwi Lama Afrika* Jan. 1932; *Izwi* 14 Aug. 1931; Kadalie and Ncwana to NEC, "Evidence" p. 5611ff.; "Natives Are Starving", "Native Unemployed" *Izwi Lama Afrika* Jan. 1932; *Umteteli wa Bantu* 10 Jan. 1931; Cobley, *Class & Consciousness* pp. 179, 215.

50 *Umlindi we Nyanga* 15 Feb. 1936; Tyamzashe, "What the White Man Doesn't Know", *Umlindi we Nyanga* 16 Apr. 1936; *Umlindi we Nyanga* 15 May, 15 Jun., 16 Aug. 1936, 15 Sept., 15 Dec. 1937, 15 Mar., 15 Sept. 1938, 16 Jan. 1939; "A Living Wage," *Umlindi we Nyanga* 15 Feb., 15 Apr. 1939; "Bantu Trade Union Movement," *Umlindi we Nyanga* 15 May 1939; "Africans on Strike," *Umlindi we Nyanga* 15 Nov., *Umlindi we Nyanga* 15 Dec. 1939.

51 Gcingca to Magistrate Nqamakwe 28 Jun. 1930; A. Madalane to CMTT, 6, 28 Apr. 1933, Magistrate Cofimvaba to CMTT 21, 28 Apr. 1933, CMTT to Madalane, 3 May 1933, CAD CMT 3/1471 42/C

52 Gcingca to Hertzog, 15 Apr. 1930, Gcingca to Magistrate Nqamakwe 28 Jun. 1930: CMT 3/1471 42/C; Magistrate Nqamakwe to NA 22 July 1932, Magistrate Nqamakwe to Magistrate Umtata 20 Jun. 1932: TAD NA 57/328; Chief Magistrate Umtata, Circular of 13 Jun. 1940: CAD 1/KNT 40/12.

53 SAP Cofimvaba to SAP Umtata, 24 Aug. 1930, M.B. Mgidlana to CMTT 25 Aug., 21 Sep. 1936, Magistrate Nqamakwe to CMTT 7 Oct. 1936, CMT 3/1471 42/C.

54 H.M. Mokoatle to Magistrate Matatiele 21 Jan. 1942. In 1947, the ANC had an office in Idutywa and claimed "members in many districts": ANC to CMTT 7 May 1947: CAD CMT 3/1471 42/C.

55 T. Mkhwanazi, "How a Schoolboy's Rage Turned Mbeki Towards Marxism", *Weekly Mail* 13 Nov. 1987; C. Bundy, "Introduction" to Mbeki, *Robben Island* pp. xi-xii; D.H. Anthony, "Max Yergan in South Africa: from Evangelical Pan-Africanist to Revolutionary Socialist", *African Studies Review* v. 34 no. 2 1991, pp. 27-55; KC v.4, p. 168; Allen, *Mineworkers* p. 334; Kantor, *Healthy Grave*, pp. 202-203.

56 *Abantu-Batho* 5 June 1930; "ANC Kimberley Congress", *Umteteli wa Bantu* 28 Jun. 1930; Modiakgotla to *Umteteli wa Bantu* 18 Oct. 1930; Skota, *African Yearly Register*, pp. 172, 427; Walshe, *African Nationalism*, p. 227. Likhing also was attracted to Garveyism: Hill, *Marcus Garvey*, p. clvi.

57 Secretary of Stand Holders No. 2 Location Kimberley to NEC; evidence of Modiakgotla, pp. 5381-5384, and Likhing, pp. 5379-5380 to NEC, 1931 "Minutes of Evidence".

58 Police reports CID Kimberley 13-17 Apr. 1931, NA49/328.

59 Likhing in *African Leader*, 19 Nov. 1932; Minutes of 1938 ANC conference, CKC 2:DA:14:30/3; Secretary ANC Kimberley to Xuma 11 Oct. 1941, XP reel 4, ABX 411011a.

"A Very, Very Wide Influence, Even When ... Dead": The Transvaal, Natal and Orange Free State in the 1930s

Congress organisations in the Transvaal, Natal and the Orange Free State exhibited considerable diversity in attitudes to and engagement with black labour. Often there was general support for black labour rights in the branches though at times there could be aloofness from radical struggles. In both the Transvaal and Natal, continuing regional rivalries tended to dissipate Congress strength. The effects of the Depression were severe throughout the country and black workers suffered most from its effects. This helped stimulate expressions of solidarity from within ANC circles. What made the 1930s different from earlier decades was firstly, the scale of economic growth and Depression, and secondly, the fact that by now Congress in the provinces had accumulated considerable political experience. Whilst they received little support from the national ANC given its relative inaction, this experience and the trust forged in earlier decades helped the ANC in these provinces, as in the Cape, survive a difficult decade and lay the basis for growth in the 1940s. In particular, the Rand continued to be the focus of urbanisation and this would gradually influence greater worker involvement in black politics.

The Transvaal

The 1930s in the Transvaal were marked economically first by Depression, then by accelerating industrialisation accompanied by greater unionisation (see Chapter 2). The rise of Afrikaner politics and cultural revivalism drove white politics further to the right, torpedoing liberal dreams of enhanced black rights. Against this backdrop, the Transvaal African Congress (TAC), mainly based on the industrialising Rand, continued to criticise oppression. In 1930, for example, it deplored the violent smashing of Western Cape ANC radicalism as "proof of the Government's inability to settle without force its oppression" of black people. To take another example, a TAC meeting at Bon Accord in 1934 expressed alarm at pass law intensification.[1] A relatively radical—in comparison with other contemporary African political organisations—TAC leadership initiated such committed stances.

Simon Peter Matseke served as TAC president from 1933 to 1941. A high-ranking ANC leader with some direct working-class experience and exposure to radical ideas as part of Gumede's executive of 1927-1930, Matseke continued to serve on Seme's executive as assistant speaker and chairman of committees. He was prominent in national ANC conferences throughout the 1930s, but was most effective at the provincial level.[2]

In June 1931, Matseke represented the Pretoria ANC before the Native Economic Commission (NEC). Here he criticised restrictions on black traders and argued in favour of communal land ownership. He also condemned pass laws and indirect "slave labour". Early the next month he acted as spokesperson for a delegation of the Marabastad branch of the Joint Committee of the Non-European Organisations that met with the acting secretary for Native Affairs. As reported by the Joint Committee's chairman, I. B. Moroe, Matseke stressed the impact on Africans of discriminatory laws, for example, criticising the extension of pass laws to women and the introduction of regulations compelling rural women moving to cities to obtain certificates from their chiefs. Interestingly, it was the government that here claimed to be acting in the interests of husbands, whereas Matseke was more concerned that "this legislation is going to cause hostilities by itself".[3]

We should not assume that Matseke was content to work with such liberal bodies. During the same year, he strongly opposed attempts by the philanthropic Pretoria Native Welfare Society to introduce recreation facilities, arguing instead that adequate housing should be top priority, thereby acting in the interests of workers who suffered especially from acute housing shortages. *Abantu-Batho* took a similar line against what it perceived as white-sponsored sports crowding out African culture and acting as a soporific anodyne to "exploit the poor native to the fullest extent". Matseke focused on such grassroots issues as housing but, by failing to grasp the growing support among black workers for popular cultures such as soccer, he lost an opportunity to widen Congress influence. By 1938, the Bantu Sports Club in Johannesburg was publicising political and trade union events in its bulletin and before long May Day rallies took place on soccer fields.[4]

Nevertheless, Matseke was more action-oriented than Seme. In 1935, Matseke held meetings on the Rand to improve the ANC's profile. *Bantu World* characterised him as "a tireless [ANC] worker and organiser". In 1938, he saw ANC success based on "permanence, action and ... readiness of people to struggle". His final act of support for workers was chairing the meeting to form the African Mine Workers' Union in 1941, the year he died.[5]

Whereas Matseke tended to avoid the political use of culture, his rival Moses Mphahlele, the TAC general secretary, was happy to exploit music for fund raising. In July 1930, for instance, he advertised a dance in honour of *The Mendi* tragedy featuring The Dark Musician of the Northern Transvaal and *Nkosi Sikelel' iAfrika*.[6] In general, however, as in other provincial branches, it would not be until the 1940s that Congress would more effectively exploit cultural avenues for recruitment and fund-raising.

The maintenance of TAC branches in working-class townships such as Alexandra, Boksburg, Germiston, Orlando and Benoni helped the TAC forge some limited worker contacts. Unionist David Bopape points to this when he recalls that to revive the Brakpan ANC he "got hold of some old [TAC] members who were workers in 1924 and 1936" to build "a powerful branch". The TAC was inclined towards workers by the geo-social proximity of different strata of African Society. In Alexandra, as the decade wore on, stand-holders frequently acted in concert (if not without class tensions) with working-class tenants against forced removals, a process that would intensify in the 1940s. Alexandra Workers' Union Chairman E. P. Mart Zulu viewed African landlords as "also victims, [who] could not be blamed for high rents".[7]

Some workers and ex-workers were active in the TAC. Farm labourer Gert Sibande formed a branch in Bethal that enrolled labourers and adopted radical policies. Ex-labourer S. B. Macheng, Randfontein Congress chairman, was a moderate who defended Seme's conservatism, yet still invoked his own working-class origins in promoting a college to train "carpenters, masons and all other kinds of artisans" and provide for "education of poor boys and girls". Carpenter J. Tladi was Benoni branch chairman. Former radicals who in 1918-1920 had defended the cause of black workers were still active. Benjamin Phooko now ran a small taxi business and served as Germiston Advisory Board secretary. Levi Mvabaza ran a small store and was more prosperous than the now-impoverished Letanka and Mabaso. According to Selby Msimang, in 1935 Mabaso "died poor in ... the material things of this world". Jeremiah Dunjwa gave a comprehensive submission to the NEC in 1931, citing many cases of evictions of farm labourers living in "dire poverty". He viewed education as a way to increase the earning capacity of Africans.

Educated Africans already worked as teachers, interpreters, and mine clerks and he foresaw further opportunities for them to find employment as engine drivers, carpenters, compound managers and doctors if the colour bar, "forcing native workers" into "poverty and migration", disappeared. High taxation had imposed "slavish conditions" upon the "workless and poorly paid" workers. Communists were important TAC members. Albert Nzula was a TAC delegate to the 1930 ANC conference. Dan Tloome, prominent in unions, and James Majoro, previously a miner and then a mine clerk, became involved with the Orlando branch. Robert Resha joined in 1939 after hearing J. B. Marks speak. Resha, from a labouring family, finished only six years of schooling and worked on the mines in the late 1930s. Armstrong Msitshana worked on the mines from 1937 until 1939, until dismissed. He joined not just the CPSA and Tin Workers' Union but also the TAC, becoming Orlando branch vice-chairman. S. M. Moema, previously a worker, rose to the TAC Executive.[8]

J. B. (John) Marks had joined the ANC in 1928. Son of a rail worker, he had led a strike as a student teacher. Banned in 1931 from teaching because of his political activities, Marks became a union, CPSA, and ANC activist. Whilst, in 1964, he claimed the ANC had "very little to do with the trade union movement. Up to … the 40s", he ironically also recalled definite ANC revival attempts by 1937 via the TAC, efforts evincing strong grassroots support, even in small "dorps". The ANC had "a very, very wide influence, even at the time when it was dead". This stark contradiction he partly explained by the ANC's "very strong ideological influence". Touring villages to signal that the ANC had "come back", he experienced little difficulty in getting the message across. Behind his espousal of proletarian and black causes were diverse influences. The CPSA encouraged members to be active in the ANC but, given Marks's expulsion from the party from 1937 to 1939 (in part for going to work for the bourgeois ANC treasurer Richard Baloyi), CPSA membership did not always directly inspire his ANC work. Thus "loosened from the bonds of [party] discipline", noted Basner, Marks "concentrated his trained mind, experience and revolutionary temper on revitalising Congress". The need for a viable instrument for black political opposition attracted people such as Marks to Congress. Similarly, Baloyi saw "that the African masses are craving for leadership and organisation". In the course of addressing meetings throughout the Transvaal, he "found remnants of the ANC" and concluded "that despite the present organisational weakness … its ideological influence" was "still predominating".[9]

In 1934, Moses Kotane noted a similar congruence between the two organisations: the party's branches in the countryside "are not really our branches at all … They are branches of the A.N.C. They do not even know that *Umsebenzi* is the communist organ."[10] Too often, historians have unfavourably compared the ANC of the period to other organisations such as the CPSA without understanding grassroots situations or without appreciating that such "CPSA" branches could be characterised by leading African communists as "ANC" branches.

Edwin Mofutsanyana continued to be active in both the TAC and CPSA. In the 1930s, he sought unsuccessfully to establish a miners' union. Hirson describes him as "a one-time miner who had some contacts on the mines". Such contacts gave the TAC added insights into worker needs. Mofutsanyana was involved in anti-pass, housing, and squatter protests. In 1935-1936, he served on the All-African Convention executive and Orlando Advisory Board. Karis argues that despite these diverse roles his "more long-term concern … was with building the ANC into an effective organisation" and in reviving the TAC.[11]

J. M. Lekhetho represented the TAC in an ANC deputation that met the Minister of Native Affairs in 1939. His perception of close ties between workers and Africans in general typified ANC attitudes. The country "derives immense profits from the cheap labour" of black workers and if they were "paid better wages there would be money in other directions, but as it is we consider that we have a share in the profits which accrue to the country as a result of the low wages paid to Natives". Lekhetho asked "for a general improvement in the salary scale of all our teachers".[12]

Such members raised the profile of Congress as a defender of black workers, and gave the TAC some contact with workers and unions. Whilst this should not be exaggerated, the ability of individual activists of the working-class movement to rise to TAC leadership indicates a lack of open hostility to such people in Congress. This does not mean that it was simply a "multi-class" movement with no internal class tensions. ANC communists did not disguise their politics. At times, they faced electoral contests against other ANC figures. Yet some, such as Kotane and J. B. Marks, appear to have already "prioritised" ANC over CPSA politics, whether by party design or personal inclination, or most probably by the sheer logic of the black predicament. With Congress receptive to the views of all who put forward the need to defend African rights, the TAC welcomed radical activists not simply because they were effective organisers but also because of its own already-established ties with the black labour movement. However, a complex web of ethnic and class forces further complicates this history.

Ethnic and chieftaincy politics intensified in the 1930s. In the Western Transvaal, challenges "from below" by commoners to Tswana chiefdoms in Rustenburg district were related to shrinking access to land and advancing (partial) proletarianisation, especially in smaller chiefdoms. The activities of African political organisations also contributed to this phenomenon.[13]

Across a wider landscape, Bonner shows how ethnic rivalries between an "Eastern Transvaal" bloc around S. M. Makgatho and a "Sotho-Tswana" bloc around S. P. Matseke influenced TAC politics and further weakened Congress, prompting a split lasting until 1941. This was "a new kind of non-traditionalist ethnicity ... rooted in the countryside and played out in the towns". In 1933, Matseke joined with Selope Thema to wrest TAC control from Makgatho. By 1934, Moses Mphahlele had organised a rival faction. Bonner cogently unpacks the previously accepted "nationalist grand narrative" and explains the reasons for these ethnic splits, including the influence of the Depression. Ethnic epithets certainly flew thick and fast in this tussle, but issues of land hunger, class, and generation also were prominent, as indeed were chiefs, traditional supporters of Congress.[14]

If there were ethnic divisions then there also was a degree of unity in action even if, as we shall see later in this chapter, divisions of a class nature also re-emerged. African political unity in the Transvaal was encouraged through media circles, cultural and community contacts and shared interests. In the period, 1930-1931, ANC radicals were still able to use their trusted weapon, *Abantu-Batho*, to champion the interests of Africans and urge inner-party democracy. L. S. Motsepe used it to assert that national ANC leaders had neglected his Pretoria branch and to suggest that Seme was plotting to undermine *Abantu-Batho*. F. Bryn of the same branch similarly wrote that as the national ANC "has no policy ... we are not going to support it"; they "are sitting tight on their seat[s] in offices ... and ignoring the oppression [and] ill-treatment ... by the white ruling class". Pretoria members pledged "emphatically our allegiance to the Independent African National Congress".[15]

After *Abantu-Batho* ceased in 1931, activists within the ANC had fewer media avenues, though some made use of Seme's *African Leader* or the CPSA's *Umsebenzi* in the mid-1930s to try to connect with local feeling. Discontent in Alexandra was one instance. Here residents held meetings to oppose evictions. Correspondent G. K. Solundwana reported to *African Leader* on such a meeting of some 100 Africans. He lamented that white people did not publish eviction notices in African languages—"they don't care who we are, or that we are this many". A different correspondent reported on another Alexandra meeting, which A. B. Xuma attended, to "unravel" the Hertzog

Bills. It was clear "something is evolving in Alexandra that is pleasing", but could Congress connect with it? The picture is unclear, but some leading TAC figures such as C. S. Ramohanoe were active in the Alexandra Standholders Protection and Vigilance Association, whilst ANC veterans, Richard Msimang and Isaiah Bud M'belle, also lived in Alexandra. By the end of the decade, Dan Gumede and Gaur Radebe led a more active branch.[16]

Popular frustration with docile leaders, including national ANC moderates such as Seme, emerges in newspaper reports, including Seme's *African Leader*. "Linga kwa Kona!" ("Don't give up, keep trying") urged one correspondent reporting on how some township people had given up on Congress. They did not want to hear anything at all about the ICU, indicating it was a spent force. People were sick of demands for money with nothing delivered, indicating they sit with folded arms and do nothing. Using an analogy, the writer recounted a story of two relatives, in which one said that he worked for white people in the "Sea" (that is, the white economy) where his father died. Yet, he stayed there, working in the same "sea" and sleeping in the same bed in which his father died: "nje kanti bonke abantu bakowabo bafela e Lwandle." The meaning was clear if the idiom was colloquial: they would die the same death in the white South African "Sea" if they did nothing; they would be cowards ("gwala"). Here then the usual blame apportioned for failure broadens out. It was not just leaders but also the masses at fault. The latter must decide whether to support the ANC or ICU. A contemporary editorial, probably written by Mweli Skota, echoes this frustration, pointing to how ICU reliance on slogans and unrealistic promises, together with ANC leaders' "spirit of self-importance" and intolerance of criticism led to a "marked failure of faith in our organisations". Instead, there was a need for the ANC to develop a clear programme of African demands, something however not achieved until the 1940s.[17]

By the late 1930s, the efforts of the activists turned to reviving Congress. TAC provincial secretary C. S. Ramohanoe stated in his provincial report to the 1938 ANC conference that in the face of a "dangerous [Afrikaner] nationalism" waged against "the discontented native masses", the TAC had decided the ANC must "be resuscitated". The ANC "is an organisation that once did a great deal for the African people". He invoked memories of past anti-pass campaigns and "the struggle against the £2.10.0 provincial tax". In this regard, the TAC did not just talk but acted. It successfully challenged sections of the 1937 Native Laws Amendment Act, proving to Africans that it could still effectively champion their interests. In 1939, Ramohanoe joined with unionist Gana Makabeni and communists Mofutsanyana and Gaur Radebe on a deputation to the Johannesburg City Council to protest grievances of African bus passengers.[18]

The TAC was well placed to lead African political revival, being more action-oriented than rival African political organisations, centrally located, and with labour-oriented members such as Marks able to liaise with unions and enter working-class communities to some extent. Politically, it was the TAC which had convened a conference in Pimville in June 1935 to discuss the Hertzog Bills, out of which the All-African Convention eventually formed. The TAC was instrumental in hosting meetings in 1937 that saw the re-launching of the ANC as a force. In doing this, it sought to *involve*, not exclude, workers. In 1938, it requested unions to send delegates to a special African unity conference. In 1939, Marks and Baloyi became leaders of the Transvaal United Front. Under Matseke's leadership, the TAC forged contacts with unionists. Communists Radebe, Marks, Mofutsanyana and Josie Mpama were active in the TAC. The latter three were credentialed TAC delegates to the 1939 ANC convention, as was unionist Daniel Koza, who in the 1940s tried to get the ANC to adopt pro-working-class policies. Pioneer communist Thibedi, who lived in Orlando, was active in the TAC, as was A. P. Mda, of Africanist as well as socialist (if anti-communist) outlook, who was an ANC organiser. Mpama was active in 1939 defending the rights of Alexandra residents, joining the TAC's Ramahanoe and other black leaders in a delegation to Johannesburg City Council's Transport Board.[19]

Josie Mpama

In 1938, with such radicals on board, Matseke led residents of Western Native Township into a CPSA-initiated boycott of the census for urban Africans. This prompted rival African leader G. Sebotsa Mabeta to allege Matseke had been elected TAC president under the "Moscow flag" and the TAC was "entirely in the hands" of the CPSA. Arguing from an extreme Africanist position, Mabeta claimed that *African Congress*, an ephemeral broadsheet edited by Thibedi would, if allowed to flourish, "throw water on the last spark of the Congress". Thibedi, no longer a CPSA member, rejected this claim, noting Congress accepted aid from anyone willing "to help us attain the necessary Unity". TAC radicalism also aroused the suspicion of *Bantu World*. Intervening in ANC politics, it warned readers against those whose "sole purpose is to capture [Congress] in order to convert it into an international body ... unable to inspire us with the spirit of nationalism". Notwithstanding such exaggeration by rivals, Matseke helped develop ANC ties with working-class forces.[20] Hence we see some working-class movement radicals finding a home in the TAC, demonstrating that this part of Congress was far from the elitist club imagined by historians.

Not all TAC contacts with workers were through radicals. Some moderates also had close ties with more traditionalist rural areas. H. Nkageleng Nkadimeng, an anti-communist, combined activity as TAC assistant secretary from 1939 with Municipal Workers Union membership. Nkadimeng, along with Elias Moretsele (a more radical TAC activist), were members of the Bapedi National Society, a group with less direct proletarian links but nonetheless aiming to support jobless Pedi migrant workers.[21] These organisational overlaps and the presence of such members with long-term ties with workers helped increase TAC-worker contacts, but on a more moderate and more ethnically-based level than that pursued by Matseke or Marks.

In north and north-eastern Transvaal, closer political ties developed between migrant workers and the TAC. Certainly, some rural areas do not seem to have attracted much ANC involvement at all, perhaps due both to stretched resources and a strategic focus on urban regions, as well as rivalries. Thus, determined black resistance to intensified labour tenancy regulations in late 1930s in Lydenburg saw neither ANC nor CPSA intervention. On the other hand, this does not mean there were no contacts elsewhere. Delius has demolished the notion of an ANC very remote from rural workers. Some workers helped "keep their home communities and chiefs informed of ANC activities". TAC leaders on the Rand "acted as a focus for a migrant constituency". Whilst the active agency of *communist* TAC members clinched the contacts, Congress was an *avenue* for worker mobilisation. These connections would flourish in the 1940s, but they had their origins in political developments in the TAC and CPSA in the late 1930s.[22]

Central figures here were TAC members Alpheus Maliba and Moretsele. Maliba was born in 1901 in Nzhelee, Zoutpansberg district. He became a worker in a Johannesburg factory from 1935. He joined the CPSA in 1936 and was active in the TAC, maintaining close contact with Venda workers and organising them through Congress meetings on the Rand and in rural areas via the Zoutpansberg Balemi Association. Maliba used oral traditions in an earthy political style that enabled rural workers to better relate to working-class and national movements.[23]

Despite such sympathy, TAC leaders made only slight inroads into mobilising the vast mass of workers on the Rand or in rural areas. In many ways, the task was overwhelming for such a small, under-resourced body. For example, in rural districts such as those around Barberton, thousands of illicit Mozambican migrants developed sophisticated networks of labour intelligence about farms, but their immigration status and cultural differences made the work of political or labour organisation doubly difficult.[24]

Many workers, and especially miners, had only limited knowledge of Congress. Walter Sisulu left school at 15 to seek work. In 1928, he travelled to the Rand, working for a dairy farmer delivering milk to the mines and as a sweeper in mines. In 1930, he cut rock below ground. He worked in kitchens and bakeries, leading a bakery strike, which led to his dismissal. Working at Germiston Rose Deep, Sisulu saw his first example of active resistance to pass laws, led by black communists. He confided to me in 1991 that he and his fellow miners did not yet know of the ANC, a fact partly explained by his comments that, working on the mines, "I was completely cut off from my people". This indicates the difficulty Congress found in penetrating the closed world of miners. Yet ironically, it also reminds us that not only Congress, but also miners, were isolated from wider society, indicative of alienation typical of capitalist and colonial societies. Although in the early 1930s he had heard East London Congress leader Richard Godlo speak, it was not until 1940 that he joined the TAC's Orlando branch. Unionist Alfred Mbele enrolled Sisulu into the ANC after they had heard A. B. Xuma speak. Also important in Sisulu's gradual politicisation was his increasing involvement in mutual aid associations such as the Orlando Brotherly Society and the Orlando Civic Society, which helped him to see connections between African culture, local conditions, and politics.[25]

Other workers, especially younger workers, similarly lacked familiarity with the political world of Congress. Naboth Mokgatle, later active in the CPSA, as a young man in 1932 felt the ANC "was no longer heard of" in Pretoria. Still, he listened to its speakers. Mark Shope, son of a rail worker, "had no chance of going to school". He worked as a farm labourer, earning three shillings and sixpence a month, and then as a kitchen worker. Shope experienced "ruthless regimented" compounds as a miner from 1935 to 1939 and worked on the railways. He became a union leader and in 1952 joined the ANC but at this time was distant from both. He took part in a strike in 1935 but told me: "it didn't mean anything to me." He only started to see problems "very clearly after the Nationalists came to power".[26]

For such reasons, historians have been wary of conceding too much township support to the ANC. Lodge agrees it is incorrect to view the ANC on Rand townships as "totally dominated by businessmen and landlords", but emphasises branch domination by non-proletarians. In the far-from-fully proletarianised Sophiatown, Congress kept its distance from poorer tenants and their anti-rent protests often led instead by CPSA activists, as in 1939. Goodhew notes that Western Areas ANC local meetings in the 1930s were "occasional, but uncoordinated". Robbie Resha joined the ANC in Western Native Township in 1939, but later recalled the Sophiatown branch as ineffective.[27]

Despite such ANC ineffectiveness, many black CPSA activists campaigning in the area were part of the broad Congress family, so in some areas we should not draw too sharp a dichotomy between the two bodies. In April 1930, the TAC held anti-pass meetings in Western Native Township, supported by residents Selby Msimang and Daniel Letanka, both still active in Congress. Some TAC members supported the CPSA pass-burning strategy; others adopted a more moderate approach. When CPSA activists in Sophiatown, such as Gaur Radebe shifted their attention to the Advisory Boards in the late 1930s, they were in one sense copying a tried-and-true Congress tactic. Historians often fail to distinguish clearly between ANC and TAC, yet the "two caps" tactic of 1980s activists can broadly apply to earlier activists. The TAC, under Matseke, took part in, or even initiated, community protests. Behind this was perceived class stratification. African plot owners in places such as Sophiatown were often in debt, forced by rising prices into a precarious reliance on renting. In the late 1930s, property-owners prominent in ANC branches in Sophiatown and Newclare, such as the doctor A. B. Xuma and the coal merchant Simon Tyeku, openly expressed support for the basic demands of black workers despite their clearly upper-middle-class status. This cross-class position was rooted in their own lives and in ANC politics.[28]

For a brief period as young men, both Xuma and Tyeku had experienced the rigours of manual labour. Tyeku had been a farm labourer and later, after victimisation for his ANC activities, returned to a life of poverty. Until the late 1930s, Xuma was not active in the ANC but his pivotal role as ANC president in the 1940s reflected an earlier interest in the problems of all Africans, including workers. In his youth, he seemed an unlikely "bourgeois". His parents received no formal schooling. At school, he helped to organise a student strike against segregation. He became a teacher, earning £14 a quarter, which he saved to go to the United States in 1913. Here he had to taste the life of a labourer to enable him to study agriculture and medicine. He worked as a labourer in a furnace for three months, "ramming the steel pipe moulds", and in coal yards, building sites and stables, and as a domestic worker and cleaner for two years. At the time, the press reported the fate of this student, "stalked for years by the spectre of grim poverty". In his correspondence, Xuma as early as 1920 had expressed an interest in black workers.[29]

Returning to South Africa in 1927, Xuma had been asked by Kadalie to "become active in the great struggle", but he "remained outside" the ICU when his enquiries about the union's finances remained unanswered, though "a most inspiring letter" from Xuma was read to the 1928 ICU conference. He was in touch with ANC leaders. He had corresponded with Plaatje, if mainly over the question of a pair of spectacles lost during Plaatje's 1923 American tour. In 1929, Seme approached Xuma to become ANC treasurer, but he declined. The next year, the ANC elected Xuma *in absentia* to its executive, but he again refused a post. Whilst declining these positions, Xuma does not appear to have objected to his name being associated with Congress. In 1935, they appointed him to its executive. By 1939, Xuma was looming as a future ANC leader. As a credentialed TAC delegate to the 1939 ANC conference, leaders asked him to respond to addresses by guests. To Durban's mayor he suggested that "African labour should be employed" on a proposed housing scheme to prevent the likelihood of increased rents if white labour was contracted. If Xuma enjoyed a very comfortable income as a doctor, he nonetheless resided on the Rand not far removed from thousands of black workers. If *petit bourgeois*, that did not seem to bother radicals. Marks, who canvassed for Xuma within the ANC, saw him as "second to none in giving evidence before commissions" and most effective in securing funds to build the ANC.[30]

At times, Xuma could seem condescending to workers. The "well-educated", he wrote, have a "sincere and heartfelt sympathy for their backward brother ... They voice his legitimate claims and interpret his wishes to the white man". Nevertheless, his sympathy for black workers was genuine and his intentions focused on practical solutions to their problems. In 1929, he urged both the Johannesburg Joint Council and the Miners' Phthisis Commission to rectify the lack of compensation paid to incapacitated African miners. In his 1930 address to the Conference of European and Bantu Christian Student Associations at Fort Hare, Xuma examined the loss of black rights. He saw a need for a revolution of thoughts, gave a detailed analysis of the role of cheap labour, and stressed the discrimination against black workers both in their wages and in the 1930 Miners' Phthisis Further Amendment Act. He debunked arguments positing a "high" black social wage. If "one complains … [that mine] wages … are low, one is, at once, told that the native miner receives more wages in kind … However [they] are never included in [phthisis] compensation".[31]

Alfred B. Xuma, 1930s

Xuma continued to speak out on the adverse effects of low wages on African lives. In 1931, he told the NEC that many black people were "working for the same wage in cash or in kind as was paid my father some 50 years ago". Today things were worse, as workers now relied on Western, not African-produced, goods. Prices were tied to white wages, hence African "wages do not allow him [to buy goods at this price, so] the native labourer must fall in debt". Xuma clearly understood that the job colour bar tended "to force all Native labourers into [the] unskilled labour class", creating "a depression of Native wages". The "oversupply of unskilled workers" created "an increasing army of unemployment" and led "to greater poverty and hardship". Pass laws limited "the black worker's bargaining power" whereas "All labour should be free to bargain collectively". A "living" wage for black labourers would extend the national market and "eliminate all reason" for white worker fear of black competition. He thus approximated the demands of contemporary black unions. Xuma told the 1931 Liquor Commission that low wages drove African women to illegal occupations. He supported demands of Klipspruit worker residents for removal of their settlement from its location adjacent to a sewage farm. For a self-proclaimed mere "student of human relations ... neither a politician or agitator", Xuma showed a keen awareness of the causes of black workers' harsh conditions.[32]

In 1932, Xuma addressed the Bantu Social Club of the University of the Witwatersrand. He condemned the appalling slum conditions and high black infant mortality on the Rand, the harsh provisions (including whipping of workers and child labour) of the 1932 Native Service Contract Act ("more akin to a state of slavery and serfdom") and the Riotous Assemblies Act, and the low salaries of African teachers (reduced by 45 per cent in the last two years). In 1933, he told the Junior South African Party that the "civilised" labour policy favoured white unemployed people at the expense of Africans and urged its abolition. He criticised the suffering of black people under pass laws, high rentals, and the long distances that they had to travel to work. He added that a more rational state economic policy would create a home market and a "progressive proletariat".[33]

By 1934, Xuma was becoming more publicly active. He told an education conference in July that Africans were "forced economically to live in crowded, squalid surroundings", with few medical facilities and inadequate diet. A poor standard of worker accommodation in compounds and locations "was common". These grim conditions he linked to their "low economic status". Addressing the Pretoria Native Welfare Association in September, he stressed the inequalities in taxation of white and black. The economic Depression and "white labour policy" pushed many black workers, initially forced to migrate to the towns to seek work, into unemployment. Yet, they were still liable for taxation and for prosecution, both for failure to produce tax receipts and for the lack of a regular contract of service. African teachers, Xuma told the Committee on Native Education in 1935, were "one of the most miserably paid and hard worked people". They "should receive serious and sympathetic consideration … [and] be paid a reasonably decent salary". Women teachers were "far worse off in pay than uneducated girls employed as nurses or domestic servants". He attended meetings of one of the first African women's labour unions: the Bantu Trained Nurses Association.[34] This was a time of increased female urban migrants, but not all African leaders matched Xuma's interest in urban women's status and well-being. The TAC continued to neglect female membership, and in the 1930s, government continued to target urban women as "undesirable". African women were still not prominent in formal African politics, but on occasion expressed their demands, as in a petition of 50 Klipspruit women against proposed charges for carrying bundles of washing on trains, a fee that would have hurt the widely commuting workers.[35]

The public condemnation of workers' harsh conditions by Xuma drew the attention of socialists. Betty Sachs, editor of the left-wing *Guardian*, wrote to him in 1939 asking him to contribute articles. *The Guardian* was not a Congress organ, but ANC demands often featured in its pages alongside worker struggles. This may have contributed to an identification of ANC and worker issues in the minds of readers, who numbered 10,000 by 1939. Xuma supported the cause of all the oppressed. He told a 1939 Mendi Memorial meeting that the Land Act left hundreds of thousands of Africans "homeless, landless, moneyless and hopeless". Various factors inclined him to focus somewhat on labour, such as personal experiences, residence adjacent to teeming numbers of workers, harsh economic times, and the tradition, established by Congress, of black leaders speaking out on labour issues. He judiciously blended moderate statements with his concerns for workers, but this does not obviate his dedication to alleviating their suffering. All this evidence indicates Xuma's interest in labour matters well before his rise to ANC leader in the 1940s, when he was to continue to back the basic human rights of black workers.[36]

The TAC continued to raise issues affecting the working class. It retained bonds with a range of organisations concerned with workers, and forged contacts with some individual workers through various TAC activists and supporters.

Natal

Congress contacts with workers in Natal at this time continued to be limited by its weak, fragmented structure, and by difficulties in recruiting migrant or casual workers, who made up a sizeable segment of the Natal labour force. The NNC reportedly had only 200 members in 1930. It lost credibility among radical working-class activists by being complimented by the government for "doing considerable good among the Natives". John Dube returned to limited activity in the NNC. Seme appointed him to his "cabinet" in 1930, but he resigned in 1931. Dube appears to have been increasingly more involved in local or regional matters of an apolitical character. He chaired and sat on the board of the Bantu Youth League, founded in 1930, a fledgling Christian youth body managed by Sibusisiwe Makhanya. Dube did attend the 1939 annual ANC meeting in Durban, but generally was distant from national ANC affairs. Such moderates dominated the NNC. However, this did not stop the NNC occasionally criticising the precarious position of African workers. For instance, in 1931 it drew the attention of the Secretary for Native Affairs to high black unemployment, and called for taxation exemptions for African workers suffering distress.[37]

Dube told the NEC in 1931 that government heavily taxed Africans who, "with our labour" had "done our share" for South African development, yet were "the poorest class". In no other country was the "poorest class" taxed so directly. Africans "have no luxuries, they are a poor people, and they earn small wages"—in Weenen they worked for only ten shillings a month, hence a £1 direct tax was "too heavy for the majority". The Depression had made them "poorer and poorer". Thus, they should not be liable for tax default fines. "I do not believe that any poor people … on the wages they receive, should be subject to direct taxation … They pay enough … through their clothes and pots and pans. ... If [taxation] is not reduced, [they] should be paid higher wages." Dube argued that African workers received only a part of their legitimate wages, the rest of which went to sustain white supremacy. An African worked for, say, £2 a month whilst a white overseer received £15. "If the wages were regulated as to benefit the natives as well, perhaps the Natives would have had more wages. But [they are] paid small wages in order to keep down the cost so that the balance can go to the overseer." This equation conveniently ignored the factor of the capitalist. African leaders, stated Dube, believed African workers should receive a higher wage, and overseers should not get inflated wages. He agreed that industrial laws should be amended to authorise African unions, claiming: "I have thought a great deal that Natives are exploited by their employers and they should organise themselves in self-defence." Nevertheless, he was aware that wage equality was only a remote possibility. Even if, in certain industries, Africans "may be as skilled as the white man ... we are not going to get the same wages as a white man". Nonetheless, "we want to compete". Dube called for a Wage Act that would apply to Africans, and for authorities to allow families of workers to live in industrial centres.[38]

Dube's emphasis on competition related to his strong, if naive, faith in capitalism. In 1930 he told a meeting in Johannesburg that, whilst white people did not care for their servants, he had "visit[ed] the mines and had seen how well cared for and fed the native workers were. He would willingly give the Chamber of Mines all credit for that." Belief in capitalism aside, Dube maintained his earlier interest in labour conditions. This was manifest in diverse forums, such as the NNC, NRC, meetings and the press. In 1931, he convened a "well-attended mass meeting" in Durban. It passed resolutions expressing "strong disapproval" of the dismissal of Africans from public and private employment, called for immediate state relief for African unemployed, and protested a "drastic" reduction by 20 per cent of African railway workers' wages, which would "produce untold misery". The meeting rejected such measures, which it stated attempted to place the burden of the Depression on Africans, as unjust and futile. The gathering delegated Dube and others to take the grievances to Pretoria. In a contribution to a 1935 pamphlet, edited by Champion, Dube criticised white peoples' opinion on black labour: "When we kept our men in Reserves you told us we were lazy niggers; when we send them as permanent labour to the towns you say we are a menace to industry."Dube's interest in labour involved more an improvisation for the benefit of listeners than a definite commitment to industrial relations change; he was in no way involved with labour unions. That did not stop him, and *Ilanga lase Natal*, from supporting wage rises for black labourers, as in 1938 when echoing a call by the Chamber of Industries, which advocated, in its own interest, increased black purchasing power.[39]

The other ANC faction in the province, the Natal ANC, "the Provincial Branch of the South African National Congress" with its headquarters in Pietermaritzburg, was more openly supportive of black workers, and broader black rights. In the early 1930s, the Natal ANC campaigned for the repeal of the Land Act "and other oppressive and repressive" anti-black legislation.[40]

The Natal ANC had more radical leaders than did Dube's Congress. Champion continued to be associated with both ICU and ANC. He espoused a highly contradictory philosophy, but one which strongly supported black labour rights. In 1930, he supported the radical Josiah Gumede's bid for re-election as national ANC president. In 1931, Champion urged total abolition of the compound system and free industrial organisation of Africans, and was in favour of mineworkers themselves giving evidence to state commissions. He was, he claimed, "the only Native ... given the privilege of going to every compound with the consent of the Chamber of Mines". Champion fell short of supporting an independent political role of workers. Instead, in 1930, he urged the creation of a black capitalist class, arguing capitalism was the main force in history. Yet in 1931, he warned that Africans might resort to "revolutionary deeds" unless Pretoria listened to their genuine leaders, not moderates who failed "to interpret the views of the masses". Nevertheless, his ICU *yase Natal* refused to support a large-scale anti-pass protest in Durban in 1930 merely because it was organised by the CPSA. Champion remained active in Congress, but was critical of its leaders. He criticised Seme for inaction in the face of deteriorating conditions of workers in the Depression, and NNC leader J. R. Msimang for favouring suspension of beer boycotts. Yet in June 1930, he organised a major ICU reception for Seme in Durban. At this time, Champion stood side-by-side with women such as Katie Makhanya and with John Dube at a Congress-led demonstration against passes for women at which he called on Makhanya to speak on behalf of women. He was also involved in helping to organise soup kitchens for the unemployed.[41]

Champion increasingly was drawn into local politics, in which he supported the rights of black workers. Following the 1929 Durban riots, he and fellow ICU official James Ngcobo won election to the Durban Advisory Board. In its meetings, they protested the low wages of Council employees, the low fares and poor working conditions of ricksha-pullers, and restrictions on African traders. Within the Board, Champion caucused a black faction, which held public meetings to attack municipal beer-halls, and circulated his pamphlet *Igazi ne Zinyebezi* ("Blood and Tears"). In it, he decried the lucrative beer-hall income of white people who took money "from the pockets of poor natives". He mixed a moderate call for "goodwill ... between the employed and the employer", with a more socialistic demand that because all people "live by the sweat of their bodies - [then the fact] that one man works for another should ... cease". In 1929, he had promised the government that he would resign from the ICU if they established an Advisory Board. However, he concluded, in similar socialist rhetoric that the ICU "is the mouth-piece of the workers. It will never die out whilst they live and are oppressed."[42]

Police reported radical speeches at ICU rallies at this time. Ngonyama ka Gumbi, ICU Pietermaritzburg secretary, told a meeting of 5,000 people in Durban in June 1930 that Africans should strike for eight shillings a day, and follow the example of Soviet communists and "cut the throats of the Government and the ministers [of religion]". Champion praised Ngonyama and was himself praised in an *izibongo* to Zulu leaders. The whole event was described by police as having an "electrical" effect on the crowd. Greatly alarmed at his growing influence, the state banned Champion from Natal from October 1930 to 1934. He revealed to the Director of Native Labour that, as his ICU monthly salary of £20 had now ceased, his wealth amounted to £82 cash and family land of 21 acres worth £230. He had considerable extended family expenses, and received no land rent. Such assets clearly distanced him from workers, but his sudden loss of income highlights the precarious foundations of many black *petit bourgeois*.[43]

Into the gap, left by Champion's banning, stepped CPSA leader Johannes Nkosi. By November 1930, police anxiously reported Nkosi was selling 100 copies of *Umsebenzi* at ICU meetings. CPSA mass meetings in mid-December attracted many workers, for example, 1,500 people attended one meeting. The CPSA's meteoric rise is evident in the burning of 3,000 passes at a rally of 1,000 people, held symbolically on 16 December 1930 at what Ndlovu calls a "counter-commemoration" of official celebrations of the 1838 settler victory over the Zulu. However, repression of the CPSA was soon to create a political vacuum. Police attacked the rally and killed Nkosi and several comrades. Communists kept Nkosi's memory alive in various ways. The Durban CPSA's Zulu news-sheet *Ndaba Zamakomanisi e Tekwini* urged workers to "revive the spirit of Nkosi" ("vuselelani umoya ka Johannes Nkosi"). The tactics it used involved linking worker and national struggles, emblemised in its masthead slogans like "Mayibuye i Afrika!" and "Workers of the World Unite!" Nkosi's widow Hetty spoke at a rally in Johannesburg. In August 1931, Durban communists erected a tombstone with the words "Our martyred dead … killed by the Durban borough police", but there is little evidence the CPSA was able to make much headway among African workers in Natal at this time.[44]

The terms of Champion's exile precluded him from taking part in ICU activities. However, authorities did not reckon with ANC-ICU connections due in part to overlapping membership. In January 1931, Champion took part in the ANC convention and in April received ANC support in Kimberley. He joined the staff of *Abantu-Batho*. Champion assisted James Shuba of the leftist African Laundry Workers' Union when police arrested its members in Cape Town. His growing disillusionment with the Joint Council influenced his temporary radicalisation. In 1931, he decided "to keep away from them" when refused permission to book the Bantu Men's Social Centre for a function.[45]

Upon his return from exile to Durban in May 1934, Champion resumed his ICU *yase* Natal organising, in conjunction with his involvement in the Natal ANC. He called a three-day ICU conference attended by 300 people including Chief Mini. At the conference remedies for the poll tax, cattle dipping, locusts, "shortage of money among working people", and replacement of black by white workers was discussed. He addressed an open-air meeting of 300 people in late May and a similar crowd at the ICU hall in early June. Together with Dube and A. N. Ntuli of the NNC, Champion addressed a crowd of 2,000 the following day concerning the illness of Chief Mshiyeni. Champion tried to mobilise Durban ricksha pullers to call for higher incomes. He also returned to political pamphleteering. In 1935, he issued a pamphlet, bringing together statements against the Hertzog Bills by black leaders, in which he outlined the discriminatory labour legislation which ensured that the African "work[ed] the hardest but is paid the lowest". Champion's 1935 New Year message called for increased wages for "every working native" and criticised discrimination against African workers and traders. Police, he stated, "do not want to collect witnesses of the native who has quarrelled with his employer". His solution to these problems was to build up the ICU and "our own businesses". He reiterated his concern over unpaid wages and loopholes in service contracts of workers in another pamphlet issued by the Natal Workers' Club. By now, he was very disillusioned with the Joint Council as it had "no power because it is controlled by biased Europeans". Worried that he was "rapidly gaining the confidence of Durban Natives", and outraged by his audacity in telling them the law, police viewed Champion as "a definite menace to peace and tranquillity", and arrested him and 90 supporters. Nevertheless, Chief Native Commissioner H. C. Lugg noted (presciently, given Champion's later conservatism) that he "may be a rogue but if properly handled there is just the possibility of him being turned to good account". We see Champion's underlying moderate politics in his letter to the Prime Minister protesting his banishment, stressing the constitutional nature of his ICU work, and pointing out that he had always "lived a European standard of living".[46]

Champion favoured financial schemes, rather than class struggle, as a solution to ICU and ANC woes and increasingly pursued his own business interests. He placed much faith in the growth of Clermont Native Village, for which he acted as an agent. In 1933, he wrote that he thought it would be a good thing for Africans "to have an opportunity to build their own village … [whereby] they would be removed from those that loathe them [white people] and only come into contact with them at work". He proposed a Bank of the Black People, or Three Years' Plan, which he had planned in exile working for the Colonial Banking and Trust Company. The idea was simple: a trust, with himself as trustee, to enable Africans to "build up businesses". He reasoned that "by the time we will have money in the I.C.U. we will have power". These schemes did not check either ICU or ANC decline. In 1935, concerned at his shrinking support, he quarrelled with Ngcobo and J. T. Gumede, attacked NNC leader John Mngadi, accusing him of corruption, and set up a rival Durban ANC. In the late 1930s Champion had an intermittent role in Congress. He served, nominally, as Mahabane's Secretary for Lands and Locations, but most of his activity centred on Durban. He returned to politics in the NRC. However, in the 1940s, as Natal ANC president, whilst maintaining a broad ANC stance, he moved to the right.[47]

Some other Natal ANC leaders continued to lobby for improved labour conditions. Selby Msimang, until then a labour adviser on the Rand, returned in 1937 to Natal as a farm manager. In Ladysmith he gave evidence to the Native Farm Labour Committee that the farm "labourer never finds time to attend to his land properly" and thus was forced into debt and six months of unpaid labour for white farmers. The following year he urged both *Ilanga* readers and the ANC executive to lobby a visiting delegation of the International Labour Office (ILO) about such matters. Pretoria had not ratified any ILO labour conventions and to advance the interests of "our labour", Africans had to give the delegation data on job colour bars and other laws discriminating against black labour.[48]

Josiah Gumede, though he never regained the level of support he enjoyed in 1927-1929, remained politically active after his defeat at Easter 1930. He unsuccessfully sought a passport to attend the aborted Conference of Negro Workers in London in May 1930. In June, he was active in an IICU-CPSA meeting in Johannesburg protesting the Riotous Assemblies Act. In December, he took part in discussions at the CPSA conference.[49]

In 1931, Gumede, with other Pietermaritzburg ANC leaders, Chief Mini and David Sioka (Natal ANC president and secretary respectively), gave evidence to the NEC. Mini, who continued to attend national ANC conferences, lamented the decline of chiefly power and loss of liberty of tenant farmers. He also opposed the "disgraceful" extension to Natal of the "tot" system, whereby employers could "pay" workers with liquor. Gumede expressed something of the consternation of traditional patriarchal authorities in his comment, "our womenfolk are getting out of hand". However, he was more directly critical, complaining government had driven Africans to towns by misrule. He condemned pass laws. Africans, added Gumede, had been "obliged to combine" in the ANC and ICU, which had succeeded in drawing to the attention of the authorities issues such as failure of employers to pay wages.

They had gained some victories in the courts, but these were short-lived. The state had responded with the draconian Riotous Assemblies Act that had turned persons pursuing these matters constitutionally into "agitators". He protested against laws that discriminated against black workers, such as provisions of the Masters and Servants' Act, which ensured that workers deserting an employer, even if motivated by harsh conditions, were gaoled, and exclusion of Africans from the Industrial Conciliation Act. Africans loyalty to the government was, he suggested, misplaced.[50]

Gumede maintained contact with the ICU and ANC. He presided at the 1932 conference of one IICU faction and was a delegate to an ICU Unity conference called by Kadalie in June 1933. In December 1933, Gumede chaired a Durban conference aimed at re-unifying ICU splinter groups under the banner of a United ICU that duly elected him president and Kadalie general secretary. At the 1934 Natal ICU conference he successfully moved resolutions calling on government to raise black workers' salaries, to institute a legal basic wage, take action on unemployment and appoint African to investigate all matters related to black labour. He stood, albeit unsuccessfully, for the NRC in 1937, and continued to attend ANC conferences until his death in 1947.[51] Gumede maintained consistent support for and involvement with bodies purporting to represent workers.

ANC support for better teacher wages encouraged them to move closer to the organisation, despite strong state discouragement of direct membership. At this time, Albert Luthuli pre-occupied himself with his work as a teachers' union leader and chief. He was not yet prominent in the ANC, yet identified with its world-view. "I was ... a part of Congress in all but the technical sense. To me ... the A.N.C. was 'the watchdog of the African people'". In retrospect, he viewed the early ANC as being far from accountable for the growing resistance seen in strikes, stating "at first it was no more than part of it, and possibly a conservative part at that - but it was there". What probably contributed to his sense of belonging to Congress was its ability to give "voice to the many day-to-day grievances of the people" at a time when he, as Natal African Teachers' Association secretary, was increasingly concerned with such matters. Giving evidence to the NEC in 1931, Luthuli criticised the meagre salaries of African teachers that were, he argued, below the cost of living. He based his claims on his own detailed survey of earnings of 120 African teachers in Natal, which revealed that many teachers were in debt and often were forced to take extra jobs to survive. Luthuli did not restrict his advocacy to teachers. Drawing on his knowledge of the fate of ex-students, Luthuli argued that African carpenters and builders received much lower wages than white people in the same trades, or were forced to work at other jobs as most Africans could not afford even to pay them trade wages. Besides his union work, one other possible reason for Luthuli's contact with workers was his engagement with African soccer, which increasingly was attracting workers as players and spectators. However, the ANC in Natal did not make the same sort of connection between sport and politics that the ICU had made in the 1920s, as there is little direct evidence of the overt use of soccer games to recruit members or raise funds for the movement.[52]

Historians have revealed little about individual worker involvement in the Natal ANC of the 1930s. Pious Mei, who later became a leader of the African Textile Workers' Union and Natal ANC, joined the ANC in 1936. Stephen Dlamini joined the CPSA in Durban in 1935. Because of discrimination, he left his teaching job, and stopped going to church. "Because of the exploitation of teachers … I decided to go and work in a garage in Durban." In the 1930s, he worked selling petrol in the Transvaal and OFS, and then as a Durban textile factory worker. On the attitude of workers to the ANC, he stressed the class dimension, that "in fact the workers were 100% behind the ANC".[53]

In 1938, ANC forces in Natal remained divided. No reports for the province reached the 1938 national ANC conference. Attempts to appoint Champion as provincial leader abated after protests from Dube, whose NNC kept its distance from the national body. Yet despite erratic growth, Congress survived—Basner claimed it remained strong in parts of Natal—and succeeded to a modest extent in protesting poor labour conditions and in keeping political protest in the mind of Africans. In 1939, S. H. D. Mnyandu wrote that Africans "very deeply resented the operation of the pass laws", and in particular recalled, "The Natal Native Congress leaders fought against them tooth and nail."[54]

The Orange Free State

ANC activity in the Orange Free State was inconsistent across the decade. Much of its work remained urban-based, although there were attempts to connect with rural workers who formed a majority of the African population of the province but who remained un-unionised. Even though some contacts developed among rural peoples, in general Congress failed to consolidate these ties. Nevertheless, Congress activity helped lay a foundation for growth in the next decade.

The position of rural-based workers remained harsh. Demands by white farmers for more cheap rural labourers increased with an agricultural revival following the 1933 drought that had driven many African farm tenants and labourers off the land. By the late 1930s, Africans outnumbered white people on farms by at least four to one (with women and children comprising the majority of workers). The increase of 87,123 in the black rural population contrasted with a decrease of 4,648 among white people adding to the pressure on African livelihoods. In the Orange Free State, many of these rural labourers were substantially divorced from land and in this sense formed a more permanent rural proletariat. At the same time, urban drift continued in the face of low wages and brutal treatment. Things, however, were changing. In 1939, the Institute of Race Relations remarked that African farm labourers were now more articulate in protesting their working and living conditions.[55]

ANC national president Z. R. Mahabane lived in Winburg, which if isolated, gave him a direct link with the province. However, the Bloemfontein branch claimed only 50 members in 1931. OFS ANC president Thomas Mapikela continued to attend national and provincial ANC conferences, but other bodies attracted his attention. In 1932, he was, simultaneously, Waaihoek location headman, Advisory Board chairman, Joint Council member, and African Life Assurance Company superintendent. In 1930, he was president of the Bantu Traders' Association. This body, which in 1931 claimed 120 OFS members, sought to "work in conjunction" with Congress. It claimed to be "capable of relieving unemployment [by employing] at least three employees [for each member]". Mapikela viewed the group as a means to raise the status of all Africans. At this time, he still had some contact with workers. He continued to train apprentice carpenters. He also served on the controlling committee of the Bantu Benevolent Fund, a group working for the relief of Africans living "below the bread line". When union organiser Max Gordon and J. D. Rheinallt Jones visited Bloemfontein in 1936 to present worker claims to the Wage Board, they wrote to Mapikela in advance to ask him to pass on questionnaires to 30 workers. However, despite his undoubted sympathy for the African poor, Mapikela tended to view unfettered commerce as a panacea for Africans' problems. If general trading rights were extended to black people, then "grievances pending and long standing communis[t] agitation etc. will disappear … Life will be worth living". He did not intend to submerge his own class interests in an undifferentiated mass of workers. He was outraged that African traders were subject to the same pass regulations as workers. It was "ridiculous" for African employers "while contracting Boys to work for them [to] have to contract themselves in return".[56]

Radicals viewed Mapikela with some suspicion. Basner in 1936 campaigned as a CPSA candidate. He travelled with a "group of stalwarts" of the "then defunct" ANC and ICU the "length and breadth" of the Orange Free State and Transvaal to "revive" the ANC. Basner saw Mapikela as dictatorial in his Bloemfontein domain, an opportunist in his rush to be a NRC candidate. Basner found support for the CPSA among ex-ICU activists and independent churches from Bloemfontein location to Witsieshoek and Kroonstad. Radical sparks flew elsewhere. In 1930, the UNIA's branch in Vrede led large-scale protests against the Riotous Assemblies Act, in which Congress radicals likely joined.[57]

Despite the distractions facing its leaders, Congress maintained a close interest in urban conditions. Some members had ties with workers or were themselves wage earners. The Bloemfontein ANC called a series of meetings between 1931 and 1934 to protest poor housing and discriminatory local government policies. At a 1934 meeting, 800 tenants and stand-holders aired grievances on housing. They instructed the ANC to send a delegation of 12 to meet the Town Council. Branch secretary Sam Lichabe, who worked as a Council caretaker, insisted on a wide representation of residents. All 12 were unable to attend at the stipulated time because they did not finish work until 6.30 pm. This indicated their plebeian status. Lichabe transmitted to the Council complaints by residents about alleged sexual exploitation by local officials of African women attempting to re-purchase their houses and the eviction of an impoverished woman who had just given birth. Branch chairman, Sam Leshoai, had worked for 25 years as a joiner/cabinet-maker. In a letter to the Native Affairs Department, he lamented the "tremendous increase of workless" at a time when the Council "retrench the labourers and keep the rates the same". He called, against the policy of Seme, for abolition of the local Advisory Board that, he claimed, denied the existence of black suffering. The ANC branch urged that the state make provision for the welfare of "widows, widowers, homeless, maimed, aged and orphans in the locations". The branch protested cases of evictions of "old and workless people", such as Elisa Matlhoko, "whose whole family and all her belongings were left right in the middle of the street ... for six weeks". Leshoai noted that, "dogs are better protected by law than our people". The ANC served a 74-point log of claims on the Council about rights of black stand-holders and tenants who risked losing houses when unemployed. It denounced increases in local taxes and lack of public amenities. Council officials put the ANC leaders under close observation. Officials noted that women were prominent ANC supporters and accused the branch of using "tactics of defiance and o[b]struction", and viewed Leshoai and Lichabe as "incorrigible agitators".[58]

These protests show not only "middle-class" concern for property, but also the ANC's representation of grievances of different social strata like the aged, the unemployed and workers. Leshoai sought the support of African herbalists. In 1937, he appealed to them to join forces with Congress. He had a particular grievance against the Council. They had failed to reimburse him for demolition of his father's house. Whilst his motives may have been personal and pecuniary, he reflected community resentment at Council housing policy: "Why can't the Dept. build its own houses ... Why should it capture our houses?" He raised issues originating with residents (including workers) such as overcrowding, dilapidated housing, and maladministration of rising lodging taxes.[59]

The Bloemfontein ANC clashed not only with Town Council officials, but also with Advisory Board and fellow ANC members, such as Mapikela (board chairman), and "Blockman" Jacob B. Sesing (board vice-chairman). Sesing, who in 1932 also was acting president of the local ICU, accused Leshoai of holding location meetings to whip up resentment against the Board, which could lead to bloodshed. The ANC in turn accused the Board of holding closed meetings and illegal elections. Congress condemned the entire "blockman" system, a demand taken up by Provincial ANC secretary, Jeremiah S. Nkoana. Based in Bloemfontein, he also was a wage earner, having worked as a railway inspector for 20 years.[60]

The ANC Bloemfontein branch elected David Mkwanazi secretary in 1931. He presented a detailed ANC submission to the NEC that squarely placed workers in the centre of its demands. The branch criticised the inequities of the pass laws for African workers. Many a worker found without a pass was imprisoned. Police were "often instructed to conduct a 'hold-up' of Native workers". It noted that most Africans were out of work "because unemployment had overpowered the world", whilst "sympathetic economists" wondered how Africans could live on their low wages. The ANC stressed the class influences on location life. Low wages badly affected health. No African could afford to build a house "unless he starves himself in order to erect the shanty". In any case, the owner soon fell into debt due to extended-family obligations. The urban African, interested in sports, must confine himself to soccer, "the cheapest of all" sports due to his "desperate struggle under a very poor earning capacity". Many of his unfortunate brothers could not afford even soccer. They suffered drunkenness, proving that the African's "expenditure complies with his earnings". Rural Africans, the ANC added, complained of their state of vagrancy and of absentee landlords. Many had to migrate to towns thanks to exorbitant taxes and low wages. The submission indicates that this ANC branch was acutely conscious of the tribulations of African working lives.[61]

Mkwanazi was born on a farm near Bethlehem. He worked as a child farm labourer, before coming to Bloemfontein in 1929. His preference for using an interpreter at NEC hearings suggests a lack of formal education. In the face of persistent questioning by commissioners, he defended ANC claims and added additional observations indicating his acquaintance with workers. Farm labourers earned "such small wages ... [that] they cannot exist". He personally knew locals who had unsuccessfully sought work on the Rand. He estimated seven shillings a day would be an adequate wage for an African worker. When Commissioner A. W. Roberts suggested that the immediate payment of this amount would be "a dangerous thing", Mkwanazi countered that, in his opinion, conditions would "gradually improve according to the class of natives that are working", and that a wage "increment ... should always be maintained" among African workers.[62]

ANC members Doyle Modiakgotla, John Mancoe, Robert Sello, Jason Jingoes and J. B. Sesing were among those nominated at a 1932 "public meeting of workers" in Heilbron to a committee charged with reconstituting the ICU. Mancoe, in Bloemfontein, had worked as a teacher in four towns before joining the ICU in 1923, quickly rising to become Bloemfontein and then provincial secretary. Critical of ANC moderation in the 1920s, he became more active in Congress in the 1930s. In 1932 he chaired the African Savings and Credit Institute, formed to "open avenues of employment" for youth. In 1931, the Federated Free State ICU had elected Sello to its executive. Sesing had worked on De Beers diamond mines for ten years, becoming an overseer. He later worked for a tobacco company, again reaching the status of foreman. In 1919, he had joined Msimang's agitation for wage rises in Bloemfontein.[63]

Keable 'Mote was ANC OFS secretary in the early 1930s. Threads tied him to the labour movement; he worked as a teacher in Kroonstad; was an IICU leader; and, in 1931, secretary of the Federated Free State ICU, which he viewed as "a working scheme to bring about mutual understanding and co-operation of the African proletariat". He attacked "all communistic tendencies" and alleged communists would return Bantu-speaking peoples to "the state of the *Lifaqane*, i.e. tribal wars". He favoured "established and orderly Christian government". Yet, he spoke forcefully on behalf of workers. He protested the dismissal of black workers in favour of white employees and the eviction of farm labourers as "violation of the fundamental ethics of Christianity". At times 'Mote applied a materialist class analysis. Giving evidence on behalf of the IICU to the NEC in 1931, he expressed socialist sentiments that South Africa "today is haunted by a spectre of *Native unrest*, and we submit that, under our present system of society, a wide and irreconcilable difference of interest exists between those who work for a living and the landlords". Black "workers fundamentally are sellers of labour power while the employers are buyers".[64]

This was not idle rhetoric but based on knowledge of actual conditions of workers. He travelled widely to gather data, speaking to rural and urban workers in Bethlehem, Harrismith, and Bloemfontein (which he termed "Sjambokfontein"). These workers, he stated, "are asking, when the I.C.U. and the African National Congress promises will be fulfilled 'to break these inhuman shackles of oppression and slavery by means of passive resistance'." 'Mote presented detailed figures on wages and conditions. Many farm labourers received only five to 12 shillings per month, or even "alms disguised as wages". If they asked for wages then they faced *sjambokking* or shooting. Farm conditions were "intolerable". There were few written contracts, "no fixed hours of work"; workers were fired at no notice, and labourers expressly forbidden "to attend any political meetings". Yet labourers, "who get nothing except verbal promises", were forced to pay tax, and received no pensions. Some white people wanted to segregate Africans so as "to exploit their labour". 'Mote suggested various solutions. Non-manual avenues of employment should be made available to Africans. To assist this, organisations such as the IICU and ANC should be "allowed a say" in administration of black education. Africans should be exempted from poll tax until after the effects of the Depression on them were ameliorated. Despite 'Mote's anti-communism, his advice to government was hardly of a conservative nature. He demanded abolition of all discriminatory legislation and an end to the "high-handed and reprehensible" pass law and poll tax raids by police. The "pernicious" Masters and Servants Amendment Bill, that allowed workers to be whipped, should be withdrawn. A 1932 memorandum on African trading rights by 'Mote, Selby Msimang, and S. G. Ndlovu (ANC branch chairperson), also raised the hardships of African workers.[65]

'Mote spent part of the 1930s involved with the Joint Council and Advisory Board. He was a signatory of a Kroonstad Advisory Board submission to the NEC that argued general labour conditions in the OFS were bad, particularly on farms, causing labourers to move to the cities and depress wages. 'Mote's knowledge of working lives was apparent in the detailed description of Africans' urban and rural wages, and the information presented on unemployment and on the plight of black semi-skilled tractor drivers, who received little compensation for their work. However, the submission also made derogatory comments against women, such as the claim that female domestic workers "waste a lot of time … and are inclined to be temperamental, sulky, noisy and often impertinent".[66]

'Mote retained his allegiance to the labour movement. In 1938, he was general secretary of the African Workers' Union, and publicised conditions of farm labourers. This allegiance was mixed with pecuniary concern, for he was also secretary of the OFS African Traders' Association. Despite involvement in other groups, he maintained a role in the ANC. In May 1938, he accompanied ANC treasurer Baloyi on a speaking tour to Cape Town. Speaking to a well-attended meeting, 'Mote stated that "the most important aspect of our life is to try and build on Trade Unions and thereby get economic betterment". 'Mote blended moderate and radical political ideas. Irrespective of the inconsistencies of 'Mote's philosophy, his support for black labour rights was constant. This we can trace to his earlier experiences in the work force and the ICU. However, Congress provided a relatively stable and sympathetic political avenue through which he could express his views.[67]

Another leader active in both the ANC and ICU was Simon Elias. In the 1940s, he would become ANC OFS Secretary. His considerable union experience included working for the ICU in the 1920s and serving as IICU OFS secretary in the early 1930s. In 1931, Elias gave evidence to the NEC on behalf of the IICU. He argued that Africans faced a sharp decline in their working and living conditions. The opportunity to ameliorate their situation was restricted by "subjugating" state policies that aimed to "check and stem" their "progress in the competitive labour market". The result was slums, unemployment, and a "poverty-stricken humanity surging to and fro [in a] desperate struggle to obtain livelihood by resorting to drunkenness, violence, murder, theft". The solution lay in providing Africans with more land and raising their wages, thereby ensuring earning capacity exceeded spending power. Elias purported to represent a labour union, and referred to the inadequacy of current wages. Yet his presentation was less focused on workers, and presented far fewer data about labour conditions than the aforementioned Bloemfontein ANC submission. Neither body was flourishing at this time, but comparison of submissions suggests the ANC were in just as close, if not closer, touch with black workers than the most prominent local black union of the time.[68]

However, few workers rushed to join the ANC. In 1938, OFS Secretary Lichabe wrote to *Bantu World*, urging readers to join, but Mapikela reported that attempts to revive the ANC had been slow. Only 28 people joined the Bloemfontein branch after a public meeting addressed by Calata. When the local ANC committee failed to meet regularly, Mapikela was compelled to work jointly with the ICU. This suggests that, at a local level, sheer lack of resources could lead to a merging of black labour and political groups, with activists wearing many "hats". By 1939, 11 OFS ANC delegates attended the national ANC convention. There was evidence of labour influences among them. Modiakgotla and James Mpinda had been ICU leaders. Mpinda, ANC assistant sergeant-at-arms, worked as a shower-bath caretaker for Bloemfontein Council. *Petit bourgeois* influences too were evident, not only in the fact both men were now more involved in trading than trade unions but also in the presence of businessman Mapikela and four Bloemfontein Traders' Association representatives. This middle-class focus was later to change with the entry into provincial Congress leadership positions of people such as Jacob Mafora, a domestic servant, who in the 1950s became OFS ANC President.[69]

Some African leaders, less in touch with the ANC, nevertheless retained an interest in labour, an interest partly related to their ANC past. Veteran leader W. Z. Fenyang continued to lobby for African land rights. He increasingly was inactive in the ANC, more interested in adding to his already substantial landholdings. Nevertheless, he was aware of worker suffering. Addressing the NEC in 1931, he lamented that many aged farm workers lacked land, and were abandoned by relatives who migrated for work. Labourers could not work for farmers forever. That ICU organiser William Ballinger in 1930 sought Fenyang's advice about meetings with Africans in Thaba 'Nchu suggests Fenyang was still active.[70]

James Moroka only turned to politics in 1936, when involved in the All-African Convention. He did not actively embrace the ANC until 1949, when he catapulted to the ANC presidency. He decried the "almost inhuman treatment of poor working men" by pass laws and "that diabolical fascist measure of Farm Prisons", arguing that the ANC "must take a very active part in the organisation of our working class movement". This rhetoric conforms to the nature of contemporary ANC politics. However, earlier, in 1931, Moroka had expressed sympathy for the position of black workers. Before the NEC, he criticised the fact that "there is no definite standard wage for a Native labourer" and that some workers were paid only in kind. By enumerating the wide variation in labourer wages in Tweespruit and Thaba 'Nchu, he displayed his knowledge of their conditions. A minimum African wage was a good idea, he stated, adding that Africans "have always demanded a higher standard of payment, but the Government has consistently turned a deaf ear to that demand". Educated Africans were attracted to teaching and the ministry "because they have known for some time" that they "never get any kind of remunerative employment outside of these two callings". A black person in any other occupation "never gets much in the way of pay. He works for a very little indeed." Even African teachers, "for the services they render ... get very little. They are not paid for the amount of work which they do... They are labouring practically for nothing".[71]

The source of Moroka's early sympathy for African workers is unclear. He was not a paid-up ANC member, had no contact with unions, and no sympathy for communism. He came from a landowning family, and had a lucrative medical practice: Peter Abrahams saw him as an "immensely wealthy ... land-owning Black capitalist". In the 1920s, Moroka was thwarted in attempts to expand his land holdings and hence was increasingly disillusioned with white rule. Given the closely interlocking nature of OFS African elites, we cannot discount the possibility that ANC stalwarts such as Mapikela, who served with Moroka on the All-African Convention executive, or Fenyang, may have impressed upon him the need for policies that attracted all Africans, including workers.[72]

Ultimately, the glaring exploitation of OFS Africans was plain for Moroka to see. The fate of black workers in the face of the rising tide of repression could leave no African unmoved. Whilst the ANC in the OFS was not numerically strong, it succeeded, directly or indirectly, in keeping before the public eye the oppressive conditions of black workers.

Conclusion

The 1930s were a particularly unstable decade for both black workers and the ANC. Depression and oppressive state policies pitilessly hammered black workers. The decade began with intense, but short-lived, commitment to labour struggles by ANC radicals. Their defeat ushered in a period of profound miasma in Congress at the very time that, with increased repression, black workers most needed support. By the late 1930s, ANC radicals favouring closer formal ANC-labour alliances once more were prominent. Under their influence, Congress again began to pay greater attention to workers.

In the 1930s, Congress gradually widened the social base of its influence. In diverse ways—from the agitation of Tonjeni to the labour protests of the Bloemfontein ANC—the image of Congress as the premier African national political forum and champion of black grievances was kept alive among Africans, including workers. ANC weaknesses and divisions helped distance it from workers. Ironically, the economic crisis and increasingly repressive legislation served to re-focus the ANC on labour issues at the same time that its rivals floundered. It continued to organise on a political front whilst simultaneously some branches were active on labour fronts. On a programmatic level, in resolutions and speeches, it retained a strong interest in labour rights.

On an individual level, some members were workers or had had tangible associations with workers.

During this decade, black labour and political movements experienced turbulent times but nonetheless found some common ground. Numerical growth of the black work force was substantial enough to spawn new trade unions. Neither the CPSA nor the black unions were able to take advantage of this growth. They all suffered long periods of instability, partly due to state repression, which also hastened the decline of ANC radicalism. What remained stable were the real and "imagined" ties between Africans, which included ANC sympathy for black workers, exhibited by practically all ANC leaders, including moderates. They simply could not ignore publicly the blatant exploitation of Africans. Moving beyond sympathy to active solidarity was not always easy for ANC figures of a moderate political disposition. Yet, even many ANC moderates sought to try and actively influence harsh state labour policies in a more humanitarian, and Afrocentric, direction. Members that were more radical were able to join and, at times, lead workers' struggles.

That the ANC, written off as dead by many of its own radicals in the early 1930s, was so easily able to re-build, suggests tenacity of its ideas among Africans. It reinforces the idea that affinity between black workers and political activists was never distant in the common spatial territory apportioned to black people in South Africa. The phoenix-like militancy of the next two decades of this seemingly dead organisation is more understandable in this light. The scale of the relationship is in this sense immaterial. Association, not membership, was important here. Despite the decrepit ANC of the 1930s, there was no lasting challenge to its legitimacy among Africans. Liberal institutions did not succeed in forging a viable alternative African party and their grip on ANC activists slipped. In the absence of a mass-based social democratic party, it is not surprising that the ANC gave support to workers. The CPSA had a clear theoretical mandate to mobilise labour, but by 1939, it had no more than a tangential link with individual black workers. The ANC could perhaps boast as many indirect contacts with black workers.

Notes

1 *Umteteli wa Bantu* 17 May 1930; "Amendments to Pass Laws: Views of the Transvaal African Congress", *Star* 31 Oct. 1934. The TAC had the "closest ties to the working class": Meier, "ANC", p. 116.

2 KC v. 4 p. 78; Skota, *African Yearly Register* p. 427; Walshe, *Rise of African Nationalism*, p. 176. *Abantu-Batho's* prospectus (1 May 1930) listed Matseke as a director. He was active on the Marabastad Advisory Board.

3   Matseke, NEC "Evidence", 4 Jun. 1931, p. 8516 ff.; I.B. Moroe, "Joint Committee of the
     Non-European Organisations, Marabastad Location Pretoria" *Abantu-Batho* 17 Jul. 1930:
     Moroe urged Africans to "march to prison behind the bars of which the Government will
     be compelled to feed them."

4   *Umteteli wa Bantu* 27 Jun. 1931; News in Brief" *Abantu-Batho* 5 Mar. 1931 (cited in
     A. Cobley, *The Rules of the Game: Struggles in Black Recreation and Social Welfare
     Policy in South Africa* [New York: Greenwood Press, 1997], p. 34,); C. Badenhorst,
     "New Traditions, Old Struggles: Organized Sports for Johannesburg's Africans, 1920-50"
     Culture, Sport, Society v. 6 (2003), pp. 116-143, pp. 136, 126.

5   *Bantu World* 12 Dec. 1936; TAC report to 1938 ANC conference, CKC 2:DA:14:30/3;
     Matseke, "Transvaal African Congress", *Mochochonono* 3 Sep. 1938; Bunting, *Moses
     Kotane* p. 129.

6   M. Mphahlele, "Ho Morena le makhla la ohle a Transvaal African Congress", *Abantu-
     Batho* 31 Jul. 1930.

7   TAC reports, 1938 ANC conference, CKC 2:DA:14:30/3; Callinicos, *Place in the City*, p.
     64; D. Duncan, "Liberals and Local Administration in South Africa: Alfred Hoernlé and
     the Alexandra Health Committee 1933-1943", *IJAHS* v. 23 (1990), pp. 475-93, p. 480.

8   Skota, *African Yearly Register*, pp. 175, 273, 248; KC v. 4 pp. 140, 63, 67, 158; Delius,
     "Zoutpansberg Balemi Association", p. 297; Macheng, "Transvaal African Congress", *Bantu
     World* 11 Sept. 1930; *Bantu World* 5 May 1934, 14 May, 4 Jun. 1932 (Letanka) 31 Aug. 1935
     (Mabaso); Verwey, *New Dictionary*, p. 61; Dunjwa to NEC; Resha interview, 1964, CKC
     13A; *Robert Mabilwane Resha* (London: Resha Memorial, 1975); M. Resha, *'Mangoana
     Tsoara Thipa ka Bohaleng: My Life in the Struggle* (Johannesburg: Cosaw, 1991), pp. 36-37;
     "Orlando A.B. Elections" CPSA flyer [1940?], *ICS Political Ephemera*.

9   Marks interview 1964, CKC XM42:94; *Sechaba* 6 10 (1972); *Mochochonono* 4 Jun. 1938;
     R. Baloyi, "ANC", *Bantu World* 2 Apr. 1938; Bunting, *Moses Kotane*, p. 87; Basner, *Am I
     an African?* pp. xii, 94-95.

10   "Minutes of Special Meeting, Johannesburg Branch, CPSA 24 May-2 Jun. 1934", in
     Davidson et al. *South Africa and the Communist International*, v. 2, pp. 94-101, p. 100.

11   KC v. 4, p. 92; "Orlando Advisory Board Elections"; Edgar, *Prophet with Honour*, pp. 23,
     201-202; Hirson, *Yours for the Union*, p. 170; Walshe, *Rise of African Nationalism*, p. 120;
     Basner, *Am I an African?* p. 236.

12   "Report of Joint Deputation of ANC/ABC ... 16 May 1939", CKC 2:DA:14:30/3.

13   Simpson, "Peasants and Politics in the Western Transvaal, 1920-1940", pp. 100, 108,

14   Bonner, "Kgatla Conspiracies, Pedi Plots", who notes that Selope Thema identified
     strongly as a Pedi.

15   L.S. Motsepe, and F. Bryn (I-ANC) to *Abantu-Batho* 9 Apr., 25 Jun. 1931, respectively.

16   Letter of "Solundwana" and "Apa na Paya: Unyatelo Oluhle e Alexandra" (meeting
     report), both in Xhosa, *African Leader* 18 Feb. 1933; Nauright, "Black Island", pp. 116,
     125-126, 294, 314.

17   "Linga kwa Kona!" (Xhosa) and "The Coalition Government", *African Leader* 15 Apr.
     1933.

18   Reports of TAC to 1938 ANC conference; official TAC Report, 1938, CKC 2:DA:14:30/3;
     "Grievances of African Passengers." *Transvaal Communist* vol. 1 no. 3 (Jun. 1939).

19   Walshe, *Rise of African Nationalism*, pp. 228, 309; TAC report, 1938 ANC conference;
     Mochochonono 3 Sep. 1938; Non-European United Front. *Minutes of Conference...April
     1939* (Cape Town, 1939) pp. 8-11; Bunting, *Moses Kotane*, p. 72; "Delegates Presenting
     Credential to the 1939 ANC conference", CKC 2:DA: 14:30/3; Thibedi to *Bantu World* 29

Jan., 2 Jul. 1938; Drew, *Radical Tradition,* v. 1, p. 390; Nauright, "Black Island", p. 262; *Transvaal Communist,* v. 1 no. 3 (Jun. 1939), p. 10.

20 G.S. Mabeta, "Transvaal African Congress: a Brand of Communism", *Bantu World* 3 Sept. 1938 and reply of T.W. Thibedi, *Bantu World* 24 Sept. 1938; "Congress Elections", *Bantu World* 30 Jul. 1938. On TAC-CPSA relations, see Maseble Majoro's "Mr Makgatho le Dr Seme", *Abantu-Batho* 3 Jul. 1930. Copies of *African Congress* have not survived.

21 J. Nkadimeng interview with the author, Lusaka, 1989; Walshe, *Rise of African Nationalism,* p. 257; Delius, "Zoutpansberg Balemi Association"; A. Phashe (*Bantu World* 23 Jan. 1937) urged "young workers of the Bapedi tribe" to join the Bapedi Union to obtain work.

22 S. Schirmer, "Land, Legislation and Labor Tenants: Resistance in Lydenberg, 1938" in A. Jeeves and J. Crush (eds.) *White Farms, Black Labor: The State and Agrarian Change in Southern Africa, 1910-1950* (Pietermaritzburg: University of Natal Press, 1997), pp. 46-60, p. 55; P. Delius, "Zoutpansberg Balemi Association", pp. 296, 303-304, Delius, *A Lion amongst the Cattle* (Johannesburg: Ravan, 1996).

23 KC v.4 p. 70; notes in CKC reel 12A 2:XM29:96/2; B. Hirson, "Rural Revolt in South Africa: 1937-51", *Présence africaine (*1978), pp. 60-68 (also SSA vol. 8); A. Maliba, *Vhudzulotia Vhatha Vhavenda=Condition of the Venda People* (Johannesburg: CPSA, 1939); Nemutanzhela, "Malivha and the Zoutpansberg Balemi Association". Maliba earlier, in 1932, joined Thibedi's short-lived and Trotskyite Communist Party of Africa: see Thibedi to Communist League of America 26 Apr. 1932, reproduced in Drew, *Radical Tradition,* v. 1 p. 125.

24 C. Mather, "Agrarian Transformation in South Africa: Land and Labor in the Barberton District, c1920-1960", PhD dissertation Queens University, 1992, Chapters 6-7.

25 N. Gordimer, "Walter Sisulu", CKC reel 14a; *New Nation* 27 Oct. 1989; W. Sisulu to the author, Perth, Aug. 1991; P. Bonner, "African Urbanisation on the Rand between the 30s and 60s", *JSAS* v. 21 (1995), pp. 115-131, p. 128; E. Sisulu, *Walter and Albertina Sisulu: In Our Lifetime* (Cape Town: David Philip, 2002), pp. 40-46; W. Sisulu, *I Will Go Singing: Walter Sisulu Speaks of His Life and the Struggle for Freedom in South Africa,* in conversation with George M. Houser and Herbert Shore (Cape Town: Robben Island Museum, 2001), pp. 38-43.

26 Mokgatle, *Autobiography,* p. 188; CKC reel 14A; my interview with Mark Shope, Lusaka, 1989.

27 T. Lodge, "The ANC in the Rand Townships 1955-7", *Africa Perspective* 8 (1978), pp. 1-15; Lodge, "Sophiatown"; Lodge, *Black Politics,* p. 83; Goodhew, *Respectability and Resistance,* pp. 51-54.

28 Goodhew, *Respectability and Resistance,* pp. 48-49, 11; S. Lebelo, "Ons Dak Nie ... Ons Phola Hierso: Politics, Protest & Proletarians in Sophiatown 1930-1955" ASI seminar 1991, pp. 10, 20. For a vivid first-hand description of 1930s Sophiatown, see B. Modisane, *Blame Me on History* (New York: Touchstone, 1986).

29 KC v. 4 p. 162; Xuma "Autobiography" ms. 1954, pp. 2-7, 16-19, 27-31, XP reel 2, AD843, P24, *Syracuse Journal* 11 Jul. 1924; KC v. 4, p. 164; Skota, *Register* p. 283; M. Work to Xuma 29 Apr. 1920, XP reel 1, ABX 200429. See P. Limb, "Introduction", *Autobiography and Selected Works of A. B. Xuma* (Cape Town: Van Riebeeck Society, forthcoming).

30 Xuma "Autobiography", pp. 27, 40-43; *Workers' Herald* 12 May 1928; Plaatje to Xuma 19 Jul. 1923, XP, ABX 230719; ANC Conference minutes, Durban 15 Dec. 1939, CKC 2:DA:14:30/3; Sheridan Johns interview with J.B. Marks.

31 *Umteteli wa Bantu* 7 Sep. 1929; Gish, "Xuma", pp. 102, 98; Xuma, "Autobiography" p. 32; Xuma, *Bridging the Gap Between White and Black in South Africa* (Lovedale: Lovedale Press, 1930), p. 10.

32 Xuma, "Evidence" to NEC 22 May 1931 pp. 2-7, XP ABX 230719; NEC "Minutes of Evidence" pp. 8362, 8342; "Minutes of Liquor Commission 1931," XP reel 2, ABX 310531.

33 A.B. Xuma, *Reconstituting the Union of South Africa; or, A More Rational Union Policy* (Lovedale: Lovedale Press, 1933); *Bantu World* 13 Aug. 1932; *Umteteli wa Bantu* 8 Jul. 1933.

34 "Native's Point of View", *Rand Daily Mail* 22 Feb. 1934; "The Native's Health", *Star* 18 Jul. 1934; "Conditions in Pretoria Location", *Star* 21 Sep. 1934. Xuma "revealed a striking sense of solidarity with South Africa's overtaxed, underpaid black working class" in a 1933 article on tax: Gish, "Xuma", p. 121; Xuma, "Evidence Submitted before Committee on Native Education 1935", XP ABX 3512316; Minutes of the Bantu Trained Nurses Association 2nd Annual Meeting, 9 Dec. 1934, XP reel 2, ABX 341209.

35 K. Eales, "Rehabilitating the Body Politic: Black Women, Sexuality and the Social Order in Johannesburg, 1924-1937", African Studies seminar paper, University of the Witwatersrand, Apr. 1990; Gaitskell, "Female Initiatives", p. 139, citing *Umteteli* 6 Oct. 1934.

36 B. Sachs to Xuma Nov. 1939, XP reel 1, ABX 391119; L. Switzer, "Socialism and the Resistance Movement: The Life and Times of the *Guardian*, 1937-1952" in Switzer, *South Africa's Alternative Press*, pp. 266-307; *Umlindi we Nyanga* 15 Mar. 1939.

37 Benson, *Struggle,* p. 59; Walshe, *Rise of African Nationalism*, p. 230; *Ilanga lase Natal* 3 Jul. 1931; S. Makhanya, *A Record of the Bantu Youth League July 1930-July 1935* (Amanzimtoti, 1935?), Makhanya Papers KCM 15959, Campbell Collections, University of KZN. Cf. Marks, *Experimental Doll*, p. 34.

38 Dube to NEC 2 Apr. 1931, "Minutes of Evidence", pp. 6255-76. Cf. *Ilanga lase Natal* 10 Apr. 1931.

39 Dube cited in *Star* ca. Jan. 1930, copy in SAIRR Newspaper Clippings; *Ilanga lase Natal* 2 Oct. 1931; *U-Sihlanganisile* (Durban: Natal Workers Club, 1935), NA 49/328: "AWG Champion: Agitator"; "Wage Board versus Chamber of Industries", *Ilanga* 10 Dec. 1938.

40 A. Magadla, Natal ANC to Magistrate Dundee 5 Dec. 1932, J.S. Gumede, Organising Secretary Natal ANC to CNC 2 Sep. 1932, CNC 64/2 N.1/9/3, "Natal Native Congress". J. S. (Jerishem) Gumede worked as an interpreter and lawyer's clerk (La Hausse, *Restless Identities*, p. 77). Archie Gumede did not join the ANC until 1941 but in an interview (2 Oct. 1997, Alan Paton & Struggle Archives, PMB 97APB13, ts. p. 9 and recording) recalled Congress was active in Sobantu, and had a Women's League organised more by the ANC.

41 Champion to NEC 1931, "Minutes", pp. 8230-8257; Walshe, *Rise of African Nationalism*, p. 146; *Cape Times* 7 Jan. 1930; *Umkosi Omkulu Etekwini* (translated) in SAP Durban to SAP Pietermaritzburg 16 June 1930: NA49/328; La Hausse, "Message", pp. 41-42; McCord, *Calling of Katie Makanya*, pp. 228-229.

42 "Report of Native Advisory Board" 22 Jan., 19 Feb., 19 Mar., 16 Apr., 21 May, 16 Jul., 1 Oct., 26 Nov. 1930: NAD Durban; Champion to NEC 1931 p. 8258; NC Durban to CNC Natal 18 Mar. 1930; *Igazi ne Zinyebezi* (Durban, 1930), translated CNC Natal to SNA 8 Nov. 1929; H. Robson (compound manager) and N. Howard (location manager) to Manager NAD Durban 13 Mar.1930: NA49/328.

43 "Native Unrest", Detective Arnold to CID Durban 2 Jun. 1930; SAP Pretoria to JUS 19 Sept. 1930; SAP Durban reports of 16, 17 Jun. 1930; C. Ngcobo affidavit 22 Nov.

1930; "Notes on an Interview ... 9th Oct. 1930 between H.S. Cooke... and ...Champion" NA49/328.

44 *Umsebenzi* 19 Dec. 1930, 9 Jan., 16 Jan. 1931; Ndlovu, "Nkosi & CPSA", pp. 119-120, who argues Zulu heritage was influential: at the rally Nkosi stated Dingaan, Shaka, and Bhambatha were communists; *Cape Argus* 15, 17 Dec. 1930; *Ndaba Zamakomanisi e Tekwini* no.2 19 Apr. 1931 no.4 24 May 1931; "Johannes Nkosi" *African Communist* 60 1975 pp. 78-84; "Our Martyred Dead", *Midland News* 22 Aug. 1931.

45 *Umteteli wa Bantu* 10 Jan.1931; Police reports CID Kimberley 13-17 Apr. 1931: NA49/328; Mancoe, *Bloemfontein Bantu and Coloured People's Directory* p. 68. Champion's exile evoked sympathy from moderates: cf. *Imvo Zabantsundu* 23 Dec. 1930 and *Umteteli wa Bantu* 4 Oct. 1930.

46 SAP to SJ 21 Mar. 1935; CID Durban to SAP PMB 4 Jun., 5 Jul. 1934; *U-Sihlanganisile*; Champion, "We Are Greeting the Year of 1935"; Champion, "Third Attempt of the ICU Natal"; Champion, "We Explain the Failure of the Meeting with Mr SWB Shepstone", translated in SAP to SJ 21 Mar. 1935; SAP Natal to SAP Pretoria 8 Dec. 1934, CID Durban to SAP PMB 5 Jul. 1934; CNC Natal to NC Durban 12 Apr. 1935, NC Durban to CNC Natal 23 Apr. 1935; Champion to Hertzog 28 Sep. 1931: NA49/328.

47 Champion, "The Three Years' Scheme" (translated) CNC Natal to SNA 8 Sep. 1934, letter to *Ilanga* 24 Nov. 1933 (translated), SNA to SJ, 27 Dec. 1935, NA49/328. He continued to speak on behalf of the, by now, largely defunct ICU: *Natal Advertiser* 25 Mar. 1937; Walshe, *Rise of African Nationalism*, p. 231; M. Swanson, "Introduction" to Champion, *Views of Mahlathi: Writings of A.W.G. Champion, a Black South African* ed. by M. Swanson (Pietermaritzburg: University; Natal Press, 1983), p. xxiii, Marks, *Ambiguities of Dependence*, p. 107.

48 Deane, *Black South Africans*; Msimang to Native Farm Labour Committee, in Record of Evidence K. 356, National Archives, Pretoria, cited in V.S. Harris, *Land, Labour & Ideology: Government Land Policy and the Relations between Africans and Whites on the Land in Northern Natal 1910-1936* (Pretoria: Archives Yearbook, 1991), p. 232; Msimang, "International Labour Delegation Coming", *Ilanga lase Natal* 3 Dec. 1938.

49 *Umteteli wa Bantu* 31 May 1930; *Umsebenzi* 20 Jun. 1930; Bunting, *Moses Kotane*, p. 52;

50 S. Mini and J. T. Gumede to NEC 10 Apr. 1931, "Evidence" pp. 6772-6782, 6825-6825; *Umteteli wa Bantu* 10 Jan. 1931.

51 *Umteteli wa Bantu* 22 Oct. 1932, 1 Jul. 1933; Ngcobo to NC Ixopo, NAD CNC 92 PMB. The IICU, based in East London, had provincial branches, headed in Natal by Jerishem Gumede and Ngcobo; Resolutions, "General Meeting of Natives in Durban, Dec. 15-17 1934" with SAP to SJ 21 Mar. 1935, CNC Natal to SNA 2 Mar. 1935: NA49/328; Wickins, *ICU* p. 198; M. Roth, "Domination by Consent: Elections under the Representation of Natives Act 1937-1948", in T. Lodge (ed.) *Resistance and Ideology in Settler Societies* (Johannesburg: Ravan Press, 1986), pp. 144-167; "Delegates Who Presented Credentials, [1939]" CKC 2:DA:14:30/3.

52 Luthuli, *Let My People Go*, pp. 34, 82-89, 34, "Let My People Go" ms., Luthuli Papers 1948-1967; Callan, *Luthuli*, pp. 24-9; evidence of Lutulo [sic] to NEC, "Evidence" pp. 6282-6300a; Alegi, *Laduma!* p. 34.

53 KC v. 4 pp. 23, 87; S. Dlamini interview with the author, Lusaka, May 1989.

54 Minutes of ANC conferences, 1938 [Handwritten] and 1939 [mimeo], CKC 2:DA:14:30/3; Basner, "Interview", pp. 16-19; letter of S. H. D. Mnyandu to *Rand Daily Mail* 3 Aug. 1939.

55 *Farm Labour in the Orange Free State* (Johannesburg: SAIRR, 1939), pp. 3, 13-15.

56 D. Mkwanazi (ANC) to NEC 1931, "NEC Minutes" p. 5053; Mancoe, *Bloemfontein Bantu and Coloured People's Directory*, pp. 2, 44, 50, 72-73; *Umteteli wa Bantu* 10 Jan. 1931; Bloemfontein JC "Memo. on the Influx of Natives from the Country into Urban Areas," B/E, NEC "Minutes"; *Umteteli wa Bantu* 16 Aug. 1930; Rheinallt-Jones to Mapikela 27 May 1936, *Rheinallt Jones Papers*, CAMP; Bantu Traders Association to NEC 24 Feb. 1931, T. Mapikela to NEC, "Minutes" p. 5217 ff. There were 84 African builders, 34 cafe owners and 25 brick-makers in Bloemfontein in 1929. Of 7,325 Africans working there, 210 were employers, 315 self-employed.

57 Basner, "Interview", p. 13; Basner to B. Hirson 27 May 1975, Basner Papers; Basner, *Am I an African?*; Hill (ed.), *Marcus Garvey*, p. clvii.

58 VAB MBL Correspondence of Town Clerk 4/8/1/80 25/43, "Grievances: ANC": ANC Bloemfontein (Lichabe) to Location Superintendent 31 Mar., 23 Apr., 7, 9 May 1934; ANC (Leshoai) to Mayor 19 Dec. 1933, and to Chairman, NA Committee 7 May 1934, appended to: J.R. Cooper, Bloemfontein Location Manager, to NA Dept. members, 28 Apr. 1934; Mancoe, *Bloemfontein Bantu and Coloured People's Directory* pp. 3, 32, 50.

59 "Native Herbalists in Free State" *Friend* 7 Jan. 1937; "Notes on an Interview between Members of the Native Affairs Committee and ... Officials of the ANC ... 11 May 1934; ANC (Leshoai) to Town Council 24 Jan. 1933": VAB MBL 4/8/1/80 25/43.

60 "Minutes Native Advisory Board ... 10 Apr. 1934"; ANC to Town Clerk 22 Feb., 21 Mar. 1934; ANC to Council 24 Jan. 1933; Nkoana to NA Pretoria 1 Mar. 1933: MBL4/8/1/80 25/43; Mancoe, *Bloemfontein Bantu and Coloured People's Directory*; J.S. Nkoana, "Lefu la Mr Albert Mothibi", *Abantu-Batho* 5 Jun. 1930.

61 Mkwanazi to NEC, pp. 5046-5050; ANC. Bloemfontein. "Evidence ..." pp. 3-5, NEC "Minutes", reel 2.

62 Evidence of Mkwanazi, ANC, to NEC, "Minutes of Evidence", pp. 5051-5052.

63 Mancoe, *Bloemfontein Bantu and Coloured People's Directory* pp. 34, 82,45; *Umteteli wa Bantu* 18 Apr. 1931.

64 *Umteteli wa Bantu* 16 Dec. 1933; "ICU Federation" *Umteteli wa Bantu* 18 Apr. 1931; K. 'Mote, "The 'Reds' and Natives", *Umteteli wa Bantu* 20 Oct. 1931, and "Plight of 'Free' State Natives", *Umteteli wa Bantu* 7 Nov. 1931. Cf. Bradford, *Taste of Freedom*, pp. 133, 163-167; *Umteteli wa Bantu* 17 Jan. 1931; 'Mote to NEC, Feb. 1931, "Minutes of Evidence", pp. 4792-4804.

65 *Umteteli wa Bantu* 7 Nov. 1931, 24 Sep. 1932; 'Mote to NEC, pp. 4792-4804.

66 Native Advisory Board Kroonstad. "Evidence ... 17 Feb. 1931, "NEC Minutes".

67 *Free State Advocate* 29 Jan. 1938; *Mochochonono* 4 Jun. 1938; 'Mote, "Evidence of the African Workers' Union on Native Farm Labour", *Mochochonono* 22, 29 Jan. 1938; Cobley, *Class & Consciousness*, p. 148.

68 Rich "Managing Black Leadership", p. 194; IICU "Evidence before the Economic Commission" (signed by S. Elias), and oral evidence of S. Elias to NEC, 1931, "Minutes of Evidence", pp. 5085-5093.

69 Lichabe to *Bantu World* 19 Feb. 1938; Report of OFS ANC to 1938 ANC conference, and list of "Delegates Who Presented Credentials" to 1939 ANC conference, CKC 2:DA:14:30/3; Mancoe, *Bloemfontein Bantu and Coloured People's Directory* pp. 2-4, 32; Cobley, *Class and Consciousness,* p. 175; CKC 2:XM1:96; KC v. 4, p. 64.

70 Fenyang to NEC, 1931, "Minutes of Evidence" p. 4929. Cf. Murray, *Black Mountain*, pp. 137-139; W.Z. Fenyang to W.G. Ballinger 25 Feb. 1930, in *W.G. Ballinger Papers*.

71 KC v. 4, pp. 97-98; "Dr. Moroka Says Congress on March" *Inkundla ya Bantu* 10, 24 Feb. 1951; Evidence of J. Moroka, 1931 to NEC, "Minutes of Evidence", pp. 4885, 4907-4914.

72 Murray, *Black Mountain*, pp. 103, 175; P. Abrahams, *Return to Goli* (London: Faber, 1953), pp. 186-191. On Moroka's later anti-communism see letter of High Commissioner 24 Sep. 1952, D.O.35/3259, PRO.

Conclusion

The early ANC did not grasp many opportunities to build stronger ties with working people. Lacking resources and facing many state restrictions, the ANC found it difficult to penetrate the mines and farms, or the equally closed-in world of domestic workers. This is not surprising, as even the CPSA and black unions, absolutely committed to the cause of such workers, also failed abysmally in these sectors. The ANC had inconsistencies in its policies, switching back and forth from a softly-softly, *hamba kahle* to a more strident protest approach. This was largely the product of the class composition of its leaders and the impact of ideologies that preached moderation. Perhaps most fundamentally, the ANC at all levels failed to mobilise more fully the human potential in African communities represented by women, to whom it still denied full membership, and by the ordinary worker. On the one hand, this reflected its inability to develop strong, vibrant, self-sustaining branches, something that only really occurred first under Xuma in the 1940s, and then in the 1950s. By then there was much better use of social and political avenues to raise funds, spread awareness of Congress policies and, with the defiance campaigns and the M-Plan of Nelson Mandela, to forge close-knit cells or networks based on localities. On the other hand, weak national leadership, regional divisions, and the determined pressure of big business and the state to push leaders away from militancy also played their part in limiting ANC popular growth.

However, at the regional and local levels, and even among some national leaders, issues of nation and class strongly influenced ANC debates and policies to the extent that labour concerns, mediated by common African national interests and articulated in specific places, appear regularly in Congress circles during these years. Indeed, throughout most of the twentieth century, the difficulties posed for all social strata of Africans by the oppressive features of South African society pushed them together, helping to transcend a degree of class stratification, without ever masking class tensions entirely.

We may say the same of geographic differences. Despite marked regional variations and urban-rural divides that I have explored in this book, the basic contradiction between white rule and black national oppression provided an impetus toward a latent supra-class unity of the ANC and organised workers. The relationship was neither smooth, nor simple. In those years, black workers faced a dilemma. The ANC seemed to offer some prospect of relief from race-defined oppression, yet often appeared little able or willing to mobilise workers. At times, some workers may have regarded Congress as too distant to be of much practical use to them in their daily class struggles. The ANC, for its part, found workers hard to mobilise, and even harder to recruit, especially on the mines and in rural areas where Congress organisation was weak. Moreover, their relations were uneven over time and from place to place. ANC-worker relations thus had their difficulties.

The level of ANC commitment to the black workers' cause and its effectiveness varied. The ANC more whole-heartedly embraced the cause of black labour from 1918 to 1920 and 1927 to 1930, whereas ANC-worker relations tended to be more distant immediately following these periods. There are four major reasons accounting for these variations. They are the intervention of the state, differences and vacillations in ANC leadership, instability of both ANC and black worker structures, and impediments to the effective use of the vehicles through which the ANC articulated its attitudes to workers.

Firstly, the ANC faced an uncompromising state never conceding to pressures of political or labour forces. On the contrary, state repression intensified. This meant that the *raison d'être* of the ANC, political equality and better economic and social conditions for Africans, did not change; its basic aims did not change, and hence its commitment to African workers, as an inherent part of the African people, never substantially wavered. We thus can see some correlation in both the level and effectiveness of state repression and periods of ANC relative aloofness from workers. Repression increased markedly to silence strikes and mass protests in 1918-1920, and again in 1929-1932. The intent of open displays of force by the state or legislation curbing African political or labour organisation undoubtedly was to intimidate. This is precisely what happened. Many ANC leaders, in the early 1920s and 1930s, abandoned any pretence of solidarity with labour and instead rushed to support comfortable, moderate bodies. In contrast, in periods of political crisis, economic depression, or temporary relaxation of repressive measures, such as during and immediately after World War I, or in the late 1920s, the ANC felt more emboldened, and was less constrained, to link up with the black labour movement.

Often, there is too little appreciation by historians of such structural barriers to a successful mass-based anti-colonial movement. Throughout Africa and the wider colonial world in this period the gun, the Bible, and educational and propaganda media depicting Africans as inferior continued to rule. African nationalists remained poorly resourced, and subject to repression despite a veneer of liberal freedoms. If cases of armed repression, as seen at Bulhoek, or in the deployment of machine-guns in the streets of Durban, were rather less common in South Africa than some other African countries, then the ongoing daily impact of pass raids, censorship, and poverty, and more subtle forms of dissuasion such as white supremacy and paternalism continued to confront political movements.

Secondly, the different attitudes of ANC leaders to workers and the nature of ANC organisation influenced these fluctuations. ANC leadership patterns present a conundrum. They exhibit both amazing shifts and great continuity. ANC ideologies such as African nationalism offered a measure of stability. A sense of black identity, which was developing into a shared African nationalism, was an increasingly powerful force helping ANC leaders recognise that workers were part of their natural constituency, and serving to attract some, such as J. B. Marks or Moses Kotane. Concomitantly, a growing sense of class could justify the remoteness of more moderate leaders from workers or drive radical leaders into the arms of militant workers. ANC leaders frequently stopped short of supporting strikes and other radical actions by workers. This strained the ANC-worker relationship, although it should be recalled that not all workers were radicals. Yet whilst strikes may have made ANC moderates feel uncomfortable, the issues they raised could promote African political unity.

Thirdly, variations in ANC labour policy or views of individual ANC leaders also contributed to chronic instability in ANC structures as well as the ephemeral nature of black unions. The intensity of repression, low levels of literacy, persistence of rural traditions and ethnic divisions among workers, and poverty in general—and hence of union and ANC branches—ensured organisational volatility. Weaknesses of unions denied the ANC a greater following among workers. Subtle changes in the class composition of the ANC, or even in the politics of the handful of delegates to its annual convention, could push Congress closer to, or further away from, the working-class movement. Ironically, the plasticity of ANC structures enabled it at times to escape from the liberal moderation that was its hallmark in this period. The loose nature of ANC structure, however, could work to alienate Congress from workers, as under Seme's more autocratic rule. In addition, ANC resources remained slender, and its theoretical understanding of the causes and likely future direction of black workers' situation was incomplete. It is therefore not surprising that ANC-labour relations were inconsistent and ill defined.

Fourthly, when the avenues used by ANC leaders to raise issues of importance to the African public or to remind authorities of mass suffering, such as commissions, the press, and union meetings, closed or malfunctioned, the ANC had less chance of developing wide social support. For the duration of its existence (1912-1931), *Abantu-Batho* supported the cause of African labour and thus contributed not only to some continuity in ANC-labour relations but also to a wider community understanding of labour's position. Its demise robbed both Congress and workers of an effective if indirect vehicle of protest and mobilisation. In its place, white-owned business graciously offered *Bantu World* as an anodyne substitute. Some leaders previously active in the ANC, notably Selope Thema, enthusiastically embraced the opportunity to banish radicalism in its pages. However, labour issues refused to go away and even moderates continued to editorialise on lamentable African working conditions. What is sometimes lost sight of, in the emphasis on Joint Councils and the cultural predilections of the black "elite" of the 1930s, is that leaders with experience in the ANC continued to keep labour issues before the public.

This does not mean that processes of political decay or disillusionment and cultural change were not at work. That the "moderate thirties" were not just a generational thing is shown by 1938 comments of Margaret Ballinger (then throwing herself into the politics of African representation) that a new love of sport was inclining youth to "play and forget rather than to remember and agitate like their elders". Nonetheless, even as she wrote, the murmurings of a youth revolt soon to transform African politics became increasingly audible.[1]

After the demise of its press, the ANC might have better deployed informal networks of communication. Whilst recent research by Delius and others has revealed migrant worker-ANC connections, notably in the 1940s, we still know relatively little about the wider political uses of the oral domain in earlier years. In any case, it is not enough for historians merely to disparage ANC "elitism", but rather to unravel more of its hidden history at a local level. Here, identity is important. The selling of membership cards was one measure of commitment, but it seems more than likely that a good many Africans simply identified with those movements, such as the ANC or ICU, that were from time to time able to articulate their demands. Such identification, of course, easily turned to disillusionment when petitioning went unheeded by government.

This substantiation indicates a degree of continuity in ANC relations with politically conscious black workers and their bodies. This liaison was twofold. The ANC looked to workers as part of its support base whilst workers could count on the ANC to keep their problems before the public and government. This affinity was rooted in national oppression and constricted labour and political rights. Even under the most moderate of its leaders, the ANC spoke out about poor black working conditions.

Relative continuity of ANC-working-class contacts could make it easier to build campaigns with workers and help offset ANC structural instability and internal divisions. The ceaseless repetition by the ANC of support for amelioration of workers' harsh conditions engendered, for Congress, a reputation for solidarity in the African community. The evidence also points to recurring patterns of social interaction in the class and national consciousness of their partners. This was due not simply to the broad socio-economic parameters set by the state. Political strategies employed by the ANC and its individual activists and by organised, politicised workers helped build concrete bridges to each other.

In this regard, the gradual development of a distinct African political culture with a constituency including workers and propertied strata was crucial in embedding Congress in the gaze and memory of African society. The weaknesses of Congress did not escape this gaze—the troubles of the 1930s diminished the legitimacy, accountability, and trust it had started to win in earlier decades—but neither did the equally chronic weaknesses of its rivals or allies gain them much kudos. The experimentation of Congress branches with political alliances, with policies on land, labour and social conditions, and with (partial) representation of women and workers if very incomplete, nevertheless gave Africans a political arena and much-needed experiences with the ebb and flow of political life. Congress helped arouse a yearning for effective power, which if in this period it was unable to satisfy then helped lay the foundations for future viable alliances. The activity of hundreds of Congress members and supporters over the first three decades of its history made ordinary people more aware of political affairs. Therefore, Congress remained on the political radar of African society, and had some effect on mass attitudes even if, as Raymond Suttner argues, it lacked "patient organisation" and was not a well "organised force".[2]

ANC history writing often is a top-down affair, moulded by over-reliance on a view privileging leaders and institutions. The tendency in the historiography to emphasise the "middle class" or "elitist" nature of the movement is rooted in theoretical perspectives that pay too little attention to *definitions* of class and nationalism and to the *specific nature* of South African society. In charting early ANC-labour ties, it is more productive to focus on the specific, confined nature of African societies in particular places and to define precisely the class, political, and cultural components of the ANC. This approach prompts a different emphasis, on the ANC as representative of the aspirations of different social classes, including the African working class. This representativeness was possible due to the lack of rigid barriers between different African social strata. It is a mistake to characterise Congress in a static way, simply as an "elite", because from its earliest years it consisted of a complex web of branches with definite, if uneven and fluctuating, contacts with workers. This is not to argue that Congress was merely a "multi-class" movement. At various times, and in various branches, it articulated demands of certain social classes more clearly than others did. Nevertheless, events never allowed the ANC the luxury of settling into a comfortable accommodation with the ruling class, even if this would perhaps have satisfied some of its more moderate leaders. National and class oppression of Africans proceeded apace. The ANC objectively was a national liberation movement even before it claimed to be.

While in some cases they could be the same person, the African worker and African nationalist did not always speak the same language. The debate of an ANC convention rarely was the same as the dialogue of a union meeting. The non-radical (some might say non-socialist or non-Marxist) ideologies of most ANC leaders set real limits to their understanding of, and commitment to, workers. However, ideology alone did not drive their lives. At times, they responded practically to crises affecting workers. Moreover, these different discourses at times were mutually understandable through mediation of "interpreters" such as pro-ANC journalists or individual leaders, such as, for example, Herbert Msane, Josiah Gumede, and Elliot Tonjeni. These three took the trouble to try to make the connections in people's minds between class and national oppression. I would argue that these seemingly so different approaches were part of a new, changing political discourse, an anti-colonial African national identity closely connected by race and place. The different worldviews of workers and the ANC mixed in the relative social intimacy of black communities to help create a definite, if limited, awareness of worker issues inside the ANC. The cited cases of interaction and exchanges between ANC members and workers in meetings, in correspondence, and in political campaigns demonstrate this argument.

This mutual, if incomplete, understanding was formed by several forces: ANC policies and ideologies; established traditions of ANC support for worker demands and, to a lesser degree, of worker support for ANC campaigns; joint resistance to state policies; and the presence of workers in the ANC. In cases where workers themselves took a leading role in organising class and national struggles, as in the Western Cape in 1929-1932, ANC-worker relations could be intimate. In cases where ANC leaders sought to mobilise workers from above, as when TNC leaders promoted action over wages in 1918-1920, they drew on common recent remembrances of the ANC's historic role. A section of politicised African workers in all probability knew something, if only a little, about this history that had passed into the everyday discourse of the African location.

To account fully for the resilience, the longevity of the ANC, and to explain why later it increasingly became the medium of mass struggles, requires consideration of the subjective, collective, individual, intellectual, and ideological realms in which ANC-worker interactions took place. These realms, taken together, generally were conducive to a form of communication involving a degree of common understanding of African history and social situations. For all their differences in education, African workers and African nationalists shared a great deal: indigenous languages and cultures; the language of a shared history that included images of contemporary and pre-colonial resistance to oppression; the shared predicament of national oppression; and often, experience as fellow wage earners or fellow residents of "slums". Too rarely do historians ask why the ANC survived when all around it dozens of other political—and labour—organisations fell by the wayside.

The ANC, for all its faults, spoke the language of the people. After 1940 it was able to communicate more effectively in many urban and some rural areas. In Sekhukhuneland, for example, the ANC employed "traditional" culture; it embodied the local saying *"Feta Kgomo o Sware Motho"* (Pass by the cattle and aim (instead) for the people). In January 1943, S. M. Molema, looking back on the first three decades of ANC history and lamenting its decline since the "years of vitality", asked: "Can you—Father Dube—first President of the Congress and Leader of English Deputations, can you tell us why our folk-moot, our Ndaba, our Pitso has fallen on evil ways?" Nevertheless, the ANC still had "prodigious strength"; it was "a giant, dormant, asleep".[3] If before 1940 Congress had its vicissitudes, then Thaele's ambitious claim that *"I-Kongilesi Lilizwi ezindi ezindlwini"* (Congress's Name is Household) generally was true, even if this notoriety often was expressed in despair at its impotence, as in Mgqwetho's 1924 stanza, "'Has anyone seen where it's gone'". Still, even at its nadir, the movement's temporary decline elicited much concern even from those convinced of its imminent demise.

Nationalism's appeal, argues Isaiah Berlin, emerges "not by rational analysis, but by a special awareness, which need not be fully conscious, of the unique relationship that binds individual human beings into the indissoluble organic whole".[4] The ANC recurrently sought to build with workers just such a relationship. They thereby contributed to awareness (not always fully conscious) among workers of the ANC's political role. The ANC based its claims to political leadership of African society on a string of implicit images and shared symbols. In the period 1912-1940, new historical images and symbols became part of ANC imagery and entered the consciousness of politicised workers. These symbols included images of resistance to oppression, symbols of national unity like the ANC flag, *Nkosi Sikelel' iAfrika,* as well as the founding of Congress, the strikes of 1918-1920 and anti-pass protests. ANC survival (and its eventual success) was rooted both in the tenacity of such images in the minds of Africans and in the essential need for a vehicle for African political demands. Congress was a vast reservoir for national aspirations. Its leaders helped nourish symbols of resistance capable of politically uniting Africans—land, historical traditions, and the ANC image itself. The ANC succeeded in cultivating a tradition of its own significance as the centre of African political resistance. Its policies always claimed to incorporate black workers' basic grievances, explicitly or implicitly, and they offered workers a way to identify their own struggles with a broader national struggle, as well as a partial explanation—injustice and national discrimination—for their own harsh lives. It filled, if imperfectly, the vacuum caused by the brittle nature of African unions. Congress thus left its mark on workers. On the other hand, its own organisation, if remarkably durable, was still weak, poorly resourced, and susceptible to internal disputes. As a result, Congress failed, at this time, effectively to combat the excesses of white minority rule. Moreover, this was the period *before* African nationalism really emerged, and so the ANC still lacked a more coherent and efficient ideology.

What did Congress mean to African society in general, and to African workers in particular? In a sense, it was a sort of national, regional, and local *kgotla,* a people's council or forum to address grievances, like a community church or an extended family, seemingly able to absorb disagreements. The national Congress was a once-a-year palaver, but provincial and local meetings were more frequent and representative of different social strata. ANC methods of articulating shared views and grievances were diverse involving conferences, branch meetings, demonstrations, leaflets, the press, word of mouth, petitions and submissions to state commissions. These were not always the best media for directly pressing labour demands. Nevertheless, some workers attended their demonstrations and wrote letters to its press. Some even found a home in the ANC, and in so doing influenced ANC labour attitudes. The social and political biographies of people like Edwin Thabo Mofutsanyana and Moses

Kotane, who joined the ANC *before* the CPSA or unions, is particularly instructive. Workers of course spoke to each other, and their discourse was perhaps the most accurate reflection of their innermost feelings. But of this discourse, little remains in the historical record. Rarely did historians record, for posterity, labour's words or thoughts. This also was a time of technological change, but we have no idea of what may have transpired between activists on, say, the telephone, which in any case few Africans could afford, or in whispered communications, despite the best efforts of the police.

At times within the ANC organisational discourse, individual workers articulated their views. This became more common in the 1950s. However, some knowledge of workers and their problems was common inside the ANC from its earliest days. In this sense, in this discourse there always were very real links between the ANC "machine" and workers. I have indicated how many ANC leaders had close direct or indirect contacts with workers. These included actual experience of being a worker, contact with workers or unions, or sympathy for, and a commitment to fighting for, worker rights. The ANC fought for the rights of all Africans but, from 1912, it also specified and demanded that white power structures accord black wage earners basic social justice.

A simplistic relationship of alienation between "workers" and "nationalists" did not exist in real society. That does not mean class divisions did not appear, or that there were not different ideologies, occupations, or cultures at work. Yet there were many connecting threads, of community, culture, race, church, and politics. In any case, in this period, the very formation of the proletariat continued apace in diverse ideological, demographic, and structural ways, just as African nationalism was rarely a coherent ideology in these years.

The implications of interaction are threefold. First, the impact of national oppression remained constant. ANC leaders had little alternative but to at least appear to support black workers. Avenues of effective, constitutional protest progressively closed. Any "black bourgeois" hope of a gentrified ANC, aloof from workers, finally died with the onset of the apartheid government. Second, workers were a significant part of the ANC's constituency, and increasingly so as structural economic changes accelerated proletarianisation and urbanisation. Third, the later transformation of the ANC into a mass-based movement was not simply due to structural causes. It also had slowly evolving causes using precedents of earlier decades when individuals forged bonds between labour and Congress.

Liberation movement-labour relationships were exceedingly complex and uneven. The period 1912-1940 saw the formation of the ANC and the first black labour bodies. Workers always have held some place within ANC ranks. However, after 1940 they would exert an expanding influence. By the 1940s, the African working class was becoming more permanent. In the next four decades, it would become a significant component of anti-apartheid alliances. ANC-worker ties stood the test of time, and in 1994 contributed to the election victory of the ANC. The quasi "social democratic" nature of the ANC reveals itself, after 1994, in the organisation's continued engagement in a Tripartite Alliance with labour unions, affiliation to the Socialist International in 1999,[5] and (temporary) flirting with the Reconstruction and Development Programme (RDP). Issues of class and class alliances strongly influenced the December 2007 election of Jacob Zuma as ANC president. Yet every alliance needs common ground and these alliances had a history, gradually developed in the formative decades that I have discussed.

This study contains enough examples of different kinds of ANC members and workers to warrant consideration when weighing my central hypothesis, that when conditions favoured their interaction, the ANC moved closer to workers and always maintained an interest in them. The ANC, in theory and practice, sought to articulate black worker aspirations. Other groups acted as conductors to enable workers and Congress to come together, but in the end did not eclipse the ANC's own determination to have a definite presence among workers. At times, specific conditions such as the nature of leadership and limited resources made these relations difficult to consummate. The ANC played the role of elder to the nascent black labour movement. It defended their right to strike, even if it did not relish the prospect of joining strikes. At times, it also succoured unions. It survived repression and offered a sense of continuity of resistance and hope. It articulated a broad-based, inclusive form of nationalism, not excluding workers, and which served a maieutic purpose—bringing out workers' latent nationalism. There was enough contact to warrant a reconsideration of the nature of the early ANC.

In Chapter 1, I asked, what was the ANC's motivation for interest in workers? The evidence adduced above shows that such an orientation was not only politically expedient, a tactical need for African nationalism to garner all possible support and a motive enhanced by the strategic position of African workers in the economy, but also grounded in a solidarity rooted in race and nation and nourished in a common oppression across class in specific places.

The wider lesson, I would draw, is that scholarly writing on political movements such as the ANC must always be alert to social complexity. There is still an enormous amount of research needed on the African language columns of newspapers with mainly African readers, on oral history, on regional histories and biographies of ANC members and supporters. ANC history at the regional and local level needs careful investigation. The formative period of 1912-1940 especially stands in need of such a corrective, so we can see ANC and worker attitudes in all their nuances. More understanding is required of the ANC as a *dynamic* movement, and not just as a monolithic structure. I hope I have done this.

It has taken many years for writers to probe ANC history of the exile period. Only recently have historians plumbed the silences of the 1960s, a decade in which the ANC completely and mysteriously disappeared in extant historiography. It now is emerging that the ferocious apartheid regime was unable to uproot all black organisational and human connections in this period. Similarly, pre-World War II influences on later periods of organisational building and defiance in the 1940s and 1950s need to be unravelled. The national liberation Alliance did not emerge out of nothing.

Events since 1990 may suggest to some that a rift between the ANC and workers is growing. There is some evidence for such views; however the shift to GEAR and abandonment of RDP were widely resisted not only by organised labour but also within the ANC. Elections since 1994 suggest that the "centre will hold" notwithstanding the 2008 split in the ANC.[6] The ANC and the black labour movement can be either complementary or antagonistic. The manner in which many ANC leaders continually return to workers' problems in their pronouncements is evidence that root ideas of equality, justice, and better working conditions, once implanted among the people, proved impossible to uproot in a society in which Africans were denied genuine labour rights, social mobility, and political freedom.

Notes

1   Ballinger, "Native Life in South African Towns", pp. 333-334.
2   R. Suttner, "African National Congress (ANC): Attainment of Power, Post Liberation Phases and Current Crisis", *Historia* v. 52 no. 1 (2007), pp. 1-46, p. 2.
3   Delius, "*Sebatakgomo* and Zoutpansberg"; C.V. Bothma, *Ntšhabeleng Social Structure: A Study of a Northern Transvaal Sotho Tribe* (Pretoria: Govt. Printer, 1962), p. 75; S.M. Molema, "Thoughts and Reflections on the African National Congress", 28 Jan. 1943, in Silas Modiri Molema Collection, 1914-1957, Yale University.
4   I. Berlin cited in J. Gray, *Post-Liberalism: Studies in Political Thought* (London: Routledge, 1993), p. 262.
5   See *Address by the Deputy President of South Africa, Jacob Zuma, to the XXI Congress of the Socialist International 8-10 Nov. 1999.*

6   D. Pillay, "Cosatu, Alliances, and Working-Class Politics", in S. Buhlungu (ed.) *Trade Unions and Democracy: Cosatu Workers' Political Attitudes in South Africa* (Cape Town: HSRC, 2006), pp. 167-198.

Select Bibliography

I. UNPUBLISHED PRIMARY SOURCES

A. OFFICIAL GOVERNMENT PAPERS

South Africa

(1) Archives

[earlier repository abbreviations are used for consistency].

National Archives Repository, Pretoria [previously Transvaal Archives Depot (TAD)]
Director of Native Labour: GNLB (Government Native Labour Bureau).
Governor General, GG.
Secretary for Justice, JUS.
Secretary for Native Affairs, NA, NTS.

Cape Town Archives Repository [previously Cape Archives Depot (CAD)]
Attorney-General, AG.
Chief Magistrate of Transkeian Territories, CMT.
Chief of the Supreme Court, CSC.
Engcobo Magistrate, 1/ECO.
Governor General, GG.
Government House, General Department, GH.
Justice, JUS.
Kentani Magistrate, 1/KNT 40.
Native Affairs, NA.
PAS D59/3 Ref. 4/337: Political Activities of Government Servants: ANC.
Sterkspruit Magistrate, 2/SPT.

KwaZulu-Natal Archives [previously Natal Archives Depot (NAD)]
Pietermaritzburg Archives Repository
Chief Native Commissioner, CNC Natal.

Pietermaritzburg, 1/PMB, Magistrate, Pietermaritzburg.
Secretary of Native Affairs, SNA.

Durban
Minutes of the Native Advisory Board.
Native Riots Commission, Minutes of Evidence, 1929, 3/DBN v. 14/5.

Free State Archives Repository [previously Orange Free State Archives, [VAB]
Bloemfontein
   Bloemfontein, MBL, Correspondence of Town Clerk/Minutes of Town Council.
   Colonial Office, CO, Colonial Secretary, ORC (1901-1911).
   Governor General, G, Governor, ORC (1900-1911).
   Native Affairs Branch, N.A.B.

(2) Collections of Official State Papers

Dept. of Justice. *Files, 1916-1928* (JUS). CAMP microfilm.
Native Affairs Department. "[Papers] 1913-1923," SOU/1 file 6. York University,
   microfilm.
Native Economic Commission 1930-1932 "[Minutes of] Evidence," SOAS,
   microfilm M4581.
"Native Separatist Churches" [1921] in *A.W. Roberts Papers,* Cory Library, Rhodes
   University, copy in University of California, San Diego Library.

United Kingdom

National Archives [previously Public Record Office]
C.O. 532/239, original correspondence.
C.O. 551/149, 151, 4892 includes: Reports from Governor General, SA.
D.O. 35/3251: "NRC" (Natives' Representative Council).
D.O. 35/3259: "Native Affairs Union: Civil Disobedience Campaign".
D.O. 116/8 : "S. African Affairs: Despatches... High Commissioner (Harlech)".
W.O. 107/37: [South African Native Labour Contingent].

B. ANC, TRADE UNION, PRIVATE PAPERS and COLLECTIONS

South Africa

University of Cape Town
Jack Simons Papers.
J.M. Smalberger Collection.
James La Guma Memorial Committee [A. La Guma] "Jimmy La Guma: A
   Biography," ms. 1964.

University of KwaZulu-Natal (Durban). Campbell Collections
John Dube Papers.
Magema Fuze Papers KCM 90/13/1/2.
Makanya Papers KCM 15959.
Marwick Papers, file 73-74, ICWU, KCM 8349-56, 3196.
Thom McClendon Interviews with Labour Tenants, Mid-Natal, 1992.
Mabel Palmer Papers, KCM 17691, files 26-27 NEC 1921, 1931.

University of KwaZulu-Natal (Pietermaritzburg). Alan Paton
and Struggle Archives
Selby Msimang Papers (Aitchison Collection).
    PC14/1/3/1 Msimang Biography.
    PC 14/1/1/1-3 Early Autobiographical Writings Pre-1972: "The Emakhosini
    Mission Station."

University of South Africa. Documentation Centre for
African Studies
Transcript of Interview with Miss Bertha Mkize, Inanda, 4.8.1979.
James Moroka Papers.

University of the Western Cape. Mayibuye Centre
ANC Papers (Lusaka and London, 1960-1991).
Brian Bunting Collection.

University of the Witwatersrand. Historical Papers.
W. Cullen Library
James Calata Papers.
Silas T. Molema and Solomon T. Plaatje Papers.
South African Institute of Race Relations. *Newspaper Clippings* [1920-1955).
—*Records Relating to the Joint Councils of Europeans and Natives... 1929-1940.*
A. B. Xuma Papers.

United Kingdom

Centre for Southern African Studies, University of York
W. Cope, *Papers (Including "Comrade Bill Notebooks").*
Food and Canning Workers' Union. *Publications.*
Baruch Hirson, *[Papers] Socialist Pamphlets (South Africa) Collection.*
Tom Lodge. *Political Documents.*
A. S. Saffery, *Papers.*
South African Materials. *"SOU/I" (Southern Africa. Research Papers, Press*
    Cuttings, Memorandum and Miscellaneous Correspondence, 1913-1979).
South African Trade Union Material. ("TRA/I") file 5.

Institute of Commonwealth Studies, University of London
Apartheid: A TV History (Granada TV), Filmed Research Interviews, Transcripts.
H. Basner, *Papers.*
James Calata, *"A History of the ANC,"* mimeo, [1957].
David Hemson. *Collection of South African Political and Trade Union Material*
     (M924).
I. Horvich, *Papers.*
ICS Political Parties (Box) Collection.
Julius Lewin, *Papers.*
Z.K. Matthews, *Papers* (M932).
S. M. Molema, *Papers* (M932).
Edward Roux, *Papers.*
A. L. Saffery, *Saffery Papers: A Selection.*
South African Mining Unions, *Papers* (M 843).
South African Unions *Papers 1927-1960* (M846).

School of Oriental and African Studies, University of London
S. Lusipo, "U-Boni Dr. Walter Benson Rubusana: Intshayebelo" Ms. of unpublished
biography in Xhosa, ca. 1969/70 (Ms.380263).
"Mendi: Correspondence, Newspaper Clippings...Relating to Sinking of the
     'Mendi.'"
H. Selby Msimang, "Autobiography," unpublished Ms. (Mss.380077).
W.B. Rubusana, *Letters, 1910-1922* (Ms. 380264).
R. V. Selope Thema, "Out of Darkness: From Cattle Herding to the Editor's Chair"
     1936 (Mss.320895).
S. M. Molema. *Collection of Political Ephemera Relating to the ANC*, M3233.

University of Oxford
Ms. Fisher, 67, Bodleian Library, Oxford.

United States

Cooperative Africana Microfilm Project (Camp)
Abdullah Abdurahman Family Papers, 1906-1962.
African National Congress Collection.
Carter-Karis Collection.
Cradock, South Africa Collected Papers, 1929-1962: Town Council Minutes.
Comintern Papers. 1928 Congress Papers. Fond 493.
Federation of South African Women Papers.
ICU. *Records, 1925-1947.*
ICU *yase* Natal. *Papers, 1905-1943.*
Sheridan Johns. *Small Collection of Anti-Apartheid Material Issued by Various*
     Groups.

J.R. Rheinallt Jones Papers. (Labour Section).
Clements Kadalie, *Papers Relating to Publication of Book, My Life ... 1943-1954.*
A.J. Luthuli, Papers, 1948-1967.
Selected Pamphlets, Handbooks, Congress and Other Reports Relating to South Africa.
South Africa: A Collection of Political Materials, 1902-1963.
South African Miscellaneous Manuscripts, 1911-1953.
South African Police and Justice Department files, 1916-1928.
South African Institute of Race Relations *"B Box" Collection.*
—. *Newspaper Clippings* (1920-1955).
—. *Records Relating to the Joint Councils of Europeans and Native:... 1929-1940.*
— *South African Institute of Race Relations Collection of Political Documents.*
Xuma, A. B. *Papers, 1918-1960.*

Emory University. Pitts Theology Library
Abantu-Batho 29 Jun., 11 Jul. 1929, in *African Orthodox Church Records, 1880-1974*, RG005.

Michigan State University Libraries
CIA Research Reports: Africa 1946-1976.
John and Eleanor Reuling Papers.

Northwestern University Archives
A.B. Xuma, *Biographical File.*

Yale University Library (microform)
Margaret and William Ballinger Papers, 1894-1964.
W. G. Ballinger Papers, 1920-1960.
Lionel Forman Papers, 1912-1944.
Silas Modiri Molema Collection, 1914-1957.

Canada

Webster Library, Concordia University, Montreal
S.A. Rochlin Collection of South African Political and Trade Union Organizations.

Australia

National Library of Australia
Federation of Mining Unions. *Collection of Miscellaneous Papers of South African Mining Unions* (microform).
J.C. Smuts, *Transcripts Made by Sir Keith Hancock of the Papers of the Clark and Gillett Families Relating to J.C. Smuts* (microform).

II. UNPUBLISHED ORAL INTERVIEWS AND DISCUSSIONS

(in possession of author unless indicated)

Lusaka, Zambia, May 1989

Stephen Dlamini.
Eric Mtshali.
John Nkadimeng.
Mark Shope.
Jack Simons.
Ray Alexander [Simons].

London April 1989

Mzala [pseudonym of Jabulani Nxumalo] April 1989.

Australia, 1985-1991

Kay Moonsamay (SACTU, ANC), Perth, 1985.
Les Stone (CPSA, ANC), Perth, 1986 (discussions).
Enid Howard (ex-CPSA), Perth, various dates.
Makhosozana Njobi, (ANCWL), Perth 1989.
Raymond Suttner, (ANC) Perth, Dec. 1989.
Sheila Suttner, various dates, Perth.
Ronald Mofokeng, (COSATU), Perth, 1991 (discussions).
Walter Sisulu, (ANC), Perth 1991 (discussion).

University of KwaZulu-Natal (Pietermaritzburg). Alan Paton and Struggle Archives

Interview with A. Gumede conducted by Ruth Lundie in Apr. 1995, 95APB1.
Interview with A. Gumede by R. Lundie and S. Mhkize, 2 Oct. 1997, 97APB13 ts. and recording.
Interview with S. Msimang [by David Hemson] 1971, Aitchison Collection, PC14/1.

Robert Edgar, Washington DC

Interview with Edwin Mofutsanyana, Roma, Lesotho, 1981.

III. PUBLISHED CONTEMPORARY SOURCES

A. GOVERNMENT PUBLICATIONS

South Africa (Colonies and Union)
South Africa. *Report of the South African Native Affairs Commission 1903-1905.* 5 v.

Cape
Census of the Colony, 1865 (G. 20-66).
Commission of Enquiry into the Public Service of the Colony, 1904-1906, Minutes of Evidence.
Dept. of Native Affairs. *Blue-Book on Native Affairs* (1900-1908).
Fourth Census of the Population of the Union of South Africa (1927-1931).
Report of the Select Committee ... Relative to the Native Question (1869) (C.3-69).
Report of the Select Committee on Introduction of Kafirs into the Colony 1859.
Report of the Select Committee on the Native Locations Act (No. 40 of 1902) (A.15-03).
Report and Proceedings of the Cape Peninsula Plague Advisory Board (1901).
Report and Proceedings of the Commission on Native Laws and Customs. (1883).
Report of Proceedings of the Annual Meeting of the Transkeian Territories General Council.
Report of the Labour Commission. Minutes and Proceedings (1893-1894) (G.39-93).
Report of the Select Committee on Master and Servants Acts (1889) (A.3-89).
Reports of Delegates, together with Correspondence relating to Visit of Native Representatives from the Colony Proper and the Transkeian Territories to Johannesburg to Enquire into the Conditions of Labour & the Treatment Accorded to Native Labourers (G.4-1904).
Results of a Census of the Colony (1905).
Third Census of the Population of the Union of South Africa (1921-1924).

Natal
Native Affairs Commission. *Evidence* (1906-1907).
Native Affairs Dept. *Annual Report.*
Papers Relating to the Case of Mr. Alfred Mangena (1908); Command 4403.

Orange River Colony
Statutes 1901.
Report of the Industrial Commission, 1904.

Transvaal
Annual Report of Government Mining Engineer.
Correspondence relating to Conditions of Native Labour Employed in Transvaal Mines. 1904.
Minutes of Evidence, Transvaal Mining Industry Commission 1907-1908 (TG2-08).

Minutes of Evidence, Transvaal Indigency Commission 1906-1908 (TG11-08).
Native Affairs Dept. Annual Report.
The Native Labour Question in the Transvaal: Extracts from the Industrial Commission of Inquiry: Report and Proceedings ... 1897 (London: P.S. King, [1901]).
Report of the Commissioner for Native Affairs 1903.
Report of the Mining Industry Commission 1907-1908.
Report of the Transvaal Labour Commission 1903-1904.
Reports of the Transvaal Labour Commission. Minutes of Proceedings & Evidence (Cd. 1897), 1904.

Union of South Africa
Blue Book on Native Affairs 1910 (U17-11).
Census 1936.
Correspondence Relating to the Recent Strike in South Africa (Cd. 7348), 1914.
Minutes of Evidence Judicial Commission of Inquiry into Witwatersrand Disturbances 1913 (G56-13).
Minutes of Evidence of the Natal Natives Land Committee (UG35-1918).
Minutes of Evidence of the Eastern Transvaal Natives Land Committee (UG32-18).
Minutes of Evidence Taken before the Select Committee on Native Affairs (SC6A-17).
Minutes of Evidence Taken before the Select Committee on Native Affairs (SC10A-20).
Minutes of Evidence Taken before the Select Committee on the Subject of the Native Bills (SC10-27).
Natives Land Commission: Minute ... by ... W. H. Beaumont (UG25-16).
Natives Representative Council. *Verbatim Report of Proceedings, 1937-1946.*
Official Yearbook of the Union of South Africa, 1910-1940.
Report from the Select Committee on Native Custom & Marriage Laws (SC6-1913).
Report of Native Churches Commission 1925 (UG39-25).
Report of the Commission Appointed to Enquire into Assaults on Women 1913. (UG39-13)
Report of the Commission of Enquiry, Native Riots at Durban, 1929.
Report of the Commission of Enquiry into Native Unrest, Johannesburg, May 1919.
Report of the Commissioner, South African Police.
Report of the Commissioners to Enquire into the Causes of and Occurrences... Native Disturbances at Port Elizabeth on 23 October 1920...1920.
Report of the Dept. of Labour.
Report of the Dept. of Native Affairs.
Report of the Economic Commission, 1914.
Report of Factories and Labour Division, Dept. Mines and Industries.
Report of the Industrial Legislation Commission, 1935.
Report of the Inter-Departmental Committee on the Native Pass Laws. 1920. (UG41-22).
Report of the Judicial Inquiry into the Witwatersrand Disturbances, 1913.
Report of the Local Natives' Land Committee (Natal Province) (UG34-18).

Report of the Low Grade Mines Commission, 1920.

Report of the Martial Law Inquiry Judicial Commission, 1922.

Report of the Native Affairs Commission, 1925-1927.

Report of the Native Economic Commission, 1925.

Report of the Native Economic Commission, 1930-1932.

Report of the Native Grievances Inquiry 1913-1914 (UG37-14).

Report of the Natives Land Commission (UG.19-16, and 22-16 (including [UG22-14]).

Report of the Natives' Land Commission 1916-1918 (UG32-18).

Report of the Natives' Land Committee, Western Transvaal (UG23-18).

Report of the Orange Free State Local Natives Land Committee (UG22-18).

Report of the Select Committee on the Industrial Conciliation (Amendment) Bill, 1930.

Report of the Select Committee on the Native Labour Regulation Bill (SC3-11).

Report of the Select Committee on Native Affairs (Natives [Urban Areas] Bill), 1923.

Report of the Select Committee on Subject-Matter of Masters and Servants Law (Transvaal) Amendment Bill (1925; SC12-25).

Report of the Select Committee on the Wage Bill (and Industrial Conciliation Bill) 1937.

Report of the Select Committee on the Wage Bill, 1925.

Reports of the Special Commissioner ... into the Boycotting of Rand Storekeepers by Natives ... (4-19)

Report of the Vereeniging Location Riots (1937) Commission, 1937.

Report of the Witwatersrand Disturbances Commission, 1913.

Report on Suppression of Stock Thefts (SC4-23).

Statutes 1913-1953.

Union Statistics for Fifty Years, 1910-1960. 1960.

Municipal

Official South African Municipal Year Book.

United Kingdom

British Documents on Foreign Affairs: Reports & Papers from the Foreign Office Confidential Print, edited by D. Throup (UPA, 1995) v. 3, (Zululand), v. 10 ("Labour Problems").

B. CONTEMPORARY NEWSPAPERS AND JOURNALS

Abantu-Batho (Johannesburg, 1918-1931, varia). *African Defender* (Port Elizabeth, 1927).

African Leader (Johannesburg, 1932-1933). *African Liberator* (1935).

African Voice (1938). *African World* (Cape Town, 1925-1926).

A.P.O. (Cape Town, 1909-1923). *Bantu World* (Johannesburg, 1932-1940).

The Black Man (Cape Town, 1920). *Bolshevist* (Cape Town, 1919-1921).

Cape Argus (1872, 1918-1931). *Cape Monitor* (1854).

Cape Times (1918-1940).

Daily Despatch (East London).

Drum.

Fighting Talk.

Frankforter (Frankfort).

Friend (Bloemfontein, clippings).

The Hammer (Johannesburg, Nov.-Dec. 1931).

Ikwesi Le Afrika (Eshowe, 1928-1932).

Imvo Zabantsundu (1912-1940).

Inkanyiso lase Natal (Pietermaritzburg, 1890-1994).

Inkululeko (Johannesburg, 1940-1950).

The International (1915-1924).

Izindaba Zabantu (Marianhill, 1926-1928).

Izwe La Kiti (Dundee, 1912-1915).

Izwi La Lentsoe La = Congress Voice.

Izwi Lase Afrika (Cape Town, 1941-1942).

Kroonstad Times.

Liberator (1937).

Mochochonono (1936-1941).

Natal Witness.

Negro Worker (Hamburg, Paris, 1928-1937).

New Africa (Johannesburg, IICU, 1929).

South African Commercial Advertiser (1834).

South African Worker (1926-1930, 1936-1938).

Sunday Times (Johannesburg, 1917-1920).

Tsala ea Batho (Kimberley, 1912-1915).

Udibi Lwase Afrika (Durban, 1927).

Umlindi we Nyanga (East London, 1936-1940).

Umteteli wa Bantu (Johannesburg, 1920-1940).

Voice of Labour (Johannesburg, 1908-1912).

Chain-Breaker (Johannesburg, 1939-1940).

Discussion (Cape Town).

Eastern Province Herald.

Forward.

The Free State Advocate (1936-1941).

The Guardian (Cape Town).

Ikaka (Johannesburg, Jul.-Aug. 1931).

Ilanga lase Natal.

Indlela Yenkululeko (Johannesburg) 1934.

Inkokeli ya Bantu (Cape Town, 1940-1942).

Inkundla ya Bantu (Verulam, 1938-1951).

Iphepa Lo Hlanga (Pietermaritzburg, 1898-1904).

Izwi La Bantu (East London, 1902-1908).

Izwi Lakiti=Our Country (1929-1930).

Izwi Lama Africa (East London, 1931).

Koranta ea Becoana (Mafeking, 1901-1903).

Liberation.

Midland News (Cradock, 1929-1932).

Natal Advertiser.

Ndaba Zamakomanisi e Tekwini (Durban, 1931).

Negro World.

Rand Daily Mail.

The South African Spectator (1901-1902).

Star (Johannesburg).

Transvaal Communist (1939).

Tsala ea Becoana (Kimberley, 1910-1912).

UmAfrika (Marianhill, 1929-1937).

Umsebenzi (1930-1938).

Umvikeli-Thebe (Cape Town, 1936-1937).

The Workers' Herald (Johannesburg, 1923-1928).

C. CONTEMPORARY PUBLICATIONS/MEMOIRS

A

Abrahams, P. *Return to Goli* (London: Faber, 1953).

—. *Tell Freedom* (London: Faber, 1954).

African National Congress (ANC). *The Powers of the Supreme Chief, under the Native Administration Act, 1927: Originally Machinery of the African Native Government and Native Social Life* (Johannesburg: Esson [for ANC], 1928).

—. "The African Bill of Rights, 1923", [adopted at 1923 ANC conference] in *The ANC and the Bill of Rights, 1923 to 1993* (Johannesburg: ANC, 1993).

—. "Resolutions of the Annual Conference ... May 28-29 1923", KC v. 1, pp. 297-298.

—. Resolutions of the Annual Conference, Dec. 15-18, 1939", KC v. 2, pp. 154-155.

—. *Africans' Claims in South Africa* (Johannesburg: ANC, 1944).

Alexander, R. *All My Life and All My Strength*. (ed.) R. Suttner (Johannesburg: STE, 2004).

—. "Johnny Gomas as I Knew Him", *SALB* v. 15 no. 5 (1991) pp. 80-83.

Allen, S.A. "Mr. Alan Kirkland Soga," *Colored American Magazine* Feb. 1904, pp. 114-116.

Andrews, W.H. *Class Struggles in South Africa* (Cape Town: Stewart, 1941).

B

Baard, F. *My Spirit is Not Banned* (Harare: Zimbabwe Pub. House, 1986).

Baartman, B. *The Autobiography of a South African Textile Worker* (London: SACTU, 1988).

Ballinger, M. "Native Life in South African Towns", *Journal of the Royal African Society* v. 37 no. 148 (1938), pp. 326-338.

Basner, M. *Am I an African? The Political Memoirs of H.M. Basner* (Johannesburg: Wits University Press, 1993).

Bridgman, F.B. "Social Conditions in Johannesburg", *International Review of Missions* v. 15 no. 59 (Jul. 1926), pp. 569-583.

A Brief Account of the Jubilee Celebrations ... Normal Training Institution, Healdtown (Healdtown: The Institution,1906).

Bud-M'belle, I. *Kafir Scholar's Companion* (Lovedale: Lovedale Missionary Press, 1903).

Buell, R. *The Native Problem in Africa* (New York: Macmillan, 1928).

Bunting, S.P. *Imperialism and South Africa* (Johannesburg: CPSA, 1928).

C

Champion, A.W.G. *The I.C.U. (the Industrial and Commercial Workers' Union): What it is, What it is Doing and What it Wants* (Durban: African Workers Club, 1927).

—. *Mehlomadala: My Experiences in the ICU* (Durban: Crown Printing, 1928).

—. *Views of Mahlathi: Writings of A.W.G. Champion, a Black South African* (ed.) by M. Swanson (Pietermaritzburg: University of Natal Press, 1983).

Close, R. *New Life* (Cape Town: Food and Canning Workers' Union, 1950).

Coka, G. "The Story of Gilbert Coka of the Zulu Tribe, Written by Himself", in M. Perham (ed.) *Ten Africans* (London: Faber, 1936), pp. 273-321.

Communist Party of South Africa. *Communism and the Native Question* (Johannesburg, 193?).

—. *Organise a People's Front in South Africa* (CPSA, 1936).

—. *Vereeniging: Who is to Blame?* (CPSA, 1937).

Coppin, L. *Observations of Persons and Things in South Africa, 1900-1904* (Philadelphia: AME, 1905?).

Cornell, P.H. et al. *Native Housing: A Collective Thesis* (Johannesburg: Witwatersrand University Press, 1939).

Cope, R. *Comrade Bill: The Life and Times of W.H. Andrews, Workers' Leader* (Cape Town, Stewart Printing, 1943).

D

de Kiewiet, C.W. *The Imperial Factor in South Africa* (Cambridge: Cambridge University Press, 1937).

Dhlomo, H.I.E. *Collected Works* (eds) N. Visser and T. Couzens (Johannesburg: Ravan Press, 1985).

Dube, J. *A Talk upon My Native Land* (Rochester, N.Y.: Swinburne, 1892).

—. *The Zulu's Appeal for Light and England's Duty* (London: Unwin, 1909).

—. and Archdeacon Lee, *The Clash of Colour* (Durban: Natal Missionary Conference, 1926)

—. "Native Political and Industrial Organizations in South Africa", in D. Taylor (ed.) *Christianity and the Natives of South Africa: A Year-Book of South African Missions* (Lovedale: Lovedale Press, 1927?), pp. 53-59.

—. "The Industrial Organisation of Native People", in *Report of the National European-Bantu Conference ... Feb.6-9 1929* (Lovedale Press, n.d.), pp. 141-147.

F

Farm Labour in the Orange Free State (Johannesburg: SAIRR, 1939).

Ford, J.W. *The Negro Industrial Proletariat of America* (Moscow : RILU, 1928).

Forman, L. *Black and White in S.A. History* (Cape Town: New Age, 1960).

—. *A Trumpet from the Housetops: The Selected Writings of Lionel Forman* (ed.) S. Forman and A. Odendaal (Cape Town: David Philip, 1992).

— ."Nationalisms in South Africa", *Viewpoints and Perspectives* v. 1 no. 2 (June 1953).

Frew, A. *Prince George's African Tour* (London: Blackie, 1934).

Fuze, M.M. 1922. *The Black People, and Whence They Came: A Zulu View,* (ed.) A. Cope (Pietermaritzburg: University of Natal Press, 1979; first published in Zulu, 1922).

G

Gebuza [pseud.], *The Peril in Natal* (London: Unwin, 1906).

Gitsham, E. and J.F. Trembath, *A First Account of Labour Organisation in South Africa* (Durban: Commercial, 1926).

Gomas J. *100 Years: 'Emancipation of Slaves': Smash the Chains of Slavery* (CPSA, 1934).

Gumede, J.T. "To All Leaders of the African People", *National Gazette* 7 Sept. 1927.

H

Haines, E. "The Economic Status of the Cape Province Farm Native", *SAJE* v. 3 (1935), pp. 57-79

Harrison, W.H. *Memoirs of a Socialist in South Africa 1903-1947* (Cape Town: The Author, 1947).

Hellmann, E. *Rooiyard. A Sociological Survey of an Urban Native Slum Yard* (Lusaka: OUP for Rhodes-Livingstone Institute, 1948).

Hill, Robert A. (ed.) *Marcus Garvey and Universal Negro Improvement Association Papers. Volume 10: Africa for the Africans 1923-1946* (Berkeley: University of California Press, 2006).

Hunter, M. *Reaction to Conquest* (London: OUP, 1936).

I

Industrial and Commercial Workers' Union. *Evidence to Economic and Wages Commission, Submitted at Johannesburg, September 19th, 1925* (Johannesburg: ICU, 1925).

J

Jabavu, D.D.T. *Native Disabilities in South Africa* (Lovedale: Lovedale Press, 1932).

—. (ed.) *Findings of the All African Convention* (Lovedale: Lovedale Press, 1935).

—. (ed.) *Minutes of the All-African Convention* (Lovedale: Lovedale Press, 1936).

—. "Native Unrest in South Africa", *International Review of Missions* v. 11 1922, pp. 248-259.

Jabavu, F. "Bantu Home Life", in Taylor, *Christianity and the Natives*, pp. 164-176.

Jingoes, S. *A Chief is a Chief by the People: The Autobiography of Stimela Jason Jingoes*. (ed.) J. and C. Perry. (London: OUP, 1975).

Johannesburg Joint Council of Europeans and Natives. *General Hertzog's Solution to the Native Question* (Johannesburg: Esson, 1927).

—. *The Native in Industry* [J.D.R. Jones (ed.)] (Johannesburg: The Council, ca. 1927-1929).

Jones, D.I. "Communism in South Africa", *Communist Review* v. 1 no. 3 (1921), pp. 15-17, no. 4 1921, pp. 63-71.

K

Kadalie, C. *The Relation Between Black and White Workers in South Africa* (Johannesburg: ICWU, 1927). (London: F. Cass, 1970).

—. *My Life and the ICU: The Autobiography of a Black Trade Unionist in South Africa* (ed.) S. Trapido (London: F. Cass, 1971).

—. "The Black Man's Labour Movement", *Foreign Affairs* (U.K.) Sept. 1927, pp. 84-85.

—. "The African Labour Movement", *Foreign Affairs* (U.K.) Apr. 1928.

Karis, T. and G.M. Carter (eds.) *From Protest to Challenge: A Documentary History of African Politics in South Africa 1882-1964* 4 v. (Stanford: Hoover University Press, 1972-1977).

Kotane, M. *The Great Crisis Ahead: A Call to Unity* (New Age: [n.d. 1957]).

—. "How a Non-European Looks at Afrikanerdom", *Freedom* no. 6 1945.

—. "Landmarks of the ANC", *Sechaba* v. 2 no. 8 (1968), pp. 10-11.

Kuzwayo, E. *Call Me Woman* (London: Women's Press, 1985).

L

La Guma, A. *Jimmy La Guma: A Biography* (ed.) M. Adhikari (Cape Town: Friends of the SA Library, 1997).

Laidler, P. *Locations: Health & Sanitation* (East London, 1936).

—. "The Relationship of the Native to South Africa's Health", *South African Medical Journal* v. 6 no. 10 (8 Oct. 1932), pp. 617-628.

Lembede, A.M. *Freedom in Our Lifetime: The Collected Writing of Anton Muziwakhe Lembede* (ed.) by R. Edgar and L. ka Msumza (Athens OH: Ohio University Press, 1996).

—. "Some Basic Principles of African Nationalism", *Inyaniso,* Feb. 1945.

Lewin, J. "The Rise of Congress in South Africa", *Political Quarterly* 24 (1953), pp. 292-307.

Luthuli, A. *Let My People Go* (London: Collins, 1962).

M

Macmillan, W. M. *Complex South Africa: An Economic foot-note to History* (London: Faber, 1930).

—. *The Land, the Native, and Unemployment* (Johannesburg: Council of Education, 1924).

Mahabane, Z.R. *The Good Fight: Selected Speeches of Rev. Zaccheus R. Mahabane* (ed.) by G. Carter and S. Johns (Evanston: Northwestern University Press, 1965).

—. "Problems of the African Church", in M. Stauffer (ed.) *Thinking with Africa* (1928), pp. 135-146.

Maliba, [Malivha] A. *Vhudzulotia Vhatha Vhavenda=Condition of the Venda People* (CPSA, 194-).

Mancoe, J. *The Bloemfontein Bantu and Coloured People's Directory* 1st. ed (Bloemfontein: A. C. White, 1934)

Mandela, N. *Long Walk to Freedom: The Autobiography of Nelson Mandela* (New York: Little, Brown, 1994)

—. "Freedom in Our Lifetime", *Liberation* (Jun. 1956), pp. 4-8.

Mann, T. *Memoirs* (London: MacGibbon, 1923).

Marks, J. B. "Breaking the Shackles", *African Communist*, no. 51 (1972), pp. 10-11.

Matthews, Z.K. *Freedom for My People: The Autobiography of Z.K. Matthews: Southern Africa 1901 to 1968.* Memoir by M. Wilson (London: Collings, 1981).

Maxeke, C. "The Progress of Native Womanhood in South Africa", in Taylor, *Christianity and the Natives*, pp. 177-182.

—. "The Native Christian Mother", in *The Evangelisation of South Africa* (Cape Town: Nasionale Pers, 1925), pp. 127-134.

—. "Social Conditions among Bantu Women and Girls", in *Christian Students and Modern South Africa* (Fort Hare: SCA, 1930: also reprinted in KC v. 1 pp. 344-6).

Modisane, B. *Blame Me on History* (New York: Touchstone, 1986 1963).

Mofutsanyana, E. T. "African Labour and Wages," in D.D.T. Jabavu (ed.) *Minutes of the All-African Convention* (Lovedale: Lovedale Press, 1936).

Mokgatle, N. *The Autobiography of an Unknown South African* (Berkeley: University of California Press, 1971).

Molema, S.M. *The Bantu Past and Present: An Ethnographical and Historical Study of the Native Races of South Africa* (Edinburgh: Green, 1920).

Msimang, H. S. *The Crisis* (Johannesburg: Express, 1936).

—. "50 Years on the Road to Liberty", *Contact* 2 Apr. 1960, pp. 9, 12 [interview].

Msimang, R.W. (comp.), *Natives Land Act 1913: Specific Cases of Evictions and Hardships, etc.* (Cape Town: Friends of South African Library, 1996, reprint 1914).

N

Natal Native Congress. *Constitution* (Pietermaritzburg, 1915).

Native and Coloured Women of the Province of the Orange Free State. "Petition ..." in M. Daymond et al (eds.) *Women Writing Africa: The Southern Region* (New York: Feminist Press, 2003), pp. 158-161.

Non-European Railway & Harbour Workers of South Africa. *We Want to Live* (S.l.: ca.1937) [written by R. Alexander].

Non-European United Front. *Minutes of the Conference...8-10 Apr. 1939* (Cape Town: NEUF, 1939).

Nzula, A., I.I. Potekhin, and A.Z. Zusmanovich, *Forced Labour in Colonial Africa* (ed.) R. Cohen (London: Zed Press, 1979; first pub. in Russian, 1933).

—. "The Struggles of the Negro Toilers in SA", *Negro Worker* v. 5 no's 2-6, 10, (1935).

O

Oliphant, S. *The Salvation of a Race* (Cape Town: The Author, 1939).

P

Palmer, M. "Note on Some Native Budgets Collected in Durban", *South African Journal of Science* v. 25 (1928), pp. 499-506.

—. "Some Problems of the Transition from Subsistence to Money Economy", *South African Journal of Science* v. 27 (1930), pp. 117-125

Peregrino, F.Z.S. *Life among the Native and Coloured Miners in the Transvaal* (Cape Town: Hodgson I Penne, 1910).

—. *His Majesty's Black Labourers: A Treatise on the Camp Life of the South African Native Labour Corps* (Cape Town: Cape Times, 1918)

Phillips, R. *The Bantu Are Coming: Phases of South Africa's Race Problem* (London: SCM, 1930).

—. *The Bantu in the City* (Lovedale: Lovedale Press, 1938).

—. "Social Work in South Africa", in Taylor, *Christianity and the Natives*, pp. 145-151.

Plaatje, S. *Native Life in South Africa, Before and Since the European War and the Boer Rebellion* (3rd ed.) (Kimberley: Tsala ea Batho, 1920; original edition, 1916).

—. *Native Life in South Africa.* (ed.) by B. Willan. (Harlow: Longman, reprint 1987).

—. *Some of the Legal Disabilities Suffered by the Native Population of the Union of South Africa and Imperial Responsibility* (London: The African Telegraph, 1918).

—. "A South African's Homage", in I. Gollancz, *A Book of Homage to Shakespeare* (1916) reprinted in *Sol T. Plaatje: Selected Shorter Writings* (Grahamstown: ISEA, 1995), pp. 9-11.

—. *The Mote and the Beam.* (New York: Youngs, 1921).

—. *Mhudi: An Epic of South African Life a Hundred Years Ago.* (Lovedale: Lovedale Press, 1930).

—. *Selected Writings*, (ed.) B. Willan (Johannesburg: Witwatersrand University Press, 1996).

—. *The Mafeking Diary of Sol T. Plaatje,* (ed.) J. Comaroff and B. Willan. (Cape Town: D. Philip, 1999).

Q

A Question of Colour: A Study of South Africa (Edinburgh: Blackwood, 1906).

R

Report of the Proceedings of the Fifth General Missionary Conference of South Africa 1921 (Durban: Commercial Printing Co., 1922).

Rich, S.G. "Notes on Natal", *International Socialist Review* v. 17 1917, pp. 723-726.

Robertson, H. "150 Years of Economic Contact between Black and White", *SAJE* v. 3 (1935), pp. 3-25.

Roux, E. *S.P. Bunting* (Cape Town: The Author, 1944).

—. *Time Longer than Rope* (London: Gollancz, 1948).

—. and W. Roux, *Rebel Pity: The Life of Eddie Roux* (London: Collings, 1970).

S

Sachs, E.S. *Rebels Daughters* (London: McGibbon and Kee, 1957).

Sachs, W. *Black Hamlet* (London: Bles, 1937)

[Saffery, A.L.] "Development of Trade Unionism in South Africa", *Social and Industrial Review* (Jan. 1926), pp. 45-48.

Schumann, C. *Structural Changes and Business Cycles in South Africa 1806-1936* (London: 1938).

Selope Thema, R.V. and H.D. Tyamzashe, *The Inequity of the Pass Laws* (Pretoria: [1945?]).

—. "Social Conditions of the Africans", in D. Taylor, *Christianity and the Natives*, pp. 45-52.

—. and J. Jones, "In South Africa", in Stauffer (ed.) *Thinking with Africa* (1928), pp. 36-65.

—. "The Union's Native Policy", *African Observer* v. 5 no. 1 (1936), p. 32.

—. "White and Black in South Africa", *African Observer* v. 6 no. 3 (Jan. 1937).

—. "How Congress Began," in M. Mutloatse (ed.) *Reconstruction: 90 Years of Black Historical Tradition* (Johannesburg: Ravan Press, 1981), pp. 108-114.

Seme, P. ka I. *The African National Congress: Is it Dead? No It Lives: The Proposed Amendment to its Constitution* (Newcastle: Newcastle Advertiser, 1932).

—. "The Regeneration of Africa," in A.L. and M.B. McLeod (eds.) *Representative South African Speeches: The Rhetoric of Race and Religion* (Mysore: University of Mysore, 1980), pp. 99-101.

Shepherd, R.H.W. *Literature for the South African Bantu* (Pretoria: Carnegie Corporation, 1936).

Sisulu, W. "The Development of African Nationalism", *India Quarterly* v. 10 1954, pp. 206-214.

Skota, T.D. Mweli (ed.) *The African Yearly Register, Being an Illustrated National Biographical Dictionary (Who's Who) of Black Folks in Africa* (Johannesburg: Esson (printer), 1931).

—. *The African Who's Who: An Illustrated Classified Register and National Biographical Dictionary of the Africans in the Transvaal*. 3rd ed. (Johannesburg: Distributed by CNA, 1966).

Soga, T. *The Journal and Selected Writings of the Reverend Tiyo Soga,* (ed.) D. Williams (Cape Town: Balkema, 1983).

Solomon, R. "Economic Conditions and Communications", in A. Herbertson (ed.) *The Oxford Survey of the British Empire: Africa* (Oxford: OUP, 1914).

South African Native Races Committee (ed.) *The Natives of South Africa: Their Economic and Social Condition* (London: Murray, 1901).

—. *The South African Natives: Their Progress and Present Condition* (London: Murray, 1908).

Stauffer, M. *Thinking with Africa: Chapters by a Group of Nationals Interpreting the Christian Movement* (London: SCM, 1928).

Stuart, J. *A History of the Zulu Rebellion* (London: Macmillan, 1913).

T

Tinley, J. *The Native Labor Problem of South Africa* (Chapel Hill: University of North Carolina Press, 1942).

Tloome, D. "Origin and Development of Non-European Trade Unions", *Viewpoints and Perspectives* v. 1 no. 1 (1953), pp. 17-23.

Transvaal Native Congress. *Constitution* (1919).

Trollope, A. *South Africa* (London: Chapman & Hall, 1878).

Tyamzashe, H.D. "Summary History of the ICU", (East London, 1941), ts. in Saffery Papers, B5.

U

University of the Witwatersrand. Dept. of Commerce. *Native Urban Employment: A Study of Johannesburg Employment Records 1936-1944* (Johannesburg: The Dept. 1948).

"Unrest in South Africa", *Round Table* v. 9 (Dec. 1918), pp. 194-200.

V

Van der Horst, S. *Native Labour in South Africa* (Cape Town: OUP, 1942).

W

Wilson, F. and D. Perrot (eds.) *Outlook on a Century: South Africa 1870-1970* (Lovedale: Lovedale Press, 1972).

X

Xuma, A.B. *Bridging the Gap Between White and Black in South Africa* (Lovedale: Lovedale Press, 1930).

—. *Charlotte Manye (Mrs. Maxeke): "What an Educated African Girl Can Do"* (Nashville: Women's Mite Missionary Society, AME Church, 1930).

—. *Reconstituting the Union of South Africa; or A More Rational Union Policy* (Lovedale: Lovedale Press, 1933)

D. SECONDARY SOURCES

A

Abbink, J., M. de Bruijn and K. van Walraven (eds.) *Rethinking Resistance: Revolt and Violence in African History* (Leiden: Brill, 2003).

Africa, E.J. *The Kimberley Malay Camp, 1882 to 1957* (Kimberley: Sol Plaatje Trust, 2006).

African National Congress.

—. *African National Congress, South Africa: A Short History* (London: ANC, 1970).

—. *The South African Trade Union Movement* (London: ANC, 1970).

—. *Unity in Action: A Short History of the African National Congress (South Africa) 1912-1982* (London: ANC, 1982).

—. *Apartheid South Africa: Colonialism of a Special Type* (London: ANC, 198?).

—. "Solomon Tshekisho Plaatje: First ANC Secretary-General (1876-1932)", *Sechaba,* Dec. 1981.

—. *Statement of the National Executive Committee of the ANC on the Occasion of the 89th Anniversary of the ANC, 8 January* (Johannesburg: ANC, 2001).

Alegi, P. *Laduma! Soccer, Politics and Society in South Africa* (Scottsville: UKZN Press, 2004).

Alexander, P. *Workers, War and the Origins of Apartheid: Labour and Politics in South Africa 1939-1948* (Cape Town: David Philip, 2000).

—. "Challenging Cheap-Labour Theory: Natal and Transvaal Coal Miners, c. 1890-1950", *Labour History* v. 49 no. 1 (2008), pp. 47-70.

Allen, V. *The History of Black Mineworkers in South Africa* (Keightly: Moor, 1992) v. 1.

Anderson, B. *Imagined Communities: Reflections on the Origin and Spread of Nationalism* (London: Verso, 1983, and rev. ed. 1991).

Anthony, D.H. "Max Yergan in South Africa: from Evangelical Pan-Africanist to Revolutionary Socialist", *African Studies Review* v. 34 no. 2 (1991), pp. 27-55.

Ashforth, A. *The Politics of Official Discourse in Twentieth-Century South Africa* (Oxford: Clarendon, 1990).

Atkins, K.E. *The Moon is Dead! Give Us Our Money: The Cultural Origins of an African Work Ethic, Natal, South Africa, 1843-1900* (London: J. Currey, 1993).

B

Badenhorst, C. "New Traditions, Old Struggles: Organized Sports for Johannesburg's Africans, 1920-1950" *Culture, Sport, Society* v. 6 (2003), pp. 116-143.

Baines, G. *A History of New Brighton, Port Elizabeth, South Africa 1903-1953* (Lewiston: Mellen, 2002).

—. "The Origins of Urban Segregation: Local Government and the Residence of Africans in Port Elizabeth, c.1835-1865", *SAHJ* no. 22 (1990), pp. 61-81.

—. "From Populism to Unionism: The Emergence and Nature of Port Elizabeth's Industrial and Commercial Workers' Union, 1918-1920", *JSAS* v. 17 1991, pp. 679-716.

—. "'In the World But Not of It': 'Bishop' Limba and the Church of Christ in New Brighton, c1929-49", *Kronos* no. 19 (1992), pp. 102-134.

—. "The Contradictions of Community Politics: The African Petty Bourgeoisie and the New Brighton Advisory Board, c1937-1952", *Journal of African History* v. 35 (1994), pp. 79-97.

—. "Masabalala, Samuel Makama Martin", in Sonderling, *New Dictionary* (1995), pp. 95-96.

Balibar, E. and I. Wallerstein, *Race, Nation, Class: Ambiguous Identities* (London: Verso, 1991).

Beall, J. and M. North-Coombes, "The 1913 Disturbances in Natal: Social & Economic Background to 'Passive Resistance'", *JNZH* v. 6 (1983), pp. 48-77.

Beinart, W. *The Political Economy of Pondoland 1860-1930* (Cambridge, 1982).

—. Delius, P. and S. Trapido, (eds.) *Putting a Plough to the Ground: Accumulation and Dispossession in Rural South Africa, 1850-1930* (Johannesburg: Ravan Press, 1986).

—. and C. Bundy, *Hidden Struggles in Rural South Africa* (Johannesburg: Ravan Press, 1987).

—. *Twentieth Century South Africa* (Oxford: OUP, 1994).

—. and C. Bundy, "The Union, the Nation and the Talking Crow: The Ideology and Tactics of the Independent ICU in East London", in Beinart and Bundy, *Hidden*

Struggles pp. 270-320 (also in *Societies of Southern Africa in the 19th and 20th Centuries Collected Seminar Papers* 28 [1981], pp. 69-76).

—. "Amafelandawonye (the Die-hards)": Popular Protest and Women's Movements in Herschel District in the 1920s", in Beinart and Bundy, *Hidden Struggles* pp. 222-269.

—. "Conflict in Qumbu: Rural Consciousness, Ethnicity and Violence in the Colonial Transkei", in Beinart and Bundy, *Hidden Struggles*, pp. 106-137.

—. "Women in Rural Politics: Herschel District in the 1920s and 1930s", in Bozzoli, *Class, Community and Conflict* (1987), pp. 324-357.

—. "Worker Consciousness, Ethnic Particularism and Nationalism: The Experience of a South African Migrant, 1930-1960", in Marks, *Politics of Race,* pp. 286-309.

—. "Transkeian Migrant Workers and Youth Labour on the Natal Sugar Estates 1918-1948," *Journal of African History* v. 32 (1991), pp. 41-63.

Benson, M. *South Africa: The Struggle for a Birthright* (London: Penguin, 1966).

—. *A Far Cry* (London: Viking, 1989).

Berger, I. *Threads of Solidarity: Women in South African Industry, 1900-1980* (London: J. Currey, 1992).

—. "Generations of Struggle: Trade Unions and the Roots of Feminism, 1930–1960", in N. Gasa (ed.) *Women in South African History* (Cape Town: HSRC, 2007), pp. 185-205.

Bergh, J.S. and F. Morton (eds.) *"To Make Them Serve ...": The 1871 Transvaal Commission on African Labour* (Pretoria: Protea, 2003).

Berman, B. and J. Lonsdale, *Unhappy Valley* (London: J. Currey 1992).

Bickford-Smith, V. *Ethnic Pride and Racial Prejudice in Victorian Cape Town* (Cambridge, 1995).

—. "Black Labour at the Docks at the Beginning of the Twentieth Century", *Studies in the History of Cape Town* v. 1 (Cape Town: UCT, 1979), pp. 75-125.

—. "Protest, Organisation and Ethnicity among Cape Town Workers, 1891-1902". in E. van Heyningen (ed.) *Studies in the History of Cape Town* v. 7 (Cape Town: UCT, 1994), pp. 84-108.

Bloch, R. "The High Cost of Living: The Port Elizabeth 'Disturbances' of October 1920", *Africa Perspective* 19 (1981), pp. 39-59.

Bonacich, E. "Capitalism and Race Relations in South Africa: A Split Labor Market Analysis", *Political Power and Social Theory* v. 2 (1981), pp. 239-278.

Bond, P. *Elite Transition* (Pietermaritzburg: University of Natal Press, 2000).

Bonner, P. ... [et al.] (eds.) *Holding their Ground: Class, Locality and Culture in 19th and 20th Century South Africa* (Johannesburg: Ravan Press, 1989).

—. P. Delius, and D. Posel, (eds.) *Apartheid's Genesis, 1935-1962* (Johannesburg: Ravan Press; Witwatersrand University Press, 1993).

—. "The 1920 Black Mineworkers' Strike: A Preliminary Account", in Bozzoli, *Labour, Townships and Protest*, pp. 273-297.

—. "The Transvaal Native Congress 1917-1920: The Radicalization of the Black Petty Bourgeoisie on the Rand", *Africa Perspective* 20 (1982), pp. 41-62; modified in S. Marks and R. Rathbone (eds.) *Industrialisation and Social*

Change in South Africa (London: Longman, 1982), pp. 270-313.

—. "Family, Crime and Political Consciousness on the East Rand, 1939-55", *JSAS* v. 14 no. 3 (1988), pp. 393-420.

—. "Desirable or Undesirable Basotho Women? Liquor, Prostitution and the Migration of Basotho women to the Rand, 1920–1945", in C. Walker (ed.) *Women and Gender in Southern Africa*, pp. 221–250.

—. and K.A. Shapiro, "Company Town, Company Estate: Pilgrim's Rest, 1910-1932", *JSAS* v. 19 no. 2 (1993), pp. 171-201.

—. "Backs to the Fence: Law, Liquor, and the Search for Social Control in an East Rand Town, 1929-1942", in Crush, *Liquor and Labor,* pp. 269-305.

—. "African Urbanisation on the Rand between the 1930s and 1960s: Its Social Character and Political Consequences", *JSAS* v. 21 no. 1 (1995), pp. 115-131.

—. P. Delius and D. Posel, "The Shaping of Apartheid: Contradiction, Continuity and Popular Struggle", in Bonner, Delius and Posel (eds.) *Apartheid's Genesis* pp. 1-41.

Bothma, C.V. *Ntšhabeleng Social Structure* (Pretoria: Govt. Printer, 1962).

Bozzoli, B. (ed.) *Labour, Townships and Protest: Studies in the Social History of the Witwatersrand* (Johannesburg: Ravan Press, 1979).

—. (ed.) *Town and Countryside in the Transvaal: Capitalist Penetration and Popular Response* (Johannesburg: Ravan Press, 1983).

—. (ed.) *Class, Community and Conflict: South African Perspectives* (Johannesburg: Ravan Press, 1987).

—. with the assistance of M. Nkotsoe, *Women of Phokeng: Consciousness, Life Strategy, and Migrancy in South Africa, 1900-1983* (Johannesburg: Ravan Press, 1991).

—. *Theatres of Struggle and the End of Apartheid* (Edinburgh: Edinburgh University Press, 2005).

—. "The Origins, Development and Ideology of Local Manufacturing in South Africa", *JSAS* v. 1 (1975), pp. 194-214.

—. and P. Delius, "Radical History and South African Society", *Radical History Review* 46 (1990), pp. 13-46.

Bradford, H. *A Taste of Freedom: The ICU in Rural South Africa 1924-1930* (New Haven: Yale University Press; Johannesburg: Ravan Press 1987).

—. "'A Taste of Freedom': Capitalist Development and Response to the ICU in the Transvaal Countryside", in Bozzoli (ed.) *Town and Countryside*, pp. 128-150.

—. "Mass Movements and the Petty Bourgeoisie: The Social Origins of ICU Leadership, 1924-1929," *Journal of African History* v. 25 (1984), pp. 295-310.

—. "'We Are Now the Men': Women's Beer Protests in the Natal Countryside, 1929," in Bozzoli (ed.) *Class and Conflict* (1997), pp. 292-323.

Bradlow, E. "The Khoi and the Proposed Vagrancy Legislation of 1834", *Quarterly Bulletin of the South African Library* v. 39 1985, pp. 99-106.

Brandel-Syrier, M. *Black Woman in Search of God* (London: Lutterworth, 1962).

Braverman, H. *Labor and Monopoly Capital: The Degradation of Work in the 20th Century* (New York: Monthly Review Press, 1974).

Breckenridge, K. "Migrancy, Crime and Faction Fighting: The Role of the *Isitshozi* in the Development of Ethnic Organisations in the Compounds", *JSAS* v. 16 (1990), pp. 55-78.

—. "'Money with Dignity': Migrants, Minelords and the Cultural Politics of the South African Gold Standard Crisis 1920-33", *Journal of African History* v. 36 (1995), pp. 271-304.

—. "'We Must Speak for Ourselves': The Rise and Fall of a Public Sphere on the South African Gold Mines, 1920 to 1931", *Comparative Studies in Society & History* v. 40 (1998), pp. 71-108.

—. "Love Letters and Amanuenses: Beginning the Cultural History of the Working Class Private Sphere in Southern Africa, 1900-1933", *JSAS* v. 26 no. 2 (2000), pp. 337-348.

Bunche, R.J. *An African American in South Africa: The Travel Notes of Ralph J. Bunche, 28 Sept. 1937-1 Jan. 1938* (ed.) by R. Edgar (Athens: Ohio University Press, 1992).

Bundy, C. *The Rise and Fall of the South African Peasantry* (London: Heinemann, 1979).

—. "The Abolition of the Masters and Servants Act", *SALB* v. 2 no. 1 (1975), pp. 37-46.

—. "'We Don't Want Your Rain, We Won't Dip': Popular Opposition, Collaboration and Social Control in the Anti-Dipping Movement, 1908-1916", in Beinart and Bundy, *Hidden Struggles*, pp. 191-221.

—. "A Voice in the Big House: The Career of Headman Enoch Mamba", in Beinart and Bundy, *Hidden Struggles*, pp. 78-105.

Bunting, B. *Moses Kotane: South African Revolutionary* (London: Inkululeko, 1986).

Burger, J. *The Black Man's Burden* (London: Gollancz, 1943).

Burns, C. "Louisa Mvemve: A Woman's Advice to the Public on the Cure of Various Diseases", *Kronos* no. 23 (1996), pp. 108-134.

C

Callan, E. *Albert John Luthuli & the South African Race Conflict* (Kalamazoo: Western Michigan University, 1965).

Callinicos, L. *A People's History of South Africa* 3 v. (Johannesburg: Ravan Press, 1981-1993).

—. "'We Are Not Alone': The Making of a Mass Movement, 1950-1960", *Staffrider* v.8 (1989), pp. 88-104.

—. "'People's History for People's Power'": Representing the Past in a Divided South Africa", *South African Historical Journal [SAHJ]* 25 (1991), pp. 22-37.

Campbell, J. *Songs of Zion: The African Methodist Episcopal Church in the United States and South Africa* (New York: OUP, 1995).

—. "'Like Locusts in Pharaoh's Palace': The Origins and Politics of African

Methodism in the Orange Free State, 1895-1914", *African Studies* v. 53 (1994), pp. 37-70.

Carter, D. "The Defiance Campaign: A Comparative Analysis of the Organisation, Leadership and Participation in the Eastern Cape and Transvaal", *Societies of Southern Africa in the 19th and 20th Centuries Collected Seminar Papers* no. 12, pp. 76-97.

Carton, B. *Blood from Your Children: The Colonial Origins of Generational Conflict in South Africa* (Pietermaritzburg: University of Natal Press, 2000).

Chandavarkar, R. *Imperial Power and Popular Politics: Class, Resistance and the State in India, c. 1850-1950* (Cambridge: CUP, 1998).

Chanock, M. *The Making of South African Legal Culture, 1902-1936: Fear, Favour, and Prejudice* (Cambridge: CUP, 2001.)

—. "The South African Native Administration Act of 1927", in O. Mendelshohn and U. Baxi (eds.) *The Rights of Subordinated Peoples* (Delhi: OUP, 1994), pp. 295-323.

Chipkin, I. *Do South Africans Exist? Nationalism, Democracy and the Identity of 'The People'* (Johannesburg: Wits University Press, 2007).

Chrisman, L. 1997. "Fathering the Black Nation of South Africa: Gender and Generation in Sol Plaatje's *Native Life in South Africa* and *Mhudi*", *Social Dynamics* v. 23 no 2: 59-73.

—. *Rereading the Imperial Romance. British Imperialism and South African Resistance in Haggard, Schreiner and Plaatje* (Oxford: Clarendon, 2000).

Christie, R. *Electricity, Industry and Class in South Africa* (London: Macmillan, 1984).

Cloete, R. "The Ideology of Self-Help in the National Native Congress from 1910 to the Early 1920s", in *Conference on the History of the Opposition in South Africa* (Johannesburg: Development Studies Group, Wits University, 1978), pp. 141-49.

Clynick, T. "Chiefs, Diggers and African Labour: The Tlaping Diamond Rush, 1920-1", *African Studies* v. 54 (1995), pp. 73-93.

Cobley, A. *Class and Consciousness: The Black Petty Bourgeoisie in South Africa, 1924 to 1950* (New York: Greenwood Press, 1990).

—. *The Rules of the Game: Struggles in Black Recreation and Social Welfare Policy in South Africa* (New York: Greenwood Press, 1997).

—. "'The African National Church': Determination and Political Struggle among Black Christians in South Africa to 1948", *Church History* v. 60 1991, pp. 356-371.

Cohen, J. "*Twatwa*: The Working Class of Benoni during the 1930s", *Africa Perspective* 20 (1982), pp. 76-96.

Comaroff, J. and J.L. *Of Revelation and Revolution* v. 1 (Chicago: University of Chicago Press, 1991).

Comaroff, J. "The Madman and the Migrant: Work and Labor in the Historical Consciousness of a South African People", *American Ethnologist* v. 14 (1987), pp. 191-209.

Cooper, F. *Colonialism in Question: Theory, Knowledge, History* (Berkeley: University of California Press, 2005).

Cope, N. *To Bind the Nation: Solomon kaDinuzulu and Zulu nationalism, 1913-1933* (Pietermaritzburg: University of Natal Press, 1993).

Coplan, D. *In Township Tonight! South Africa's Black City Music and Theatre* (Johannesburg: Ravan Press, 1985).

—. "The Emergence of an African Working-Class Culture," in Marks and Rathbone (eds.) *Industrialisation and Social Change,* pp. 358-375.

Couzens, T. *The New African: A Study of the Life and Work of H.I.E. Dhlomo* (Ravan Press, 1985).

—. "Introduction", in *R.R.R. Dhlomo: 20 Short Stories,* special issue, *English in Africa* v. 2 no1 (1975).

—. "The Black Press and Black Literature in South Africa 1900-1950" *English Studies in Africa* v. 19 no 2 (Sep. 1976) pp. 93-99.

—. and B. Willan, (eds.) *Solomon T. Plaatje, 1876-1932,* special issue *English in Africa* v. 3 no. 2 (1976).

—. "Robert Grendon: Iris Traders, Cricket Scores and Paul Kruger's Dream's", *English in Africa* v. 15 no. 2 (1988), pp. 49-91.

—. "Solomon Plaatje's Vision of a Just South Africa", in *A Collection of Solomon T. Plaatje Memorial Lectures 1981-1992* (Mafikeng: University of Bophuthatswana, 1993), pp. 107-119.

Crush, J., A. Jeeves, and D. Yudelman, *South Africa's Labor Empire: A History of Black Migrancy to the Gold Mines* (Boulder: Westview, 1991).

—. and Ambler, C. (eds.) *Liquor and Labor in Southern Africa* (Scotsville: University of Natal Press, 1992).

D

Dadoo, Y. (ed.) *South African Communists Speak* (London: Inkululeko, 1981).

Davidson, A.B. *Iuzhnaia Afrika: Stanovlenie sil protesta 1870-1924* (Moscow: Nauka, 1972).

—. I. Filitova, V. Gorodnov, and S. Johns, (eds.) *South Africa and the Communist International: A Documentary History* (London: Cass, 2003). 2 v.

—. "The Foundation of the ANC", *Narodni Azii i Afriki,* 6 (1962), pp. 78-84 (in Russian).

Davidson, B. *The Black Man's Burden* (London: J. Currey, 1992).

Davies, R. *Capital, State and White Labour in South Africa 1900-1960: An Historical Materialist Analysis of Class Formation and Class Relations* (London: Harvester, 1979).

—. "Capital Restructuring and the Modification of the Racial Division of Labour in South Africa ", *Societies of Southern Africa in the 19th and 20th Centuries Collected Seminar Papers, SSA* 26 (1981), pp. 121-132.

Davis, R. H. "John L. Dube: A South African Exponent of Booker T. Washington", *Journal of African Studies* v. 2 (1976), pp. 497-528.

—. "'Qude Maniki!': John L. Dube, Pioneer Editor of *Ilanga Lase Natal*", in Switzer, *South Africa's Alternative Press,* pp. 83-98.

De Kock, L. *Civilising Barbarians: Missionary Narrative and African Textual Response in Nineteenth-Century South Africa* (Johannesburg: Witwatersrand University Press, 1996).

Deane, D.S. *Black South Africans: A Who's Who* (Cape Town: OUP, 1978).

Delius, P. *A Lion amongst the Cattle: Reconstruction and Resistance in the Northern Transvaal* (Johannesburg: Ravan Press, 1996).

—. "*Sebatakgomo*; Migrant Organisation, the ANC and the Sekhukhuneland Revolt", *JSAS* v. 15 (1989), pp. 581-616.

—. "*Sebatakgomo* and the Zoutpansberg Balemi Association: The ANC, the Communist Party and Rural Organization 1939-1955", *Journal of African History* v. 34 (1993), pp. 293-313.

—. and S. Trapido, "*Inboekselings* and *Oorlams*: The Creation and Transformation of a Servile Class", in Bozzoli, *Town and Countryside*, pp. 53-88.

Denoon, D. *A Grand Illusion: The failure of Imperial Policy in the Transvaal Colony during the Period of Reconstruction 1900-1905* (London: Longman, 1973).

—. *Settler Capitalism* (Oxford: OUP, 1983).

Diamond, C. "The Natives' Grievances Enquiry 1913-1934", *SAJE* v. 36 (1968), pp. 211-227.

Diepen, M. van (ed.) *The National Question in South Africa* (London: Zed Press, 1988).

Drew, A. (ed.) *South Africa's Radical Tradition* (Cape Town: UCT Press, 1996-1997).

—. *Discordant Comrades: Identities and Loyalties on the South African Left* (Pretoria: Unisa, 2000).

—. *Between Empire and Revolution: A Life of Sidney Bunting, 1873-1936* (London: Pickering, 2007).

—. "Events Were Breaking Above Their Heads: Socialism in South Africa, 1921-1950", *Social Dynamics* v. 17 no. 1 (1991), pp. 49-77.

—. "Bolshevizing Communist Parties: The Algerian and South African Experiences", *International Review of Social History* v. 48 (2003), pp. 167-202.

—. "The New Line in South Africa: Ideology and Perception in a Very Small Communist Party", in M. Worley (ed.) *In Search of Revolution* (London: Tauris, 2004), pp. 337-359.

Dreyer, L. *The Modern African Elite of South Africa* (London: Macmillan, 1989).

Dubow, S. "African Labour at the Cape Town Docks 1900-1904: Processes of Transition," *Studies in the History of Cape Town* v. 4 (1984), pp. 108-134.

—. *The African National Congress* (Sutton: Thrupp, 2000).

Duin, P. "Artisans and Trade Unions in the Cape Town Building Industry 1900-1924", in W. James and M. Simons (eds.) *The Angry Divide* (Cape Town: D. Philip, 1989), pp. 95-110.

Duncan, D. *The Mills of God: The State and African Labour in South Africa, 1918-1948* (Johannesburg: Wits University Press, 1995).

—. "Liberals and Local Administration in South Africa: Alfred Hoernlé and the Alexandra Health Committee 1933-1943", *IJAHS* v. 23 (1990), pp. 475-493.

—. "The State Divided: Farm Labour Policy in South Africa 1924-1948", *SAHJ* v. 24 (1991), pp. 67-89.

—. "The State and African Trade Unions 1918-1948", *Social Dynamics* v. 18 no. 2 (1992), pp. 55-74.

—. "Wage Regulation for African Workers 1918-1948", *South African Journal of Economic History* v. 8 (1993), pp. 24-45.

Dunn, J. "The Politics of Representation and Good Government in Post-Colonial Africa," in P. Chabal (ed.) *Political Domination in Africa* (Cambridge: Cambridge University Press, 1986), pp. 158-174.

E

Eales, K. "Patriarchs, Passes and Privilege: Johannesburg's African Middle Classes and the Question of Night Passes for African Women, 1920-1931", in P. Bonner, ed. *Holding their Ground*, pp. 105-140.

—. "'Good Girls' vs 'Bad Girls'", *Agenda* no. 4 (1989), pp. 1-22.

Edgar, R. *Prophets with Honour: A Documentary History of Lekhotla la Bafo* (Johannesburg: Ravan Press, 1987).

—. *The Making of an African Communist: Edwin Mofutsanyana and the Communist Party of South Africa 1927-1939* (Pretoria: Unisa Press, 2005).

Edgecombe, R. and B. Guest, "'The Coal Miners' Way of Death': Safety in the Natal Collieries, 1910-1953", *Journal of Natal and Zulu History,* v. 8 (1985), pp. 63-83.

—. and B. Guest, "The Black Heart of the Beautiful Mountain: Hlobane Colliery, 1898-1953", *SAHJ* v. 18 (1986), pp. 191-221.

Elphick, R. and V. Malherbe, "The Khoisan to 1828", in R. Elphick and H. Giliomee (eds.) *The Shaping of South African Society 1652-1840* (Middletown: Wesleyan University Press, 1988), pp. 3-65.

Erlank, N. "Gender and Masculinity in South African Nationalist Discourse, 1912-1950", *Feminist Studies* v. 29 no. 3 (2003), pp. 653-671.

Etherington, N. *Preachers, Peasants and Politics in Southeast Africa, 1875-1880* (London: Royal Historical Society, 1978).

—. "Mission Station Melting Pots as a Factor in the Rise of South African Black Nationalism", *IJAHS* v. 9 no. 4 (1976), pp. 592-605.

—. "African Economic Experiments in Colonial Natal 1845-1880", *African Economic History* 3 (1978), pp. 1-15.

Everatt, D. "Alliance Politics of a Special Type: The Roots of the ANC/SACP Alliance, 1950-1954", *JSAS* v. 18 no. 1 (1991), pp. 19-39.

F

Feinberg, H. M. "The 1913 Natives Land Act in South Africa: Politics, Race, and Segregation in the Early 20th Century", *IJAHS* v. 26 no. 1 (1993), pp. 65-109.

—. "Protest in South Africa: Prominent Black Leaders' Commentary on the Natives Land Act, 1913-1936" *Historia* v. 51 no. 2 (2006), pp. 119-144.

Feinstein, C.H. *An Economic History of South Africa* (Cambridge, 2005).

Feit, E. *South Africa: The Dynamics of the African National Congress* (OUP, 1962)

—. *African Opposition in South Africa: The Failure of Passive Resistance* (Stanford: Stanford University Press, 1967).

Filatova, I. "Indoctrination or Scholarship? Education of Africans at the Communist University of the Toilers of the East in the Soviet Union, 1923-1937", *Paedagogica Historica* 35 (1999), pp. 41-66.

Fine, R. and D. Davis, *Beyond Apartheid: Labour and Liberation in South Africa* (London: Pluto Press, 1991).

Fisher, F. "Class Consciousness among Colonized Workers in South Africa," in T. Adler (ed.) *Perspectives on South Africa : A Collection of Working Papers* (Johannesburg: African Studies Institute, University of the Witwatersrand, 1977), pp. 300-352.

Fortescue, D. "The Communist Party of South Africa and the African Working Class in the 1940s", *IJAHS* v. 24 no. 3 (1991), pp. 481-512.

Freund, B. "The Social Character of Secondary Industry in South Africa: 1915-1945", in A. Mabin (ed.) *Organisation and Economic Change* (Johannesburg: Ravan Press, 1989), pp. 78-119.

Friedgut, A.J. "The Non-European Press", in E. Hellmann (ed.) *Handbook of Race Relations* (Cape Town: OUP, 1949), pp. 484-510.

Friedland, E. "The South African Freedom Movement: Factors Influencing its Ideological Development 1912-1980s", *Journal of Black Studies* v. 13 (1983), pp. 337-354.

G

Gaitskell, D. "Devout Domesticity? A Century of African Women's Christianity in South Africa" in C. Walker (ed.) *Women and Gender in Southern Africa to 1945*, pp. 251-272.

—. "'Christian Compounds for Girls': Church Hostels for African Women in Johannesburg, 1907-1970", *JSAS* v. 6 (1979), pp. 44-69.

—. "Housewives, Maids or Mothers: Some Contradictions of Domesticity for Christian Women in Johannesburg, 1903-1939", *Journal of African History* v. 24 (1983), pp. 241-256.

Gasa, N. "'Let Them Build More Gaols'", in Gasa (ed.) *Women in South African History: Basus'iimbokodo, Bawel'imilambo=They Remove Boulders and Cross Rivers* (Cape Town: HSRC, 2007), pp. 129-151.

Gebhard, W. *Shades of Reality: Black Perceptions of South African History* (Essen: Blaue Eule, 1991).

Geiger, S. "Tanganyikan Nationalism as 'Women's Work': Life Histories, Collective Biography and Changing Historiography", *Journal of African History* v. 37, (1996), pp. 465-478.

Gerhart, G. *Black Power in South Africa: The Evolution of an Ideology* (Berkeley: University of California Press, 1978).

Giddens, A. *The Nation-State and Violence* (Oxford: Polity Press, 1985).

Ginwala, F. "Women and the ANC 1912-1943", *Agenda* no. 8 (1990), pp. 77-93.

Gish, S. *Alfred B. Xuma: African, American, South African* (New York: NYU Press, 1999).

Goedhals, M. "African Nationalism and Indigenous Christianity: A Study in the Life of James Calata (1895-1983)", *Journal of Religion in Africa*, v. 33 (2003), pp. 63-82.

Goode, R. "May Day: International Labour Day", *SALB* v. 9 (1984), pp. 58-76.

Goodhew, D. *Respectability and Resistance: A History of Sophiatown* (Westport: Praeger, 2004).

Gooptu, N. *The Politics of the Urban Poor in Early Twentieth-Century India* (Cambridge: Cambridge University Press, 2001).

Gottschalk, K. and J. Smalberger, "The Earliest Known Strikes by Black Workers in South Africa," *SALB* v. 3 no.7 (1977), pp. 73-75.

Grundlingh, A. *Fighting Their Own War: South African Blacks and the First World War* (Johannesburg: Ravan Press, 1987).

Guha, R. "Discipline and Mobilize", in P. Chatterjee and G. Pandey (eds.) *Subaltern Studies VII* (Delhi: OUP, 1992) pp. 69-120.

Guy, J. *Remembering the Rebellion: The Zulu Uprising of 1906* (Scottsville: UKZN Press, 2006).

Guy, J. and M. Thabane. "Technology, Ethnicity and Ideology: Basotho Miners and Shaft-Sinking on the South African Gold Mines", *JSAS* v. 14 (1988), pp. 257-278

H

Haasbroek, J. "Die Verhouding Tussen die Swart Inwoners en die Stadsraad van Bloemfontein Gedurende die Oranjerivierkolonie-Tydperk, 1902-1910", *Navorsinge van die Nasionale Museum* v. 15 no. 1 (1999) pp. 1-28.

—. "Die Rol van Henry Selby Msimang in Bloemfontein, 1917-22", *Navorsinge van die Nasionale Museum* v. 16 no. 3 (2000), pp. 33-66.

—. "Founding Venue of the African National Congress (1912): Wesleyan School, Fort Street, Waaihoek, Bloemfontein," *Navorsinge van die Nasionale Museum* v. 18 no. 7 (2002), pp. 125-160.

Haines, R. "The Opposition to General Hertzog's Segregation Bills: 1929-1934" in *Conference on the History of Opposition in South Africa* (Johannesburg: Development Studies Group, 1978), pp. 150-182.

Harries, P. *Work, Culture, and Identity: Migrant Laborers in Mozambique and South Africa, c.1860-1910* (Johannesburg: Witwatersrand University Press, 1994).

—. "Capital, State & Labour on the 19th Century Witwatersrand: A Reassessment", *SAHJ* v. 18 (1986), pp. 25-45.

Harris, V.S. *Land, Labour and Ideology: Government Land Policy and the Relations between Africans and Whites on the Land in Northern Natal 1910-1936* (Pretoria: Archives Yearbook, 1991).

Heerma van Voss, L. (ed.) *Petitions in Social History* (Cambridge: Cambridge University Press, 2001).

Hemson, D. "In the Eye of the Storm: Dock-Workers in Durban", in Maylam, *People's City*, pp. 145-173.

Higgs, *The Ghost of Equality: The Public Lives of D.D.T. Jabavu of South Africa, 1885-1959* (Cape Town: David Philip, 1996).

—. "Zenzele: African Women's Self-Help Organizations in South Africa, 1927-1998" *African Studies Review* v. 47 no. 3 (2004), pp. 119-141.

Hill, R.A. and G.A. Pirio, "'Africa for the Africans': The Garvey Movement in South Africa, 1920-1940", in Marks and Trapido (eds.) *The Politics of Race*, pp. 209-253.

Hindson, D. *Pass Controls and the Urban African Proletariat in South Africa* (Johannesburg: Ravan Press, 1987).

Hirson, B. *Yours for the Union: Class and Community Struggles in South Africa, 1930-1947* (London: Zed Press, 1990).

—. *Frank Glass: The Restless Revolutionary* (London: Porcupine, 2003).

—. *A History of the Left in South Africa: Writings of Baruch Hirson* (London: Tauris, 2005).

—. "Rural Revolt in South Africa: 1937-51," *Présence africaine* (1978), pp. 60-68.

—. "Tuskegee, the Joint Councils and the All-African Convention", *Societies of Southern Africa in the 19th and 20th Centuries Collected Seminar Papers* 10 (1981), pp. 65-75.

—. "The Bloemfontein Riots, 1925: A Study in Community Culture and Class Consciousness", *Societies of Southern Africa in the 19th and 20th Centuries Collected Seminar Papers* 11 (1982).

—. "The General Strike of 1922" *Searchlight South Africa* 11 (1993), pp. 63-93.

Hobsbawm, E. *Nations and Nationalism since 1780: Programme, Myth, Reality* (Cambridge: Cambridge University Press, 1990).

Hoffman, J. and N. Mzala, "'Non-Historical Nations' and the National Question: A South African Perspective," *Science and Society* v. 54 no. 4 (1990/91), pp. 408-426.

Hofmeyr, W. "Rural Popular Organisation and its Problems: Struggles in the Western Cape, 1929-1930", *Africa Perspective* no. 22 1983, pp. 26-49.

Holland, H. *The Struggle: A History of the ANC* (London: Grafton, 1989).

Honwana, R. *The Life History of Raul Honwana* (Boulder: L. Rienner, 1988).

Horton, J.W. "South Africa's Joint Councils: Black and White Co-operation between the Two World Wars", *SAHJ* no 4 (1972), pp. 29-44.

Houghton, H. "Economic Development, 1865-1965", in Wilson, *Oxford History of South Africa*, v. 2, pp. 1-49.

Hyslop, J. "The Imperial Working Class Makes Itself 'White': White Labourism in Britain, Australia, and South Africa before the First World War", *Journal of Historical Sociology* v.12 no. 4 (1999), pp. 398-421.

J

Jeeves, A. *Migrant Labour in South Africa's Mining Economy: The Struggle for the Gold Mines' Labour Supply 1890-1920* (Montreal: McGill-Queen's University Press, 1985).

Jenkins, R. *Pierre Bourdieu* (London: Routledge, 1992).

Johns, S. *Raising the Red Flag: The International Socialist League and the Communist Party of South Africa, 1914-1932* (Cape Town: Mayibuye Books, 1995).

—. "Trade Union, Political Pressure Group, or Mass Movement? The Industrial and Commercial Workers Union of Africa", in R.I. Rotberg and A. Mazrui (eds.) *Protest and Power in Black Africa* (Oxford: OUP, 1970), pp. 695-754.

Johnson, D. *Shakespeare and South Africa* (Oxford: Clarendon, 1996).

Johnstone, F.A. *Class, Race and Gold: A Study of Class Relations and Racial Discrimination in South Africa* (London: Routledge and Kegan Paul, 1976).

—. "The IWA on the Rand: Socialist Organising among Black Workers on the Rand, 1917-1918", in Bozzoli, *Labour, Townships and Protest* (1979), pp. 248-272.

Jones, G.S. *Languages of Class: Studies in English Working Class History 1832-1982* (Cambridge: Cambridge University Press, 1983).

Jones, S. and M. Müller, *The South African Economy, 1910-1990* (Basingstoke: Macmillan, 1992).

Jordan, Z.P. "The South African Liberation Movement and the Making of a New Nation", in Diepen, *The National Question in South Africa*, pp. 110-124.

K

Kantor, J. *A Healthy Grave* (Berlin: Seven Seas, 1967).

Katz, E. *A Trade Union Aristocracy: A History of White Workers in the Transvaal and the General Strike of 1913* (Johannesburg: African Studies Institute, 1976).

—. "Revisiting the Origins of the Industrial Colour Bar in the Witwatersrand Gold Mining Industry, 1891-1899", *JSAS* v. 25 no. 1 (1999), pp. 73-88.

Keegan, T. *Facing the Storm: Portraits of Black Lives in SA* (London: Zed, 1988).

—. "The Restructuring of Agrarian Class Relations in a Colonial Economy: The Orange River Colony 1902-1910", *JSAS* v. 5 (1979), pp. 234-254

Kelley, R. "The Religious Odyssey of African Radicals: Notes on the CPSA, 1921-1934", *Radical History Review* no. 51 (1991), pp. 5-24.

Kennedy, B. "Missionaries, Black Converts, and Separatists on the Rand, 1886-1910: From Accommodation to Resistance", *Journal of Imperial and Commonwealth History* v. 20 (1992), pp. 196-222.

Khumalo, V. "Ekukhanyeni Letter Writers: A Historical Enquiry into Epistolary Network(s) and Political Imagination in KwaZulu-Natal, South Africa", in K. Barber (ed.) *Africa's Hidden Histories: Everyday Literacy and Making the Self* (Bloomington: Indiana University Press, 2006), pp. 113-142.

—. "Political Rights, Land Ownership and Contending Forms of Representation in Colonial Natal 1860-1900", *Journal of Natal and Zulu History* v. 22 (2004), pp. 109-148.

Kiloh, M. and A. Sibeko, *A Fighting Union: An Oral History of the South African Railway and Harbour Workers' Union* (Randburg: Ravan Press, 2000).

Kimble, J. and E. Unterhalter, "'We Opened the Road for You, You Must Go Forward': ANC Women's Struggles 1912-1982", *Feminist Review* 12 (1982) pp. 12-35.

Kirk, J. *Making a Voice: African Resistance to Segregation in South Africa* (Boulder: Westview, 1998).

Koch, E. "'Without Visible Means of Subsistence': Slumyard Culture in Johannesburg 1918-1940", in Bozzoli, *Town and Countryside in the Transvaal*, pp. 151-175.

Krikler, J. *Revolution from Above, Rebellion from Below: The Agrarian Transvaal at the Turn of the Century* (Oxford: Clarendon Press, 1993).

—. *White Rising: The 1922 Insurrection and Racial Killing in South Africa* (Manchester: Manchester University Press, 2005).

—. "Agrarian Struggle and the South African War", *Social History* v. 14 (1989), pp. 153-176.

Kros, C. *Urban African Women's Organisations, 1935-1956* (Johannesburg: Africa Perspective, 1982).

Kuper, L. *An African Bourgeoisie: Race, Class and Politics in South Africa* (New Haven: Yale University Press, 1965).

—. "African Nationalism in South Africa, 1910-1964", in M. Wilson and L. Thompson (eds.) *Oxford History of South Africa,* v. 2,(Oxford: Clarendon, 1971) pp. 424-476.

Kuumba, M.B. "African Women, Resistance Cultures & Cultural Resistances" *Agenda* 68 (2006), pp. 112-121.

L

Lacey, M. *Working for Boroko: The Origins of the Coercive Labour System in South Africa* (Johannesburg: Ravan Press, 1981).

La Hausse, P. *Restless Identities: Signatures of Nationalism, Zulu Ethnicity and History in the Lives of Petros Lamula (c. 1881-1948) and Lymon Maling (1889-c. 1936)* (Pietermaritzburg: University of Natal Press, 2000).

—. "Drinking in a Cage: The Durban System and the 1929 Beer Hall Riots", *Africa Perspective* no. 20 (1982), pp. 63-75.

—. "The Message of the Warriors: The ICU, the Labouring Poor and the Making of a Popular Political Culture in Durban, 1925-1930", in Bonner (ed.) *Holding Their Ground*, pp. 19-58.

—. "'The Cows of Nongoloza': Youth, Crime and Amalaita Gangs in Durban 1900-1936", *JSAS* 16 (1990), pp. 79-111.

—. "So Who Was Elias Kuzwayo? Nationalism, Collaboration and the Picaresque in Natal", *Cahiers d'études africaines* v. 22 no. 127 (1992), pp. 469-507.

—. "Drink and Cultural Innovation in Durban: The Origins of the Beerhall in South Africa, 1902-1916", in Crush and Ambler (eds.) *Liquor and Labor*, pp. 78-114.

Lalu, P. *The Communist Party Press and the Creation of the South African Working Class: 1921-1936* (Cape Town: Centre for African Studies, 1993).

Lambert, J. *Betrayed Trust: Africans and the State in Colonial Natal* (Pietermaritzburg: University of Natal Press, 1995).

—. and R. Morrell, "Domination and Subordination in Natal, 1890-1920", in Morrell (ed.) *Political Economy,* pp. 63-95.

Lambert, R. "Trade Unionism, Race, Class and Nationalism in the 1950s Resistance Movement", in Bonner (ed.) *Apartheid's Genesis, 1935-1962,* pp. 275-295.

Lawrence, B., E. Osborn and R. Roberts (eds.), *Intermediaries, Interpreters and Clerks: African Employees in the Making of Colonial Africa* (Madison: University of Winconsin Press, 2006).

Le Roux, C.J.P. *Die Verhouding tussen Blank en Nie-Blank in die Oranjerivierkolonie, 1900-1910* (Pretoria: Argiefjaarboek vir Suid-Afrikaanse Geskiedenis, 1986).

—. "The Role of T.M. Mapikela in the Municipal Administration of Black Affairs in Bloemfontein 1902-1945", *Historia* v. 42, no. 2 (1997), pp. 67-79.

Legassick, M. *Class and Nationalism in South African Protest: The South African Communist Party and the 'Native Republic' 1928-1934* (Syracuse: Syracuse University Press, 1973).

—. "Race, Industrialization and Social Change in South Africa: The Case of R.F.A. Hoernlé", *African Affairs* v. 75 (1976), pp. 224-239.

Lenin, V.I. *On Trade Unions* (Moscow: Progress, 1978).

Lever, J. "Capital and Labour in South Africa: The Passage of the Industrial Conciliation Act 1924", *SALB* v. 3 no. 10 (1977), pp. 4-31.

Lewis, J. *Industrialisation and Trade Union Organisation in South Africa 1924-1955: The Rise and Fall of the South African Trades and Labour Council* (Cambridge: Cambridge University Press 1984).

—. "The New Unionism: Industrialisation and Industrial Unionism in South Africa 1925-1930", *SALB* v. 3 no. 5 (1977), pp. 25-49

—. "South African Labor History: A Historiographical Assessment", *Radical History Review* 46/47 (1990), pp. 213-257.

Lewis, J. "Rural Contradictions and Class Consciousness", *Africa Seminar 5* 1985, pp. 38-58.

Limb, P. (ed.) *Autobiography and Selected Works of A.B. Xuma* (Cape Town: Van Riebeeck Society, forthcoming).

—. "The ANC and Black Workers", in N. Etherington (ed.) *Peace, Politics and Violence in the New South Africa* (London: H. Zell, 1992) pp. 284-305.

—. "'Representing the Labouring Classes': African Workers in the African Nationalist Press 1900-1960", in L. Switzer and M. Adhikar (eds.) *South Africa's Resistance Press: Alternative Voices in the Last Generation under Apartheid* (Athens OH: Ohio University International Studies Center, 2000), pp. 79-127.

—. "Early ANC Leaders and the British World: Ambiguities and Identities", *Historia* 47 (2002), pp. 56-82.

—. "'No People Can Be Expected to Be Loyal under Such Difficulties': Ambiguities and Identities among Early ANC Leaders", *Social Dynamics* v. 29 no. 1 (2003), pp. 1-26.

—. "Sol Plaatje Reconsidered", *African Studies* v. 62 no. 1 (2003), pp. 33-52.

—. "'I-Kongilesi Lilizwi ezindi ezindlwini* (Congress' Name is Household)': Politics and Class in the Cape Province during the 1920s", *Historia* vol. 51, no. 1 (2006): 49-86

—. "Intermediaries in South African Labour Relations, 1890s-1920s: Class, Nation, Gender" in P. Limb, N. Etherington and P. Midgley (eds.) *Indigenous Southern*

African Responses to Colonialism (Leiden: Brill, 2009)

Lodge, T. *Black Politics in South Africa since 1945* (London: Longman, 1983).

— ."The ANC in the Rand Townships 1955-1957," *Africa Perspective* 8 (1978), pp. 1-15.

—. "The Destruction of Sophiatown," *Journal of Modern African Studies* v. 19 (1981), pp. 107-132.

—. "Political Organisations in Pretoria's African Townships, 1940-1963," in Bozzoli (ed.) *Class, Community and Conflict* (1987), pp. 401-417.

—. "Political Mobilisation during the 1950s: An East London Case Study", in Marks and Trapido, *Politics of Race*, pp. 310-335.

—. "Charters from the Past: The African National Congress and its Historiographical Traditions", *Radical History Review* no. 46/47 1990, pp. 161-188.

Lonsdale, J. "Some Origins of Nationalism in East Africa", *Journal of African History* v. 9 (1968), pp. 119-146.

Lubanga, N. "Nursing in South Africa: Black Women Workers Organize", in M. Turshen (ed.) *Women and Health in Africa* (Trenton: Africa World Press, 1991), pp. 51-78.

M

Mabin, A. "The Rise and Decline of Port Elizabeth", *IJAHS* v. 19 (1986), pp. 275-303.

Machin, I. *Antbears and Targets for Zulu Assegais: The Levying of Forced African Labour and Military Service by the Colonial State of Natal* (Howick: Brevitas, 2002).

Macmillan, H. "A Nation Divided? The Swazi in Swaziland and the Transvaal, 1865–1986", in L. Vail (ed.) *The Creation of Tribalism in Southern Africa* (California: University of California Press, 1989), pp. 289-323.

McClendon, T. *Genders and Generations Apart: Labor Tenants and Customary Law in Segregation-Era South Africa, 1920s to 1940s* (Cape Town: David Philip, 2002).

McCord, M. *The Calling of Katie Makanya* (Cape Town: David Philip, 1995).

MacKenzie, D.J. "Influx Control, Health Regulation and African Women in Durban c. 1917-1949", in *Natal, 1909-1961: A Collection of Papers* (Pietermaritzburg: University of Natal, 1983).

Magubane, B. *The Political Economy of Race and Class in South Africa* (New York: Monthly Review Press, 1979).

—. "Whose Memory-Whose History? The Illusion of Liberal and Radical Historical Debates", in H.E. Stolten (ed.) *History Making and Present Day Politics*, pp. 251-279.

Malherbe, V.C. "Indentures and Unfree Labour in South Africa: Towards an Understanding", *SAHJ* v. 24 (1991), pp. 3-30.

Mantzaris, E. "The Promise of the Impossible Revolution: The Cape Town ISL 1918-1921", *Studies in History of Cape Town* v. 4 (1984), pp. 145-173.

Marable, M. "John L. Dube and the Politics of Segregated Education in South Africa", in A. Mugomba (ed.) *Independence without Freedom* (Oxford: Clio, 1980), pp. 113-128.

Marais, G. "Structural Changes in Manufacturing Industry 1916-1975", *SAJE* v. 49 (1981), pp. 26-46.

Marks, S., *Reluctant Rebellion: The 1906-1908 Disturbances in Natal* (Oxford: Clarendon, 1970).

—. and R. Rathbone (eds.) *Industrialisation and Social Change in South Africa: African Class Formation, Culture and Consciousness 1870-1930* (London: Longman, 1982).

—. *Ambiguities of Dependence in South Africa: Class, Nationalism, and the State in Twentieth-Century Natal* (Baltimore: Johns Hopkins University Press, 1986).

—. *Not Either an Experimental Doll* (London: Women's Press, 1987).

—. and S. Trapido, (eds.) *The Politics of Race, Class and Nationalism in Twentieth Century South Africa* (London: Longman, 1987).

—. "The Ambiguities of Dependence: John L. Dube of Natal," *JSAS* v. 1 (1975), pp. 162-180.

—. "Class, Ideology and the Bambatha Rebellion", in D. Crummey (ed.) *Banditry, Rebellion and Social Protest in Africa* (London: Currey, 1986), pp. 351-369.

Marx, K. *Capital*, v. 1 (Moscow: Progress Publishers, 1976).

Masilela, N. *The Cultural Modernity of H.I.E. Dhlomo* (Trenton: Africa World Press, 2007).

Mason, J. *Social Death and Resurrection: Slavery and Emancipation inn South Africa* (Charlottesville: University of Virginia Press, 2003).

Matthews, J. "The Roaring Years: The History of the African National Congress", *Fighting Talk* (June 1961).

Maylam, P. and I. Edwards (eds.) *The People's City: African Life in Twentieth-Century Durban* (Pietermaritzburg: University of Natal Press, 1996).

—. "The Changing Political Economy of the Region, 1920-50" in R. Morrell (ed.) *Political Economy & Identities in KwaZulu-Natal* (Durban: Indicator, 1996), pp. 97-118

Mbeki, G. *Let's Do It Together: What Co-Operative Societies Can Do* (African Bookman, 1944).

—. *Learning from Robben Island: The Prison Writings of Govan Mbeki* (Cape Town: David Philip, 1991).

—. *The Struggle for Liberation in South Africa: A Short History* (Cape Town: David Philip, 1992).

—. *Sunset at Midday* (Johannesburg: Nolwazi, 1996).

Meer, F. *Women in the Apartheid Society* (New York: UN Notes and Documents; 4/1985).

Meintjes, S. "The Early African Press in Natal: *Inkyaniso yase Natal*, April 1889-June 1896", *Natalia* 16 (1986), pp. 5-11.

—. "Family and Gender in the Christian Community at Edendale, Natal, in Colonial times" in C. Walker (ed.) *Women & Gender in Southern Africa to 1945* (1990), pp. 125-145.

Meli, F. [A. Madolwana], *South Africa Belongs to Us: A History of the ANC* (Harare: Zimbabwe Publishing House, 1988).

—. "The Comintern and Africa," *African Communist* no. 43 (1970), pp. 81-99.

—. "A Nation is Born" *African Communist* no. 48 (1972), pp. 17-36.

—. "South Africa and the Rise of African Nationalism", in M. van Diepen (ed.) *The National Question in South Africa* (1988), p. 66-76.

Metz, K. "Solidarity & History" in K. Bayeertz (ed.) *Solidarity* (Dordrecht: Kluwer, 1999), pp. 191-207.

Millard, J. "Charlotte Manye Maxeke: Agent for Change", in J. Malherbe, M. Kleijwegt and E. Koen (eds.) *Women, Society and Constraints: A Collection of Contemporary South African Gender Studies* (Pretoria: Institute for Gender Studies, 2000), pp. 167-176.

—. "Charlotte Makgoma Manye Maxeke: Her Legacy Lives On," *Studia Historiae Ecclesiasticae* v. 345 (2008), pp. 75-89.

Minkley, G. "'I Shall Die Married to the Beer'", *Kronos* 23 1(996), pp. 135-157.

—. "'Did Not Come to Work on Monday': The East London Waterfront in Comparative Perspective, c.1930-1963," in P. Alexander and R. Halpern (eds.) *Racializing Class, Classifying Race: Labour and Difference in Britain, the USA and Africa* (New York: St. Martin's Press, 2000), pp. 193-212.

Minnaar, A. "Labour Supply Problems of Zululand Sugar Planters 1905-39", *JNZH* 12 (1989), pp. 53-72

Moodie, T. *Going for Gold: Men, Mines and Migration* (Johannesburg: Wits University Press, 1994).

—. "The Moral Economy of the Black Miners' Strike of 1946", *JSAS* v. 13 1986, pp. 1-35.

Moroney, S. "Mine Workers' Protest on the Witwatersrand 1901-1912," *SALB* v. 3 no. 5 (1977), pp.5-24.

—. "The Development of the Compound as a Mechanism of Worker Control 1900-12", *SALB* v. 4 no. 3 (1978), pp. 29-49.

Morrell, R. (ed.) *Political Economy and Identities in KwaZulu-Natal: Historical and Social Perspectives* (Durban: Indicator Press, 1996).

—. "African Land Purchase and the 1913 Natives Land Act in the Eastern Transvaal", *SAHJ* v. 21 (1989), pp. 1-18.

Morris, M. and D. Kaplan, "Labour Policy in a State Corporation: A Case Study of the S.A. Iron and Steel Corporation", *SALB* v. 2 no. 6 (1976) pp. 21-33.

Morris P. "The Early Black South African Newspaper and the Development of the Novel", *Journal of Commonwealth Literature* v. 15 no.1 (1980), pp. 15-29.

Morton, F. "Female *Inboekelinge* in the South African Republic, 1850-1880", *Slavery & Abolition* v. 26 2 (2005), pp. 199-215.

Mpe, P. "Orality, Mediation and Subversion in Sol Plaatje's *Mhudi*", *African Studies* v. 57 (1998), pp. 79-91.

Mphahlele, E. "Landmarks", in M. Mutloatse, (ed.) *Reconstruction: 90 Years of Black Historical Tradition* (Johannesburg: Ravan Press, 1981), pp. 1-20.

Mtimkhulu, P. "Mass Movements of the 70s and 80s and the Liberation Struggle", in S. Buthelezi (ed.) *South Africa: The Dynamics and Prospects of Transformation* (Harare: Sapes, 1995), pp. 93-110.

Mulaudzi, C. and S. Schirmer. "Land Struggles in the 20ᵗʰ Century" in P. Delius, (ed.) *Mpumalanga: History and Heritage* (Scottsville: UKZN Press, 2007), pp. 351-391.

Murray, C. *Black Mountain: Land, Class and Power in the Eastern Orange Free State: 1880s to 1980s* (Edinburgh: Edinburgh University Press, 1992).

Murray, M. "The Formation of the Rural Proletariat in the South African Countryside: The Class Struggle and the 1913 Natives' Land Act", in M. Hanagan (ed.) *Confrontation, Class Consciousness and the Labor Process* (New York: Greenwood, 1985), pp. 97-121.

—. "'Burning the Wheat Stacks': Land Clearances and Agrarian Unrest along the Northern Middleburg Frontier, c.1918-1926", *JSAS* v. 15 (1988), pp. 74-95.

—. "'The Natives Are Always Stealing': White Vigilantes and the 'The Reign of Terror' in the Orange Free State, 1918-24", *Journal of African History* v. 30 (1989), pp. 107-123.

Musson, D. *Johnny Gomas: Voice of the Working Class: A Political Biography* (Cape Town: Buchu, 1989).

Mutloatse M. *Umhlaba Wethu: A Historical Indictment* (Johannesburg: Skotaville, 1989).

N

Nasson, B. *Abraham Esau's War: A Black South African War in the Cape 1899-1902* (Cambridge: Cambridge, 1991).

Nattrass, J. *The South African Economy* (Oxford: OUP, 1981).

Ndabula, T.Z. and M. Tsedu, *Epainette Nomaka Mbeki: A Humble Journey in her Footprints* (Johannesburg: Zazi's Productions, 2008)

Ndebele, N. "Actors and Interpreters: Popular Culture and Progressive Formalism," in *A Collection of Solomon T. Plaatje Memorial Lectures* (1993), pp. 51-71.

Ndlovo, S. "Johannes Nkosi and the Communist Party of South Africa: Images of 'Blood River' and King Dingane in the late 1920s-1930", *History and Theory*, v. 39 (2000), pp. 111-132.

S.N.[Neame, S.], "The ICU of Africa", *Sechaba* (Nov. 1979), pp. 28-32.

Nemutanzhela, T.J. "Cultural Forms and Literacy as Resources for Political Mobilisation: A.M. Malivha and the Zoutpansberg Balemi Association 1939-1944", *African Studies* v. 52 (1993), pp. 89-102.

Newbury, C. *The Diamond Ring: Business Politics and Precious Stones in South Africa, 1867-1947* (Oxford: Clarendon, 1989).

Newton-King, S. *Masters and Servants on the Cape Eastern Frontier* (Cambridge: Cambridge University Press, 1999).

Nimni, E. "Marx, Engels and the National Question," *Science and Society* v. 53 (1989), pp. 297-326.

Ntsebeza, L. *Democracy Compromised: Chiefs & the Politics of the Land in South Africa* (Leiden: Brill, 2005).

Nxumalo, J. ["Mzala"], "The National Question in the Writing of South African History: A Critical Survey of Some Major Tendencies", *Journal of Social Studies* (Dacca), v. 58 1992, pp. 17-91.

Nyquist, T.E. *Toward a Theory of the African Upper Stratum in South Africa* (Athens OH: Center for International Studies, 1972).

Nzimande, B. "Class, National Oppression and the African Petty Bourgeoisie: The Case of African Traders", in R. Cohen, Y. Muthien, and A. Zegeye (eds.) *Repression and Resistance: Insider Accounts of Apartheid* (London: H. Zell, 1990), pp. 165-210.

O

Odendaal, A. *Vukani Bantu! The Beginnings of Black Protest Politics in South Africa to 1912* (Cape Town: David Philip, 1984).

—. "'Even White Boys Call Us "Boy"': Early Black Organisational Politics in Port Elizabeth", *Kronos* no. 20, (1993), pp. 3-16.

O'Meara, D. "The 1946 African Mineworkers' Strike in the Political Economy of South Africa", *Journal of Commonwealth and Comparative Politics* v. 12 (1975), pp. 146-173.

Opland, J. *The Nation's Bounty: The Xhosa Poetry of Nontsizi Mgqwetho* (Johannesburg: Wits UP, 2007).

—. "Nontsizi Mgqwetho: Stranger in Town", in G. Furniss and L. Gunner (ed.) *Power, Marginality and African Oral Literature* (Wits University Press, 1995), pp. 162-184.

P

Packard, R. *White Plague, Black Labor: Tuberculosis and the Political Economy of Health and Disease in South Africa* (Berkeley: University of California Press, 1989).

Padayachee, V. S. Vawda and P. Tichmann, *Indian Workers and Trade Unions in Durban 1930-1950* (Durban: ISER, 1985).

Page, C. "Charlotte Manye Maxeke," in R. Keller, L. Queen and H. Thomas (eds.) *Women in New Worlds: Historical Perspectives on the Wesleyan Tradition* (Nashville: Abingdon, 1982), pp. 281-289.

Pampalis, J. *Foundations of the New South Africa* (London: Zed Press, 1991).

Parnell, S. "Racial Segregation in Johannesburg: The Slums Act 1934-1939", *South African Geographical Journal* v. 70 (1988), pp. 112-126.

—. "Race, Power and Urban Control: Johannesburg's Inner City Slum-Yards, 1910-1923". *JSAS* v. 29 no. 3 (2003), pp. 615-623.

Parsons, Q. N. "F. Z. S. Peregrino (1851-1919) : An Early Pan-Africanist", *Tinabantu* v. 1 no. 1 (2002), pp. 104-115 (written 1970).

Peires, J. *The House of Phalo* (Johannesburg: Ravan Press, 1981).

Perrings, C. *Black Mineworkers in Central Africa: Industrial Strategies and the Evolution of an African Proletariat in the Copperbelt 1911-1941* (London: Heinemann, 1979).

Perrot, M. *Workers on Strike: France, 1871-1890* (New Haven: Yale University Press, 1987).

Peteni, R.L. *Towards Tomorrow: The Story of the African Teachers Association of South Africa* (Morges, 1978).

Peterson, B. *Monarchs, Missionaries, and African Intellectuals: African Theater & the Unmaking of Colonial Marginality* (Trenton NJ: Africa World Press, 2000).

—. *"The Bantu World* and the World of the Book: Reading, Writing, and 'Enlightenment'." in K. Barber (ed.) *Africa's Hidden Histories* (Bloomington: Indiana University Press, 2006), pp. 236-257.

Phoofolo, P. *"Zafa! Kwahlwa! Kwasa!* African Responses to the Rinderpest Epizootic in the Transkeian Territories, 1897-1898", *Kronos* 30 (2004), pp. 94-117

Pillay, D. "The Congress Movement in Historical Perspective 1912-92", in S. Buthelezi (ed.) *South Africa: Dynamics and Prospects of Transformation* (Harare: Sapes, 1995), pp. 23-41.

—. "Cosatu, Alliances, & Working-Class Politics," in S. Buhlungu (ed.) *Trade Unions and Democracy: Cosatu Workers' Political Attitudes in South Africa* (Cape Town: HSRC, 2006), pp. 167-198.

Posel, D. "The Durban Ricksha Pullers' 'Strikes' of 1918 and 1930", *Journal of Natal and Zulu History* v. 8 (1985), pp. 85-106.

—. "Marriage at the Drop of a Hat: Housing and Partnership in South Africa's Urban African Townships, 1920s–1960s", *History Workshop* 61 (2006), pp. 57-76.

Poulantzas, N. *Classes in Contemporary Capitalism* (London: Verso, 1978).

Proctor, A. "Class Struggle, Segregation and the City: A History of Sophiatown, 1905-1946", in Bozzoli (ed.) *Labour, Townships and Protest*, pp. 49-89.

R

Ranger, T. "The Invention of Tradition in Colonial Africa," in E. Hobsbawm and T. Ranger (eds.) *The Invention of Tradition* (Cambridge: Cambridge University Press, 1983), pp. 211-262.

—. "Faction Fighting, Race Consciousness and Worker Consciousness: A Note on the Jagersfontein Riots of 1914", *SALB* v. 4 no. 5 (1978), pp. 66-74.

Redding, S. *Sorcery and Sovereignty: Taxation, Power, and Rebellion in South Africa, 1880-1963* (Athens OH: Ohio University Press, 2006).

—. "Peasants and the Creation of an African Middle Class in Umtata, 1880-1950", *IJAHS* v. 26 no. 3 (1993), pp. 513-539.

Reid, D. *Paris Sewers and Sewermen* (Cambridge MA: Harvard University Press, 1991).

Resha, M. *'Mangoana Tsoara Thipa ka Bohaleng: My Life in the Struggle* (Johannesburg: Cosaw, 1991).

Reynolds, G. "'From Red Blanket to Civilization': Propaganda and Recruitment Films for South Africa's Gold Mines, 1920-1940", *JSAS* v. 33 no. 1 (2007), pp. 133-152.

Rich, P. *White Power and the Liberal Conscience: Racial Segregation and South African Liberalism 1921-1960* (Manchester: Manchester University Press, 1984).

—. *Hope and Despair: English-Speaking Intellectuals and South African Politics 1896-1976* (London: British Academic Press, 1993).

—. *State Power and Black Politics in South Africa, 1912-1951* (London: Macmillan, 1996).

—. "Ministering to the White Man's Needs: The Development of Urban Segregation in South Africa, 1913-1923," *African Studies* v. 37 no. 2 (1978), pp. 177-191.

—. "Managing Black Leadership: The Joint Councils, Urban Trading and Political Conflict in the OFS, 1925-1942," in P. Bonner (ed.) *Holding Their Ground*, p. 177-200.

—. "Reviewing the Origins of the Freedom Charter", in N. Etherington (ed.) *Peace, Politics and Violence in the New South Africa* (London: Zell, 1992), pp. 254-283.

Richards, C. *The Iron & Steel Industry in South Africa* (Johannesburg: Wits University Press, 1940).

Richardson, P. *Chinese Labour in the Transvaal* (London: Macmillan, 1982).

Ringrose, H.J. *Trade Unions in Natal* (Oxford: OUP, 1951),

Rive, R. and T. Couzens, (eds.) *Seme: The Founder of the ANC* (Johannesburg: Skotaville, 1991).

Robert Mabilwane Resha (London: Resha Memorial, 1975).

Rosenthal, E. *Bantu Journalism in South Africa* (Johannesburg: Society of Friends of Africa, 1949).

Ross, R. *Status and Respectability in the Cape Colony 1750-1870* (Cambridge: Cambridge University Press, 1999).

—. *A Concise History of South Africa* (Cambridge: University Press, 1999).

—. "Emancipations and the Economy of the Cape Colony", *Slavery & Abolition* v. 14 (1993), pp. 130-148.

Roth, M. "Domination by Consent: Elections under the Representation of Natives Act 1937-1948", in T. Lodge (ed.) *Resistance and Ideology in Settler Societies* (Johannesburg: Ravan, 1986), pp. 144-167.

—. "Josie Mpama: The Contribution of a Largely Forgotten Figure in the South African Liberation Struggle", *Kleio* 28 (1996), pp. 120-136.

—. "The Wide-Ranging Influence of the 1928 Decree of the Communist International", *Acta Academica* v. 34 (2002), pp. 114-136.

S

Sapire, H. "African Political Organisation in Brakpan in the 1950s", *African Studies* v. 48 no. 2 (1989), pp. 183-207.

Saunders, C. "F.Z.S. Peregrino and the *South African Spectator*", *Quarterly Bulletin of the South African Library* v. 32 no. 3 (1978), pp. 82-87.

—. "Pixley Seme: Towards a Biography," *SAHJ* no. 25 (1991), pp. 196-217.

—. "Ngcongco, Jabavu, and the South African War," *Pula* v. 11 no. 1 (1997), pp. 63-69.

—. "African Attitudes to Britain and the Empire before and after the South African War," in D. Lowry (ed.) *The South African War Reappraised* (Manchester: Manchester University Press, 2000), pp. 140-149.

—. "Four Decades of South African Academic Historical Writing: A Personal Perspective" in H.E. Stolten (ed.) *History Making and Present Day Politics*, pp. 280-291.

Scanlon, H. *Representation & Reality: Portraits of Women's Lives in the Western Cape, 1948-1976* (Cape Town: HSRC Press, 2007).

Schirmer, S. "Land, Legislation and Labor Tenants: Resistance in Lydenberg, 1938", in A. Jeeves and J. Crush (eds.) *White Farms, Black Labor: The State and Agrarian Change in Southern Africa, 1910-1950* (Pietermaritzburg: University of Natal Press, 1997), pp. 46-60.

Schoeman, K. *Bloemfontein: Die Ontstaan van 'n Stad 1846-1946* (Pretoria: Human and Rousseau, 1980).

Scully, P. *Liberating the Family?: Gender and British Slave Emancipation in the Rural Western Cape, South Africa, 1823-1853* (Cape Town: D. Philip, 1997).

Seabury, R. *Daughter of Africa* (Boston: Pilgrim, 1945).

Simons, H.J. and R. *Class and Colour in South Africa 1850-1950* (London: Penguin, 1989 and IDAF, 1983).

—. *Struggles in Southern Africa for Survival and Equality* (London: Macmillan, 1997).

—. "Masters and Servants," *Fighting Talk* Nov. 1956, pp. 3-4.

Sisulu, E. *Walter & Albertina Sisulu: In Our Lifetime* (Cape Town: D. Philip, 2002).

Sisulu, W. *I Will Go Singing: Walter Sisulu Speaks of His Life and the Struggle for Freedom in South Africa* (Cape Town: Robben Island Museum, 2001).

Sitas, A. "Class, Nation, Ethnicity in Natal's Black Urban Working Class", *Societies of Southern Africa in the 19th and 20th Centuries Collected Seminar Papers* 38 (1990), pp. 257-278.

Smith, A.D. *Nationalism: Theory, Ideology, History* (Oxford: Polity, 2001).

—. "The Nation: Invented, Imagined, Reconstructed?" in M. Ringrose and A. Lerner (eds.) *Reimagining the Nation* (London: Open University, 1993), pp. 9-28.

Sonderling, N. (ed.) *New Dictionary of South African Biography* (Pretoria: Vista University, 1995).

Southall, H. "British Artisan Unions in the New World", *Journal Historical Geography* 15 (1989), pp. 163-182.

Starfield, J. "'Not Quite History': The Autobiographies of H. Selby Msimang and R.V. Selope Thema and the Writing of South African History", *Social Dynamics* v. 14 no. 2 (1988), pp. 16-35.

—. "A Dance with the Empire: Modiri Molema's Glasgow Years, 1914–1921", *JSAS* 27 (2001) pp. 479–504.

Stein, M. "Max Gordon and African Trade Unionism on the Witwatersrand, 1935-1940", *SALB* v. 3 no. 9 (1977), pp. 41-57.

Stolten, H.E. (ed.) *History Making and Present Day Politics: The Meaning of Collective Memory in South Africa* (Uppsala: Nordic African Institute, 2007).

Suttner, R. "Masculinities in the African National Congress-led Underground Organisation", *Kleio* 37 (2005), pp. 71-106.

—. "African National Congress (ANC): Attainment of Power, Post Liberation Phases and Current Crisis", *Historia* v. 52 no. 1 (2007), pp. 1-46.

Swan, M. "The 1913 Natal Indian Strike", *JSAS* v. 10 (1984), pp. 239-258.

Swanson, M. "'The Fate of the Natives': Black Durban and African Ideology", *Natalia* 14 (1984) pp.59-68.

—. "The Joy of Proximity: The Rise of Clermont", in Maylam, *People's City*, pp. 274-298.

Switzer, L. *Power and Resistance in an African Society: The Ciskei Xhosa and the Making of South Africa* (Madison: University of Wisconsin Press, 1993).

—. (ed.) *South Africa's Alternative Press: Voices of Protest and Resistance, 1880s-1960s* (Cambridge: Cambridge University Press 1997).

—. and M. Adhikari (eds.) *South Africa's Resistance Press: Alternative Voices in the Last Generation under Apartheid* (Athens OH: Ohio University, International Studies Center, 2000).

—. "The African Christian Community and its Press in Victorian South Africa", *Cahiers d'études africaines,* 96 (1984), pp. 455-476.

—. "Moderate and Militant Voices in the African Nationalist Press during the 1920s", in Switzer (ed.) *South Africa's Alternative Press*, pp. 147-188.

—. "Socialism and the Resistance Movement: The Life and Times of the *Guardian,* 1937-1952", in Switzer (ed.) *South Africa's Alternative Press,* pp. 266-307.

T

Tankard, K. "Urban Segregation: William Mvalo's 'Celebrated Stick Case,'" *SAHJ* 34 (1996), pp. 29-38.

Thompson, A. "The Languages of Loyalism in Southern Africa, c. 1870-1939", *English Historical Review v.* 117 (2003), pp. 617-650.

Thompson, E.P. *The Making of the English Working Class* (London: Penguin, 1968).

Torr, L. "Lamontville: A History 1930-1960", in Maylam, *People's City*, pp. 245-273.

Trapido, S. "The Origin and Development of the African Political Organization," *Societies of Southern Africa in the 19th and 20th Centuries Collected Seminar Papers* v. 1 no. 10 (1969/70), pp. 89-111.

Turok, B. "A Peasant's Son Turned Trade Unionist," *Sechaba* v. 5 no. 4 (1971), p. 16.

Turrell, R. *Capital and Labour on the Kimberley Diamond Fields 1871-1890* (Cambridge: Cambridge University Press, 1987).

Twala, C. "'Ulundi-Kaya': The Dwelling of Thomas Mtobi Mapikela in Bloemfontein (Mangaung): Its Historical Significance", *South African Journal of Cultural History* v. 18 no. 1 (2004), pp. 63-79.

V

Vahed, G. "'African Gandhi': The South African War and the Limits of Imperial Identity", *Historia* 45 (2000), pp. 201-219.

Van der Walt, L. "'The Industrial Union is the Embryo of the Socialist Commonwealth': The International Socialist League and Revolutionary Syndicalism in South Africa, 1915-1920", *Comparative Studies of South Asia, Africa and the Middle East,* v. 19 (1999), pp. 5-28.

Van Diemel, R. *"In Search of Freedom, Fair Play and Justice": Josiah Tshangana Gumede 1867-1947: A Biography* (Cape Town: The Author, 2001).

Van Onselen, C. *Chibaro: African Mine Labour in Southern Rhodesia 1900-1933* (London: Pluto, 1976).

—. *The Seed is Mine: The Life of Kas Maine, a South African Sharecropper 1894-1985* (Cape Town: D. Philip, 1996).

—. "Reaction to Rinderpest in Southern Africa 1896-1897", *Journal of African History* v. 13 (1972), pp. 473-488.

Verwey, E.J. (ed.) *New Dictionary of South African Biography* v. 1 (Pretoria: HSRC, 1995).

Vinson, R. "'Sea Kaffirs': 'American Negroes' and the Gospel of Garveyism in Early Twentieth Century Cape Town," *Journal of African History* v. 47 (2006), pp. 281-303.

Von Holdt, K. *Transition from Below: Forging Trade Unionism and Workplace Change in South Africa* (Pietermaritzburg: University of Natal Press, 2003).

W

Walker, C. (ed.) *Women and Gender in Southern Africa to 1945* (Cape Town: D. Philip, 1990).

Walshe, P. *The Rise of African Nationalism in South Africa: The African National Congress, 1912-1952* (London: Hurst, 1970).

—. *Prophetic Christianity & the Liberation Movement in South Africa* (Pietermaritzburg: Cluster, 1995).

—. "The Origins of African Political Consciousness in South Africa," *Journal of Modern African Studies* v. 7 (1969), pp. 583-610.

Warwick, P. *Black People and the South African War 1899-1902* (Cambridge: Cambridge University Press, 1983).

Webster, E. *Cast in a Racial Mould: Labour Process and Trade Unionism in the Foundries* (Johannesburg: Ravan Press, 1985).

—. (ed.) *Essays in Southern African Labour History* (Johannesburg: Ravan Press, 1978).

—. "Champion, the ICU and the Predicament of the African Trade Unions" *SALB* 1 6/7 (1974), pp. 6-13.

Wells, J. *We Now Demand! The History of Women's Resistance to Pass Laws in South Africa* (Johannesburg: Witwatersrand University Press, 1993).

—. "Why Women Rebel: A Comparative Study of South African Women's Resistance in Bloemfontein (1913) and Johannesburg (1958)", *JSAS* v. 10 (1983), pp. 55-70.

—. "The War of Degradation: Black Women's Struggle against Orange Free State Pass Laws, 1913" in D. Crummey (ed.) *Banditry, Rebellion and Social Protest in Africa* (London: Currey, 1986), pp. 253-270.

Wickins, P. *The Industrial and Commercial Workers Union of Africa* (Cape Town: OUP, 1978).

—. "General Labour Unions in Cape Town 1918-20," *SAJE* v. 40 (1972), pp. 275-301.

Wildt, A. "Solidarity: Its History and Contemporary Definition", in K. Bayertz (ed.) *Solidarity* (Dordrecht: Kluwer, 1999) pp. 209-220.

Willan, B. *Sol Plaatje: South African Nationalist, 1876-1932* (Johannesburg, Ravan Press, 1982).

—. "Sol Plaatje, De Beers and an Old Tram Shed: Class Relations and Social Control in a South African Town, 1918-1919," *JSAS* v. 4 (1978), pp. 195-215.

—. "An African in Kimberley: Sol T. Plaatje, 1894-1898", in S. Marks and R. Rathbone (eds.) *Industrialisation and Social Change in South Africa* (London: Longman, 1982), pp. 238-258.

Williams, D. "African Nationalism in South Africa: Origins and Problems," *Journal of African History* v. 11 no. 3 (1970), pp. 371-384.

Wilson, F. *Labour in the South African Gold Mines 1911-1969* (Cambridge, 1972).

Wolpe, H. *Race, Class and the Apartheid State* (London: J. Currey, 1988).

—. "The Theory of Internal Colonialism: The South African Case", in I. Oxaal, T. Barnett and D. Booth (eds.) *Beyond the Sociology of Development* (London: Routledge, 1975), pp. 229-252.

Worden, N. *Slavery in Dutch South Africa* (Cambridge, 1985).

—. and G. Groenewald (eds.) *Trials of Slavery: Selected Documents Concerning Slaves from Criminal Records of the Council of Justice at the Cape of Good Hope, 1705-1794* (Cape Town: Van Riebeeck Society, 2005).

Worger, W. *South Africa's City of Diamonds: Mine Workers and Monopoly Capitalism in Kimberley, 1867-1895* (New Haven: Yale University Press, 1987).

Wright, C. G. *Beneath the Southern Cross: The Story of an American Bishop's Wife in South Africa* (New York: Exposition Press, 1955).

Z

Zania, T. [S. Neame], "The ICU", *African Communist* no. 38 (1969), pp. 62-79.

—. [S. Neame], "70th Anniversary of ICU", *African Communist* no. 116 (1989), pp. 33-48.

Zug, J. *The Guardian: The History of South Africa's Extraordinary Anti-Apartheid Newspaper* (Pretoria: Unisa Press; East Lansing: MSU Press, 2007).

E. UNPUBLISHED THESES and SEMINAR/ CONFERENCE PAPERS

Theses

Baines, G. "The Port Elizabeth Disturbances of October 1920", M. A. Rhodes University, 1988.

Baker, J.J. "'The Silent Crisis': Black Labour, Disease and the Economics and Politics of Health on the South African Gold Mines 1902-1930", Ph.D. Queens' University, 1989.

Burns, C. "Reproductive Labors: The Politics of Women's Health in South Africa, 1900-1960" Ph.D. Northwestern University, 1995.

Caldwell, M. "Struggle in Discourse: *The International's* Discourse against Racism in the Labour Movement in South Africa, 1915-1919", M.A. Rhodes University, 1997.

Cele, N. "Between AmaZulu and AmaMpondo: Community Building at KwaMachi, Harding, 1820s-1948", Ph.D. Michigan State University, 2006.

Cherry, J. "The Making of an African Working Class, Port Elizabeth 1925-1963", M.A. UCT, 1992.

Clack, G. "The Changing Structure of Industrial Relations in South Africa with Special Reference to Racial Factors and Social Movements", Ph.D. University of London, 1962.

Cobley, A. "'On the Shoulders of Giants': The Black Petty Bourgeoisie in Politics and Society in South Africa, 1924 to 1950", Ph.D. SOAS, University of London, 1986.

Cope, N.L.G. "The Zulu Royal Family under the South African Government, 1910-1933: Solomon kaDinuzulu, Inkatha and Zulu Nationalism", Ph.D. University of Natal, 1985.

Couzens, T. "The 'New African': Herbert Dhlomo and Black South African Literature in English 1857-1956," Ph.D. University of the Witwatersrand, 1980.

Curry, D. "Community Culture and Resistance in Alexandra, 1912-1985", Ph.D. Michigan State University, 2005.

Daniel, A.J.C. "Radical Resistance to Minority Rule in South Africa: 1906-1965", Ph.D. Buffalo, 1975.

Dube, T.M. "A Study of African Reaction to Apartheid 1910-1966", MA University of Chicago, 1972.

Eales, K.A. "Jordan Ngubane, *Inkundla ya Bantu* and the African National Congress Youth League, 1944-1951", B.A. (Hons.) University of Natal, Pietermaritzburg, 1984.

Gaitskell, D. "Female Mission Initiatives: Black and White Women in Three Witwatersrand Churches, 1903-1939", Ph.D. University of London, 1981.

Ginwala, F.N. "Class Consciousness and Control: Indian South Africans 1860-1946", D.Phil. University of Oxford, 1975.

Gish, S. "Alfred B. Xuma, 1893-1962; African, American, South African", Ph.D. University Stanford, 1994.

Goode, R. "A History of the FCWU 1941-1975," M.A. UCT, 1986.

Grossman, J. "Class Relations and the Policies of the CPSA, 1921-1950", Ph.D. University of Warwick, 1985.

Hadebe, M. "A Contextualisation and Examination of the *Impi Yamakhanda* (1906 Uprising) as Reported by J.L. Dube in *Ilanga Lase Natal*, with Special Focus on Dube's Attitude to Dinuzulu as indicated in His Reportage on the Treason Trial of Dinuzulu", M.A. University of Natal, 2003.

Haines, C.G. "A Political History of the Congress Alliance in South Africa 1947-1956", Ph.D. SOAS, University of London, 1981.

Hawley, S.J. "The African National Congress and the Urban Black South African 1912-1930", M.A. Queens University, 1986.

Hemson, D. "Class Consciousness and Migrant Workers: Dock Workers of Durban", Ph.D. University of Warwick, 1979.

Hendricks, J.P. "From Moderation to Militancy: A Study of African Leadership and Political Reactions in South Africa, 1936-1960", Ph.D. University of Michigan, 1983.

Hofmeyr, W. "Agricultural Crisis and Rural Organisation in the Cape, 1929-1933", M.A. UCT, 1985.

Ibokette, I.S. "Labour Strategies in the Transvaal Gold Mining Industry, 1890-1910", M.A. Queens University, 1983.

Johns, S.W. "Marxism-Leninism in a Multi-Racial Environment: The Origins and Early History of the Communist Party of South Africa, 1914-1932", Ph.D. Harvard University, 1965.

Jordan, E. "From Time Immemorial: Washerwomen, Culture and Community in Cape Town, South Africa", Ph.D. Rutgers University, 2006.

Khumalo, V. "Epistolary Networks and the Politics of Cultural Production in KwaZulu-Natal, 1860 to 1910", Ph.D. University of Michigan, 2005.

Kingwill, R. "The African National Congress in the Western Cape: A Preliminary Study", B.A. (Hons.) UCT, 1977.

Kinkead-Weekes, B. "Africans in Cape Town: The Origins and Development of State Policy and Popular Resistance to 1936", M.Soc. Sc. UCT, 1985.

Kirk, J.F. "The Formation of an African Working Class in South Africa : Workers' Protest and 'Consciousness' 1900-1930", M.A. University of Wisconsin, 1980.

Lahouel, B. "The Origins of Nationalism in Algeria, the Gold Coast and South Africa". Ph.D. Aberdeen University, 1984.

Lambert, R.V. "Political Unionism in South Africa: The South African Congress of Trade Unions: 1955-1965", Ph.D. University of the Witwatersrand, 1988.

Lowe, C. "Swaziland's Colonial Politics: The Decline of Progressivist South African Nationalism and the Emergence of Swazi Political Traditionalism, 1910-1939", Ph. D. Yale University, 1998.

MacNamara, J. "Black Workers Conflict on South African Mines 1973-1982", Ph.D. University of the Witwatersrand, 1985.

Magagula, J. "*Inkanyiso yase Natal* as an Outlet of Political Opinion in Natal, 1889-1896", BA (Hons.), University of Natal, 1996.

Mahali, V. "Contradiction, Conflict and Convergence of Class and Nation in Black South African Politics, 1925-1985", Ph.D. University of Illinois, 1996.

Marable, M. "African Nationalist: John Langalibalele Dube", Ph.D. University of Maryland, 1976.

Mather, C. "Agrarian Transformation in South Africa: Land and Labor in the Barberton District, c.1920-1960", Queens University, 1992.

Matsepe, I.F. "African Women's Labor in the Political Economy of South Africa", Ph.D. State University of New Jersey, 1984.

McCullough, P.B. "The Growth of Assertive Action: The African National Congress and Urban Issues, 1930-1948", M.A. Queens University, 1988.

McNamara, J. "Black Workers Conflict on South African Mines 1973-1982", Ph.D. University of the Witwatersrand, 1985.

Meier, J. "The African National Congress and the Black Working Class, 1937-1948", M.A. Queens University, 1994.

Meintjes, S. "Edendale 1850-1906: A Case Study of Rural Transformation and Class Formation in an African Mission in Natal", Ph.D. University of London, 1988.

Moroney, S. "Industrial Conflict in a Labour Repressive Economy: Black Labour on the Transvaal Gold Mines 1901-1912", B.A. Hons. University of Witwatersrand, 1976.

Mindry, D. "'Good Women': Philanthropy, Power, and the Politics of Femininity in Contemporary South Africa", Ph.D. University of California, Irvine, 1999.

Minkley, G. "'To Keep in Your Hearts': The IICU, Class Formation and Popular Struggle, 1928-1932", B.A. (Hons.) University of Cape Town, 1985.

Morrell, R. "Rural Transformation in the Transvaal: The Middelburg District, 1919 to 1930", M.A. University of the Witwatersrand, 1983.

Motala, M.E.S. "Theories of the Rule of Law in South Africa with Special Reference to the Control of Labour", M.Phil. University of Warwick, 1981.

Mulaudzi, M. "'*U Shumu Bulasi*': Agrarian Transformation in the Zoutpansberg District of South Africa to 1946", Ph.D. University of Minnesota, 2000.

Nauright, J. "'Black Island in a White Sea': Black and White in the Making of Alexandra Township, South Africa, 1912-1948", Queens University, 1992.

Ndlovu, S. "The Changing African Perceptions of King Dingane in Historical Literature: A Case Study in the Construction of Historical Knowledge in 19th and 20th Century South African History", Ph.D. University of the Witwatersrand, 2001.

Ngqongolo, S. "Mpilo Walter Benson Rubusana 1858-1910: The Making of the New African Elite in the Eastern Cape", M. A. University of Fort Hare, 1996.

Ntsebeza, L. "Divisions and Unity in Struggle: The ANC, ISL and the CP, 1910-1928", B.A. (Hons.) UCT Economic History, 1988.

Odendaal, A, "African Political Mobilisation in the Eastern Cape, 1880-1910", Ph.D. University of Cambridge, 1983.

Page, C. "Black America in White South Africa: Church and State Reaction to the A.M.E. Church in Cape Colony and Transvaal, 1896-1910", Ph.D. University of Edinburgh, 1978.

Peel, H. "Sobantu Village: An Administrative History of a Pietermaritzburg Township 1924-1959", B.A. (Hons.) University of Natal, Pietermaritzburg, 1987.

Phillips, H. "'Black October': The Impact of the Spanish Influenza Epidemic of 1918 on South Africa", Ph.D. UCT, 1984.

Redding, S. "The Making of a South African Town: Social and Economic Change in Umtata, 1870-1950", Ph. D. Yale University, 1987.

Sapire, H. "African Urbanisation and Struggles against Municipal Control in Brakpan, 1920-1958", Ph.D. University of the Witwatersrand, 1988.

Scully, P. "The Bouquet of Freedom: Social and Economic Relations in Stellenbosch District, 1870-1900", M.A. University of Cape Town, 1987.

Simpson, G. "Peasants and Politics in the Western Transvaal, 1920-1940", M.A. University of the Witwatersrand, 1986.

Stein, M. "African Trade Unionism on the Witwatersrand, 1928-1940", B.A. Honours, University of the Witwatersrand, 1977.

Swanson, M. "The Rise of Multiracial Durban: Urban History and Race Policy in South Africa 1850-1930", Ph.D. Harvard University, 1964.

Tetelman, M. "We Can: Black Politics in Cradock, 1948-1985", Ph.D. Northwestern University 1997.

Ticktin, D. "Origins of the South African Labour Party, 1880-1910", Ph.D. UCT, 1973.

Trapido, S. "A Preliminary Study of the Development of African Political Opinion 1884-1955", B.A. (Hons.) University of the Witwatersrand, 1959.

—. "White Conflict and Non-White Participation in the Politics of the Cape of Good Hope, 1853-1910", Ph. D. University of London, 1970.

Vinson, R. "In the Time of the Americans: Garveyism in Segregationist South Africa, 1920-1940", Ph.D. Howard University, 2001.

Wells, J. "The History of Black Women's Struggle Against Pass Laws in South Africa 1900-1960", Ph.D. Columbia University" 1982.

Unpublished Seminar/Conference Papers

Bonner, P. *"'Siyawugobha, Siyawugebhola Umbhlala ka Maspala'":* ('We Are Digging, We Are Seizing Great Chunks of the Municipalities' Land'): Popular Struggles in Benoni, 1944-1952", African Studies Institute (ASI), University of the Witwatersrand, seminar paper, 28 Oct. 1985.

—. "'Home Truths' and the Political Discourse of the ICU", paper to the South African Historical Society conference, Cape Town, 1999.

—. "Kgatla Conspiracies, Pedi Plots: African Nationalist Politics in the Transvaal in the "Dead" Decade of the 1930s", UKZN History Seminar, 2002.

—. "Decompartmentalizing South African History", WISER seminar paper, Feb. 2007.

Breckenridge, K. "Fighting for a White South Africa: White Working Class Racism & the 1922 Rand Revolt", UKZN History, seminar paper, Mar. 2007.

Eales, K. "'Jezebels': Good Girls and Mine Married Quarters, Johannesburg, 1912", African Studies seminar paper, University of the Witwatersrand, Oct. 1988.

—. "Rehabilitating the Body Politic: Black Women, Sexuality and the Social Order in Johannesburg, 1924-1937", African Studies seminar paper, University of the Witwatersrand, Apr. 1990.

Edgecombe, R. and B. Guest, "Labour Conditions on the Natal Collieries: The Case of the Dundee Coal Company, 1908-1955", African Studies seminar paper, University of the Witwatersrand, May 1986.

Erlank, N. "Masculinity and Nationalism in ANC Discourse in the Twentieth Century", paper to Canadian Association of African Studies Annual Conference, Quebec, 2001.

Hadebe, M. "Pleading for Clemency through Poetry: Discursive Issues in the 1906 Poll Tax Rebellion", paper to UKZN History seminar May 2007; African Studies Conference, East Lansing, Sep. 2007.

Hirson, B. "The Reorganisation of African Trade Unions in South Africa, 1936-1942", ICS, Feb. 1975.

La Hausse, P. "The Dispersal of the Regiments: Radical African Opposition in Durban, 1930", ASI seminar paper Mar. 1986.

Lebelo, S. M. "Ons Dak Nie ... Ons Phola Hierso: Politics, Protest and Proletarians in Sophiatown, 1930-1955", ASI seminar paper, 25 Mar. 1991.

Limb, P. "Attitudes to Class, Nation and Gender in the Early African National Congress", paper to North American Labor History Conference, Wayne State University, Detroit, Oct. 2002.

—. "The African National Congress and the Indian National Congresses: A Comparative History of Strategies, Relationships and Identities", paper to ASA, Washington DC, 2003.

—. "Apartheid, Solidarity, and Globalisation: Lessons from the History of the Anti-Apartheid Movements", paper to International Conference on a Decade of Freedom, Durban 10-13 Oct. 2004.

Lowe, C. "'The Tragedy of Malunge,' or, the Fall of the House of Chiefs: *Abantu-Batho,* the Swazi Royalty, and Nationalist Politics in Southern Africa, 1894-1927", paper to the African Studies Association (U.S.) Boston, Dec. 1993.

—. "*Abantu-Batho* and the South African Native National Congress in the 1910s", CRCSA, May 1998.

Mabin, A. "Strikes in the Cape Colony, 1854-1899," ASI seminar paper 9 May 1983.

Mills, W. "Intra-African Hostilities among Educated Africans in the Cape Colony, 1890-1925" paper to Canadian Association of African Studies conference, 1975.

Ntantala, P. "Black Women Intellectuals & the Struggle for Liberation", University of the Witwatersrand, Aug. 2006.

Roth, M. "Black Councils, White Parliaments, 1920-87", ASI seminar paper, 29 Apr. 1991.

Starfield, J. "The Lore and the Proverbs: Sol Plaatje as Historian", ASI seminar paper, 26 Aug. 1991.

Swanson, M. "Champion of Durban: An African Politician and the ICU", ASA conference paper Los Angeles, 18 Oct. 1968, copy in National Archives of Zimbabwe.

Index

Numbers in *italics* refer to illustrations

B

C

D

G

H

J

K

L

M

N

Q

R

S

T

U

X

Y

Z